Classical Scholarship and Its History

Trends in Classics – Scholarship in the Making

―

Edited by
Franco Montanari and Antonios Rengakos

Advisory Board
Constanze Güthenke · Stephen Harrison
Luigi Lehnus · Irmgard Männlein-Robert
Filippomaria Pontani ·Stefan Rebenich

Volume 1

Classical Scholarship and Its History

—

From the Renaissance to the Present

Essays in Honour of Christopher Stray

Edited by
Stephen Harrison and Christopher Pelling

DE GRUYTER

ISBN 978-3-11-111513-9
e-ISBN (PDF) 978-3-11-071921-5
e-ISBN (EPUB) 978-3-11-071932-1
ISSN 2701-1100

Library of Congress Control Number: 2021931473

Bibliographic information published by the Deutsche Nationalbibliothek
The Deutsche Nationalbibliothek lists this publication in the Deutsche Nationalbibliografie;
detailed bibliographic data are available on the Internet at http://dnb.dnb.de.

© 2022 Walter de Gruyter GmbH, Berlin/Boston
This volume is text- and page-identical with the hardback published in 2021.
Editorial Office: Alessia Ferreccio and Katerina Zianna
Cover image: © Acropolis Museum, 2009. Photo by Nikos Daniilidis
Printing and binding: CPI books GmbH, Leck

www.degruyter.com

Preface

The germ of this volume was a day conference celebrating the work of Chris Stray and his 75th birthday, held at Corpus Christi College, Oxford, in October 2018. We are most grateful to Corpus and its Centre for the Study of Greek and Roman Antiquity (especially its Director, Constanze Güthenke) for hosting and sponsoring the event, to Mary Beard, who was a key part of the occasion but was sadly unable to contribute to the volume, and to those who attended for their lively comments and discussion.

We are most grateful to the contributors to this volume for their agreement to participate and for their patience and practical assistance with the editorial and publication process, and especially to De Gruyter for taking on this volume in their new strand 'Scholarship in the Making' in the series Trends in Classics; we thank Franco Montanari and Antonios Rengakos as editors of Trends in Classics for their kind acceptance, and Marco Acquafredda at De Gruyter for his efficient management of the publication.

Our fuller tribute to Chris Stray appears in the introduction below, but we would like to thank him for his full support of this project: it is unusual indeed for the recipient of a Festschrift not only to read and comment on most of the volume's papers before publication but also to write a paper in it, but we think the book is much the better for both these elements.

SJH & CBRP

Contents

Preface —— V
List of Figures —— IX
List of Tables —— XI

Stephen Harrison and Christopher Pelling
Introduction —— 1

Part I: Orientation and Origins

Lorna Hardwick
Tracking Classical Scholarship: Myth, Evidence and Epistemology —— 9

Part II: Early Modern

Edith Hall
Classics Invented: Books, Schools, Universities and Society 1679–1742 —— 35

Robert A. Kaster
The Vulgate Text of Seneca's *De beneficiis*, 1475–1650 —— 59

Michael Clarke
From Dares Phrygius to Thomas Jefferson, via Joseph of Exeter: A Study in Classical Reception —— 81

Part III: Victorian Cambridge and Oxford

David Butterfield
The Shilleto Phenomenon —— 101

James Clackson
Dangerous Lunatics: Comparative Philology in Cambridge and Beyond —— 131

Stephen Harrison
John Conington as Corpus Professor of Latin at Oxford —— 155

Part IV: History of the Book/Commentary

Roy Gibson
Fifty Years of Green and Yellow: The Cambridge Greek and Latin Classics Series 1970–2020 —— 175

Christopher Pelling
Gomme's *Thucydides* and the Idea of the Historical Commentary —— 219

Christina Shuttleworth Kraus
'Pointing the moral' or 'Adorning the Tale?' Illustrations and Commentary on Caesar's *Bellum Gallicum* in 19th and Early 20th-century American Textbooks —— 249

Part V: International Connections

Ward Briggs
The Founding of the American Philological Association —— 277

Judith P. Hallett
Gender and the Classical Diaspora —— 301

Jaś Elsner
Room with a Few: Eduard Fraenkel and the Receptions of Reception —— 319

Part VI: Academic Practices

Graham Whitaker
Congratulations and Celebrations: Unwrapping the Classical Festschrift —— 351

Christopher Stray
Working Together: Classical Scholars in Collaboration —— 377

Complete List of Publications of Christopher Stray —— 401
List of Contributors —— 411
Index —— 413

List of Figures

Fig. 1: Chris Stray (photo: Margaret Kenna). —— XII
Fig. 2: Peter Paul Rubens, *The Death of Achilles* (The Courtauld Institute Gallery, London; image courtesy of the Courtauld Institute Gallery and Art UK). —— **93**
Fig. 3: Richard Shilleto around sixty (1809–76) (photo c. 1869, CUL CAS G.256). —— **102**
Fig. 4: Arnold Wycombe Gomme (reproduced by courtesy of Susan Gomme). —— **222**
Fig. 5: Head from the Acropolis (reproduced by courtesy of Susan Gomme). —— **223**
Fig. 6: Gomme's Commentary, vol. 1 (1945), Table of Contents (reproduced by permission of the Secretary to the Delegates of Oxford University Press). —— **231**
Fig. 7: Gomme's Commentary, vol. 1 (1945), p. 1 (reproduced by permission of the Secretary to the Delegates of Oxford University Press). —— **233**
Fig. 8: Gomme's Commentary, vol. 1 (1945), Commentary on 1.138.6–139.1 (reproduced by permission of the Secretary to the Delegates of Oxford University Press). —— **239–40**
Fig. 9: Arrival of Caesar at the River Sambre, from C. Anthon, *Caesar's Commentaries on the Gallic War* (1838). —— **258**
Fig. 10: Battle at the Sambre, from F.W. Kelsey, *C. Iuli Caesaris de bello Gallico libri vii* (1886). —— **260**
Fig. 11: Walls, from C. Anthon, *Caesar's Commentaries on the Gallic War* (1838). —— **265**
Fig. 12: Bridge over the Rhine, from A. Palladio, *I quattro libri dell'architettura* (1570, 3.14). —— **266**
Fig. 13: Bridge over the Rhine, from J. Lipsius, *Poliorcheton* (1596, 108). —— **267**
Fig. 14: Charles Henri Graux (1852–1882); photograph (Mun, Madrid, December 1875). —— **359**
Fig. 15: Paolo Brezzi, Léopold Sédar Senghor, Robert Schilling; presentation of Festschrift, Dakar, 13 April 1977. Reproduced with the permission of L'Erma di Bretschneider, Rome. —— **368**
Fig. 16: *The Dilettanti Society* (1777–8), print after oil by Sir Joshua Reynolds: public domain. —— **378**

List of Tables

Tab. 1: Number of students receiving instruction in the subjects of Part II in June 1883. —— 150
Tab. 2: Firsts in Part II of the Classical Tripos. —— 150
Tab. 3: CGLC Volumes 1970–2020, including Imperial Library Volumes. —— 208
Tab. 4: Thucydides Commentaries. —— 227
Tab. 5: Speech and Narrative. —— 227
Tab. 6: Herodotus Commentaries. —— 228
Tab. 7: Selected editions of Caesar 1838–1918. —— 249
Tab. 8: British classical societies and archaeological schools. —— 389

Fig. 1: Chris Stray (photo: Margaret Kenna).

Stephen Harrison and Christopher Pelling
Introduction

This volume celebrates the career and scholarly achievements of Christopher Stray, and originated in a conference held in Oxford in 2018 to celebrate his 75th birthday; that year also saw the publication by OUP of his collected papers on the history of UK scholarship, *Classics in Britain: Scholarship, Education, and Publishing 1800–2000* (Stray 2018a).[1]

It is unusual for a single scholar practically to reorient an entire sub-field of study, but this is what Chris Stray has done for the history of UK classical scholarship. His remarkable combination of interests in the sociology of scholars and scholarship, in the history of the book and of publishing, and (especially) in the detailed intellectual contextualisation of classical scholarship as a form of classical reception has fundamentally changed the way the history of British classics and its study is viewed. His co-editorship of *A Companion to Classical Receptions* with Lorna Hardwick, the doyenne of UK classical reception studies (Stray and Hardwick 2008), rightly identifies him as a key figure in that currently lively and central discipline.

As Constanze Güthenke has noted (Güthenke 2018), a generation ago the history of classical scholarship still consisted largely of accounts of particular scholars and groups of scholars written by other scholars (e.g. Sandys 1903–8, Wilamowitz-Moellendorf 1921 and 1982, Pfeiffer 1976, and Brink 1986), from a broadly biographical and 'heroic individual' perspective. In these works scholars often sought to find their own place in the great tradition, choosing to praise or blame those whose work they admired or deprecated, and to identify with particular schools or trends, and there were few attempts to provide a broader, more nuanced and less prosopographical perspective.

Stray's epoch-making monograph *Classics transformed: schools, universities, and society in England, 1830–1960* (Stray 1998a) came into the debate as a wholly fresh voice. Informed by sociology (it was a revised version of his 1994 Swansea PhD in that discipline), coal-face classroom experience (at both secondary and tertiary level), an impressive grasp of the history of classical publishing (both high scholarship and humble textbooks) and of UK educational institutions (both schools and universities), and a rich knowledge of many archival sources, it pro-

---

[1] All references to Chris Stray's works in this introduction refer to the full bibliography of his scholarship at the end of this volume.

https://doi.org/10.1515/9783110719215-001

vided a history of classical teaching and scholarship which for the first time integrated it with larger social and cultural patterns in the UK of the period covered, a time in which British classics was shaped as a formal discipline, grew to its apogee, and suffered some eclipse and decline. It was warmly reviewed, won the Runciman Award of the Anglo-Hellenic League for a publication on a Greek topic from antiquity to the present, and is still available in print more than twenty years later.

Remarkably, this book was published in the author's fifties, after a quarter-century of research in which he had never held a substantive university post, a telling index of the marginality of the history of classical scholarship in that period. After undergraduate study at Sidney Sussex College, Cambridge (1963–6) and a Postgraduate Certificate in Education at the London Institute of Education (1966–7), he taught classics at the independent Latymer Upper School in West London (1967–9) and then at North-Western Polytechnic, now the University of North London (1969–70).

In 1970 he met and married Margaret Kenna, anthropologist of Greece, already then at the University of Wales, Swansea (now Swansea University), where she taught for forty years, and moved to Wales, commuting to the University of Bristol for a Diploma in Social Science (1971–2). Thereafter at Swansea he gained an MSc Econ. by thesis (1977) entitled 'Classics in crisis: the changing forms and current decline of Classics as exemplary curricular knowledge, with special reference to the experience of Classics teachers in South Wales' (this involved teaching Latin for several terms at a local comprehensive school), and the PhD in Sociology (1994) which underlay his 1998 book, entitled 'Culture and Discipline: The reconstruction of Classics in England 1830–1930'.

This rich breadth of education and experience underlies his remarkable expertise in the sociological and pedagogical context of UK classics. Alongside this sits a profound knowledge of classical publications of every kind, which has been a continuing strand in his research and publications, from his establishment with Ian Michael of The Textbook Colloquium (1988–2009) and its journal *Paradigm* (see Michael 1997) through his splendid pamphlet *Grinders and Grammars: A Victorian Controversy. The Text of Thirty-Six Letters Printed in The Times following the Publication of Kennedy's Public School Latin Primer in September 1866, with an Introduction and Notes* (Stray 1995a) to a set of major edited volumes over the last decade or so: *Classical Books: Scholarship and Publishing in Britain Since 1800* (Stray 2007a), *Classical Dictionaries: Past, Present and Future* (Stray 2010a), *Expurgating the Classics: Editing Out in Greek and Latin* (Harrison and Stray 2012), *Sophocles' Jebb: A Life in Letters* (Stray 2013), *Classical Commentaries: Studies in the History of an Academic Genre* (Kraus and Stray 2015), and *Liddell and Scott:*

The History, Methodology and Languages of the World's Leading Lexicon of Ancient Greek (Stray, Clarke and Katz 2018).

Stray's revisionary and richer perspective has also been effectively applied in the re-evaluation of some of the heroic individuals traditionally identified in the history of scholarship, firmly contextualising them in their broader cultural and social environment: *Gilbert Murray Reassessed. Hellenism, Theatre, and International Politics* (Stray 2007) and *Rediscovering E.R. Dodds: Scholarship, Education, Poetry, and the Paranormal* (Stray, Pelling and Harrison 2019) look at the fascinating range of activities of the UK's two most famous twentieth-century Greek scholars, while *A.E. Housman: Classical Scholar* (Butterfield and Stray 2009) does the same for its most celebrated twentieth-century Latinist.

His lens has also been trained on the chief institutions of UK classical learning, including both Oxford and Cambridge: there are volumes on *Classics in 19th and 20th Century Cambridge: Curriculum, Culture and Community* (Stray 1998), *The Owl of Minerva. The Cambridge praelections of 1906* (Stray 2005), and *Oxford Classics: Teaching and Learning 1800–2000* (Stray 2007), and he was the natural choice for editing the centenary history of the national UK body for the promotion of classics, *The Classical Association: The First Century 1903–2003* (Stray 2003). The international reception of UK scholarship has also been important for him, e.g. in *British Classics Beyond England: Its Impact Inside and Outside the Academy* (Hallett and Stray 2009).

Appropriately, these and other volumes were often written with the aid of prestigious attachments to leading academic institutions: as a Visiting Fellow at Wolfson College, Cambridge (1996–8), as a Jackson Brothers Fellow at the Beinecke Library, Yale University (2005) and as a Member of the School of Historical Studies of the Institute for Advanced Study in Princeton (2012). He was an Associate Fellow at the Institute of Classical Studies, University of London (2010–18) and has been Honorary Research Fellow in the Department of History and Classics at Swansea University since 1988; he is a welcome regular visitor at Oxford, where he is a well-known figure at a range of archives and libraries and has co-organised a number of memorable colloquia underlying some of the volumes listed above.

****

The main business of this volume opens with a chapter by Lorna Hardwick which looks at the assumptions behind and systems that underlie modern studies of the ancient world, and where the discipline might be heading against the broader background of contemporary public intellectual discourse. After this orientation, we find a group of three chapters focussed on the early modern period. Edith Hall examines the origin of the term 'classics' in English from its origins in the later 17C in reference to the Delphin series of Greek and Latin authors in France to its emergence as a label for a subject of study in 18C Britain, in a period of greater self-consciousness about education and ambitions to distinguish the new Anglican gentlemanly classical curriculum from the Continental model, and one where the discussion of Dryden's 1697 translation of Virgil followed by Pope's Homer are inseparable from that cultural dispute, while Robert Kaster looks at the emergence of the vulgate text of Seneca's *De beneficiis* from its first printing in 1475 to Gronovius' magisterial edition of 1649, which dominated subsequent scholarship and led to a two-century fallow period where few advances were made. Michael Clarke looks at Thomas Jefferson's surprising pairing of Dares Phrygius and Homer as poets of Troy in his assessment of contemporary classical education, showing that the founder of the University of Virginia actually meant the twelfth-century Anglo-Latin epic adaptation by Joseph of Exeter, which in fact circulated under Dares' name in the period; this is a splendid example of how serendipitous and surprising the history of scholarship and classical publishing can be.

A following trio of chapters then looks at the history of classical scholarship in the Cambridge and Oxford of the Victorian period, through 'thick' analysis of academic figures and frameworks (see especially Stray 2018a). David Butterfield considers the career of Richard Shilleto (1809–76), the leading classical coach of Victorian Cambridge (as well as being a 'friend of ale' and a Tory activist) while James Clackson looks at the history of comparative philology and its embedding in Cambridge classics since 1883, an important motivation behind key interactions between classicists and linguists which remain fundamental to the field. On Oxford, Stephen Harrison considers the career arc of John Conington, the first Corpus Professor of Latin at Oxford (1854–69), who began as a Hellenist but produced key work on Virgil and other Latin topics in a relatively short tenure of his chair; his popular verse translations of Horace and Vergil served to diffuse his subject most effectively by appealing to contemporary literary fashion.

A further trio of chapters then looks at commentaries. Roy Gibson considers the history of the 'green and yellow' Cambridge Greek and Latin Classics now it has reached more than 100 volumes in just under half a century, and how it has developed and responded to changes in classical education and research over that period. Christopher Pelling considers the genre of 'historical commentary' in the form of A.W. Gomme's Thucydides, looking at it through comparison and contrast with both its predecessors and the successor Thucydides commentaries of Andrewes/Dover and Hornblower. Finally, Christina Shuttleworth Kraus looks at US editions of school and college commentaries on Caesar's Gallic War, a mainstay of the curriculum, especially showing how the illustrations and other graphic content help organize information, communicate authority, and regulate the ways in which students consumed the 'classics'.

This US turn leads to a section of three chapters with strongly international perspectives. Ward Briggs looks at the foundation of the American Philological Association, now the Society for Classical Studies, in New York in 1868 by a lecturer in aesthetics, George Fisk Comfort (1833–1910), who ten days later was instrumental in founding the Metropolitan Museum of Art, and the early history of what is now the largest classical organisation worldwide. Judith Hallett reflects on how to think and theorize about the role played by gender in the emigration of classical scholars from Nazi-controlled Europe to England, Canada and the United States during the 1930's and 1940's, a diaspora which transformed the international discipline and profession of classics demographically and intellectually. Jas' Elsner discusses the very recent history of the Fraenkel Room at Corpus Christi College, Oxford, and its change of name to the Refugee Scholars Room, a story which incorporates the impact of *#MeToo* on the history of classical scholarship in the case of Eduard Fraenkel.

A final pair of chapters considers two types of scholarly practice. Graham Whitaker looks at the traditional and worldwide practice of the Festschrift, its history and development, and attempts to establish a typology of the genre. In last place, Chris Stray himself addresses the issue of scholarly collaboration, in which he himself has been such a prominent participant; though most research in Classics has been produced by individuals, he shows how collaborative scholarship has produced important results, and demonstrates its roots in universities, societies, journals — and friendships.

****

Chris Stray has been a true scholarly pioneer, but he has rarely been isolated in his efforts; as he himself points out in his essay in this volume, collaboration in classical scholarship, though less common than in some other disciplines, has had important results. It is notable that most of his twenty-plus books have been co-edited, and he has a remarkable capacity for effective, harmonious and sometimes hilarious teamwork to which the editors of the current volume can warmly testify. We are delighted to present to him and to the world a collection of papers which we hope will not only do honour to perhaps the most distinguished living historian of classical scholarship but also itself make a range of impressive and stimulating contributions to that discipline, as well as bringing pleasure to the honorand's many friends, collaborators and admirers throughout the worldwide classical community.

Bibliography

Brink, C.O. (1986), *English Classical Scholarship: Historical Reflections on Bentley, Porson, and Housman*, Cambridge.
Michael, I. (1997), 'The Textbook Colloquium', *Henry Sweet Society for the History of Linguistic Ideas Bulletin* 28, 50–51.
Güthenke, C. (2018) 'Introduction', in: Stray, C.A. (ed.), *Classics in Britain: Scholarship, Education, and Publishing 1800–2000*, Oxford, 1–12.
Pfeiffer, R. (1976), *History of Classical Scholarship from 1300 to 1850*, Oxford.
Sandys, J.E. (1903–8), *A History of Classical Scholarship* [3 vols], Cambridge.
Wilamowitz-Moellendorff, U.von (1921), *Geschichte der Philologie*, Leipzig.
Wilamowitz-Moellendorff, U.von (1982), *A History of Classical Scholarship* [trans. and ed. H. Lloyd-Jones], London.

Part I: Orientation and Origins

Lorna Hardwick
Tracking Classical Scholarship: Myth, Evidence and Epistemology

> The past is rubbish till scholars take the pains
> to sift and sort and interpret the remains.
> This chaos is the past, mounds of heaped debris
> just waiting to be organised into history.
>
> Harrison 1990, 79
>
> Memory runs a marathon, a human mind relay
> From century to century to recreate our play.
> Memory, mother of the Muses, frees
> from oblivion the 'Ichneftes' of Sophocles.
>
> Harrison 1990, xxii

As so often over the years my starting point for a new project is the result of a jog supplied by Chris Stray.[1] He has identified a gap in research and thinking and has pointed me to 'the part played in the transmission of classical culture by scholarship and teaching', which is 'but rarely reflected in the pages of the journals and monographs devoted to classical reception studies' (Stray 2018a, xv). The theory and practice of classical scholarship, including classical reception, is a huge field. The history of scholarship is now increasingly recognised as an area that is not only important for analysing classical receptions and classical traditions but is also a necessary tool in reflecting on research and teaching in any aspect of classics and ancient history. Scholarship is itself a 'reception' practice that in its turn shapes all parts of the field. Stray's comments prompt investigation of norms, modes of communication, measures of authority and means of persuasion that have shaped the interpretation of texts, the development of the study of ancient Greece and Rome, and its role in wider cultural and intellectual histories.

The histories of classical scholarship present a challenging mix of systemic assumptions, paradoxes and shifts in values, epistemology and practice, some of

---

[1] It is a pleasure and a privilege to be invited to contribute to this volume in honour of Chris Stray and I would like to thank him and the editors for making the publication possible. The main inspiration for this essay has been Stray's work, although he is in no way responsible for its contents. I would also like to thank audiences at the universities of Durham, Oxford, Queen's Belfast and the Institute of Classical Studies in London for their comments on earlier versions.

https://doi.org/10.1515/9783110719215-002

which are openly proclaimed, some of which are assumed, and some of which lurk beneath the surface. All scholarship has cultural parameters and norms. Historically, these have usually been based on aspirations to objectivity and emotional neutrality. Modern scholarship also includes but is not confined to the currently prominent categories of gender, sexuality, class and ethnicity. 'Engaged' scholarship is a slightly fuzzy concept that nods commitment to values that are thought to extend beyond the subject area itself. However, comparatively little attention has been given to investigating how and why research questions are formed, how questions shape research methods and how scholars persuade others that the questions are important and the judgements convincing. How are colleagues, students and readers to be persuaded, rather than drilled and dragooned? Looking at these processes in no way implies 'bad faith' on behalf of scholars, merely an acknowledgement that very few scholarly 'truths' are self-evident and that sometimes scholars do not explain how they have arrived at the questions that frame their investigations and hence shape the conclusions.

In this short essay I shall try to put a toe in the water of this ocean by focusing on issues around personal voice scholarship, identity scholarship and modes of persuasion. In the closing section I will move outward to suggest how it might be possible to build on those analyses and will make some suggestions about the future role of classical scholarship, both within the field of classics and in the wider public sphere. I hope this tentative exploration may lead to some future discussion.

****

Where better to start than with a quotation from Stray's most recent book, his collection of essays *Classics in Britain: Scholarship, Education and Publishing 1800–2000* (Stray 2018a). Chapter 16 of this book is an essay on 'Edward Adolf Sonnenschein and the Politics of Linguistic Authority in England, 1880–1930'. As with many of Stray's essays, it was published in a cross-disciplinary collection that might have escaped the attention of classicists. It is structured round an argument that is richly informed by evidence from archives and publications dating from the time under consideration. It also exemplifies the importance of the critical evaluation of evidence in building a bridge between the 'case-study' and the bigger picture.

In a section of the essay headed *Grammatical Terminology and the Politics of Knowledge*, Stray addressed issues of academic ideology that were involved in the late-nineteenth and early-twentieth century construction of a university curriculum of separate specialist subjects. He argued that what was created was an 'idea that any subject, studied in the search for truth, had a moral worth' (Stray 2018a,

301). I am preaching to the converted when I say that in these days of instrumentalism and blurring of the distinctions between education and training, classicists are at the forefront of those who argue that intellectual acuity and integrity, underpinned by the weighing of evidence and of arguments and especially by the exposure of weak arguments and untruth, is the prime aim of education at all levels.

This is a noble aspiration, but the rhetoric is easier than the practice. I need to probe a little at the interfaces between the study of antiquity, conceptualisation, judgement and anachronism. As a graduate student, I had the good fortune to spend some time supervised by Moses Finley.[2] The initial six months were, to put it mildly, somewhat gruelling. I remember in particular one session in which I made the mistake of mouthing the then fashionable mantra about the difference between ancient and modern concepts (in particular between status groups and class categories; such distinctions underlay Finley's research on slavery). I then spent a challenging couple of hours being grilled about how concepts were generated and how they might be tested. I was made to reflect on the difference between sources and evidence and to give examples of the questions that sources must bear before they could be regarded as providing evidence. There followed an inquisition about the ways in which scholars alighted on questions (including the personal and social histories involved) and how they formulated questions and tested the results. It seems to me that not only historians of scholarship but also any practising classicist or ancient historian faces similar challenges today.

Scholars aspire (and I do not denigrate the role of aspiration in scholarship, as in life). They aspire to validate and vindicate in some way the importance of studying antiquity. They aspire to share in the *gravitas* of scholarship and also to wield its spotlights without fear or favour. They aspire to spread knowledge of the texts, ideas and material cultures of Greece and Rome in ways that both honour the ancient cultures and also inculcate critical thinking about antiquity and about subsequent times and places. Scholars face particular challenges because the worlds of antiquity and the present day are multi-faceted, culturally and politically, and are both distant and in various metaphorical and material ways still present. Attempts to engage with these problems without attention to the histories of scholarship and to the interaction between scholarship and the public imagination are surely doomed.

****

---

[2] It was M.I. Finley who first advised me that I should meet and discuss with a (then) youthful researcher called Christopher Stray.

A look at some recent debates is salutary. There has been a certain amount of reflection on the perspectives that frame scholarly enquiry, the types of authority that they imply and the language of scholarship and its communications. A good example is the recognition of Personal Voice scholarship. This has surely exploded the assumption that the scholar has or could have a professional carapace insulated from his/her own life experiences, let alone that this would be a desirable state. Perspectives of gender, sexuality, ethnicity, class, physical and mental states are recognised as infusing critical thinking.

Judith Hallett, a pioneer in that field, has followed the lead of Nancy Miller and categorized the Personal Voice as entailing an 'explicitly autobiographical performance within the act of criticism' (Hallett 2001, 134). Hallett also aimed to situate this mode of self-expression within a larger intellectual framework. She has noted that individual biographies draw on lived experiences — for example as immigrants or children of refugee parents, Holocaust survivors, people of faith (Jews, Christians).[3] Ground-breaking work by Hallett and Van Nortwick related the personal voice to style as well as to content and was instrumental in the recognition that powerfully felt emotions were important drivers of scholarship (Hallett and Van Nortwick 1997). The essays collected by Hallett and Van Nortwick also stressed the value of personal voice scholarship for the analysis and interpretation of Greek and Latin texts and their reception in various historical and cultural contexts and raised questions about the personal and professional implications of writing in a personal voice, which would be judged by sometimes hostile peers. To the issues they raised I would add the value of considering covert as well as overt aspects of the personal voice, which after all was not first invented in 1997. This repays some detective work, not only in respect of literary scholarship but also to search out ways in which personal voices can be embedded in historiography and commentaries. The kinds of questions asked by scholars — the underlying as well as the prominent — also shape the methods used and the tones and registers in which judgements are communicated. The personal voice analysis developed in the last quarter of the twentieth century by Hallett and van Nortwick and their collaborators provides an important benchmark for assessing how scholarly norms have shifted in subsequent years, and for identifying by comparison the focus and implications of more recent concerns. One of these concerns is the debate about the relationship between lived experience and the status and analysis of historical sources.

---

[3] Hallett 2001, 133–4. Since the initial explorations of personal voice scholarship more attention has been paid to insights from Muslim traditions, from war veterans and other marginalized groups. The borders between personal and group experience are complex and mutually porous.

****

In 2013 the historian David Reynolds published a book, *The Long Shadow: the Great War and the Twentieth century*, a well-received contribution to the plethora of publications marking the run-up to the one hundredth anniversary of the outbreak in 1914 of the First World War. In his Introduction he commented:

> In Britain we have lost touch with the Great War ... *1914–18 has become a literary war, detached from its moorings in historical events* [italics added] ... by reducing the conflict to personal tragedies, however moving, we have lost the big picture: the history has been distilled into poetry ... This process has been accentuated by the 'cultural turn' in academic history as a whole, which in the case of 1914–18, has resulted in a fascination with the public memory and memorialisation of the conflict (Reynolds 2013, xv).

In seeking to remove the 'distilling' effects of poetry from 'scientific history' Reynolds implicitly raised important questions about the relationship between poetry (and the arts more generally) and other ways of looking at the world. His enterprise involved not only questioning (justifiably) the umbrella term 'war poets' but also questioning whether some of the most influential writers could be regarded as truly representative, in their experiences and backgrounds, of the wider body of soldiers as well as of soldiers who wrote poetry:

> we now reserve the term 'war poets' for a few celebrated soldiers such as Siegfried Sassoon and Wilfred Owen ... atypical soldiers as well as unrepresentative poets, being young, unmarried officers, sometimes uneasy about homosexual leanings and uncertain about their own courage — who often ended up with a martyr complex (Reynolds 2013, 187).[4]

By extension, Reynolds' approach denies validity as historical evidence to the 'personal voice' of lived experience.

In contrast, the relationship between personal voice scholarship and lived experience, the questions prompted by both and the judgements to which they lead has been given a new turn by the work of Jonathan Shay. Shay (who has professional qualifications in both classical scholarship and psychiatry — PhD

---

4 Ivor Gurney and Isaac Rosenberg were actually private soldiers. They and the officers Owen, Sassoon, and Sorley had substantial experience of front-line fighting. Their letters as well as their poems and art work refer to the experience of soldiers in general. Reynolds' thesis and the relationship between the lived experience of the war poets and artists and their aesthetics is discussed in more detail in Hardwick 2018. The forthcoming *Oxford Classical Receptions Commentaries* (*OCRC*) digital project will include detailed analysis of the reception of classical texts in a range of WW1 poetry. See also Hardwick, Harrison and Vandiver forthcoming.

and MD), has authored two studies of Homeric epic. In the first, *Achilles in Vietnam: Combat Trauma and the Undoing of Character* he discussed affinities between the psychological trauma of Achilles and that of military personnel who fought in Vietnam (Shay 1994). In the second, *Odysseus in America: Combat Trauma and the Trials of Homecoming*, he discussed the problems of homecoming and reintegration into a society that had changed from the one that the veterans had left (Shay 2002). The books were motivated and constructed in a frame that involved interaction between three spheres of personal voice (Shay's; the veterans'; figures and focalisations in Homer) and three corresponding spheres of lived experience. The 2002 book was published with a Foreword by Senators John McCain (1936–2018) and Max Cleland (1942–). McCain, a Republican, was a Navy veteran and Cleland, a Democrat, served in the Army, so their experience and standpoints bridged generational and political differences. Their Foreword made a specific link between ancient and modern experience and also distinguished between different strands in those experiences: 'Those of us who have witnessed, taken part in, and suffered the tragedies of war know that the ancient Greek epics offer compelling insights into our own experiences' (McCain and Cleland in Shay 2002, xi).

In his Introduction, Shay took up those aspects in a nuanced reflection on the polyfocal structure of his book:

> You already know that this book is written in a 'personal voice'. I don't, or won't, or can't hide behind an expressionless mask of professionalism. But this personal voice is somewhat different in each of the three parts of the book. The voice of the first part is the labor of love voice, telling readers about veterans, about the *Iliad* and the *Odyssey*. In Part 2 I notice that my voice changes because I am trying to persuade my professional colleagues [sc.in psychiatry] to think differently. In Part 3 I address military professionals and the policy makers who are their bosses, and, most important, the American people, who are their boss's bosses. It is an effort in democratic persuasion — because I have authority over no-one but myself (Shay 2002, 7).

It seems to me that Shay's reflection illuminates comparable processes in the subject areas of Classics and Ancient History, notably in (i) the relationship between personal voice and lived experience; (ii) communication with academic peers; and (iii) reaching out to the public sphere. In published work these aspects are infrequently articulated in direct authorial comment and may need to be tracked down by historians of scholarship who have access to paramaterial.

There is a further major leap to be made from the initial step that recognizes these perspectives and the experiences underlying them as starting points for asking questions of the sources. The next step requires formulating and investigating key questions about 'how can this be done?' and 'what difference is then made and to whom?'. Do different scholarly approaches involve the *same* criteria of evaluation both of good questions and of good answers, even though they may use a different lens (whether that of veterans or other individuals or groups)? In other words, is it the personnel and the agenda which change or the substance of the discipline? Similar questions might be posed about the effects of the admission of scholars of different genders, cultures, ethnicities and class backgrounds. Is classical scholarship changing continually or are the new voices assimilated into what is already an established, even rigidly defined, project?

****

Identity politics has become a shorthand term that masks a complex inter-relationship of different things. For example, an increasing perception of the gap between government and people has generated more and more pressure groups that concentrate on getting particular issues on to the political agenda. Their determination to make their voices heard can be powerful, but the downside is that starting from a position of perceived marginalisation can restrict the wider public's ability and willingness to integrate such issues into the common fabric, and hence preclude addressing underlying causes. For example, the impact of war and peace is not only a matter for veterans. These are issues for all — as citizens and as human beings. There is also a tension between the value of the voice of lived experience and a potentially restricting sense that it is *only* people who are in that situation who have the right or duty to speak about it. This can result in a denial that others can understand the situation and by extension fragments responsibility for ameliorating it, with the result that the underlying causes may go unchallenged and unresolved. I mention these tensions because it seems to me that they provide some analogies with problems affecting communities of classical scholars.

In the area of classics there has been forceful debate in various spheres around identity issues. Lianeri and Zajko's edited collection (2008) pioneered theoretical aspects, focusing on the relationship between identity and change in the history of culture, with special studies of translation of Greek and Latin texts. Some disturbing events at recent conferences and informal and less public email exchanges between practitioners working in the field have revealed deep fractures within and between subject communities. One email discussion was initiated by Nathaniel, who has kindly given me permission to quote from his comments. Nathaniel was a student in Oxford and was a director of the Oxford Greek Play. In brief, his emails reflected on the history of how antiquity had been appropriated by scholarship — and through scholarship diffused into the public imagination — to create, underpin and sustain the association between Greek and

Roman antiquity and the validation, even vindication, of colonialism and racism.[5]

Nathaniel also stated his view that, in spite of having been admitted to the exclusive society of Oxford, gaining a double first in 'Mods' and 'Greats' (the Oxford undergraduate classics course) followed by a PhD in the United States (Michigan) and taking a prominent part in classical activities, he was nevertheless racialized as a black man and felt powerless to change the prevailing ethos and practice in the field. This led him, *inter alia*, to challenge the rather tentative suggestions I had made in a book chapter to the effect that classics was gradually being decolonised, that is liberated from its appropriation in predominantly western and imperialist narratives (Hardwick 2004). As a result of his doubts, Nathaniel took a gloomy view of the future of ancient Greece and Rome as a subject of study (other than for a small antiquarian residue who might claim its lack of utility as a virtue).[6]

'I was not encouraged to see, let alone critique, the colonial power struggle [that was imbricated in] the Classical Tradition in which we were working… Even though I got a double first *I feel cheated of a rigorous education*' (personal emails, January – October 2018, quoted with permission; italics added).[7]

These are hard words. Although I tried to persuade Nathaniel that there is an alternative and positive future for classics, while not denying the validity of his own experiences and his concerns, his intervention compelled me to take a look at the reverse side of the coin: firstly, to consider the question of the norms associated with the sense of identity of the scholarly community in classics as a whole; and secondly to consider how to construct and communicate a scholarship that neither represses nor privileges strands that contend with one another

---

[5] To that might be added the validation and vindication of misogyny, a trope exposed by Emily Wilson's analysis of how Victorian translators of Homer's *Odyssey* added moral condemnation to the narrative of the hanging of the serving maids in *Od.* 22 after their sexual exploitation by the suitors. The effect was not only to blame the victims but also to misrepresent the text by repressing readers' awareness of the objectification in Homer of women as the property of males (Wilson 2017, 91). Wilson thus exposed a double untruth.

[6] He subsequently became a teaching assistant at a University Centre for Black Humanities and not a lecturer in a Classics department. At the time of writing my essay he holds honorary research fellowships in the UK at the University of Birmingham Centre for West Midlands History and at the University of Warwick and is currently researching Black Perspectives in Birmingham's Memorials.

[7] Other observations on the future of Classics made from a similar perspective can be found on the *Eidolon* Blog (*www.eidolon.pub*). The mission statement of *Eidolon* is a significant statement in the history of classical scholarship.

(including those which some might wish were not there but which are nevertheless part of its history).

I found it quite hard not to fall into the 'identity trap' myself. Robin DiAngelo's studies have discussed the social environment that protects and insulates white people from race-based stress, exposure to which generates anxiety, triggering a range of defensive moves (DiAngelo 2011 and 2018). These include outward display of emotions such as anger, fear, guilt[8] and behaviours such as argumentation, silence and leaving the stress-inducing situation. DiAngelo argued that these behaviours in turn function to retain and reinstate white racial equilibrium. She referred initially to interpersonal situations. She then shifted the responsibility for perpetuation of racial hierarchies from people of colour to white people and argued that whites do not need to be *active* supporters of racist social practices to be *complicit* in them. Silence is complicity. This is, according to DiAngelo, the result of a 'failure of imagination' rather than necessarily a moral flaw. For me, the notion of 'failure of imagination' immediately turns the lens back on to the effects and potential (both liberating and repressing) of an education that includes study of Greek and Roman texts, ideas and material culture.[9] The other side of that coin is the cultural defensiveness of some classicists in the face of what they regard as a 'blame project' that imbricates them in the vindication and perpetuation of colonial attitudes, racism, misogyny, fascism and violence.[10] This brings me to take a closer look at shifts in the parameters of how classicists self-define and how they seek to ensure the survival and future development of their discipline.

****

In talking about the identity of the community of classical scholars (senior, junior and students) I stress that I am not here talking about statistics or composition of

---

8 To which it seems that those who self-identify as liberal humanists may be particularly prone?
9 See for example, Richard Armstrong's discussion of how translation can involve an imaginative approach to the future possibilities of epic (Armstrong 2008).
10 I am grateful to an anonymous external reader who posed the additional question of why classically educated scholars of colour have often been marginalised or 'invisible' outside their own peer group, despite their contributions to research and teaching. S/he cited the 2009 Greek language course published by James Ezzueduemhoi the Nigerian-born classicist, as an example. See also Rankine 2006 and Malamud 2013 for discussions of cultural and political exclusion/inclusion, and Goff/Simpson 2007 for creative practices and their receptions. Goff (2013b, 163 n. 14) refers under the sub-heading 'Educational Slavery' to public policy predispositions towards technical and agricultural education rather than to Black Colleges that had a classical curriculum, such as Howard and Fisk.

the community or its demographics, nor about the persisting problems in the UK of access to study of classical subjects at school and university and to professional appointments in the subject area.[11] There are two aspects to analysing identity definitions in particular subject areas. The first aspect requires recognition that identity in respect of individuals is likely to be multi-faceted. Most people simultaneously hold several identities, personal, social, cultural, professional. In some contexts one identity may be paramount (either as the result of self-definition or externally imposed). The second aspect concerns how an academic or subject community defines itself and how it is regarded externally (including how it projects itself). Group identity may constrain, enhance or shape the senses of identity of the individual members and sub-groups (and by extension their relationship with wider society). How individuals perceive their own identities and the extent to which they judge that they are pushed to proclaim or repress these is increasingly recognised as important. I have already made clear my view that having any particular class, cultural, ethnic or gender identity is by no means a *sine qua non* for speaking on problems of exclusion, oppression or limitation of academic aspiration.[12]

In a recent article Kenan Malik has explored how identity politics can become a means rather than an end in itself:

> I discovered I could find more solidarity with those whose ethnicity and culture was different to mine [sic], but who shared my values, than with those with whom I shared an ethnicity or culture but not the same political vision. Politics was not shackled to my identity but *helped me reach beyond it*. (Malik 2020, italics added)

Politics and scholarship are not co-terminous but Malik's comments offer a heuristic spur. Once it is clear that identity can function as a springboard for formulating questions and methods of investigating them, identity scholarship can become a radical tool rather than an end in itself. The values and practices of the scholarly community and openness to extending its reach then enter the debate. To investigate the trends for classics, it is helpful not just to look at the work done on cultural and political identity by critics such as Stuart Hall and Kwame Antony Appiah (Hall 1990; Appiah 1993), but also to consider analyses that have been

---

11 These areas have been the focus of detailed studies published in the Bulletin of the UK Council of University Classical Departments (https://cucd.blogs.sas.ac.uk).
12 For the record, I am female, white, no longer young, born a Bristolian, and probably assimilated to whatever kinds of 'middle-class' labels are now attached to professional academics, but those are externally imposed categories that I would not necessarily select if self-describing.

made of organisations as sites of identity. Here I draw on Andrew Brown's analysis, published in an international journal devoted to Management (Brown 2015). I want to emphasise that in referring to 'identity scholarship' I do not mean scholarly investigation of issues of identity, but rather scholarship that is informed and shaped, wittingly or unwittingly, by the identity of the teacher or researcher, and/or is regarded as such and evaluated accordingly. This can be a positive factor when it leads to the inclusion of marginalised issues or new research questions and data or it can be negative when used to limit the application of the hypotheses that have been tested by the researcher. There is a parallel with the potential and shortcomings of identity politics that I referred to earlier.

Brown uses a working definition of identities as: 'people's constructively construed understanding of who they were, are and desire to become'. In terms of desire to study antiquity and work towards become a professional scholar (teaching and/or research) that provides a general definition. Brown also identifies five interconnected debates in contemporary identity research, centred on notions of: Choice, Stability, Coherence, Positivity, Authenticity.

You may well comment that the summary I have included contains some unargued assumptions about the content and value of all these terms and you would be right. In terms of becoming a professional scholar they are all problematic. They involve some sub-texts. Choice is conditioned by agency and structure; Stability is counter-balanced by fluidity and by openness to challenge and change; Coherence has to accommodate debate, even fragmentation; Positivity is counterbalanced by doubt (an essential for scholarship although, as I have pointed out, doubt can collapse into a more generalised anxiety and pessimism); and as for Authenticity … In terms of scholarship I would characterize this as entailing a scrupulous transparency in identifying questions and methods, evaluating evidence and presenting the conclusions in a manner that is respectful to those who have laboured with equal integrity but have arrived at different judgements.[13] The scholar's duty to 'follow the argument where it leads' will sometimes unearth troubling material and lead to unforeseen (and perhaps unwelcome) conclusions.

My point in querying Brown's categories is to make the point that although identity in classical scholarship is (sometimes) categorised by a strong sense of shared scholarly values and community, in order to achieve that it also has to

---

13 For example, Harloe 2013 and Hardwick 2013 endeavoured in different ways to address thorny questions in current debates about shifts in paradigms and practices in the subject area. The Editors' 'Introduction: Making Connections' to Hardwick and Stray 2008, 1–3, offered a preliminary sketch of some of these issues.

accommodate – and indeed encourage – debates, challenges, difference. It therefore differs in important respect from the kinds of potentially coercive and rigid norms and structures that make up much of the 'business model' deployed in management theory and practice, in which those initiated may be expected to embrace the totality of the 'Brand'.[14]

However, even if admission to the community of classical scholars does not depend on coercion, it is worth glancing at the ways in which norms are established and communicated both within scholarship and beyond. One of the helpful tools in tracking such processes is Nudge Theory. The concept is found in behavioural science, political theory and behaviour economics and it is frequently theorized using models derived from psychology. At their simplest Nudge models describe systems of positive reinforcement and indirect suggestion, suggestions that are intended to influence the decision-making, behaviour and actions of groups and individuals (so linking back to the third of the categories identified by Shay). The term Nudge is commonly applied to a wide range of contexts and issues. The best known specific example of a Nudge situation is probably that of the fly etched in men's urinals with the aim of encouraging accurate aim. However, Nudge practice has also migrated to politics. For example, in 2010 UK Prime Minister David Cameron set up a Nudge Unit to explore and test ways of communicating the advantages and disadvantages of compliant behaviour in payment of taxes and other social priorities.[15] This influenced US President Barack Obama to experiment along the same lines.[16] Obama consulted the Harvard law professor Cass Sunstein and in 2014 the White House launched a Social and Behavioural Science team (SBST) to lead a cross-agency initiative to bring behavioural science into policy making.[17] Similar Units are based in the OECD, the World Bank and the United Nations. All these have in common a wish to promote compliance without enforcement, either because enforcement is not plausible (e.g. in terms of resources or democratic and civic values) or (more sinisterly) because the point of the exercise is that the subjects must not be aware that they are

---

14 There is, however, some relevance to scholarship here in that universities increasingly use business and marketing models in which research and teaching are characterised and regulated in ways derived from management theory. Furthermore, these sometimes involve promotion of the Brand of a particular institution.
15 The Editors have pointed out to me the 'benevolent' potential in employment of Nudge techniques to promote awareness and positive action in respect of the climate emergency.
16 Wright 2015 records that the President signed an executive order directing the federal government to make use of behavioural science to 'improve the efficiency and effectiveness of government programmes'.
17 Vinik 2015 offers an account and critique of this experiment.

being nudged in a particular direction. The possible lack of transparency associated with Nudge can be partially contrasted with other means of bringing about desired behaviour, such as education and legislation.

The best-known theorization of Nudge is probably in Richard Thaler and Cass Sunstein's book *Nudge: Improving Decisions about Health, Wealth and Happiness* (Thaler and Sunstein 2008). They coined two terms that have stuck with the concept. The first is *libertarian paternalism*, which implies both the liberty not to do what one is being nudged towards and the assumption that 'those who know best' are nudging one in a good direction. The second term they coined, and the one that is most important for my argument here, is *choice architecture*. In that scenario, Nudgers are the architects of choice. That is, they design and populate spaces that frame what people may choose to do (and think). In scholarship the concept of 'choice architecture' is readily applicable to curricula, to the structure and content of research projects, commentaries and much else besides. It subtly shapes what people experience, intellectually and materially, how they respond to it and relates that to their own future decisions, what they do — and by extension, the outcomes for them (including gaining high grades, appointments and promotions and the approbation of their colleagues, research funders and publishers).

Nudging involves appealing to senses of identity, whether based on experience or aspiration. This may involve a simple use of triggers such as 'we' and 'our' to massage readers' and listeners' identification with the judgements being communicated. Even apparently dispassionate scholarly work is inevitably infused with persuasion to accept arguments and observations. For example, in his influential commentary on Sophocles' *Antigone*, Richard Jebb's persuader words include 'naturally' (to describe Creon's irritated response to a woman's defiance, line 679: Jebb 2004, 129). Other nudges given at this point in the commentary depend on words such as 'tact' and 'deference'. The values are those of Jebb's time and it is equally salutary to identify and reflect on the persuader words that are used in present-day commentaries to shape users' responses. As with reading translations, reading commentaries requires a critical distance (which students can and should be encouraged to develop). Even the best scholarly work cannot be detached from its language and context.[18]

Critique of Nudge theory and practice may suggest that Nudge is a euphemism for psychological manipulation. Critics make the points that Nudging can

---

[18] See comments in the Preface to Harrison 2001. Kraus and Stray 2016 includes essays on the history and evaluation of commentaries.

be short-term in its effects and that it diminishes autonomy. In terms of scholarship that would be a serious criticism, since academic freedom is so highly valued. Therefore, I do want to probe a bit further and ask about the extent to which the famed intellectual rigour of the classical (or any other) scholarly community can actually be somewhat cosmetic. There is a certain *cursus honorum* (although it is not unknown for a *res publica* to mutate into empire). Identity can be 'caught'; it can also be imposed. Put bluntly, does acceptance into the company of professional scholars involve a smoothing out of other potentially overlapping identities that are part of the individual *persona* and of lived and inherited experience? Can this involve a suppression of aspiration for the setting of alternative agendas (intellectual and cultural)? What difference is made when perceived and historically evident barriers of gender, race, or sexuality are dismantled or rendered negotiable? And how can any differences made to classical scholarship be identified and described?

There are many double-binds involved in trying to answer these questions. For instance, there has been distinguished work done in both teaching and research to retrieve female classicists from the historical limbo to which most of them had been consigned. Female scholars have been appointed to senior positions. Yet to ask whether the theory and practice of scholarship itself has been changed by this risks on the one hand falling into the trap of essentialism (i.e. assuming that women think and work in particular ways precisely because they are women) and so on *vel sim.* in terms of race and ethnicity. The trap on the other hand is equally awkward: if the norms and aspirations of scholarship remain unchanged, it can be said that the 'outsiders' have been normalised into the (predominantly white) patriarchy that set and developed those scholarly practices and criteria, including the topics for research and teaching and the questions asked of received wisdom about them. Indeed, access to the power systems at play may be part of the attraction of work in classics — and, as the 2015 essay collection edited by Stead and Hall as part of the *Classics and Class* project has shown, initiates may use classical resonances to embrace enthusiastically the values of the powerful rather than to challenge the *status quo* (Hardwick 2015). Do new topics and different kinds of evidence require not only new questions but also experiments in ways of interrogating and evaluating sources before they can be accepted as providing 'evidence' that supports judgements? In the long term investigating 'what difference was made' will require strong powers of Stray-like detection to locate and work through archival material, including annotated texts, letters and other unpublished sources.[19]

****

I would now like to move on to the third area identified by Shay, the public realm. There is some encouragement to be found in current projects generated by neighbouring subject areas and I will mention just two of those before commenting on the extent to which classical studies in general has the potential to 'come out of the closet' and make a distinctive contribution.

Professor Mona Baker, a leading translation studies teacher and researcher, heads an international project on the Genealogies of Knowledge, which has implications not just for how scholarship itself is framed and transmitted but also for how scholars operate in the wider public domain. The Genealogies Project hosted a conference in Manchester in 2019 which, *inter alia*, aimed to challenge Edward Said's ideal of the public intellectual as a beacon of fiercely independent incorruptibility and an expression of the norms of liberal democracy. It aimed to generate critical examination of his view as a product of place and time. There are bound to be implications for the corresponding myth of the classical scholar as embodying similar qualities.

Chris Stray has already raised questions about the extent to which admission into classical scholarship involves admission into shared codes. 'Shared codes' can imply something that could be described as 'classical values' as well as pointing to methods of categorising and interrogating sources and the criteria for making judgements in response to specific questions. However, these issues are not confined to one discipline, nor to academic life. Sometimes looking outside one's own immediate intellectual environment aids clarity. As Arundhati Roy put it in her 2018 Sebald Lecture at the British Library on the topic 'What is the Morally

---

19 Wyles and Hall, in the Introduction to their edited collection of essays on women and scholarship have started to engage with these questions (Wyles and Hall 2016), as have Cox and Theodorakopoulos 2019. To my knowledge at present, systematic investigation of the long-term effects on scholarship of senses of racial and ethnic identity has yet to be undertaken, although prosopographical studies are opening the way to this, notably Ronnick 2006 and 2011. The essays in Hardwick and Gillespie 2007 and Cox 2011 and 2018 primarily address the work of creative practitioners in the arts and literature rather than that of scholars, as does Hurst 2006. Stephens/Vasunia, 2010 focuses on national identities. Hall/Stead 2020 focuses on class, with some discussion of gender and ethnicity. The Postclassicisms Collective 2020 unfortunately appeared too late to be discussed here. Its chapters on 'Knowing' (2.5) and 'Situations' (2.7) are particularly relevant. The authors identify their driving question as 'how does who you are affect how you engage with antiquity?' (144). See also Goff (2013a).

Appropriate Language in which to Think and Write': 'people who speak the same language are not necessarily those who understand one another best'.[20] Roy self-identifies as the opponent of 'one nation, one religion, one language' and points to schisms within as well as between communities. She picks up Mona Baker's term 'a companionship of languages', which was coined to represent the mutuality of source and target languages in translation studies. Roy adapts this to image an 'infusion' of languages, not as a scattering of quotes or tags from different languages but as a mutually enhancing relationship. For example, she refers to her novel *The Ministry* as 'written in English but imagined in several languages'. Her approach might equally well prompt examination of the dialogue between languages, modes of discourse and underlying assumptions in subject communities of scholars.[21] This is relevant to two key questions for practising classicists and ancient historians: (i) in what language(s) do classical scholars think and imagine, as well as write?[22] (ii) given that Greek and Latin make even imperial languages, such as English, become subaltern, does this assist classicists to achieve polyphonic perspectives on debates inside and outside their field? In her lecture Roy commented that: 'my English has been widened and deepened by the rhythms and cadences of my alien mother's other tongues'.

Following on once more from Shay's encouragement to engage with public issues, the next area to mention is this: how can classical scholarship best engage with wider debates about the past — in terms of analysis, judgements (intellectual and ethical) and in terms of how the past is represented and communicated in the present? This is a huge and challenging question that permeates many current issues — for example, disputes about the naming of buildings and philanthropic projects (as in debates in the city of Bristol about the Colston Hall and in

---

20 The 2017 W.G. Sebald Lecture was given by Michael Longley, who deploys Greek and Roman texts in many of his poems. The 2019 Lecture was given by Emily Wilson (see n. 5 above).
21 'Words and the Company They Keep' was the subject of the Oxford seminar series in autumn 2019 co-hosted by the *Classics And Poetry Now* network and the *Archive of Performances of Greek and Roman Drama*.
22 In a forthcoming essay I hope to reflect on the 'inner translations' that take place in the intellects and imaginations of authors of commentaries and other scholarly works (Hardwick forthcoming). These 'inner translations' involve movements across and between ancient and modern languages and, especially in the case of multi-lingual scholarship, *between* modern languages (including in translations of academic presentations and publications). This is an area of intersection between scholarship, hermeneutics and reception that has been under-researched.

Oxford's Corpus Christi College about the renaming of the Fraenkel Room to become the Refugee Scholars' Room);[23] the siting of statues; the award and retention of blue plaques and other marks of historical recognition.

Underlying these debates are deep questions about how a society and its institutions recognise and characterize their historical involvement in empire, slavery, misogyny, genocide and their effects in the present. These are sites for struggle. Usually the victors get to decide, although their dominance may not last. For example, the toppling of the statue of Sadaam Hussein in Iraq was widely presented in TV news films in the West in the context of defeat for Sadaam and victory for Western forces and Iraqi dissidents. More recently there has been extensive interest in the fate of statues of Confederate generals in the US and of colonialist icons such as Cecil Rhodes in South Africa and in the UK. You may have your own examples.

For the purposes of this essay two aspects of these struggles seem to me to be especially important. The first is that the history of the statues and of the debates surrounding them provide an index to political and cultural shifts. Within that frame the second important aspect is that who erected the statue and how it was designated can itself involve an element of appropriation of the past in the service of subsequent values. For example, in 2020 the toppling of the statue of Edward Colston in Bristol involved a complex set of issues. Colston (1636–1721) was a slave trader who had devoted a substantial proportion of his fortune to philanthropic educational and cultural work in Bristol and elsewhere. The Royal Africa Company with which he was associated had trafficked over 84,000 people (including 12,000 children) from West Africa to the Americas. The statue of him was a late nineteenth-century installation, commissioned and erected in 1895 long after the slave trade itself was abolished. The Bristol city authorities who authorized this were fully aware of the origins of Colston's wealth but chose to inscribe with the statue a eulogy assimilating him to Victorian values:[24] 'Erected by the citizens of Bristol as a memorial of one of the most virtuous and wise sons of that city'. The statue was unveiled by the then Mayor of Bristol and the Bishop of Bristol. In 1977 it was given the architectural and historical status of Grade 2 listing. In the late twentieth and early twenty-first centuries there were petitions asking for the addition of a detailed explanatory plaque and suggesting resiting in the city's Museum. Alternative art installations were created as a form of challenge

---

23 See Elsner's essay in this volume.
24 A summary, with images of the statue and supporting Bibliography, can be found at wikipedia.org.wiki/statue_of_Edward_Colston

and protest. The requests for removal of Colston's statue were resisted.[25] In 2020 the Black Lives Matter movement provided a catalyst and on 7 June Colston's statue was toppled and thrown into Bristol Dock.[26] The example of Colston and the debates and events surrounding the statue provide a microcosm for study of the threads involved in assessing and commemorating the past and the successive appropriations that occur.[27] In that respect, the episode also provides a heuristic metaphor for some of the challenges revealed in the history of scholarship.

Illuminating this field, there is important work being done in Memory Studies.[28] As the *Trackers* epigraph to this essay suggests 'Memory runs a marathon'. In theoretical terms, three influential models of memory have been identified: antagonistic, cosmopolitan, agonistic (Bull *et al.*). The last of these has specific resonances with Greek literature and history. *Agonistic* memory serves as a contrast to concepts of *antagonistic* memory (i.e. 'them and us', 'goodies and baddies') and *cosmopolitan* memory (that seeks a consensual judgement that implies 'universal' collective belonging and can result in confrontation with those who are excluded). Agonistic memory involves listening to arguments and recognising that there are different experiences of past events. It underlies and informs practices of restorative justice, of truth and reconciliation commissions, for instance as developed in post-apartheid South Africa.[29] The deployment of an agonistic memory model is also found in recent approaches to curating in War Museums (for example, the Imperial War Museum's *Lest We Forget* project); in the collaboration between Nottingham Trent University and the Ulster Museum in

---

[25] A city councillor described the aims as 'revisionist'.
[26] This action was, in effect, a performative irony, as not only was the statue thrown into the waters near where slave ships had sailed but the action also recalled the fate of many of the enslaved Africans who were thrown overboard alive during the Atlantic crossing if sickness or shortage of food threatened the success of the traders. Olivette Otele, Professor of the History of Slavery at Bristol University has drawn attention to the fact that many other slave traders are still uncritically celebrated in Bristol and elsewhere, while the legacy of poverty, racism and modern slavery remain to be tackled (Otele 2019).
[27] For an example which draws on complicated colonial histories and the use of classical sculpture, see Evans (2007) which discusses histories surrounding the Voortrekker monument in South Africa. At the time of publication, the inclusion of an essay on that topic in a volume on classical receptions was considered questionable by some critics.
[28] On antiquity and its reception this includes a substantial project *Memoria Romana*, led by Karl Galinsky (Galinsky 2014; https://www.press.umich.edu/6421151/memoria.romana; www.laits.utexas.edu/memoria).
[29] Yael Farber's play *Molora* (published text 1998) contributed to this through her re-imagining of Aeschylus' *Oresteia*, in which the Areopagus of *Eumenides* was replaced by a framework based on the Truth and Reconciliation process (Van Zyl Smit 2010; Hardwick 2010).

the *Voices of 68: Contested Pasts* project; and in the UNREST project — *Unsettling, Remembering, Social Cohesion in Transnational Europe*.

Understanding why people thought and acted as they did can bring contexts and value judgements into dialogue and support aspirations for a better future without repressing or sanitizing the past. Classics and ancient history provide important threads that run through these. I could cite, for example, how the subject area and its scholars have been imbricated in the struggles through which Germany has had to come to terms with its past; how creative writers such as Derek Walcott and Seamus Heaney have deployed and sometimes repositioned material from Greece and Rome.[30] However, I also want to suggest that the potential contribution of classics and ancient history scholarship and teaching goes beyond case studies and beyond classical reception research. The subject matter of classics and ancient history is based on societies and cultures founded on slavery, xenophobia and misogyny, preserved through force and by various kinds of empire and class/status denigration, transmitted via privilege and subsequently frequently, although not exclusively, deployed in the service of values based on oligarchy and colonialism (internal and external). That it is the discipline's research that has revealed this, and that much significant work has been done to reconstruct lost and neglected evidence and to retrieve lost voices, does serve to redress imbalance but does not change the basic truths.

What is important is how such unpalatable facts are faced; how scholars can best assess how and to what extent these situations were identified, explored and challenged in antiquity; how judgements can best be made about the extent to which the ancient texts, ideas and values seeded subsequent ones; how the extent to which subsequent values were grafted back onto antiquity (that equally includes what might be described as 'progressive' values) can be assessed and communicated (and to whom). All these are the fabric of the study of Greek and Roman antiquity and its receptions. I suggest we can also put this work to greater use.

The histories of classics and ancient history scholarship and public engagement provide a prototype for the kind of 'facing up to the past' that present societies as a whole now have to do. Classical scholars and students have the advantage of critical distance because the past of Greece and Rome is both distant and different, and yet is also an agent in the development of subsequent cultural and political frames and attitudes. The histories of the discipline also offer the

---

30 See further the essays in Harrison 2009; Parker and Mathews 2011, Harrison *et al.* 2019. The essays in Richardson 2019 examine the role of classical receptions in times of crisis.

opportunity to use comparative perspectives — different times, places, languages, cultures. For all of these sites Greek and Roman antiquity is important but is neither a totally defining characteristic nor confined to any one place, time or receiving culture. Of course there is a risk — this time of appearing to claim exceptionalism for the study of Greek and Roman antiquity.[31] So I prefer to use the term 'distinctive contribution' to cover the role of classics research and public engagement in addressing these deep issues.[32]

One final point. It is often said that the job of scholars in the public domain (and in the academic community with which they identify) is to discuss complex ideas in a straightforward way. Lucidity is an honourable aspiration but it is not the same as simplicity. There is another side to the coin. The job of scholars is also to undermine easy assumptions about simplicity (whether rhetorical or substantive). They should not be afraid of trying to analyse and communicate complexity and nuance (lucidly of course). In so doing scholars will also make a contribution to the current public debates about how best to recognise, explain and debate the awful strands in everyone's histories, rather than to deny, repress and erase them.

Bibliography

Appiah, K.A. (1993), 'Thick Translation', *Calaloo* 16 (4), 808–819.
Armstrong, R. (2008), 'Classical Translation of the Classics: The Dynamics of Literary Tradition in Retranslating Epic Poetry', in: Lianeri/Zajko 2008, 169–202.
Brown, A. (2015), 'Identities and identity work in organizations', *International Journal of Management Reviews*, 17, 20–40.
Brown, A./Coupland, C. (2015), 'Identity threats, identity work, and elite professionals', *Organisation Studies* 36.10, 1315–1336.
Bull, A., *et al.*, https://researchportal.bath.ac.uk/en/publications/on-agonistic-memory

---

[31] 'Exceptionalism' brings adverse connotations because of its use, laden with associations of value, power and entitlement, to vindicate imperial and racial hegemonies and, more parochially, its associations with the grand narratives associated with classics and classicism.

[32] The poet, translator and critic Josephine Balmer has characterized scholarship as potentially 'poetic' in its imagination and 'inspirational' in its effects (in a paper that examined 'Poetic Inspiration from non-literary Texts', Oxford 28 October 2019). Holmes 2016 makes an inspirational case for *cosmopoiesis* which she interprets as: 'the building of worlds that bring sometimes unusual constellations of ancient texts together with live elements in the present in creative symbiosis'. Holmes acknowledges that this process is 'processual, partial and contingent' and yet by virtue of those qualities is also 'integral to the world of living together and living well' (Holmes 2016, 285).

Butler, S. (ed.) (2016), *Deep Classics: Rethinking Classical Reception*, London.
Classics and Class Research Project, dir. Professor E. Hall, www.classicsandclass/about-us/ (now *The People's History of Classics*).
Cox, F. (2011), *Sybilline Sisters: Virgil's Presence in Contemporary Women's Writing*, Oxford.
Cox, F. (2018), *Ovid's Presence in Contemporary Women's Writing*, Oxford.
Cox, F./Theodorakopoulos, E. (eds.) (2019), *Homer's Daughters: Women's Response to Homer in the Twentieth Century and Beyond*, Oxford.
DiAngelo, R. (2011), 'White Fragility', *International Journal of Critical Pedagogy* 3, 54–70.
DiAngelo, R. (2018), *White Fragility: Why it's so hard for White People to talk about Racism*, Boston.
Evans, R. (2007), 'Perspectives on Post-Colonialism in South Africa: The Voortrekker Monument's Classical Heritage', in: Hardwick/Gillespie 2007, 141–156.
Ezzueduemhoi, J.I.A. (2009), *A Fundamental Greek Course*, Lanham MD.
Galinsky, K. (ed.) (2014), *Memoria Romana: Memory in Rome and Rome in Memory*, Ann Arbor.
Genealogies of Knowledge (AHRC funded project directed by Professor Mona Baker) genealogies of knowledge.net
Goff, B. (2013a), *Your Secret Language: Classics in the British Colonies of West Africa*, London.
Goff, B. (2013b), 'Classics in African Education: The Rhetoric of Colonial Commissions', in: Hardwick/Harrison 2013, 157–169.
Goff, B./Simpson, M. (2007), *Crossroads in the Black Aegean: Oedipus, Antigone and Dramas of the Africa Diaspora*, Oxford.
Hall, E./Harrop, S. (eds.) (2010), *Theorising Performance: Greek Drama, Cultural History and Critical Practice*, London.
Hall, E./Macintosh, F./Wrigley, A. (eds.) (2004), *Dionysus Since 69: Greek Tragedy at the Dawn of the Third Millennium*, Oxford.
Hall, E./Stead, H. (2020), *A People's History of Classics: Class and Graeco-Roman Antiquity in Britain and Ireland 1689 to 1939*, London.
Hall, S. (1990), 'Cultural identity and Diaspora', in: Rutherford 1990, 222–237.
Hallett, J. (2001), 'The Personal Voice in Classical Scholarship: Literary and Theoretical Reflections', *Arethusa* 34, 133–135.
Hallett, J./Van Nortwick, T. (eds.) (1997), *Compromising Traditions: The Personal Voice in Classical Scholarship*, London/New York.
Hardwick, L. (2004), 'Greek Drama and Anti-colonialism: Decolonizing Classics', in: Hall *et al.* 2004, 219–42.
Hardwick, L. (2010), 'Negotiating Translation for the Stage', in: Hall/Harrop 2010, 192–207.
Hardwick, L. (2013), 'Against the 'Democratic Turn': Counter-texts; Counter-contexts; Counter-arguments', in: Hardwick/Harrison 2013, 15–32.
Hardwick, L. (2018), 'The poetics of cultural memory: World War 1 refractions of ancient peace' *Classical Receptions Journal* 10.4 [Special Issue: *Classics and Classicists in World War One*, ed. E. Pender], 393–414.
Hardwick, L. (forthcoming 2021), 'Epic /between translation and reception: Translation writes back', in: Lianeri/Armstrong 2021.
Hardwick, L./Gillespie, C. (eds.) (2007), *Classics in Post-Colonial Worlds*, Oxford.
Hardwick, L./Stray, C. (eds.) (2008), *A Companion to Classical Receptions*, Oxford/Malden, MA.
Hardwick, L./Harrison, S. (eds.) (2013), *Classics in the Modern World: A 'Democratic Turn'?*, Oxford.

Hardwick, L./Harrison, S./Vandiver, E. (forthcoming 2021), *Classical Warriors: Greece and Rome in Some Poets of the First World War*, Oxford.
Harloe, K. (2013), 'Questioning the Democratic and Democratic Questioning' in: Hardwick/Harrison 2013, 3–13.
Harrison, S. (ed.) (2001), *Texts, Ideas and the Classics; Scholarship, Theory and Classical Literature*, Oxford.
Harrison, S. (ed.) (2009), *Living Classics; Greece and Rome in Contemporary Poetry in English*, Oxford.
Harrison, S./Macintosh, F./Eastman, H. (eds.) (2019), *Seamus Heaney and the Classics: Bann Valley Muses*, Oxford.
Harrison, T. (1990), *The Trackers of Oxyrhynchus*, London.
Holmes, B. (2016), '*Cosmopoiesis* in the Field of "The Classical"', in: Butler 2016, 269–289.
Hurst, I. (2006), *Victorian Women Writers and the Classics: The Feminine of Homer*, Oxford.
Jebb, R.C. (2004) [originally 1900], *Sophocles: Plays:* Antigone, Bristol.
Lianeri, A./Zajko, V. (eds.) (2008), *Translation and the Classic: Identity as Change in the History of Cultures*, Oxford.
Lianeri, A./Armstrong, R. (eds.) (2021), *A Companion to the Translation of Greek and Latin Epic*.
Malik, K. (2020), 'The Rise of White Identity Politics', *Prospect Magazine*, July 13.
Malamud, M. (2013), 'Classics as a Weapon: African Americans and the Fight for Inclusion in American Democracy', in: Hardwick/Harrison 2013, 89–103.
Kraus, C.S./Stray, C. (eds.) (2016), *Classical Commentaries: Explorations in a Scholarly Genre*, Oxford.
Otele, O. (2019, 2020 hb forthcoming), *African Europeans: An Untold Story*, London.
Parker, J./Mathews, T. (eds.) (2011), *Tradition, Translation, Trauma*, Oxford.
Rankine, P. (2006), *Ulysses in Black: Ralph Ellison, Classicism and Africa American Literature*, Madison.
Reynolds, D. (2013), *The Long Shadow: The Great War in the Twentieth* Century, New York.
Richardson, E. (ed.) (2019), *Classics in Extremis: The Edges of Classical Reception*, London.
Ronnick, M. (ed.) (2006), *The Works of William Saunders Scarborough: Black Classicist and Race Leader*, New York.
Ronnick, M. (2016), 'Classical Education and the Advancement of African American Women, from the Eighteenth Century to the Twentieth Century', in: Wyles/Hall 2016, 176–193.
Roy, A. (2018), 'What is the Morally Appropriate Language in Which to Think and Write?', *WG Sebald Lecture in Literary Translation*, delivered at the British Library, 5 June 2018. Video link to You Tube at the British Centre for Literary Translation website, www.bclt.org.uk/sebald-lecture-2018; text (no pagination) at www.lithub.com/what-is-the-morally-appropriate-language-in-which-to-think-and-write/
Rutherford, J. (ed.) (1990), *Identity, Community, Culture, Difference*, London.
Shay, J. (1994), *Achilles in Vietnam: Combat Trauma and the Undoing of Character*, New York.
Shay, J. (2002), *Odysseus in America: Combat Trauma and the Trials of Homecoming*, with foreword by Senators John McCain and Max Cleland, New York/London/Toronto/Sydney/Singapore.
Stead, H. (2019), 'Classics Down the Mineshaft: A Buried History', in: Richardson 2019, 136–156.
Stead, H./Hall, E. (eds.) (2015), *Greek and Roman Classics in the British Struggle for Social Reform*, London.
Stephens, S./Vasunia, P. (eds.) (2010), *Classics and National Cultures*, Oxford.

Thaler, R./Sunstein, C. (2008), *Nudge: Improving Decisions about Health, Wealth and Happiness*, London.
The Postclassicisms Collective (2020), *Postclassicisms*, Chicago/London.
Unsettling, Remembering, Social Cohesion in Transnational Europe (UNREST), unrest.eu
Van Zyl Smit, B. (2010), 'Orestes and the Truth and Reconciliation Commission', *Classical Receptions Journal* 2, 114–135.
Voices of 68: Contested Pasts Ulster Museum and Nottingham Trent University, nmni.com/news/voices-of-68-exhibition
Vinik, D. (2015), Politico.com 15 October.
Wilson, E. (2017), *The Odyssey: Homer*, New York.
Wright, O. (2015), *Independent*, 16 September, 'Barack Obama to bring Whitehall's 'nudge' theory to the White House: US to embrace behavioural science technique popularised in Britain'.
Wyles, R./Hall, E. (eds.) (2016), *Women Classical Scholars: Unsealing the Fountain from the Renaissance to Jacqueline de Romilly*, Oxford.

Part II: **Early Modern**

Edith Hall
Classics Invented: Books, Schools, Universities and Society 1679–1742

In 1740 an anonymous novel was published in London which purported to be an English translation of a manuscript travelogue penned by a French Lesbian.[1] The ironically named Mademoiselle Alithia ('Truth') de Richelieu, cousin of the Duke Richelieu, had allegedly travelled across Europe dressed as a nobleman, accompanied by her maid Lucy attired as her male valet. At the town of Blois in the Loire valley, Alithia is a participant in a pseudo-Platonic dialogue held at the house of the local bishop. After one lengthy peroration by a Marquis on the human passions, the Count with whom our heroine is travelling suggests that the Marquis continue tomorrow, 'as my Friend here, pointing to me, is very fond of the Poetical Works of the Ancients and Moderns, and is forever poring on the Classics, I hope you'll favour us To-morrow with your Thoughts upon the Passions in Poetry'.[2] The Marquis does not wait, but continues immediately; 'the Classics' he discusses include the *Aeneid*, the *Iliad*, Ovid's *Metamorphoses*, Cicero's *In Catilinam*, the *Fables of Phaedrus and Aesop,* and Seneca's tragedies.

Shortly afterwards, 'Alithia' inserts into her first-person account a treatise on morality penned by a Scotsman by name of Mr Somers whom she encountered at Montpellier, a city with one of the oldest universities in Europe, and a longstanding association with Protestant intellectual culture. His discourse recommends to statesmen that they observe religion and practise public piety:

> The World is much influenced by Example, especially the Lower Class of Men, by that of their betters; so that the former (who in every State make the Bulk of the People) are much strengthened in their Belief of Religion.[3]

Within a very few pages, the terms *Classics* and *class* have been used to denote something equivalent to what they mean today, and the Greek and Latin classical

---

[1] My title, as a tribute to his pioneering volume *Classics Transformed*, is intended to express my profound intellectual debt to Chris Stray, who has been a mentor and staunch friend for more than thirty years. He taught me to love old Classics textbooks, and it is that enthusiasm which prompted the intensive investigation of early 18th-century volumes in this article. Some of the discussion here overlaps with parts of chapters 1 and 2 of Hall and Stead 2020, a book resulting from an AHRC-funded project, *Classics and Class 1689–1939*, on which Chris proved a most valuable consultant and contributor to an earlier volume; see Stray 2015.
[2] Richelieu 1740, vol. II, 68.
[3] Richelieu 1740, vol. II, 72.

https://doi.org/10.1515/9783110719215-003

authors have been identified by leisured aristocrats as their preferred reading matter. This seems to be only the second known instance in English printed texts of the two terms in proximity.

In 1736, we find the first use of term 'class' in its modern, socio-economic sense being used alongside 'Classics', but the social distinction here is not the typically French one of nobility versus 'the bulk' of the nation's people as constituted by the lower class. It is used to make a distinction between two types of British people prosperous enough to purchase their sons an education (it is imperative that we keep in mind that nearly half of the children of Britain, two million, were given even rudimentary schooling only by the passing of the Elementary Education Act 1870). A Georgian polemicist questions the point of boys spending most of the hours available for education on acquiring proficiency in the ancient languages, when reading relevant material had a more obvious application to the aspiring businessman. Teachers are 'as capable of contributing to the Welfare or Prejudice of a State, as any of the several Classes of Men of which it is composed'; learning Latin, especially how to compose verses in Latin, inculcates no skills useful to commerce. Better to read newspapers instead: several famous writers 'spell and write English perfectly (better than others who have read the Classics), tho' they are quite ignorant of Latin.'[4]

Neither term had ever been used in such a sense a mere sixty years earlier. There had of course been precursors of the curriculum suggested by the term Classics, notably the list of Christian books supplemented by pagan authors constituting the *Ratio atque Institutio Studiorum*. This was designed by Jesuits in Rome in 1599 and exported across the planet by the Society of Jesus' missionaries.[5] But the anti-Jesuit paranoia ever after the Gun Powder Plot of 1605 had helped to prevent any such systematised set of recommended texts taking hold in the British Isles.

Christopher Stray's *Classics Transformed* (1998) has itself transformed our understanding of the sociology of British Classics education in the 19th and earlier 20th centuries.[6] Other studies of the social context of Victorian Classics have subsequently appeared, including Stephen Harrison's fine (2017) *Victorian Horace: Classics and Class*.[7] But the present chapter delves into a previous era in British Classics. By looking at a substantial number of school and university textbooks, it argues that the emergence of Classics as a distinct curriculum under that

---

4 Stonehouse 1736, 4, 10. My emphases.
5 See Cueva, Byrne, and Benda 2009.
6 Stray 1998a; see also Stray 1998b and 1999.
7 Harrison 2017. See also, amongst others, Vasunia 2005.

name, comprising the study of the Latin and Greek authors in their original languages with complementary publications relating to 'classical' history, religion, myth, geography, artefacts and 'antiquities', emerged in England (after 1707 Britain) between the 1670s and about 1715. This was partly in response to the famous French series of editions *Ad Usum Delphini* originally designed for Louis de France, 'Le Grand Dauphin' (1661-1711), the eldest son of Louis XIV. But in Britain, the invention of Classics took place in a different social context, where the power of the monarchy had been curtailed by the Bill of Rights 1689, and the power of the nobility was being challenged by an ambitious mercantile middle class. The term 'class' acquired its precise modern sense slightly later than 'Classics', but (as we have seen) by the mid-1730s sprang naturally enough to the mind of an author discussing the appropriate education for the male offspring of Britons with means.

In 1635 the word 'classics' could still mean 'trumpets' or 'trumpets-calls', as the neuter noun *classicum*, plural *classica*, did in canonical ancient authors.[8] In 1635 King Charles I commissioned an epic poem on the achievements of his ancestor King Edward III from Thomas May, renowned translator of Lucan's *Civil War*. In one passage May draws a comparison with the impact made by Julius' Caesar's army in France long ago,

> When dreadfull Classicks in all parts were heard,
> And threatning Eagles every where appear'd.[9]

By 'dreadfull Classicks' being heard in all parts, May clearly does not mean that Caesar subjected the Gauls to long recitations of ancient Greek and Latin literary works.

When the Romans heard their Latin noun *classis*, it contained a resonance that we do not hear when we say class: deriving from the same root as the verb *clamare* ('call out'), a *classis* consisted of a group of people 'called out' or 'summoned' together by trumpets. The word has always been associated with Servius Tullius, the sixth of the legendary kings of early Rome, who was thought to have held the first census in order to find out, for the purposes of military planning, what assets his people possessed (Livy I.42–4). Yet, by the second third of the 18th century, the term was adopted in order to distinguish different strata within English society. The plural *Classics*, meanwhile, had been used in English by 1679, as we shall see, to designate the corpus of Greek and Latin writings. But it

---

8 See e.g. Livy 28.27.15, Caesar, *Civil War* 3.82; Virgil, *Aeneid* 7.637.
9 May 1635, book VII, n.p.

is to the legendary first census that the origins of the term Classics must also be traced. In Servius' scheme, the men in the top of his six classes — the men with the most money and property — were called the *classici*. The Top Men were 'Classics'. By the time of the late second-century AD Roman miscellanist Aulus Gellius, the Top Authors could by metaphorical extension be called 'Classic Authors', *scriptores classici*, to distinguish them from inferior or metaphorically 'proletarian' authors, *scriptores proletarii* (*Noctes Attici* 19.8.15). The involvement, historically, of the study of Greece and Rome with the maintenance of socio-economic hierarchies is thus transparent in the label Classics.[10]

The *Attic Nights* was a favourite Renaissance and Early Modern text, first printed in 1469. By 1602, the adjective classic, variously spelt classick, classicke and classique, is found occasionally, if only in scholarly contexts, to describe a canonical text: William Perkins writes in a theological work written in 1602, 'Neither Plinie (who writ after Paul) nor any other ancient classique author, doth make mention of Phrigia.'[11] He needs to distinguish between 'ancient' classic authors and more recent ones, and he also seems to include St. Paul's epistles amongst 'classical' works. We find the term 'classic' used of a 'folio' in 1628,[12] and a 'word' in the Latin language in 1646.[13] And by 1645, with the increasing familiarity of the Greek treatise *On the Sublime* in European literary circles, Sir Dudley North fuses the idea of a top literary *class* derived from Aulus Gellius with the new interest in sublimity: 'Farre more sublime and better Authours have discovered as little order, and as much repetition; witnesse the Collections of Marcus Aurelius, St. Augustines Confessions, and some of a higher Classe.'[14] By 1694, the former Archbishop of Canterbury, Willian Sancroft, can be praised posthumously by another learned divine for having being 'an admirable Critic in all the Antient and Classic Knowledge, both among the Greeks and Romans', although here, too, the words 'antient and classic' probably include biblical literature.[15]

The tendency to include biblical literature and patristic writers in the category of 'classic' authors persisted in some quarters for decades.[16] Erasmus' *Colloquies* also find themselves in catalogues of 'Classics' until at least 1714.[17] But,

---

10 See further Hall 2008.
11 Perkins 1604, vi. 657. Perkins was incorrect; Phrygia is ubiquitous in ancient authors.
12 Earle 1630, xxxiii.
13 Browne 1646, vol. V.xiii, 253.
14 North 1645, vol. III, 181.
15 'M.M.', in Sancroft 1694, xiii.
16 Bentley 1713, 62.
17 Anon. 1714, 'Advertisement'.

by late in the 17th century, the plural noun with a definite article, 'the Classics', begins at least occasionally to mean, without further qualification, texts written in antiquity by non-Christian ancient authors in Latin and ancient Greek. The 17th-century examples, however, remain few.

The earliest I have identified appears in a text where one schoolmaster writes to an implied specialist audience of teachers. It is a guide to Latin syntax published in 1679, written by one Jonathan Banks. The author's intention was to simplify the famous 16th-century Latin grammar of William Lyly: the full title is *Januae clavis: or, Lilly's syntax explained its elegancy from good authors cleared, its fundamentals compared with the Accidence, and the rules thereof more fitted to the capacity of children*. In the Preface, Banks explains the system he has used for explaining the different types of verb: 'The Rules...are explain'd by adding the *Verbs*...whose variety is shewn, and whose difficulties are cleared by contracted sentences out of the *Classics*.'[18] So there it is, although of course 'the Classics' here means books, or possibly authors, writing in classical Latin rather than in Latin and Greek.

Yet, in 1684, 'the Classics' first occurs meaning ancient authors, certainly including Greek ones, as studied by well-to-do junior males. That year an English translation of Eutropius' *Breviarium historiae Romanae* was published, and its authorship credited to 'several young gentlemen privately educated in Hatton-Garden'; Hatton Garden was a new residential development off Holborn with splendid houses. It was favoured by the rich and aristocratic wishing to flee the squalor of the old city, which had succumbed to a bout of plague in 1665 and gone up in the flames of the Great Fire of 1666. The Eutropius translation was intended to serve as an advertisement for the school. It was prefaced by a poem entitled 'To the ingenious translators' praising the efforts of these 'Auspicious Youths, our Ages Hope, and Pride, / Exalted minds'. The dedicatory verses are by the Irish poet Nahum Tate, whose adaptations of Shakespearean plays were currently all the rage in London. He praises their teacher while regretting his own less happy experience of reading ancient authors: he had been

> by Pedants led astray,
> Who at my setting out mistook the way.
> With Terms confounded (such their methods were)
> Those rules my Cloud, that should have been my Star:
> Yet groping forwards **through the Classicks** went,
> Nor wholly of my Labors may repent.

---

18 Banks 1679, 'Preface', n.p.

Later in the poem, Tate recommends that they move on to read not only Cicero but Demosthenes.

This Preface by the Hatton Garden schoolmaster Lewis Maidwell is dedicated to Baronet John Lowther, whose two sons attended the school and were amongst the translators (the experience did not prevent them leading degenerate lives!).[19] Its list of excellent things the boys may find in ancient authors include material which shows they might expect to study, in addition to Latin, Homer, Plutarch and Dionysius of Halicarnassus, who is quoted, albeit briefly, in Greek. Maidwell expresses the interesting viewpoint that England is lacking a system of education for boys which makes sufficient use of their intellectual potential: if more fathers thought so hard about the right education for their sons, 'the sleepy Genius of our Nation would rouse itself... Your nice assistance in Education well imitated, might adorn our Country within itself, and save many the trouble of dry-nursing their Youth abroad'. He specifies France and Italy.

The impact of French scholarship can be seen at work even in Mr Maidwell's school for proudly English boys, however. It is no coincidence that this 1684 translation was published the year after an edition of Eutropius had come out, the work of a young French prodigy, Mademoiselle Anne Le Fèvre, the daughter of a celebrated Protestant academician in Saumur; she is better known by her married name, Madame Dacier.[20] Her Eutropius was one of the early volumes in the Paris-published 'Delphin' series, which was destined to transform educational practice and intellectual life across Europe, as April Shelford has meticulously argued.[21] Another author already published *ad Usum Delphini*, a little earlier in 1681, had been Aulus Gellius of the 'classici' and 'proletarii' authors himself.[22]

This 'Delphin' volumes were the joint brainchild of two eminent Frenchmen with exalted positions in the court of Louis XIV. Charles de Sainte-Maure, duc de Montausier (1610–1690), a fascinating character whose career combined military

---

19 Maidwell 1684. He was a correspondent of Dryden's. The boys were named Christopher and James and in 1684 were about 18 and about 11 respectively. Christopher's gentlemanly classical education did not prevent him from succumbing to alcoholism and gambling debts; he was disinherited by his father in favour of James, who also fought a drink problem. See Beckett 1980.
20 This book was also printed by a woman, who called herself on the title page 'widow of Antonius Cellier' (Apud viduam Antonii Cellier). Like the Daciers, Antoine Cellier was a Protestant who had converted, and his wife's name seems to have been either Anne or Florence. On Dacier see further Wyles 2016.
21 Shelford 2007.
22 Proust 1681.

and administrative service with literary pursuits,[23] was raised Protestant but converted in adulthood. A severe but persuasive figure, supposedly the inspiration behind Molière's *Le Misanthrope* (1666),[24] he gained the monarch's trust. He was appointed official Governor of Louis, le Grand Dauphin, who was, while he lived, the heir to the throne. Montausier was then involved in the appointment of Pierre-Daniel Huet to the post of assistant *précepteur* to the Dauphin in 1670.

Huet was a Jesuit-trained intellectual from a nouveau-riche family, born in 1630 in Caen, Normandy. He built up networks with other French and Dutch scholars, including several learned women, transforming the Roman ideal of political friendship, especially as defined in Cicero's *de Amicitia*, into an intellectual and spiritual idiom.[25] He edited Origen and acquired a reputation for his brilliant neo-Latin poems, as well as writing an important essay on the ancient novel.[26] Louis XIV was himself keen on Latin and taking private lessons in it himself;[27] as soon as he was appointed, Huet began work on the Latin texts edited *Ad Usum Delphini*.[28] In this role he became one of the key 'Ancients' in the first round of the French *querelle des Anciens et des Modernes*, which began in about 1687, as his protégée Anne Dacier was to kick off the second round in 1699 with her translation of the *Iliad*.

The series *Ad Usum Delphini* was conceived as the curriculum for the studious young Dauphin, as Huet wrote to Henry Oldenburg in London, the Secretary of the Royal Society, who was in charge of all its foreign correspondence.[29] Huet was concerned about finding sufficient editors of a high enough standard, but fell on his feet with the prodigious Dacier, with whose scholarly father Tanneguy le Fèvre he had been a regular correspondent. She was a fine Hellenist, as her father had been; she had published an edition of Callimachus in 1674. To her Huet entrusted no fewer than four volumes. Before her Eutropius, she had previously published three other Delphin editions — Publius Annius Florus (1674), Dictys and Dares (1681), and Sextus Aurelius Victor (1681).

Huet threw so much energy into the series because it was his primary weapon in the war that advocates of classical erudition were waging against the combined

---

23 Lopez 1987.
24 Seward 1798, vol. IV, 374.
25 Shelford 2007, 43, 80–6.
26 See Whitmarsh 2018, 11.
27 Shelford 2007.
28 Shelford 2007, 3–4.
29 Quoted in Shelford 2007, 86.

modernising forces of Cartesianism and vernacular literary production. The series was thus designed as an intervention in a cultural crisis.[30] The 'branding' of the series by the frontispiece dolphin image and the motto 'Trahitur dulcedine cantus' ('he is drawn along by the sweetness of the song') is suggestive of the story of Arion, the inspired singer who was attacked by barbarous pirates but saved by a music-loving dolphin. The series is allegorically represented by Arion, who charmed the ears of a rich ruler; the moderns, it is implied, are but ignorant pirates.

The series was not intended for the Dauphin alone. Montausier recommended to the King that the editions be published so that his subjects could all share in the education enjoyed by royalty (illiterate French peasants do not seem to have registered in Montausier's thoughts); Louis agreed, decreeing that the volumes were all to be published, for the good of the French public and 'all the world'.[31] Eminent intellectuals lavished praise on the initiative. Leibniz saw an opportunity to attack modernising Cartesian education, and declared the series would 'revivify the nearly extinguished light of antiquity, and then give the best authors a third life, as after the course of barely one century, contempt for them has revived'.[32] At the Royal Society in London, Oldenburg predicted that the series would achieve lasting celebrity, since it reconciled young men, put off by the difficulty of the ancient texts, to liberal studies once again.[33]

The books soon arrived in England, to play their role in the invention of 'Classics' as we know it. The forty-three Latin authors, some (e.g. Cicero and Ovid) spread across several volumes each, edited with Latin paraphrase, commentary and copious appendixes and indexes by thirty-nine scholars, made a colossal impact. Enterprising publishers swiftly printed facsimiles of the Delphin editions: Benjamin Tooke and Thomas Cockerill in 1688 published the 1675 Phaedrus edited by Pierre Danet; Quintus Curtius, as edited by Michel le Tellier (1678), was published by A. & J. Churchill in 1705; Louis Desprez's 1675 edition of Juvenal and Persius was published in 1699 by John Nicholson (on whom see below); the Clarendon Press at Oxford in 1716 published Cicero's oratorical treatises as edited in 1687 by Jean Proust.[34]

---

30 Shelford 2007, 172.
31 Shelford 2007, 172.
32 In a letter to Huet of 15th April, 1673, reproduced in Leibniz 2006, 363, translated by Shelford 2007, 173.
33 Oldenburg 1975, 343–46.
34 Danet 1688, Le Tellier 1705, Desprez 1675. Proust 1716.

Lists of gentlemanly personal libraries put up for auction in 18th-century Britain rarely do not include several Delphin volumes alongside the editions of Latin authors by Gronovius (Johann Friedrich Gronow), the Hesiod of William III's favourite Graevius (Johann Georg Greffe, 1667), or (for both Latin and Greek authors) the Dutch Elzevir editions, for example the Elzevir Dionysius of Halicarnassus (1627), selections from the *Iliad* (1642) and Xenophon's *Cyropaedia* (1647).[35] The popularity of the Delphin editions is shown by the plethora available on the 19th-century second-hand book market, after they were supplanted by A.J. Valpy's extensive new *The Latin Writings after the System of the Delphin Classics, with Variorum*, editorially overseen by George Dyer, the first of which was published in 1819.[36] In Thomas Hardy's *Jude the Obscure*, Jude Fawley's attempts to teach himself Classics draw on Hardy's own experience as the son of a rural stonemason who struggled to further his classical education while apprenticed to an ecclesiastical architect. In Chapter 5, Jude is given a decrepit horse and a creaky cart to deliver bread near Marygreen. He sits with a dictionary on his knees, and a crumbling Delphin edition of a Latin author, Caesar, Virgil or Horace, which he could just about afford 'because they were superseded, and therefore cheap'.[37]

Publishers also commissioned translations into English of the Delphin authors, correctly assuming that the youths reading these texts at school might want some help in construing them. In 1714 the entrepeneurial Smithfield printer and bookseller John Nicholson, having already profited from several Classics books including a new, expanded 1706 edition of John Potter's popular *Archaeologiae Graecae: or, the Antiquities of Greece*, and synoptic English translations of moral essays by Seneca and Plutarch,[38] published an anonymous translation he had commissioned of Florus, almost certainly inspired by Anne Dacier's renowned 1674 Delphin edition. It includes an Advertisement, presumably penned by Nicholson himself, with this declaration: 'It is design'd to do all the Classicks of Value in these Volumes, publishing one every Month, till most of the Greek and Latin Authors are finish'd, if encouragement be given'.[39] A list of the first texts Nicholson planned to have translated include the Delphin Sallust and Elder Pliny, and only one Greek author, Thucydides. The Advertisement invites not only subscribers to contact him, but also 'Any Eminent

---

35 E.g. Curll 1714, Symon 1723, Unwin 1743.
36 See further Hall and Stead 2020 chapters 2, 8.
37 Hardy 1995 (1895) 22–3.
38 Anon. 1702 and 1704.
39 Anon. 1714 'Advertisement',

Scholars, that have done, or will do any, if their Performance be approv'd, by the Persons that read these things over'. Sadly, the only other ancient author to see the light in this projected series was Tacitus, 'Made English by several Hands' in 1716, because Nicholson died in 1715 before reaching the age of thirty.[40] But there were hundreds of other translations of this kind published between about 1705 and the 1740s, often by one or more anonymous and now unidentifiable scholars, some of whom are likely to have been women.[41] The schoolboy's and undergraduate's 'crib' was born. There are far more English translations of classical authors than there are Delphin editions or any other untranslated ancient texts in the catalogue of books auctioned in 1729 that had belonged to the prematurely deceased Mr. Lusher, of Pembroke College, Oxford.[42]

A fine example of an early crib is the reading aid of 1712 prepared by David Watson, a teacher at St. Leonard's College, St. Andrews, whose long title shows exactly what was needed in addition to Latin texts: *The Odes, Epodes, and Carmen Seculare of Horace, Translated into English Prose, As near as the Two Languages will admit, together with the original Latin from the best editions. Wherein The Words of the Latin Text are put in their Grammatical Order; the Observations of the most Valuable Commentators, both antient and modern, represented; and the Author's Design and Beautiful Descriptions fully set forth in a Key annexed to each Ode and Poem; with Notes both Geographical and Historical. The Whole adapted to the Capacities of Youth at School, as well as of Private Gentlemen.*[43] Watson specifies the people he imagines will benefit most from his book: 'those of lower capacities' and 'younger Persons'.[44]

In the wake of Dryden's Virgil (1697), the 18th century soon became the great age of vernacular translation from classical authors into English — a development which was not greeted with universal enthusiasm, especially when fairground showmen started adapting bits of the *Aeneid* into vulgar English rhyming couplets to entertain plebeian audiences at the London fairs.[45] Translations were criticised both by those who had paid large sums to educate their sons in the ancient languages and by prudish Christians who were horrified when the racier passages of Ovid or Martial became accessible in English: a vehement controversy between advocates of reading in translation or in the

---

40 Anon. 1716; Plomer *et al.* 1922, 218.
41 Hall and Wyles 2016, 21–22; Hall 2016.
42 Curll 1729.
43 Watson 1712.
44 Watson 1712, 'Preface' pp. v and viii.
45 See Hall 2018.

ancient texts is demonstrated in many polemics of this era.⁴⁶ So are altercations between proponents of literal and free translation of classical authors, informed by Dryden's famous 'Preface' to the 1680 translation of Ovid's *Epistles*.⁴⁷ The wittiest supporter of paraphrase was Aaron Hill, who wrote in 1709 that he wholeheartedly respects 'the Classics', but that

> Literal Translation *commonly appears* Confin'd, Uneasy, Close *and* Aukward, *like a* Streght-Lac'd Lady *in her* New Made Stays, *but when* the Version *has put on an* Easy Paraphrase, *and and the* Fine Lady *is completely* Dres'd, *with* Ribbons, Manteau, *and her* Looser Ornaments, *tho' they are* still *the* same, *they were before, they brightly double* Former Graces, *and become* Adorn'd *with an* Attractive Majesty.⁴⁸

The Delphin series, which expurgated all passages regarded as too obscene for the young Dauphin, was an important stimulant to these debates and the whole publishing sector.

Its impact can be seen from a different perspective in 1712. In that year Richard Steele published a satirical article in the *The Spectator* containing what he claimed were letters he had recently received from two schoolboys. One of them, a fourteen-year-old, complains that his father, although wealthy, does not think that training in ancient authors will do his son any good, and will not buy him the (expensive) books he needs to further his studies of Latin authors: our teenager laments, 'All the Boys in the School, but I, have the Classick Authors in usum Delphini, gilt and letter'd on the Back.'⁴⁹ By 1712, acquisition of Delphin Classics had become indispensable to what was beginning to be called 'a classical education'.

The series did not include Greek authors, which can help us understand the difference between the French and the British educational versions of classical education at this time. The image of Greek was ambivalent. On the one hand, it was sometimes seen as an arcane and sinister language, associated with evil Jesuits and even witchcraft.⁵⁰ On the other hand, after the Glorious Revolution, reading some carefully selected classical Greek authors alongside the New Testament was deemed helpful in distinguishing British boys in their happy liberty from their Latin-focussed, feudal, monarchical, Roman Catholic equivalents in

---

46 See Coney 1722, 19, 'The most Debauch'd of the *Classics* have been turn'd into our Language with some additional Strokes to their *Original Obscenity*; and appeared in a more loose dress in *England*, than they ever dar'd to in *Rome*'. See further Hall and Stead 2020, ch. 2.
47 Dryden *et al.*, 1680.
48 Hill 1709, xiv.
49 *The Spectator*, Wednesday March 19th 1712, no. 330.
50 Hall and Stead 2020, ch. 16.

France. Greek was also associated with enlightened Continental Protestants, especially the Huguenots who poured into London after the revocation of the Edict of Nantes.[51] Some of them became prominent in printing and publishing: the refugee Luc du Guernier, who engraved most of the frontispieces to versions of Greek tragedy published in Britain during this period, and Abel Boyer, the Marylebone polymath whose *Achilles*, an adaptation of *Iphigenia in Aulis*, was performed at Lincoln's Inn Fields in 1699–1700 and revived at Covent Garden, under the title *Iphigenia*, as late as 1778.[52] Moreover, the two greatest classical scholars at the beginning of the seventeenth century had been Joseph Scaliger and Isaac Casaubon, both Protestant refugees (one in Holland and one in England), whose erudition engendered enormous respect for the Huguenot study of Greek Classics. The brilliant French scholars of Greek, Anne Dacier and her husband André, had both been born and raised in humanist Protestantism before expediently converting.

The celebrated Michel Maittaire, moreover, was a French Huguenot whose parents had fled to England. He won a King's scholarship at Westminster School in 1682, studied at Christ Church, Oxford, and thereafter worked as a schoolmaster and later tutor to Lord Chesterfield's son. He produced a series of Latin Classics for the publisher Jacob Tonson between 1713 and 1719, in a deliberate challenge to the Delphin editions, as well as his much-reprinted *Græcæ Linguæ Dialecti* (1706), his Greek New Testament (1714), *Batrachomyomachia* (1721), *Anacreontea* (1725) and Plutarch's *Apophthegmata* (1740).

New books to help in the contextual study of the Classics were already being published in the 1690s. In 1695, Basil Kennett published his *Romanae Antiquae Notitia, or, The Antiquities of Rome*, which he tells us in the Preface offered information, 'gather'd from the Classicks and other Writers',[53] on Roman religion, festivals, politics, warfare, education and erudition, 'with copper cuts of the principal buildings' and a fold-out map. This was followed swiftly by John Potter's 1697 *Archaeologiae Graecae: or, the Antiquities of Greece*.[54] But we begin to see the word 'classic' appearing on title-pages in 1700, when Kennett was also involved in the publication of the English translation of Pierre Danet's *Dictionarium Antiquitatum Romanarum et Graecarum* as *A Complete Dictionary of the Greek and*

---

51 See Hall and Macintosh 2005, 34–5 and Alonge 2019.
52 Hall and Macintosh 2005, 35.
53 Kennett 1695, 'Preface' n.p.
54 Potter 1697.

Roman Antiquities Explaining the Obscure Places in Classic Authors and Ancient Historians.[55]

A key agent in shaping the early 18th-century fashion for the classical curriculum was Henry Felton, in his *A Dissertation on Reading the Classics, and Forming a Just Style*, written in 1709 and published four years later. Felton had been educated at Charterhouse and St. Edmund Hall, Oxford. He wrote the work as domestic chaplain to the Duke of Rutland, and dedicated the work to his pupil, John, Lord Roos, later the third Duke. It embeds its recommendations for imitating the example of the classic writers not only in style but in the morality of the great men they portrayed and the distinctive new vocabulary surrounding the new 18th-century concept of the gentleman: civility and politeness.[56]

The book cites the rhetorical handbooks of Cicero, Quintilian, Longinus and Aristotle as its ancient forerunners, but places itself at a specific time and place in its advocacy of the Classics. It celebrates the Duke of Marlborough's successes in Belgium and France; it talks at length about the need for a new, politer, more civil style of British speaking and writing than had prevailed in the Restoration period. It insists that all education needs to be subservient to the duties of the Christian religion, but also that 'humane' education can be immeasurably enriched by study of the Classics:[57]

> Your Lordship will meet with great and wonderful Examples of an irregular and mistaken Virtue in the *Greeks* and *Romans*; with many Instances of Greatness of Mind, of unshaken Fidelity, Contempt of human Grandeur, a most passionate Love of their Country, Prodigality of Life, Disdain of Servitude, inviolable Truth, and the most publick disinterested Souls, that ever threw off all Regards in Comparison with their Country's Good...[58]

Felton advises that his Lordship could 'extract a generous and noble Spirit from the Writings and Histories of the Ancients' and especially recommends 'the *Classic Authors*' to his favour.[59] This pedagogical handbook was popular for decades, running into five editions and numerous reprints over the next forty years, despite the publication of rival volumes such as *Advice to a Young Student*, with its section 'General Directions for the Study of Classicks' by Daniel Waterland, then Master of Magdalene College, Cambridge.[60]

---

55 Danet 1700.
56 Felton 1713, xv, xx.
57 Felton 1713, 13–14, 9–10, 17.
58 Felton 1713, 18–19.
59 Felton 1713, 19.
60 Waterland 1730, 9–11.

Fenton played a seminal role in the establishment of the Classics as the polite and refined curriculum for any aspiring gentleman, and putting that key-word 'Classics' on his title page was an influential act of disciplinary branding that was imitated by many. When a revised version of the famed Latin grammar of Samuel Shaw, the Tamworth schoolmaster, was re-published in 1726, the title page made the claim that it had been in the private possession of the friend to whom he had sent it; the second title page consists of a dedication purportedly written by Shaw himself in old age, 'To all the Young Gentlemen and Scholars in England', promising that this volume 'WILL MAKE THEM MASTERS OF THE CLASSICKS (those Fountains of Learning and Philosophy)'.[61]

The modish new syllabus prompted diverse Classics publishing ventures. The title-page of John Pointer's textbook *Miscellanea in Usum Juventutis Academicae* of 1718 boasted that it provided everything a schoolmaster might need — instructions for 'Reading the Classick Authors', 'A Chronology of the Classick Authors', 'A Catalogue of the Best Classick Authors and their Best Editions', information on pagan mythology and Latin exercises. The maturing discipline prompted a flood of books designed for the classroom, now even exploring the aesthetic value of ancient texts and their authors' biographies as well their factual content.[62] The appreciation of classical literature was also much enhanced by John Stirling's 1733 *A System of Rhetoric, in a Method Entirely New: containing all the tropes and figures necessary to illustrate the Classics, both Poetical and Historical*.[63]

But *why* did Classics/the Classics acquire its new name, identity and function in this precise period of English/British history? One factor is that education was being discussed with a new self-consciousness. Influential thinkers from Locke to Rousseau and Shaftesbury to Johnson were united in stressing the importance of education, whatever their views of what its contents should be. But British educators, while imitating the French, were also keen after the Glorious Revolution to *distinguish* the new Anglican gentlemanly classical curriculum from the Continental model, *especially* the French one. The French *querelle* between the ancients and the moderns was transformed to suit local English literature,[64] and the

---

61 Shaw 1726.
62 E.g. the multiple reprintings of François Pomey's *Pantheon* translated into English and substantially revised and supplemented by Andrew Tooke 1698, on which see Hall and Stead 2020 ch. 3; Echard 1694; Kennett 1713; Dunster (1729).
63 Stirling 1733.
64 See Levine 1991 and 1999.

rise of the Classics and Dryden's 1697 translation of Virgil followed by Pope's Homer are inseparable from that cultural dispute.[65]

There was also a debate on whether boys should be educated at home or at school. Robert Ainsworth, author of a famous Latin-English dictionary (1736) which was used to educate countless schoolboys for over a century, staunchly defended a 'domestic education' in his 1698 *The Most Natural and Easie Way of Institution*, but his proposals assume phenomenal wealth. A house needs to be hired 'a small distance from London, with a large garden', and TWO masters hired to speak Latin with the boys round the clock. Ainsworth warns against sending children to school. From dame schools, boys only learn to make errors in spelling and punctuation like 'Vulgar People'. At 'Publick School', 'for the sake of a little Latin', boys are exposed out of hours to the 'Common, if not impious Sayings, of Porters, Car men, and Kitchen-Wenches.'[66]

On the other hand, the *Spectator*'s educational expert, Budgell, found the preference for home-schooling unrealistic.[67] Swift strongly favoured school education.[68] Even the über-aristocrat Lord Chesterfield sent his son to Westminster for three years. The most significant factor was socio-economic: the rise of a new Whiggish mercantile segment of the ruling class. This process, which was beginning to transform Britain, is often subsumed by historians under terms like 'emergence of the bourgeoisie': it entailed the appearance of the anonymous-exchange market and the evolution of what Jürgen Habermas defined as the 'bourgeois public sphere' (*bürgerliche Öffentlichkeit*), accompanied by an explosion in printed communication and accelerating urbanisation.[69]

Most importantly, a new ruling order was being created and collectively trained.[70] The Whiggish sons of tradesman and the Tory sons of hereditary nobles were increasingly being schooled *together*.[71] Classics emerged to provide a curriculum which could bestow a shared concept of gentlemanliness upon them all. The eighteenth century saw an exponential growth in private boarding schools, mostly small and run by Anglican priests, offering a classical curriculum aiming to provide the patina of gentlemanliness and access to Oxford and Cambridge.[72]

---

65 Hall 2018.
66 Ainsworth 1698, 9, 17–18.
67 *Spectator* no. 313, Thursday, February 28, 1712.
68 See e.g. Gill 2016, 74–5.
69 Habermas 1989 (1962); see Wahrman 1995, 6–7.
70 On the economic, social and political aspects of this development, see the excellent study of Rosenheim 1998.
71 See the cogent and detailed study of Bründl 2003, 69–151.
72 Hans 2014 (1951), 117–35; see also Miller 1997, 64–70 and Stray 1998b.

In early 17th-century England, the sons of gentry had often been educated beside merchants' children at town grammar schools, but after the Restoration they were educated at home by tutors, or sent to one of the tiny group of richly endowed public schools.[73] Divisions had become very visible in education. A fresh tone and inclusive model of manliness were required for the new and heterogeneous audience after the Bill of Rights 1689.

A new species of gentry among the merchant sector bought land and wanted prestige and a high 'class'. In this context of the contestation of status and social mobility, substantial wealth had become attainable by a wider sector of the literate population and they wanted cultural capital and the status of gentlemen to match: 'In a society which has become more superciliously class-conscious than in earlier centuries, those already privileged to belong to this class, guard its frontiers with a fastidious sensitiveness to the subtleties of class distinctions; at the same time, an increasing number of new aspirants made attempts to climb into the privileged territory'.[74] And once they had made it, they usually began to exclude those who had not, to ensure themselves safe positions high up the social hierarchy. Classics was useful to exclusion.

Ideas about good breeding, honesty and sound character were scrutinised as they gave shape to a revised idea of the 'Gentleman' which was different from the gentlemanly consummate courtier of the Renaissance. This is reflected in the fiction of the period.[75] Samuel Richardson's *Sir Charles Grandison* 'is a systematic attempt to devise every conceivable kind of situation in which an English gentleman may be called upon to display his gentlemanliness',[76] an explicit aim which Richardson formulated in his Preface. Fielding portrays depraved town gallants and brutal country 'gentlemen', but set against him a range of heroes of the squirearchy — Parson Adams, Dr Harrison, Squire Allworthy — whose moral characters, civility and kindness qualified them, even if they were less highly born, for the soubriquet of ideal gentlemen. And they are classicists: Parson Adams is obsessed with Aeschylus.[77] Both Smollett's titular heroes Roderick Random and Peregrine Pickle desire at all costs to establish themselves as gentlemen, in novels where the author fulminates 'against the depravity vulgarity and sycophancy' of the born-and-bred upper classes in both Bath and London.[78]

---

73 Monod 2009, 37.
74 Shroff 1983, 117.
75 Shroff 1983.
76 Shroff 1983, 11.
77 See Dudden 1952, vol. I, 157–9, 357–63, and 398–100.
78 Shroff 1983, 12.

Addison and Steele moulded the idea of the gentleman through *The Spectator* from 1711 onwards. Addison wanted *The Spectator* to proselytise for good breeding and for 'wit tempered with morality' (no. 10), 'effective among all the different sections of a rapidly growing middle class, as well as among the established upper class.'[79] He deliberately aimed at the whole male reading public, including longstanding rivals and antagonists — men of the court, the town, the city and the country. The place where these values were discussed and promulgated were public coffee houses and private clubs.[80] The concept of taste emerges at this time, a strange fusion of the aesthetic and the ethical, but closely tied to classicism, new forms of consumerism, including the book trade, and a burgeoning entertainment industry.[81]

Henry Fielding's *Joseph Andrews* is especially illuminating. In the second chapter, Fielding directly asks whether a low-born man with a noble character and refined education was not as admirable as one who was genteel by birth: 'But suppose, for argument's sake, we should admit that he had no ancestors at all... Would not this *autokopros* have been justly entitled to all the praise arising from his own virtues?'[82] But it turns out that it really *was* only for the sake of argument that this possibility has been raised. Joseph is refined and genteel in his manners and conduct, but can never, as an *autokopros*, become fully a gentleman. The use of the term *autokopros* (never instanced in ancient Greek but invented by Fielding and glossed by him as 'sprung from a dunghill') links the idea of failure to be properly a gentleman with knowledge of the ancient Greek language. Only someone who knew Greek, and was therefore familiar with the term he is imitating, the Athenians' own title glorifying the antiquity of their bloodline and its intimate relationship to the land they occupied, *autochthōn*, could fully understand why Joseph Andrews could never be a true gentleman in every sense, after all.

This piece began with two texts published in 1736 and 1740 where the terms *Classics* and *class* are found in proximity meaning virtually the same things as they do today, with a man's class being identifiable partly through his mastery of Classics. Late 17th- and 18th-century school novels and plays, the latter usually thought to be a genre founded by Daniel Defoe in his allegorical *The Quarrel of the School-Boys at Athens* (1717),[83] are a rich potential source of information about

---

79 Shroff 1983, 38.
80 Maurer 1998, 15–18.
81 Maurer 1998, 16–17.
82 Fielding 1742, vol. I, 6–7.
83 Reprinted with commentary in Sill 2003, 201–14 and 257–61. Although the object of Defoe's satire is actually the Whig Party in disguise, he incidentally provides many interesting details about the organisation of contemporary boys' schools.

Classics teaching.⁸⁴ One didactic play for performance in schools published in 1742 required pupils to act out the way their knowledge of Classics would dictate the entire arc of their lives until the day they died. Thomas Spateman's *The School-Boy's Mask* was designed for use on important days in a school's calendar. It is a dramatic lesson teaching a simple moral: boys who work hard at Classics will be rewarded in terms of career and money. Boys who don't will die impecuniously in the social gutter. Spateman was Prebendary of St. Paul's Cathedral as well as Rector of St Bartholomew's and took an interest in the indigent children of deceased clergy. His only other publication is a sermon he preached at St Paul's to a congregation partially consisting of such fatherless sons, on what was an annual occasion used to fund-raise towards their financial support.⁸⁵

The four acts in the play depict the situations of a set of pupils from professional, mercantile and aristocratic backgrounds, who together attended an imaginary school, as children, students, mature adults and old men respectively. Time delivers the prologue, standing in a school yard; he laments that so many people waste their time on silly pastimes. He offers books to a group of boys, with the admonition to use them well, so that they may one day become a bishop or a judge.⁸⁶ The principal characters are divided into two groups by rank, but within each rank there are successes and failures, dictated by their attitudes to classical study, which is presented as inseparable from good taste, refined manners, and virtue.

Amongst the professional-class boys, the dissipated Guzzle and Wild-Rogue insult Time. Wild-Rogue intends to be an army Captain. He can't see what use book-learning would be for such a profession, but Time reminds him that both Caesar and Hannibal were good scholars as well as brave.⁸⁷ Wild-Rogue's faults include being aggressive to his father's manservant and asking if Time has a pretty daughter. There is an additional subplot involving a boy called Fondle who refuses to go away to school, is spoiled completely by his mother and never reads a book.⁸⁸ As an undergraduate, Guzzle bemoans his hangover.⁸⁹ Later in life, we find him drinking in Covent Garden. A near-destitute curate, he dies in acute debt, while Fondler got a servant pregnant and died miserably young, having achieved nothing.⁹⁰

---

84 I have learned much from Kirkpatrick 2005.
85 Spateman 1731.
86 Spateman 1742, 1–3.
87 Spateman 1742, 2.
88 Spateman 1742, 4–6, 14–16.
89 Spateman 1742, 24–5.
90 Spateman 1742, 34–6, 42–4.

In contrast, there are three rather sanctimonious middle-class boys who do apply themselves to the Classics and enjoy successful careers. Bookish and Goodwill rebuke their playmates for showing disrespect to Time and accept his gifts of books gratefully. The plot thickens with the introduction of a new boy, Rival, who is envious of the praises bestowed on Bookish and Goodwill by the master. He knows that he is less clever than they are, but nevertheless resolves to work hard in order to take third place in the master's esteem.[91]

Goodwill is rewarded by being the first to be sent off to university in Oxford. In Act II, he travels from Oxford to Cambridge, where Bookish is now studying. He says that Bookish's room is

> as full of Books as Crownfield's Shop.
> Not like Charles Guzzel's, who by shameful Sale
> Has all his Books converted into Ale;
> Swallow'd the authors, that he should have read,
> And got them in his belly, not his head.[92]

Goodwill launches into a rhapsodic encomium to Cicero, hoping that he can be inspired 'with Philippic rage / Against the Antonii of the present age'. Bookish tops this with a panegyric to Fénelon, Homer, Virgil and religious writers. But they both agree that the Bible is more important than all these books, for it is the record 'of Sacred authors wise'.[93]

Fortified by these elevated thoughts, they go to seek refreshment and run into Rival. He is envious that Bookish has already taken his first degree, but resolves to keep on applying himself, since 'Perseverance oft its Ends attains'.[94] In Act III, we meet the same men again as mature adults. Bookish was made Master of his College at an unusually young age. He has also been given a Deanery followed by a Bishopric and publishes famous sermons. He earns six hundred pounds a year in preferments. Goodwill becomes a famous lawyer, because he studied Cicero's orations in his youth, and was then appointed Lord Chancellor. He also married an heiress with twelve thousand pounds. Even Rival became a Doctor of Medicine and is much admired.[95]

Alongside these sons of professionals and businessmen, there are three young landed aristocrats, only one of whom respects the Classics and therefore

---

91 Spateman 1742, 3–4.
92 Spateman 1742, 17.
93 Spateman 1742, 19.
94 Spateman 1742, 19–20.
95 Spateman 1742, 34, 28, 39, 35, 37.

makes a success of his life. The two decadent nobles, Lords Tinsel and Rakish, rudely dismiss Time and his books because they are going to grow up to be members of the nobility. Rakish is a cheat who even pays one of the studious boys to compose verses for him on the theme *fugit irreparabile tempus*, and is seen in later life dying in drunken penury because he has failed to find an heiress to marry.[96]

Lord Grand-clerck, however, provides a contrast with these nefarious aristocrats. At breakfast in his chambers at Cambridge, he is attended by a Bookseller's apprentice, who has brought him Plutarch, Cornelius Nepos, and Perrault's *Lives*. 'What an Assembly of illustrious Personages are here! How I burn to be better acquainted with each of them; to partake of his Adventures, learn Greatness of Soul from him, and make the Love and Emulation of his Virtue Fewel to feed the sacred Spark of my own!'[97] He is interrupted by Lord Tinsel, who has chosen travelling in pursuit of pleasure over university. Tinsel tells him to stop reading and play cards with him; they argue about whether aristocrats need educating. Lord Grand-clerck says he has no need to travel except to the 'delightful Land' of Learning. Its entrance is surrounded by thorns, 'to keep off the great Vulgar, and the small'; its fruits 'are too delicious to be gather'd by those who are not willing to be at some Labour to obtain them'.[98] Tinsel refuses to give money to Grand-clerck's charity, which he has established to found an Infirmary. Later in life, Grand-clerck is now Duke of Kingsdown and an acclaimed philanthropist, while Tinsel is in massive debt. But he is at least given the explicit moral of the show to pronounce when he recognises that he 'fell into all this Misconduct for want of a better Education' because he refused the opportunity to study in his youth.[99]

Spateman's play taught boys that if they studied classical authors hard they would be enabled to attain wealth and status, or, as Thomas Gaisford, Dean of Christ Church, was said to have told his congregation one Christmas Day a century later, the study of Greek literature, 'not only elevates above the vulgar herd, but leads not infrequently to positions of considerable emolument.'[100] Gaisford's supposed apophthegm is the most concise statement available that *financial* capital can be accumulated through acquisition of a classical education. But Spateman's play shows that, by the 1740s, capital of other kinds, including the moral capital that makes a gentleman happy in his virtue, distinguishable from the vul-

---

[96] Spateman 1742, 7, 34–5.
[97] Spateman 1742, 21.
[98] Spateman 1742, 23.
[99] Spateman 1742, 49.
[100] Quoted in Tuckwell 1907, 24. The story is very likely apocryphal — cf. Stray 2018a, 76–80.

gar and admired by his peers, along with the social capital that makes him attractive to rich heiresses, was already understood to be conferred by what Lord Grand-clerk calls the laborious, thorny but delightful study of those Classics textbooks, too.

Bibliography

Abbamonte, G./Harrison, S. (eds.) (2019), *Making and Rethinking the Renaissance*, Berlin/Boston.
Ainsworth, R. (1698), *The most Natural and easie way of institution containing proposals for making a domestic education less chargeable to parents*, London.
Alonge, T. (2019), 'Rethinking the Birth of French Tragedy', in: Abbamonte/Harrison 2019, 143–156.
Anon. (1702, trans.), *Seneca's Morals by way of abstract* [8th edition], London.
Anon. (1704, trans.), *Plutarch's Morals by way of abstract: done from the Greek*, London.
Anon. (1714, trans.), *Lucius Annæus Florus, his Epitome of Roman History, from Romulus to Augustus Cæsar. Made English from the best editions and Corrections of Learned Men*, London.
Anon. (1716, trans), *The Annals and History of Cornelius Tacitus; his account of the ancient Germans, and the life of Agricola. Made English by several hands* [3 volumes], London.
Bankes, J. (1679), *Januae Clavis: or, Lilly's Syntax Explained*, London.
Beckett, J.V. (1980), 'The disinheritance of Sir Christopher Lowther in 1701', *Transactions of the Cumberland and Westmorland Antiquarian and Archaeological Society* 80, 131–136.
Bentley, R. (1713), *Remarks upon a late Discourse of free-thinking: in a letter to F. H. D. D. By Phileleutherus Lipsiensis*, London.
Browne, T. (1646), *Pseudodoxia Epidemica*, London.
Bründl, S. (2003), *The Gentleman Ideal*, Göttingen.
Cueva, E.P./Byrne, S.P./Benda, F. (eds.) (2009), *Jesuit Education and the Classics*, Newcastle-upon-Tyne.
Curll, E. (1714), *For the year 1714, a catalogue of books, sold by Edmund Curll, at his shop at Tunbridge-Wells*, Tunbridge Wells.
Curll, E. (1729), *A Young Student's Library or, A catalogue of books belonging to the late Mr. Lusher*, Tunbridge Wells.
Danet, P. (1688), *Phædri Augusti Cæsaris liberti Fabularum Æsopiarum libri quinque*, London.
Danet, P. (1700), *Dictionarium Antiquitatum Romanarum et Graecarum, A Complete Dictionary of the Greek and Roman Antiquities Explaining the Obscure Places in Classic Authors and Ancient Historians*, London.
Dryden, J. et al. (1680), *Ovid's Epistles Translated by Several Hands*, London.
Dudden, F.H. (1952), *Henry Fielding: His Life, Work and Times*, Oxford.
Dunster, S. (1729), *Horace's Satires, Epistles, and Art of Poetry, Done into English, with Notes*, London.
Earle, J. (1630), *Microcosmographie*, London.
Echard, L. (1694), *Plautus' Comedies*, London.

Fielding, H. (1742), *The History of the Adventures of Joseph Andrews, and his Friend Mr. Abraham Adams. Written in Imitation of The Manner of Cervantes, Author of Don Quixote*. [2nd edition in two volumes], London.

Felton, H. (1713), *A Dissertation on Reading the Classics, and Forming a Just Style. Written in the Year 1709, and Addressed to the Right Honourable, John Lord Roos, the Present Marquis of Granby*, London.

Gill, E. (2016), *Naval Families, War and Duty in Britain, 1740–1820*, Rochester, NY.

Habermas, J. (1989 [1962]), *The Structural Transformation of the Public Sphere: An Inquiry into a Category of Bourgeois Society* [trans. Thomas Burger], Cambridge, MA (originally published in 1962 as *Strukturwandel der Öffentlichkeit: Untersuchungen zu einer Kategorie der bürgerlichen Gesellschaft*, Berlin).

Hall, E. (2008), 'Putting the class into classical reception', in: Hardwick/Stray 2008, 386–397.

Hall, E. (2016),'Intellectual pleasure and the woman translator in 17th- and 18th-century England', in: Wyles/Hall 2016, 103–131.

Hall, E. (2018), 'Classical Epic at the London Fairs: Elkanah Settle's *The Siege of Troy*, 1707–1734', in: Macintosh et al. 2018, 439–460.

Hall, E./Stead, H. (2020), *A People's History of Classics: Class and Greco-Roman Antiquity in Britain and Ireland 1689–1939*, London.

Hall, E./Macintosh, F. (2005), *Greek Tragedy and the British Theatre 1660–1914*, Oxford.

Hall, E./Wyles, R. (2016), 'Introduction: approaches to the fountain', in: Wyles/Hall 2016, 1–28.

Hans, N. (2014 [1951]), *New Trends in Education in the Eighteenth Century*, London.

Hardwick, L./Stray, C. (eds.) (2008), *A Companion to Classical Receptions*, Oxford.

Harrison, S. (2017), *Victorian Horace: Classics and Class*, London.

Hill, A. (1709), *A Full and Just Account of the Present State of the Ottoman Empire*, London.

Kennett, B. (1695), *Romae Antiquae Notitia: Or The Antiquities of Rome*, London.

Kennett, B. (1713), *The Idylliums of Theocritus…To which is prefix'd, the Life of Theocritus*, London.

Kirkpatrick, R. (2005), *Before Tom Brown: the Birth and Development of the Boys' School Story*, Cambridge.

Le Tellier, M. (1705), *Q. Curtii Rufi De rebus gestis Alexandri Magni*, London.

Leibniz, G.W. (2003), *Sämtliche Schiften und Briefe I* [ed. Heinrich Schepers, Martin Schneider, Philip A. Beeley, Gerhard Biller, Stefan Lorenz, Herma Kliege-Biller], Berlin.

Levine, J. (1991),*The Battle of the Books: History and Literature in the Augustan Age*, Ithaca, NY.

Levine, J. (1999), *Between the Ancients and the Moderns: Baroque Culture in Restoration England*, New Haven.

Lopez, D. (1987), *La plume et l'épée: Montausier (1610–1690)*, Paris/Seattle/Tübingen.

Macintosh, F./McConnell, J./Harrison, S./Kenward, C. (eds.) (2018), *Epic Performances from the Middle Ages into the Twenty-First Century*, Oxford.

Maurer, S.L. (1998), *Proposing Men: Dialectics of Gender and Class in the Eighteenth-Century English Periodical*, Stanford, CA.

May, T. (1635), *The Victorious Reigne of King Edvvard the Third Written in Seven Bookes*, London.

Miller, T.P.(1997), *The Formation of College English*, Pittsburgh, PA.

Monod, P.K. (2009), *Imperial Island: A History of Britain and its Empire, 1660–1837*, Malden, MA/Oxford.

North, D. (1645), *A Forest of Varieties*, London.

Oldenburg, H. (1975), *The Correspondence of Henry Oldenburg Vol. X* [ed. and trans. A.R. Hall and M.B. Hall], London.
Perkins, W. (1604), *A Commentarie or Exposition, vpon the Fiue First Chapters of the Epistle to the Galatians*, Cambridge.
Plomer, H.R. (1922), *A Dictionary of the Printers and Booksellers who Were at work in England, Scotland and Ireland from 1668 to 1725*, Oxford.
Potter, J. (1697), *Archaeologiae Graecae: or, the Antiquities of Greece*, Oxford.
Proust, J. (1681), *Auli Gellii Noctes Atticae Interpretatione et notis illustravit Jacobus Proust e Soc. Jesu. Jussu Christianissimi Regis, ad usum serenissimi Delphini*, Paris.
Proust, J. (1716), *M. T. Ciceronis liber de claris oratoribus, qui dicitur Brutus. Ad M. Brutum orator. Ad C. Trebatium topica. Oratoriæ partitiones. Liber de optimo genere oratorum. Cum interpretatione ac notis, quas in usum Serenissinu Delphini edidit Jacobus Proust*, Oxford.
Richelieu, A. de (1740), *Travels and Adventures Vol. 1* [2nd edition], London.
Rosenheim, J.M. (1998), *The Emergence of a Ruling Order: English Landed Society 1650–1750*, London.
Sancroft, W. (1694), *Occasional Sermons Preached by the Most Reverend Father in God, William Sancroft*, London.
Seward, W. (1798), *Anecdotes of Distinguished Persons, chiefly of the present and two preceding centuries* [4th edition], London.
Shaw, S. (1726), *A Grammatical Dictionary, containing the heteroclites of the Latin tongue, collected from the classicks themselves*, London.
Shelford, A.G. (2007), *Transforming the Republic of Letteres: Pierre-Daniel Huet and European Intellectual life, 1650–1720*, Rochester, NY.
Shroff, H.J. (1983), *The Eighteenth-Century Novel: The Idea of the Gentleman*, London.
Sill, G. (2003), *Satire, Fantasy and Writings on the Supernatural by Daniel Defoe: Vol. III*, London.
Spateman, T. (1731), *A Sermon Preach'd before the Sons of the Clergy, at their anniversary-meeting in the Cathedral Church of St. Paul, February 25. 1730*, London.
Stirling, J. (1733), *A System of Rhetoric, in a Method Entirely New: containing all the tropes and figures necessary to illustrate the Classics, both Poetical and Historical*, London.
Stead, H./Hall, E. (eds.) (2015), *Greek and Roman Classics in the British Struggle for Social Reform*, London.
Stonehouse, S. (1736), *A Rational Method of Fitting Youth for Business*, London.
Stray, C. (1998a), *Classics Transformed: Schools, Universities, and Society in England 1830–1960*, Oxford.
Stray, C. (1998b), 'Schoolboys and gentlemen: classical pedagogy and authority in the English public school', in: Too/Livingstone 1998, 29–46.
Stray, C. (ed.) (1999), *Classics in 19th- and 20th-Century Cambridge: Curriculum, Culture and Community*, Cambridge.
Stray, C. (2015), 'Classics and social closure', in: Stead/Hall 2015, 116–137.
Symon, E. (1723), *Catalogus librorum in omni ferè arte & scientia præstantium; or, a catalogue of the library of a very Eminent Gentleman lately deceas'd*, London.
Too, Yun Lee/Livingstone, N. (eds.) (1998), *Pedagogy and Power: Rhetorics of Classical Learning*, Cambridge.
Tuckwell, F.W. (1907), *Reminiscences of Oxford* [2nd ed.], London.

Unwin, M. (1743), *A Catalogue of Books. Divinity, history, law, physick, mathematicks, poetry, classicks*, Leicester.

Vasunia, P. (2005), 'Greek, Latin and the Indian Civil Service', *Cambridge Classical Journal* 51, 35–71.

Wahrman, D. (1995), *Imagining the Middle Class: The Political Representation of Class in Britain, c. 1780–1840*, Cambridge.

Waterland, D. (1730), *Advice to a young student. With a Method of Study for the Four First Years*, London.

Watson, D. (1712), *The Odes, Epodes, and Carmen Seculare of Horace*, London.

Whitmarsh, T. (2018), *Dirty Love: The Genealogy of the Ancient Greek Novel*, Oxford.

Wyles, R. (2016), 'Ménage's learned ladies: Anne Dacier (1647–1720) and Anna Maria van Schurman (1607–1678), in: Wyles/Hall 2016, 61–77.

Wyles, R./Hall, E. (eds.) (2016), *Women classical scholars: unsealing the fountain from the Renaissance to Jacqueline de Romilly*, Oxford.

Robert A. Kaster
The Vulgate Text of Seneca's *De beneficiis*, 1475–1650

If in 1830 you opened E.F. Vogel's new edition of Seneca's *De beneficiis*, the text you encountered would be all but identical to the text you would read had you been transported back to 1650 and opened what was then the most recent edition, published in 1649 by J.F. Gronovius. After the *editio princeps* appeared in Naples in 1475, its text was passed along, virtually unchanged, through the next four editions, published down to 1503. Serious critical engagement with the text began with the Basel edition of 1515 and continued so robustly for the next four generations that with the appearance of Gronovius' edition the text carried over 2000 readings — roughly, one every twenty-two words — that had not stood in the *editio princeps*. But after that vulgate text had emerged, the critical impulse went dormant: for nearly two hundred years there were no significant advances and not much variety. Two Bipontine editions, of 1782 and 1809, F.R. Ruhkopf's edition of 1808, and Vogel's already mentioned differed only in very minor ways from their predecessors and among themselves;[1] a new period of vigorous critical activity was marked only by the appearance of Friedrich Haase's Teubner of 1852 and, especially, M.C. Gertz's edition of 1876.[2] The following pages attempt to demonstrate how that enormously influential early modern vulgate text emerged.

My first book had barely appeared when I received a letter (typed, thank God: those who know his hand will understand) from a man in Swansea saying that it had piqued his interest, and would I mind a few questions? The letter began a friendship of more than thirty years, which has brought countless opportunities to enjoy his curiosity, humor, and warm humanity: it is a joy to offer this essay in honor of Chris Stray, a pioneer in the fields of classical reception and the sociology of knowledge, and a *uerus amicus*.

---

1 In what follows, I regard any reading that appears in at least three of these four editions as a continuation of the 17th-century vulgate.
2 A change was already signaled by Fickert 1843, an edition remarkable not so much for its criticism as for the effort devoted to reporting the text's documentary basis, including the manuscripts cited in previous editions. The second edition of Carl Hosius' Teubner (1914) has been the standard text for the last century; I am preparing a new critical edition for the Oxford Classical Texts series.

https://doi.org/10.1515/9783110719215-004

1 The Earliest Editions, 1475–1503

Seneca's philosophical works were transmitted in four distinct units: *De beneficiis*, accompanied by *De clementia*; the *Dialogi*; the *Naturales Quaestiones*; and the *Epistulae Morales*.[3] *De beneficiis* and *De clementia* are doubly distinguished: among the *philosophica* they re-emerged earliest after the passage from late antiquity, and the manuscript that ensured their survival — the archetype of the tradition — still survives. Vatican Pal. lat. 1547 was written around 800 in northern Italy, in a version of the script that became renowned as "Beneventan": it is known today as **N** (for *Nazarianus*), having spent the Middle Ages in the church of Saint Nazarius in Lorsch. After **N** had been corrected, a copy was made: this copy — Vatican Reg. lat. 1529 (**R**, ca. 825–850) — was the ultimate source of all later copies.[4]

Then matters took an unhappy but familiar turn: in the words of Leighton Reynolds, "The history of the text is a study in degeneration, as the primitive text of **N** recedes behind successive layers of corruption".[5] Surely among the most interpolated of the archetype's descendants is the unknown manuscript that served as the source of the *editio princeps*, and so of the other early editions that reproduced its text.[6] These are:

Naples 1475: "Incipit lucii annei Senecae cordubensis liber de moribus" (the book begins with the pseudo-Senecan *Liber de moribus*), published by Mathias Morauus, who produced other editions of Latin texts in Naples, including a *De inuentione* the following year; *De beneficiis* begins on p. 75 (unnumbered).

Treviso 1478: Same incipit as the preceding; the colophon records the date and place of publication, "per Bernardum de Colonia". *De beneficiis* begins on fo. 33ᵛ (unnumbered).

---

[3] Reynolds 1983b and Hine 1983 concisely survey the four units' traditions; on the *EM*'s descent in two distinct traditions, Reynolds 1965.

[4] Gertz 1876 is based on the view that the text descends exclusively from **N** (or "ex codice plane gemino"); Buck 1908, 1–38, demonstrated the relationship between **N** and **R**; Mazzoli 1982 traced the ramifications of the subsequent tradition in three families (φ, π, γ). Readings of **N** *ante correctionem* are cited below as **Nac**, readings *post correctionem* as **Npc**.

[5] Reynolds 1983b, 364.

[6] 'Unknown manuscript': beyond Mazzoli 1982, the 14th- and 15th-century manuscripts of *Ben.* largely remain *terra incognita*; but the egregiously bad readings of Naples 1475 are so numerous that it should be possible to identify, if not the precise manuscript, then the corrupt corner of the tradition from which the readings emanate.

Venice 1490: "Seneca moralis"; the colophon records the date and place of publication, "per Bernardinum de Cremona & Simonem de Luero". *De beneficiis* begins on fo. xxiii^r.

Venice 1492: "Senece opera omnia"; the verso of the first folium records the place and date of publication, "per Bernardinum de Coris de Cremona"; *De beneficiis* is printed on fo. lxxx^r-cviii^v.

Venice 1503: Same title page; the colophon records the date and place of publication, "per Bertholomeum de Zanis de Portesio". *De beneficiis* begins on fo. 87^r.

It is proper to acknowledge at the outset that the *editio princeps* did contribute positively to the print tradition, most notably in the form of eighteen good readings first found in Naples 1475 that would subsequently become part of the vulgate text.[7] These readings are innovations relative to the text of **N** and the tradition derived from it: in other words, they are good conjectures, most if not all of which probably were circulating among the *recentiores* before they landed in the unknown manuscript that was the *editio princeps*' immediate source. I feel some confidence in making this suggestion, because of the many cases where we do find Naples 1475 sharing a good conjecture with just such a manuscript long known to editors of *De beneficiis*: **V** (Wrocław, Biblioteka Uniwersytecka IV.F.39, s. XIV), which includes among its countless interpolations many readings that have been accepted as good corrections of a faulty paradosis.[8]

But the text Naples 1475 took from its manuscript source is, overwhelmingly, much less attractive. It is well known that incunabular editions of the Latin classics do not generally set a high standard, since they are typically little more than typeset copies of whatever manuscript happened to be closest to hand, with little critical attention given to the result. Yet judged against even that low standard, the text that Naples 1475 derived from its source was very bad indeed: beyond the many hundreds of errors that subsequent editions corrected, more than 330 inferior readings remained embedded in the text long after the story told in this chapter ended.[9] And then there are the grotesques.

---

[7] E.g., 2.5.3 qui Naples 1475 : ut **Nac**, ł dū **Npc**; 3.28.4 spectemus Naples 1475 : expectemus **N**; 4.2.1 inquis Naples 1475 : iniquis **N**.

[8] E.g., 1.2.5 reducet V Naples 1475 : reducetur **N**; 5.24.1 Iulium V Naples 1475 : filium **N**; 6.3.1 si cito V Naples 1475 : scito **N**; 6.25.4 sua Naples V 1475 : suo **N**. Another 14th-century manuscript, not previously reported — Vatican, Archivio del Capitolio di S. Pietro C.121 — uniquely shares an even larger number of interpolations with Naples 1475, though it is clear that it cannot be the edition's proximate source.

[9] These 300-odd readings are in addition to the more than 2000 readings in the vulgate text that did not appear in the *editio princeps*.

Consider 6.6.2, where Seneca explains that — unlike matters governed by positive law, where individual discretion has little scope — judging *beneficia* is nuanced and flexible. Seneca wrote,

> In illis [sc. certis legibus] nihil est nostrae potestatis, eundum est qua ducimur; in beneficio tota potestas mea est, *ego iudico. Itaque non separo illa* nec *diduco*, sed iniurias *et beneficia* ad eundem iudicem mitto.

This appears in Naples 1475 as:

> In illis nihil est nostrae potestatis, eundum est, qua ducimur; in beneficio tota potestas mea est, ego itaque iudico illa, non separo, nec deduco nec diuido distribuo separo discerno distinguo secerno segrego dissotio disgrego dimoueo distendo distraho distorqueo seiungo, sed iniurias ad beneficia ad eundem iudicem mitto,

where (lesser matters aside) the reader has a predecessor to thank for tipping a glossary into the margin of his manuscript, whence its contents were swept into the text. Compare 1.2.1 institueris, perdenda] institueris, *remunerationem muneris non expectant*, perdenda; 1.2.1 ponas bene] ponas bene, *quasi dicat non est curandum si multa perdantur: dummodo aliquid bene detur munere*; 3.35.1 Iam tempus est quaedam ex nostra … moneta *proferre*] Iam tempus est quaedam ex nostra … moneta *proferri si quid milius [sic] uita est et a patre sola uita datur, potest beneficiis a filio uinci pater*.

These enormities and many others persisted as the four successor-editions passed along the *editio princeps*' text in nearly monolithic fashion. By my count the four editions combined to introduce a mere fifty innovations, twenty-one of which made the text worse: only Venice 1490 — which introduced fourteen superior readings that became the vulgate, against two inferior readings — causes one to wish that the hand responsible had done more.

In a sense, then, these first five editions represent one kind of vulgate text, established by the dependence of Naples 1475 on a very poor source and retained virtually without change for the next generation. Now we can turn to the critical work that over the next century and a half cumulatively produced a common text of a very different sort.

2 The Age of Criticism, 1515–1650

It is one of the striking features of the early modern history of *De beneficiis* — and of Seneca's *philosophica* more generally — that so few editions count for so much. To take another text I know well, Suetonius' *De uita Caesarum*, the same period

(1516–1651) saw sixteen new editions that I needed to cite in my critical apparatus. In the case of Seneca, the editions number eight,[10] of which I will need to cite only seven:

Basel 1515: "Ioannes Frobenius verae philosophiae studiosis s. d. En tibi lector optime, Lucii Annaei Senecae ... philosophi lucubrationes omnes ... Erasmi Roterodami cura, si non ab omnibus, certe ab innumeris mendis repurgatae: ... In inclyta Germaniae Basilea. An. M. D. XV. Mense Iulio"; *De beneficiis* begins on p. 8. The margins occasionally display variant readings, and asterisks mark points of textual difficulty, but more was evidently intended, since Erasmus later complained, "that part of the copy which had the most notes went astray".[11] Though Erasmus' name appears on the title page, he subsequently disavowed the edition, for reasons discussed below.

Basel 1529: "L. Annae Senecae opera ... per Des. Erasmum Roterod. ex fide ueterum codicum, tum ex probatis autoribus, postremo sagaci non nunquam diuinatione, sic emendate, ut merito priorem aeditionem, ipso absente peractam, nolit haberi pro sua. ... Basileae in officina Frobeniana. Anno M. D. XXIX"; cf. the colophon, "Basileae in officina Frobeniana per Hieronymum Frobenium & Ioannem Heruagium, Mense Martio. Anno M. D. XXIX". *De beneficiis* begins on p. 1; Erasmus' brief text-critical notes follow each book. For reasons made plain below, Erasmus also inserted a brief critical apparatus relevant to *De beneficiis* on pp. 271–73, after the *Epistulae Morales*. Erasmus was the first scholar to use the archetype, **N**, which he called the "Lombard book" (*codex Longobardicus*), after its distinctive northern Italian script; but as we shall see, circumstances prevented him from exploiting it fully.

Basel 1557: "L. Annaei Senecae Philosophi ... opera quae extant omnia, Coelii Secundi Curionis uigilantissima cura castigate"; the colophon records the date and place of publication "per Ioannem Heruagium, et Bernardum Brandum". *De beneficiis* begins on p. 1; a selection of the notes by Erasmus and Pincianus (below) follows each book.

Rome 1585: "L. Annaeus Seneca a M. Antonio Mureto correctus et notis illustratus. ... Romae, apud Bartholomaeum Graßium. M. D. XXCV". *De beneficiis* begins on p. 1; Muretus' notes follow each book. A prefatory epistle reveals that the

---

10 Counting Lipsius' 4th edition separately from the first three: see below. I ignore here, e.g., the many reprintings of Muretus' edition of 1585, which offer texts that contain little or no revision and so do not contribute to this chapter's theme.

11 Letter 1341A Allen, 30 January 1523 (to Johann von Bozheim), trans. in Mynors and Estes 1989, 311: he suspected the bad faith of a collaborator in Basel, while he himself was in England; on this letter see below at n. 42.

edition appeared posthumously: Muretus died in Rome on 4 June 1585, after he had completed a draft of *Naturales Quaestiones*, the antepenultimate work in the volume, leaving only notes for the text of the elder Seneca's *Controversiae* and *Suasoriae* and the *Apocolocyntosis*.

Basel 1590: "L. Annaei Seneca Philosophi ... opera, quae extant, omnia, ... authore Dionysio Gothofredo I(uris)C(onsulto). Basileae ... Anno, M. D. XC"; *De beneficiis* begins on p. 1. There are no notes, but Gothofredus separately published many conjectures (*Coniecturarum et variarum lectionum libri V*, Basel 1590) that are — certainly for *De beneficiis* — often arbitrary and always negligible.[12] The edition essentially reproduces the text of Basel 1557: because only one of its innovations — a trivial error — joined the vulgate text, it plays no role in this discussion.[13]

Lipsius: "L. Annaei Senecae Philosophi opera, quae exstant, omnia: a Iusto Lipsio emendata, et scholiis illustrata. Antuerpiae ex officina Plantiniana, apud Ioannem Moretum, M. DC. V". *De beneficiis* begins on p. 260; the scholia accompany the text as footnotes, where Lipsius often signals his emendations rather than placing them in the text. Three later editions were published in Antwerp, all posthumously (Lipsius died on 23 March 1606): the second (1615) and third (1632) are essentially reprints of the first, while the fourth (1652) incorporates a number of good readings from Gruter and Gronovius.[14]

Leiden 1649: "L. Annaei Senecae Philosophi opera omnia, ex ult. I. Lipsii & I. F. Gronovii emendat. ... Lugd. Batav. Apud Elzeviros 1649".[15] *De beneficiis* begins on p. 364 (vol. 1 of 3); there are no notes, but in 1649 Elzevir also published Gronovius' *Notae*, with acute and detailed textual observations on select passages (pp.

---

12 Gruter pointed out many of their shortcomings in his *Suspicionum extraordinariarum liber singularis* (Wittenberg 1591) and — receiving in exchange Gothofredus' scorching polemic, *Pro coniecturis in Senecam, breuis ... responsio* (Frankfurt 1591) — delivered a *Confirmatio suspicionum* (Wittenberg 1591) and continued the polemics — quite exceptionally, relative to the work's overall tone — in his *Animaduersiones* (1594, discussed below). Nearly ten years later, when he was well-established at Heidelberg, Gruter wrote that he considered leaving after Gothofredus was offered a chair there (Weber 1894, 63: Epist. 49, 21 Sept. 1600); but there was evidently a later reconciliation (cf. Weber 1894, 81: Epist. 62, 15 Febr. 1614, "Recte mihi tradidit tuas [sc. literas] Gothofredus noster").
13 4.10.3 eligimus (elegimus **N**, *recte*): after appearing in the *editio princeps*, the error was corrected in Basel 1515 but gained a new lease on life thanks to Gothofredus.
14 On the work of the unknown scholar responsible for these changes, see Malaspina 2000.
15 I cite the edition of 1649, where Gronovius' name first appears on the title-page; but he evidently served as "ghost-editor" (*editore fantasma*, in the happy phrase of Malspina 2000) of the Elzevir edition of 1640, "L. Annaei Senecae Philosophi Opera omnia ex ult. I. Lipsii emendation".

112–78 on *Ben.*), occasionally approving readings different from those printed in the edition.¹⁶

To these editions it is necessary to add two other text-critical sources that play a vital role in the story:¹⁷

Pincianus: "Fernandi Pinciani ... in Salmanticensi Gymnasio professoris ..., In omnia L. Annaei Senecae philosophi scripta ... castigationes utilissimae. Venetiis M.DXXXVI": this compilation, including many hundreds of notes on *De beneficiis* alone, was produced by Hernán Núñez de Toledo y Guzmán, known as *Pincianus*, "the man of Pintia", the Latin name of his birthplace, Valladolid in northwest Spain. Drawing his lemmata primarily from Basel 1529, he introduces the readings he favors — often clearly right and regularly worthy of reflection — in several different ways. Of some he simply says *scribendum* (or the like), without reference to a source: these are presumably his own conjectures. Some he ascribes to specific manuscripts now unidentifiable (e.g., *exemplar Franciscanum*) or to undifferentiated *correctioria exemplaria* or *castigatissimi codices*. Very often they are said to represent or be drawn from the *uetus lectio*, a thoroughly opaque phrase: it cannot (or cannot simply) refer to the "old text" found in printed editions earlier than Basel 1529; some have suspected that the phrase is a cover for his own conjectures,¹⁸ though as already noted he does not shrink from a magisterial *scribendum*; perhaps, since he cites only half a dozen specific manuscripts but says in his prefatory letter that he used "exemplaria scripta et peruetusta quindecim", the phrase gestures at the books he does not name. In any case, both readings merely reported and those explicitly favored greatly influenced all the scholars who subsequently worked on the text.

Gruter: "Iani Gruteri Animaduersiones in L. Annaei Senecae opera. In quibus ... quam plurima loca supplentur, confirmantur, corriguntur, illustrantur ope M.SS. quae in Bibliotheca Elect. Palat. ... Ex typographeio Hieronymi Commelini,

---

16 E.g., 1.10.1 omne nefas **Npc** Leiden 1649 : omne fas **Nac** Gronovius' *Notae* (after Gruter's report; the earlier editions printed *in omne nefas*). A second edition of the *Notae* appeared in 1658, with some notes drawn from Albert Rubens, including two excellent emendations: 6.25.5 equus obsequens facile et parens, 6.35.5 uoti tui an uis?

17 Several good readings were also proposed or defended by Franciscus Modius (*Nouantiquae lectiones tributae in epistolas centum*, Frankfurt 1584) and Henricus Stephanus (*Ad Senecae lectionem proodopoeia* and *Epistolae*, in one volume, *sine loco* 1586), but these had little direct impact on the printed editions; notes by Johannes Opsopoeus (first published in a reprint of Muretus, Paris 1587) and Franciscus Juretus (first published in another reprint of Muretus, Paris 1598) made no large contribution.

18 E.g., Fickert 1842, xv.

Anno M. D. XCIIII".[19] First incorporated in a version of Muretus' edition published at Heidelberg and running to 400 pages of minute type set two columns to the page, the *Animaduersiones* was among the earliest in a long series of monumental commentaries on and editions of Latin prose authors that Janus Gruter produced before his death in 1627:[20] together with his *Inscriptiones antiquae* (Heidelberg 1602) — the standard collection before the creation of the *Corpus Inscriptionum Latinarum* — these works established him as one of the most consequential Latinists of his time; as a critic of Seneca's *philosophica* in this period, he alone is worthy of comparison with Erasmus. Because of his stature, and because he will not be at the center of the discussion below, which focuses on the editions strictly so called, we should pause here briefly to appreciate his work.

Born in 1560 to a wealthy mercantile household of Antwerp, he fled with his family to Norwich, England, in 1567, to escape the religious persecutions led by the Duke of Alba. After enrolling in Gonville and Gaius College, Cambridge, in 1577, he left without taking a degree to join his family in returning to the Continent. He studied ancient history at Leiden with Lipsius and was made a Doctor of Law in 1584; he assumed the chair of ancient history at Wittenberg in Fall 1590 and in February 1593 was called to the corresponding chair in Heidelberg. There his connections at the court of the Elector Palatine of the Rhine gave him access to its fabulous library (he became librarian in 1602), with enormous consequences for our story.

Although Gruter's comments on *De beneficiis* address topics other than the text — especially law — the vast majority are textual, and for these he relied on five manuscripts, which (in a notable advance over his predecessors) he cites absolutely consistently, explicitly, and specifically throughout, as he cites the conjectures and interpretations of others. One manuscript, now unknown, came from Cologne; four belonged to the Palatinate's library. The three that he termed Palatinus primus, secundus, and tertius survive as Vatican, Palatinus latinus 1538 (s. XIV/XV, Italy, excerpts only), 1539 (s. XIV, northern Italy), and 1540 (s. XIV, northern Italy).[21] The fourth was **N**, which like Erasmus he recognized as a product of northern Italy,[22]

---

19 Notes by Nicolas Faber on the elder Seneca's declamatory works and the *Apocolocyntosis* follow Gruter's commentary on *Naturales Quaestiones*.
20 Kühlmann *et al.* 2005 provides an exhaustive bibliography.
21 The Palatinate's library was transferred to the Vatican for safekeeping during the Thirty Years War: the Greek and Latin manuscripts remained there, as the Palatini Graeci and Latini.
22 *Longobardicae literae*: e.g., 1594, 518 (1.2.3), 519 (1.3.4).

though his citations make clear that he took Erasmus' *Longobardicus* and his *Nazarianus* ("Naz.") to be distinct witnesses.[23] While he attributed special authority to **N**, sometimes in extravagant terms (1594, 519, on 1.3.9 minores: "Naz. cuius fidei credo atque si ab ipsa descriptus fide"), he was very far from simply swearing allegiance to its text. In fact, it is typical of his critical procedure that he first tries to understand the main point at issue in any given passage, taking Muretus' text as his starting point, then compares that understanding with the record of the manuscripts and draws his conclusion.

That procedure often led him to conclude that emendation was needed, and though his misses outnumber his hits, as with any conjectural critic, over thirty of his emendations are printed in the standard modern text.[24] More generally, his critical approach often sounds thoroughly modern: he offers a tongue-in-cheek recognition of the principle of *lectio difficilior*;[25] registers his awareness that collections of excerpts, which often lapse into paraphrase, are less authoritative;[26] notes that unfamiliar words are more likely to prompt variations;[27] diagnoses an error caused by *saut du même au même* in one of his manuscripts;[28] acutely explains how two variant readings ultimately derive from an abbreviation found in **N** and his Palatinus secundus; and makes a number of other shrewd diagnoses of the same sort.[29]

---

[23] See, e.g., 1594, 560, on 6.16.6. It seems that the equivalence was not recognised until Fickert wrote the preface to his edition (1843, vii, on Erasmus' manuscripts: "*Cod. Langobardicus* ... idem esse videtur ac *Nazarianus* Gruteri"), though notes in the edition's body regularly cite them as though they were different books (e.g., 1843, 213, on 6.23.2 inbecillitate).

[24] E.g., 3.11.1 Cui des, elige; ipse tecum, si deceptus es, querere; dignum adiuua (a brilliant repunctuation of the print vulgate, Cui des elige ipse tecum. Si deceptus es, querere, dignum adiuua); 7.25.1 qui tam bellam rem, admonitionem (quam bellarem admonitionem **N**, qui tam bellam admonitionem Naples 1475 *et al.*).

[25] 1594, 555, correctly choosing the impersonal passive *proficitur* at 5.17.6, where Muretus read *proficit*: "Naz. & Col. nihil *proficitur* ... uix est ut non admiserim qui sit quo cerebrum findatur Grammaticis".

[26] E.g., 1594, 566 (on 6.43.3): "*tamquam quae non ducere, sed sequi debeat*] ita Mureti editio, secuta quosdam codd. Pinc(iani), cum prius esset, *tanquam non ducere*. quod etiamnum remanet in mss. meis quattuor: solum comparet illud *quae* in scidis Palat. pr. [sc., the collection of excerpts], quarum sublestior esse debet fides".

[27] 1594, 536, on 3.16.4 ingratus plures ...

[28] 1594, 539, on the text of 3.29.3 in his Palatinus secundus.

[29] 1594, 544, on 4.11.5 cura sanctiore: noting that the variant *curatiores* had been previously reported, he says, "credo: & originem mendi hanc dico, quod scriberetur olim *cura scīōre*. quomodo adhuc est in Pal. sec. & Naz. unde est quod praeferat Pal. tert. *cum sanctione*". Cf. also, e.g., 1594, 544 (4.12.5 uices suas), 555 (5.17.5 praeterito), 556 (5.21.2 quis tam ingratus), 557 (6.1 cognoscere), 562 (6.32.4 solitos), 574 (7.31.5 in irritum).

And all the while he maintains a scholarly persona that is thoroughly attractive and engaging. With the exception already remarked,[30] he does not engage in polemics, nor does he cite predecessors only to refute them while appropriating their contributions as his own (the latter a trait he especially regrets in Muretus); rather, he makes a point of painstakingly acknowledging his debts.[31] And for every note in which he exuberantly claims, "I'd bet anything [sc. that I'm right]", there are ten in which he simply acknowledges, "I'm stuck here".[32] In short, in his notes — far more copious than Erasmus' and more detailed than Pincianus' — Gruter's voice allows one to form a clear view of both his critical practices and his character, and the view in both respects is admirable.

Returning now to the main line of our story: before tracing the path that led to the mid-seventeenth century vulgate, we should note that the unanimity achieved was, not surprisingly, imperfect, for there remained passages where divisions can be found among the early modern editions and their late-eighteenth- and early-nineteenth-century successors. What perhaps does surprise is that there are so few sites of division: in my census, just under sixty. These run heavily to passages of two sorts: where there is real textual difficulty going back to the archetype, or where frivolous tinkering early in the printed tradition inserted difficulty where there was none. Two examples are enough to illustrate the point: I set out the standard text for each, with the record of the editions, then comment briefly.

> 3.22.1 Seruus, ut placet Chrysippo, perpetuus mercennarius est. Quemadmodum ille beneficium dat, ubi plus praestat quam <in> **quod operas** locauit, sic seruus, ubi beneuolentia erga dominum fortunae suae modum transit ...
> in quod operas Gruter 1594, 537, Leiden 1649, Ruhkopf, Vogel : quod operas **Nac** (quot **Npc** manu posteriore) Pincianus ('omnis antiqua lectio') Bipont. 2 : quo operis Neap. 1475 : quos operis Treviso 1478–Venice 1503 : quod operis Basel 1515–Basel 1590 Lipsius Bipont. 1 : ad quod operas Muretus
>
> 4.6.6 Noting how changes in our bodies occur at certain regular stages, Seneca instances the way baby teeth are lost and the teeth of adulthood arise: ... nunc puerilium dentium lapsus, nunc ad surgentem iam aetatem et in robustiorem gradum transeuntem pubertas et ultimus ille dens **surgenti iuuentae** terminum ponens.

---

30 Cf. n. 12, on Gothofredus.
31 Two examples chosen at random from many: 1594, 543 (4.1.3 damni), 570 (7.12.4 equestribus [2º]).
32 "Quouis contenderim pignore": 1594, 542 (4.6.6 dens). "Haereo" uel sim.: 1594, 569 (on 7.9.3 propinauerint) "ego hic haereo. tu lector, ipsum te expedi, si potes", with, e.g., 1594, 522 (1.10.5 sine ullo meo), 525 (2.5.3 gratus esse?), 526 (2.10.1 in sumptum), 528 (2.14.5 in nullum malum ...).

surgenti iuuentae **N** (defend. Gruter, Lipsius ad loc., Gronovius 1658, 165, recip. Ruhkopf Bipont. 2) : surgenti uiuente edd. usqe ad Venice 1503 : fugienti uitae Basil. 1515 — Lipsius : urgenti iuventae Lugd. Bat. 1649 Bipont. 1 Vogel : uergenti iuventae Gronovius 1649, 142

In the first, *quod operas* of the archetype's first hand seems clearly deficient, though it unaccountably was accepted by the first Bipontine edition; so too the bad guess of **N**'s late corrector (*quot operas*) and the readings of the *editio princeps* (*quo operis*) and the other editions down to Venice 1503 (*quos operis*). The rest of the tradition is divided between *quod operis* of Basel 1515, thereafter frequently read, and Gruter's supplement of *in* before *quod* (inspired by Muretus' *ad*, but as Gruter noted, the loss of *in* after *m* is easier to explain), adopted by Gronovius and others, as it probably will be by me. In the second case, the archetype's *surgenti* might seem awkward so soon after *surgentem*, but Seneca's appetite for repetition was greater than ours;[33] if a change were wanted, either of Gronovius's initial efforts, *urgenti* (printed in his text and adopted by Bipont. 1 and Vogel) or *uergenti* (mooted in his notes), would be preferable to *surgenti uiuente* (unintelligible) or *fugienti uitae* (too far from the *ductus litterarum* in form and too bathetic in sense). But Gronovius himself came around to *surgenti* in the end.

In other words: we have a relative handful of cases the likes of which one can find in any tradition. Turning now to the 2000-odd readings that came to define the vulgate, and proceeding as briskly as possible edition by edition, I note any special issues that a given edition raises, offer a few comments on its critical approach, then summarize the edition's influence by answering three questions: how many new readings introduced in the edition were then shared by all or virtually all subsequent editions? how many of those readings were good, and how many were bad?[34] And — as a final rough metric — what is the edition's "textual improvement average", the percentage of new readings introduced that actually improve the emerging vulgate text.

Basel 1515 begins with a letter addressed to Thomas Ruthall, bishop of Durham and secretary to Henry VIII of England, in which Erasmus compares the king's defeat of his enemies, the French and the Scots (June and September 1513, respectively), with the successful battle he had simultaneously fought against the forces hostile to literate culture:[35] "I have rescued the divine Jerome and Seneca, two of the best authors but also the most corrupted, from the faults — surely the

---

33 Cf. Albrecht 2008, 77–78.
34 Here "good" and "bad" reflect my judgment, which for the readings at issue is generally in line with the now-standard text of Hosius. Opinions might differ in any given case, but that cannot affect the overall picture that emerges.
35 Basel 1515, 3–4 = 325 Allen, dated 7 March 1515.

foulest foes of literature — by which they had been, not contaminated, but absolutely destroyed (*prorsus extincti*)", adding that he had removed over 4000 "monstrosities" from Seneca alone. He also goes on to give a general idea of his working method. He had received two manuscripts, from the archbishop of Canterbury and from King's College, Cambridge:[36] though these were "even more corrupt than the published copies" (*uulgata exemplaria*), yet — because their corruptions did not overlap — Erasmus could proceed "like an experienced and alert judge" to "conjecture the true text (*uera lectio*) from their diverging flaws ..., sniffing out a good deal from the traces of the letters and strokes"; in some cases — but more sparingly, he stresses — the truth had to be conjectured (*diuinandum*).

Erasmus was writing in England, where he had been toiling under a crushing load, not just purging Seneca of the massed monstrosities but also preparing two other monumental works, the editions of Jerome's *opera omnia* and the New Testament that began to appear the following year. Though he speaks of the Senecan edition as a *fait accompli*, it was still being seen through the press by two collaborators in Basel, Beatus Rhenanus, serving as Erasmus' proxy-editor, and the proofreader Wilhelm Nesen: a letter from Rhenanus to Erasmus, dated just weeks after the prefatory letter quoted above, gives a fascinating glimpse of the process:[37]

> Nesen is most careful in reading proof, and I wish I were as successful in emending the text as he is "right keen of scent" in sniffing out errors. ... I happened lately on that chapter in the *De beneficiis*, book 4, which begins:
>> Non ideo per se non est expetendum, cui aliquid extra quoque emolumenti adhaeret. *Eero* enim pulcherrima quaeque multis et aduentitiis comitata sunt *dolis*, sed illas trahunt, ipsa praecedunt. Num dubium est ... quin alterius [sc. solis] calore alantur corpora, terrae relaxentur, immodici humores comprimantur, *alligatis* omnia hyemis tristitia *frangantur*, alterius [sc. lunae] *tempore* efficaci ac penetrabili *rigatur* maturitas frugum? quin ad huius cursum foecunditas humana respondeat, quin ille *animum* obseruabilem fecerit circumactu suo?
>
> On the spur of the moment, when that sheet had already begun to be printed, I emended it like this; whether I was as clever as I was brave, I do not know:
>> *Fere* enim pulcherrima quaeque multis et aduentitiis comitata sunt *dotibus*, sed illas trahunt, ipsa praecedunt. Num dubium est ... quin alterius calore alantur corpora, terrae relaxentur, immodici humores comprimantur, *alligantis* omnia

---

[36] These seem to correspond to no manuscripts of *Ben.* known today.

[37] 328 Allen, of 17 April 1515; trans. in Mynors *et al.* 1976, 80. Ellipsis points replace clauses I have omitted, and in the quoted extract of Seneca (= 4.22.4–23.1) words to which Rhenanus' textual remarks refer are in italics; several clauses in the last paragraph are underlined for emphasis. On the genesis of this edition and that of 1529, see Trillitzsch 1965.

> hyemis tristicia *frangatur*, alterius *tepore* efficaci et penetrabili *rigetur* maturitas frugum? quin ad huius cursum foecunditas humana respondeat, quin ille *annum* obseruabilem fecerit circumactu suo?'
>
> There that passage ends; but I have done the same in many places, restoring, for instance, *dementissime* for *clementisse* [sic], *peierat* for *perierat*, *detestabili uia* for *de stabili uia*, *uota* for *nota*, and much else of the same sort. But **I do not like always relying on my own judgment**, especially extempore, and under pressure from men [viz., the typographers] who cannot stand delay. **If only we had an ancient copy, there is nothing I should enjoy more than to emend this text in the places that are still left uncorrected**, for by so doing I should be of use to scholars and advance your reputation, although you do say in your preface that you have removed most of the mistakes but not all.

Rhenanus' suggestion that his own conjectures could advance the reputation of Erasmus is perhaps striking, but it is not the most striking thing about the passage. Of the seven conjectures recorded in the extract, all but one are correct (for *rigatur* or *rigetur* read *regatur*, the correct text of **N**, which was still unknown); but of the six good corrections, four were already circulating in earlier editions and only two, *tepore* and *animum*, were new emendations.[38] In other words, Rhenanus is recounting his improvised correction, while the text was literally in press, of the errors that Froben's typographers introduced; and the four other readings he mentions tell the same tale.[39]

Basel 1515, then, was something of a hybrid, in which it is often impossible to know exactly who is responsible for a given reading. Erasmus drafted his text while working in England with the support of the manuscripts loaned to him and, evidently, some of the earlier printed editions — the *uulgata exemplaria* to which he refers — applying his analysis and resorting to "divination" where necessary. After his draft was received in Basel, it was typeset in a manner that — if Rhenanus' letter is any indication — introduced errors with hair-raising frequency, leaving Rhenanus and Nesen to correct them by conjecture, under time-

---

38 *Fere, dotibus,* and *frangatur* appear in all the earlier editions; *alligantis* stood in Naples 1475 and Treviso 1478 but was displaced by *alligatis* in the Venetian editions.

39 *Dementissime* (also the reading of **N**) corrects *clementissime*, the reading of the earlier editions at 4.27.5; *peierat* corrects *perierat*, the reading of both **N** and the editions at 6.8.2; *de stabili uia* (for *destestabili uia* at 6.25.5) is not otherwise attested as a reading and must be a new typographer's error; while *nota* is the correct reading of **N** at 6.19.4, where Rhenanus' conjectured *uota* is an impossible trivialization also found in the late manuscript **V** and the earlier editions (Seneca ventriloquizes a Gaul granted citizenship by the *princeps* as one among all other Gauls: "cum [sc. princeps] cogitauit Gallis omnibus prodesse, et mihi cogitauit prodesse; eram enim Gallus et me, etiam si non mea, publica tamen nota conprendit", where accusative plural *uota*, for ablative singular *nota*, can be construed only if one ignores *me*).

pressure, with reference to no other text, manuscript or print, and with the occasional epistolary appeal to Erasmus for clarification.[40] And that is consistent with the character of the edition's innovations that thereafter become the standard text. On the one hand, some of them correct "uncorrectable" errors found in the earlier editions — omissions, intelligible interpolations, transpositions of word-order, substitution of lexically or grammatically plausible innovations — that could not be corrected or often even detected without reference to an independent manuscript source, for example:

> 1.1.10 at male cesserit (**N**) *om. edd. prior.* (at male cessit Basel. 1515)
> 1.6.3 est honor (**N**) *om. edd. prior.* (est honos Basel. 1515)
> 2.2.1 qui roganti dedit (**N** Basel 1515) *om. edd. prior.*
> 2.21.1 cum obsceno (**N** Basel. 1515) : non obscuro *edd. prior.*
> 4.36.3 repetam (**N** Basel. 1515) : repetam, errori fidem non esse praestandum *edd. prior.*

Such corrections are almost certainly owed to Erasmus. On the other hand, there are many places where a superficial fault found in the earlier editions was removed but a core difficulty, which careful comparison with an independent source would have revealed, was allowed to remain, for example:

> 1.4.6 at qui ... *fidem* in rebus humanis retinere... uolunt **N** : at qui ... *praepositum poetarum fidem* in rebus humanis retinere ... uolunt *edd. prior.* : at qui ... *praepositam fidem* in rebus humanis retinere ... uolunt Basel 1515 —where the irrelevant poets are exiled and the gender of *praepositam* is adjusted, but the intrusion of the latter word is not noticed;

> 2.8.1 "Tamen" inquit "*effugere* Tiberius ne hoc quidem modo *quod uitabat* potuit" **N** : Tamen *inquietudinem effugere* Tiberius ne hoc quidem modo *putabat* potuit *effugere edd. prior.* : Tamen *inquietudinem* Tiberius ne hoc quidem modo *quo* potuit *putabat effugere* Basel. 1515 —where a superfluous *effugere* is deleted, but in the wrong place, and an attempt is made to make *putabat potuit effugere* at least look like Latin, but *inquietudinem* (probably owed to an initial corruption of *inquit* to *inquiet*) is allowed to stand.

In short, Basel 1515 is not a distinguished edition, but it does represent a real effort at correction for the text of *De beneficiis*; and in fact if the two manuscripts that Erasmus used were at least moderately more faithful in reflecting the text transmitted from the archetype than the terrible text established by the *editio princeps*, many errors could easily have been removed — a matter of plucking

---

40 Reference to no other text: this must be what Froben had in mind when he wrote in the edition's colophon, "I will not say that [the text] has been purged of all flaws, something that could not happen without recourse to *exemplaria*". Epistolary appeal: see 329 Allen, sent by Nesen to Erasmus around the same time, asking Erasmus about a marginal note in his draft.

low-hanging fruit. Perhaps that is at least partly why of the 437 readings that were introduced by Basel 1515 and remained part of the print tradition, 348 were improvements, while 89 were new deformations (textual improvement average: 79.6%).[41]

In his prefatory epistle Erasmus had written with equanimity that despite all the errors he had removed, "I have left a great deal for others to scrutinize". And yet, according to the prefatory epistle he wrote to introduce the edition of 1529, that earlier edition had caused him shame "within a few months". That claim might be a product of hindsight; but certainly by early 1523 he was venting his frank dissatisfaction:

> I had entrusted to scholarly friends [presumably, Rhenanus and Nesen] the task of choosing out of my marginal annotations what they thought worth using, and they – generously, to be sure – undertook it. But I then learned ... that even among those who are thought to be true as steel ..., there are some who cannot be relied on; and it was useless to regret that I had not followed the advice of the crested lark in the fable: Do not wait for your friends to do what you can do yourself.[42]

And so he resolved to take on the job of "scrutinizing" himself. Work began in earnest at the end of 1525, after the edition of Jerome was complete, and printing began in September 1528, with *De beneficiis* standing first in the volume, as it had in Basel 1515.[43] Erasmus' notes on the text of *De beneficiis* mention throughout the use of multiple *codices*, some of them *uetustissimi*, and he refers specifically to manuscripts he received from England and Basel.[44] But two important sources seem to have reached him only after the work was well advanced. One, certainly, was a copy of Treviso 1478 in which the Dutch humanist Rodolphus Agricola had entered valuable marginal notes: since this book reached Erasmus only when *De beneficiis* and much of the *Epistulae Morales* was already typeset, he decided to

---

[41] Of course, a very large majority of those 348 good readings are innovations relative only to the print tradition. The good readings of Basel 1515 that are absolutely new tend to be slight and obvious adjustments (e.g., 1.15.2 exaudit : exaudiat **N**), though there are exceptions (e.g., 2.1.2 frontis : fortes **N**).

[42] Letter 1341A Allen, 30 January 1523 (to Johann von Bozheim), trans. in Mynors and Estes 1989, 310–11, similarly ibid. 356; Nesen is obliquely criticized in 1257 Allen. Crested lark: from a fable of Aesop quoted in the satires of Ennius in a fragment preserved at Gellius 2.29.20; it reappears in the preface to Basel 1529.

[43] On the chronology of Basel 1529 see Allen's introduction to the prefatory epistle (= 2091 Allen: Allen *et al.* 1906–1958, 8:25–26), with Trillitzsch 1965.

[44] Basel 1529, 29 (on 3.14), 42 (4.18).

incorporate the notes in a critical appendix inserted after the *Epistulae*.⁴⁵ It is probable that another latecomer was **N** itself, which Erasmus first cites, as the *Longobardicus uetustissimus*, in a note on 4.36: since he cites the *Longobardicus* twenty-six more times in the notes down through the end of the work, and never before, it seems reasonable to infer that he did not have the manuscript when the text of the first three books, and most of the fourth, was being revised and set in type. If this is right, then **N** could make its mark directly on the text and margins only of *Ben.* 5–7 (and the end of 4); but in *Ben.* 1–3 (and most of 4) it could contribute only indirectly, in the later appendix that carries Agricola's notes, where it doubtless stands behind at least some of the notes — a mere sprinkling in any case — that cite a *uetus* or *uetustissimus codex*.⁴⁶

If, as seems to be the case, **N** reached Erasmus too late for him to bring it to bear on the text as thoroughly as he might have done, he nonetheless had his critical brilliance to rely on. He proceeded circumspectly, eager where appropriate to assure readers that he was not acting arbitrarily: so, for example, he invokes the testimony of two manuscripts at 4.18.2 to support a two-word supplement in the text, and he repeatedly offers similar assurances elsewhere.⁴⁷ But where he saw the need to emend, he did so: I count over 120 places where a certainly or probably conjectural reading became part of the vulgate, of which nearly fifty have been accepted

---

45 Readings of Agricola that joined the vulgate include 1.12.2 deterat (dederat **N**) and 6.17.1 institoribus (institutoribus **N**).

46 In the appendix, where the epithet *Longobardicus* does not occur, 36 notes to Books 1–4 cite a *uetus* or *uetustissimus codex* (the notes to Books 5–7 have only 10 such citations). Certain or likely references to **N** include 1.12.3 obseruet personas **Nac**, obseruet et personas **Npc** (superscript & added): "Vetustus [sc. codex] habebat *et personas*, sed ascripta super uersum coniunctione"; 1.15.4 quolibet **Nac**, ƚ quod liber **Npc** (superscript note): "uetustum exemplar habebat annotatum, *liber*"; 3.29.4 aspice Rhenum] aspicer henum **N**: "uetus codex habebat *Henum*"; 4.13.1 facere **Nac,** ƚ farcire **Npc**: "in uetustissimo codice ... pro *facere*, subnotatum erat *farcire*". Other such citations cannot look to **N**: e.g., 2.23.3 clientium **N**: "uetus codex melius habebat *debentium*"; 3.4.2 futurorum **N**: "*praeteritorum* ... exemplar uetustissimum"; 3.7.1 in illo **N**: "*in illo* abest in uetusto codice". In most cases we simply cannot judge, since at any given point any "old codex" was far more likely than not to have **N**'s text: e.g., at 1.15.3, where the earlier editions had the nonsensical *tecum potiri* for the correct *nepotari*, Erasmus noted, "quod (sc. *nepotari*) prius diuinaueramus repperimus expresse scriptum, in uetusto codice, manu descripto"; and though **N** does indeed read *nepotari*, so do Florence, BML San Marco 286 (γ), Paris, BnF lat. 6382 (π), and Paris, BnF 15085 (φ), twelfth-century representatives of the medieval tradition's three branches, here chosen at random.

47 "Ea [sc. uerba] restituimus ex fide duorum exemplariorum, ... ne quis suspicetur a nobis adiecta" (Basel 1529, 42); for similar scruples expressed later in the same book, see 4.28.1, 4.40.3, 4.40.5.

as correct by editors since the nineteenth century.⁴⁸ In all, 462 readings in Basel 1529 were retained in all future editions: 378 of these are certainly to the good, yielding a textual improvement average of 81.8% — a figure remarkably similar to the record of Basel 1515 (79.6%), despite Erasmus' dismay at the latter.

The Basel editions of 1515 and 1529 put their stamp on the tradition as no subsequent edition managed to do, and for that reason the latter can be treated more summarily, starting with the two weakest editions, Curio's of 1557 and Muretus' of 1585. The former contributed 139 good readings to the developing vulgate, and 190 readings overall, for a respectable textual improvement average of 73.2%. But that record is due almost entirely to the fact that Curio imported so many readings from Pincianus' *Castigationes* (120) or the margins and notes of Basel 1529 (53) or both (3). To his credit, Curio acknowledges this debt in the second sentence of his introductory letter to the reader ("adhibitis Erasmi & Pinciani annotationibus & scholiis"). But when he goes on to stress the critical rigor of his selections ("ad exactam iudicii trutinam singula expendentes"), he claims a virtue that I confess I cannot find in the work. His superficiality, in contrast to Erasmus' penetration, is typified in a case like 2.35.3, where Seneca, having introduced the familiar Stoic category of the " unwise" (*stulti*), makes the equally familiar remark, *insanire omnes dicimus*. That is what **N** and its medieval descendants tell us he wrote, whereas the earlier printed editions inserted an obvious gloss, *insanire omnes scilicet stultos dicimus*: Erasmus accordingly wrote, "Some smarty-pants (*eruditulus*) had inserted the two words *scilicet stultos*, which I have removed in accordance with an ancient book's testimony: let no one rashly replace [them]" — but replace them Curio did, and there they remained for two and half centuries. It is therefore not surprising that on the rare occasions when Curio seems to have struck out on his own, adding fourteen conjectural readings to the vulgate, he was clearly wrong in all cases but four.⁴⁹

By contrast, Muretus was one of the finest Latinists of his time and a critic who had displayed his talents over a wide range in the fifteen books of *Variae lectiones* that he published down to 1580, among other works. But his edition of

---

48 E.g., 3.36.3 partam (paratam **N**, peractam edd.), 4.23.3 quam tu (quantum **N** edd.), 4.28.5 percussores (persecutors **N** edd.), 5.20.6 plectere (flectere **N** edd.), 7.19.2 quidem habeat (quidam debeat **N** edd.).

49 1.14.1 quis patitur sibi imputari <uulgaria> (plugging a certain lacuna with a plausible stopgap, after Agricola's equally plausible *communia*), 1.14.4 excogitet (an easy correction of the mood, found also in some *recentiores*), 6.5.2 sed aliud pro illo. Reddere (correcting the punctuation), 7.15.3 huic uero qui et (huic uero debes et qui et **N**: Curio's reading blends Erasmus' *huic uere debes qui et* and Pincianus' *huic uero qui*).

Seneca, certainly in the case of *De beneficiis*, is a desultory affair,[50] peppered with dyspeptic outbursts — "locum hunc, ut alios sane quam multos, deprauauerat Erasmus" (provoked by his own misreading of Erasmus' note at 7.19.4) — that prompted Gruter's mild rejoinders ("Muretus carpit ... Erasmum tanquam huius loci corruptorem. iniurie"). It is probably just to suppose that as he worked on the edition his failing health affected its quality. His ability as a critic is still attested by the good conjectures, just over thirty, that he produced.[51] But overall the edition's contribution to the vulgate is weak: it adds 283 new readings (101 drawn from Erasmus' marginalia and annotations, or Pincianus, or the marginalia of Basel 1557, or some combination of the three); and of those added readings, 117 are inferior to the readings they displaced (textual improvement average: 58.6%).

The last two editions we have to consider, Lipsius' of 1605 and Gronovius' of 1649, did not so much stand in Gruter's shadow as flourish in the light he cast. Lipsius of course was one of the very greatest scholars of the sixteenth century, and his running annotations amounted to the most thorough commentary that Seneca's *philosophica* had yet received; and both men were estimable textual scholars who made valuable contributions to the text of *De beneficiis* through their conjectures.[52] Yet the success that both editions enjoyed in improving the text reflects the guidance provided by Gruter's shrewdness as a critic in the *Animaduersiones* and, above all, the access to **N** that its reports provided. In the case of the 203 new contributions to the vulgate made by Lipsius' text, the way was pointed by Gruter alone eighty-nine times and by the combined judgment of Gruter and Pincianus in another forty-two; since those new contributions included only thirty-nine inferior readings, the edition's textual improvement average (80.8%) reached a level not seen since Basel 1529. And the point emerges even more clearly in the case of Leiden 1649. In his reception of **N** from Gruter's reports, Gronovius sounds very much like a nineteenth-century critic embracing the doctrine of the *codex optimus*: "nihil lubrici, nulla titubatione opus, modo

---

50 In the Heidelberg edition of 1594, where his annotations are followed by Gruter's in the identical format, his notes on *Ben.* run to eleven and a half columns, Gruter's to 116.

51 E.g., 2.30.2 iners <sine> opera (ineas operam **N**, in ea opera Naples 1475 — Venice 1503, iners opera Basel 1515–1557), 3.25 crudelitate mitem (crudelitatem item **N** edd.), 4.12.2 legem dicimus (legem scimus **N** edd.).

52 Lipsius: e.g., 3.18.1 *post* superiori *lacunam statuit*, 4.21.6 audiat (audiam **N** edd.), 4.30.2 inpudici (inpodiri **N**, impediret edd.). Gronovius: e.g., 1.5.2 tangi: res (tangiles **Nac**, sed **Npc** edd.), 2.12.2 licet it (licit **Nac**, ł litiget **Npc**, dicit edd.), 4.12.3 paraturus (paratus **Nac**, ł pratum uł portus **Npc**, emere paratus edd.).

adhaereamus Naz(ariano)" could be his motto.⁵³ The impact of this view on the text is clear: 250 new readings of Leiden 1649 join the now-bulging vulgate text; in those cases, a note by Gruter alone is the starting point 144 times and a note by Gruter combined with Lipsius and/or Pincianus another 54 times.⁵⁴ With only twenty-one inferior readings included in the mix, the result is the highest textual improvement average (91.6%) of all the editions.

A brief coda to the discussion will throw into even greater relief the importance of Gruter's work at this stage of the tradition. In all the many hundreds of cases relevant to the discussion so far, the development of the vulgate is simple and unidirectional: that is, a reading (good or bad) that stood in the *editio princeps* was passed along from one edition to the next until another reading (good or bad) displaced it and remained as the vulgate text. But there is a smaller but significant set of cases in which the movement instead has a back-and-forth dimension: the reading that stood in the *editio princeps* was passed along until it was displaced, and the new reading remained until it was displaced in turn, either by its predecessor or by a new reading, which then became the vulgate.⁵⁵ For example (correct reading in italics):

> 1.1.9 cuncta interque illa Naples 1475–Basel 1515 : *et cuncta interque illa* Basel 1529 : cunctanterque Basel 1557 : *et cuncta interque illa* Rome 1585, which becomes the vulgate;

---

53 Gronovius *Notae*, 119 (on 1.10.1); cf. ibid. 120, 135, 139, 152, 157 ("liber omnium princeps"), 157, 159, 162, 167. In fact Malaspina (2000, 760 n. 40) hypothesized that Gronovius had direct knowledge of **N**, but the hypothesis derives no support from anything that Gronovius says, while what he does say in his *Notae* demonstrates his dependence on Gruter: e.g., in his note on *Ben.* 6.8.3 *causae ... gratiae* (**N** : *causae ... gratia* ψ Naples 1475 – Venice 1503, *causa ... gratia* **G** and the editions from Basel 1515) — where Gruter approved *causae ... gratiae* and noted, "legerim cum mss. plerisque" — Gronovius wrote (1649, 162), "uellem magnopere, expliquisset nobis Gruterus, an in illis 'plerisque' esset Naz[arianus]. Nam ei forte aliquid deferrem: caeterum, si uere auguror, non fuit: certe non est in Rot. [= our **G**] & multo Latinius ad aures meas accidit uulgatum."
54 By contrast a note by Lipsius alone provides the precedent eleven times; by Pincianus alone, twice; by Lipsius and Pincianus together, twice.
55 Two displacements is the norm, three the exception, more than three all but unexampled: see 2.4.1 (correct reading in italics) quam ubi quodque quod impetrasti Naples 1475 Treviso 1478 : quam ubi quoque quod impetrasti edd. Venice 1490–1503 : quamque ubi quid impetrasti Basel 1515 (so later Pincianus) : *quam ubi quod impetrasti* Basel 1529–Rome 1585 : quam ubi quoque cum impetrasti Lipsius : quam ubi quoque quod impetrasti Leiden 1649 (Gronovius *Notae*, 125, after Gruter 1594, 525), which then remains the vulgate.

1.3.5 adscripti Naples 1475–Basil. 1515 : *adstricti* Basel 1529–Rome 1585 : adscripti Lipsius, which becomes the vulgate.

The following table records the editions' contributions to this form of vulgate-formation; an entry in the form "21/1" means that twenty-one superior readings were added to the vulgate, against one inferior:

Basel 1515 2/0
Basel 1529 6/1
Basel 1557 16/1[56]
Rome 1585   21/1[57]
Lipsius   45/6[58]
Leiden 1649 75/2[59]

Since such back-and-forth movements typically require time to unfold, the results — 165 good readings gained for the vulgate vs. 11 inferior readings — cluster at the latter end of the chronological range and lead to two perfectly obvious observations: first, the editions of Lipsius and Gronovius, which typically correct inferior readings introduced by Curio and Muretus, were by far the most influential; second, by far the greatest influence on those two editions was the work of Janus Gruter.

* * *

To the obvious question raised by all that precedes — "Why did critical progress on the *De beneficiis* halt so suddenly, to be replaced so long by critical inertia?" — I can think of two possible answers. It might be that critics came to a judgment that anticipated the famous remark of E.R. Dodds, "Our editions ... are good enough to live with".[60] But surely a more important factor was the absence of any stimulus comparable to Gruter's placing so much of **N**'s text before his readers; and this hunch receives some confirmation from a comment made in 1852 by Friedrich Haase, in the preface to the second volume of his edition. After remarking

---

[56] A good reading is restored 13 times after Pincianus, twice after the margins of Basel 1529, once after both; the inferior restoration follows Pincianus.
[57] A good reading is restored 4 times after Pincianus, 9 times after the text or margin of Basel 1529, once after both.
[58] A good reading is restored 35 times after Gruter, 6 times after Pincianus, twice after both; of the 6 inferior restorations, one follows Gruter's judgment, two are contrary to Gruter's judgment.
[59] A good reading is restored 60 times after Gruter and another 6 when Gruter's note is combined with a note by Pincianus and/or Lipsius.
[60] Quoted at Tarrant 2016, 145, with the probably apocryphal rejoinder attributed to D.R. Shackleton Bailey, "Maybe, maybe not; it all depends on one's standard of living".

that he had left many passages of *De beneficiis* in the corrupt or at least imperfectly corrected state in which he had found them, he added, "multum tamen ibi ad inueniendam ueram scripturam profuit praestantissimus cod. Nazarianus, plus etiam profuturus ille, si post Gruterum denuo conferri potuisset". The counterfactual in the last clause was shifted to the indicative two decades later — *tandem post Gruterum denuo conferri potuit* — when M.C. Gertz gained access to a complete collation of **N**, published a new edition based on the premise that **N** is the archetype, and initiated intense discussion of the text that continued for two generations and more.⁶¹

Bibliography

Albrecht, M. von (2008), 'Seneca's Language and Style. I', *Hyperboreus* 14, 68–90.
Allen, P.S., *et al.* (1906–1958), *Opus Epistolarum Des. Erasmi Roterodami*, 8 vols., Oxford.
Buck, J. (1908), *Seneca de Beneficiis und de Clementia in der Überlieferung*, Tübingen.
Fickert, K.R. (1842), *L. Annaei Senecae opera*, vol. 1, Leipzig.
Fickert, K.R. (1843), *L. Annaei Senecae opera*, vol. 2, Leipzig.
Gertz, M.C. (1876), *L. Annaei Senecae Libri De beneficiis et De clementia,* Berlin.
Gronovius, J.F.(1649), *Joh. Fred. Gronovii ad L. & M. Annaeos Senecas Notae,* Leiden.
Gruter, J. (1594), *Iani Gruteri Animaduersiones in L. Annaei Senecae opera*, Heidelberg.
Kühlmann, W., *et al.* (2005), *Die deutschen Humanisten: Dokumente zur Überlieferung der antiken und mittelalterlichen Literatur in der frühen Neuzeit*, Abteilung I: *Die Kurpfalz*, Band I/2: *Janus Gruter*, Turnhout.
Hine, H.M. (1983), 'The Younger Seneca: *Natural Questions*', in: Reynolds 1983a, 376–378.
Malaspina, E. (2000), 'J.F. Gronovius, *Editore fantasma* delle opere senecane *Ex ultima I. Lipsii emendatione* (Leida 1639–40)', *Aevum* 74, 751–761.
Mazzoli, G. (1982), 'Ricerche sulla tradizione medievale del *De beneficiis* e del *De clementia* di Seneca: III, Storia della tradizione manoscritti', *Bolletino dei classici* 30, 165–223.
Mynors, R.A.B., *et al.* (1976), *The Correspondence of Erasmus: Letters 298 to 445 (1515–1516),* Toronto.
Mynors, R.A.B./Martin, J. (1989), *The Correspondence of Erasmus: Letters 1252 to 1355 (1522 to 1523)*, Toronto.
Reynolds, L.D. (1965), *The Medieval Tradition of Seneca's Letters*, Oxford.
Reynolds, L.D. (ed.) (1983a), *Texts and Transmission: A Survey of the Latin Classics,* Oxford.
Reynolds, L.D. (1983b), 'Seneca the Younger: *De beneficiis* and *De clementia*; *Dialogues*; *Letters*', in: Reynolds 1983a, 357–360, 363–375.

---

61 The collation was made by R. Kekulé for Moritz Haupt, who in turn made it available to Gertz: Gertz 1876, iii. I have on my hard drive digital copies of 89 monographs, articles, and reviews, published between 1876 and 1930, that bear on the textual criticism of the works we owe to **N**.

Tarrant, R.J. (2016), *Texts, Editors, and Readers: Methods and Problems in Latin Textual Criticism*, Cambridge.
Trillitzsch, W. (1965), 'Erasmus und Seneca', *Philologus* 109, 270–293.
Weber, E. (ed.) (1894), *Virorum clarorum saeculi XVI et XVII epistolae selectae*, Leipzig.

Michael Clarke
From Dares Phrygius to Thomas Jefferson, via Joseph of Exeter: A Study in Classical Reception

One of the salutary lessons of reading Chris Stray's *Classics Transformed*[1] is to see with sudden clarity how the set of authors canonised by taste and curricula has changed over the generations, often narrowing rather than widening in the process. This awareness is essential not only as a corrective to the all-too-common belief that to learn or teach Latin and Greek is to pass on a stable tradition, but also as a reminder of the countless once-famous texts that are waiting to be brought back out of the shadows. My aim is to explore one such story, in which a forgotten poet from a once-vibrant tradition of Latin hexameter composition can be found lurking behind the familiar figure of Homer.

1 Jefferson's Homer

As a starting-point, I want to look at a celebrated letter written in 1800 by Thomas Jefferson to the radical English scientist, educationalist and theologian Joseph Priestley, who had recently settled in America as a political and intellectual exile.[2] The letter follows upon an earlier one in which Jefferson had been describing his plan to found a new university. In the first letter he had written only of applied and scientific studies, and he now sets out to emphasise the study of 'the languages', meaning primarily or exclusively Latin and Greek. He begins with their usefulness as sources of 'models... of fine composition', plainly directed at the practical task of training future leaders and politicians in the art of rhetoric, but goes on to make a more idealised claim:

---

1 Stray 1998, 7–29 and *passim*. There is an interesting contrast in the approach taken by Silk, Gildenhard and Barrow 2014, where the authors tend to construct the Classical canon as a stable edifice over time.
2 See Jefferson 1999, 263–5 for the text of the letter (January 27th, 1800, following on that of January 18th). This and other correspondence with Priestley can be found at https://founders.archives.gov/documents/Jefferson/01-31-02-0289, last accessed 8th August 2019.

> To all this I add, that to read the Latin & Greek authors in their original, is a sublime luxury; and I deem luxury in science to be at least as justifiable as in architecture, painting, gardening, or the other arts. I enjoy Homer in his own language infinitely beyond Pope's translation of him, & both beyond the dull narration of the same events by Dares Phrygius; & it is an innocent enjoyment. I thank on my knees, him who directed my early education, for having put into my possession this rich source of delight; and I would not exchange it for anything which I could then have acquired, & have not since acquired.

There is a certain defensiveness in this, and in the next sentence Jefferson pleads 'With this regard for those languages, you will acquit me of meaning to omit them' — in other words, his silence about the Classics in the earlier letter was simply because it was so obvious that they would be part of the curriculum.

In this evocation of the value of a youthful immersion in ancient literature, the word 'sublime' invokes the pivotal term of critical approbation used by Jefferson and his generation.[3] He evidently uses it here in the same sense as he does (for example) with regard to Macpherson's Ossian, of which he writes that 'the tender and the sublime emotions of the mind were never so finely wrought up by human hand'.[4] In his commonplace book he even annotated Ossianic passages with Homeric parallels in Greek, following the precedent set by Hugh Blair in the essay accompanying the published text of Macpherson's work.[5] As far as Homer is concerned, all this seems fairly conventional as expressing the sensibilities of an educated 'man of taste' of Jefferson's generation. The problem is the other name: who is Dares Phrygius, and why does he stand for a *contrast* with the excellences to which Jefferson is paying homage?

Dares Phrygius' star has sunk low in our time, so a brief explanation is in order.[6] He is a minor character in the *Iliad*, a priest of Hephaestus who fights on the Trojan side (*Il.* 5.9–10), and his name was chosen — for reasons no longer recoverable — for the supposed author of a fictitious eyewitness account of the Trojan War, written perhaps in the fifth century CE (though this dating is guesswork). The *De Excidio Troiae* that goes under the name of Dares Phrygius survives only in Latin, but the prefatory letter that introduces it — purportedly written by

---

3 See Brown 2012.
4 Cited by Hayes 2009, 134.
5 Blair's essay is available at Macpherson 1996, 343–400. On the international influence of Ossianic poetry see Gaskill 2005; on Jefferson's Ossian, Johnson 2016 is a thoughtful essay.
6 The authoritative edition of Dares and Dictys is now Lelli 2015. An outstanding survey treatment is Merkle 1996, alongside the many subsequent articles on Dares by Frederic N. Clark; the publication of Clark's monograph on Dares is eagerly awaited as I write this.

the historian Cornelius Nepos in the generation of Cicero — asserts that he is giving an exact translation from the author's original Greek.[7] Of course the Greek version may never have existed; but it is worth remembering that the generically similar (but much more elaborate) account of the war by another participant, ascribing itself to Dictys of Crete, was thought to have been composed in Latin as a forgery until papyrus fragments of the Greek original were found in modern times.

Reading the *De Excidio Troiae* is a strange and shadowy challenge. The plan seems to have been to re-imagine what the historical realities of the Trojan War *might* have been, stripped of the poetic extravagance and divine apparatus that Homer added to them when he composed the *Iliad* long after the events. The gods are absent from the action, and the Judgment of Paris is narrated by Paris himself as something he saw in a dream. Everything that happens on the battlefield is the behaviour of mortal fighting men, not demigods: when Achilles quarrels with the other Greek leaders he does so because he has been passed over for promotion, not because of a god-like wrath as in the *Iliad*. This resentment is compounded by falling in love with the Trojan princess Polyxena; Hecuba uses the promise of Polyxena's hand in marriage to lure him to a meeting at the Trojan temple of Apollo, where he is ambushed by Paris. In due course the city falls because Aeneas and other Trojan leaders betray it to the Greeks in return for safe passage into exile afterwards; but Dares mentions that the gate through which they admitted the Greeks was carved with the image of a horse's head — the detail, it is implied, that would emerge garbled as the story of the Wooden Horse.[8]

One wonders whether the author was following the clues laid by Plato's celebrated condemnation of the Homeric gods in the *Republic*, or even those of other Classical authors with a 'revisionist' bent. It is striking, for example, that the war begins as part of a tit-for-tat series of abductions of princesses between Greeks and barbarians (Medea, Hesione, Helen), reminiscent of the sequence evoked by Herodotus at the beginning of his *Histories*. Similarly the story of Achilles lured into the temple to marry Polyxena is briefly mentioned in Servius' commentary on the *Aeneid*,[9] and it is a fair guess that this was the basis on which the author of the *De Excidio* worked for this episode. The same principle explains why the work is written in such spare and formless prose, entirely without apparent artistry or significant form: a soldier's straightforward account of the war he fought in, barely forty printed pages in Latin. If the power of Homer's account of Helen

---

7 On the compositional technique, cf. Ní Mheallaigh 2008.
8 *De Excidio Troiae* §40.
9 Servius on *Aeneid* 3.321.

lies in her intangibility, her goddess-like aura of mystery, then what a climb-down it is to read Dares telling us exactly what she looked like:

> ...Helenam similem illis formosam animi simplicis blandam cruribus optimis notam inter duo supercilia habentem ore pusillo. (*De Excidio Troiae* § 12)

> Helen was similar to them [sc. Castor and Pollux]: she was beautiful, with an honest mind, kindly, with very fine legs, having a mark between her two eyebrows, and with a gentle mouth.

It is a fair guess that the work began its life as a Second Sophistic *jeu d' esprit*, akin to the more artistically complex *Heroicus* of Philostratus[10] and even comparable (however distantly) to the pseudo-historical narratives of the Gospel story that survive among the New Testament apocrypha. Precisely because it is supposed to resemble the unvarnished truth, it reads as if it barely counts as literature at all.

2 Jefferson's Dares

When we turn back to Jefferson's letter, we are left with a puzzle. Why express Homer's excellence by the contrast with Dares? On the face of it, the juxtaposition is absurd — as if one were to say that London is a fine city, much more lively and vibrant than Luton, or that Shakespeare's greatness is revealed by the contrast with the crude Tudor comedy *Gammer Gurton's Needle*. Yet the letter as a whole is not quirky, or satirical, or casually written: its style is that of one writing to impress, choosing his words carefully and with deference. A solution can, I believe, be found through a closer look at the strange fortunes of the *De Excidio Troiae* in the medieval and Early Modern periods.[11]

Almost the only record of the early reception of the *De Excidio Troiae* is a notice in the *Etymologies* of Isidore of Seville (about 630 CE), where it is appears in the treatment of History: on the principle that History deals with what has been seen by the writer with his eyes, Dares among the pagans and Moses among the believers are identified as the art's first practitioners.[12] After Isidore, however, there is a gap until the work suddenly reappears in Francia in the eighth century CE. Once rediscovered, and evidently taken to be the authentic account of the

---

10 Cf. Kim 2010, 175–215.
11 See the excellent introductory survey by Solomon 2007.
12 Isidore, *Etymologies* 1.41–42.

ancient war, it took on new relevance because of the claim of the Franks to be lineally descended — like the Romans — from Trojan fugitives, led by the eponymous Francus or Francio. Manuscripts from this period preserve a further fictitious history, *Daretis Phrygii De Origine Francorum Liber*, in which Dares' narrative of the Trojan War is extended to become an account of the wanderings of Francio and his people's eventual settlement in what would become the historical homeland of the Franks.[13] Successive re-elaborations and emulations of this origin legend appeared through the Middle Ages and beyond,[14] and other nations looked to rival articulations of the same basic narrative of Trojan origins, among them that of the British descended from Brutus the grandson of Aeneas.[15]

Despite this evidence for historiographical interest in Dares in the Carolingian period, his influence on poetry only becomes discernible two centuries later.[16] A new interest in the revival and emulation of Classical poetry on the Trojan War is evident in the work of Baudri de Bourgeuil and other poets of the 'Loire Valley school' in the second half of the eleventh century, and this bears further fruit afterwards in two full-scale hexameter poems, the *Ylias* of Simon Aurea Capra (Simon Chèvre d' Or) and the *Anonymi Historia Daretis Frigii*.[17] In its opening lines, this poem declares the source of its own authority: poetic inventions (*figmenta poetica*) confuse (*turbant*) the true history of the Trojan War, but the present work will preserve that history by following the 'trustworthy footsteps' (*vestigia fida*) of Dares Phrygius himself.[18] In effect, the poem claims both the grandeur of poetry and the authenticity of eyewitness historiography.

3 Twelfth-century experiments

The full flowering of this movement came in the later twelfth century, when the Dares tradition fed into the development of a new mode of heroic verse narrative in the form of French romance. From the ferment of multi-lingual creative activity that developed around the Angevin court of Henry II of England and under the

---

13 Gerberding 1987 remains the best study of the sources.
14 See further Innes 2000, with Keller 2008, 104–128, Clark 2010.
15 For the underlying discourse of national myth-making, cf. Geary 2002.
16 On the Trojan revival in literature of the West (esp. the Francophonic world) from c. 1050 onward, see the recent summary treatment by Mora-Lebrun 2018, with Tilliette 1999, Ziolkowski 2009.
17 The *Anonymi Historia* is edited by Stohlmann 1968.
18 *Anonymi Historia* 1–5.

patronage of his queen, Eleanor of Aquitaine, comes the astonishingly ambitious *Roman de Troie* of Benoît de Sainte-Maure.[19] This is the first, in all likelihood, of the great *romans d' antiquité* (the others being the *Roman de Thèbes, Roman d' Alexandre* and *Histoire d' Éneas*) that form, with the cycles of Charlemagne and Arthur, the central subject-matter of chivalric romance in the transnational culture of later medieval Europe.[20] The expansion and re-imagining of the war plays tricks on the reader's imagination, and one is left disorientated by the realisation that Hector and Achilles have become mounted knights, charging at each other with lances, or that the captive women Briseis and Chryseis have become the pivotal figures in a tale of the conflict between erotic love and military duty. But Dares Phrygius is still in control. Like the Latin poets in the previous generation, Benoît appeals to Dares' primal authority, and despite his own baroque innovations he allows the sequence of events in the ancient work to remain as the skeleton of his narrative. In the opening lines, Benoît explains his work in the same terms as his predecessors had done: Homer's version is famous but is marred by the absurdity of his gods, and he was not an eyewitness of the war, but in the text of Dares we have the exact translation of what he wrote when 'each day he would record exactly what he had witnessed with his own eyes'.[21]

The afterlife of Benoît's work is staggeringly complex.[22] It was translated into numerous languages, including even Byzantine Greek,[23] and was also reduced back to prose as pure historiography, becoming absorbed into the second recension of the authoritative compendium of francocentric world history, the thirteenth-century *Histoire ancienne jusqu'à César*. Separately, it was rendered into Latin prose as the *Historia destructionis Troiae* of Guido de Columnis, which then became the basis for a series of prose and verse translations in many languages including French, German, and English, eventually becoming captured in the

---

19 The authoritative edition remains that of Constans 1904–1912, with the recent full translation by Burgess and Kelly 2017. See Burgess and Kelly 2017, 1–31 for an introductory survey of the composition and reception of the work.
20 See Green 2002, 153–68, Mora-Lebrun 2008; for the wider context in chivalric mythology, Keen 1984, 117–113.
21 Chascun jor ensi l'escriveit/ cum il a sez oilz le veeit (Roman de Troie 105–6, tr. Burgess and Kelly).
22 Jung 1996 is the standard survey.
23 On the Greek *War of Troy* see Beaton 1996, 135–6, with the discussion of sources in the *editio princeps*, Papathomopoulou and Jeffreys 1996, xli–lxviii, demonstrating the precision of the dependence on the French source.

canon of English literature as the ultimate source of much of Shakespeare's *Troilus and Cressida*.[24]

The Angevin court in Benoît's time was the setting for the creation of poetic historiography in many languages,[25] and alongside the *Roman* may be placed such diverse works as Layamon's *Brut* in English alliterative verse, the *Roman de Brut* of Wace in Old French rhyme, and the imaginative fantasy of Geoffrey of Monmouth's *Historia Regum Britanniae* in Latin prose[26] — all centred on a conception of national and cultural origins that looks back to the Trojan War and the fate of the people of the vanquished city. Among this range of literary production, the closest thematic analogue to Benoît is an epic on the Trojan War in six books of Latin hexameters, composed at Rheims about 1180 by a young cleric called Joseph — customarily known, although without good authority, as Joseph of Exeter — and dedicated to his uncle Baldwin, who would later become Archbishop of Canterbury.[27]

Joseph again takes the skeleton offered by Dares and builds it up in the poetic and even visual forms of a different and entirely medieval cultural, military and ethical world.[28] His proem poses a rhetorical question on the theme that we have already seen articulated by his predecessors:

> Maeoniumne senem mirer Latiumne Maronem
> An vatem Phrygium, Martem cui certior index
> Explicuit praesens oculus, quem fabula nescit?
>
> Joseph I 23–25

> Should I admire the Maeonian elder or Latian Maro, or the Phrygian seer, for whom that more certain witness, the eye, makes things plain — the one who is a stranger to Myth?

To call Dares a 'seer', *vates*,[29] might seem hyperbolic until we recognise the underlying assertion, which looks back ultimately to Isidore: as an eyewitness, Dares and Dares alone gives us the truth of the war and avoid the *figmenta* that

---

24 See the overview by Desmond 2016.
25 See Gillingham 2006.
26 See Ingledew 1994.
27 On the evidence for the authorship of Joseph there is useful survey by Bate 1986, 3–28, drawing on the authoritative account by Gompf 1970, 5–73. The association with Exeter is doubtful and lacks medieval authority, but will be retained here as it has become conventional in the scholarship.
28 For a comparative study of expansive stylistic strategies in Joseph and Benoît see Kelly 1999, 121–170.
29 Stephen Harrison points out to me that this could also be a reference to the fact that Dares was a priest of Hephaestus (already at *Iliad* 5.9–10).

have infected the tradition since Homer (I 29–32). The similarity in spirit between Benoît and Joseph is so close, and the circumstances of composition so closely intertwined, that it is tempting to speculate that there may be an intertextual linkage between them; but this remains unproved,[30] and the best we can say is that both works must have contributed, explicitly or implicitly, to the promotion of the cultural and political authority of the Angevin courts, both because of their claim to Trojan ancestry and their ongoing involvement in the ideology of the Crusades. It is not coincidental that Joseph himself was part of an attempt to participate in the Third Crusade, and afterwards embarked on the composition of an epic on the subject, from which a fragment survives that opens as follows with a reference to Brutus and the origins of Britain:[31]

> His Brutus, avito
> Sanguine Troianus, Latiis egressus ab oris
> Post varios casus consedit finibus, orbem
> Fatalem nactus, debellatorque gigantum
> Et terrae victor dedit.

In this land Brutus, Trojan by his grandfather's blood, after leaving the shores of Latium, settled after many chances, after finding the circle of his fate; he fought the giants to submission, and gave his name to the land.

The identity of the people of Britain — and, ultimately, the glory of its crusaders — is tied up with the fact that they are defined as Trojan exiles like the Franks.

4 The reception of Joseph of Exeter

Joseph's epic seems to have acquired the status of a classic in its own time: Alan of Lille calls him *Ennius noster*[32] and two of the six surviving manuscripts carry an elaborate gloss commentary.[33] In the transmission, however, its actual author's name is less prominent than that of his ancient model: a writer of 1216 refers to *Ioseph in Darete suo*, and elsewhere the work is called *Daretis historia*

---

30 *Pace* Mora 2003, who argues that Joseph wrote in reaction to Benoît; cf. Kelly 1999, 121–45, comparing the texts without a hypothesis of direct influence.
31 Gompf 1970, 61–67, 212.
32 *Anticlaudianus* 1.165–6.
33 The principal manuscripts cited by the editors are Admont, Stiftsbibliothek 128; Cambridge, CCC 406; Oxford, Bodleian Library, Digby 157; Paris, BnF fonds lat. 15015; London, Westminster Abbey 18. The Admont and Paris manuscripts contain the glosses.

Troiana or *Daretis Phrygii Ylias*.[34] This had extraordinary consequences when the epic emerged in print,[35] first in the edition published at Basel in 1541 with a preface by the polymath Albanus Torinus (Alban Thorer, 1489–1550).[36] Here the name of the real author does not appear at all, and the title-page reads as follows:

> DARETIS
> PHRYGII POETARUM ET
> Historicorum omnium primi, de bello
> Troiano, in quo ipse militavit, Libri
> (quibus multis seculis caruimus) sex, a
> CORNELIO NEPOTE Latino
> carmine heroico donati, & CRISPO
> SALLUSTIO dedicati,
> nunc primum in lucem
> editi.

The six books (which we lacked for many centuries) by Dares Phrygius, first of all poets and historians, on the Trojan War, in which he himself fought, endowed with Latin heroic verse by Cornelius Nepos and dedicated to Crispus Sallustius, now for the first time brought into the light.

The poem has been misidentified as Sallust's original translation from Dares' Greek. Accordingly, the letter of Sallust from the *De Excidio Troiae* has been moved out of its original context and placed immediately before the poem, so that it seems to be referring to the six books of hexameters when it announces that what follows will be a faithful Latin rendering of what Dares wrote.

Torinus' preface suggests that the editor genuinely believes that this poem is Sallust's translation of Dares. He has perhaps misconstrued the information in the title-page or prefatory *accessus* of his manuscript,[37] or he may be following the assessment of another scholar of his own time — significantly, the Italian Rafaello Volterrano in his *Anthropologia* (1526) had already referred to the Latin translation of Dares as a work in 'six books', which corresponds to Joseph's poem

---

34 See sources collected by Gompf 1970, 6–10.
35 Useful survey of the published editions by Riddehough 1947, 254–255; see also Gompf 1970, 57–60. Clark 2011 and Prosperi 2019 have been extremely helpful in dealing with the difficult history of these Early Modern publications.
36 A copy is available at www.archive.org.
37 This must remain guesswork, as stemmatic analysis shows that this manuscript was not closely related to any of those that survive (Gompf 1970, 31–35, 45).

rather than the original prose, which could not possibly be given a six-book structure.[38] Revealingly, Torinus interrupts his extravagant praises of the eyewitness validity of the work, identical in spirit to those of the medieval celebration of Dares proper, with the admission that 'some people say' (*sunt qui dicunt...*) that the Latin translator responsible for the poem was a Briton or Englishman (*Britannus*);[39] but he immediately dismisses this doubt by reasserting the excellence of the poetry.

In Torinus' edition, the epic is followed in sequence by the original Latin prose of Dares, then two further works in Latin hexameters: the *Ilias Latina* summarising the story of the Homeric *Iliad*,[40] here as usual ascribed to Pindar of Thebes, and finally the complete Latin translation of the *Iliad* in elegant hexameters by Nicolò delle Valle and Vincentius Opsopoeus (Vinzenz Heidecker, d. 1539).[41] Perhaps the most disconcerting thing about this book is that the Homeric text is allowed to remain in a secondary position, as an addendum to the Dares version rather than the other way around.

The next stage in this history is marked by the publication in 1583 of the monumental edition of Homer by Johannes Spondanus, *Homeri quae extant omnia*.[42] Here the Greek text is the central object of attention, just as one would expect in a modern edition, and it is accompanied not only by a copious marginal commentary but also by a Latin translation facing the Greek. Significantly, this is no longer a polished metrical work but a crib, tracking the Greek word for word as an aid to study.[43] After the *Iliad* we find a sequence that has clearly been copied from Torinus: first the *Ilias Latina* and then the poem of Joseph, with the same title *Daretis Phrygii poetarum et historicorum omnium primi...*[44] The all-important change is that these two works are now presented as if secondary to Homer

---

38 Clark 2011, 193–200. Clark shows how the error was repeated by later encyclopaedists and editors.
39 Torinus 1541, 3.
40 Modern references to this poem too often seem to suggest that it is a translation of the *Iliad*: rather, it is a very brief summary of the sequence of events, passing over many that would seem crucial to us, such as Achilles' account of his choice between life and glory in Book 9.
41 Torinus 1541, 177ff.
42 There is an easily-accessed copy on the Bayerische Staatsbibliothek website at https://reader.digitale-sammlungen.de/resolve/display/bsb10138706.html, last consulted 13th August 2019.
43 This is a revision of Andreas Divus' translation first published in 1537. On the relationship between this and other contemporary Latin versions of the *Iliad* see Sowerby (1996).
44 For the ascription see Spondanus 1583, 444.

proper, printed in two columns without apparatus or commentary, and their authenticity is explicitly questioned. In the *Argumentum* heading his *Iliad*, Spondanus mentions[45] that the works of Dares Phrygius and Dictys of Crete are well-known but are considered by many to be spurious (*nothi ac adulterini*): he will admit them into his book by 'suspense of judgment' (*iudicio suspenso*), and will print Sallust's versified version — that is, Joseph's — at the end of the *Iliad* without declaring a position on the question of authenticity.

Doubts about the genuineness of Dares Phrygius the 'eyewitness' were emerging as early as 1400, when Coluccio Salutati in his *De tyranno* argued against Dares' version of the fall of Troy, in which Aeneas is a traitor to his people, by asserting that he and Dictys should be placed *inter apocriphos* and that Livy's account should be trusted instead.[46] Nonetheless, it was only with the rise of scientific philology from Spondanus' time onward that Dares and Dictys began to retreat into the debatable lands of Classical scholarship. As for the epic poem of Joseph, its subsequent publication history divides into two branches in the course of the seventeenth and early eighteenth century.[47] Numerous editions based ultimately on the Basel version of 1541 continued to be published under Dares' name, treating the work as genuinely ancient, while Samuel Dresemius of Frankfurt in 1620 produced an edition restoring the authorship of the twelfth-century poet, naming him *Josephus Iscanus* ('of Exeter'). After several reprintings this was remodelled to become Valpy's Delphin Classics edition, where Joseph's epic is printed in a companion volume to the prose texts of Dares and Dictys themselves. This edition is explicit about the twelfth-century origin of the work, but includes it for the sake of its poetic quality, *heroici argumenti excellentia*.[48]

In this tangled history we have, I suggest, the explanation for Jefferson's words in the letter with which we began this essay. What he is remembering seems to be the experience of studying Homer in an edition derived from that of Spondanus — which, indeed, was very frequently reprinted, adapted and pirated, and whose facing translation made it ideal for those who would have embarked on the study of Greek after first acquiring good Latin. When he writes of 'him who put into my possession this rich source of delight', he is probably remembering the Classical school of the Rev. James Maury, which he attended from 1758 before going up to William and Mary College.[49] Although nothing is known of the details

---
45 Spondanus 1583, 44, discussed by Prosperi 2019.
46 Clark 2011, 185–6.
47 Gompf 1970, 57–60.
48 Valpy 1819, vol. 1 p. 1.
49 See Hayes 2008, 30–36, 42.

of Maury's book collection,[50] there is good corroborating evidence in the surviving catalogue of the book collection that John Adams (1735–1826), Jefferson's friend and rival and his predecessor as President of the United States,[51] donated to the city of Quincy, Massachusetts, for the express purpose of founding a new Classical school. Here we find a copy of Spondanus' edition of Homer with Joseph of Exeter under the name of Dares Phrygius at the back, as well as a 1606 copy of the Basle edition of the poem whose title-page we examined above.[52]

When Jefferson contrasts Homer with the dullness of Dares Phrygius, by the latter he means what we now know to be the poem of Joseph of Exeter, masquerading as Dares as he does in these editions. It is intriguing to wonder whether Jefferson has recognised that the poem is a work of the Middle Ages, in which case his rejection would carry even greater import in the overall context of the correspondence with Priestley, concerned as it is with plans for an enlightened new university with anti-traditional aspirations. Even without that added angle, however, the point remains that the Homeric original is being set in contrast with the grimness of the obscure Latin texts that had filled the bookshelves of earlier generations.

5 Rubens' Homer

Does Joseph of Exeter matter? Only a very crude approach to the meaning of authorship would dismiss his epic on the grounds that it is a derivative work built on the model of the *De Excidio Troiae*, or that it is a hybrid production poised between the authenticity of Homeric origins and the imagined worlds of twelfth-century courtly literature. A more real complaint might be that the works on which we have depended for this discussion are marginal to the mainstream of cultural history. Against this, I would argue that Joseph of Exeter is a valid and sophisticated response to the Trojan War tradition, from a world far closer than ours to the real-life ethics and psychology of heroic warfare; and, perhaps more important, that his witness is an integral part of how the Homeric poems themselves have been read and imagined all along in the tradition.

---

50 So far as I know, the only surviving record of the books read in Maury's school is in a catalogue of the book collection of Jefferson's classmate Dabney Carr, but the only Greek books listed there are grammars and the New Testament (cf. Hayes 2008, 35 n. 20).
51 On the relationship between Jefferson and Adams see Wood 2017, *passim*.
52 See Swift 1917, 123 for the Spondanus edition of Homer, and p. 69 for the Basel Dares.

To illustrate this, I conclude with an exhibit that seems at first sight utterly different in kind to the mode of Classical reception exemplified by Jefferson. In the gallery of the Courtauld Institute in London there is a fine painting by Peter Paul Rubens, *The Death of Achilles*.

Fig. 2: Peter Paul Rubens, *The Death of Achilles* (The Courtauld Insitute Gallery, London; image courtesy of the Courtauld Institute Gallery and Art UK).

This is the *modello* (preliminary oil painting) for one of a set of tapestries on the subject of *The Life of Achilles* that Rubens produced in the early 1630's, examples of which can be found in many galleries in Europe and America. As one would expect from an artist distinguished among his contemporaries for his exceptional level of learning, the designs of Rubens' tapestries reflect a close knowledge of the ancient sources, and the subjects appear to have been newly developed by the artist, not borrowed from an existing iconographic tradition.[53] The first three in the series are from the infancy and boyhood of Achilles — dipped in the Styx, carried on Cheiron's back, hidden among the girls on Lemnos and are familiar

---

[53] The fundamental study of the sources of the tapestries by Haverkamp Begemann 1975, 20–41, has been effectively superseded by the work of subsequent scholars, especially Elizabeth Healy and Elizabeth McGrath. McGrath 1997, esp. 55–67, McGrath 2009, Healy 2005, and McGrath *et al.* 2016 have been invaluable sources for what follows.

from the mythographic tradition, including Statius' *Achilleid* with its copious medieval commentary tradition.[54] Then come four based closely on the *Iliad*: the Wrath of Achilles, the return of Briseis, Thetis receiving arms for Achilles, Achilles slays Hector. But the scene in the final tapestry and in our London painting is more puzzling: it shows the death of Achilles, shot with the familiar arrow in the heel, but the scene is located not on the battlefield but in the temple of Apollo. Achilles is not dressed for battle, and Paris is ambushing him from behind a pillar: and who are the other figures in front of the altar? This of course corresponds not to the Homeric version but to the account of Dares Phrygius, in which (as we saw above) Achilles was lured to his death in the temple of Apollo by the promise of marriage to Polyxena.

Rubens read Latin and Greek and owned and used a sophisticated Classical library, whose contents have been reconstructed with confidence.[55] According to the specialist research on this subject, these included a Homer closely akin to, or identical with, Spondanus' edition described above.[56] Since the four central tapestries in the series are unmistakeably derived from the Homeric version, subject to the artist's characteristic techniques of selection and re-shaping, it makes sense to look further in Spondanus for a narrative of Achilles' death: and we find it in our poem *De Bello Troiano*, placed as we have seen after the end of the *Iliad*. Joseph describes how Achilles was lured by Hecuba to come unarmed to the temple of Apollo outside the walls to be married in secret to Polyxena:

> Huc Hecuba in facinus audax invitat Achillem
> Coniugii factura fidem. Venit ille, sed arma,
> Sed comites nulli, solum sibi Nestore natum
> Iungit vix gladio cingi memor; omnia linquit,
> Dum miser optatos properat visurus amores.
> Quin vetat insidias credi fraudesque timeri
> Ipse locus templique fides. At matris adulter
> Dardanus imperio post laesa cubilia saevum
> Nil reputans pacemque deum delubraque turbans
> Occulit armatas post ipsa altaria turbas.
>   Joseph 6.410–419

---

54 Clogan 1968.
55 See McGrath 1997, esp. 63–6 on Rubens' reading of Greek authors in the original and/or in Latin translations, with the survey in McGrath et al. 2016, 11–71. Much of the evidence comes from Rubens' surviving letters, in which are found references to purchasing and/or using such works as Homer, Vergil, Servius, Philostratus *Imagines*, and Boccaccio's *Genealogia Deorum*. See further Arents 2001, with the detailed case study in McGrath 2009.
56 Healy 2005, 47 n. 15, with McGrath 1997, 118 n. 29.

> To this place Hecuba, eager for the deed, invites Achilles
> To make the pledge of marriage. He comes, but without
> Weapons or companions, he joins with himself Nestor's son
> Alone, barely remembering to gird himself with his sword; he leaves all
> As he hurries, sorry one, to meet his chosen beloved.
> Indeed the place itself and the trust of the temple forbid any thought
> Of an ambush, any fear of deceit. But the Dardan lecher,
> Thinking nothing in his mother's realm to be wretched after defiling
> The marriage bed, disrupting the peace of the gods and the temple,
> Has hidden armed companies behind the very altar...

Rubens has simplified the scene of combat that follows, removing the 'armed companies' and leaving Paris and Apollo alone as the attackers, but the elements of the scene clearly correspond to those in Joseph's poem — there is of course no source or authority for it in Homer, where Achilles's death is foreseen as coming on the battlefield, 'at the Scaean gate'.[57] Although it remains possible that Rubens is drawing on an extraneous source — perhaps the account of the ambush in the original prose of Dares,[58] or the paraphrase of that passage in Natale Conti's *Mythologies*[59] — it is more economical and more plausible to hypothesise that he is remaining with his Spondanus, and drawing here on the text that we know to be that of Joseph of Exeter.

By using the materials in Spondanus' edition together, the student of the Trojan War is encouraged to assimilate the *Iliad* and the epic supposedly by Dares as a single, sequential whole — a whole that must, for the likes of Rubens at least, have been held together all the more tightly if one's eye was following the Latin verse translation of the *Iliad* as closely as the Greek original. Jefferson, by contrast, is a man of his time in the way he sets them up in contrast rather than in continuity: but in their different ways these two men of learning are witnesses to the fact that the *literati* of the Middle Ages are present all the time among the modes of Classical reception in the Early Modern and Enlightenment worlds. Joseph of Exeter, in short, is thoroughly enmeshed in the reception of the Classical canon, even when his presence is obscured and his identity forgotten. For that reason above all, he deserves to be taken seriously again, even (or especially)

---

57 *Il.* 22.360 etc., on which see Burgess 2009. In the Western mythographic tradition, at least since the high Middle Ages, this version was mediated through the account in Ovid's *Metamorphoses* (12.580–619).
58 *De Excidio Troiae* §34. As early as the 1320's we find the Bologna scholar Giovanni del Virgilio in his *Expositio* on Ovid asserting the correctness of Dares' version over that in the *Metamorphoses*: see Huber-Reinich 2009, 180, and text at p. 188.
59 Mulryan and Brown 2006, 2.861.

when he keeps us guessing as to where the imagined world of the poem belongs, somewhere between the ancient heritage of Classical epic and the contemporary mythology of chivalric warfare.[60]

Bibliography

Arents, P. (2001), *De Bibliotheek van Pieter Pauwel Rubens: een reconstructie*, Antwerp.
Bate, A.K. (1986), *Joseph of Exeter, Bellum Troianum Books I–III*, Liverpool.
Beaton, R. (1996), *The Medieval Greek Romance* [2nd ed.], Cambridge.
Brown, C.M. (2012), 'The first American Sublime', in: Costelloe, T.M. (ed.), *The Sublime: From Antiquity to the Present*, Cambridge, 147–170.
Burgess, G./Kelly, D.N. (2017), *The Roman de Troie by Benoît de Sainte-Maure*, Cambridge.
Burgess, J.S. (2019), *The Death and Afterlife of Achilles*, Baltimore.
Clark, F.N. (2010), 'Reading the "First pagan historiographer": Dares Phrygius and medieval genealogy', *Viator* 41, 203–226.
Clark, F.N. (2011), 'Authenticity, antiquity and authority: Dares Phrygius in early modern Europe', *Journal of the History of Ideas* 72, 183–207.
Clogan, P.N. (1968), *The Medieval Achilleid of Statius*, Leiden.
Constans, L. (1904–1912), *Le Roman de Troie par Benoît de Sainte-Maure*, 6 vols., Paris.
Desmond, M. (2016), 'Trojan itineraries and the matter of Troy', in: Copeland, R. (ed.), *The Oxford History of Classical Reception in English Literature I (800–1558)*, Oxford, 251–268.
Duits, R./Quiviger, F. (2009), *Images of the Pagan Gods: Papers of a Conference in Memory of Jean Seznec*, London.
Gainsford, P. (2012), 'Diktys of Crete', *Cambridge Classical Journal* 58, 58–87.
Gaskill, H. (ed.) (2005), *The Reception of Ossian in Europe*, London.
Geary, P. (2002), *The Myth of Nations: The Medieval Origins of Europe*, Princeton.
Gerberding, R.A. (1987), *The Rise of the Carolingians and the Liber Historiae Francorum*, Oxford.
Gillingham, J. (2006), 'The cultivation of history, legend and courtesy at the court of Henry II', in: Kennedy/Meecham-Jones 2006, 25–52.
Gompf, L. (1970), *Josephus Iscanus, Werke und Briefe*, Leiden.
Green, D.H. (2002), *The Beginnings of Medieval Romance: Fact and Fiction, 1150–1220*, Cambridge.
Haverkamp Begemann, E. (1975), *The Achilles Series*, Corpus Rubenianum Ludwig Burchard X, London.
Hayes, K.J. (2008), *The Road to Monticello: The Life and Mind of Thomas Jefferson*, Oxford.
Healy, F. (2005), '"This is Homer and more than Homer": Rubens's depiction of the *Life of Achilles*', in: Lammertse/Vergara 2005, 43–55.

---

[60] I am grateful to Enrico dal Lago for comments and discussion on an early version of this paper, and to Michele Valerie Ronnick for valuable suggestions at a later stage.

Huber-Reinich, G. (2009), 'A lecture with consequences: tracing a trecento commentary on the *Metamorphoses*', in: Duits/Quiviger, 177–198.

Ingledew, F. (1994), 'The Book of Troy and the genealogical construction of history: the case of Geoffrey of Monmouth's *Historia regum Britanniae*', *Speculum* 69, 665–704.

Innes, M. (2000), 'Teutons or Trojans? The Carolingians and the Germanic past', in: Y. Hen/ M. Innes (eds.), *The Uses of the Past in the Early Middle Ages*, Cambridge, 227–249.

Jefferson, T. (1999), *Political Writings*, edited by J. Appleby and T. Ball, Cambridge.

Johnson, A.L. (2016), 'Thomas Jefferson's Ossianic romance', *Studies in Eighteenth-Century Culture* 45, 19–35.

Jung, M.-R. (1996), *La Légende de Troie en France au moyen age*, Basel.

Keen, M. (1984), *Chivalry*, New Haven.

Keller, W.R. (2008), *Selves and Nations: The Troy Story from Sicily to England in the Middle Ages*, Heidelberg.

Kelly, D.N. (1999), *The Conspiracy of Allusion: Description, Rewriting and Authorship from Macrobius to Medieval Romance*, Leiden.

Kennedy, R./Meecham-Jones, S. (eds.) (2006), *Writers of the Reign of Henry II: Twelve Essays*, New York.

Kim, L. (2010), *Homer Between History and Fiction in Imperial Greek Literature*, Cambridge.

Lammertse, F./Vergara, A. (eds.) (2004), *Peter Paul Rubens: The Life of Achilles*, exhibtion catalogue, Rotterdam.

Lelli, E. (ed.) (2015), *Ditti di Creta, L' Altra Iliade... con la Storia della Distruzione di Troia di Darete Frigio e i testi bizantini sulla Guerra Troiana*, Milan.

McGrath, E. (1997), *Subjects from History I*, Corpus Rubenianum Ludwig Burchard XIII, London.

McGrath, E. (2009), 'Artists and mythographic handbooks', in: Duits/Quiviger 2009, 389–420.

McGrath, E./Martin, G./Healy, F./Schepers, B./Van de Velde, C./De Clippel, K. (2016), *Mythological Subjects I: Achilles to the Graces*, Corpus Rubenianum Ludwig Burchard XI.1, Turnhout.

Macpherson, J. (1996), *The Poems of Ossian and Related Works*, edited by H. Gaskill with an introduction by F. Stafford, Edinburgh.

Merkle, S. (1996), 'The truth and nothing but the truth: Dares and Dictys', in: G. Schmeling, (ed.), *The Novel in the Ancient World*, Leiden, 563–580.

Mora, F. (2003), 'L'*Ylias* de Joseph d'Exeter: une reaction cléricale au *Roman de Troie* de Benoît de Sainte-Maure', in: E. Baumgartner/L. Harf-Lancner (eds.), *Progrès, reaction, décadence dans l' occident médiévale*, Geneva, 199–213.

Mora-Lebrun, F. (2018), 'Joseph of Exeter: Troy through Dictys and Dares', in: R. Simms (ed.), *Brill's Companion to Prequels, Sequels, and Retellings of Classical Epic*, Leiden, 115–133.

Mora-Lebrun, F. (2008), *"Mettre en romanz": les romans d'antiquité du XIIe siècle et leur posterité (XIIIe-XIVe siècle)*, Paris.

Mulryan, J./Brown, S. (2006), *Natale Conti's Mythologiae*, 2 vols., Tempe, Arizona.

Ní Mheallaigh, K. (2008), 'Pseudo-documentarism and the limits of ancient fiction', *American Journal of Philology* 129, 403–431.

Papathomopoulou, M./Jeffreys, E.M. (1996), *O Polemos tes Troados (The War of Troy)*, Athens.

Prosperi, V. (2019), 'The place of the father: the reception of Homer in the Renaissance', in: E. Morra (ed.), *Building the Canon through the Classics: Imitation and Variation in Renaissance Italy (1350–1580)*, Leiden, 47–69.

Riddehough, G.B. (1947), 'A forgotten poet: Joseph of Exeter' *Journal of English and Germanic Philology* 46, 254–259.

Silk, M./Gildenhard, I./Barrow, R. (2017), *The Classical Tradition: Art, Literature, Thought*, London.
Solomon, J. (2007), 'The vacillations of the Trojan myth: popularization and classicization, variation and codification', *International Journal of the Classical Tradition* 14, 482–534.
Sowerby, R. (1996), 'The Homeric *Versio Latina*', *Illinois Classical Studies* 21, 161–202.
Spondanus, J. (1583), *Homeri quae extant omnia*, Basel.
Stohlmann, J. (1968), *Anonymi historia Daretis Frigii*, Düsseldorf.
Stray, C.A. (1998), *Classics Transformed: Schools, Universities and Society in England, 1830–1960*, Oxford.
Swift, L. (ed.) (1917), *The Catalogue of the John Adams Library in the City Library of Boston*, Boston.
Tilliette, J.-Y. (1999), '*Troie ab oris*: Aspects de la revolution poétique de la seconde moitié du XIe siècle', *Latomus* 58, 405–431.
Torinus, Albanus (1541), *Daretis Phrygii...libri sex*, Basel.
Valpy, A.J. (1829), *Dictys Cretensis et Dares Phrygius De Bello Troiano... accedunt Josephi Iscani De Bello Troiano libri sex*, London.
Wood, G.S. (2017), *John Adams and Thomas Jefferson: Friends Divided*, New York.
Ziolkowski, J.M. (2009), 'Cultures of authority in the long twelfth century', *Journal of English and Germanic Philology* 108, 421–448.

Part III: **Victorian Cambridge and Oxford**

David Butterfield
The Shilleto Phenomenon

> It would be difficult to name a Continental Scholar whose judgment in questions of criticism is superior to his. His power of Greek composition is truly marvellous, and unequalled, I take upon me to say, by any living Scholar in Europe.

That is to say, for an Englishman writing in 1862, any living scholar in the world. We here have the considered judgment of the Regius Professor of Greek, writing of a Cambridge colleague he had known for 34 years. But while W.H. Thompson (1810–1886) sung the praise of his learned friend from the comfort of the foremost classical chair in the land, his subject — the Reverend Richard Shilleto (1809–1876) — was perched in a converted haybarn, teaching for a dozen hours per day the unfeeling, unchanging facts of the Greek and Latin languages, punctuating that drudgery with tea, snuff and stout. This paper will explore how two exact contemporaries, both formidable Hellenists, could exist in the same city in such different ways.[1]

To study the life of Shilleto is to unravel the tale of a classicist who embodied the change from one scholarly culture to another. Having arrived at Cambridge in the 1820s, he came at the tail end of the school of Richard Porson (1759–1808), devoted to the minute verbal criticism of texts, especially in Attic Greek.[2] But with the marked growth of the university in the nineteenth century, we find a man who taught so much that he struggled to find time to write. We also meet one long deprived of any formal college life by his early marriage. All the while, we have a man committed to resisting the increasing influence of the outside world on the delicate microcosm of university academia. We are thus considering a man who, though being very much of his time, faced several obstacles that resonate with our own.

---

[1] Chris Stray is, undoubtedly, the first person I heard pronounce the name Shilleto, which I had mistakenly endowed with the prosody of women's footwear. In treating a subject whom Chris has himself tackled, directly and indirectly, in several pieces of scholarship, I am doubtless in danger of sending Owls to Athens or Swans to Swansea. But, inspired by Chris's disarming ability to reconstruct the human scholar out of the fog of hazy hagiography or anachronistic misanthropy, there seem few better figures to revisit than the curious character we have here. There really has been none in classical scholarship quite like Shilleto, and, at one remove, in the history of classical scholarship, none quite like Stray.

[2] See esp. Stray 2018, 82–107.

https://doi.org/10.1515/9783110719215-006

Our subject, much indeed like Porson, is a man well known but little studied. The core facts of his life can be swiftly told: born in 1809, Shilleto came to Cambridge aged eighteen and stayed there until he died 48 years later, committed throughout to studying and teaching the Classics. But a much more complex picture emerges when we retrace that career arc at a more cautious pace.

Fig. 3: Richard Shilleto around sixty (1809–76) (photo c. 1869, CUL CAS G.256).

Shilleto[3] was born in Ulleskelf, in the West Riding of Yorkshire, where his father John, although not high born, would later serve as Deputy Lieutenant. The second of twelve children, Richard soon learned that he would have to strike out to make his own way. After a spell at Repton, he moved to Shrewsbury for his last three years, a school transformed under the visionary headmastership of Samuel Butler (1774–1839, HM 1798–1836). Both he and a 22-year-old Benjamin Hall Kennedy (1804–1889), testing the water as a sixth-form master, were struck by Shilleto's linguistic facility. His school record was a broad success, crowned by his becoming head boy, even ahead of Robert Scott (1811–1887) — later of lexicon fame.[4]

He followed his father in entering Trinity College Cambridge as a pensioner in October 1828, becoming a scholar in 1830. Shilleto was one of the early cohorts to take the Classical Tripos (first examined four years before his entry). However, the right to sit examinations for Classical Honours was limited to those who passed the Mathematical Tripos: to compound the difficulty, since the Classical examinations followed soon after the Senate House Examinations for Mathematics, classicists effectively had to study for a joint-honours degree. Shilleto's own passage from one to the next was a textbook case of doing the bare minimum: he took the wooden spoon for the lowest mark deserving honours in Mathematics (i.e. the bottom candidate of that year's 24 Junior Optimes). Although the mathematical examiners were especially merciful towards those known to have potential for a career in the Classics, it was later reported that another examinee (Charles Davidson, later a Fellow of Christ's and Middle Temple barrister) had allowed Shilleto to copy his answers.[5] As it was, Shilleto was bracketed for the

---

3 The surname — sometimes Shillito(e) — originates in the West Riding, but its rarity would earn Richard the nickname 'Silly Toes' (a.k.a. *Morodactulos*). His tormentors were presumably unaware that the name actually does mean 'scaly' or 'shelly' toe(s), which was later assimilated to the adjective 'silly'.

4 Of the few anecdotes that survive from the time, perhaps the most relevant concerns Butler himself. As part of his forlorn attempt to ban schoolboys from boating on the Severn, the headmaster declared his hard-line strategy to deal with unscrupulous locals: 'If the men will let the boys have boats, I will have them up before the magistrates.' Within seconds Shilleto had scribbled on a scrap of paper the decree in Latin elegiacs: *quando velint homines pueris conducere cymbas | ante magistratus Butler habebit eos*. When this was slipped onto his desk, Butler gave the characteristically non-committal response of 'psha, boy, psha', but folded the paper carefully and put it in his pocket. Shilleto ruefully recalled, 'I knew *conducere* was wrong, but it was the nearest thing I could get at the moment, and I have never been able to set it right since without spoiling the whole thing: so it must stand.'

5 M.G. Davidson on his uncle Charles, see Vaizey 1895–1907, IV.160.

spoon equally with Matthew Chapman (1796–1865), who had come late to Trinity after earning an M.D. at Edinburgh.

Shilleto's acceptance of his own hard-won degree became the stuff of legend. Just before its conferral, he proclaimed the following elegiac distich to the Vice-Chancellor at the Senate House congregation:

> Ligneus haud ego sum spoonus, neque Chapman; uterque
>   Dimidium capiat, nos sumus ergo pares.
>
> I am not the wooden spoon, nor Chapman; let each | Take half of it, and thus we are equals.

Simultaneously he produced a small wooden spoon from his pocket, broke it in two, and handed half to Chapman.[6] This was nothing new: Shilleto had already revealed his flair for *ad hoc* Latin humour, when keeping an Act — i.e. conducting one of the two Latin debates enjoined by University Statutes — earlier that year. Tasked with the unenviable role of supporting the motion *recte statuerit Paleius de Suicidiis* ('That [William] Paley reached the correct decision about suicides'), Shilleto managed to make light of both the subject and his opponent. Well aware of the barbarous character of such post-scholastic Latin, he decided to reanalyse the words on Classical principles. To the bafflement of his opponent, his defence of suicide began with the pleasures of the table: *Si sues omnino non caedemus, unde, quaeso pernam, hillas, sumen, unde inquam petasonem sumus habituri. Est profecto judaicum.* ('If we don't slaughter pigs at all, from where, I ask, could we get ham, sausages, udder, from where indeed bacon? It's completely Jewish.') When pressed to explain this bizarre tangent, Shilleto asked *quid est ergo suicidium nisi suum caesio*? ('What is *sui*cide other than the slaughter of swine [*sues*]?') His adversary, a mathematician of St John's, was far out of his depth. But the moderator, Francis Martin (1802–1868, a Fellow of Trinity), well apprehended the puckish undergraduate's dig at Johnian 'hogs', and took over to join in the fun of the discussion.[7]

---

[6] Since Shilleto told this story to a friend at the very end of his life (1875), which was printed 31 years later, it is highly probable that details had acquired a romantic patina from repeated telling: see J.D.H. Dickson in the *Cambridge Review*, 6 June 1906, 449. For broader context, see Stray 2015, 176–177.

[7] The tale is told by Christopher Wordsworth (1877, 41–42) who had heard the tale from Shilleto; a shorter version is given by Rouse Ball 1880, 181–182.

Shilleto's performance in the Classics was appreciably more successful. Although not a prize winner, this 'Shrewsbury fine animal'[8] graduated with a different kind of near miss, coming Second Classic to the prodigious Edward Law Lushington (1811–1893), later Professor of Greek at Glasgow. He edged into third William Dobson (1809–1867), later Fellow of Trinity and Principal of Cheltenham College, and into fourth William Hepworth Thompson (1810–1886), later not just Regius Professor but Master of Trinity. Unusually for those who showed such academic firepower in the Tripos, Shilleto married. In 1834, a year before taking his M.A., he wedded Isabella S.H. Snelgar, then 22. The two literally fell in together, when Isabella — then a complete stranger — collapsed in fear at a fire alarm; Shilleto, visiting the Congregational Church on Green Street where her father was then pastor, fell in love. Perhaps, on hearing that she had 'Homer' for a middle name, romance was inevitable. One may assume that the pending arrival of their first son in 1834 intensified the desire to marry. But any happy wedding bells tolled ill for Shilleto's career at Cambridge: no college, from his grand *alma mater* Trinity (1546–) to the most recently founded Downing (1800–), could admit any married fellow into its ranks.

With no bar to pursuing a domestic life, Shilleto soon became the head of a large family. Despite the infant deaths of a daughter and two sons (Isabella 1836, Edward 1841–1842, and William 1842), and the loss of two daughters in their teens (Isabella 1838–1855, Catherine 1840–1855), seven children survived into adulthood: five sons (Richard 1834–1878, John 1837–1895, Edward 1846–1913, Arthur 1848–1894 and William 1849–1915) and two daughters (Ellen 1844–1920, Mary 1851–1900). After Isabella's father (Jacob Snelgar, a dissenting minister who was later rehabilitated as vicar of Royston) lapsed into insanity, he and his wife (Isabella senior) moved in with the Shilletos. But in 1843, Jacob hanged himself. Not long after, Isabella's brother (also Jacob) was detained in the mental hospital until his death; she herself was also reported to have periodic mental outbreaks that traumatised her children.[9] Even by Victorian standards, this was a family fraught with private tragedy.

With Shilleto solely responsible for the family's finances, there was intense pressure to find a career that paid profitably. The obvious routes available to one so well versed in the Classics were to pursue the life of a schoolmaster, or take holy orders and enter the Church. Shilleto initially favoured the latter, becoming

---

8 Arthur Henry Hallam to his father, 4 Feb. 1829: see Kolb 1981, 271.
9 A glimpse is given in the diary entry for 1857 by a friend of the family: 'Mrs Shilleto is sometimes out of her mind, shuts up the children in the watercloset, and treats them with great severity.' See Bury & Pickles 2000, 287.

ordained as a deacon in the Gloucester diocese in 1838, and being priested the following year. He lived for a while at the vicarage in Ware, Hertfordshire, very probably through the aid of Revd Snelgar eighteen miles north. But Shilleto gravitated back to Cambridge, where in 1839–1840 he served as officiating minister at St Botolph's. Being once more in the hubbub of academic life, it was perhaps unsurprising that his expertise was called upon: in 1839–1841 he examined the Classical Tripos, and managed to become in 1841 a Lecturer in Classics and (rather brazenly) Mathematics at King's College. Although this post gave him some regular teaching, it was several rungs below a fellowship proper. Perhaps dissatisfied with the few options available to him when debarred from the close-knit community of dons, Shilleto looked for options elsewhere: soon enough he became an assistant master at Harrow in 1843, having failed in his rather optimistic pitch to become Head of Rugby in 1842, following the great Thomas Arnold (1795–1842). After one year on Harrow Hill, which ended in financial ruin and the permanent closure of his house (the Grove), Shilleto returned perforce to the life of a private tutor in Cambridge.

Although his reputation as a Classical teacher was already strong, the climate in Cambridge was not entirely welcoming. In a system where private tutors earned up to ten times the salary of college lecturers,[10] whose own teaching was often snubbed by undergraduates, many college tutors felt the balance had been upset. In 1844, James Hildyard (1809–1887), a Classical Fellow of Christ's, issued a pamphlet *The University System of Private Tuition examined, In an Intellectual, Moral, and Pecuniary Point of View*. The three evils hinted at by the subtitle were explained as follows: private tuition is intellectually wrong, because it focuses on narrow cramming to the detriment of individual exertion; morally wrong, because it attracts students away from their public teachers, thus undermining the collegiate system; and financially wrong, because the prodigious sums earned by teachers outside the university system dwarf the income of those teaching within it. Hildyard conjectured that £50,000 (in modern terms, some £6.5m) was spent each year on private tuition by Cambridge students.

This was not a new problem. In 1781, to limit the undue influence of private tuition, a grace was passed to prohibit candidates from sitting honours examinations if they had taken a tutor outside college in the previous two years. (A simultaneous move to limit their use only to fellow commoners and the aristocracy happily failed.)[11] Over the next 40 years, this period of tuition-free study was

---

10 A college Fellow might receive £10 for teaching each pupil per annum, while a top private tutor could charge anywhere between £70 and £100.

11 Grace of 24 Jan. 1781.

steadily whittled down to six months, although even that restriction was breached frequently enough.[12] This development suggests a reaction to an inconvenient truth — that the steady growth of the university, and the increasing demands of the Senate House examinations, exceeded the teaching that college fellows could or would provide. Like it or not, by the mid-nineteenth century the strained University ecosystem could only survive with private support.

But Hildyard's pamphlet reopened old wounds. Unsurprisingly, Cambridge newspapers ran a lively correspondence for the weeks that followed its appearance, with impassioned cases made from either side of the divide. A former-fellow (signing himself only as *Ex-Socius*) echoed Hildyard's worries:

> The public tutor is now released from the duty of watching over and preparing for the Senate House the richer students, while the poorer are left to struggle or sink, as they may; or to wring from the scanty income of self-denying parents... The payment to the public Tutors has been increased above twenty per cent. on the same number of pupils. The payments to the private Tutors have been increased by a curious mode of division of labour, not mentioned by Adam Smith — of taking the same sum for performing half the duty; and thus rendering it requisite for the Student to have one Tutor for Mathematics and another for Classics.[13]

'An Undergraduate' — evidently an active customer in the burgeoning trade — wrote in to make clear the need for private tutors, although he drew a distinction between what rich, idle students sought compared with the genuinely diligent. For the former, the duty of a private tutor 'is to make himself as agreeable as possible — an end not to be attained by "coaching," but by the exercise of his capabilities at whist, and other pleasant pastimes.' For the latter, 'as long as there is a difficult examination to prepare for, and the way can be smoothed by Private Tutors, Private Tutors will exist.'[14]

Hildyard was himself soon put in an awkward position. He had alleged in his pamphlet that the mathematical tutor he took as an undergraduate was a complete waste of time: but that tutor in turn published the letter that came his way after he had worked his customary magic. In it, the young Hildyard took the

> opportunity of adding how exceedingly I feel indebted to you for the very kind and patient manner in which for upwards of a year you have borne with my infirmities... Possibly without considerable attention and assistance I should never have had courage to face each

---

12 Graces of 25 Jan. 1781 (two years), 9 Apr. 1807 (eighteen months), 3 July 1815 (a year), and 19 May 1824 (six months).
13 *Cambridge Independent Press*, 16 Nov. 1844.
14 *Cambridge Chronicle*, 7 Dec. 1844.

difficulty, which will now present themselves in not only a palatable but even an interesting shape.[15]

Hildyard the tutee and Hildyard the tutor both appeared to be looking out for themselves.

Shilleto, as Cambridge's dominant Classical tutor, found himself a lead figure in this strikingly public and ill-tempered debate. Other than Hildyard, he was the only correspondent of a dozen or more to sign his real name — perhaps gentlemanly conduct when opposing his successor as head boy at Shrewsbury.[16] In particular, he rejected Hildyard's allegation that it was a conflict of interest for private tutors to be involved in the public examinations of the University, where bias for their own candidates could corrupt the outcome. Shilleto's letter remarked breezily that he had not read Hildyard's pamphlet, having only glanced at the correspondence emerging from it. Nor, he added, could he claim knowledge of 'a certain paper drawn up by sundry Public Tutors, who after drinking her Majesty's health in their respective Combination-rooms drop into Mr. Hildyard's apartments to discuss tea, toast, and tuition.'[17] But, to the 'gross insinuation' of dispensing improper favour, he made the fair objection that

> it has never been imagined heretofore that an Examiner appointed from this body [of private tutors] has been influenced by unworthy motives in determining the position of any candidate presented to him for examination. If it would be unjust to charge a Public Tutor acting in a similar capacity with an undue bias towards a student of his own college, surely the insinuation is equally uncharitable when brought against a Private Tutor.

All in all, the dispute was an unsavoury affair from which no palpable change emerged.[18]

Anyhow, ever busy, Shilleto had bigger fish to fry. Around the same time as his letter appeared, so did his only completed book, a commentary on Demosthe-

---

15 Letter of 4 June 1832 to the anonymous mathematical tutor, published in *Cambridge Chronicle*, 16 Nov. 1844.
16 Shilleto was head boy in 1827, Hildyard (who had eight years at the school to Shilleto's three) in 1828.
17 *Cambridge Chronicle*, 23 Nov. 1844.
18 Rounding off the debate, a correspondent signing himself 'M.A. &c., &c., and Conservative Reformer', regretted the wasted energy: 'Anyone would tell [Shilleto] that, for the sake of his own reputation, he *ought not* to have examined his own pupils. He voluntarily put himself into a trying position, and, therefore voluntarily rendered himself liable to be suspected of being biased in favour of those candidates who had carried out his system of reading.' (*Cambridge Chronicle*, 7 Dec. 1844.)

nes' excoriating attack on Aeschines: Περὶ τῆς παραπρεσβείας = *De Falsa Legatione* = *On the False Embassy*. His edition went on to be one of the best-selling commentaries of nineteenth-century Greek scholarship, in school and university alike: it passed through four editions during his lifetime (1844, 1853², 1864³, 1874⁴), and many thereafter. Unquestionably the royalties from Deighton, later Deighton Bell, did plenty to keep HMS Shilleto afloat. And yet the work had been produced at an absurd turnaround: Shilleto had agreed to produce the edition in late June, only to find himself 'under an obligation, notwithstanding the most pressing and constant demands upon my time, to bring it out before the end of November, perfectly unconscious, being a complete tyro in publishing, of the arduous work I had before me.'[19] The result was nevertheless a triumph of erudition, in both its elucidation of Attic history and its no-nonsense linguistic clarity. No minor benefit to the student reader was the unusual decision to write the commentary in English — a practice still markedly rare among classical editions published in Britain. On this point, Shilleto candidly revealed his own steady development of thought:

> I have long convinced myself that the affinity between the Greek tongue and our own is so much closer than that which the Latin bears to either, that I have frequently wondered why so few Scholars have broken through the usage of their forefathers, that a vast majority still continue to explain the Greek idioms and structure through a medium no longer necessary even for foreign readers. And surely one would hope it is from no fear of the cuckoo cry of some δοκησίσοφοι, that English note-writing produces slip-shod and slovenly Scholars. If this charge has any foundation, it will equally apply to oral lectures in English, and Lexicons in English, and Grammars in English.[20]

Shilleto goes on to say that, when he was once preparing an (unnamed and certainly unpublished) edition of a Greek tragedy, he attempted the experiment of writing in English, but found that Latin was still favourable because of its well-established technical vocabulary for textual criticism. He ended up with the 'deliberate persuasion that explanatory notes ought to be written in one's own language, critical in the Latin,' while simultaneously confessing that 'several of the notes written originally in Latin were, on second thoughts, rewritten in English,

---

19 Shilleto 1844, vi.
20 *Ibid.*, v. A nod is naturally made to Liddell and Scott's Greek lexicon, which had chosen to translate entries entirely into English on its first appearance the previous year. See Williamson 2019.

and *vice versa*'.²¹ The preface also reveals a sharp-minded critic, who had taken unusual care in analysing the manuscript evidence for a project of this scale.²²

The success of a book that showed mastery of the most admired Attic orator only added to Shilleto's appeal as a tutor. It rendered him unquestionably the most sought-after private coach in the country, whom even ambitious Oxford scholars chose to employ outside Full Term. His influence within Cambridge was transformative. As Benjamin Kennedy later recalled, 'in some years all the first class men without exception had read with him.'²³ To list Shilleto's pupils would thus be to list anyone who studied Classics in Victorian Cambridge and enjoyed success in the university or beyond. Among star pupils were Lord Lyttelton, Richard Jebb, Sir William Harcourt, Henry Jackson, J.E.B. Mayor, John Sandys, and Samuel Butler (grandson of Shilleto's headmaster). Henry Montagu Butler, who studied with Shilleto thrice a week, wrote of him in 1852: 'He is certainly a wonderful scholar, infinitely superior in the extent and accuracy of his knowledge to any one I had before seen.' Shilleto, in turn, would later say of this pupil that 'during my very long career of private tuition I cannot call to mind a pupil who was more exact and faultless'.²⁴

With his lecturing duties at King's (resumed in 1846) limited primarily to linguistic matters, he was able to run his days from a single room at his home — which steadily moved around the streets of central and southern Cambridge.²⁵ For most of his life as a private tutor, Shilleto taught eleven or twelve hours, every day of the week except Sunday. This was conducted as one-on-one tuition, thus allowing for the sort of bespoke teaching that multi-person lectures could not provide within the college system. The focus throughout was upon the core staples of the Classical Tripos: reading set texts, honing linguistic precision, and

---

21 Shilleto 1844, vi.
22 For one thing, he was well aware of the fallacy of the 'best manuscript' a generation before A.E. Housman: 'The Zurich editors [Baiter and Sauppe, 1850] would seem to have extended their regard for this MS. [Paris. gr. 2934] beyond the rational and calm esteem of unimpassioned Critics, and to have hugged it to their bosoms with "prodigal devotedness" of a tender passion. It omits a word, and to their eye the word becomes at once an interpolation: it presents a new reading, and forthwith the old is condemned; grammar and sense may be violated by the novelty, but "Codex Parisiensis SIGMA" is *unus instar omnium*.' (*ibid.*, vii–viii).
23 Kennedy 1876, 166.
24 Letter to George Butler, cited in Graham 1920, 125.
25 Shilleto shifted his family around Cambridge — from Hills Road, to Park Terrace, to Trumpington Street, and later Scroope Terrace just off it, before spending his final years on Bateman Street. Five members of the immediate family, along with Isabella senior, now rest together beneath a cruciform stone vault in Mill Road cemetery.

composing prose and verse in Greek and Latin with as much flair as possible. A former pupil summarises Shilleto's *modus docendi* as follows:

> Criticism of an exercise consisted chiefly in telling you what you had done wrong and what you had better have written; that is, what would have been sound Latin or Greek according to the usages of the language (particularly Greek) recognized by scholars. He spoke with authority, and the outpouring of references (by chapter, section and line) without opening a book, simply took your breath away. If you turned them out afterwards, lo they were correct. Truly an astounding feat of memory. In his own kind he was unrivalled, and other teachers bowed before the first Greek scholar in England. But whether it would have been well to enjoy a great deal of this instruction may be doubted.[26]

This same pupil, William Heitland (Roman historian and Fellow of St John's), recalls how Shilleto toiled away in his Scroope Terrace garret. Following the caveat that this 'experience was perhaps somewhat abnormally grotesque' — because he met Shilleto at the end of a full day's slog — he paints a striking picture of the man in the 1860s:

> His habits had told upon an originally tough constitution, and he looked older than his real age. He did not smoke, but took snuff freely. Several snuff-boxes were about the room, presents from old pupils, but he could never lay his hand on them when wanted, so generally drew his pinch from a large tinfoil packet that stood in the middle of the table. On each such occasion he needed a handkerchief, and that speedily. It was somewhere on the floor, among the books with which the whole room was littered. In the search for it he was apt to catch his foot in a book, and sneeze prematurely; I have known him get an awkward fall in the attempt. Found and used, the handkerchief was dropped on the floor again in the line of traffic as he wandered to and fro. It was understood that during the day he drank a quantity of tea: at night, when I saw him, a pint pot of beer stood handy on a pedestal. When it was low ebb in this vessel, he placed it in a pigeon-hole close to the door, and rang the bell. Soon a stealthy hand withdrew it and put it back refilled. So much liquid refreshment entailed other embarrassing phenomena. [!] Among these various doings the work went on.[27]

The steady flow of beer may surprise — and it is true that teaching across pints of foaming ale was not the done thing, even in Victorian Cambridge. But the combination of late-hour teaching and domestic freedom allowed Shilleto to operate on his own favoured terms. A typically honest note to a student reads, 'Will you come on Thursday evening, and, if you have such strange tastes, take a cup of tea? It

---

26 Heitland 1926, 128–129.
27 Sir Sidney Colvin, a pupil in the 1860s, recalled Shilleto behind a 'table littered with snuff-boxes and bandana handkerchiefs' (Colvin 1921, 12); Lord Stanley, 15th Earl of Derby, remembered a 'little round, red man' who 'used to talk by the hour instead of sticking to his business' (Gardiner 1923, I.38).

will undoubtedly be followed by a Tankard if not of Audit at least of Guinness.'[28] Tales of his boisterous drinking escapades sometimes did the rounds. It does not bode well when a pupil (a future Regius Professor of Greek) can record that 'Shilleto nearly poisoned himself on Monday: just before going to bed he drank a glass of furniture varnish by mistake for his ale, and was so frightened that he telegraphed to his sister that he should not be surprised if he were dead tomorrow.'[29]

Reporting the talk of the town, Joseph Romilly (1791–1864, University Registrary and Fellow of Trinity) recorded in 1851 that 'the quantity of ale drunk by [John] Hind [Mathematical Fellow of Sidney] and Shilleto is quite appalling'.[30] Yet he joined Shilleto in feeling aggrieved some years later when, at a King's luncheon to welcome the Prince of Wales in 1864, they both failed to get served some beer. Shilleto composed for Romilly a Latin poem in the voice of the Provost, whose accompanying translation can be quoted in part:

> When late a Guest in K.C. Hall
> For beer as usual you did call
> You had, 'tis said, my worthy Malter,
> A flat refusal...
> It chanc'd that Romilly, dear Man,
> Was near and under the same ban,
> In midst of Sherry, Champagne, Hock,
> And other wines which only shock.

Romilly then pipes up:

> I say, let's go, we're both alike
> Against the Gunter [the Butler] we must strike.
> You thirst as I do, for some beer;
> Without it we both shall be queer:
> We must remove th' absurd obstruction
> This rascal puts to our free suction...
> If we must die (we must some day)
> I'd rather die with moisten'd clay.

Finally, the Provost responds with the answer they had hoped for:

> If ever I am call'd again
> To King's Coll. feast to ask you twain
> (Familiars both & worthy men)

---

28 Letter to G.O. Trevelyan, cited by Trevelyan 1932, 40–41.
29 Henry Jackson (writing in 1860), quoted in Parry 1926, 15.
30 Bury & Pickles 2000, 91.

> I promise I will be more heedful —
> You, Romilly, shall have your needful,
> And you, most constant friend of Ale
> Shall have your 'usual' without fail.[31]

The difference, in the event, between Romilly and Shilleto was that only the latter wandered off to the buttery to fetch a pint of beer himself.

That Shilleto was a 'friend of ale' was something he did not trouble to hide. This was true throughout his life: a 'well-informed Cambridge correspondent' could later summarise the man's 'singular character' as 'simple and innocent — proud of three things: his reading of the Church service, his handwriting, which was exquisite beyond belief, and his knowledge of beer.'[32] All these require some dedication to the cause. Still, his repute as a 'crack coach'[33] remained first-class — rivalling the famous Edward Routh (1831-1907), top-notch tutor in Mathematics.[34] And Shilleto was evidently held in sufficient repute to be on hand as the University's go-to figure as Deputy Proctor, when either the appointed Senior or Junior Proctor was temporarily absent or incapacitated. He held the post nine times, doubtless being pleased for the additional stipend available for comparatively little exertion.[35]

At any rate, Shilleto was not afraid to have an outspoken attitude to politics. An episode early in his career reveals what this could mean in practice. In May 1839, he had attended a public meeting called by the Mayor of Cambridge to vote on an address to the Queen. This was a largely Whig gathering to express dissatisfaction at the Bedchamber Crisis — where (for political reasons) the Tory leader Robert Peel had asked Victoria to dismiss her Ladies of the Bedchamber (without success). At the meeting both Peel and Wellington were mocked, and even Henry Gunning — the venerable Esquire Bedell of Christ's — held aloft a sign reading 'Three groans for the King of Hanover!'. Shilleto was alleged to be part of the rioting group who turned up to spoil the party. Gunning claimed, by contrast, that the Reverend was in fact one of three heavies who waved sticks while they

---

[31] 'To Richard Shilleto M.A.', *ibid.*, 457. The Latin verses remain unpublished in Romilly's manuscript diary for 7 June 1864

[32] *Aberdeen Press and Journal*, 11 Oct. 1876.

[33] Henry Jackson to his mother, 30 Nov. 1858, quoted in Parry 1926, 13.

[34] For a detailed account of Routh, see Warwick 2003, 229–247.

[35] In 1850 and 1852, in lieu of William Nind of St Peter's; in 1853, of H.A.J. Munro of Trinity; in 1855, of Joseph Edleston of Trinity; in 1857, of Henry Latham of Trinity Hall; in 1860, of Thomas Brocklebank of King's; in 1862, of John Hays of Christ's; in 1868 and 1871, of James Porter of St Peter's.

scrapped for a fight. For his part, Shilleto claimed — in a letter sent for good measure to three local papers — that he only cried 'Shame! Disgraceful', and that his stick-wielding was solely for self-defence.[36]

A far greater public controversy was to arrive in 1851, one which was no less self-willed. That year, Shilleto published *Thucydides or Grote?*, a 32-page pamphlet that set one great historian of Greece against another.[37] It was an explicit attack on George Grote, the radical politician and classical historian, who had cast aspersions on Thucydides in the sixth volume of his *History of Greece* (12 vols, 1846–1856). More worryingly, some felt, Grote had shown an unusual sympathy with the demagogue Cleon. The pamphlet set out its twin goal of rescuing Thucydides from unwarranted aspersions and interpretations. Should the nineteenth-century man of letters side with the Classical writer, or his anti-Classical interpreter?

Shilleto's prefatory remarks instantly make clear that some broader issues lay behind the pamphlet's appearance. In challenging a former radical MP, Shilleto declared that he wrote with the prejudice of 'one not ashamed to call himself a Tory against one not (I believe) ashamed to call himself a Republican — of one proud of an Academical Education against one disregarding such a position' (p.1). True enough, Shilleto was indirectly providing a defence of academically sanctioned scholarship against the intrusion of gentlemanly amateurs or heavy-handed political meddlers. While observing that 'it is always an invidious task to expose blunders', Shilleto expressed regret that 'Mr Grote has furnished me with many — blunders of grave moment.' With some even-handedness, however, he followed his survey of Grote's errors of Greek (pp. 16–17) with his own (largely typographical) errors in the first edition of *De falsa legatione*. But the tone is very much *de haut en bas*:

> I have before me so many inaccuracies and solecisms, even where there appears no wish to support a theory, and my task is becoming more and more wearisome, the more I become convinced of Mr Grote's unsoundness of scholarship and his rashness in obtruding it. (p.24)

On an impossible usage of the reflexive pronoun mistakenly alleged by Grote, Shilleto was only too happy to grandstand:

---

36 Letter of 29 June 1839, to the *Cambridge Chronicle and Journal*, *Cambridge Independent Press*, and *Huntingdon, Bedford and Peterborough Gazette*. It was later remarked of Shilleto that he was a 'Tory of the old type, who was ready to die for the unblemished reputation of Anne Boleyn and Mary, Queen of Scots' (Harcourt Butler, cited in Gardiner 1921, I.38).
37 See further Stray 1997.

> Now if any Oxford or Cambridge First-Class man will come forward and say Mr Grote's rendering of ἑαυτῶν is admissible, I will own all my teaching for twenty years has been in vain, or in other words that such of my pupils as have received the highest rewards at the hands of my university have stolen laurels which others had duly earned. I cannot refrain from saying — if only by way of a safety-valve — that I am thankful that the author of the above rule is not a member of either of the old Universities of our land. (p.21)

His readers will have known full well that, having passed through Sevenoaks Grammar and Charterhouse, Grote was sent by his father straight into the grubby world of banking.

Although many aspects of Shilleto's pamphlet are convincing, its aim is too narrow, its position too partial, and its tone too rasping for mainstream scholarship. The *Edinburgh Review* fairly suggested that the pamphlet would have been better entitled '*Shilleto or Grote?*'.[38] Certainly Shilleto's rhetorical swagger was only doubled by the closing apologia:

> It is not impossible that the foregoing strictures may provoke an unfriendly reader to say that I have been dipping my pen in gall as well as in ink. It may be so, but I would not desire to re-write a single sentence. I own that I am a feeble champion, yet I am confident that my unintermitting devotion to these studies qualifies me to come forward, in the absence of an abler, as the champion of Thucydides — as the champion of sound scholarship [*a loaded phrase*]... I believe that all lovers of sound scholarship [*it must follow*] will not object to these comments upon a new historian of Greece, who, not content with giving newfangled interpretations of Greek words and phrases, attempts to justify himself by lengthened notes that only aggravate the original blunder. (p.32)

Stern stuff indeed. But this was of nothing compared to what came in response: *A Few Remarks on a Pamphlet by Mr Shilleto*, issued without attribution on its title-page.[39] The preface revealed that the author had 'a near intimate connection' with Grote, and had briefly been Shilleto's pupil. The mystery disappeared with the turn of the page: 'J.G.' of 'Trumpington Vicarage' was manifestly the younger brother of the defendant, the clergyman and philosopher John Grote. The pamphlet ran to 86 pages, exhaustively and exhaustingly castigating Shilleto's 'worthless' pamphlet for its 'childishness' and 'senile narrow-mindedness', in tones still the more harsh. As a reviewer in the *Athenaeum* put it, the author

> has even out-Heroded Herod in all his worst faults, especially his bad spirit. The close relationship between him and Mr. [George] Grote may be thought an excuse by some of his readers: — we should rather say that it ought to have deterred him from touching the subject

---

38 *Edinburgh Review* 191 (July 1851) 113.
39 Shilleto 1851, 1, 84.

at all. Certain it is, he could not have chosen a more effectual means of increasing the discredit already brought on the university by Mr. Shilleto... Mr. Shilleto's pamphlet was needless, rambling and tiresome, thought it only extended to thirty pages: — this is more than three times as long, quite as useless, and ten times as spiteful.[40]

Yet, despite this rather inconclusive salvo, Shilleto was not to be done with Thucydides. At some point in the 1850s — perhaps spurred on by this unsatisfactory public dispute — he conceived the idea of a full-scale edition of and commentary on his *History of the Peloponnesian War*. Work was undertaken seriously — but with his days allowing almost no time to read and write — few were surprised when nothing appeared that decade, or the next.

What free time he had, friends and colleagues must have noticed, seemed to be directed towards another of his great loves — verse composition. Shilleto had long enjoyed especial renown for his flair in writing Latin and Greek. A not negligible advantage of these feats of skill and artistry was that they could be published in popular collections, thereby showcasing the linguistic powers at his fingertips, advertising the services of a tutor-for-hire. Although Shilleto's compositions did not appear in the first nationally successful volume of Greek and Latin versions — *Arundines Cami* (1841) — he did provide a couple of pieces for the fourth edition of that collection (1851), no doubt helped by his connections with King's and Harrow.[41] The previous year, Benjamin Kennedy had gathered together the famous Salopian collection *Sabrinae Corolla* (1850), in which no fewer than ten compositions featured from the star pupil Shilleto — translations (composed long after his schooldays) into Greek and Latin lyric, Greek hexameters and iambics, Latin elegiacs and scazons.[42]

For tuition in composition, Shilleto was as good as it got.[43] His philosophy was simple and unshaking: it was linguistic precision that made a great classicist,

---

40 Anon., 31 Jan. 1852.
41 Henry Drury, the editor, was a Kingsman and Old Harrovian; he was also an Old Etonian, a school where Shilleto had examined the Newcastle Scholarship in 1849. In the 4th ed., we find a translation from Shakespeare into Greek iambics, and a riddle about heat (by Drury) into Latin elegiacs. Erroneously, however, Shilleto is described as 'Collegii SS. Trinitatis olim Socius', which perhaps many assumed was the case from his eminence in the university. Come the fifth edition (1865), nine compositions appeared from Shilleto's hand.
42 What seems to be the manuscript of one of these compositions — Latin elegiacs in thanks for a snuff box — survive in CUL Cam.a.500.9.32. They were written in 1849, 21 years after Shilleto left Shrewsbury.
43 Even the likes of Algernon Swinburne chose to send the elegiacs preceding his *Atalanta in Calydon* (1865) to Shilleto, who is reported to have responded that 'though there was not a line

and it was Latin and Greek composition that gave the greatest linguistic precision. Even in his screed against Grote he had found cause to remark 'that an accomplished English scholar can hardly even by accident make the mistakes which occasionally deform the pages of continental scholars, who, I believe, comparatively neglect "composition".'[44]

Yet Shilleto did not limit his composing to the Tripos-mandated exercise of translation. Instead, he was fired by a passion for off-the-cuff epigram that was truly Porsonian — as was his memory of facts and events. In reworking the news of the day into Greek and Latin dress, his skill and wit were legendary on the Cambridge scene and beyond. Most of his ephemera, circulated for the occasion in manuscript, have perished permanently. Those printed privately survive in only one or two copies preserved by provident friends. The magpie-minded John Willis Clark, Fellow of Trinity, collected several in a large scrapbook, which survives in Cambridge University Library (CUL Cam a.500.9). A fair specimen of Shilleto's lively and inventive style is given by his scazons on the election of H.A.J. Munro (another Salopian) as the first Latin (later Kennedy) Professor in 1869.[45] (A translation, usually his own, was often circulated in tandem, presumably to underline to the less linguistically deft his own cleverness.)

NOVUS PROFESSOR *Cui bono?*[46]

"Latin Professor" — you, who know no
Latin, or little say — "cui bono?"
What mean the Latin words? Good Sir,
I'll kindly be interpreter.
For meanings there I've ample room —
"In honour of a good man — Whom?"
Him, on the banks of Cam whose name
Lives blazoned in his pupils' fame,
While thrice ten years their favourite Shrine
Nigh Severn own the Muses Nine.

Sciens Latine perperam, "Latinarum
Novus Professor cui bono," rogas, "iste
Sit litterarum"? Visne sim tibi interpres?
Interpretabor plures. Sonent Anglis
"Viro bono cui?* verba. Melior an quisquam est
Viro, refers cui, Granta, tu quot accepta?
Propter Sabrinam qui novem colit Musas,
Placuitque senos quinquies colens annos?
Aliud sonent haec verba — "quid boni fiat?"
Humaniores literae magis cultae.

---

without a mistake, he wished he could have written the poem himself' (quoted by H. Bryan Donkin, *Spectator*, 14 Oct. 1911).
44 Shilleto 1851, 16.
45 Also worthy of citation are verses in close imitation of *Epodes* 2.8, in praise of an unnamed tutor (13 Feb. 1849): 'Beatus ille qui procul novantibus, | Ut Cantabrorum prisca gens, | Libris alumnus fidus instruit suos | Solutus a Duello. | Neque excitatus Syndicorum ineptiis, | Neque horret indoctum Caput; | Aulamque vitat et molesta Teutonum | Potentiorum limina. | Ergo aut Latinis atque Graecis literis | Suos maritat liberos. | Aut disciplinis in severioribus | Custodit errantes greges: | *Inutilesve falce ramos amputans* | *Feliciores inserit*.' (CUL Cam.a.500.9.21).
46 Cam.a.500.9.114a.

We'll say the words might mean "What good?"	Satis Juventus nostra jam sciens Graece
Classics will more be understood.	Sciet Latine; quo quid est bono majus?
Our youth in Latin now to seek	Adhuc, amice, barbarus fui interpres.
Shall Latin know as they know Greek.	Loquar Latine — scire si velis quid sit
I've hitherto been, my good Sir,	Interpretabor — "cui bono." Bono Grantae
A barbarian interpreter.	Nobis et ipsis et nepotibus seris.
I'll give the Latin meaning true.	Ne forte quaeras cui potissimum, judex
Good unto me, good unto you,	Pronuntiato Cassius — brevi absolvet;
Good to all coming Cantabs too.	"Quicumque Carum novit is lubens dicet;
Good most to — whom? A Daniel, yea	Esto Professor carus editor Cari,
A Daniel, honoured judge, shall say.	Carus Sabrinae, carior suae Grantae."
"To him, who holds Lucretius dear,	
Him, who has made Lucretius clear.	*Vir bonus est *quis?*
Place in the Chair of Latin here,	
Him, who no greater hath — no fear —	
Whom, dear to all both far and near,	
Severn and Cam alike revere."	

Stray Shilletoiana elsewhere in this Clark gallimaufry include Horatian Latin hexameters criticising the University's creation of sub-caucuses (Dec. 1853, Cam.a.500.9.38a); Latin elegiacs on the disbanding of the University's Caput Senatus in favour of a Council (7 Nov. 1856, Cam.a.500.9.51); English verses against the title A(ssociate) of C(ambridge) as a middle class awarded by Local Examinations (1860, Cam.a.500.9.62a); Greek iambics on the Great Hippocampus Question, ridiculing T.H. Huxley for believing that humans could be closely related to apes (1862, Cam.a.500.9.69); Greek elegiacs on the plagiaristic prize verses of F.W.H. Myers (1863, Cam.a.500.71); Latin saturnians [!!] rehashing the wording of a University Grace about a coming ball into the form of the *Carmen Saliare* (2 June 1864, Cam.a.500.72); an imitation of Athenaeus citing Theocritean hexameters about the prospect of women joining the university (16 Dec. 1865, Cam.a.500.9.86); Aristophanic anapaestic tetrameters on the ignorance displayed by those placed by examination in the second class (1868, Cam.a.500.9.103). All these were for the public (if elite) sphere; for the private, Shilleto circulated Greek verses to friends at every Christmas, and his *ad hoc* congratulatory verses were legion. It is a great shame that the majority of his compositions of this nature have been permanently lost, since they would have shed unique light on university and national politics. Instead, what survives plentifully are Shilleto's formal translations, into Greek and Latin prose and verse, which enjoyed wide circulation almost immediately after manuscript fair copies were handed to his pupils. In fact, so potent were the initials 'R.S.' as a mark of quality that many unattributed compositions doing the general rounds — especially if of Attic Greek prose — were optimistically branded with those initials. After several years, Britain's universities and schools were rife with pseudo-Shilleto versions among their materials — a problem of inauthenticity which only intensified after his death.

When, 25 years later, a former pupil (Rev. C.E. Graves of St John's) produced an approved collection of some 220 compositions, his two surviving sons — Edward and William (both then in their mid-fifties) — provided the prefatory note and dedication: *Patri amantissimo hunc libellum d. d. d. filii superstites.*[47] They recorded their previous worry that 'there was no guarantee for the genuineness of those pieces which were floating about in various schools and colleges, but which were yet credited with being his actual work.' They therefore turned to those in the domestic Shilleto archive: 'Most of these, indeed almost all of them, were in Mr Shilleto's own handwriting; and we satisfied ourselves, in regard to the few exceptions, that they also were really genuine.'[48] Since the fetish for publishing compositions in the nineteenth century rarely encompassed Greek proses (an omission overturned in subsequent decades), Shilleto's book became an essential teaching tool. Still, its practical origin could be spotted by the trained eye: one celebrated schoolmaster described it as the 'stock-in-trade of a hard-worked classical coach, and though, of course, every translation contains many examples of words aptly chosen and phrases ingeniously turned, yet *tours de force* are hardly to be expected.'[49]

When time allowed, Shilleto was also a regular contributor to *Notes & Queries*, under the anagrammatic *nom de plume* of Charles Thiriold — although one observer noted that 'Richard Shilleto' was a 'name much more like an anagram surely'. From 1851 until his death, tart and learned contributions appeared, always signed from Cambridge. Within a few years, Shilleto felt the need to reveal himself as the author, to bolster his virulent defence of Walter Scott's authorship of the *Waverley Novels*.[50] But perhaps his most famous epistolary salvo was a letter, proudly above his own name, bidding *The Times* to reject the linguistic neologisms of 'telegram' and (represented by the rival daily paper founded in 1855)

---

47 Shilleto 1901, [v].
48 *Ibid.*, [vii].
49 James Gow (HM of Nottingham High School), *CR* 16.6 (July 1902) 328. F.T. Rickards had already started publishing dozens of Shilleto's Greek proses (many with questionable attributions) in the early volumes of his *Translations into Greek Prose* (8 vols, Bombay, 1893–1911). However, at the end of this slightly unhinged global exercise in version-collecting, Rickards took care to correct various minutiae and misattributions of Shilleto's pieces on the basis of the evidence he had collated: see *CR* 25.3 (May 1911) 94.
50 *N&Q*, 1 Dec. 1855. His main adversary, W.J. Fitzpatrick, went on to publish a full pamphlet: *Who Wrote The Waverley Novels?* (London, 1856), which broaches Shilleto — and his unusual name — at p. 25.

'telegraph'.⁵¹ As a sample of his remorseless linguistic logic, it is worth quoting in full:

> Sir, — "Telegram" may possibly be a useful word. I have heard the same utilitarian apology offered for the vile Americanism "reliable." But there are times when etymologers must protest.
>
> An "Oxford First Classman" is bold enough to affirm of "telegram" that it is "a word constructed, as every Greek scholar knows, on perfectly sound principles." I venture, a Cambridge First Classman, to dispute this doctrine.
>
> What does the ending, "gram," signify?
>
> The following words are all which I can now remember:
>
> -1. Anagram, diagram, epigram. 2. Chronogram, monogram, parallelogram. (Possibly there are other mathematical terms with the same ending.)
>
> Every Greek scholar knows (I hope I do not offend your Oxford correspondent by adopting his phrase) that the words given above form two classes: that class 1 consists of Greek words constructed according to precise rule (ἀνά-γραμμα, διά-γραμμα, ἐπί-γραμμα); and that class 2 presupposes and ending in -γραμμος.
>
> Now, is τηλέγραμμα a possible form? Does τηλέγραμμος convey a possible sense?
>
> May I continue my research? What does the ending "-graph" signify?
>
> Clearly either the "writer" ("painter," &c.) or the "written" ("painted," &c.). Usage, until at the close of the last century "telegraph" was coined, limited its significance; *e.g.*, autograph, chirograph, holograph, paragraph, pseudograph. (Photograph is a 19th century word, but constructed according to strict analogy.)
>
> Arbitrary law must, however, be obeyed; and as "telegraph" cannot now mean the "despatched," may I suggest to such as are not contented with, "Telegraphic Despatch," the rightly constructed word "telegrapheme"? I do not want it, but in the name of etymological common sense I protest against such a barbarism as "telegram."
>
> I am, Sir, your obedient servant,
>
> Cambridge, Oct. 12 [1857]   RICHARD SHILLETO

A lively correspondence ensued. Edward Walford, 'late scholar of Balliol,' weighed in to defend 'telegram' on the basis of a hypothetical τηλεγράφω (17 Oct.). J.W. Donaldson immediately wrote in to declare that a 'gross barbarism', 'blunder' and 'solecism which, if allowed to pass without a rebuke, might bring discredit on the scholarship of England' (20 Oct.). Shilleto wrote in once more (23 Oct.) to point out that the adverbial prefix made it akin to Latin *procul-script, before suggesting a fresh neologism: 'telepomp' — perhaps shortened to 'pomp' like 'bus' from 'omnibus'. Alas, neither Shilletoian coinage gained traction, although 'telegrapheme' made a most gentle impression on James Murray's *Oxford*

---

51 It may be rivalled by the long letter to the same paper (24 Sep. 1869) that argued that 'the Bishops of Rome are no more successors of St. Peter than are all other bishops duly consecrated'.

New English Dictionary. It seems, however, that Shilleto knew when to pick his pedantic battles. He could trouble to rib the Latinity of J.W. Donaldson in his *Jashar* (London, 1854) — much the least interesting thing about that truly bizarre book[52] — but bite his tongue when the Provost of Eton held court incorrectly on Latin usage, because of the quality of beer then on offer.[53]

Despite his success as a tutor, it seems that Shilleto longed for a more canonical academic life. When the Revd John Edwards brought to a close his singularly undistinguished term as Professor of Greek at Durham (1841–1862), Shilleto decided to throw his hat into the ring. It may be that this post held the additional appeal of bringing him into closer contact with his wider family still in Yorkshire; perhaps he was excited by the combination of a steep rise in salary with a sharp drop in teaching hours. Although he was pitching for a post without any formal academic position behind him, Shilleto was able to secure twelve varied testimonials, elegantly collected in print to seduce the Lord Bishop of Durham.[54]

His lead referee was W.H. Thompson, then enthroned as Cambridge's Regius Professor of Greek. Thompson spoke admiringly of 'the reputation which had preceded [Shilleto] from the place of his education' — a reputation that 'has been steadily increasing, and never stood higher than at present. For knowledge of the Greek usage and idioms of the best times Mr. Shilleto is second certainly to no one in this country.' Appointing such a man would bring both 'lustre' and more students to Durham. 'For,' Thompson reasoned rather bluntly, 'he could hardly fail to raise the scholarship of both pupils and teachers.' Speaking of his own environs, he added that Shilleto's 'influence on the Scholarship of Cambridge has been great and unmistakeable — insomuch as an experienced examiner will detect his pupils by their accuracy, and the subtle perception of usage and construction which they have derived from his instruction.' The longed-for Thucydides, worked on in 'his few spare hours', is also mentioned: the 'comparative leisure of a professorial chair would probably enable him to bring to a prosperous ending labours which have hitherto been interrupted by his avocations as College and private Tutor.'

---

52 In the back pages of his own copy (CUL Adv.c.94.205), Shilleto records the letter he sent to Donaldson pointing out – in rather jaunty fashion — his solecism of *utrum... annon*; Donaldson's response, tipped in, is evidently unamused. Still, Shilleto notes on the same flyleaf, because of Donaldson's 'admirable temper' he 'never saw him angry'.
53 When in 1849 Edward Hawtrey was holding forth about the pronoun *iste* to Shilleto, who was examining the Newcastle Scholarship at Eton, he kept quiet. Afterwards he said to his friend and co-examiner James Lonsdale, 'Old Hawtrey talked insufferable rot about *iste*, but he keeps uncommonly good beer.' (Duckworth 1893, 207).
54 Shilleto 1862.

Francis France, Archdeacon of Ely and former President of St John's, noted that Shilleto had 'long had nearly a monopoly of the private tuition in Classics of the most promising scholars among our undergraduates'. A former Regius Professor of Law averred that his knowledge of Latin and Greek probably 'could only be matched by the acquirements of a race of Scholars now almost extinct'.[55] J.E.B. Mayor, Fellow of St John's, bolstered his claim that there is 'no man in England who has so profound a knowledge of the facts of the Greek language' with the belief 'that a majority of the editions of classical authors, which have appeared of late years in England, has been more or less indebted to his supervision.' Shilleto's friend Romilly observed that 'he is as familiar with Greek as with English. He seems to think in Greek, and every passing event of interest in the University is by him immediately clothed in the choicest Attic dress.' On the broader subject of character, James Lonsdale, Fellow of Balliol (and formerly of Durham), noted that all Shilleto's friends 'must love him, as much as they admire him, for his unselfishness, his hearty kindness, his simplicity and unworldliness of character, and his true Christian charity, which hopeth and believeth all things of others.'

Other testimonials came from Churchill Babington, Fellow of St John's, Joseph Edleston, Fellow and Bursar of Trinity, William Johnson (later Cory), Fellow of King's and Assistant Master at Eton, William Gunson, Fellow of Christ's, Charles Scott, Head Master of Westminster and former Fellow of Trinity, and Arthur Holmes, celebrated prize winner and former Fellow of St John's. But, despite the range of firepower on show, it was not to be: the chair fell to Thomas Evans, a man even more felicitous and fertile in composition — at least in Latin. Yet more remarkably, whereas Shilleto had scraped honours in Mathematics, Evans had failed to convince the examiners — and accordingly failed to take honours in Classics.[56] Unable to proceed at Cambridge, he went on to teach at Shrewsbury and Rugby. If Shilleto published little, Evans published nothing — other than astoundingly elegant verses.

At the close of Shilleto's own copy of his testimonials (CUL Cam.d.862.22), he has transcribed a letter from his former teacher Benjamin Kennedy. It reveals that Shilleto had decided not to approach this long-standing friend on the (correct) suspicion that Evans and Riddell had already received 'strong testimonials' from

---

55 H. Sumner Maine, member of the Supreme Council of India.
56 *Mathematogonia, or the Mythological Birth of the Nymph Mathesis* (Cambridge, 1839), a mock-Hesiodic poem that depicts how Mathematics came to reside by the Cam. Samuel Butler and Edward Maltby, Bishops of Lichfield and Durham, adjudged them 'decidedly the very best Greek verses either of them had ever read'; J.E.B. Mayor said that they 'would not have disgraced a Tragedian in the days of Athens'. (cited by Joseph Waite, in the 'Memoir' to Evans 1893, viii, which reproduces *Mathematogonia* at pp. 32–9).

him. But Kennedy stated that Shilleto had an 'equal claim' to his support, asking him plainly, 'Why were you too modest to advance it?' Nevertheless, it is unlikely that such a letter would have tipped the balance.

Undeterred, Shilleto returned to his daily tuition. But five years later, in 1867, he decided to make a push for an even higher goal than the Durham Chair, though one for which he stood a better chance.[57] When Thompson stepped into the role of Master of Trinity, the Regius Professorship of Greek fell open. Shilleto soon found himself arrayed against three Cambridge Hellenists: Benjamin Kennedy (four years retired from the headmastership of Shrewsbury), Edward Cope (1818–1873, Fellow of Trinity) and Arthur Holmes (1836–1875 Fellow of Clare, previously St John's). Tellingly or troublingly, all four candidates were also Salopians. Their lecture topics for the election contest all had a firm grip on the canon: 'The *Prometheus Vinctus* of Aeschylus' (Kennedy), 'The Nemean Odes of Pindar' (Holmes), 'The *Ethics* of Aristotle' (Cope), and 'Mythus in dialogo qui Phaedrus inscribitur' (Shilleto). These were delivered on Friday 15 and Saturday 16 February, with the election occurring on the following Monday. Of these lectures Shilleto's Latin oration was to match Holmes' Pindaric presentation in winning the fewest votes: none. It may not have been a matter of simple scholarship – for none could seriously suppose that Shilleto was outgunned *qua* Greek philologist. But one distinguished pupil may have reflected the private view of many that his drink problem told against him – not least since the position was still attached to a canonry at Ely Cathedral.[58] It was hardly a shoo-in for Kennedy: his tally of eight votes matched Cope's, which meant that the matter was referred to the Master of Trinity (i.e. the ex-Regius) and the Vice-Chancellor, each of whom favoured a different candidate; it was therefore passed up to the Chancellor, William Cavendish, 7th Duke of Devonshire, who favoured the older man Kennedy (then 62 to Cope's 48).

This must have been a harsh blow for Shilleto. But, eight months later, on 29 October, he was the first to profit from a seismic change in the new statutes of St Peter's (later Peterhouse) College. Statute XXII of the 1860 revision, on 'choosing Professors and Eminent Men as Fellows', set out how two thirds of the Fellowship

---

[57] Shilleto's solid chances were set out in an anonymous but well-informed letter to a Cambridge paper. After rehearsing Shilleto's world-class knowledge of Greek, the writer moves to consider what the position would bring the scholar. A professor's stipend would allow him 'to leave us, instead of fragmentary adversaria and unavailing regret, a critical edition of the greatest Greek author by probably the most correct Greek scholar of our time. Surely it would be a pity to lose such a work... One would wish to interpose a little ease amidst the remaining labours of a hard-tasked life, and not to have it said that we let our modern Porson sink into his grave unrewarded and unacknowledged.' (Letter from 'Cratinus', *The Light Blue*, 1 Sep. 1866.)
[58] Heitland 1926, 131.

could elect 'any person (whether married or not, and whether or not he may be a member of the College or of the University) eminent for science or learning, not holding any ecclesiastical preferment out of the precincts of the University, and not being Master or Fellow of another College.' Suddenly a married man had a route into the college's secluded cloisters, which had been guarded by celibate fellows for some 600 years.

An identical or similar statute had been simultaneously introduced at five other Colleges: Gonville and Caius, Trinity Hall, Clare, Christ's, Pembroke and St John's; the similar statutes at Trinity, St John's and King's, however, expressly stated that such a person must be unmarried. His fellow no-voter in the Regius competition, Arthur Holmes, was the first married fellow to be admitted in Cambridge, to Clare in 1864; three years earlier he had been compelled to vacate his Fellowship at St John's by marriage. What seems little known, if not entirely forgotten, is that Shilleto had himself circulated a set of Greek verses in 1857 criticising the younger fellows who were increasingly pro-marriage: his *Fragmentum ex satyri* φιλογάμοις Ἑταίροις ('A fragment from the satyr-play *The Marriage-hungry Fellows*').[59] Over 41 iambic trimeters A (a student who has failed his exams) explains to B (a fellow student willing to let him rant) the disasters that married Fellows bring about: College is full of 30,000 babies crying and whimpering (βρέφη | τρισμύρι' ἀνακράζοντα καὶ κνυζούμενα, 14–15), and of women's prattling mockery, as they hurl abuse like fishwives (lit. bakesters: γυναικῶν κερτόμου γλωτταλγίας... διαλοιδορουσῶν ὥσπερ ἀρτοπωλίδων, 17–19). A tutor is said to have stopped some students from having a dinner party because their shouting would distract his little woman (γύναιον, 27) who was due to give birth (24-9). Finally, the tale is told of a Johnian Fellow (ἀνὴρ Ἰωνικός, 31) who had to leave College after accidentally kicking the child of his young gyp (31–6). After B expresses the rather uncharitable wish that Zeus destroy this gyp and his brat (37–8), A ends by gesturing to a 'host of other woes' that have come since 'the Fellows betrayed the sacred rites they had inherited and rejected the bachelor life' (ἱερὰ καταπροδόντες τὰ πάτρια | ἀπέπτυσαν μονόκοιτον οὑταῖροι βίον, 40–1).[60] And

---

59 A copy survives as CUL Cam.a.500.9.52.
60 Conversely, a poem that did the rounds in the 1860s touched upon some of the social strains between married and unmarried fellows: 'Alas! These Private Tutors lead such comfortable lives,| They can enjoy the luxury of houses for their wives, | Surely no greater evil can exist beneath the sun, | That Private Tutors should have wives, where we, alas have none! | Then in their pleasant dwellings one sight the eye appals, | A race of joyous little ones are trained within their walls; | Why should they have a privilege from which we are debarred? | No wonder that these happy men with pupils toil so hard! | For it is a fact notorious that men are apt to take | More pleasure in their duties for a wife and children's sake, | Yet it is but general interest these married

yet, a mere decade later, Shilleto's mind had evolved, and he happily became Peterhouse's first married Fellow. The decision was made suddenly: a pupil recalls failing to find him one evening for his appointed supervision. The next day, he recalls, Shilleto 'buttonholed me with a grin and said 'Very sorry — elected Fellow of Peterhouse only yesterday — had to go and wet it.'"[61]

The release from tuition must have been welcome, since Shilleto's health was starting to flag: as he wrote to a pupil in 1866, 'I am not in the best of humours, for I have gout blindness deafness and all manner of complications of maladies.'[62] From a professional point of view, he perhaps also realised that new figures were rising up in the world of Classical coaching: Samuel Butcher, Henry Jackson, Richard Jebb — and even Shilleto *minor*. More to the point, this new wave of dons sought to end the influence of the private tutor by increasing the quality of the provision within college walls. Shilleto was thus content to throw himself into life at his late-won college, serving variously as dean, librarian, praelector and assistant tutor, along with new responsibilities as an examiner for University Scholarships. The change in circumstances was excellent news for those hoping for an improvement upon the glacial pace that his Thucydidean edition had made. In 1868, subscribers gave Shilleto a three-year annuity of £600 to support his researches, thus replacing the money that he would have earned from teaching. Aided by the special dispensation to borrow two manuscripts of Thucydides from the University Library for extensive collation, Shilleto could at last beaver away.[63]

In 1872, the first book appeared. Its preface made clear how he could now, at last, pursue research as he wanted. Describing his academic life prior to his Fellowship, he recalled that 'a very great portion of this time was spent in work continued, with brief intervals, from early morning to midnight, work hard, still work intellectual, but leaving scanty space for extra work.' But a Fellowship, despite his wavering health, had made a stark difference:

---

tutors feel, | They cannot have a *single* eye to every pupil's weal. | Great men are still among us who gratefully will say, | How much the private tutor once had helped them on their way: | The system has wrought well they say, and some will deem it strange | That a good consistent Tory should ask for needless change. | We might feel some small scruples when we try to crush the race, | For we own they faithfully promote the studies of this place, | But when so near our lonely rooms the married tutors live, | They experience audacity no *fellows* can forgive.' (First printed in *Oxford and Cambridge Reporter*, 30 Oct. 1862.)

61 Heitland 1926, 131.
62 To J.E. Sandys on 1 May 1866: cited in Hammond 1933, 12.
63 Exemplary collations were made of manuscript T (KK v 19, s.xv) in his copy of Bekker's edition (Oxford, 1824: CUL Adv.c.94.169) and N (Nn iii 18) in his copy of Arnold's edition (Oxford, 1830–5: CUL Adv. 170–2).

> Within the last four years the position given to me by my adopting College, and the liberality of friends — for both of which this short Notice allows but a passing expression of gratitude — might have enabled me with more leisure to produce more results, if hard incessant work had not been followed by bodily ailments, and increasing years given to a constitution naturally robust less vigour to resist such attacks.[64]

The result was a good text, supported by a critical apparatus that was well-stocked for the time, and a parallel-heavy English commentary on the language (but little else) of the book. Given the philological acumen on show, two oddities remain. First, Shilleto had carefully collated the two fifteenth-century mss in the University Library (see n. 63), and had travelled earlier in his life to make some collations of the manuscripts in Paris; but there was little to no statement of the method on which his choice of collations relied. The Cambridge manuscripts are of little value, and the evidence he cites from other sources is scanty and/or derivative. Second, for all his expertise in Attic Greek, Shilleto emerges as a surprisingly conservative critic: although well aware of the niceties of Thucydidean style, he is content to treat one or two divergences from a particular rule as part of the author's variation in practice, rather than as evidence for possible corruption.[65] If one were to ask how Shilleto differs from the Porson with which he was so regularly compared, the answer would be simple: the one could read without emending texts, the other could not. For this reason, if no other, the name of Shilleto is relatively rare in the critical apparatus of Greek literature.

His close friend James Lonsdale privately echoed the view of many competent critics: 'Shilleto's Thucydides (lib. I that is) is come out. What there is seems extremely good; the only pity is that there is not more of it.'[66] The *Athenaeum* concluded its lengthy review with a pointed pair of sentences: 'The book is one of which its erudite author may well be proud. We trust that it will not be very long before we have occasion to record its completion and to consider it in its integrity.'[67] Unhappily, on this score Shilleto did indeed follow in the footsteps of Porson and many other celebrated scholars, by failing to complete his great single-author edition.

On 24 September 1876, Shilleto's life ended, aged 66. The second book appeared posthumously (in 1880), but had to be reconstructed by an anonymous editor (in reality F.A. Paley) from chapter 72, where Shilleto's notes tapered off.

---

64 Shilleto 1872, [v].
65 This attitude is in keeping with the remark in his *Thucydides* (1872, x): 'the longer one lives and reads the more one is conscious of one's ignorance, and shrinks from dogmatism.'
66 To Rev. W. Bulmer, 20 July 1872 (Duckworth 1893, 208).
67 10 Feb. 1872.

The rest of the project does not languish unpublished, nor scattered between disparate notes: it never reached written form at all. As a result, the total impact of 'Shilleto's Thucydides' is unhappily small.

Although he had been in poor health for a while,[68] Shilleto's end came sufficiently fast for him to die intestate, leaving behind some £3,000. In a large family this did not go far: the following year Shilleto's library was sold *in toto*, although there was little of great value.[69] Mercifully, however, Sir William Harcourt (a former pupil) successfully persuaded Disraeli, then Prime Minister, to grant Shilleto's widow Isabella a civil-list pension of £150 'in recognition of the eminent attainments of Mr. Shilleto as a Greek scholar'.

Those corners of the press that could sympathise with the genius of a figure little known beyond Classical students, marked his death with regret. 'He has not left a Greek scholar in England fit to black his boots... Except [Carel Gabriel] Cobet of Leyden, there was probably no Greek scholar equal to him in the world.'[70] His first entry in the *Dictionary of National Biography* noted that he was 'justly pronounced the 'Greatest Greek scholar in England since the death of Gaisford'.[71] An anonymous writer in a Gloucestershire paper chose to channel Horace: 'We may say of him that there were heroes before Agamemnon, but there was no Homer to sing their exploits.'[72] But his longstanding boon-companion James Lonsdale preferred to see the funnier side:

> Styx office has no post, no lines he can now write us,
> Yet doubtless still he jokes e'en by the sad Cocytus,
> On Pluto and on Cerberus he makes his pleasant squibs,
> And pokes old Aeacus and Minos in their ribs.[73]

When Henry Jackson came to inspect Shilleto's marginal adversaria, donated posthumously to Cambridge University Library, he confessed himself to be 'drearily disappointed with them... I have to admit that most of the things which I saw in the books were trivial. In fact, he had not much in reserve besides what

---

68 In 1874, Lonsdale had confided of his friend that 'time and domestic troubles have sadly altered his old animation and damped the fire of his old genius'. Letter to R. Duckworth, 26 Dec. 1874 (Duckworth 1893, 82).
69 Sold by John Swan and Son, Cambridge, 16 May 1877, along with an 18-foot mahogany bookcase (copy in CUL Munby c. 60).
70 *Aberdeen Press and Journal*, 11 Oct. 1876.
71 E.C. Marchant, *DNB* 52 (1897) 106.
72 *Stroud News and Gloucestershire Advertiser*, 29 Sep. 1876.
73 Duckworth 1893, 208.

he used to teach us, and a great deal of this teaching has been made familiar by his pupils.'[74]

It is indeed the pupils who helped pass the torch. Shilleto's great gift to nineteenth-century Cambridge was to serve as a free-flowing fount of precise and correct linguistic knowledge: standards were kept high which would certainly have slid into over-simplified, rule-bound dogmatism, had he stayed an active man of the cloth. But his life, as a whole, is manifestly not a happy tale of success.[75] It is, if anything, a test-case of how societal norms can prove a life-changing fork in the road for the course of a career. Because of an early marriage, one of Cambridge's most formidable Classicists was forced to live outside the college system for 35 years; the cost, financial and emotional, led him to spend all but the Lord's Day teaching those who had the means to pay him; his brain was kept from the research of which he was capable, and his body was drawn to rely upon the pacifying crutch of alcohol. He died with one rushed book to his name, alongside a narrowly-focused portion of a larger project that he could never grasp with both hands.

It is perhaps now clear that the Shilleto phenomenon is one created out of an unusual combination of features: linguistic brilliance, personal charm, prodigious memory, epigrammatic flair, and committed bibulosity. Given the void left when the Porsonian school dispersed from Cambridge and the life terrestrial, Shilleto was willing and able to be cast in his form, albeit as a very scaled-down model. But while Porson could not or would not teach, Shilleto's life was literally built upon that exchange. His more astute pupils drew their own conclusions:

---

[74] Letter to F.J.H. Jenkinson, 27 July 1890, quoted in Parry 1926, 228.
[75] His children were a more mixed bunch. Although Arthur Shilleto would become a successful translator of Greek classics (including Polybius, Pausanias and Aristotle) and also contribute to *Notes and Queries* under an anagram (Erato Hills), and although William followed his father in graduating as Second Classic (1873) before becoming a tutor, not all were in the image of their father: John, the second son, headed to Christ's, where he found himself plucked three years in a row for the preliminary examination ('Little-Go'), in the first case coming bottom of the heap, before he at last escaped with a B.A. five years later (1856–61); Richard, the eldest, somehow found himself in his thirties charged with assaulting the librarian of the Free Library in 1871. (It is a calumny, no less, that the editors of Romilly's diary [Bury & Pickles 2000, 91 n.24] misattribute this crime — of a drunkard who looked like he had been rolling in dirt — to Richard Shilleto senior!)

On the whole old Shill was a pathetic figure. Into the notorious troubles of a mismanaged career I will not enter. You could not help liking him or feeling sorry for him... The Fellows of Peterhouse saved Cambridge from the disgrace of ignoring a great scholar.[76]

Bibliography

Bury, M.E./Pickles, J.D. (eds.) (2000), *Romilly's Cambridge Diary, 1848–1864: Selected Passages from the Diary of the Rev. Joseph Romilly*, Cambridge.
Colvin, S. (1921), *Memories & Notes of Persons & Places, 1852–1912*, London.
Duckworth, R. (1893), *A Memoir of the Rev. James Lonsdale*, London.
Evans, T.S. (1893), *Latin and Greek Verse*, Cambridge.
Gardiner, A.G. (1923), *The Life of Sir William Harcourt*, 2 vols., London
Graham, E. (1920), *The Harrow Life of Henry Montagu Butler, D.D.*, London.
Hammond, N.G.L. (1933), *Sir John Edwin Sandys: 1844–1922*, Cambridge.
Heitland, W.E. (1926), *After Many Years: A Tale of Experiences and Impressions Gathered in the Course of an Obscure Life*, Cambridge.
Kennedy, B.H. (1876), 'Richard Shilleto', *Journal of Philology* 7, 163–168.
Kolb, J. (ed.) (1981), *The Letters of Arthur Henry Hallam*, Columbia, OH.
Parry, R. St J. (1926), *Henry Jackson, O.M.*, Cambridge.
Rouse Ball, W.W. (1889), *A History of the Study of Mathematics at Cambridge*, Cambridge.
Shilleto, R. (ed.) (1844), *Demosthenis De Falsa Legatione*, Cambridge.
Shilleto, R. (1851), *A Few Remarks upon a Pamphlet by Mr. Shilleto entitled, 'Thucydides or Grote?'*, Cambridge.
Shilleto, R. (ed.) (1862), *The Rev. R. Shilleto's Testimonials to the Lord Bishop of Durham*, Cambridge.
Shilleto, R. (ed.) (1872), *Thucydidis I. With Collation of the Two Cambridge MSS and the Aldine and Juntine Editions*, Cambridge.
Shilleto, R. (1901), *Greek and Latin Compositions*, Cambridge.
Stray, C.A. (1997), '"Thucydides or Grote?" Classical Disputes and Disputed Classics in Nineteenth-Century Cambridge', *TAPA* 127, 363–371.
Stray, C.A. (2015), 'The Wooden Spoon: Rank (Dis)order in Cambridge 1753–1909', *History of Universities* 26, 163–201.
Stray, C.A. (2018), *Classics in Britain: Scholarship, Education, and Publishing 1800–2000*, Oxford.
Stray, C./Clarke, M./Katz, J.T. (eds.) (2019), *Liddell & Scott: The History, Methodology, and Languages of the World's Leading Lexicon of Ancient Greek*, Oxford.
Trevelyan, G.M. (1932), *Sir George Otto Trevelyan: A Memoir*, London.
Vaizey, J.S. (ed.) (1895–1907), *The Institute: A Club of Conveyancing Counsel. Memoirs of Former Members*, 4 vols., London.
Warwick, A. (2003), *Masters of Theory: Cambridge and the Rise of Mathematical Physics*, Chicago.

---

76 Heitland 1926, 131.

Williamson, M. (2019), 'Dictionaries and Translations: English in the Lexicon', in: Stray/Clarke/Katz 2019, 25–44.
Wordsworth, C. (1877), *Scholae Academicae*, Cambridge.

James Clackson
Dangerous Lunatics: Comparative Philology in Cambridge and Beyond

Henry Sweet (1845–1912)[1] is generally regarded as one of the founders of modern linguistics in the UK.[2] A brilliant practical linguist and phonetician, he was a model for Prof. Henry Higgins in Shaw's *Pygmalion*. Sweet was very much an Oxford man, although his relationship with the university was not straightforward. He graduated with a fourth in Greats from Balliol in 1873, a result that played a role in his failure to be appointed either to the Merton professorship of English Language and Literature in 1885 or the chair of Comparative Philology in 1901. Sweet lived in Oxford as a private scholar from 1894, receiving, in the year he failed to win the second professorship, some recompense from the university in the form of the post of Reader in Phonetics, annual stipend £200. The title of this paper is taken from a passage of his Presidential address to the Philological Society, delivered on 18 May 1877, which well illustrates 'that rigorous candour which was alike a virtue and a defect of his character'.[3]

> An undergraduate of an English University who were to announce to the Head of his College his intention of devoting himself to English philology would be regarded as a dangerous lunatic — to be repressed by any means. If he persisted, in the face of ridicule and opposition of every kind, he would be branded with the terrible epithet of 'specialist,' no matter how wide the range of his culture, and that by men who only escape the epithet themselves by not possessing a scientific knowledge of any subject whatever.[4]

For Sweet, it was students of English philology, rather than of classical philology, who were perceived to be the object of ridicule and opposition. As I shall show, however, his caustic comments might have hit home in Cambridge also where the "specialism" of classical philology and linguistics would be examined for the first time in the new Part II of the Tripos in 1883.

---

1 An earlier version of the paper was presented as an inaugural lecture in Cambridge on 19 May 2017. It has become a commonplace to say that this would not have been written without the unstinting encouragement, help and advice from Chris Stray, but that does not make it any less true. There are few people I hold in higher esteem than Chris as a scholar and a friend, and it is a privilege to be able to contribute to this volume in his honour.
2 For accounts of Sweet's life and achievements, see Wrenn 1946, MacMahon 2006 and Momma 2013, 157–84.
3 Wrenn 1946, 194.
4 Sweet 1879, 12.

https://doi.org/10.1515/9783110719215-007

The chair of Comparative Philology at Cambridge University was founded in 1937, the last to be founded in the British Isles. Chairs of Comparative Grammar, and later of Comparative Philology, had been founded in London in 1842,[5] at Owens College in Manchester in 1851,[6] Edinburgh in 1862,[7] Oxford in 1868[8] and University College of Wales, Aberystwyth in 1872.[9] This might be seen to indicate that comparative philology was a peripheral subject, only arriving late at Cambridge, an impression reinforced by recent histories of the discipline, where Cambridge comparative philologists are scarcely mentioned.[10] It is the purpose of this chapter to show that Cambridge's role in the development of the discipline took place earlier than is generally recognised.[11] Many departments not just of classics and comparative philology, but also Celtic studies, Sanskrit and later linguistics across the UK were initially populated by scholars educated at Cambridge. The first two holders of the chair of Comparative Philology at University College London were Cambridge men,[12] as were three of the first four holders of the chair in Manchester,[13] and the

---

[5] Bellot 1929, 87, Morpurgo Davies 1992, 8, Stray 2004a.
[6] Hartog 1900, 44. The chair at Owens College was held initially by Alexander John Scott (1805–1866) first Principal of the College and also Professor of English language and literature and moral and mental philosophy; from 1873 by Augustus Samuel Wilkins (1843–1906) who held the chair at the same time as the chair of Latin (Charlton 1951, 172).
[7] The full title of the chair was Sanskrit and Comparative Philology; the first holder was Theodor Aufrecht (1821–1907), see Jacobi 1907.
[8] Morpurgo Davies 1992, 9, Momma 2013, 150.
[9] Ellis 1972, 332.
[10] Morpurgo Davies 1992 has only two passing references to Cambridge, both from the period before 1850; in the accounts of Aarsleff 1983 and Momma 2013 Cambridge features more prominently, but these narratives are also largely confined to the first half of the nineteenth century.
[11] The first calls for a chair of Comparative Philology in Cambridge were as early as 1876, see CUR 19 March 1876, 303f., cited by Beard 1999, 115.
[12] Thomas Hewitt Key (1799–1875), Professor of Comparative Grammar from 1842 at University College London, and his successor, John Percival Postgate (1853–1926), Professor of Comparative Philology 1880 to 1910 (Chambers 1939, 356f., Bellot 1929 Chart 1, Owen 1926, 337; for Postgate see below). After Postgate's departure, the post was replaced by a lectureship in Comparative Philology, held by the Cambridge graduate Frederick William Thomas (1867–1956), who was subsequently Boden Professor of Sanskrit at Oxford (Bellot 1929 Chart 1). Cecil Bendall (1856–1906) and Edward James Rapson (1861–1937) were successively Professors of Sanskrit at University College London between 1885 and 1907 (Bellot 1929 Chart 2).
[13] Wilkins was succeeded at Manchester by John Strachan (1862–1907) who was Professor of Greek from 1885 and also Comparative Philology from 1889. After Strachan's early death, Robert Seymour Conway (1864–1933) added the renamed chair of Indo-European Philology to the Hulme professorship of Latin, which he had held since 1903 (Charlton 1951, 172). A further Cambridge philologist in Manchester was James Hope Moulton (1863–1917) Greenwood Professor of Hellenistic Greek and Indo-European Philology (Peake/Macquiban 2006).

third holder of the Oxford chair.[14] Indeed, Cambridge philologists made their mark further afield: Thomas Tucker was appointed Professor of Classical and Comparative Philology at the University of Melbourne, Australia, in 1885.[15] After the Second World War, as new universities and new departments of linguistics were founded across the UK, several of those who took papers in Group E ('Language') in Part II Classics at Cambridge went on to play leading roles in the propagation and expansion of the discipline.[16]

I shall begin my account of the rise of comparative philology at Cambridge from a conventional place to start the story of modern linguistics, the 'discovery' of the Indo-European language family. Even before the advent of British rule in India, European scholars developed an awareness and interest in the languages of India, in particular Sanskrit, the language of Hindu scriptures and religious texts, of literary genres such as verse, drama, epic and of the technical sciences.[17] We are fortunate that one of those who came to India as a judge was himself a polyglot, Sir William Jones (1746–1794). Jones set out the theory that Sanskrit was a sister language to Latin and Greek in a famous passage of his 'Third Anniversary Discourse, on the Hindus' to the Asiatic Society of Calcutta.[18] Jones was not the first to point out the similarities, but his lecture captured the attention of the scholarly community in Europe. The study of this language family was enthusiastically taken up, particularly in Germany, with founding works by Bopp and Schlegel, whose lead was followed by the investigations of the brothers Grimm

---

[14] Gustav Ernst Karl Braunholtz (1887–1967) Professor of Comparative Philology, University of Oxford from 1925 to 1952. His father Eugen Gustav Wilhelm Braunholtz (1859–1941), MA of King's College, was Cambridge University Lecturer in French (1884–1900) and Reader in Romance (1900–1939).

[15] Thomas George Tucker (1859–1946), matriculated St John's College 1878, Senior Classic 1882, Fellow of St John's 1882. His publications ranged from editions and commentaries on Aeschylus to works on comparative philology and linguistics, including *Introduction to the Natural History of Language* (1908) and *Concise Etymological Dictionary of Latin* (1931) (McKay 1990).

[16] See Brown/Law 2002 for an insightful collection of personal reminiscences by key figures in the field. Over a quarter of the individuals included in the volume took papers in Group E: Jean Aitchison (b. 1938), W. Sidney Allen (1918–2004), N.E. Collinge (1921–2011), Sir John Lyons (1932–2020), Peter Matthews (b. 1934) and John Wells (b. 1939). Three others, who studied Modern and Medieval Languages — Richard Hudson (b. 1939), Neil Smith (b. 1939) and Peter Trudgill (b. 1943), took the inter-faculty 'Principles of Language' paper, lectured by the Professor of Comparative Philology, Sidney Allen.

[17] Simone 1998, 212f.

[18] See Franklin 2011, 35–8 for the passage and discussion in the context of Jones's life and its impact. The passage is cited in many histories and handbooks of linguistics (e.g. Aarslef 1983, 133, Morpurgo Davies 1992, 65, Simone 1998, 213f., Hock 1991, 556, Szemerényi 1996, 4).

into the history of German.[19] In 1813 the name by which this language family is now generally known in the English-speaking world, Indo-European, was first used in print by a Cambridge-educated polymath, Thomas Young (1773–1829).[20] The discovery of Sanskrit acted as the key which unlocked the history and affiliations of language. Sanskrit and comparative philology thus became a way to understand better, or even "scientifically", both the grammar and texts of ancient languages as well as the connections of ancient peoples.

One of the first people in England to give lectures on language using the newly found science of comparative grammar, and heavily in the debt of German scholars, in particular Jacob Grimm, was John Mitchell Kemble (1807–1857), known as 'Jack' or even 'Black Jack' to his friends. Kemble's life is full of adventure, and has been ably researched by Professor Simon Keynes, to whom I am very grateful for allowing me to cite his unpublished manuscript.[21] Kemble was an undergraduate at Trinity College Cambridge (1825–9) and was elected a member of the Cambridge Conversazione Society, better known as the Apostles, in 1825. In 1829 he sat the Cambridge Tripos, but his unorthodox opinions meant that he was not awarded a degree that year but was asked to take the exams again the next year. In 1829–30 on a trip to Munich he discovered philology, writing in a letter to a friend, dated March 1830, 'My great object is to give a History of the English Language, in which its changes, with their causes, shall be distinctly brought before the reader, and in which it shall be shown that Philology is a great Science, collaterally related to all that is interesting in the History and opinions of a people.'[22] Remarkably, he kept up this interest in 1830–1, during his participation in an abortive attempt to foster a revolution in Spain starting in Gibraltar. The story is too long to tell here, but, in the words of Keynes (p. 18) it is 'a tale of high-minded principles gradually giving way to Germanic philology, and Spanish women'.[23]

Kemble then returned to Cambridge, with occasional visits to Göttingen to consort with the brothers Grimm. It was in Cambridge that he gave the first lectures on the new subject of philology in 1834, although he had no university or college position. Around ninety people reportedly turn out for the first lecture,

---

19 Morpurgo Davies 1992, 59–82 and 129–50.
20 Young 1813, 256.
21 Unpublished working notes (dated 2013), 'The Compleat Anglo-Saxonist, John Mitchell Kemble (1807–57)'. Hereafter cited as Keynes with page number. See also Wiley 1971, 5–18, Momma 2013, 68–94) and Haigh 2015.
22 Cited in Keynes p. 15.
23 See further Nye 2015.

but then the audience dwindled; one report claimed that just five or six loyal Fellows of Trinity were left at the end.[24] The series did not last the advertised twenty lectures. After a few years, disappointed by the lack of success in his search for a university or college post, Kemble left Cambridge but continued to work on Anglo-Saxon, producing the first editions of Anglo-Saxon charters and later incorporating archaeology into his researches. With the enthusiasm and confidence of youth, Kemble thought that he had set ablaze the flame of philology in Cambridge 'my lectures have been eminently successful, and have awakened an interest that will long survive me and my labours'.[25] Indeed, the conditions in Cambridge, in particular at Trinity College, were perfect for philology to catch light. In the years immediately before Kemble's lectures, William Whewell (1794–1866), together with his friends Julius Charles Hare (1795–1855) and Connop Thirlwall (1797–1875), all currently or formerly Trinity Fellows, started an Etymology Society, publishing in the short-lived journal the *Philological Museum*.[26]

In his later life, while Kemble's interests ranged towards the historical and archaeological, the philological fire burnt steadily in Cambridge, and brightest at Trinity. In the early years of the Philological Society of London (founded in 1842), there was a preponderance of Cambridge men. Thirlwall was President until 1868, when he was succeeded by Thomas Hewitt Key, (a former Fellow of Trinity, then Professor of Comparative Grammar at University College London); two of the first three Vice-Presidents of the Philological Society were also former Trinity Fellows.[27] After Kemble's early death in 1857, his former friends and admirers in Cambridge put together a subscription for a memorial bust of him; among the donors there are those whose philological interests we have already encountered, such as Whewell, since 1841 Master of Trinity.[28] There are also a number of classical scholars who subscribed to the Kemble memorial, men who were to become important in the incorporation of comparative philology into the still relatively young Classical Tripos. Note the following: Benjamin Hall Kennedy (1804–1899) an undergraduate at St John's College, but also, like Kemble, an Apostle in the

---

24 Momma 2013, 90.
25 Undated letter to Jacob Grimm, Spring 1834, published by Wiley 1971, 57, cited in Momma 2013, 72.
26 Aarslef 1983, 216–21, Stray 1999, 3. Hare's maternal aunt was Sir William Jones's widow (Distad 2016). For the *Philological Museum* see Stray 2004c, 299–305 = 2018a, 156–64.
27 Aarslef 1983, 213–6 gives further details of the close connections between the Philological Society and Cambridge, particularly Trinity College.
28 Yeo 2009. The subscribers' names, with the amount each contributed, are listed on a leaflet, entitled 'Kemble Memorial', produced by William Bodham Donne and W. Ll. Birkbeck in 1867. I thank Professor Simon Keynes for showing me copies of the leaflet in his personal possession.

1820s, elected Regius Professor of Greek in 1867; Kennedy's former student, Hugh Andrew Johnstone Munro (1819–1885), first occupant of the new chair of Latin (later to be called the Kennedy chair) and also a Fellow of Trinity; and William Hepworth Thompson (1810–1886), Kennedy's predecessor in the Greek chair and appointed Master of Trinity in 1866. Munro was too young to have heard Kemble lecture, but his interest in comparative philology had been sparked by private lectures given by Kemble's pupil John William Donaldson (1811–1861), as were those of Thompson and the next occupant of the Latin chair, John Eyton Bickersteth Mayor (1825–1910).[29]

After his election to the professorship of Greek, Kennedy was heavily involved in the numerous educational reforms in the university, in particular those affecting the Classical Tripos, which took place in the second half of the nineteenth century.[30] I shall not trace here the various different proposals made to ensure that philology earned its place in the new Tripos, between the suggestion that a paper in Latin or Greek philology was offered as an alternative to Latin or Greek Verse composition[31] and the scheme that the Tripos be limited to Greek and Latin language, comparative philology and Sanskrit — "the elaborate fantasy of a philological ideologue".[32] During the discussion of Tripos reform, there were always strong advocates for comparative philology.

The reformed Tripos was finally passed in 1879; in effect, it showed a way to answer the dilemma over specialisms that Henry Sweet had identified in his address to the Philological Society in 1877. Despite, or perhaps because of, the great advances made by German universities in the nineteenth century, there was a mistrust of specialisms in England. Reform-minded individuals, among whom Fellows of Trinity were conspicuous, realised the value of specialist research and the willingness of students to engage with recent developments in learning. The two-part Tripos allowed students to show their linguistic knowledge and "skill" in Part I, largely translation from and into Latin and Greek. In Part II, which remained optional until the reform of 1918, they could display "knowledge" and study various specialisms. Part II was divided into five sections: Section A, compulsory until 1895, originally comprised more translation, but after 1895 was devoted to Literature and Criticism; Section B

---

[29] See Todd 2004, s.v. for Donaldson. On Mayor see Henderson 1998.
[30] On the reforms of the Classical Tripos in these years, see Winstanley 1947, 209–23, Stray 1998, 146–9, 1999, 5–9, 2018a, 110–17, Henderson 1998, 3–5, and Beard 1999, 105–13.
[31] Winstanley 1947, 214.
[32] Beard 1999, 107; the philological ideologue was Augustus Arthur Vansittart (1824–1882), Fellow of Trinity College from 1848.

was entitled 'Ancient Philosophy'; Section C 'Ancient History'; Section D 'Archaeology';[33] and Section E 'Language'.

Despite the catch-all designation, which is retained to the present day, Section E dealt with what would now be called comparative philology and classical linguistics. The four papers prescribed for Section E were originally as follows:[34]

1. Paper containing (α) Questions on Greek etymology, and the history of the Greek dialects, with illustration from inscriptions or other sources: (β) Questions on Greek syntax, together with passages from Greek authors for translation, comment, or emendation: (γ) Questions on the etymology and usages of the Greek and Latin languages as compared with one another.
2. Paper containing (α) Questions on Latin etymology, and the history of the cognate Italian dialects, with illustration from inscriptions or other sources: (β) Questions on Latin syntax, together with passages from Latin authors for translation, comment, or emendation: (γ) Questions on the etymology and usages of the Greek and Latin languages as compared with one another.
3. Paper containing (α) Simple questions on the Sanskrit grammar, with special reference to those forms which illustrate the history of the Greek and Latin languages: (β) Easy passages from selected Sanskrit authors for translation and comment.
4. Paper containing (α) General questions on the comparative grammar of the Indo-European languages with special reference to the Greek and Latin languages: (β) Questions on the history of Alphabets: (γ) Questions on some selected portion or portions of the comparative grammar of the Indo-European languages, which the Board shall from time to time define either by suggesting the books to be read or otherwise.

Until 1895 candidates could offer more than one section alongside Section A, although not many did. On 13 June 1883, the Board of Classical Studies reported to the General Board of Studies that currently 96 students were intending to take Part II in either 1883 or 1884, of these only 14 were taking a combination of

---

33 Although originally with a much wider brief than is understood by the term today (Beard 1999, 113).
34 *CUR* 11 March 1879, 439. In 1901 the papers were slimmed down with the loss of section (γ) from papers 1 and 2, and the loss of section (β) from paper 4, *CUR* 14 May 1901, 865–6. Paper 3 was optional, and candidates also had the opportunity to submit a dissertation (Beard 1999, 101).

sections B, C, D and E.³⁵ Table 1 shows the numbers of students receiving instruction in the subjects of Part II in June 1883 as given in the report.³⁶

The majority of students reading Classics avoided Part II as long as it remained optional. In the report of 1883 it was noted that 330 students had taken Part I in 1882 and 343 were due to sit the exams in 1883. This means that 13% of those eligible were taking Part II in 1883; a higher figure of 16% had the aspiration to sit the exam in the following year, but of course once Part I results were known many would lose their enthusiasm. Over the period from 1885–1914, the cumulative figures show that no more than 11% of all students who took Part I went on to Part II.³⁷ Given that some students came as affiliated students from other universities and only sat the Part II exams, the true figure is probably even lower.

As Table 1 shows, in 1883 Section E was the most popular of any section of the Tripos. This reflects the enduring popularity of the subject in the 1880s and early 1890s. It is impossible to give exact figures for what proportion of those who took Part II chose E, given that the class lists only indicated the Section chosen by those awarded firsts, but the number of firsts awarded across the different sections, given in Table 2, is suggestive.³⁸

As can be seen, in the twentieth century popularity of the optional Part II declined across all subjects, but the contrast in Section E is particularly noteworthy. The report of the Board of Classical Studies dated 8 March 1883, which gave the numbers reproduced in Table 1, brought to light the strained situation of teaching for the specialist subjects: 'which cannot be described as either adequate or perfectly organised, while much of it is, from the tenure of the appointments held by the teachers, necessarily precarious'.³⁹ In particular, for Section E 'At least one permanent teacher free to devote the whole of his time to the study and teaching of this section is needed' and there was hope for others, including remuneration

---

35 *CUR* 13 June 1883, 865f. Of those double-dipping, seven were taking a combination involving E (B+E, 5; C+E, 1; D+E, 1).

36 In this and subsequent counts, I include men and women together in the counts for students, although women were of different status and always indicated separately in the reports and class-lists (Breay 1999).

37 Figures calculated using the totals given by Breay 1999, 64, 69.

38 There is no figure in the A column before 1895, since all candidates took Section A and no candidate was awarded a first solely on the basis of work done in it. Although the class lists indicate candidates who excelled in Section A, all candidate who did so also excelled in one or more of Sections B-E. I have consequently decided that indicating the numbers of those who excelled in Section A before 1895 would give the misleading impression that some candidates opted to take Section A.

39 *CUR* 13 June 1883, 863.

for those giving special classes on technical subjects such as phonetics.[40] The pleas of the Board were heard and immediately acted upon. On 11 June 1883 the General Board approved the creation of a new post, a readership in Classical Philology, to which Peile was elected in 1884, and a lectureship was created in the same year. I shall turn later in this chapter to look at the reasons for the decrease in numbers offering Section E, but first it is worth saying something about who taught the subject in its golden age, what was taught and who were the students.

First, the teachers. The driving force behind the early days of Section E was undoubtedly John Peile (1838–1910), elected Fellow of Christ's College in 1860 and Master in 1887. Peile had long been interested in Sanskrit and comparative philology, studying under Theodor Benfey (1809–1881) in Göttingen in 1865 and 1866, and publishing on both topics (Peile 1869, 1881).[41] Peile had been seen as a candidate for the new chair of Sanskrit, but stood aside to allow the election of Edward Byles Cowell (1826–1903) in 1867; Cowell had held various posts in India including that of Principal of the Sanskrit College in Calcutta.[42] No doubt Peile's self-sacrifice was remembered later when it came to the competition for the readership. Cowell, the first recorded President of the Cambridge Philological Society,[43] threw himself into philology in Cambridge. He was able to relieve Peile of much of the Sanskrit teaching and some of the comparative philology classes as well, continuing to lecture on Sanskrit texts for Section E until his death.[44] Many of the classical Part II students were inspired by Cowell to embark on careers in Sanskrit, and these included three professors of Sanskrit already mentioned, Bendall, Rapson and Thomas. Robert Alexander Neil (1852–1901), another student of Cowell, became classical lecturer at Pembroke College, University Lecturer in Sanskrit and a frequent lecturer and examiner for Section E. Like Peile, Neil successfully kept a foot in both the classical and Sanskrit camps, publishing editions of Greek and Indian texts.[45] Others who taught or examined for E in the 1880s and 1890s included Ernest Stewart Roberts (1847–1912), University Lecturer in Comparative Philology from 1883 and later Master of Caius College,

---

40 *CUR* 13 June 1883, 863f.
41 See Giles/Pickles 2004 for an account of Peile's life.
42 See Thomas/Katz 2004 for an account of Cowell.
43 Cowell was elected as President of the Cambridge Philological Society on 23 February 1872 (*CUR* 14 January 1873, 22).
44 Beard 1999, 107 says that regulation that firsts could still be given to those who did not take the Sanskrit paper "effectively sounded its death-knell", but its demise was not actually to occur until the reframing of the E papers in 1950.
45 Cowell/Neil 1883, Neil 1901; for Neil's life see Giles/Hardy 2004.

whose main interests were Greek dialects and epigraphy,[46] and J.P. Postgate.[47] The teaching staff was soon increased by some of those who took the Part II in the 1880s, R.S. Conway, John Strachan, J.H. Moulton, F.W. Thomas and Peter Giles (1860–1935), who became Peile's successor as Reader in Comparative Philology in 1891 and was from 1911 Master of Emmanuel College.

What was taught? We have some idea of the original syllabus for E from the reading lists published annually in the Reporter. In 1880 the recommended books included Curtius *Griechische Etymologie* (tr. Wilkins and England),[48] Peile's own *Introduction to Greek and Latin Etymology* (first edition 1869, third 1875) and Schleicher's *Compendium der vergleichenden Grammatik* (tr. Bendall).[49] To modern eyes, these works clearly belong to the stage of comparative philology before the paradigm shift in the subject in the mid-1870s, which was closely associated with a circle of young German scholars active in Leipzig, later styled the *Junggrammatiker* or neogrammarians. In modern linguistics the neogrammarians are associated with the idea that sound change is regular and exceptionless, bringing a new rigour (which they proclaimed more scientific) to the study of the Indo-European languages, together with an understanding that the parent language was not as close to Sanskrit as earlier scholars had thought.[50] By the end of the century neogrammarians had largely won the field in comparative philology; the older grammars and works of Schleicher, Peile and Curtius had been swept aside by newer productions. Indeed, according to his successor Giles, Peile never offered a fourth edition of his *Introduction to Greek and Latin Etymology* since he realised it was out of date.[51] In the account of Conway, cited in full below, it was Sir William Ridgeway (1858–1926), Disney Professor of Archaeology from 1892, but a seasonal visitor to Cambridge since 1883, who first brought the neogrammarians to Cambridge:

---

46 Brooke 2004. Roberts's main focus of study is revealed by the lecture title for his series advertised in Michaelmas 1879: 'Comparative Philology (illustrated by Greek Inscriptions)' (*CUR* 10 June 1879, 656).
47 I discuss Postgate's life and career at the end of this chapter.
48 See *CUR* 1 June 1880, 588; the correct bibliographic details are Georg Curtius *Grundzüge der griechischen Etymologie*, Leipzig, first edition 1860, fifth edition 1879; translated by Augustus S. Wilkins and Edwin B. England as *Principles of Greek Etymology*, London, 1875.
49 i.e. August Schleicher *Compendium der vergleichenden Grammatik der indogermanischen Sprachen*, Weimar, first edition 1861, third edition 1871; translated by Hubert Bendall as *A Compendium of the Comparative Grammar of the Indo-European, Sanskrit, Greek and Latin Languages*, London, 1874–7.
50 See Morpurgo Davies 1992, 226–78 for the neogrammarian school. The first notice of neogrammarian work in England was in Sweet 1879.
51 Giles/Pickles 2004.

He was one of the first, if not the first, of English scholars to recognize the importance of the new scientific school of comparative philology in Germany, for in 1881 he correctly applied Brugmann's great discovery of the sonant nasals to explain certain Ionic and Attic terminations (-αται and -ατο in the 3rd plur.) before this had been done even by Brugmann himself. This was in marked contrast with the attitude prevailing at Cambridge where, as late as 1890, the official teaching was still hostile to the scientific methods of the "new school" now universally accepted. But the help of the Cambridge Philological Society more than counterbalanced, for him as for many other young scholars, the frown of his official seniors...[52]

This view of hidebound Cambridge comparative philology is not fully justified if one looks at what the students were being set in their examination papers. In 1883 students were asked about the sonant nasal, one of the most celebrated discoveries of the neogrammarians, with reference to the radical (and later acknowledged to be transformative) work of the young Swiss linguist Ferdinand de Saussure (1857–1913).[53] In 1884 students were asked about Verner's Law, a cornerstone of the new neogrammarian concept of regular sound change.[54] If the reading lists centred on the works before the neogrammarians, that probably reflected the fact that these were the only available grammars and compendia.

The picture of engagement with all recent German scholarship is further evident in work produced by Cambridge scholars in the 1880s and in papers read at the *Proceedings of the Cambridge Philological Society*. At the second meeting of Lent Term 1887, for example, J.H. Moulton read a paper looking for regularity in sound change which showed a deep acquaintance with the works of two leading neogrammarians, Karl Brugmann and Hermann Osthoff.[55] After graduation, Peter

---

52 Conway 1926, 328. See also Beard 2005 and Conway/Snodgrass 2008 on Ridgeway. Conway took the Part I exams in 1885, so cannot have been present in 1881 when Ridgeway read a paper on the "Ionic 3rd plural terminations -αται, -ατο, and -ιατο (-οιατο, -αιατο)" at the Cambridge Philological Society that year (*Transactions of the Philological Society* vol. II, 186–7). The summary of Ridgeway's paper does not, however, mention the sonant nasal; moreover, this explanation of the Greek third plural forms had already been published by Saussure 1879, 38f. As shown by Joseph 2012, 134f., scholars before the neogrammarians had said similar things about these Greek terminations.
53 Question C1 on the Section E paper sat on 2 June 1883: 'Saussure says (Système Primatif des Voyelles p. 24 [= Saussure 1879]) that "le Lat. *densus* indique que δασύς est pour δṇσύς" (By ṇ a *nasalis sonans* or *vocalic nasal* is meant). Discuss the theory of which this is an example (a) on phonetic grounds, (b) by giving evidence of a similar history.' The theory of the *nasalis sonans* is normally associated with Brugmann, although the young Saussure had arrived at the same idea independently (Joseph 2012, 186).
54 Question 12 on the paper sat on 3 June 1884: 'What is meant by Verner's Law? Give other examples of the importance of the Vedic accent to the general study of Indo-European Philology'.
55 *Proceedings of the Cambridge Philological Society* XVI–XVIII 21f.

Giles attended the lectures of Brugmann in Freiburg in 1886 and then again the following year, after Brugmann had taken up the chair in Leipzig.[56] On 3 January 1890 Peile himself read a paper discussing ideas of sound change in the work of Brugmann and another prominent neogrammarian, Hermann Paul, which received extensive discussion and a unanimous vote of thanks.[57] Brugmann's reputation in Cambridge was confirmed when he was elected an Honorary Member of the Philological Society in 1893, joining Mommsen, Zupitza, Goodwin and Gildersleeve, all of whom had been elected in 1881. In short, Cambridge was open to the latest German scholarship throughout the 1880s; the reliance on the works of Schleicher and Curtius in the reading lists merely reflects the fact that these were the only complete works available at the time (the first volume of Brugmann's monumental *Grundriß* appeared in print in 1886).[58]

Who were the students of the Section E in the nineteenth century? As we have already seen, many of these early comparative philologists at Cambridge went on to have successful careers, both inside and outside Cambridge, across different fields of study. Among the students in the 1880s and 1890s who won firsts including work in Section E were Rapson and Pearson (Part II 1883),[59] Adam (Part II 1884),[60] Strachan (Part II 1885), Rouse[61] and Moulton (Part II 1886), Conway and Giles (Part II 1887), and Thomas (Part II 1889). There were also others less well known, but of similar calibre. A brief look at two now almost completely forgotten individuals will be instructive to fill out the picture, while also giving voice to the marginalised.

---

[56] Dawkins 1935, Dawkins/Pickles 2004. Giles himself claims that sheets of the first edition of his neogrammarian manual of comparative philology had already been printed in 1890, although the work was first published only in 1895 (Giles 1901, v).

[57] *Proceedings of the Cambridge Philological Society*, XXV 1f.

[58] In the preface to the first edition of his *Short Manual* Giles emphasises the continuities between Curtius and Schleicher and the work of neogrammarians such as Brugmann: "There is no doubt a difference, but it is a difference not of character but of degree." (Giles 1901, viii). Conway and Rouse translated volumes 2–4 of the *Grundriß* into English soon after their publication. The first volume had been translated by the Professor of Comparative Philology in Oxford, Joseph Wright.

[59] Alfred Chilton Pearson (1861–1935), Regius Professor of Greek at Cambridge 1921–8. He taught for a time at Dulwich College: "It is amusing to learn that his school nickname was due to his pronunciation of the word for 'snow' in some Indo-European language", Richards (1935, 451), who leaves posterity to guess what the nickname was.

[60] James Adam (1860–1907), editor of Plato and Senior Lecturer in Classics at Emmanuel College.

[61] William Henry Denham Rouse (1863–1950), headmaster of the Perse School, Cambridge 1902–1928.

First, let us consider the career of Eleanor Purdie (1872–1929) of Newnham College. In 1894 Purdie became the second woman to be given a first in section E, but the first awarded with a star of distinction (she was placed ahead of the two men who were given firsts in E that year, Lionel Horton-Smith of St John's and Alfred Welford of Emmanuel).[62] Following her Part II Purdie was the first woman admitted to the University of Fribourg / Freiburg in Switzerland to take the PhD (a qualification not available in Cambridge at the time for men or women), working under Wilhelm Streitberg (1864–1925), later to become famous for his work on Gothic.[63] Her thesis, modestly titled the "The Perfective Aktionsart in Polybius" (published as Purdie 1898), although actually dealing with the wider topic of Greek verbal aspect, is still referred to in modern scholarship.[64] Although she held a one-year fellowship at Bryn Mawr College, on her return to England she took up schoolteaching, becoming a mistress at Cheltenham Ladies College from 1898 to 1923. She retired because of ill-health, publishing two introductory readers on Latin (Purdie 1924 and Purdie 1925) before her death at the age of 58. It is perhaps reading too much into one of the opening sentences for translation in Purdie's elementary Latin schoolbook to see anything autobiographical in the text: *Penelopa femina misera est, sed callida* "Penelope is an unhappy woman, but she is clever" (Purdie 1925, 2).

The second unknown figure is Herbert Dukinfield Darbishire (1863–1893), who entered St John's College in 1884 (during the lifetime of Kennedy), won a first in Part II with Section E in 1888, then published widely before his early death.[65] Darbishire was a candidate for the readership in Comparative Philology when Peile retired in 1891 but Peter Giles, three years older and perhaps a safer pair of hands, got the job. Darbishire was, in modern parlance, disabled, following a childhood accident, remaining sickly throughout life. Such was the regard in which he was held by the members of the Cambridge Philological Society that after his death money was raised for a collection of Darbishire's published and unpublished papers (Darbishire 1895), edited by Conway and Eleanor Purdie (although the latter's name does not appear on the title page). Darbishire's work is largely forgotten now, but he is, I believe, the first scholar in the UK to make a systematic use of Armenian not only in the reconstruction of Indo-European but

---

62 See http://venn.lib.cam.ac.uk for skeleton information on Purdie's life.
63 Streitberg had been a student in Leipzig when Giles studied there in 1887 (Adrom/Hartmann 2001, 35); the two remained friends, with Streitberg reading the proofs of Giles's *Short Manual* (Giles 1901, x).
64 See for example Giannakis 2015.
65 For Darbishire's life see Sandys 1893, reprinted in Darbishire 1895.

also to elucidate the Greek language, as part of an attempt to explain a long-standing (and still not perfectly understood) point of Greek etymology.[66] Unfortunately, later research has shown that Darbishire's brilliant hypothesis linking Greek and Armenian is not correct, although it was hailed at the time as 'by far the greatest achievement of British Comparative Philology'.[67]

Aided by the provision in the early Regulations for Part II which allowed candidates in Section E to submit an essay (not allowed to other sections),[68] the young Cambridge philologists were encouraged to publish.[69] The Cambridge Philological Society provided a setting for them to deliver papers and the *Transactions of the Cambridge Philological Society* a venue for publication, together with a growing number of journals including the *Journal of Philology* (founded 1868), *Journal of Hellenic Studies* (founded 1880), *American Journal of Philology* (founded 1880) and the *Classical Review* (founded 1887), all of which carried work by Cambridge comparative philologists.[70] Indeed, in volume III of the *Transactions of the Cambridge Philological Society*, covering the years 1886–1893, over half of the articles (and over half of the pages in the journal) were devoted to comparative philology of one form or other. The 1880s and 1890s has a good claim to be the time when there was the largest density of British publications on Indo-European linguistics.

Although there is a sense of something happening in Cambridge in the 1880s and early 1890s. that promise drops away later in the decade. If we look back to Table 2, it is clear that there is a reduction in the number of firsts in E after 1894, which mirrors a more general decline in numbers taking the papers (the majority of students who took the optional Part II won firsts). How can we explain the apparent decline? It is not the case that would-be philologists are now taking literature and criticism, the no-longer compulsory Section A, since, apart from a sudden burst of enthusiasm for the new subject, numbers soon drop back there as well. There are probably several causes: one is the dispersal of many of the

---

66 Darbishire 1889, 100f.; note that Darbishire anticipated the system for the transliteration of Armenian now in common use, but which did not become standard until the 1970s.
67 Fennell 1895, 119. Charles Augustus Maude Fennell D.Litt. (1843–1916), Fellow of Jesus College from 1866, is noteworthy as a vehement opponent to the neogrammarians, and an enthusiastic proponent of British comparative philology. Fennell was also disabled, suffering 'grievous bodily infirmities' which meant that 'for him, walking was laborious, writing difficult' (*The Cambridge Review* Volume 37, 26 January 1916, 164).
68 Beard 1999, 101.
69 Conway 1887 and Darbishire 1889 both originated as Tripos dissertations.
70 For the early history of the *Transactions of the Cambridge Philological Society*, the *Proceedings of the Cambridge Philological Society* and the *Journal of Philology* see Henderson 1998, 70–7.

younger teachers of the subject, those who would be termed post-graduates in today's language. After Peile's resignation, Giles had won the prize of the readership in 1891 and there was no incentive for others to stay around. Strachan had left in 1885; Thomas was headmaster's assistant at King Edward's School, Birmingham, from 1891 to 1888 (although he still held a fellowship at Trinity College); Rapson was employed at the British Museum from 1887; Rouse taught at Bedford Modern School from 1888 to 1890 and then at Cheltenham College; Darbishire died in 1893 and Conway was appointed Professor of Latin at University College, Cardiff in the same year. Perhaps also there was a sense that the new philology was too austere, with technical signs and phonetic terms that discouraged students. Whereas Peile had encouraged debate, his antiquated views giving the young something to spar with, Giles' presentation of comparative philology, which scarcely deviated from Brugmann, left little to argue with. Despite the flurry of articles that greets the first volume of Brugmann's *Grundriß* in 1886, British scholars were later left mostly left to dot the *i*s, cross the *t*s (and put the dots under the *s*s).

During Giles's long tenure of the readership in Comparative Philology (1891–1935), the number of students taking the subject continued to be low, even after Part II was made compulsory. Even so, many of those who took Group E (as it came to be known) went on to distinguished careers: Richard MacGillivray Dawkins (1871–1955),[71] Bywater and Sotheby Professor of Byzantine and Modern Greek at Oxford from 1920 to 1939; John Fraser (1882–1945),[72] Jesus Professor of Celtic at Oxford from 1921 to 1945; G.E.K. Braunholtz (1887–1967), Professor of Comparative Philology at Oxford from 1925 to 1952; Norman Brooke Jopson (1890–1969) the first holder of the Cambridge chair of Comparative Philology from 1937;[73] Basil Ferris Campbell Atkinson (1895–1971), Keeper of manuscripts in Cambridge University Library; Peter Scott Noble (1899–1987), later Regius Professor of Humanity at Aberdeen from 1938 to 1952, then Principal of King's College, London and Vice-Chancellor of the University of London; Thomas Burrow (1909–1986), Boden Professor of Sanskrit in Oxford from 1944 to 1976 and A.C. Moorhouse (1910–2000), later Lecturer in Classics at University College, Swansea.

Giles was by all accounts an excellent teacher, but himself published little beyond reviews, encyclopaedia entries and updates of his manual. His promised works on Latin etymology, his book on language and his edition of Theocritus

---

71 Halliday/Gill 2009.
72 See further *Aberdeen University Review* 31 (1944–1946), 122, 193–5.
73 Auty 1969.

never materialised.⁷⁴ He followed developments in the field but his efforts and interests were taken up more with administration, particularly after his election as Master of Emmanuel in 1911. There was little change or innovation in what was taught. The set texts for Sanskrit remained much the same as they had been in 1883, alternating every ten years between earlier and later passages of the Story of Nala. Despite this apparent stagnation, comparative philology had some strong allies in the Faculty in the twentieth century: Ridgeway, Reid⁷⁵ and Sandys⁷⁶ were all supporters, as was Pearson while he held the Regius chair of Greek.⁷⁷ The Faculty Board of Classics continued to list comparative philology as one of its areas which needed for further support.⁷⁸

The opportunity to create a chair at last arose in the 1930s. After the Sir Perceval Maitland Laurence bequest to the Faculty in 1931, followed by the timely resignation of Rapson from the chair of Sanskrit and death of Giles in 1935, the Faculty repeatedly petitioned the university for a new chair in comparative philology, eventually offering to put up money from its own trust funds in support.⁷⁹ A new professor, Norman Brooke Jopson, was quickly appointed and took up office in October 1937. Jopson was in some ways a surprising appointment; he had taken Section E in Part II, after a Part I in Modern and Medieval Languages, not Classics. At the time of his appointment he was Reader at the School of Slavonic Studies in London and his few publications were on Slavonic.⁸⁰ But Jopson had been teaching the comparative philology papers at Cambridge since the death of Giles in 1935, together with the recently appointed Professor of Sanskrit Harold Bailey, and examining with Braunholtz, the Professor at Oxford (who was the only external member of the Cambridge appointments panel). Jopson gave serious thought to the reorganisation of the papers in E, scaling back the large quantities of Sanskrit that students had been reading since the first days of Part II and

---

74 Dawkins 1935.
75 James Smith Reid 1846–1926, Professor of Ancient History at Cambridge from 1899 to 1925. Giles thanks him for reading the proofs of the first part of the first edition of his *Short Manual* (Giles 1901, x).
76 John Edwin Sandys (1844–1922), Public Orator of the University of Cambridge from 1876.
77 Alfred Chilton Pearson (1861–1935), see n. 59 above.
78 Board of Classics minutes 23 February 1928.
79 Requests are recorded in the Faculty Board minutes of 17 October 1935 and 19 November 1936. The minutes of 21 January 1937 record the offer of '£715 from Laurence II for Chair, if the Professor was responsible for teaching in the Tripos'.
80 Jopson's publications include his inaugural lecture in London *The Distribution and Inter-relations of the Slavonic Peoples and Languages* (London 1922, 28 pp.); the textbook *Spoken Russian* and a few articles, including a handful in the *Journal of the Gypsey Lore Society*. 'Of his immense linguistic erudition Jopson put little on paper' (Auty 1969, 305).

finally abandoning the set books that had been first taught by Cowell. At the same time, he broadened the scope of Greek and Latin on the papers through the inclusion of literary texts and other material spanning the period from the first recorded texts down to the Christian period. Furthermore, he convinced the Faculty Board to commit to dedicated lecturers in both the Greek and Latin languages (something also recommended in the 15 June 1883 report of the Board of Classics).[81] Jopson's reforms have been largely carried through into the current day in Cambridge, where the chair and three lectureship positions are dedicated to the teaching of the subject.

I shall conclude this overview of the history of comparative philology in Cambridge by considering the impact Cambridge philology has had on the wider world. At first sight this might seem negligible. Although Cambridge Section E provided many of the individuals who taught comparative philology, Sanskrit and Celtic around the UK and elsewhere, there was never a recognisable Cambridge or even British 'school', in the way that other European nations have had distinctive approaches to, and even different notations for, reconstructed Indo-European. In the period from the 1880s to the Second World War Cambridge, indeed anglophone philologists in general, closely followed the lead of the German neogrammarians, in particular Brugmann. Until 1933, with the publication of Buck's *Comparative Grammar of Greek and Latin*, (Buck 1933), Giles's handbook (Giles 1901) was the only manual of Indo-European comparative grammar originally written in English;[82] despite this, it has had no lasting impact and is ignored in those works which give surveys of the major publications in the discipline.[83]

This verdict on the impact of Cambridge philological studies is, however, not entirely fair. Although there was never a distinctly Cambridge account of reconstructed Indo-European, perhaps that is because students were trained to read and comment on actual texts, rather than to engage in discussions of hypothetical proto-languages. Many of those who went on to university posts in Classics or other languages devoted their time to work on editions of texts, on dictionaries or grammars of languages across an enormous range which included Old Irish, Oscan and Umbrian, Pali and the Tibetan language Nam, as well as Latin and

---

81 Faculty Board Minutes, 26 January 1950, see also the Report of the Faculty Board on the papers in Group E (Language) of Part II of the Classical Tripos, *CUR* 2 May 1951, 1186f.
82 Not counting the more elementary Edmonds 1906 or Guṇe 1918, which is aimed at Indian students. John Maxwell Edmonds (1875–1958) had won a first with Section E in Part II in 1898 and was later University Lecturer in Classics at Cambridge and Fellow of Jesus College.
83 For example, Buck 1933, 364–7, Szemerényi 1996, 3–9.

Greek.[84] The importance of philology for understanding of the language is shown by the involvement of those who took Group E in writing textbooks and introductory works for use in schools and for beginning students in other languages.[85] Cambridge comparative philologists led the way in taking a greater interest in attested languages and texts in preference to the more abstract realms of reconstructed Proto-Indo-European.

Cambridge students and teachers in Section E also are responsible for the continued presence of the subject in Britain. Accounts such as Momma 2013 make much of Henry Sweet's influence on the emerging disciplines of language study and English philology. Sweet had little time for the classical languages, instead promoting "living philology", with the study of speech rather than text-based languages.[86] The *Transactions* of the London based Philological Society similarly had by this time stopped publishing on classical topics, a development welcomed by Sweet.[87] The fact that the study of comparative philology and the philology of the classical languages found a home in the new discipline of Classics is largely thanks to the publications and examples of several of the Cambridge philologists active at the end of the nineteenth century.

An example to consider here is John Percival Postgate (1853–1926), who has already been mentioned as Professor of Comparative Philology at University College from 1880 to 1910, a role that he combined with a college lectureship at Trinity.[88] Postgate is of course well-known for his many scholarly editions of Latin poetic texts, principally the *Corpus poetarum latinorum*, but he also wrote a Latin primer (Postgate 1888) and guides to Latin prose composition (Postgate 1889) and

---

84 For Old Irish, see Stokes/Strachan 1901–1903, for Oscan and Umbrian, see Conway 1897, for Pali, see Rouse 1905, and for Nam, Thomas 1948. For Latin and Greek texts note, for example, Conway 1902, Neil 1901. The contributions of Postgate will be discussed further below.

85 Mention has already been made of Purdie's Latin readers (Purdie 1924 and 1925) and Edmonds 1906, note also, for example, Rouse 1909, Walters/Conway/Daniel 1916, Strachan 1905.

86 Sweet 1879, 13. Sweet repeated his call for "living philology" when invited to speak to the Cambridge Philological Society on 13 November 1884, with the recommendation that "Dead languages were to be treated as nearly as possible in the same way as living" (Sweet 1884, 37). The paper is followed by the record of an unusually large number of comments by members of the Society, with the vote of thanks proposed by Conway and seconded by Peile.

87 Sweet 1879, 3, Stray 1998, 110f., Henderson 1998, 74f.

88 Postgate was a Fellow of Trinity from 1878, and Professor of Latin at Liverpool from 1909 to 1920 (Stray 2004b). He held the London and Liverpool chairs concurrently in 1909–10, presumably in a year when there were no students at London. Chambers, 1939, 356, recounts how Postgate 'sometimes found great difficulties in forming a class'; when he was a student, Postgate would travel to London from Cambridge by train to lecture to him alone. Postgate's lecturing style was 'not lively' (Owen 1926, 346).

Greek accentuation (Postgate 1924).[89] For Postgate, philology and comparative philology were more than useful background for writing grammars; the language itself was the way to approach the past and philology the way to understand the language. His inaugural lecture for the Liverpool chair (Postgate 1910, delivered on 10 December 1909) is as eloquent a riposte to Sweet's call for 'living philology' as has ever been made. If Latin is dead, then the language of Shakespeare is also dead.[90] Latin is just an earlier point in an ever-flowing river of linguistic change which leads to French, Italian and the other Romance languages. We must, however, do we all we can to avoid being misled by our vantage point, drawing on all the information we have and employing all our efforts to relocate our understanding of earlier stages of languages to their point in time.[91]

Postgate had spoken on a similar theme at the British Academy in the previous year, in a paper entitled 'Flaws in Classical Research' (Postgate 1908), which began with a prefatory apology for not discussing the latest discoveries of a new Indo-European language 'Tocharisch'.[92] In this paper Postgate expands on his theme of how preconceptions or the desire to favour their own ideas can lead scholars to disregard all the ancient evidence. These methodological insights are not, however, as important for my purposes here as a more rhetorical passage where Postgate discusses specialisms and generality, worth citing in full:

> The dissensions of different departments are perhaps more in evidence. Archaeologists, comparative mythologists, textual critics, philologers and literary critics shake their fists at each other from opposite sides of a channel, over which as a rule they do not adventure... They cross at times with disastrous results... There is something wrong here. We are not entitled to assume that one set of inquirers is as a class intellectually less competent than another. The facts of linguistics are facts just as much as the facts of archaeology and so forth; and if the interpretation of facts tends inevitably to discord, it is the mode of interpreting that must be blamed.[93]

Striking in this passage is what Postgate includes in his category of "Classical Research": archaeology, comparative mythology, textual criticism, philology and literary criticism. These are not the divisions of the Sections of the Cambridge Part II, but they are indicative that these specialisms in the discipline had become accepted

---

89 '*The* unsung hero of British Latin studies' (Henderson 1998, 24).
90 Postgate 1910, 9.
91 Postgate 1910, 16f.
92 Postgate 1908, 161; the newly discovered language branch is now known as Tocharian in English.
93 Postgate 1908, 163. Note the collocation of Sir William Jones's "philologer" with the modern term "linguistics" within the same passage.

as part of Classics, in a way that they were not when Postgate was an undergraduate. Despite the image of the isolation of the specialists from each other, Postgate himself, many of his contemporaries, students and successors would themselves happily keep astride the divide between philology and the other subjects. Most importantly, it is largely due to the Cambridge philologists that of the last 150 years in the UK the subject is still considered part of 'Classical Research'.

Tables

Tab. 1: Number of students receiving instruction in the subjects of Part II in June 1883.

	Section B Ancient Philosophy	Section C Ancient History	Section D Archaeology	Section E Language
With a view to examination in 1883	8	19	4	12
With a view to examination in 1884	18	11	2	22
Total	26	30	6	34

Tab. 2: Firsts in Part II of the Classical Tripos.

	A Literature & Criticism	B Philosophy	C Ancient History	D Art & Archaeology	E Language
1883–1886		20	12	6	15
1887–1890		18	11	5	12
1891–1894		12	12	10	7
1895–1899	8	10	9	5	3
1900–1903	2	9	3	12	2
1904–1907	1	11	6	7	2
1908–1911	2	7	8	9	3
1912–1915	3	5	6	3	1
1916–1921	2	3	3	8	1

Bibliography

[*CUR* = Cambridge University Reporter]

Aarslef, H. (1983), *The Study of Language in England, 1780–1860*, Minneapolis.
Adrom, H./Hartmann, M. (2001), *Indogermanistik in München 1826–2001: Geschichte eines Faches und eines Institutes*, Munich.
Auty, R. (1969), 'Norman Brooke Jopson (1890–1969)', *Slavonic and East European Review* 47, No. 109, 303–307.
Beard, M. (1999), 'The invention (and re-invention) of 'Group D': an archaeology of the Classical Tripos, 1879–1984', in: Stray (ed.), 95–134.
Beard, M. (2005), 'While RIDGEWAY lives, Research can ne'er be dull: Professor Ridgeway, Aeschylus, *Supplices* 340ff.', in: C. Stray (ed.), *The Owl of Minerva: the Cambridge Praelections of 1906*, Cambridge, 111–141.
Bellot, H.H. (1929), *University College, London, 1826–1926*, London.
Breay, C. (1999), 'Women and the Classical Tripos, 1869–1914', in: Stray (ed.), 49–70.
Brown, K./Law, V. (eds.) (2002), *Linguistics in Britain. Personal Histories*, Oxford.
Buck, C.D. (1933), *Comparative Grammar of Greek and Latin*, Chicago.
Chambers, R.W. (1939), *Man's Unconquerable Mind: Studies of English Writers, from Bede to A.E. Housman and W.P. Ker*, London.
Charlton, H.B. (1951), *Portrait of a University, 1851–1951: To Commemorate the Centenary of Manchester University*, Manchester.
Conway, R.S. (1887), *Verner's Law in Italy: an Essay in the History of the Indo-European Sibilants*, London.
Conway, R.S. (1897), *The Italic Dialects: Edited with a Grammar and Glossary*, Cambridge.
Conway, R.S. (1902), *Livy Book II*, Cambridge.
Conway, R.S. (1926), 'Sir William Ridgeway (1853–1926)', *Proceedings of the British Academy* 12, 327–336.
Conway, R.S./Snodgrass, A. (2008), 'Ridgeway, Sir William (1858–1926), classical scholar', in: *Oxford Dictionary of National Biography*, Oxford.
Cowell, E.B./Neil, R.A. (1886), *Tripiṭaka. Sūtrapiṭaka. Avadāna. Divyāvadāna*, Cambridge.
Darbishire, H.D. (1889), 'Notes on the *spiritus asper* in Greek', *Transactions of the Cambridge Philological Society* 3.2, 77–118.
Darbishire, H.D. (1895), *Relliquiae Philologicae, or Essays in Comparative Philology*, edited by R.S. Conway, Cambridge.
Dawkins, R. (1935), 'Peter Giles (1860–1935)', *Proceedings of the British Academy* 21, 406–432.
Dawkins, R./Pickles. J. (2004), 'Giles, Peter (1860–1935), philologist and college head', in: *Oxford Dictionary of National Biography*, Oxford.
Distad, N. (2016), 'Hare, Julius Charles (1795–1855), author and Church of England clergyman', in: *Oxford Dictionary of National Biography*, Oxford.
Ellis, E.L. (1972), *The University College of Wales, Aberystwyth, 1872–1972*, Aberystwyth.
Edmonds, J.M. (1906), *An Introduction to Comparative Philology for Classical Students*, Cambridge.
Fennell, C.A.M. (1895), *Indo-Germanic Sonants & Consonants*, Cambridge.
Franklin, M.J. (2011), *Orientalist Jones: Sir William Jones, Poet, Lawyer, and Linguist, 1746–1794*, Oxford.

Giannakis, G.K. (2015), 'Review of Annamaria Bartolotta (ed.)', in: *The Greek Verb. Morphology, Syntax, and Semantics. Proceedings of the 8th International Meeting on Greek Linguistics. Agrigento, October 1–3, 2009. Journal of Greek Linguistics* 15 (1), 171–178.
Giles, P. (1901), *A Short Manual of Comparative Philology for Classical Students*, second edition, London.
Giles, P./Hardy, J. (2004), 'Neil, Robert Alexander (1852–1901), classical scholar and orientalist', in: *Oxford Dictionary of National Biography*, Oxford.
Giles, P./Pickles, J. (2004), 'John Peile (1838–1910), college head and philologist', in: *Oxford Dictionary of National Biography*, Oxford.
Guṇe, P.D. (1918), *An Introduction to Comparative Philology*, Poona.
Haigh, J. (2015), 'Kemble, John Mitchell (1807–1857), philologist and historian', in: *Oxford Dictionary of National Biography*, Oxford.
Halliday, W./Gill, D. (2009), 'Dawkins, Richard MacGillivray (1871–1955), scholar of classical and modern Greek', in: *Oxford Dictionary of National Biography*, Oxford.
Hartog, F.J. (1900), *The Owens College, Manchester: A Brief History of the College and Description of its Various Departments*, Manchester.
Henderson, J. (1998), *Juvenal's Mayor: the Professor who Lived on 2d a Day*, Cambridge.
Jacobi, H. (1907), 'Theodor Aufrecht', *The Journal of the Royal Asiatic Society of Great Britain and Ireland* October 1907, 1121–1125.
Joseph, J.E. (2012), *Saussure*, Oxford.
MacMahon, M.K.C. (2006), 'Henry Sweet (1845–1912), phonetician and comparative philologist', in: *Oxford Dictionary of National Biography*, Oxford.
McKay, K.J. (1990), 'Thomas George Tucker', in: *Australian Dictionary of Biography*, Volume 12, Melbourne, 277–278.
Momma, H. (2013) *From Philology to English Studies. Language and Culture in the Nineteenth Century*, Cambridge.
Morpurgo Davies, A. (1992), *Nineteenth-century Linguistics*, (= G. Lepschy (ed.), *The History of Linguistics. Volume IV*), London/New York.
Neil, R.A. (1901), *The Knights of Aristophanes*, Cambridge.
Nye, E. (2015), *John Kemble's Gibraltar Journal: The Spanish Expedition of the Cambridge Apostles, 1830–1831*, Basingstoke/New York.
Owen, S.G. (1926), 'John Percival Postgate (1853–1926)', *Proceedings of the British Academy* 12, 337–347.
Peake, A./Macquiban, T. (2006), 'Moulton, James Hope (1863–1917), biblical and Zoroastrian scholar', in: *Oxford Dictionary of National Biography*, Oxford.
Peile, J. (1869), *An Introduction to Greek and Latin Etymology*, London.
Peile, J. (1881), *Notes on the Nalopākhyānam: or Tale of Nala, for the Use of Classical Students*, Cambridge.
Postgate, J.P./Vince, C.A. (1888), *The New Latin Primer*, London.
Postgate, J.P. (1889), *Sermo Latinus: a Short Guide to Latin Prose Composition*, London.
Postgate, J.P. (1908), 'Flaws in Classical Research', *Proceedings of the British Academy* 3, 1–54.
Postgate, J.P. (1910), *Dead Language and Dead Languages, with Special Reference to Latin: an Inaugural Lecture Delivered before the University of Liverpool*, London.
Postgate, J.P. (1924), *A Short Guide to the Accentuation of Ancient Greek*, Liverpool.
Purdie, E. (1898), 'The Perfective 'Aktionsart' in Polybius', *Indogermanische Forschungen* 9, 63–153.

Purdie, E. (1924), *Liviana: a Second Year Latin Reader & Writer Based on Livy I and II*, Cambridge.
Purdie, E. (1925), *Fabulae Heroicae: a First Year Latin Reader & Writer*, Cambridge.
Richards, G.C. (1935), 'Alfred Chilton Pearson 1861–1935', *Proceedings of the British Academy* 21, 449–463.
Rouse, W.H.D. (1905), *Jinacarita*, London.
Rouse, W.H.D. (1909), *Lucian's dialogues*, Oxford.
Sandys, J.E. (1893), 'In Memoriam H.D. Darbishire' *The Cambridge Review* Volume 5, 12 October 1893, 6–7.
Saussure, F. de (1879), *Mémoire sur le système primitif des voyelles dans les langues indo-européennes*, Leipzig.
Simone, R. (1998), 'The Early Modern Period', in: G. Lepschy (ed.), *History of Linguistics. Volume III: Renaissance and Early Modern Linguistics,* London/New York, 149–236.
Stokes, W./Strachan, J. (1901–1903), *Thesaurus Palaeohibernicus: a Collection of Old-Irish Glosses, Scholia, Prose and Verse*, Cambridge.
Strachan, J. (1905), *Old-Irish paradigms*, Dublin/London.
Stray, C. (1998), *Classics Transformed: Schools, Universities, and Society in England, 1830–1960*, Oxford.
Stray, C. (1999), 'The First Century of the Classical Tripos (1822–1922): High Culture and the Politics of Curriculum', in: Stray (ed.), 1–14.
Stray, C. (ed.) (1999), *Classics in 19th and 20th Century Cambridge: Curriculum, Culture and Community*, Cambridge.
Stray, C. (2004a), 'Key, Thomas Hewitt (1799–1875), Latin scholar', in: *Oxford Dictionary of National Biography*, Oxford.
Stray, C. (2004b), 'Postgate, John Percival (1853–1926), classical scholar', in: *Oxford Dictionary of National Biography*, Oxford.
Stray, C. (2004c), 'From One Museum to Another: The 'Museum Criticum' (1813–26) and the 'Philological Museum' (1831–33)', *Victorian Periodicals Review* 37, 289–314.
Stray, C. (2018a), *Classics in Britain. Scholarship, Education, and Publishing 1800–2000*, Oxford.
Stray, C. (no date), 'Postgate unrolled', Unpublished paper.
Sweet, H. (1879), 'Sixth Annual Address of the President to the Philological Society', *Transactions of the Philological Society* 17, 1–122.
Sweet, H. (1884), 'Practical Study of Languages', *Proceedings of the Cambridge Philological Society* 9, 36–39.
Szemerényi, O. (1996), *Introduction to Indo-European Linguistics*, Fourth revised edition, Oxford.
Thomas, F.W. (1948), *Nam, an Ancient Language of the Sino-Tibetan Borderland: Text, with Introd., Vocabulary and Linguistic Studies*, Oxford.
Thomas, F.W./Katz, J. (2004), 'Cowell, Edward Byles (1826–1903), orientalist', in: *Oxford Dictionary of National Biography*, Oxford.
Todd, R.C. (ed.) (2004), *Dictionary of British Classicists*, Bristol.
Walters, C.F./Conway, R.S./Daniel, C.I. (1916), *Deigma: A first Greek book*, London.
Wiley, R.C. (1971), *John Mitchell Kemble and Jakob Grimm: a Correspondence*, Leiden.
Winstanley, D.A. (1947), *Later Victorian Cambridge*, Cambridge.
Wrenn, C.L. (1946), 'Henry Sweet', *Transactions of the Philological Society* 45, 177–201.

Yeo, R. (2009), 'Whewell, William (1794–1866), college head and writer on the history and philosophy of science', in: *Oxford Dictionary of National Biography*, Oxford.

Young, T. (1813), 'Review of Adelung, *Mithridates, oder Allgemeine Sprachenkunde. Mithridates*', *Quarterly Review* 10.19, 250–292.

Stephen Harrison
John Conington as Corpus Professor of Latin at Oxford

John Conington (1825–69), despite his relatively short professional life, was a prominent figure in UK classical scholarship as the first holder of the Corpus Chair of the Latin Language and Literature at the University of Oxford (1854–69). This paper considers the arc of his career within the academic and cultural context of his own time, and in particular how his appointment to the Corpus Chair redirected his scholarly and literary activity from Greek tragedy to Latin poetry and towards presentation of Latin literature to a wider audience as well as scholarly engagement with his academic peers.[1]

1 Conington's early career

Conington's education[2] was typical of the able middle-class British scholarship boy of his time. His father was a country clergyman;[3] he studied at the distinguished independent Rugby School, where he was an exhibitioner (minor scholar) in the last days of Thomas Arnold's headmastership (1838–43), and won a demyship (scholarship) to Magdalen College, Oxford, 1843–6. In October 1846 he took up a scholarship at University College, where he graduated BA at the end of that year and was elected to a fellowship in 1848. As an undergraduate he achieved distinction in both academic and non-academic fields; in 1844 he won both the Ireland Scholarship and the Hertford Prize (the two most important classical awards, both mainly for composition) and in 1847 served as President of the

---

[1] It is an especial pleasure to include this piece in a volume dedicated to my friend and longtime collaborator Chris Stray, second to none in his knowledge and analysis of 19C UK classical scholarship (see especially Stray 2018a), as well as to thank him for his advice and help on a number of points.
[2] For accounts by contemporaries the most substantial source is Smith 1872, followed by Nettleship 1887 and (less positive) Pattison 1969, 245–52; more recently see Smail 2004. Conington is memorialised at Oxford in the form of the substantial (£1000) Conington Prize, offered annually since 1871 for the best doctoral dissertation (or book version of a recent dissertation) in classical literature, ancient history or ancient philosophy (by rotation).
[3] The Rev. Richard Conington (d.1861) was (1827–34) Rector of Fishtoft, a country parish close to Boston in Lincolnshire (Smith 1872, ix), and Conington (who never married) generally spent his Oxford vacations in Boston with his widowed mother (Smith 1872, xlviii).

https://doi.org/10.1515/9783110719215-008

Oxford Union debating society, then as now a cradle of future politicians (W.E. Gladstone had held the same office in 1830); in the summer of the same year he briefly visited the aged Gottfried Hermann (1772–1848), doyen of German Greek scholars, in Leipzig.

In his early days of his tenure as a fellow of University College (1848–54) he was clearly still considering a non-academic career, not least because he did not wish to be ordained, and at that point most Oxford fellowships were only open long-term to those in holy orders. In 1848–9 he was elected to an Eldon Law Scholarship and began training as a barrister in London, but soon returned to Oxford. In this early period he was a strong advocate of the liberal reforms of Oxford which eventually came about in the 1850's, writing in London newspapers in 1849–50 on means of opening up the competition for fellowships at Oxford more widely and of democratising the governance structures of the University and its colleges.[4]

2 Initial work in Greek

The young Conington's earliest mentors and publications suggest a primary profile in Greek rather than Latin; in addition to his visit of homage to Hermann (above), as an undergraduate his private tutor had been the Rev. William Linwood of Christ Church, author of a standard edition of Sophocles and an lexicon to Aeschylus (Linwood 1846 [with other later editions], Linwood 1843). Indeed, Conington has been plausibly suggested as the 'iuvenis ingeniosus' mentioned by Linwood as the author of a conjecture in his edition of Aeschylus' *Eumenides* (Linwood 1844, 200; West 1988).[5] Very soon after his election as a fellow of University College in 1848, Conington published *The Agamemnon of Aeschylus: the Greek text, with a translation into English verse and notes critical and explanatory* (Conington 1848). The similar edition of Sophocles' *Antigone* published the same year by the headmaster and former Cambridge academic J.W. Donaldson (Donaldson 1848) makes it clear that this kind of edition of a Greek tragedy with facing translation was then new to England but came from Germany; the most prominent precedent was the edition of

---

[4] See e.g. Nettleship 1887, Mackail 1925, 25–6. Following his religious experience of 1854 (see n. 34 below) he became more conservative in his views — see the somewhat jaundiced presentation of Pattison 1969, 245–52.

[5] This is αἰδουμένους for αἱρουμένους at line 483, rightly printed by all modern editors, though until West 1988 it was generally attributed to the German scholar Carl Prien who suggested it four years later (Prien 1848).

Aeschylus' *Eumenides* by Karl Otfried Müller (Müller 1833).⁶ Müller's edition, focussed on mining the play for historical information, was the cause of a famous quarrel with Hermann, more concerned with philological and textual criticism.⁷ In Conington's edition, the parallel translation and notes in English rather than Latin (another recent innovation)⁸ made it clear that it aimed at a wider audience than the textually oriented editions of Greek tragedies which had appeared in England in the previous half-century under the influence of the Cambridge scholar Richard Porson,⁹ an interesting adumbration of his later popularising work in Latin. But its text and annotations showed that it kept a foot in the textual camp,¹⁰ while its preface refers to frequent editions in Germany where proper critical attention to the text and literary appreciation of its poetry through a suitably literary translation are found together (iii). This seems to refer not so much to Müller's parallel edition as to Wilhelm von Humboldt's 1816 translation of the *Agamemnon* (highlighted at Conington 1848, vii), which, although it did not include a Greek text, fully incorporated Hermann's latest textual work in its notes.¹¹

Conington's further early ambitions in Greek tragedy are clear not only from his edition of Aeschylus' *Choephoroe*, published in 1857 after his move to the Corpus Chair but begun in the early 1850s,¹² but also from his *Epistola critica de quibusdam Aeschyli Sophoclis Euripidis fragmentis* of 1852.¹³ This ten-page Latin epistle

---

6 Donaldson 1848, x n. 6; xi n. 7 looks forward to the imminent publication of Conington's parallel edition, suggesting that the two are the first of their kind in English. On Donaldson, previously author of *The New Cratylus* (1839) and *Varronianus* (1844), see Garnett and Smail 2004.
7 See especially Most 1998.
8 Conington 1848, ix–xii implies that the English notes in Peile 1839 are a novel feature, and spends much space justifying them as providing a better means of literary analysis than Latin and a means to show that classical literature is relevant to the current age. The use of English for the translations in the first edition of Liddell and Scott's Greek lexicon (1843; for this feature see Williamson 2019) may also be relevant.
9 On the 'Porsoniasm' of this period see Stray 2018, 82–107.
10 For example on its first page excising line 7, citing Dindorf and Blomfield (a decision followed by Fraenkel 1950, I.90, but not by West 1998, 191).
11 See Fraenkel 1950, I.48. Conington's own best emendation (λέοντος ἶνιν for λέοντα σίνιν, *Agamemnon* 717), described as 'unassailable' by Fraenkel (1950, I.52) and printed by all modern editors, was made a little later and published in the short-lived journal *Terminalia* (Anon. 1851, 83).
12 Conington 1857a, vi. This commentary (highly praised by Fraenkel 1950, I.52) has notes in English but no translation. Smith 1872, xxx states that Conington had extensive notes towards an edition of Aeschylus' *Supplices*, but was diverted from this by his agreement to edit Virgil in 1852 (see below) and his appointment to the Corpus chair in 1854. Conington's review of Nauck's important edition of the Greek tragic fragments (Conington 1857b), along with other publications in the area, showed that he continued to work on Greek tragedy in the 1850s.
13 Reprinted in Conington 1872, 449–59.

on textual issues in tragic fragments, separately published as a pamphlet, was addressed to Thomas Gaisford (1779–1855), Dean of Christ Church, Regius Professor of Greek, Delegate of Oxford University Press and the doyen of English Greek scholars.[14] It arguably echoes on a much smaller scale the impressive and capacious scholarly debut of the young Richard Bentley in his 1691 *Epistola ad Ioannem Millium*,[15] another epistolary series of classical emendations addressed by a rising scholar in his late twenties to a senior scholarly and ecclesiastical figure (John Mill was Principal of St Edmund Hall at Oxford and later editor of the Greek New Testament).[16] The preface to this essay cites with approval as its model the short critical papers found in Germany, especially Hermann's eight-volume *Opuscula* (1827–39), but not then so common in Britain;[17] this short work thus seems to frame its author implicitly as a successor of both Bentley and Hermann as textual critics, no mean company.

3 The Corpus Chair

Still seeking an academic post which did not require eventual ordination into the Church of England,[18] in 1852 Conington was an unsuccessful candidate for the chair of Greek at Edinburgh; he was defeated by J.S. Blackie, recent author of a verse translation of Aeschylus (Blackie 1850). In 1854 another opportunity arose in Oxford with the establishment of the new Chair of the Latin Language and Literature at Corpus Christi College as part of the general reforms of the era.[19] The duties of the new professor included the obligation to 'explain the language philologically and philosophically, and expound the best authors, using means to test the proficiency of his hearers',[20] and the requirements to reside the full eight weeks of each term, give 24 private lectures in each of them (for which fees were

---

14 See Stray 2018, 54–81 on Gaisford's career and importance.
15 For the *Epistola* see the tercentennial edition by Goold 1962.
16 For Mill see Handley 2004. Conington's admiration for Bentley is clear from his later remark on Bentley's 'immortal work on Phalaris' (Conington 1872, I.412).
17 Conington 1872, II.449. See further n. 39 below.
18 At University College it was only in 1857 that most fellowships were available to those who did not intend to be clergymen; Conington's own William of Durham Fellowship carried this restriction until then — see Darwall-Smith 2008, 363, 369.
19 See Charles-Edwards and Reid 2017, 303–5. Corpus paid £300 of the professor's £600 salary, belatedly ensuring the teaching of the Latin praelector provided for in its original 1517 statutes.
20 See Conington 1872, I.198 n. 2.

payable by students other than those of Corpus Christi College), and two free public lectures a year. Corpus was a college well known to Conington, since his younger brother Francis Thirkill Conington had been a fellow there since 1849.[21]

Though as we have seen Conington's published work before 1854 had been in Greek, his capacity in Latin was well known in Oxford. Apart from winning the Hertford Prize (dedicated to Latin) in 1844 as an undergraduate, in 1846 he contributed two versions in Latin elegiacs to his tutor William Linwood's *Anthologia Oxoniensis*, while in 1847 his 200+ hexameters on the history of the Tower of London (*Turris Londoniensis*, published as Conington 1848) won the Chancellor's Prize for Latin Verse in 1847 and in 1849 he carried off the Chancellor's Prize for Latin Prose with an essay on Plato's intentions in the *Republic* (Conington 1849). Such awards counted for a good deal in the Oxford of this period, and were often the prelude to a permanent academic post; the Latin form of his 1852 *Epistola Critica* to Gaisford also advertised his capacity in the language. Most significantly, he had also in 1852 signed up (initially with his friend and University College colleague Goldwin Smith)[22] to edit the works of Virgil (see further below). These credentials in Latin were clearly enough to convince the electors to elect him on June 14th 1854, aged only 28.

In his inaugural lecture, delivered in December of the same year, 'The Academical Study of Latin', Conington made it clear that there was a job to be done in Latin literature to match what his compatriots had recently achieved in Greek (he is thinking of scholars in the tradition of Porson, see above): 'Greek literature has of late been successfully cultivated by Englishmen, while in Latin we have still to depend on the Continent' (Conington 1872, 204). He may have been thinking of such recent milestone editions as Karl Lachmann's Lucretius (1850) or F.W. Ritschl's Plautus (1849–53); he is certainly keen to urge their type of detailed analysis, arguing that 'the way to study literature is to study the authors who gave it its characters: the way to study those authors is to study them individually in their individual works, and to study each work, as far as may be, in its minutest details. ... the peculiar training which is sought from the study of literature is only to be obtained, in anything like its true fullness, by attending, not merely to each paragraph or each sentence, but to each word, not merely to the general force of an expression, but to the various constituents which make up the effect produced

---

21 For his career (degrees in Classics followed by the study and teaching of chemistry) see Cooper and McConnell 2004.

22 Later Regius Professor of Modern History at Oxford (1858–66) and professor of English and Constitutional History at the newly-founded Cornell University (1868–72), then finally a major journalist and newspaper-owner in Canada – see Kent 2004.

by it on a thoroughly intelligent reader' (Conington 1855, 220). There follows a detailed discussion of *Aeneid* 1.1–7 (221–6), an early anticipation of his commentary; a combination of various modes of detailed analysis (linguistic, grammatical, historico-cultural)is urged, leading finally to a 'full appreciation' (225) by the student.

4 Virgil edition

Conington's edition of Virgil appeared (initially in 1858–71) in the series Bibliotheca Classica, edited for the London publisher George Bell by two scholarly schoolmasters, Arthur Macleane and George Long, which provided commentaries on texts central to the school and university curriculum of the time.[23] Its many editions during and after Conington's lifetime, often revised and (for one part) written by Conington's former student and Corpus successor Henry Nettleship,[24] who completed the commentary on the *Aeneid*, are as follows:[25]

– Vol. 1 *Eclogues* and *Georgics*: edition 1 1858, edition 2 1865, [posthumous] edition 3 1872 [revised by H. Nettleship and G. Long], edition 4 1881 [revised by H. Nettleship]
– Vol. 2 *Aeneid* Books I–VI: edition 1 1863, [posthumous] edition 2 1871, edition 3 1876 [both revised by H. Nettleship and G. Long], edition 4 1881 [revised by H. Nettleship]
– Vol. 3 *Aeneid* Books VII–XII: edition 1 1871 [edited by H. Nettleship, who did notes on books 10 and 12, and G. Long], edition 2 1874, edition 3 1882 [both revised by H. Nettleship]

As this continuous history of re-edition over a quarter-century suggests, the work was very useful and much used: as Anne Rogerson has noted, 'it was, in the late nineteenth and early twentieth centuries, hardly possible to read the *Aeneid* without the aid of Conington's commentary'.[26] At the time the edition was praised for

---

23 For Macleane see Harrison 2017, 25–6, for Long see Wroth and Jones 2004.
24 For Nettleship's career see Harrison 2007.
25 These can be interestingly compared with the similar complex publication profile of another multi-volume classic commentary on Latin poetry of the succeeding generation (1884–1930), that by Adolf Kiessling and Richard Heinze on Horace – for the details see Harrison 2016.
26 Rogerson 2007b, 94. For more detailed accounts of the edition in general (not possible here) see Rogerson 2007a and 2007b.

its extensive noting of Homeric and other sources, including Greek tragedy[27] (unsurprising given Conington's previous interests; here especially it made considerable advances on its predecessors) and its interest in poetic style, but criticised for its relative lack of interest in grammar and in the advances of continental scholarship, its relative unconcern for textual criticism, and its relative weakness on the poem's historical context. These last three points were emphasised by Nettleship himself, who was a Latin lexicographer, had studied at Göttingen with Hermann's son-in-law Moriz Haupt, a major textual critic, and was strong on the poem's historical background.[28] In considering these issues, more account should perhaps be taken of the needs of students at school and university, the primary readership of the series in which the commentary appeared (see above). Even if its austere page setup generally shows more notes than text on most pages, the commentary is always clear and helpful, without too much technical complexity. Moreover, it can discuss textual points in an acute way — for example Latinus' phrase at *Aeneid* 7.598–9 *nam mihi parta quies, omnisque in limine portus / funere felici spolior*, where Conington (though he prints an unlikely punctuation) discusses *rapta* as a possible alternative for *parta*, introducing a metaphor which goes very well with the image of robbery in *spolior*.

Conington's views on the *Aeneid*, the central text of Latin literature, are set out in his introduction to that poem in the commentary's second volume (cited from Conington 1876, 3–28). This reading of the poem is very much of its time in regarding the *Aeneid* as not 'original' because of its relationship to the Homeric epics, and holding that the poem was composed for political motives and that Virgil was 'venturing beyond the province of his genius' (2); these accorded with the views of Gladstone as recently expressed in his work on Homer.[29] On the other hand, Conington defends Virgil in several respects, presenting his difference from Homer (plausibly) as a result of his different historical context (12), and as a genuine rivalry rather than a colourless imitation: 'he is an artist, an Italian antiquary, a Roman of the Augustan period, speaking to the average educated intelligence of his own day'. He objects to Gladstone's view that Aeneas has a poor moral character (12–14), plausibly suggesting that the poem's hero shows both 'tenderness and grace' and 'the savage, indomitable spirit of the hero of the Iliad' (13); he labels this 'an essential want of consistency' in characterisation (12), but in fact he has put his finger on a key feature of Aeneas' complex and intriguing

---

27 See Conington's own emphasis on this in his introduction to the second volume (Conington 1876, 28).
28 See Nettleship 1887; for Nettleship's own work on Virgil see Harrison 2007.
29 Gladstone 1858, III.500–35.

character which is still discussed by critics. He points out that Aeneas' treatment of Dido, often attacked in the Victorian period, is little different from that of Odysseus' treatment of Calypso, and rightly points out that it the brilliant and passionate characterisation of Dido which leads the reader to think badly of Aeneas, who comes out as 'traitorous' to modern readers: 'the reason lies in the depth of colouring with which Virgil ... has painted the agonies of the abandoned queen' (14). Here we can see penetrating and suggestive analysis of the poem's key issues which are still worth consideration. This is a major edition which has much to offer to readers of Virgil a century and a half after Conington's death.

5 Virgil translations

Alongside generating a Virgilian commentary of wide use to classical students who could read Virgil's poetry in the original, Conington had clear interests in promoting the translation of Virgil for the use of a broader audience. In 1861 he published the first substantial study of 'The English Translators of Virgil' from Caxton to his own times.[30] This was no doubt motivated by Matthew Arnold's 1860–1 lectures as Oxford Professor of Poetry *On Translating Homer*, published in the same year, but provides more of a historical survey than Arnold on Homer, showing clear interest in classical reception as a feature of English literary history, an interesting anticipation of more recent work. In this essay Conington, after discussing various forms of verse for translating Virgil, finally recommends the medium of prose.

However, in 1866 he published a verse version of the *Aeneid* in a metre associated with Sir Walter Scott's poems: largely four-stress rhyming couplets, though a four-stress line was sometimes followed by a three-stress shorter line which then gave a rhythmical effect very similar to the fourteener used by some earlier translators such as Thomas Phaer discussed in Conington's 1861 essay (above) – compare e.g. 'The ancient sires of Alba's blood / and lofty-rampired Rome' (below). Conington himself claimed that the use of this ballad metre was primarily in order to ensure the rapidity suitable for a long epic narrative (as stressed by Arnold for Homer), but the enormous popularity of Scott's poetry in the Victorian period[31] must also have been significant.

Here is the opening of the poem:

---

30 Conington 1872, II.137–97.
31 See e.g. O'Hayden 1970.

> Arms and the man I sing, who first,
> By fate of Ilian realm amerced,
> To fair Italia onward bore,
> And landed on Lavinium's shore: –
> Long tossing earth and heaven o'er,
> By violence of heaven, to sate
> Fell Juno's unforgetting hate:
> Much laboured too in battle-field,
> Striving his city walls to build
>   And give his gods a home:
> Thence come the hardy Latin brood,
> The ancient sires of Alba's blood,
>   And lofty-rampired Rome.
>
> *Arma virumque cano, Troiae qui primus ab oris*
> *Italiam fato profugus Lavinaque venit*
> *litora—multum ille et terris iactatus et alto*
> *vi superum, saevae memorem Iunonis ob iram,*
> *multa quoque et bello passus, dum conderet urbem*
> *inferretque deos Latio; genus unde Latinum*
> *Albanique patres atque altae moenia Romae.*

The version combines a modern verse-structure (an element of 'domestication' into contemporary culture in translation theory)[32] with archaic diction appropriate to an ancient epic (an element of 'foreignisation'): 'amerced' = 'deprived' is from Milton (*Paradise Lost* 1.609), 'rampired' = 'ramparted' is from Shakespeare (*Timon of Athens* V.4). The translation was a literary success, running to three editions in Conington's lifetime (1866, 1867, 1868) and twelve impressions by 1907; this can be seen as highly effective wide outreach by the holder of the Corpus chair, bringing Virgil to the Latinless.

Conington did also follow his own advice in writing prose translations of all Virgil's works as part of his work of commentary; these were published posthumously.[33] Here again is the opening of the *Aeneid*:

> Arms and the man I sing, who at the first from Troy's shores the exile of destiny, won his way to Italy and her Latian coast — a man much buffeted on land and on the deep by violence from above, to sate the unforgetting wrath of Juno the cruel — much scourged too in war, as he struggled to build him a city, and find his gods a home in Latium — himself the father of the Latian people, and the chiefs of Alba's houses, and the walls of high towering Rome.

---

32 For these terms in translation theory see e.g. Venuti 1995.
33 First in Conington 1872, II.3–445.

This is a much more straightforward version aimed primarily at elucidating the meaning, without literary ambition or striking archaisms; 'much scourged' perhaps brings out the Christ-like suffering which a serious Christian such as Conington might see in the figure of Aeneas, enduring personal tribulation for a larger cause.[34]

6 Horace translations

Even before the publication of his *Aeneid* translation, Conington had launched another poetic version of a classic Latin poet for a larger audience from the platform of the Corpus chair — that of Horace's *Odes* (Conington 1863, seven editions by 1877, the one cited below).[35] This shows quite a different approach from the *Aeneid* translation. For Conington, Horace's sententious brevity can only be captured by a 'stanza … in some sort analogous to the metre of Horace' (Conington 1877, ix), and the result is a series of versions which all show a quatrain or distich stanza structure, carefully calculated to mirror key features of the original complex lyric metres; where a metre is repeated between Horatian poems, it is repeated in Conington's versions. This seems to be part of an overall strategy of stressing the alien and historical nature of Horace and his Augustan period in the Victorian age: 'it will not, I think, be disputed that between our period and the Augustan period the resemblances are very few, perhaps not more than must necessarily exist between two periods of high cultivation' (1877, xxix). This can be seen as opposing attempts of Theodore Martin and others to make Horace a Victorian contemporary, and as a more scholarly/historicised approach.[36] Conington in fact aims at making his versions eighteenth-century 'Augustan' rather than Victorian in style, 'believing the poetry of that time to be the nearest analogue of the poetry of Augustus' court that England has produced' (1877, xxxi). Cf. e.g. *Odes* 1.10.1–4:

> Grandson of Atlas, wise of tongue,
> O Mercury, whose wit could tame
> Man's savage youth by power of song
> And plastic game!

---

34 For Conington's intense Christian beliefs (especially following a conversion experience in the summer of 1854) cf. Smith 1872, xxxii–iv.
35 I have discussed Conington's verse translations of Horace in more detail in Harrison 2017, 41–44, with which this section shares some material.
36 See further Harrison 2017, 37–55.

> *Mercuri, facunde nepos Atlantis,*
> *qui feros cultus hominum recentum*
> *uoce formasti catus et decorae*
> *more palaestrae.*

'Savage youth' is a phrase from Gray's 'The Progress of Poesy' (1754) [line 60], while 'plastic game' recalls Pope's 'plastic care' from 'The Dunciad' (1728) [1.103]. The metre is carefully calculated to echo the original Sapphic stanza: the short last line (iambic dimeter) recalls the five-syllable adonean, as in Martin's version, but iambic tetrameters are used for the three hendecasyllables rather than pentameters, a choice carefully discussed in Conington's introduction (1877, xii–xv).

Following the success of this version of Horatian lyric, Conington followed up with another volume containing the *Satires* and *Epistles* (1869, nine editions by 1902, the one cited below); he left out the *Epodes*, which Victorians (and indeed others earlier) found difficult because of their often earthy subject-matter.[37] Here again he sought to render Latin Augustan poems by their English Augustan equivalent, using the heroic couplet of Dryden and Pope, though treating it in the later and looser manner of Cowper, which suits Horace's flexible and conversational style in these works (Conington 1902, x–xiv). The need to impart vitality means it is less close to the original than the *Odes* and the Virgil verse translations (1902, xxi), and Conington hopes that it is 'not without its use as a sort of free commentary' (1902, xxi). It omits *Satires* 1.2 (on adultery) and *Satires* 1.8 (Priapic obscenity), often excluded by translators and editors in this period and before.[38] It reads fluently and attractively — e.g. *Satires* 1.9.1–11:

> Along the Sacred Road I strolled one day,
> Deep in some bagatelle (you know my way),
> When up comes one whose name I scarcely knew —
> 'The dearest of dear fellows! How d'ye do?'.
> He grasped my hand — 'Well, thanks: the same to you'.
> Then, as he still kept walking by my side,
> To cut things short, 'You've no commands?' I cried.
> 'Nay, you should know me: I'm a man of lore.'
> 'Sir, I'm your humble servant all the more'.
> All in a fret to make him let me go,
> I now walk fast, now loiter and walk slow,
> Now whisper to my servant, while the sweat
> Ran down so fast, my very feet were wet.

---

37 See Harrison 2017, 3–9, 40.
38 See Harrison 2012.

> *Ibam forte via sacra, sicut meus est mos,*
> *nescio quid meditans nugarum, totus in illis:*
> *accurrit quidam notus mihi nomine tantum*
> *arreptaque manu 'quid agis, dulcissime rerum?'*
> *'suaviter, ut nunc est,' inquam 'et cupio omnia quae vis.'*
> *cum adsectaretur, 'numquid vis?' occupo. at ille*
> *'noris nos' inquit; 'docti sumus.' hic ego 'pluris*
> *hoc' inquam 'mihi eris.' misere discedere quaerens*
> *ire modo ocius, interdum consistere, in aurem*
> *dicere nescio quid puero, cum sudor ad imos*
> *manaret talos.*

Thus in his tenure of the Corpus chair Conington published verse versions of the two greatest Latin Augustan poets for a broad literary audience, showing a clear determination to promote their reading outside the traditional academic establishment.

7 Essays on Latin literature

As noted above, the Corpus chair obliged its holder to give two free public lectures annually; in the nineteenth century, these were regularly occasionally published as pamphlets. Several of them were collected in Conington's posthumous *Miscellaneous Writings* (Conington 1872, 1.198–411) alongside a few other essays from other contexts, which represent almost all his work of this kind; it is clear that the article or essay form of academic publication was only occasionally used by Conington compared with some contemporary German Latinists,[39] and that most of the 1850s and early 1860s were taken up with his commentary work on Virgil and his translations of Virgil and Horace.

This short-form output shows Conington taking his public role as professor earnestly, with a concern to cover the wider literary history of Rome in writing on early and late texts as well as the Augustan poets, and to engage with the output of distinguished Latinist peers in the UK and beyond. His 'The Later Roman Tragedy — Seneca' (an Oxford lecture of 1857) argues (in an anticipation of later work

---

39 Contrast e.g. the five volumes of F.W. Ritschl's *Opuscula Philologica* (Leipzig, 1866–79), though it is worth noting that Conington did publish a lengthy paper in 1861 on the textual criticism of the Greek poet Babrius (in Latin) in the German journal *Rheinisches Museum*, of which Ritschl was then one of the joint editors (reprinted in Conington 1872, II.460–91).

such as that of Friedrich Leo) that Seneca's tragedies destroy pathos through rhetoric and are works 'which, though not wanting in a certain kind of ability, are chiefly remarkable for the gross and glaring faults which they exhibit' (410, harsh) and 'sacrifice propriety to effect, the consistency of the whole to the brilliancy of the parts' (411, perceptive). Here we see Conington's interest in tragedy applied on the Roman side, and the usual low opinion of Seneca's dramas after his popularity in the early modern period, something which was to change only in the next century.[40]

His 1864 piece 'Early Roman Tragedy and Epic Poetry' (1864) is a substantial response to W.Y. Sellar's 1863 *The Roman Poets of the Republic* on the earliest period of Latin literature, the first of several attractive volumes by Sellar, then just elected as Professor of Humanity (Latin) at Edinburgh, which have some claim to be the earliest modern-style Latin literary criticism.[41] Here Conington again focusses on Roman tragedy, a natural link with his earlier work on its Greek counterpart, and on Ennius' *Annales* (a key background for his simultaneous work on the later books of the *Aeneid*). Another 1864 piece, 'The Later Roman Epic — Statius' '*Thebaid*', gives an extensive account of Statius' poem but ends up like most criticism of its time by comparing Statius unfavourably with Virgil: Statius' strengths are those of a miniaturist (he has good similes, but like Seneca *tragicus* cannot control larger literary structures), and the *Thebaid* is 'an elaborate failure' (354), 'a medley of confused and exaggerated effects' with 'disproportioned incidents and underdrawn characters' (370); 'all is noise, glare and confusion' (376).

In 1865–7 Conington engaged in some controversy with H.A.J. Munro, to be elected a few years later (1869) to the parallel newly-established Chair of Latin at Cambridge.[42] His extensive 1865 'Review of Munro's Lucretius' saw Munro's edition, the first British one to rival German scholarship in its philological rigour,[43] as of high quality if a little too technical and in a compressed and sometimes 're-pellant' (238) style (fair comment for modern readers); here as elsewhere Conington emphasises the need for Latin literary criticism to be expressed in an English which appeals to the literary world (237), showing his persistent concern with the broader impact of scholarship. Most of the piece is in fact taken up with an account of Lucretius' poem, which is said to to be rough in style and to share the

---

40 See Harrison 2009.
41 See Sellar 1877 and 1892, and for his career Lang and Curthoys 2004.
42 For Munro's career see Duff and Stearn 2004.
43 So Stray 2018, 219, with a useful account of its complex publication history.

failure of all didactic poetry in trying to combine technical exposition with attractive verse (241, a view with which few moderns would agree), though its poet shows 'extraordinary powers' (248), and with a comparative survey of five translators from Thomas Creech's verse version (1682) to the prose of Munro himself, echoing his much longer 1861 account of the English translators of Virgil. Here as in that piece Conington shows himself a pioneer in translation and reception studies. In Munro's second edition of 1866, he engaged with Conington's criticisms of Lucretius' style; Conington replied in an Oxford lecture of 1867, 'The Style of Lucretius and Catullus as compared with that of the Augustan Poets', re-iterating that Lucretius is prosaic and hence inferior to Vergil as a poet, Catullus rough and redundant in style, more dependent on Greek predecessors and hence inferior to Horace. Here as elsewhere Conington is typical of his time (and of most classical scholarship until recently) in setting a special premium on Virgil and Horace as the classical and canonical poets and the natural standard of literary comparison.

8 Posthumous edition of Persius

One of Conington's earliest Corpus lectures (1855) was on the difficult Neronian satirical poet Persius, again venturing outside the Augustan poetic canon; this and his other Persius lectures were apparently particularly popular.[44] In 1872 Conington's successor Nettleship published posthumously his edition of Persius prefixed by the 1855 lecture, with Latin text, prose translation and commentary (there were two further editions in 1874 and 1893). This was in the same Clarendon Press series as E.C. Wickham's two-volume edition of Horace (1874, 1891) but that had no translation; Persius was perhaps deemed to need one as a less-known and more difficult author, but again this points to Conington's general interest in translation.

The lecture gives quite an elaborate biography of Persius based on the ancient Life and stresses his strongly Stoic nature and links with Cornutus. Befitting its didactic context, it provides a history of Roman satire from its beginnings, pointing to Persius' links with Lucilius and Horace. The view of Persius is very positive (Conington 1874, xxx 'it is his own excellence that has made him a classic'); while admitting the poet's obscurity, Conington admires (xxx) 'the distinct and individual character of his writings, the power of mind and depth of feeling

---

44 As noted by Nettleship at Conington 1874, v.

visible throughout, the austere purity of his moral tone, relieved by frequent outbreaks of genial humour, and the condensed vigour and graphic freshness of a style where elaborate art seems to be only nature triumphing over obstacles. Probably no writer ever borrowed so much and yet left on the mind so decided an impression of originality'. He holds that Persius 'has to write the tragi-comedy of his day, and he writes it in a dialect where grandiose epic diction and philosophical terminology are strangely blended with the talk of the forum, the gymnasia and the barber's shop' (xxxi); Persius is compared to the stylistically quirky and rhetorical (and very popular) Victorian moralist Thomas Carlyle (apt as well as a contemporary touch); here as so often we see Conington concerned to connect Latin scholarship with the larger literary world.

9 Conclusion

Conington's premature death at 44 in 1869 (unexpectedly, of a 'malignant pustule')[45] cut his career cruelly short. It came at a time of renaissance of Latin studies in the UK: the establishment of his chair in the subject in Oxford, matched in the year of his death by a parallel post in Cambridge, gave Latin literature the prominence Greek had attained under the influence of Porson and his followers in the previous half-century. Unlike his Cambridge counterpart Munro, and more like his Edinburgh counterpart Sellar, Conington promoted Latin literature as part of more general literary culture, presenting the classic texts of Latin poetry in attractive and suitable forms for literary study at school and university (his Virgil commentary and Oxford lectures) and for wider consumption (his verse translations of Virgil and Horace), while still engaging in the business of traditional philological scholarship in editing texts (Virgil and Persius).

His initial interest in Greek tragedy was turned to Latin by his election to the Corpus chair with its very specific statutes enjoining discussion of the 'best' Latin authors, which Conington pursued closely by working on the most famous Latin poets, and can be seen to underlie some of his work on Latin poetry, both in identifying Greek tragic elements in Virgil and in investigating early and imperial Roman tragedy; his interest in translation (criticised unfairly by one contemporary as a lazy choice for a real scholar)[46] and the larger literary aspect of classical poets was a key and pioneering strand in his work which looks ahead to the future

---

45 Smith 1872, lxx.
46 Pattison 1969, 251 'the laziest of all occupations with the classics'.

prominence of Latin literary studies, translation studies and reception studies. He took seriously his national public profile as Corpus professor, not just in producing translations for a wider audience but also in engaging with his academic peers in reviews and the like;[47] he was perhaps not as close to the important contemporary advances in Latin scholarship in Germany as his successor Nettleship,[48] but his inaugural lecture (see above) and his Virgil commentary show that he was fully aware of continental work.[49] His translations still merit study as Victorian receptions of Virgil and Horace, and his edition of the works of Virgil still has real value 150 years after his death.[50]

Bibliography

Anonymous [various hands] (1851), *Terminalia, or notes on the subjects of the Litterae Humaniores and Moderation Schools*, Oxford.

Calder, W.M. III/Schlesier, R. (eds.) (1998), *Zwischen Rationalismus und Romantik: Karl Otfried Müller und die antike Kultur*, Hildesheim.

Charles-Edwards, T.M./Reid, J. (2017), *Corpus Christi College, Oxford: A History*, Oxford.

Conington, J. (1848), *The Agamemnon of Aeschylus: the Greek text, with a translation into English verse and notes critical and explanatory*, London.

Conington, J. (1849), *Quænam fuerit Platonis idea in politia sua conscribenda : oratio in Theatro Sheldoniano habita, die Junii XXI MDCCCXLIX*, Oxford.

Conington, J. (1852), *Epistola critica de quibusdam Aeschyli Sophoclis Euripidis fragmentis*, Oxford.

Conington, J. (1857a), *The Choephoroe of Aeschylus: with notes, critical and explanatory*, London.

Conington, J. (1857b), review of A. Nauck, *Tragicorum Graecorum Fragmenta*, Journal of Classical and Sacred Philology 4, 98–106.

---

[47] It is clear from obituaries published in the USA that his work was influential there too: see *New York Times*, 26 October 1869, 5 and *Harper's Magazine* 40 (1869) 311.

[48] On Nettleship's own important German links (especially with Moriz Haupt) see Harrison 2007.

[49] Nettleship's criticism of Conington (in Nettleship 1887) for not being interested enough in the work of German Latinists (repeated by Pattison 1969, 251) is perhaps overplayed. Conington certainly knew and used the most important German Virgil scholarship in his edition, (not mentioned by Pattison), as its various prefaces make clear, and a letter to Mark Pattison of 2nd January 1860 preserved in the Bodleian Library (MSS. Pattison 53) shows him anxious to publish in the Bonn journal *Rheinisches Museum*, then edited by Ritschl, doyen of German Latinists (see n. 39 above), though he needed Pattison's connections to direct the article to the right place.

[50] Shown by its recent multi-volume reprint in six volumes (Conington 2007).

Conington, J. (1872), *Miscellaneous Writings of John Conington*, ed. J.A. Symonds [2 vols.], London.
Conington, J. (1874), *Persius* [ed. by H. Nettleship; 2nd ed.], Oxford.
Conington, J. (2007), *Conington's Virgil* [six volumes, reprint], Exeter.
Cooper, T./McConnell, A. (2004), 'Conington, Francis Thirkill (1828–1863)', *Oxford Dictionary of National Biography* https://www.oxforddnb.com/.
Darwall-Smith, R. (2008), *A History of University College, Oxford*, Oxford.
Donaldson, J.W. (1848), *The Antigone of Sophocles in Greek and English*, London.
Duff, J.D./Stearn, R.T. (2004), 'Munro, Hugh Andrew Johnstone (1819–1885), *Oxford Dictionary of National Biography* https://www.oxforddnb.com/.
Fraenkel, E. (1950), *Aeschylus: Agamemnon*, 3 vols., Oxford.
Garnett, R./Smail, R. (2004), 'Donaldson, John William (1811–1861), *Oxford Dictionary of National Biography* https://www.oxforddnb.com/.
Gladstone, W.E. (1858), *Studies on Homer and the Homeric Age*, 3 vols., London.
Goold, G.P. (1962), *Richard Bentley: Epistola ad Joannem Millium*, Toronto.
Handley, S. (2004), 'Mill, John (1644/5–1707)', *Oxford Dictionary of National Biography* https://www.oxforddnb.com/.
Harrison, S.J. (2007), 'Henry Nettleship and the beginning of modern Latin studies', in: Stray 2007, 107–116.
Harrison, S.J. (2009), 'Modern Versions of Senecan Tragedy', *Trends in Classics* 1, 148–170.
Harrison S.J. (2012), 'Expurgating Horace 1660-1900', in: Harrison/Stray 2012, 115–125.
Harrison, S.J./Stray, C.A. (eds.) (2012), *Expurgating the Classics: Editing Out in Latin and Greek*, London.
Harrison, S.J. (2016), 'Two-author Commentaries on Horace: Three Case Studies', in: Kraus/Stray 2016, 71–83.
Harrison, S.J. (2017), *Victorian Horace: Classics and Class*, London.
Kent, C. (2004), 'Smith, Goldwin (1823–1910)', *Oxford Dictionary of National Biography* https://www.oxforddnb.com/.
Kraus, C.S./Stray, C.A. (eds.) (2016), *Classical Commentaries; Explorations in a Scholarly Genre*, Oxford.
Lang, A./Curthoys, M. (2004), 'Sellar, William Young (1825–1890)', *Oxford Dictionary of National Biography* https://www.oxforddnb.com/
Linwood, W. (1843), *A Lexicon to Aeschylus*, London.
Linwood, W. (1846), *Sophoclis tragœdiæ superstites*, London.
Linwood, W. (1844), *Aeschyli Eumenides*, Oxford.
Mackail, J.W. (1925), *James Leigh Strachan-Davidson, Master of Balliol: A Memoir*, Oxford.
Most, G.W. (1998), 'Karl Otfried Müller's Edition of Aeschylus' *Eumenides*', in: Calder/Schlesier 1998, 349–373.
Nettleship, H.L. (1887), 'John Conington, 1825–1869', in: *Dictionary of National Biography* 12, 13–17.
O'Hayden, J. (1970), *Walter Scott: The Critical Heritage*, London.
Pattison, M. (1969), *Memoirs*, Fontwell.
Peile, J.W. (1839), *The Agamemnon of Aeschylus*, London.
Rogerson, A. (2007a), 'An Introduction to Conington's *Aeneid*', in: Conington 2007, xvii–xxxix.
Rogerson, A. (2007b), 'Conington's "Roman Homer"', in: Stray 2007, 94–106.
Sellar, W.Y. (1863), *The Roman Poets of the Republic*, Oxford.
Sellar, W.Y. (1877), *The Roman Poets of the Augustan Age: Virgil*, Oxford.

Sellar, W.Y. (1892), *Horace and the Elegiac Poets*, Oxford.
Smail, R.C. (2004), 'Conington, John, 1825-1869', *Oxford Dictionary of National Biography* https://www.oxforddnb.com/.
Smith, H.J.S. 'Memoir', in: Conington 1872, I.i–lxxi.
Stray, C.A., (ed.) (2007), *Oxford classics: teaching and learning, 1800–2000*, London.
Stray, C.A. (2018), *Classics in Britain: Scholarship, Education and Publishing 1800–1900*, Oxford.
Stray, C.A./Clarke, M./Katz, J. (eds.) (2019), *Liddell and Scott: The History, Methodology, and Languages of the World's Leading Lexicon of Ancient Greek*, Oxford.
Venuti, L. (1995), *The Translator's Invisibility*, London.
West, M.L. (1988), 'Conington's First Emendation', *Classical Quarterly* 38, 555.
West, M.L. (1998), *Aeschylus: Trageodiae*, Stuttgart/Leipzig.
Williamson, M. (2019), 'Dictionaries as Translations: English in the Lexicon', in: Stray *et al.* 2019, 25–44.
Wroth, W.W./M.D.W. Jones (2004), 'Long, George (1800–1879)', *Oxford Dictionary of National Biography*, http://www.oxforddnb.com

Part IV: **History of the Book/Commentary**

Roy Gibson
Fifty Years of Green and Yellow: The Cambridge Greek and Latin Classics Series 1970–2020

In memoriam E.J. Kenney (1924–2019)

This chapter is more than usually indebted to Chris Stray:[1] he encouraged the topic, went on to identify, inspect and contextualise the relevant archives at Cambridge University Library and Cambridge University Press,[2] and throughout offered an example of how to do research in a field he has himself largely created.

1 CGLC at 50

'Cambridge Greek and Latin Classics' (CGLC) commentaries, popularly known as the 'green and yellow' or 'green and gold' series, reached their fiftieth year of publication in 2020. With over 120 editions in print or in production, and nearly

---

[1] With characteristic modesty, Chris firmly declined to be credited as co-author: he cannot therefore be blamed for anything in this chapter; all errors of fact and judgement are my own responsibility. I am grateful to Chris not only for his gentle encouragement over a number of years, but also for the example set by his generosity and humanity. Extensive aid was received also from both Michael Sharp, the current Classics editor at CUP, and his predecessors Jeremy Mynott and Pauline Hire, as well as from the series editors of CGLC: Pat Easterling, Richard Hunter, Philip Hardie, Stephen Oakley, and Neil Hopkinson. To each I express my gratitude for comments, clarifications, and permissions to quote from documents. Searching questions were also asked by Chris Kraus and Tony Woodman and the editors of this volume, Stephen Harrison and Chris Pelling. Finally, I am grateful to around 20 Classicists from the UK, Ireland and North America who responded to my queries about their experience of the series, and whose insights guided and focused my attention. Their anonymity has been preserved. Note: in the short delay between submission of this chapter and publication, three new CGLC volumes appeared: they are incorporated in Appendix 1, but it has regrettably not been possible to include them in the statistics that appear throughout the paper (and which they do not greatly affect).
[2] Particular thanks are due to Ros Grooms (CUP archivist) and Michael Sharp for their generosity in providing access to these Press files. Frequent reference to, and quotation from, documents in these files occur throughout the chapter, albeit largely without identification of individual documents and /or authors. More information is given on the contents of these files at the conclusion of the chapter.

50 more under contract, the green and yellows have proven a remarkable academic and commercial success. By 2013, 312,000 volumes had been sold for c. £3.6 million, with sales divided more or less equally between UK/Europe and the USA/Rest of World. Outside the UK, sales have been particularly strong in the USA, Germany and the Netherlands.[3] The half-centenary of the series presents an opportunity to look back over the history and significance of a set of commentaries with firmly local roots in Cambridge, but an evidently inter-continental reach. In the highly variegated field of publishing in Greek and Latin literature, the commentaries have instant 'brand recognition'. More significant has been the tenacity of the founding editors, P.E. Easterling and E.J. Kenney, in designing and promoting a series of commentaries whose consistent aim has been to 'provide the student with … guidance … for the interpretation and understanding of the book as a work of literature'.[4]

Readers will, I trust, find this history of the green and yellow series properly critical. Its author is doubly implicated: educated at Cambridge and, like many authors in the Cambridge Greek and Latin Classics series, long possessed of a contract for a commentary which he is yet to deliver. The patience of the editors and their willingness to take a long view will form part of the story. In fact, if this chapter tackles an issue larger than the CGLC series itself, that issue is the advantage, for publishers, series editors and authors, of assuming a lengthy perspective. Between the planting of a series and its flowering in full, decades of editorial patience and a willingness to experiment might be necessary; between the commissioning of the right commentary from the right commentator and its actual delivery, most of a professional career might elapse. And between 1970 and 2020, the field of classics changed beyond recognition: what was needed was a vision that commentaries on texts would continue to be required in times of inevitable and necessary changes in intellectual culture.

2 Beginnings: 1966–70

The first green and yellow appeared in 1970. Fourteen years earlier, in his inaugural lecture as Kennedy Professor of Latin at Cambridge in 1956, C.O. Brink anticipated the birth of a rather different series, in his lament for the 'present dearth

---

[3] Figures supplied by the 'Impact Case Study' submitted by the Cambridge Classics Faculty to the UK 'Research Excellence Framework 2014' exercise: Hardie, Hunter, and Oakley 2013.
[4] *Cambridge Greek and Latin Classics: Notes for Editors* (rev. 1971): published in full in Easterling 2007.

of really dependable large editions, both textual and explanatory, of the major Latin writers'.[5] The sterility of the crop could not be overlooked, 'the more so because the other type of edition — *in usum Delphini* — is not so badly represented ... and it is easy to put the cart of sixth-form teaching before the horse of sound scholarship'.[6] Six years later, in 1962, Brink established the Cambridge Classical Texts and Commentaries 'orange' series.[7]

By the time of the appearance of the first 'orange' volumes in 1965, Brink perhaps had less reason to feel complacent about the teaching of classical texts at secondary level. Cambridge and Oxford had both abolished Latin as a general entrance requirement in 1960.[8] This action was ultimately to have 'deep and far reaching consequences for the teaching of Latin and Classics in schools' in the UK.[9] Latin had been disestablished: the classical languages would have to compete for customers in an open marketplace. The Joint Association of Classical Teachers (JACT) came together in 1962–3 in the wake of the Oxbridge abolition, and Brink eventually served as its President 1969–71, having himself taken a prominent role in immediate responses to the 1960 reform.[10] School teachers also now began publicly to express unhappiness with the quality of the commentaries available to them (whatever Brink might have thought in 1956). 'Old and unsatisfactory editions', were the substance of the complaint, according to a Cambridge University Press (CUP) report of 1966, 'and the lack of good new ones'. From the distance of over half a century, such discontent appears surprising at first. Series long established in the field were continuing to produce volumes of good quality: W.B. Stanford's 1958 edition of Aristophanes' *Frogs* had replaced the 1906 volume by T.G. Tucker in the Macmillan series of classical commentaries for schools; while Methuen had supplied a serviceable series of commentaries with vocabu-

---

5 Brink 1957, 18–19.
6 Brink 1957, 8.
7 The 'orange' series is the subject of a companion piece to the present contribution: Gibson 2016 — which appeared in a volume on the classical commentary co-edited by Chris Stray.
8 On this event, its broader context and cultural significance, see Stray 1998, 270–97.
9 Forrest 2003, 42.
10 On the origins of JACT in the context of the abolition of Latin as an Oxbridge entrance requirement, and Brink's attempts at reform of O-level Latin in the immediate aftermath, see Forrest 2003. For a brief history of JACT itself (a national organization with lively local branches until its merger with the UK Classical Association in 2015), see Lister 2015. On Brink's tenure at JACT 1969–71 and involvement with the Cambridge Latin Course from 1970, see also Jocelyn 1997, 339–42.

laries throughout the 1950s and early 1960s. The OUP 'red' series of commentaries, which could trace its origins to the 1920s,[11] had produced eight new or revised editions of commentaries on Latin texts alone between 1960 and 1964.[12]

But a world in which Latin had been dethroned from its previously assured position as an entrance requirement for leading universities, was evidently one in which action and innovation were required.[13] An informal conference of school and university teachers and a number of publishers met under the auspices of JACT in May 1966. A JACT sub-committee on publishing was subsequently set up, chaired by Norma Miller of Royal Holloway and including one of the future editors of the green and yellow series.[14] It was tasked with assessing possibilities for 'liaison between English-speaking countries to establish common policy on styles and levels of commentary, and to exchange lists of texts in print', as well as looking at the potential for JACT to act as a 'clearing house' designed to 'disseminate information about projected editions to avoid overlapping' and even 'arrange the meeting of publisher and editor'. A list of annotated editions in print was subsequently prepared and made available to schools and universities in the UK and abroad, in advance of a formal conference early in the following year. Eighteen representatives from schools, universities and publishers met at the Institute of Classical Studies in London in January 1967. A paper on 'Texts for A-level Candidates' based on comments collected from teachers was circulated to aid discussion. It noted, with unpretentious profundity, that 'it is easier to say what is not wanted'. Alongside requests for the inclusion of illustrations and a

---

11 On the Oxford 'red' series of commentaries on Latin texts, see Henderson 2006, including a list of the c. 23 volumes regarded as part of the series 1926–77 at 2006, 163–4; on the Greek editions in the same series, see Henderson 2006, 152 (roughly 14 volumes), 2007 (specifically on the 'Euripides reds' series 1938–84). See also Henderson 2002 on Austin's edition of Cicero's *Pro Caelio* and Oakley 2016 on E.R. Dodds' edition of Euripides' *Bacchae* 1940 (rev. ed. 1960).

12 R.G. Austin on Cicero, *Pro Caelio* 1960 (rev. ed.); R.D Williams on Virgil, *Aen.* V 1960; A.E. Douglas on Cicero, *Brutus* 1962; R.G.M. Nisbet on Cicero, *In Pisonem* 1961; C.J. Fordyce on Catullus 1961 (rev. ed. 1965); Williams on Virgil, *Aen.* III 1962; Austin on Quintilian, *Inst.* XII 1964 (rev. ed.); Austin on Virgil, *Aen.* II 1964. On Fordyce and his bowdlerization of Catullus, see Henderson 2006, 70–110; cf. Trimble 2012.

13 The demand for change documented in the 1966 CUP report makes an interesting contrast with the conservatism of initial responses (documented in Forrest 2003) to a suggested need for reform of Latin teaching in the wake of Oxbridge abolition of 1960.

14 Pat Easterling served on the sub-committee. N.P. Miller: commentator and translator of Tacitus: https://en.wikipedia.org/wiki/Norma_Miller_(classicist). An edition of some books of Tacitus' *Histories* by Miller for CGLC would be mooted in the 1980s; but she died before it could be completed.

full Introduction (*excluding* comment on the transmission of the text), the document added that 'genuine literary comment is needed and often sadly lacking'. (Cross-references to other authors were not to be overdone, however.) The inclusion of a vocabulary was 'absolutely essential'.

The CUP representative at the conference, T.F. (Tim) Wheatley, prepared a report for his employers. The proposal for JACT to act as a clearing house, with the hope of avoiding 'wasteful duplication', had been accepted. Publishers agreed to inform the Association when contracts for new editions were signed, while JACT undertook to pass on the names of potential editors to publishers. Other matters proved less amenable to consensus. A 'general disagreement' between secondary schools and universities emerged 'on the weight of annotation and the need for vocabularies'. A further proposal for 'plain text, with commentaries and notes in a separate pamphlet', where 'commentaries could be graded according to level with different versions for school and university use' was discouraged by publishers on the ground of expense and practicality.

This is the context for the birth of the Cambridge Greek and Latin Classics series: the disestablishment of Latin by Oxbridge; dissatisfaction with long outmoded editions; idealistic aspirations to co-operation between schools, universities, publishers, and the 'English-speaking' countries; and a desire for 'genuine' literary engagement with texts rather than unadorned grammatical explication or (worse) concentration on textual criticism. Some, but by no means all, of the hopes of the 1967 conference would be realized in the green and yellows of the 1970s and 1980s, not least the aspiration to 'genuine literary comment' and, over time, a general demotion of textual criticism (it did not take place instantly). Other features of the new series would eventually serve to widen the 'general disagreement' between schools and universities.

Wheatley had been busy, even before the JACT conference of early 1967, and had grasped early the opportunities opening up in this new era of co-operation and change. The May 1966 conference hosted by JACT, in fact, had already 'relieved ... the fear of wasteful competition' between publishers. The market, it appeared, might be stabilized. Shortly afterwards, in July 1966, Wheatley drafted an internal memorandum for CUP, recommending 'a new Pitt series concentrating first on the most widely read authors' (something will be said on this ancient series in a moment.) The proposal was eventually accepted by CUP, and in the interim E.J. (Ted) Kenney of Peterhouse was approached with a view to his acting as general editor of the Latin texts of the series. In late 1966, Wheatley added the suggestion that P.E. (Pat) Easterling of Newnham be brought in to act as general editor of a proposed set of commentaries on Sophocles within the renewed Pitt

Press series. Kenney was then in his early 40s, Easterling a decade younger. Kenney eventually succeeded Brink in the Kennedy Chair of Latin in 1974; Easterling was the first woman to become Regius Professor of Greek at Cambridge, in 1994.[15]

Wheatley was able to attend the January 1967 conference organized by JACT safe in the knowledge that Kenney and Easterling were minded to take up their roles of general editors as proposed. Other publishers came away from the same conference newly energized: Macmillan now seriously considered a fresh classical series, consisting of introduction, commentary and vocabulary without a text; the imprimatur of JACT was sought for the cover of volumes in the new format. By then, plans at CUP for *its* new series were already well advanced. Among names of scholars earlier put forward as potential editors, Kenney suggested that he might edit Lucretius, *De Rerum Natura* III himself. By early autumn 1967, the Syndics had approved contracts for a further four commentaries, including two on Sophocles (with three more on the tragedian at the planning stage).

Before further progress could be made, a local difficulty had to be cleared up. The Pitt Press series traced its origins to 1874, and consisted of editions of texts in mainly ancient and foreign languages set for examination by the University's Local Examinations Syndicate.[16] The series would eventually include around 200 volumes. Editions were often produced in some haste, to meet the syllabus under examination; annotation might be correspondingly light. A continuation in this tradition was *not* what the new editors had in mind. Easterling wrote to Wheatley in September 1967 to make clear that their preferred model was the Oxford 'red' series: these commentaries had 'achieved a really distinguished status both here and abroad, and it is something of this order of seriousness that we have in mind'.

The bureaucratic and institutional history and context for the series are of interest in themselves; but they also illustrate a larger point. The exchange between Easterling and Wheatley encapsulates a dilemma that perhaps has never quite been entirely resolved in the fifty years of the series, or in the field of 'literary' commentaries in general. Who are the volumes written for and aimed at?

---

15 Kenney was University lecturer in Classics at Cambridge and fellow of Peterhouse until 1974, when he became the Kennedy Professor of Latin, before taking early retirement in 1982. Easterling was University lecturer in Classics and fellow of Newnham until 1987, when she became Professor of Greek at UCL (1987–94), before returning to Cambridge as Regius Professor of Greek in 1994 and retiring in 2001. Kenney's inaugural lecture in 1975 had as its title 'New frameworks for old: the place of literature in the Cambridge classical course'. It argued for a widening of the undergraduate curriculum to include neglected authors such as Lucan, and envisaged the closer prescription of set texts within better defined papers. Both arguments have relevance for understanding the development of CGLC.

16 On the early decades of the series, see McKitterick 2004, 79–82, 110.

CUP, for their part, thought they were getting a revived Pitt Press series, perhaps roughly along the lines that JACT had outlined. Guy Lee's well-received 1953 edition of Ovid, *Metamorphoses* I for the Pitt Press series provided a reference point. Easterling and Kenney emphatically preferred the Oxford 'red' series as their ideal. The Press would continue to advertise the suitability of the green and yellow series for a joint constituency: 'intended for use by students at school and university' according to the jackets of early members of the series.[17] But a sixth-form audience was never at the heart of what the editors of the series conceived as their mission.[18] Over time, not a few editions eventually drifted beyond the actual needs and real capabilities even of most undergraduates. Such developments lay many years in the future; but the course was already set in the late 1960s.

Confirmation of the extent to which the green and yellow series was concentrating primarily (but not exclusively) on the university market rather than on JACT's constituency, arrived in the early 1970s with the reappearance of the issue of 'absolutely essential' vocabularies. Easterling and Kenney had already won an initial battle against their inclusion, taking the view that 'at the university level certainly and at the A level in most cases the students ought to use dictionaries': so Jeremy Mynott, the successor of Wheatley at CUP, reported. But JACT continued to press the issue, and in 1971 Mynott considered allowing schoolteachers to produce and distribute their own vocabularies for green and yellow volumes (the initiative proved too difficult to implement).[19] The vision of Easterling and Kenney for their series had prevailed with CUP.

One further issue had had to be negotiated with the Press, even before the publication of the first green and yellow volume in 1970. Having been given the go-ahead for the series in early 1967, Kenney and Easterling acted with vigour.

---

17 Cf. the 1971 'Notes for Editors': 'These editions are intended to be suitable for sixth-form and undergraduate students' (Easterling 2007); cf. the understanding by Griffin 1995, 14 of the target audience of the series.

18 In recognition of this fact, perhaps, CUP soon joined forces with JACT to produce the very successful two-volume coursebook *Reading Greek* 1978 and its follow-up partners *A World of Heroes* 1979 and *The Intellectual Revolution* 1980.

19 For demands in an earlier generation that the Oxford 'red' series include vocabularies, see Henderson 2006, 19–20, 157–8. JACT, nevertheless, continued to be useful to CUP (and other publishers) in acting as the promised 'clearing house' for news on proposed, planned and contracted editions: the discovery in 1970–71 of rival proposals for CGLC and OUP editions of the *Cena* of Petronius sharpened minds in this regard. Throughout the 1970s, CUP would avoid commissioning rivals to readily available editions in the 'spirit of the informal agreement' between publishers and JACT. The latter eventually reconvened a Working Party on classical publishing in 1981, under John Betts.

Contracts had been obtained for some editors, and new editors were being lined up in the expectation of more. In March 1968, the Syndics agreed a contract for T.B.L. Webster's edition of Sophocles, *Philoctetes*, but now asked for a pause in all commissioning activity. With the aim of regulating 'the pattern and growth of ... business', the Syndics planned to 'give editors of series a quota of rates of publication for their books', so as to avoid committing 'themselves too heavily in any one direction'.[20] The Press, of course, was subject to changing financial pressures – some of them rather severe from time to time.[21] At any rate, Easterling and Kenney would be encouraged to make the case for the extension of quotas for the series on several occasions in the coming decades.

3 The 1970s: the first decade

Easterling had initially been brought in as prospective general editor solely for a set of editions of Sophocles. That idea had quietly been dropped and Easterling was now general editor for Greek texts in the series. Sophocles would in fact feature strongly in the first decades of the series, with editions of four of the plays in print by 1982.[22] The very first volume in the series would also be taken by a play of Sophocles. Only two years intervened between issue of a contract for Webster's *Philoctetes* in spring 1968 and publication in early 1970.[23] And there lay part of the problem. Webster (1905–1974) produced around fifty books and monographs

---

20 Mynott speculated that two to three volumes a year would be appropriate for the series, although, in the event, no new volumes would be taken on for almost a decade; see later in this chapter. That quota, if fulfilled, would have seen the production of somewhere between forty and sixty green and yellows by 1990. In fact, the series would produce just over twenty volumes in this period. Perhaps still expecting a revived Pitt Press series, the Syndics had not reckoned on the amount of time it would take editors to actually produce commentaries equal to the seriousness of the OUP 'red' series.

21 For an excellent one-volume history of the Press and its vicissitudes up to 1984, see Black 1984; on financial crises at CUP, cf. n. 42 later in this chapter.

22 The comparative rush of Webster's *Philoctetes* 1970, Kells' *Electra* 1973, Dawe's *Oedipus Rex* 1982 and Easterling's *Trachiniae* 1982 was followed by a long pause before the arrival of Griffith's *Antigone* 1999. On the fate of the Sophocles mini-series, see later p. 192. The obvious comparator here is the series of editions produced in the late nineteenth century by R.C. Jebb; on the enduring appeal of Jebb as critic and commentator, see Easterling 2005, Stray 2005b, 2013 and Finglass 2016.

23 Based in London since 1948, Webster had been instrumental in the foundation of JACT. He left London for Stanford in 1968; see Todd 2004, III.1039–41.

during his lifetime: 'some felt that he worked too quickly'.²⁴ The commentary on Sophocles appears to have been his first since a 1931 edition of Cicero's *pro Flacco* for Oxford, although numerous works on Greek drama had appeared in the interval. Reviewers were not impressed. Writing in the *American Journal of Philology*, Pietro Pucci contrasted the advertised aims of the new series (quoted at the outset of this chapter and found in Webster's own preface) with the actual content of the commentary: 'The reader will find virtually nothing of what is called literary criticism'.²⁵ The edition confined itself largely to mundane explication of the text, without comment even on such fundamental issues as 'Sophocles' unmistakable language ... the succession of scenes, tragic irony'.²⁶

A couple of green and yellows acquired full second editions in the following decades.²⁷ Webster's *Philoctetes* was replaced after a respectful interval of 43 years.²⁸ Rather longer in the making than its predecessor, Seth Schein's *Philoctetes* (2013) met reviewers' expectations for a modern commentary that both explains the Greek and gives full attention to literary and dramatic aspects of the play.²⁹ The physical differences between the two editions also tell much about the development of the series over five decades. Not only does the larger format of Schein's volume allow c. 43 lines of commentary per page (Webster c. 35), but his Introduction is a hefty 59 pages (Webster 9), while the commentary proper fills 235 pages (Webster 95). The page ratio of Greek text to commentary to is particularly telling: Webster 1 : 1.8 vs Schein 1 : 5.0. (The gradual increase in the girth of volumes in the series will be a matter for reflection later in the chapter.)

A further six commentaries would appear in the CGLC series before the 1970s were out, of which five were on Latin texts.³⁰ A second commentary on Sophocles, by J.H. Kells on *Electra* (1973), ultimately proved a disappointment — although that experience would be redeemed around a decade later by the appearance of

---

24 Todd 2004, III.1040.
25 Pucci 1973, 197; cf. Lloyd-Jones 1972.
26 Pucci 1973, 197. The volume still sold well; see later for the 1978 sales figures for Webster's edition. Of course, sales often reflect recommendations from academics to students based on 'what is available', and are not necessarily a sign of professional approval as such.
27 Dawe on Sophocles, *Oedipus Rex* 1982 (rev. ed. 2006); Kenney on Lucretius III 1971 (rev. ed. 2014).
28 McGill's 2020 edition of *Aeneid* XI also replaces Gransden's slim volume of 1991.
29 See (e.g.) Finglass 2013a, who notes Schein's correction of Webster's denial of a notorious pun at *Phil.* 931: 'perhaps the most notorious note in any Sophoclean commentary'.
30 See Appendix 1, also later n. 54 on the balance of editions in Latin and Greek in each decade.

Easterling's own volume on the *Trachiniae* (1982).[31] A number of the 1970s Latin commentaries acquired classic status very rapidly, notably Kenney on Lucretius III (1971) and Robert Coleman on Virgil's *Eclogues* (1977). Kenney's edition, in particular, initiated a period of reappraisal for its subject, and allowed Lucretius an assured position on graduate and undergraduate teaching syllabuses at anglophone universities. Research on the *De Rerum Natura* eventually flowed from those who had first encountered the poet in Kenney's sympathetic edition, which took the argument of the poem seriously and offered incisive analysis.

It can be added that the green and yellow jacket in which this edition was clothed met some early criticism from within CUP. The origins of the design and name of its composer have left no record in the Press files, although the ease and economy of printing a two-tone colour scheme must explain its initial attraction for CUP.[32] A production note from early 1971 accompanying Kenney's Lucretius III remarks: 'Series design. But can't we have different colours each time? This particular colour scheme will get a bit monotonous, I think'. The green and yellow covers survived the criticisms also of influential external reviewers: '… a small text book, unpromising in form and unappetizing in appearance'.[33] Perseverance was required from the editors, who had perhaps grasped from the Oxford 'red' series the importance of a stable and unifying design.[34] As the series grew, the colours became a brand and allowed individual editions the mutual support and quality assurance of their fellows — irrespective of individual virtues or, occasionally, flaws.

---

[31] In his review of commentaries on Sophocles for the Oxford Bibliographies series, Finglass 2013b passes judgement on Kells: 'Generally unhelpful notes; one-sidedly anti-Electra in its interpretation'; Easterling receives notice as 'excellent modern introduction and commentary'. R.D. Dawe's edition of *Oedipus Rex* appeared alongside Easterling in 1982: its revised second edition in 2006 is judged by Finglass to be 'occasionally brilliant … occluded by wilful textual choices and inconsistent coverage'.

[32] The resemblance of the scheme to the fields of Cambridgeshire in spring - with their characteristic mixture of greenery and oilseed rape — was remarked at the Press.

[33] Peter Levi, reviewing Macleod's Homer *Iliad* XXIV 1982, in *The Spectator* for 17 April 1982. 'Unappetizing in appearance' is a phrase perhaps better reserved for the large birthday cake in green and yellow icing served at the party to mark the 100th volume in the series, in February 2018.

[34] In the words of the Assistant Secretary of OUP, addressed to D.L. Page (who had asked that his Oxford 'red' adopt a blue cloth binding): 'The outside world recognizes series chiefly by their colour': K. Sisam, 25.07.38, quoted as epigraph by Henderson 2007, 143. More will be said at the end of this chapter on the production values of CGLC and changes in design and format.

4 Easterling and Kenney

The editions of the 1970s were soon joined by a succession of high-quality commentaries in the 1980s and 1990s. Two elements in the success of the series can be discerned — quite apart from the skill of individual commentators. The first is the vision for the commentary format shared by the editors of the series and set out in the 'Notes to Editors' dispatched to all those holding a contract for a volume.[35] The existence of such detailed and explicit guidelines is a rarity within the commentary genre.[36] And, as anyone who has successfully evaded explicit editorial directions will know, guidelines are useless without editors willing to enforce them. The second element is the fact that, remarkably, both Easterling and Kenney tried to read and comment on all submissions to the series in their entirety, whether Latin or Greek. Prefaces to CGLC volumes repeatedly place emphasis on direct editorial contributions and guiding hands. The process, as we shall see, did not suppress considerable diversity of practice amongst commentators.

The 'Notes for Editors' (1971) stated emphatically that 'the emphasis in both introduction and commentary should be on the book concerned as a work of literature'.[37] Editors must aim to provide a good critical text, whether their own or that of another, but 'textual problems should be discussed only where they are of real critical interest: i.e. when they have implications for style or content'. There is an obvious contrast here with the contemporary CUP 'orange' series, which regarded the establishment of a fresh critical text as fundamental, in the tradition of Housman.[38] 'Important points of usage' in style, grammar and metre were to be illustrated by 'carefully selected parallels', but where 'important' bore a precise meaning: 'having a bearing on the understanding and literary appreciation of the text'. Basic comprehension of the text was not neglected, and translation of lemmata was urged as often the 'most economical way' of 'elucidat[ing] sense'. Economy in the citation of parallels was encouraged; the illustration of general points was to be made in the introduction rather than the notes.

---

35 For the intellectual context in the Cambridge Classics Faculty at the time, see later n. 93.
36 E.g. formal written guidelines have always played a rather less important role in the Cambridge 'orange' series CCTC. A set of guidelines was drawn up in 1981–82 (described by Brink in a note as 'much-discussed and much-altered'); but, beyond an insistence on a survey within the commentary's Introduction of transmission and the manuscripts, and on the independent establishment of a text (with *apparatus criticus*), the guidelines have nothing to say on what should (or should not) be in the commentary.
37 Easterling 2007.
38 Gibson 2016, 351–2, 361–3.

These guidelines naturally underwent development over the decades, although the emphasis on the elucidation of sense and literary comprehension remained. The 1996 version of the 'Notes' added an important supplement to the original advice that volumes in the series were intended primarily for schools and universities: 'they are also designed to answer the more general needs of scholars' (although 'the learned element should not be overdone'). Confirmation here, if it were needed, of a divergence from the old JACT agenda: an eventual parting of the ways already foretold in the guidelines of 1971. It was also now part of the commentator's job to 'bring out the structure and design of the whole work as it may emerge from the analysis of its parts'. A new clarification on how to handle the job of interpretation proved useful to numerous commentators and their readers:

> The material should be presented in the order that will be most helpful to the intended reader. In particular it is recommended that notes should *begin* with the preferred interpretation or — when textual variants are discussed — the preferred reading, and only then proceed, in so far as it is useful to do so, to discuss rejected alternatives. What readers generally find most useful is a firm steer from the commentator.[39]

At the same time, commentators were firmly discouraged from referring to themselves in the first person.[40] Their names had also recently been removed from the spines of editions, and placed at the bottom of the front cover in reduced font and subdued tone. Commentaries, of course, are never impersonal:[41] the desiderated 'firm steer' effectively enshrined personal preference at the heart of the commentator's approach. The marketing of the series dictated that the identity of the commentator take second place to the subject of the commentary all the same.

5 An editorial history: 1980s–2010s

Changes in the guidelines variously reflect, codify and foretell developments within the character of editions in the series (on which more will be said later). There were also significant developments on the editorial side of CGLC as the 1970s gave way to the 80s and 90s. After the requested pause in commissioning

---

39 On the other hand, a case can be made for the view that this practice is potentially (at least) anti-intellectual: readers need to see the stages by which a problem is discussed and worked out. For the example of a commentator who exemplifies a practice quite different from that required by the CGLC series guidelines, see Pelling on Gomme in this volume.
40 Tortuous periphrasis is the occasional and unintended consequence of this rule.
41 See Kraus 2002, esp. 3–7.

in 1968, CUP remained cautious about extending the series beyond the dozen or so volumes either in print or under contract.[42] By the late 1970s, sales had proven encouraging: even Webster's poorly reviewed *Philoctetes* had sold an impressive 3,000 copies in hardback and over 1,000 in paperback.[43] Whatever its drawbacks, Webster was clearly preferable to the competition; it certainly looked and felt modern to the touch (and it *was* Sophocles.) The go-ahead to commission six more volumes arrived in 1977.

From the perspective of 2020, the path of CGLC to its current eminent position in the field looks assured. Increasing its rate of production markedly in nearly every decade since inception, the Cambridge series has now secured a place in the popular consciousness of anglophone Classics.[44] Yet the progress of the series has not always been entirely smooth. The Press was generally willing to take the long view. An internal CUP series review in 2002 remarked that sales might fluctuate wildly depending on the level of uptake for a particular title in any one academic year, and that initial purchases might often fall below what was normally considered desirable. Nevertheless, it was accepted that the life of editions was to be measured 'at least in decades'. The lengthy perspective extended to editorial toleration of an interval between issue of contract and delivery of edition. Several recent additions to the series were first proposed or given contracts in the 1980s. A lengthy gap can offer benefits. Rather than ossifying a project, the interval in years may provide time for reflection by a commentator who has kept up with developments in the field. Noting a space of almost two decades between the commission of his *Three Homeric Hymns* and publication in 2010, Nicholas Richardson suggested that the appearance in the interim of editions by younger scholars of all three of his chosen texts, 'made it easier for [him] to see [his] own work as a stage in the process, rather an attempt to offer a final verdict on all the possible questions which might arise'.[45]

For all the willingness of CUP and the editors of CGLC to take the long view, and for all the value clearly placed by the Press on CGLC and the series editors with whom it worked so closely, it was not expected that the green and yellows would simply go on forever. It was standard practice for the Press to supply clear

---

[42] For the severe financial crises experienced by the Press in the early 1970s, see McKitterick 2004, 410–28, Black 2011, 165.
[43] By May 1978, Kenney's Lucretius III had sold 3770 in HB and 539 in PB; Kells' *Electra* had sold 570 in HB and 1810 in PB. The series was published in hardback alone till 1973, with simultaneous publication in paperback and hardback thereafter.
[44] See later n. 106.
[45] Richardson 2010, ix.

quotas and time limits to established series, and to invite applications from editors for extensions to both. Fifteen slots for new titles were approved (e.g.) for the period 1992–97, and, when this proved insufficient, ten more were added in 1995 and a further five in 1996. The series was renewed for another five-year period in 1997, with a limit of twelve titles to be offered contracts by 2002. And so on. Applications for renewal were encouraged, but the case for each had to be argued in front of the Syndics of the Press. A particularly intense period of soul-searching took place just after the 25th anniversary of the series in 1995.[46] In that year, Jasper Griffin published a long review article on CGLC in the *Times Literary Supplement*, titled 'The guidance that we need'. There were by now thirty-nine volumes in the series, and, as Griffin noted, all were still in print.[47] Among a series of provocative and occasionally alarming assertions, Griffin hailed the green and yellow series as 'one of the success stories of the subject', and praised its commitment to covering both poetry and prose, including the two volumes so far published on Attic oratory.[48] He added a remark on the division of labours between CGLC and the Oxford 'red' series: 'Sophocles is a Cambridge man, Euripides and Aristophanes are left to Oxford University Press'.[49] In fact, it was around this time that CGLC quietly slipped the bonds of the informal publishers' agreement brokered by JACT almost thirty years before.[50]

---

46 For a different set of trouble affecting the CUP 'orange' series in the mid-1990s — under-recruitment rather than over-recruitment — see later in this chapter.
47 Griffin 1995, 13. The commitment to keeping all titles available simultaneously was a key factor in the initial success of the series: a commitment greatly aided in recent decades by the development of Digital Print on Demand. Griffin 1995, 14 rightly drew the contrast with the 'orange' series, where editions were allowed to go out of print, including 'one or two notoriously unobtainable' editions, such as H.D. Jocelyn's *Ennius*; cf. Gibson 2016, 365–6 with n. 84.
48 Carey and Reid on Demosthenes 1986 and Carey on Lysias 1989.
49 Griffin 1995, 14.
50 At the start of the 1990s, enquiries about whether a commentary on Euripides would be welcomed as a submission to CGLC were still being met with the 'Oxford author' response. By the mid-1990s, Euripidean enquiries began to be more positively received. The first Euripides volume in the series would be Mastronarde's *Medea* 2002 — by common agreement one of the finest editions in CGLC. The CGLC *Medea* was followed by Allan's *Helen* 2008, Battezzato's *Hecuba* 2018, Gibert's *Ion* 2019, and most recently Hunter and Laemmle's *Cyclops* 2020. OUP had produced a series of Euripidean commentaries in the 1980s (Seaford, *Cyclops* 1984; Bond, *Heracles* 1988; Willink, *Orestes* 1989), but the 1990s would see only Wilkins on the *Heraclidae* 1993, before the publication of Parker's editions of *Alcestis* 2007 and *Iphigenia in Tauris* 2016, of Kovacs on *Troades* 2018, and of Liapis on *Rhesus* 2012.

Encroaching on old OUP territory no longer perturbed CUP; but the prospect of potentially limitless expansion to the series did occasion some serious reflection. From its inception, CGLC had been ready to commission commentaries as widely as possible across the works of a handful of classic authors, including Homer, Herodotus, Sophocles and Virgil. The works of other authors were largely confined to a commentary on one representative book of a poem or prose work. That pattern began to change with the issue of contracts for two commentaries on Ovid's *Heroides* by Peter Knox (selections from 1–15) and Kenney himself (on 16–21). The pair appeared, months apart, in the first quarter of 1996. Was this pattern to continue? What did it mean for the future direction of the series? What audience was presupposed by this development? And would the availability of two titles for the same text split the student market and ensure that both took longer to sell?

CGLC came up for renewal in 1997 with CUP. It was already apparent that with around fifty volumes in print or production (including the new Imperial Library — a subject for later in the chapter), a further thirty-five under contract, and a significant series expansion likely to be granted later in 1997, the series had now reached sight of a total of 100 volumes. The immediate issue at hand was obvious: with Kenney in his early 70s, Easterling around four years from retirement, and the same number of commentaries scheduled to appear as had been already commissioned and published in three previous decades of operation, this was a good moment to think of bringing in successors. The new recruits could be trained in the onerous task of editing drafts as they arrived for comment in their customary successive 'chunks'. It was eventually suggested that Philip Hardie, then of New Hall in Cambridge, and Richard Hunter of Pembroke should join the editorial board with a view to eventual succession at some date yet to be fixed (the issue of gender balance on the board and — more significantly — across the volumes of the series will be taken up later). Both had published well-received volumes in the series: Hunter on Apollonius' *Argonautica* III (1989) and Hardie on *Aeneid* IX (1994).[51] But what of the future of the series itself? CUP took the eminently reasonable position that *this* was the occasion to ask whether new editors might think of developing a fresh style of commentary adapted to the needs of the students of the next quarter-century. Should a halt be called to commissions for CGLC once one hundred contracts had been reached, in order to avoid dilution of the strength of the series?

---

51 Hunter succeeded Pat Easterling as Regius Professor of Greek at Cambridge in 2001, while Hardie took up the Corpus Christi Chair of Latin in Oxford in 2002, before returning to Cambridge as Senior Research Fellow at Trinity in 2006.

In the event, in early 1999, it proved challenging to convince the putative new editors to take over a series with an inbuilt end-date. The sudden axing by OUP of its entire modern poetry list around the same time hardly helped matters.[52] And, as one of the new CGLC editors soon wrote to Pauline Hire, successor to Jeremy Mynott as Classics editor at CUP, 'I always enjoy picking up a new green and yellow in the confidence that it will give me a thoroughly up-to-date way into a text'. Clearly, this was an important moment for the life of the series and character of its volumes. Was this a lost opportunity to change direction and rethink the commentary for the new millennium? Opinions will differ. What is certain is that commissions and sales boomed in the first two decades of the new era. The new editors were unveiled in early summer 1999, and a satisfactory strategy for commissioning new texts was agreed in time for the renewal of the series in 2002, now under Michael Sharp, successor to Pauline Hire as Classics editor at CUP. Hardie and Hunter were joined as editors of CGLC in 2008 by Stephen Oakley, successor in the Kennedy Chair of Latin to Michael Reeve, and by Neil Hopkinson of Trinity in Cambridge in 2015.[53]

6 A series overview (1): eras and genres

By 2020/21, CGLC will have 123 volumes published or in production: 58 Greek commentaries, 64 Latin commentaries, and one edition devoted equally to Greek and Latin epistolography.[54] In his 1995 review of the series, Jasper Griffin had expressed the apprehension that 'the study of Greek and Latin literature in school

---

52 On this highly controversial action, widely reported in the press at the time, see Robbins 2017, 471–8.

53 Kenney and Easterling began the process of retirement from the series after the recruitment of Oakley and Hopkinson respectively. Oakley is a distinguished commentator on Livy who also serves on the editorial board of the CUP 'orange' series of commentaries; Hopkinson holds the record for number of editions by a single commentator in the series: *A Hellenistic Anthology* 1988; *Greek Poetry of the Imperial Period* 1994; Ovid, *Metamorphoses* XIII 2000; Lucian, *Selected Works* 2008; and *Hellenistic Anthology* (2nd edition) 2020.

54 Trapp, *Greek and Latin Letters* 2003. (In compiling statistics for the series, I generally exclude Trapp's volume, since it cuts across the divides of prose / verse, Greek / Latin, and classical / late antique. Second editions are also generally reckoned as one volume, not two.) Rates of production for the series in each decade: 2 Greek + 5 Latin (1970s); 11 Greek + 5 Latin (1980s); 11 Greek + 17 Latin (1990s); 10 Greek + 13 Latin + 1 hybrid (2000s); 24 Greek + 23 Latin (2010–20).

and college will become exclusively a study of poetry, preferably of short poems'.[55] His confidence that CGLC might be part of a solution to the 'problem' of the absence of prose texts from syllabuses proved to be well founded. It is undoubtedly true that poetry remains more popular than prose at universities, but the green and yellow series has devoted around two-fifths of both its Greek and Latin volumes to prose authors. Within Greek texts, drama and epic have proven the most popular genres for commentary, with around a fifth of editions devoted to each of these broad areas respectively, followed by the prose genres of philosophy, historiography and oratory, which each attract about a tenth of Greek volumes. Amongst Latin texts, epic leads the pack, with around one-sixth of editions focused on this genre, followed by drama, elegy, and the various hexameter subgenres developed by innovative Latin poets (satire, epistolography) — each also with around a tenth of Latin volumes to their name. Prose texts are spread across a wide range of genres, including oratory, historiography, epistolography, philosophy and a number of less readily classifiable categories, including forms of satire and of the novel. In both Latin and Greek, examples of commentaries on ancient biographies remain among the least well represented genres — despite the riches on offer from both Plutarch and Suetonius.[56] There are other obvious gaps in coverage of areas currently popular in both teaching and research. The Greek novel has belatedly entered the CGLC catalogue with Bowie's *Daphnis and Chloe* (2019) and Tim Whitmarsh's edition of the first two books of the *Leucippe and Clitophon* of Achilles Tatius (2020). Flavian epic is currently confined to an edition of a single book of Valerius Flaccus by Gesine Manuwald (2015) — although Valerius, Statius and Silius Italicus are reasonably well catered for in commentaries from Brill, De Gruyter and OUP (even if those commentaries often have a more obviously scholarly focus).

Of course, the commissioning of commentaries must deal with a number of factors beyond the control of editors. Who is available? Will they deliver on time? Will their manuscript reach the required standard?[57] And the series has always

---

55 Griffin 1995, 14.

56 The editions of both Pelling on Plutarch's *Antony* 1988 and Hurley on Suetonius' *Claudius* 2001 were important milestones within the study of ancient biography (now joined by Woodman's *Agricola* 2014). It may well be that Plutarch's Greek is perceived as too challenging, and the Latin of Suetonius as falling too far below the standards set either by Cicero or Tacitus (Suetonius, of course, was not trying to be either).

57 The CUP and Cambridge University Library files on CGLC contain numerous examples of (notably humane and considerate) 'rejection' letters from the first three decades of the series in the hand of either Easterling or Kenney. Nothing can be said here of such recent history. Equally, nothing will be said here of promised volumes that failed to materialise and whose contracts

relied on a combination of attempts by series editors to commission commentaries on desirable texts, of reactions to suggestions from target editors of some text other than that suggested, and of responses to proposals sent in by prospective editors on their own initiative. The inherently difficult nature of the enterprise is demonstrated by the fact that the initiative to produce editions of all seven plays of Sophocles, central to the founding of the whole series, enthusiastically supported by both editors and the Press, and eagerly anticipated by university teachers, has so far produced commentaries on five plays in fifty years.[58] Perhaps take the long view (editions of the *Ajax* and *Oedipus at Colonus* in fact *are* contracted to CGLC)?[59] At any rate, a glance at the spread of texts currently covered by the series suggests that it is much harder to commission editions of texts at the very heart of the traditional Latin 'canon' — e.g. the first half of Virgil's *Aeneid* — than it is to get scholars to write about some of Ovid's less popular texts. The research interests of the commentators are far from irrelevant, as we shall see.

There is more to be said about CGLC and the canon. But the range of periods covered by the series is worth some reflection first.[60] The archaic and especially classical periods dominate volumes on the Greek side of the series, with rather less space given to the Hellenistic and imperial eras. There are no Greek volumes devoted exclusively to texts from late antiquity — here defined as the era that begins with Constantine's edict of toleration in the early fourth century.[61] Latin volumes are more equally distributed across the eras of the republic, Augustus and early empire. Two volumes of the *Confessions* of Augustine allow Roman late antiquity to register a score of representation above zero percent.[62] An initiative in the early 1990s to establish the 'Cambridge Greek and Latin Classics Imperial Library' as a parallel series, in a distinctive purple and pink livery, did produce a short run of volumes. Critical acclaim was not matched by the sales required to

---

were cancelled by mutual agreement: something of their history can be followed by inspection of the back covers of the earlier titles in the series.

58 See earlier n. 22.

59 The Aris and Phillips series of classical commentaries, now published by University of Liverpool Press, likewise covers four out of the seven plays, plus editions of the fragmentary plays.

60 On notions of and the effects of the 'canon' and 'periodization' in the modern study of Latin literature, see the essays by Garrison-Peirano 2021 and Kelly 2021.

61 Hopkinson's *Greek Poetry of the Imperial Period* 1994 includes selections from the Christian era, although these tend to allow continuities with the classical period to emerge, rather than ruptures and discontinuities; see the review by Lamberton 1995. Trapp's *Greek and Latin Letters* 2003 — originally commissioned for the Imperial Library series — includes extensive selections from the Christian letter-writers of late antiquity.

62 Clark on *Confessions* I–IV 1995 and White on *Confessions* V–IX 2019.

sustain a separate series and the attendant quotas for commissioning of titles that would be entailed. The project was eventually absorbed within the main CGLC series, and all existing contracts were honoured. The desire of the editors to commission new titles from the later imperial and early Christian centuries remained.[63]

7 A series overview (2): commentary creep

The first decade of the series offered two volumes apiece on Sophocles and Virgil, two on Roman comedy and one on a poet of the late republic: all verse authors. Thereafter CGLC gradually expanded to achieve the fuller coverage in eras and genres outlined above. A change also eventually came over the series while that spread was taking place. That development is most easily grasped by focusing on changes in the ratio of text to commentary over time. Commentaries from more recent decades regularly display larger ratios between text size and commentary than their counterparts in the early years of the series. These ratios point to a very definite increase in the importance allotted to commentary over the life of the series.[64]

The average ratio between text and commentary stayed steady between c. 1 : 4 and 1 : 5 for the first four decades of the series, before rising to an average of around 1 : 7 in the 2010s. (Further detailed information can be found in Appendix 2.) It was not until the late 1980s and early 1990s that commentaries began regularly to outweigh text by ratios of five to one or more. A clear sign of future developments arrived in 1995 with the publication of David Mankin's edition of Horace's *Epodes*. With a text of only just over 600 verses (22 pages) and a commentary of 245 pages, the ratio between the two suddenly accelerated to 1 : 11. It looked enormous when placed beside the next publication in the series. Gillian Clark's commentary on Augustine, *Confessions* I–IV (1995), the final member of the 'Imperial

---

[63] See later on 'canons and conservatism'.
[64] That importance, in fact, is even greater than the ratios themselves can indicate, since the ratios may be even larger than I present them. CGLC has employed — roughly speaking — two differently sized formats, where the format used from around the mid-2000s is significantly wider and taller than its predecessor; see the section on design at the end of this chapter. The greater number of lines and words per page allowed by the enlarged format of the 2000s mean that commentators regularly have rather more space to play with in their commentaries, with the result that the ratios produced below may somewhat underplay the increased size of commentary versus text.

Library' family, offered a relatively restrained 106 pages of commentary on 55 pages of text (ratio: 1: 1.9). Mankin went just over the formal upper limit of 320 pages in total; Clark stopped short of 200 pages. The latitude allowed by the editors of the series to their commentators is perhaps most strongly evident here. The *Confessions* were no less unfamiliar a text to most classicists than the *Epodes*. Clark perhaps had less room for manoeuvre than Mankin. As the latter observed in his preface, 'The *Epodes* have received less attention than Horace's other works': the most clichéd trope in the commentator's introduction,[65] yet undoubtedly true in this instance. By contrast, the *Confessions* have been intensively studied since the Renaissance, and — no less importantly — Jim O'Donnell's major commentary on the work had appeared with OUP only three years before Clark's edition, in 1992. Mankin saw it as his task to cover the full range of 'grammatical and linguistic material, historical context, and literary background', as well as to set his own interpretations beside those of his predecessors.[66] Clark, by contrast, concentrated on the area where she perhaps had the best chance of making a distinctive contribution, on 'explaining theological and philosophical questions', as well as bringing out the scriptural and classical sources that formed Augustine's thinking.[67] As in O'Donnell, relatively little space is devoted to explicating Augustine's Latin and such elements of it as might be unfamiliar to those trained in Classical Latin. CGLC commentators evidently interpret and adapt the 'Notes for Editors' to suit their own needs. After all, an edition that a commentator is actually interested in writing will always be better than one composed to a strictly enforced formula. Peter White's new CGLC commentary on *Confessions* V–IX (2019), nevertheless, reveals the amount of help that students do actually need with Augustine's distinctive Latin.[68]

Ratios continued to fluctuate in the decade and a half following the publication of Mankin's *Epodes*. Yet the steady supply of impressively detailed commentaries on a range of Greek and Latin texts had its own impact on perceptions of the green and yellow series. Such perceptions tended to tally with the revised 1996 'Notes for editors', which advised that editions in the series 'are also designed to answer the more general needs of scholars'. A further explanation for the greater amount of space taken up by commentators is surely the need to take account of the vast increase in scholarly literature witnessed in recent decades.

---

65 As noted by Kenney 1996, ix, quoting Kingsley Amis' *Lucky Jim* on 'strangely neglected' topics.
66 Mankin 1995, vii.
67 Clark 1995, vii.
68 With 267 pages of commentary on 64 pages of text, White's ratio is 1 : 4.2.

One additional factor, at least in the UK, is the operation of the Research Excellence Framework, and its predecessor the Research Assessment Exercise. These competitive government exercises for funding and reputation set standards of achievement for scholars that only more fully developed commentaries are likely to satisfy. If an academic is going to spend five or six years writing a commentary — a length of time that matches the interval between iterations of the REF / RAE assessments — then that commentary will need to meet the published criterion of 'a primary or essential point of reference'.[69] Yet US-based scholars exempt from the REF have also begun to write longer commentaries.

Kenney's second edition of his commentary on Lucretius III (2014) offers some insight into how CGLC commentaries have expanded their range over the fifty years of the series. In his preface, Kenney describes the new volume as 'extensively revised and enlarged', partly to take account of the comments of reviewers and partly in recognition of the fact that 'students now come to Lucretius less well prepared linguistically than was the case in the 1970s'.[70] A comparison of the 1971 and 2014 notes on the fifteen lines following Lucretius III.830 *nil igitur mors est ad nos* — 'surely the most heavily loaded conjunction in all Latin literature'[71] — reveals that there is now more help with straightforward translation (III.843 *si iam ... sentit*) and with points of grammar, such as the impersonal use of the neuter of the gerundive at III.836–7 *utrorum ad regna cadendum | ... esset*. But a good grounding in basic syntax continues to be assumed. The rarity of *uniter* (III.839) and of *comptus* signifying 'union' (III.845) is established with newly added or supplemented material. A heightened interest in questions of style is matched by an increased focus on more purely literary matters. The well-known reference at III.834–5 to Ennius is now fitted with more data on the original Ennian context and elaborated with quotation from Catullus 64 to demonstrate the engagement by that poet with Lucretius. Particular care is taken to provide fresh explication of the details of Lucretius' argument (III.834 *animi natura animaeque potestas*)

---

69 The Introductions to green and yellow editions, however, have not grown so markedly in size as the commentaries proper. Over the lifetimes of the series, Introductions have occupied between twenty and forty pages, broadly speaking. Rutherford's 1992 edition of *Odyssey* XIX–XX was the first to go substantially beyond the norm, with 92 pages of Introduction on Books XIX–XX in the context of the poem as a whole, and on general issues of Homeric composition: a classic contribution in its own right. Other Homeric commentators in the series have also written extended Introductions (Graziosi and Haubold on *Iliad* VI 2010, Bowie on *Odyssey* XIII–XIV 2013); they are joined (e.g.) by Christenson on Plautus, *Amphitruo* 2000, Allan on Euripides, *Helen* 2008, and Sommerstein on Menander, *Samia* 2013.
70 Kenney 2014, xi.
71 Kenney 2014, 183: a new note.

and to provide illumination from other parts of the poem for features of that argument (III.842 *non si terra mari miscebitur* ...). And so on.

There are clear concessions here to those linguistically 'less well prepared' students; but equally Kenney capitalizes on the boom in the literary study of Lucretius (which his edition helped to initiate four decades previously) to extend interests in style, intertextuality, and intratextuality. Reviewers attest to the usability of the edition with advanced undergraduates,[72] although postgraduates and established critics will also find it their first port of call for Lucretius III. The 2007 revision of the series 'Notes for Editors' added to the envisaged audience of school, university and 'general needs of scholars', the observation that CGLC editions 'are regularly used in the graduate schools of American universities'.[73] Graduate schools are perhaps now the modern 'middle ground' in terms of audience for a CGLC edition. Recent commentators, it can be observed, initiate personal decisions on whether to privilege either undergraduates or fellow scholars alongside this *de facto* central constituency. Emily Gowers' edition of Horace, *Satires* I (2012), in common with several other volumes in the series, is notable for the way in which its absorption of the full range of earlier scholarship is combined with advancement of its own set of literary interpretations – including, in this instance, a distinctive focus on the 'plot' of the Horatian book. But help with translation and points of grammar tends towards the concise.[74] Christopher Whitton's edition of Pliny, *Epistles* II (2013), remarkably, manages to combine patient explanation of almost every subjunctive in his text with a drive towards literary comprehension that ultimately represents a major critical advance in the field of Roman epistolography.[75] In his commentary on Herodotus VIII (2007), Angus Bowie highlights the introduction of English subtitles into his Greek text: an innovation for the series that alongside 'the emphasis on grammatical questions make this edition rather like nineteenth-century editions'. He connects these features of the commentary with his teaching of the Herodotean book at the annual

---

72 E.g. Beale 2016, Nelis 2016.
73 The absence of facing translations is a recognized factor in the popularity of the series with this constituency. Only a handful of CGLC editions feature such translations: e.g. Eden on Seneca's *Apocolocyntosis* 1984; Kenney on Apuleius, *Cupid and Psyche* 1990, and Trapp, *Greek and Latin Letters* 2003. The relative difficulty of construing these texts appears to be a factor in the inclusion of translations in each instance. (Russell's edition of Dio Chrysostom 1992 might have benefited from inclusion of a translation on precisely these grounds.)
74 See (e.g.) the review by Keane 2014.
75 Felix Budelmann's *Greek Lyric: A Selection* 2018 likewise sets itself the task of appealing to all three main constituencies: Budelmann 2018, vii.

summer school for Greek-learners in the UK run by JACT.[76] Yet even those CGLC editions which clearly are more at home with a constituency of fellow scholars and aspiring graduate students could not be published virtually unchanged in the Cambridge 'orange' series.[77] Woodman's recent edition of Tacitus, *Annals* IV (2018) for the latter series gives some idea of what an audience composed entirely of fellow scholars may be supposed to demand from a commentary, when compared with Woodman's and R.H. Martin's edition of the same Tacitean book published nearly three decades before in the green and yellow series (1989).

The decade that witnessed these developments in the CGLC series also saw, perhaps not coincidentally, the foundation of a number of new commentaries by other publishers. Series such as Dickinson College Commentaries (founded 2011) and Oxford Greek and Latin College Commentaries (founded 2015) have to a large extent met JACT's original vision of extensive help with grammar and vocabulary alongside basic commentary on literary aspects of the texts.[78] In 2007, CUP had tried its own hand at hand at catering for an audience in need of more systematic help in the basics, with the launch of the online tool *Lectrix*. The project had taken nearly a decade to develop in partnership with the Cambridge Classics Faculty, and became available to users by annual subscription. The tool featured eight texts chosen from the CGLC series:[79] the user could simultaneously obtain help on individual words (via on-screen dictionary and grammatical parser), access a newly commissioned translation of the whole text, and make use of both a basic and advanced commentary on the text.[80] The more advanced commentary was

---

76 Bowie 2007, ix; cf. the preface to his edition of Homer, *Odyssey* XIII–XIV 2013, ix. In their edition of Herodotus IX (2002, ix), Flower and Marincola declare their practice as one of 'work[ing] outwards from grammatical explanation to larger issues and questions': a practice inherently more suited to the undergraduate end of the spectrum. The relative latitude allowed to CGLC commentators means it is always worth reading editorial prefaces, where authors generally spell out in carefully nuanced terms the particular audiences they believe themselves to be aiming at. Naturally one must make allowances for self-delusion or acquaintance only with students who possess a thorough grounding in the ancient languages.
77 Hardbacks in the two series are of exactly the same dimensions now. For transition in design for the hardback green and yellows from dust-wrappers to bindings in a single colour, see the final section of this chapter.
78 Dickinson College Commentaries: dcc.dickinson.edu; Oxford Greek and Latin College Commentaries: https://global.oup.com/academic/content/series/o/oxford-greek-and-latin-college-commentaries-oglcc/.
79 The eight advertised texts were: Lysias, *Orations* (selection), Plato, *Ion*, Sophocles, *Antigone*, Euripides, *Medea*; and Cicero, *Catilinarians* I–II, Virgil, *Aeneid* IX, Ovid, *Heroides* (selection), Apuleius, *The Tale of Cupid and Psyche*.
80 For *Lectrix*, see http://assets.cambridge.org/052193/6861/full_version/0521936861_pub.pdf.

taken from the relevant CGLC edition. *Lectrix* was well received by both teachers and students, but eventually fell victim to the financial and commercial problems which appear to characteristically afflict digital publications.

8 A series overview (3): a literary focus

Amidst all this effective diversity of practice, one thing has remained constant: a clear focus on the 'literary' aspects of texts. This is most easily seen in the CGLC commentaries on Homer or the historians of antiquity. In her edition of *Odyssey* XVII–XVIII (2010), Deborah Steiner emphasizes her concentration on the 'stylistic and structural over the more strictly technical aspects of the poem', that is to say on (e.g.) 'the purposeful deployment of formulas, similes, modes of address, apostrophe', etc.[81] In this she acknowledges the example set by the practice of previous Homeric commentators in the series, including Macleod on *Iliad* XXIV (1982), Rutherford on *Odyssey* XIX–XX (1992), and Garvie on *Odyssey* VI–VIII (1994). Rutherford had emphasized that his focus was on 'the shaping of a scene ... techniques of anticipation, misdirection' rather than on 'more 'realistic'' concerns, such as the architecture and layout of Odysseus' house'.[82] Bronze age archaeology — and much else besides of a traditional technical bent — can be found in the multi-authored Lorenzo Valla edition published in six volumes between 1981 and 1986, and translated into English for the three volume OUP edition of 1988–92.[83] Nor need one look for up-to-date archaeology in Woodman's commentary on Tacitus' *Agricola* (2014). R.M. Ogilvie and I. Richmond had included copious information on the remains of Roman Britain in their standard edition of 1967 for OUP. This content was 'in many ways intellectually misleading', as Woodman points out: 'Tacitus provides ... very few specific details of events or localities which can be illustrated by reference to evidence on the ground'.[84] Woodman goes on to undersell his own intellectual agenda: 'to explain the nature and meaning of Tacitus' Latin'.[85] Rhiannon Ash, fellow commentator

---

[81] Steiner 2010, ix.
[82] Rutherford 1992, ix.
[83] Edited by S. West, J.B. Hainsworth, A. Heubeck, A. Hoekstra, J. Russo, and M. Fernandéz-Galiano.
[84] Woodman 2014, vii, who nevertheless thanks A.R. Birley for 'the benefit of his unrivalled knowledge of Roman Britain'. For a history of commentaries on *Agricola*, and the growth of archaeological comment therein, see Kraus 2016.
[85] Woodman 2014, vii.

on Tacitus, elucidates her own purpose (and largely that of Woodman) more fully: 'to elucidate how Tacitus' style and arrangement of material impose meaning on complex historical events'.[86] Chris Kraus' commentary on Livy VI (1994) likewise focuses firmly on the historiographical and narratological rather than historical,[87] while Donna Hurley's edition of Suetonius' life of Claudius (2001) takes seriously the distinctive rubric structure that the ancient author deploys to marshal and present material to the reader.[88] Such thoroughgoing commitment to a literary reading of ancient historiographical texts is not quite uniform across the series, however. CGLC editors of Herodotus give space and serious consideration to the insights that the text might provide into (e.g.) Achaemenid Persia and its relationship with Greece.[89] The relative positions of Herodotus (near the foundation of an ancient historiographical genre in prose) and of Tacitus (the inheritor of an already sophisticated tradition) are perhaps important to understanding the different sorts of commentary they might attract.

9 Canons and conservatism in CGLC

Reflection earlier in this chapter on eras and genres favoured by CGLC raises important questions about ideas on the ancient literary canon potentially embodied by the series. Hardie, Hunter and Oakley have publicly stated that 'the series has helped to change ideas about the 'canon' of texts that are central to the study of the ancient world', citing as examples the fact that 'major works of Hellenistic poetry and Plutarch, for example, are now readily accessible, and in Latin, Lucan

---

86 Ash 2007, vii on *Annals* II. For a brief historical overview of approaches to commentaries on Tacitus, see Bartera 2016.
87 Contrast the more thoroughly historical interests of S.P. Oakley's edition of the same book for OUP in 1997.
88 Contrast the emphasis on political and social history found in the editions of the lives Suetonius produced for the Bristol Classical Press series, e.g. Jones 1996 on the life of Domitian. Pelling's CGLC edition of Plutarch's *Antony* 1988 emphasizes the literary over the historical via a distinctive emphasis on the Shakespearian reception of the Plutarchan life; contrast the more thoroughly historical interests of Pelling's edition of Plutarch's *Caesar* 2011 for the Clarendon Ancient History Series.
89 E.g. Flower and Marincola on Herodotus IX 2002, Bowie on Herodotus VIII 2007, Hornblower on Herodotus V 2013, and Hornblower and Pelling on Herodotus VI 2017. On the phenomenon of the 'historical commentary', see Davies 2016 and Pelling in this volume.

and Statius are examples of poets now easily available to students'.[90] The story is more complicated than even this carefully nuanced statement suggests.

The first of four volumes in the CGLC 'Imperial Library' series appeared in 1990. Kenney on the *Cupid and Psyche* episode of Apuleius' 'novel' (1990) was followed by D.A. Russell on three orations of Dio Chrysostom (1992), Hopkinson's anthology of *Greek Poetry of the Imperial Period* (1994), and Clark's edition of Augustine, *Confessions* I–IV (1995). The contents of this new library appeared curious, in one sense, because the regular CGLC series had already published one edition of an exact contemporary of Dio, namely Pelling on Plutarch's *Antony* (1988). The new series began with high hopes, at any rate. 'The time seems ripe for new developments', announced the blurb on the back cover of editions, 'in response to the trends of current teaching and research'. The Imperial Library had a clear remit: 'to accommodate titles which fall outside the conventional canon but are works of genuine interest and literary quality'. A range of authors and texts was considered by the editors for inclusion, including Plutarch and Galen, and (on the Latin side) the poetry of Ausonius, Prudentius and Claudian, plus the prose works of Tertullian and the letters of Sidonius Apollinaris. An edition of the letters of Jerome had long been a target for a CGLC volume, well before the launch of the Imperial Library series. But a proposal for an edition was ultimately turned down by the 'Higher Command' at CUP, despite support from Easterling, Kenney, and Hire. The reasons were not far to seek. Despite encouraging reviews and apparent enthusiasm in the Classics community for the extension of the canon into late antiquity, including patristic authors, sales for two of the volumes were low by the standards of the series, and somewhat sluggish for a third. The editions, it appears, were finding a place on the shelves of scholars, but not being adopted quite widely enough in the classroom. In 1999, the series was not renewed, although, as Pauline Hire noted, 'it has been welcomed as a concept and probably done good in intangible ways'. Subsequent editions of texts from the later imperial period or Christian antiquity, such as Bowie on *Daphnis and Chloe* (2019) or White on Augustine, *Confessions* V–IX (2019), were published as part of the regular green and yellow series.

One story that could be told on the basis of this episode is of a radical editorial project colliding with the innate conservatism of a Classics audience that kept its money in its wallet in the hope and expectation of more Sophocles. Yet, at other times, the story of CGLC has been one of perhaps belated editorial response to pressures from that same audience. The preface to Stephen Heyworth's edition of Ovid, *Fasti* III (2019) reveals that in the 1980s 'an initial informal approach [was

---

90 Hardie, Hunter and Oakley 2013, 2.

rejected by the editors] on the grounds that the *Fasti* was not a much read text and Elaine Fantham, already signed up to do book 4, was likely to produce her commentary rather sooner'.[91] A formal proposal was greeted more positively by a widened editorial board in 2009. Caution at CUP about two editions of separate books from the same work has been glimpsed before now. The perception that the *Fasti* was 'not a much read text' proved to be unfounded, however. The Press files have several stories to tell about editions (or types of edition)[92] proposed for the series that, having been gently turned down on the ground of the lack of a student market (sometimes twinned with the failure of the proposed text to reach standards of literary quality requisite for that audience), would eventually appear decades later between green and yellow covers. Yet the same files also reveal that one of the major obstacles to the expansion of the canon further into the imperial era or late antiquity has been the difficulty of persuading or finding editors with the right skills to take editions on.

In his 1995 review of the series for the *TLS*, Jasper Griffin expressed himself content with the principles of exegesis enshrined in the just under forty volumes of the series then published: 'No general problem of hermeneutics is raised; we all know what it is to understand a text. The British reader, unless contaminated by Continental notions, will generally feel well content'. His ultimate target here was the contemporary Cambridge Classics Faculty: 'The side of Cambridge classics which seems so close to Paris is not represented in these ... volumes'.[93] From a distance of a quarter of a century, these concerns appear phrased in distinctly

---

[91] Heyworth 2019, ix–x. Fantham produced her edition in 1998.
[92] E.g. editions of fragmentary texts.
[93] Griffin 1995, 14. CGLC achieved lift-off in 1980s Cambridge at the very moment that the literary caucus of the Cambridge Classics Faculty entered a lengthy phase of vigorous and often rancorous internal debate on the future development of the field. Commentaries fell out of fashion amongst Cambridge graduate students during the 'Theory Wars'. Newly minted PhDs, perhaps, were not the primary recruiting ground for the green and yellow series. And serving Cambridge staff would author over 20% of CGLC volumes between inception and the mid-1990s. It is also largely coincidental that Kenney retired from the Kennedy chair in 1982, and Easterling left for UCL in 1987 — to return to as Regius Professor of Greek in 1994. Even so, the series did not reflect the kind of research associated with the literary caucus of the Cambridge Classics Faculty and its graduate students in these decades — just as the *Cambridge Ancient History*, then powering its way through a completely rewritten second edition, hardly mirrored the kinds of historical research fostered in the history caucus of the Faculty. The hostility of the intellectual climate to commentaries can be over-emphasized (although the remarks of Watson and Watson 2014, ix should not be disregarded); but the editors did need to hold their nerve. Buoyant sales, good reviews, and a very appreciative CUP no doubt provided fortitude in abundance.

parochial terms.⁹⁴ There is no doubt, however, that commentaries — particularly those that have some role in the classroom or seminar — tend to partake in, and reinforce, a generally conservative hermeneutics. And the characteristic focus of the CGLC series on the book unit rather than the themed selection,⁹⁵ can act to privilege a rather traditional way of reading a text. In an addendum to the Introduction of his edition of Horace, *Odes* I (2012), Roland Mayer appealed to a dictum of Elaine Fantham, herself a commentator in the CGLC series: 'commentators have a responsibility to privilege literal or traditional interpretation'.⁹⁶ Few recent commentators might sign up explicitly to this position. And Richard Thomas's editions of the *Georgics* (1988) and Chris Kraus's commentary on Livy VI (1994), among several others, clearly stand apart from it: they are prime examples of volumes that continue to challenge the traditional interpretation of their texts. The depth, quality and freshness of a commentator's insights are perhaps the more useful standard against which to measure the value of a CGLC edition.

If the hermeneutics of the commentary, including the green and yellow series, ultimately tend towards the conservative, the genre has an important role to play in challenging certain readings or styles of reading. In the Introduction to his green and yellow edition of Virgil, *Aeneid* XII (2012), Richard Tarrant makes a highly significant observation:

> ... the main advantage for the reader is that the commentator must engage continuously with the text as it progresses and so cannot choose to pass over aspects of it that might pose problems for a given interpretation. In other words, the commentary form provides some protection against tendentious readings or at least makes it harder to present such readings without the fact becoming obvious through significant omissions or over-interpretations.⁹⁷

There is a manifesto here for how commentaries might constructively be used to teach methodologies of reading.

---

94 But for serious engagement with the hermeneutics implicit in Griffin's article, see Kraus 2002.
95 However, neither anthologies nor selections are absent from the series: e.g. — on the Greek side alone — Maehler on Bacchylides 2004, Carey and Reid on Demosthenes, *Selected Private Speeches* 1985, Russell on Dio Chrysostom 7, 12, 36 1992, Budelmann on Greek Lyric 2018, Hopkinson's anthologies of Greek poetry of the Hellenistic and Imperial periods 1988, 1994, Richardson on *Three Homeric Hymns* 2010, Hopkinson on Lucian, *Selected Work* 2008, Carey on Lysias, *Selected Speeches* 1989, Willcock on Pindar, *Victory Odes* 1995, Denyer on the *Apologies* of Plato and Xenophon 2019, Murray on *Plato on Poetry* 1996, Hunter on Theocritus, *Select Poems* 1999, and Gray on *Xenophon on Government* 2007.
96 Mayer 2012, 20, citing Fantham 2002, 408.
97 Tarrant 2012, 44. This resonates with my own experience as a commentator: see Gibson 2003, 186–7 on attempts to read Ovid, *Ars Amatoria* 3 as the manifesto of an 'anti-Pygmalion'.

10 CGLC commentators: gender, institution, national affiliation

Commentaries, like textual-critical editions of texts, are often perceived as 'conservative' in one further respect: they are usually authored by men. An overview of the gender of editors within the CGLC series offers a useful snapshot of more general developments within the field of Classics, although one ought to begin by saying that, during the commissioning of volumes in the now distant decades of the 1960s and 1970s, the editors were presumably aiming at a diverse coverage of texts rather than diversity and inclusion amongst commentators. The general editorship of the series, of course, maintained a perfect gender balance between the mid-1960s and the millennium. After that point, not so much.

Over the fifty years of the series, around 17% of CGLC volumes have been edited by women, although the proportion is higher for Latin texts (c. 24%) than for Greek (c. 10%). These bare statistics are not quite the whole story. The first two decades of the series saw very low numbers of editions produced by women (none in the 1970s, only one in the 1980s), although that would change in the decades from 1990–2020, where women would regularly edit around one fifth of all green and yellow volumes produced in those years. Women currently hold a little under 40% of contracts for all CGLC yet to appear in the series.

Analysis of editors by national affiliation at the time of publication also tells a story of gradually increasing diversity, in certain respects.[98] Roughly 60% of CGLC volumes have been authored by UK scholars, with the US accounting for all but a small percentage of the rest. Again, a breakdown of the numbers gives a more nuanced view of the situation. Latin volumes in the series show an almost equal 50–50 split between UK- and US-based editors. This rather undermines the perception that Americans don't 'do' commentaries (the late Elaine Fantham revealed her active discouragement of US graduate students from pursuing commentaries, on the ground of future employment prospects, in 2002).[99] Or at least it undermines the perception that Americans don't do Latin commentaries. UK editors account for nearly three-quarters of CGLC Greek texts overall, with US scholars contributing only just over a fifth. The first decade of the series featured

---

98 By national affiliation is meant: to which institution in which country was the editor attached at the time of publication? British and Irish scholars in the US lurk amongst those counted as US scholars; equally, American, Irish and continental European scholars working in Britain count for these purposes as UK-based. The statistics are therefore necessarily approximate.
99 Fantham 2002, 417–19.

only one US-based scholar (and at that in a very qualified sense: Webster had moved to Stanford in 1968, at the very end of his career), although numbers of US-based editors would gradually rise to hit roughly the 40% mark in the two most recent decades.[100] This growth in US numbers reflects, in part, the fact that it was only in the 1970s that representatives from UK presses, including CUP, began to visit north America on a regular basis. Finally, how many CGLC editors were employed at either Oxford or Cambridge at the time of publication?[101] Again, there is a story of an ultimate divergence between Greek and Latin volumes in the series. Just over one third of CGLC volumes have been produced by 'Oxbridge' editors: half of all Greek editions emanate from this source, compared with around a fifth of all Latin editions.[102]

Different readers will take away different messages from these statistics, and feel modest hope, disheartenment, or indifference according to their analyses. One thing is clear: unlike the Cambridge 'orange' series, CGLC did not start out as a club exclusively for a small band of Cambridge-educated academics and their doctoral students, focused on a narrow agenda bound up with the practice of textual criticism. The pursuit of that agenda led to problems of recruitment for the 'orange' series in the mid-1990s (before its renewal in the following decade), at precisely the time that the green and yellow volumes were causing CUP to worry about over-expansion.[103]

---

[100] US scholars currently hold 48% of contracts for all future Greek volumes in series and 43% of all Latin volumes, compared with figures of 48% and 38% respectively for contracts held by UK-based scholars. CGLC is rapidly becoming an Anglo-American series, particularly on the Latin side — which also now features an increasing number of scholars based in continental Europe.

[101] Unlike information on employment / national affiliation (which is normally recorded either in CGLC volumes themselves or in CUP catalogues), easily accessible and reliable information on where editors were educated is not consistently available. Were an Oxbridge education to be added to these statistics, their complexion would undoubtedly alter.

[102] The proportion of editions produced by editors employed at Oxbridge has fluctuated over the decades: from just under a third in the 1970s, it rose to around 40% in the 1980s, and eventually returned to that higher figure in the most recent decade after a dip down to around a quarter in the 1990s and 2000s. Oxbridge editors currently hold 5% of all contracts for future Latin volumes, compared with 25% of contracts held for Greek volumes by the same constituency.

[103] See Gibson 2016, 358–9, 369 on the troubles of the 'orange' series at this time.

11 Sales and design of CGLC

Sales figures are far from uniform for titles in the series. Sales in the big-selling genres, such as Greek tragedy, support the ability to publish volumes with a readership that is one-fifth the size of the former. The books remain moderately priced in their paperback versions, but still account for around 10% of the revenue generated by the total CUP Classics list. A look at historic sales for individual volumes and genres within the series offers some interesting perspectives on the readership for CGLC. Most green and yellows can expect to sell at least 2,000 copies in the first two decades of publication. It can take time for 'adoptions' to materialize in significant numbers, as noted earlier. Many volumes sell considerably more in this time period; few sell less. For comparison, lifetime sales of the average academic monograph tend to stall somewhere between 350 and 700 copies. In general, Greek volumes tend to sell particularly well: tragedy, Homer, Plato, even oratory. CGLC has in fact been successful in persuading more Greek than Latin editors to write commentaries on texts that are 'staples' on university courses (perhaps, also, those who study Greek have more money to spend).[104] Fourteen volumes in the series, i.e. more than a tenth of all editions, have sold over 7000 copies, including (from recent decades) Mastronarde on Euripides, *Medea* (2002) and Griffith on Sophocles, *Antigone* (1999). Volumes in this same class notable for breaking out beyond the more restricted readership that genres other than drama and epic normally attract, include Carey on Lysias (1990), Martin and Woodman on Tacitus, *Annals* IV (1989), Shackleton Bailey on Cicero's letters (1980), and Martin on Terence's *Adelphoe* (1976). Given the policy of keeping all titles in print, it is inevitable that the list of bestsellers is crowded with titles from the first decade or so of the series. Dawe's *Oedipus Rex* (1982/2006), Macleod's *Iliad* XXIV (1982), Coleman's *Eclogues* (1977) and Kenney's Lucretius III (1971/2014) have all sold over the 10,000 mark — as have the combined two volumes of Thomas' *Georgics* (1988). Sir Kenneth Dover's edition of Plato's *Symposium* (1980) is the leading title for sales, with over 16,000 copies shifted. Seasoned Dover watchers think of this as perhaps his least satisfactory book: rather short (ratio 1 : 1.68); somewhat underpowered in its help with the Greek; and of limited insight into the core issues raised by the text. A thought suggests itself: some edi-

---

[104] More seriously: while Roman historians have decisively turned away from Latin historians to (e.g.) epigraphy as their preferred 'sources' (see Lavan 2021), it is perhaps the case that Greek historians, particularly those of the archaic and early classical eras, are perforce more reliant on historical and 'literary' texts.

tions may sell, and keep on selling, largely because of the popularity of the ancient text itself, the perceived authority of the commentator, *and* the very strength of the green and yellow 'brand' (there may also be nothing better on the market).

CGLC volumes have never been 'luxury' items in their physical format — unlike the editions produced for the Cambridge 'orange' series, particularly in its first two decades of operation.[105] They have, like the Oxford 'reds', nevertheless inspired in their users an affection that is easier to document than it is to understand (in oneself or others).[106] The hardbacks produced by CUP at the very start of the series are only now coming to the end of their much-handled working lives in libraries now, fifty years after first publication. For the first few titles, a 'Ratchford' cloth binding was used for the hardbacks, replaced by a cheaper cloth substitute 'Linson, light stone' after the publication of Kells' *Electra* in 1973. Libraries, the main purchasers of hardbacks, inevitably threw the accompanying dustjackets away, but it was not until 1997 that CUP decided to dispense with these complicated and expensive items. The Press opted for a deep shade of green for the cloth-substitute binding, and gold lettering for the author, title and series title on front and spine. The handsome result was a distinct improvement on the unattractive grey and gold of previous hardbacks. John Barsby on Terence's *Eunuchus* (1999) and Richard Hunter on Theocritus (1999) were the first hardback editions to appear in this new livery.

Simultaneous publication in paperback and hardback began at the same time as the move to a cloth substitute for the hardback. The design of the cover on both paperback and hardback remained largely the same for around two decades after 1973, with its design of a yellow box within a green border on the cover and a yellow spine — both with offset green or yellow lettering. The hue of the green and yellow shades did vary somewhat — a result no doubt of change and development in printing inputs, suppliers and technology — but always remained recognizable. In the mid-1990s, a simpler and more striking design was developed, with the top third of spine and front cover shaded in green and offset against a lower two-thirds in yellow. The hue of the green and yellow continues to vary — as also for reprints of the purple and pink livery of the Imperial Library series. Standards of paper and binding have inevitably also shown distinct highs

---

105 See Gibson 2016, 367–8.
106 See (e.g.) the 'Green and Yellows' rap on youtube.com attributed to kziggurat (27 April, 2011), or the photo of a fancy dress competition (winner: green and yellow Cicero, *Catilinarians*) submitted as part of the Impact Case Study evidence of Hardie-Hunter-Oakley 2013.

and lows.[107] In recent decades, both 80 gsm uncoated and 90 gsm coated paper have been used: the latter is both more expensive and thinner than its uncoated counterpart. Coated paper is standard at CUP for all books regarded as 'textbooks', although the editorial board of CGLC has taken the view that uncoated paper is preferable on the ground that it is easier to make notes on, with one eye also on the fact that inkjet printing on uncoated paper helps to keep costs down (coated paper is nicer to the touch). For printing Greek, CGLC uses the striking 'New Hellenic' font: the legibility, elegance and simplicity of the type are part of the attractions of using the series for readers accustomed to the rather uninspiring 'Porsonic' Greek type[108] (use of New Hellenic has been distinctive to CUP since the 1930s). Font size and spacing of the commentary in CGLC volumes, however, has (again) varied considerably: some commentaries pack more on the page than others of comparable girth.[109]

The biggest change in the design of CGLC, from a smaller format of c. 18.5 x 12 cm to taller and wider format of 21.6 x 13.8 cm, took place almost by accident. The advent of 'Print on Demand' made it easier and cheaper to keep titles in print; but the technology was unable to reproduce the format of the smaller size, and so a text suitable for a book with dimensions of 18.5 x 12 cm was printed within the new larger format (hence the outsize footers and headers in reprints of older titles in the series). In the mid-2000s, Michael Sharp recommended that all new titles in the series accommodate themselves fully to the dimensions of the larger format. Whereas the older format generally allowed the inclusion of 323–5 lines

---

[107] To take an example from my own library: the good quality coated paper and robust binding of Hopkinson's *Hellenistic Anthology* 1988 makes a strong contrast with the browned paper and disintegrating gathers of the reprint of Gransden's *Aeneid* VIII from the very same year. Both were printed at the University Press. Since the latter ceased to operate in 2012, printing has been outsourced, first to MPG (based in Cornwall until its demise in 2013) and then to Clays Ltd in Suffolk (sold to an Italian conglomerate in 2018) and TJ International in Cornwall. On-demand reprints are manufactured by Lightning Source (a subsidiary of Ingram) at its various operations around the world.

[108] This type had been invented by Victor Scholderer in the 1920s, apparently at the instigation of the Society for the Promotion of Hellenic Studies, in order to replace the 'Porsonic' Greek type that had been designed for CUP in 1813 (and based on the handwriting of the former Professor of Greek, Richard Porson); for a history of the New Hellenic type, see Bowman 1991. Since New Hellenic Greek is less compressed than Porsonic, more words can be fitted onto a line in a prose text: this caused problems for the setting of the first prose text in the series, Plato's *Symposium*, whose standard reference system is by printed line (a system maintained for the Porsonic Greek of the standard Oxford Classical Text edition).

[109] For the main text of Introduction and commentary, the standard font is New Baskerville 9.5 / 11.5 pt.

of text per page (depending on the presence or absence of an apparatus) and around 36–38 lines of commentary per page, the larger format allowed c. 36–43 lines of text per page and a more regular 43 lines of printed commentary. The increased width also facilitated the admission of more words per line. One immediate result was physical: commentaries of a length standard for the old format immediately became thinner. Less pressure was now put on the spine of the book, and volumes in the series became less likely to disintegrate in the hands — as some of the fatter commentaries in the old format threatened to do — and easier to use.

12 The (personal) long view

It may well be that, had I chosen to spend the bulk of 2019 on my own green and yellow, rather than on writing this chapter, I would be a good deal closer to fulfilling the CGLC contract now signed so long ago. However, in addition to the pleasure of expressing gratitude (to the best of my abilities) for the example set by Chris Stray and his scholarship, it has been a joy to spend time thinking about a commentary series that has been lodged in my consciousness since I first saw a copy of Kells' *Electra* in the hand of a teacher at my secondary school in Belfast around 1979. CGLC as a series is not without imperfections or some persistent contradictions. But I emphatically look forward to each new instalment, in the expectation that (to echo an earlier sentiment) 'it will give me a thoroughly up-to-date way into a text'.

13 Appendix 1

Tab. 3: CGLC Volumes 1970–2020, including Imperial Library Volumes.

Short title	Author	Published
Sophocles, *Philoctetes*	T.B.L. Webster	1970
Lucretius, *De Rerum Natura* Book III	E.J. Kenney	1971
Sophocles, *Electra*	J.H. Kells	March 1973
Plautus, *Casina*	W.T. MacCary and M.M. Willcock	May 1976
Terence, *Adelphoe*	R.H. Martin	May 1976

Short title	Author	Published
Virgil, *Aeneid* Book VIII	K.W. Gransden	July 1976
Virgil, *Eclogues*	R.G.G. Coleman	May 1977
Plato, *Symposium*	K.J. Dover	Feb. 1980
Cicero, Select Letters	D.R. Shackleton Bailey	July 1980
Homer, *Iliad* Book XXIV	C.W. Macleod	March 1982
Sophocles, *Oedipus Rex*	R.D. Dawe	Oct. 1982
Sophocles, *Trachiniae*	P.E. Easterling	Oct. 1982
Aeschylus, *Prometheus Bound*	Mark Griffith	May 1983
Seneca, *Apocolocyntosis*	P.T. Eden	March 1984
Demosthenes, Selected Private Speeches	C. Carey and R. Reid	July 1985
A Hellenistic Anthology	Neil Hopkinson	Feb. 1988
Plutarch, *Life of Antony*	C.B.R. Pelling	May 1988
Virgil, *Georgics* (2 vols.)	R.F. Thomas	Aug. 1988
Thucydides, *The Peloponnesian War* Book II	J.S. Rusten	March 1989
Apollonius of Rhodes, *Argonautica* Book III	R.L. Hunter	June 1989
Aeschylus, *Eumenides*	A.H. Sommerstein	Nov. 1989
Horace, *Epistles* Book II and 'Ars Poetica'	Niall Rudd	Dec. 1989
Tacitus, *Annals* Book IV	R.H. Martin and A.J. Woodman	Jan. 1990
Lysias, Selected Speeches	C. Carey	Jan. 1990
Seneca, *Phaedra*	M. Coffey and R.G. Mayer	March 1990
Apuleius, *Cupid and Psyche*	E.J. Kenney	Dec. 1990
Virgil, *Aeneid* Book XI	K.W. Gransden	Nov. 1991
Homer, *Odyssey* Books XIX and XX	R.B. Rutherford	April 1992
Lucan, *De Bello Civili* Book II	Elaine Fantham	July 1992
Dio Chrysostom, *Orations* 7, 12 and 36	Donald Russell	Oct. 1992
Plautus, *Menaechmi*	A.S. Gratwick	July 1993
Plato, *Phaedo*	C.J. Rowe	Sept. 1993
Greek Poetry of the Imperial Period	Neil Hopkinson	Sept. 1994
Horace, *Epistles* Book I	R.G. Mayer	Sept. 1994
Livy, *Ab Vrbe Condita* Book VI	C.S. Kraus	Nov. 1994
Virgil, *Aeneid* Book IX	P.R. Hardie	Nov. 1994
Homer, *Odyssey* Books VI–VIII	A.F. Garvie	Dec. 1994

Short title	Author	Published
Cicero, *De re publica*	James E.G. Zetzel	April 1995
Pindar, Victory Odes	M.M. Willcock	April 1995
Horace, *Epodes*	David Mankin	Oct. 1995
Augustine, *Confessions* Books I-IV	Gillian Clark	Nov. 1995
Ovid, *Heroides* Select Epistles	Peter E. Knox	Jan. 1996
Plato on Poetry	Penelope Murray	March 1996
Juvenal, *Satires* Book I	Susanna Morton Braund	March 1996
Ovid, *Heroides* XVI–XXI	E.J. Kenney	March 1996
Antiphon, The Speeches	Michael Gagarin	Feb. 1997
Ovid, *Fasti* Book IV	Elaine Fantham	May 1998
Theocritus, *Select Poems*	R.L. Hunter	Feb. 1999
Terence, *Eunuchus*	John Barsby	Feb. 1999
Sophocles, *Antigone*	Mark Griffith	Sept. 1999
Plautus, *Amphitruo*	David Christenson	July 2000
Ovid, *Metamorphoses* Book XIII	Neil Hopkinson	Nov. 2000
Suetonius, *Diuus Claudius*	Donna Hurley	March 2001
Tacitus, *Dialogus de Oratoribus*	Roland Mayer	June 2001
Demosthenes, *On the Crown*	Harvey E. Yunis	June 2001
Plato, *Alcibiades*	Nicholas Denyer	Sept. 2001
Euripides, *Medea*	Donald J. Mastronarde	Aug. 2002
Herodotus, *Histories* Book IX	Michael A. Flower and John Marincola	Dec. 2002
Tacitus, *Histories* Book I	Cynthia Damon	Dec. 2002
Seneca, *De Otio*; *De Brevitate Vitae*	G.D. Williams	Jan. 2003
Greek and Latin Letters: An Anthology, with Translation	M.B. Trapp	March 2003
Martial, Select Epigrams	Lindsay Watson and Pat Watson	June 2003
Cicero, *De natura deorum* Book I	Andrew Dyck	July 2003
Cicero, *Philippics* I-II	John Ramsey	Sept. 2003
Bacchylides, A Selection	Herwig Maehler	June 2004
Sophocles, *Oedipus Rex* (rev. ed.)	R.D. Dawe	July 2006
Propertius, *Elegies* Book IV	G.O. Hutchinson	Aug. 2006
Xenophon on Government	Vivienne Gray	May 2007
Tacitus, *Histories* Book II	Rhiannon Ash	Nov. 2007
Herodotus, *Histories* Book VIII	Angus Bowie	Dec. 2007

Short title	Author	Published
Euripides, *Helen*	William Allan	Feb. 2008
Cicero, *Catilinarians*	Andrew Dyck	April 2008
Plato, *Protagoras*	Nicholas Denyer	Sept. 2008
Lucian, Selected Works	Neil Hopkinson	Oct. 2008
Ovid, *Metamorphoses* Book XIV	K. Sara Myers	Dec. 2009
Three Homeric Hymns	N. Richardson	April 2010
Cicero, *Pro Sexto Roscio Amerino*	Andrew Dyck	April 2010
Homer, *Odyssey* Books XVII-XVIII	Deborah Steiner	June 2010
Homer, *Iliad* Book VI	Barbara Graziosi and Johannes Haubold	Nov. 2010
Statius, *Silvae* Book II	Carole Newlands	Feb. 2011
Cicero, *De oratore* Book III	David Mankin	March 2011
Plato, *Phaedrus*	Harvey Yunis	May 2011
Plutarch, *How to Study Poetry*	Richard Hunter and Donald Russell	June 2011
Horace, *Odes* Book IV and *Carmen Saeculare*	Richard F. Thomas	July 2011
Homer, *Iliad* Book XXII	Irene de Jong	Jan. 2012
Horace, *Satires* Book I	Emily Gowers	Jan. 2012
Horace, *Odes* Book I	Roland Mayer	April 2012
Virgil, *Aeneid* Book XII	Richard Tarrant	July 2012
Cicero, *Pro Marco Caelio*	Andrew Dyck	April 2013
Sophocles, *Philoctetes* (new ed.)	Seth Schein	Sept. 2013
Terence, *Hecyra*	Sander Goldberg	Nov. 2013
Pliny the Younger, *Epistles* Book II	Chris Whitton	Nov. 2013
Herodotus, *Histories* Book V	Simon Hornblower	Dec. 2013
Homer, *Odyssey* Books XIII-XIV	Angus Bowie	Jan. 2014
Menander, *Samia*	Alan Sommerstein	Jan. 2014
Ovid, *Epistulae ex Ponto* Book I	Garth Tissol	March 2014
Juvenal, *Satire* 6	Lindsay Watson and Pat Watson	May 2014
Lucretius, *De Rerum Natura* Book III (2nd ed.)	E.J. Kenney	Aug. 2014
Tacitus, *Agricola*	A.J. Woodman with C.S. Kraus	Sept. 2014
Apollonius of Rhodes, *Argonautica* Book IV	Richard Hunter	Aug. 2015
Valerius Flaccus, *Argonautica* Book III	Gesine Manuwald	Oct. 2015

Short title	Author	Published
Horace, *Odes* Book II	S.J. Harrison	April 2017
Tacitus, *Annals* Book XV	Rhiannon Ash	Dec. 2017
Herodotus, *Histories* Book VI	Simon Hornblower and Chris Pelling	Dec. 2017
Euripides, *Hecuba*	Luigi Battezzato	Jan. 2018
Greek Lyric	Felix Budelmann	May 2018
Homer, *Iliad* Book XVIII	R.B. Rutherford	Jan. 2019
Xenophon, *Anabasis* Book III	Luuk Huitink and Tim Rood	March 2019
Plato, *Apology* and **Xenophon,** *Apology*	Nicholas Denyer	April 2019
Ovid, *Fasti* Book III	S.J. Heyworth	May 2019
Lucan, *De Bello Civili* Book VII	Paul Roche	May 2019
Seneca, Select Letters	Catharine Edwards	June 2019
Demosthenes, Selected Political Speeches	Judson Herrman	July 2019
Longus, *Daphnis and Chloe*	E.L. Bowie	July 2019
Greek Elegy and Iambus	William Allan	Aug. 2019
Homer, *Iliad* Book III	Angus Bowie	Sept. 2019
Augustine, *Confessions* Books V-IX	Peter White	Sept. 2019
Aeschylus, *Suppliants*	A.H. Sommerstein	Sept. 2019
Euripides, *Ion*	John C. Gibert	Nov. 2019
Virgil, *Aeneid* Book XI	Scott McGill	Jan. 2020
Achilles Tatius, *Leucippe and Clitophon* Books I–II	Tim Whitmarsh	June 2020
Euripides, *Cyclops*	Richard Hunter and Rebecca Laemmle	July 2020
Plautus, *Pseudolus*	David Christenson	July 2020
A Hellenistic Anthology (2nd ed.)	Neil Hopkinson	Sept. 2020
Plato, *Menexenus*	David Sansone	Aug. 2020
Livy, *Ab Vrbe Condita* Book XXII	John Briscoe and Simon Hornblower	Oct. 2020
Hellenistic Epigrams	Alex Sens	Nov. 2020

14 Appendix 2

CGLC: Text to Commentary Ratios

The average ratio between text and commentary, as noted earlier, stayed steady between c. 1 : 4 and 1 : 5 for the first four decades of the series, before rising to an average of around 1 : 7 in the 2010s. The recognized upper page limit for an edition eventually settled at around 320 pages, although authors regularly produced commentaries below this maximum, and less frequently beyond it. However, the apparent steady state of ratios between the 1970s and the first decade of the new millennium conceals some important developments. Editions such as Martin on Terence's *Adelphoe* (1976), Dover on Plato's *Symposium* (1980), and Shackleton Bailey on Cicero's letters (1980) perhaps embody the less intensive commentaries produced in the first decade or so of the series. With an average ratio of 1 : 2 between text and commentary, none of these editions went far beyond 250 pages in total; Dover reached only 185 pages, in an edition notoriously unsympathetic to its ancient author.[110] Through inclusion of a large amount of Latin text (92 pages) and a characteristically patchy commentary (108 pages), Shackleton Bailey achieved a ratio of only c. 1 : 1.2: the lowest in the half-century of the series.[111] Kenney on Lucretius III (1971) and Coleman on Virgil's *Eclogues* (1977) demonstrated the true capabilities of the series: with longer commentaries on shorter texts, Kenney's edition reached a ratio of c. 1 : 4.6 and Coleman's a ratio of c. 1 : 8.1. The greater intensity of exposition achieved by these editions is part of the explanation for their later success.

Mark Griffith's well-received edition of Aeschylus' *Prometheus Bound* (1983) followed the same path as Kenney and Coleman in opting for a longer commentary on his text (ratio: 1 : 5.3). This was the harbinger of an upwards trend. Richard Thomas' two-volume commentary on the four relatively short books of Virgil's

---

[110] As was noted by Griffin 1995, 14; cf. Dover 1980, vii–viii.

[111] On the patchiness of Shackleton Bailey's 'orange' commentaries on Cicero's letters, cf. Gibson 2016, 355 n. 33. With 144 pages of text and 133 pages of commentary, Trapp on *Greek and Latin Letters* 2003 has a technically lower ratio of c. 1 : 0.9; but half of that text is taken up by a translation that effectively acts as a commentary on texts rather unfamiliar to most classicists. As such, the more accurate ratio for text vs commentary in this edition is c. 2.8. (For the inclusion of translations in CGLC volumes, see above n. 73.) With only 76 pages of commentary, Gransden on Virgil *Aeneid* XI 1991 may appear rather slight, but the ratio of text to commentary is in fact c. 1 : 2.5, i.e. roughly the same as Kells' *Electra* at c. 1 : 2.8. (The 915 verses of *Aeneid* XI take up 30 pages, whereas the 1510 lines of the *Electra* take up 54 pages of text.) Gransden's *Aeneid* VIII 1976, however, had a much higher text vs commentary ratio of c. 1 : 4.75.

Georgics (1988) demonstrated ratios of 1: 6.2/6.3, while (e.g.) Alan Sommerstein on Aeschylus' *Eumenides* (1989), Christina Kraus on Livy VI (1994), and A.F. Garvie on Homer, *Odyssey* VI–VIII (1994) all reached ratios between 1: 5 and 1: 6.75. At the same time, there were plenty of editions content with a deliberately less thorough treatment of their chosen texts.[112] Yet the general trend remained upwards. Susanna Morton Braund's commentary on a single book of Juvenal's satires (I–V, 1996; ratio 1 : 8) was followed by Richard Hunter on selections from Theocritus (1999; ratio 1: 8.6), Gareth Williams on two relatively unfamiliar dialogues of Seneca (2003; ratio 1 : 7.4), and Lindsay and Patricia Watson on selections from Martial (2003; ratio 1 : 9.2).[113] In the second decade of the new millennium, ratios of text to commentary rose in unison across volumes published in the series. Barbara Graziosi and Johannes Haubold devoted 159 pages of commentary to the short 15 pages of text that constitute *Iliad* VI (2010; ratio: 1 : 10.5). Numerous other commentaries achieved similar levels of coverage, including Harrison on Horace, *Odes* II (2017: ratio 1: 11.8).[114]

14.1 Archive Sources

Since the early-2000s and the rise of email to dominance, only contracts and the minutes of meetings held at the highest level, such as Syndicate Meetings, are archived at CUP. Fuller archives for earlier decades of the series are listed below.

---

[112] E.g. Hopkinson's *Hellenistic Anthology* 1988: 1: 2.9; Rusten on Thucydides II 1989: 1: 2.5; Coffey and Mayer on Seneca's *Phaedra* 1989: 1 : 2.65; Russell on Dio Chrysostom 1992: 1: 1.75.

[113] Authors of commentaries on Greek texts were more routinely continent in terms of length – or perhaps they thought their readers needed less help than Latinists. Appearances can also be deceptive: Rhiannon Ash's edition of Tacitus' *Histories* II 2007 is widely assumed to be the very largest in the CGLC canon; but with a text of 36 pages and a commentary of 309 pages (ratio 1 : 8.9) it falls below the 245 pages devoted by Mankin to just 22 pages of text (1 : 11), even while Ash's total of 415 pages exceeds that of Mankin's 321 pages. (This is not the whole story: Ash 2007 appears to use a smaller font size than Mankin 1995, at least in the commentary; and the broader and taller format of Ash allows significantly more words per page in other ways. But with its short iambus lines, Mankin's Latin text is considerably shorter than the margin-swamping *Histories* of Tacitus.)

[114] Woodman came close to overhauling Mankin's ratio with his edition of Tacitus' *Agricola* 2014; Ash finally achieved it with her commentary on Tacitus, *Annals* 15 2018. Other notably large commentaries include: Newlands on Statius *Silvae* II (2011; 1 : 9.5); Thomas on Horace, *Odes* IV (2011; 1 : 8.4); Irene de Jong on Homer, *Iliad* 22 (2012; 1 : 8.4); Gowers on Horace, *Satires* I (2012; 1 : 10.4); Tarrant on Virgil, *Aeneid* XII (2012; 1 : 9.25); Whitton on Pliny, *Epistles* II (2013; 1: 9.9); the Watsons on Juvenal, *Satires* VI (2014; 1 : 10.3); Manuwald on Valerius Flaccus III (2015; 1 : 8.8); and Roche on Lucan VII (2019; 1 : 8.3).

14.2 Series files at Cambridge University Library

- Press 3/1/5/326: 2 folders. Folder 1: CGLC general editorial correspondence 1966–85; folder 2: CGLC general editorial correspondence 1986–92.
- Press 3/1/5/619: 1 folder: correspondence on the CUP publications of K.J. Dover.
- Press 3/1/5/645: 1 folder: correspondence on P.E. Easterling's CGLC edition of Sophocles, *Trachiniae*.
- Press 3/1/5/1136: 1 folder: correspondence on the CUP publications of E.J. Kenney.
- Press 3/1/6/268: 2 folders: CGLC general editorial correspondence 1990–96.

14.3 Series files at Cambridge University Press

Two files held by the Classics editor at CUP cover editorial correspondence mostly from 1996–2005, with some additional later material.

Bibliography

Publication details of CGLC commentaries are given earlier in Appendix 1.

Austin, R.G. (1960), *Cicero, Pro Caelio* (rev. ed.), Oxford.
Austin, R.G. (1964a), *Virgil, Aeneid II*, Oxford.
Austin, R.G. (1964b), *Quintilian, Inst. XII* (rev. ed.), Oxford.
Bartera, S. (2016), 'Commentary writing on the *Annals* of Tacitus: different approaches for different audiences', in: Kraus/Stray 2016, 113–134.
Beale, A. (2016), review of E.J. Kenney, Lucretius, *De Rerum Natura III* (2nd ed.), *Classics for All Book Reviews*, https://classicsforall.org.uk/book-reviews/lucretius-de-rerum-natura-book-3/.
Black, M. (1984), *Cambridge University Press 1584–1984*, Cambridge.
Black, M. (2011), *Learning to be a Publisher: Cambridge University Press 1951–1987: Personal Reminiscences*, Cambridge.
Bond, G.W. (1988), *Euripides, Heracles*, Oxford.
Bowman, J. (1991), 'The 'New Hellenic' Greek type', *Printing Historical Society Bulletin* 30, 2–8.
Brink, C.O. (1957), *Latin Studies and the Humanities: an Inaugural Lecture*, Cambridge.
Davies, J. (2016), 'The historical commentary', in: Kraus/Stray 2016, 233–250.
Dodds, E.R. (1960), *Euripides, Bacchae* (rev. ed.), Oxford.
Douglas, A.E. (1962), *Cicero, Brutus*, Oxford.
Easterling, P.E. (2005), ''The speaking page': reading Sophocles with Jebb', in: Stray 2005a, 25–46.

Easterling, P.E. (2007), 'A note on Cambridge Greek and Latin Classics', in: Stray 2007, 177–179.
Fantham, E. (2002), 'Commenting on commentaries: a pragmatic postscript', in: Gibson/Kraus 2002, 403–422.
Finglass, P.J. (2013a), review of S. Schein, Sophocles, *Philoctetes*, *Bryn Mawr Classical Review* 2013, 11.31.
Finglass, P.J. (2013b), 'Sophocles: editions and commentaries' [indexed by individual play], in: *Oxford Bibliographies*, www.oxfordbibliographies.com/.
Finglass, P.J. (2016), 'Jebb's Sophocles', in: Kraus/Stray 2016, 21–38.
Fordyce, C.J. (1961), *Catullus* (rev. ed. 1965), Oxford.
Forrest, M. (2003), 'The abolition of compulsory Latin and its consequences', in: C.A. Stray (ed.), *The Classical Association: the First Century, 1903–2003* (Greece & Rome Supplement), Oxford, 42–66.
Garrison-Peirano, I. (2021). 'Canon(s)', in: Gibson/Whitton 2021.
Gibson, R.K. (2003), *Ovid, Ars Amatoria 3*, Cambridge.
Gibson, R.K. (2016), 'Fifty shades of orange: Cambridge Classical Texts and Commentaries', in: Kraus/Stray 2016, 346–375.
Gibson, R.K./Kraus, C.S. (eds.) (2002), *The Classical Commentary: Histories, Practices, Theory*, Leiden.
Gibson, R.K./Whitton, C.L. (eds.) (2021), *The Cambridge Critical Guide to Latin Literature*, Cambridge.
Griffin, J. (1995), 'The Guidance that we Need,' *Times Literary Supplement* 4.4.95, 13–14.
Hardie, P./Hunter, R.L./Oakley, S.P. (2013), 'The Cambridge Greek and Latin Classics series' (REF 2014 Impact Case Study), [https://results.ref.ac.uk/(S(x2gokgbmfal3hsryb22bxg5i))/Submissions/Impact/533].
Henderson, J.G.W. (2002), 'The way we were: R.G. Austin, *in Caelianam*', in: Gibson/Kraus 2002, 205–234.
Henderson, J.G.W. (2006), *'Oxford Reds': Classic Commentaries on Classic Texts*, London.
Henderson, J.G.W. (2007), 'The 'Euripides reds' series: best-laid plans at OUP', in: Stray 2007, 143–175.
Jocelyn, H.D. (1969), *The Tragedies of Ennius: the Fragments*, Cambridge.
Jocelyn, H.D. (1997), 'Charles Oscar Brink 1907–1994', *PBA* 94, 319–354.
Joint Association of Classical Teachers (1978), *Reading Greek*, Cambridge.
Joint Association of Classical Teachers (1979), *A World of Heroes*, Cambridge.
Joint Association of Classical Teachers (1980), *The Intellectual Revolution*, Cambridge.
Jones, B.W. (1996), *Suetonius: Domitian*, London.
Keane, C. (2014), review of E. Gowers, Horace, *Satires I*, *CR* 64, 128–130.
Kelly, G. (2021), 'Periodization', in: Gibson/Whitton 2021.
Kenney, E.J. (1975), *New Frameworks for Old. The place of Classical literature in the Cambridge Classical course. An inaugural lecture*, Cambridge.
Kovacs, D. (2018), *Euripides, Troades,* Oxford.
Kraus, C.S. (2002), 'Introduction: reading commentaries / commentaries as reading', in: Gibson/Kraus, 1–28.
Kraus, C.S. (2016), 'Agricolan paratexts', in: Kraus/Stray 2016, 318–344.
Kraus, C.S./Stray, C.A. (eds.) (2016), *Classical Commentaries: Explorations in a Classical Genre*, Oxford.

Lamberton, R. (1995), review of N. Hopkinson, *Greek Poetry of the Imperial Period*, Bryn Mawr Classical Review 95, 04.09
Lavan, M. (2021), 'Latin literature and Roman history', in: Gibson/Whitton 2021.
Lee, A.G. (1953), *P. Ovidi Nasonis Metamorphoseon Liber I*, Cambridge.
Levi, P. (1982), review of C. W. Macleod, *Homer, Iliad XXIV 1982, The Spectator*, 17 April.
Liapis, V. (2012), *Commentary on the Rhesus attributed to Euripides*, Oxford.
Lister, B. (2015), 'In memoriam JACT, 1963-2015', G&R 62, 206–217.
Lloyd-Jones, H. (1972), review of T.B.L. Webster, Sophocles, *Philoctetes*, CR 22, 102.
McKitterick, D. (2004), *A History of Cambridge University Press, volume 3*, Cambridge.
Nelis, D.P. (2016), review of E.J. Kenney, Lucretius, *De Rerum Natura III* (2nd ed.), CR 66, 292.
Nisbet, R.G.M. (1961), *Cicero, In Pisonem*, Oxford.
O'Donnell, J.J. (2012), *Augustine, Confessions*. Oxford.
Oakley, S.P. (1997), *A Commentary on Livy, Books VI-X, Vol. I, Book VI*, Oxford.
Oakley, S.P. (2016), 'Dodds' *Bacchae*', in: Kraus/Stray 2016, 84–109.
Ogilvie, R.M./Richmond, I. (1967), *Tacitus, Agricola*, Oxford.
Parker, L.P.E. (2007), *Euripides, Alcestis*, Oxford.
Parker, L.P.E. (2016), *Euripides, Iphigenia in Tauris*, Oxford.
Pelling, C. (2011), *Plutarch: Caesar*. Oxford.
Pucci, P. (1973), review of T.B.L. Webster, Sophocles, *Philoctetes*, AJP 94, 197–201.
Robbins, K. (2017), *The History of Oxford University Press, Volume IV: 1970-2004*, Oxford.
Seaford, R. (1984), *Euripides, Cyclops*, Oxford.
Stanford, W.B. (1991), *Aristophanes, The Frogs*, London/New York.
Stray, C.A. (1998), *Classics Transformed: Schools, Universities, and Society in England, 1830–1960*, Oxford.
Stray, C.A. (ed.) (2005a), *The Owl of Minerva: The Cambridge Praelections of 1906*, Proceedings of the Cambridge Philological Soc., Supp vol. 28, Cambridge.
Stray, C.A. (2005b), 'Reading Jebb: life and afterlife', in: Stray 2005a, 13–24.
Stray, C.A. (2007), *Classical Books: Scholarship and Publishing in Britain since 1800*, London.
Stray, C.A. (2013), *Sophocles' Jebb: A Life in Letters. Cambridge Classical Journal*, Supplement 38, Cambridge.
Todd, R.B. (ed.) (2004), *The Dictionary of British Classicists*, 3 vols., Bristol.
Trimble, G. (2012), 'Catullus and 'comment in English': the tradition of the expurgated commentary before Fordyce', in: S. Harrison/C.A. Stray (eds.), *Expurgating the Classics: Editing Out in Greek and Latin*, London, 143–162.
Tucker, T.G. (1906), *The Frogs of Aristophanes*, London.
Webster, T.B.L. (1932), *M. Tulli Ciceronis Pro L. Flacco Oratio*, Oxford.
West, S./Hainsworth, J.B./Heubeck, A./Hoekstra, A./Russo, J./Fernandéz-Galiano. M. (1988–92), *A Commentary on Homer's Odyssey*, Oxford.
Wilkins, J. (1993), *Euripides, Heraclidae*, Oxford.
Williams, R.D. (1960), *Virgil, Aeneid V*, Oxford.
Williams, R.D. (1962), *Virgil, Aeneid III*, Oxford.
Willink, C.W. (1989), *Euripides, Orestes*, Oxford.

Christopher Pelling
Gomme's *Thucydides* and the Idea of the Historical Commentary

This is a tale of two cities, and a tale that starts in the 1930s. The first city is Oxford, especially that small part of it consisting of Oxford University Press. The 1930s were a bumper decade for Oxford commentaries: commentaries coming out,[1] commentaries being commissioned,[2] and commentaries on the stocks.[3] There is a lot of serious thought in the Press itself about what form commentaries ought to take. Cyril Bailey is playing a large role behind the scenes as a Delegate, as (inevitably) is Maurice Bowra at first, but even more energy is being put into it by the Press professionals. There were not yet designated 'Classics editors', but the senior figures W.D. 'Billy' Hogarth at the beginning of the thirties and Kenneth Sisam towards the end certainly knew their Classics stuff.[4] John Henderson's research in the OUP files has cast a lot of light on this,[5] and we can now see how the plan for the red Euripides series formed in 1932 and 1933.[6] Four appeared by the end of the thirties (after a fair amount of scuffling in the correspondence), including two that became classics, Page's *Medea* and Denniston's *Electra*. The Latin reds — never quite planned as a 'series' but destined to end up as something

---

[1] Besides the 'Oxford Reds' there were big ones from the senior and revered, like Butler and Barber's *Propertius* (1933), Ross's *Physics* (1936), and Anderson's *Germania* (1938), and also from the odd rising star in Dodds' *Proclus* (1933) — Ross had a hand in that commission, Dodds 1977, 91 — and in Webster's shorter but still scholarly *Pro Flacco* (1931). The 1920s had been thinner. Ross's massive *Metaphysics* was published in 1924 and Hunter/Handford's *Aeneas Tacticus* in 1927, but most were slighter and clearly targeted on undergraduates: thus, explicitly, Braithwaite's Suet. *Vesp.* (1927) and Denniston's Cic. *Phil.* 1–2 (1926). Butler and Cary's *de Prouinciis Consularibus* (1924) and Suet. *Diu. Iul.* (1927) are on a similar scale. Monro's *Livy 25* (1929) is clearly a school-text, including a vocabulary.
[2] Including some that never materialised, including an *Orestes* from Page (noted in the Delegates' Order Book, Feb. 1939) and a Plutarch *Alexander* from Enoch Powell (Order Book, November 1937).
[3] In Corpus Fraenkel's *Agamemnon* seminar was underway (Stray 2016), and in Balliol Bailey was at work on his Lucretius (1947): his unpublished memoir in Balliol library (pp. 124–5) makes it clear that this was his 'ultimate goal' when publishing on the Greek atomists and Epicurus (1928) and on Roman religion (1932, 1935).
[4] Chris Stray points out to me that this was not the only area of classical energy in the early 1930s: the *Oxford Latin Dictionary* also had a big push, with an initiative starting in 1931 and 55 volunteers set to their task in 1933–5 (Henderson 2010).
[5] Henderson 2006, 2007, and 2013.
[6] Henderson 2006, 152 and 2007.

of one — were also getting started, and the correspondence with Roland Austin in particular again shows how engaged and thoughtful, even if initially sceptical, a response he got from the Press: Henderson again is fascinating on this.[7] It was not just Oxford, of course: Pease's massive *Aeneid* 4 came out from Cambridge MA in 1935, and there were many others. But there is a lot of serious thinking going on within what was one day to be the ring road about what commentaries ought to look like, and particularly in the Press itself.

The second city is Glasgow. It is extraordinary what a galaxy of commentators — commentators past, commentators present, and commentators yet to come — are to be found in the Glasgow Classics department. The Greek professor was William Rennie, whose *Acharnians* commentary came out as early as 1909; Roland Austin was there when the first edition of his *Pro Caelio* came out in 1933, and stayed till 1937; C.J. Fordyce arrived in 1934; R.G. Nisbet was beavering away at Cicero's *de Domo*, to be published in 1939; less well known is Gilbert Davies, who had published a Cambridge commentary on Demosthenes back in 1907. The traditional close link of Glasgow Classics with Cyril Bailey's Balliol may have played a part here: Austin and Fordyce had both been Bailey's pupils there. And perhaps we can count another, teenage Nisbet, growing up in 'in a house where Cicero was not just a name but a real person',[8] and destined to follow that path to Balliol and to write a decent commentary or so himself. (John Henderson speculates that 'Cicero' was the name of the family cat.)

And then there was Gomme: Arnold Wycombe Gomme, born 1886, died 1959, at that time lecturer in Greek History (he was not promoted to Reader and then Professor until his late fifties, after the publication of the first volume of the commentary): an Englishman in a Scots university, and a contented one. There is no indication that he tried to move to a chair elsewhere, though he would have been an immensely strong candidate. The story goes[9] that, once he was Professor, he encouraged two colleagues, Henry Chalk and Jim Carnegie, not to call him 'Professor': the Englishman Chalk assumed that meant 'call me Gomme', so he did; the Scot Carnegie took it as 'call me Arnold', so he did; and so it continued on both sides, with Gomme reciprocally calling the one 'Chalk' and the other 'Jim' for evermore.

The first volume of the Thucydides commentary was published in 1945, one of only nine books going through the Clarendon Press in 1944 when most were being

---

[7] Henderson 2006, chs. 1 and 2.
[8] Personal communication of R.G.M. Nisbet quoted by Henderson 2006, 128.
[9] Told to me by Ronald Knox.

held back till after the war.[10] The 'Informal History' of the Press comments on how all nine proved to be 'of the enduring kind'.[11] It was envisaged as the first volume of three, but the second had to expand into two, published in 1956, and then the planned third into two more in the Andrewes and Dover continuation after his death (1970 and 1981). That is the way of such things — Walbank's Polybius, Bosworth's Arrian, and Hornblower's Thucydides were all planned as two and expanded into three, Oakley's Livy as three and expanded into four. The appearance of the second and third volumes was delayed by one of scholarship's famous calamities. In summer 1945[12] Gomme was taking the train from Glasgow to London, and chose to stow his case with the guard's van. I gather from his daughter-in-law that this preference was an odd personal foible of his, not imposed on him by train regulations. The case was never found, and it contained not only his draft manuscript but most of his notes on the scholarship he had read, much of it in German libraries that had subsequently been destroyed in the war.[13] Just imagine.

A painting by his wife Phyllis shows him at work (Fig. 4). He was especially fond of it because of the pile of books on the desk in front of him. 'To copy from one book is plagiarism,' he would say, 'to copy from several is scholarship.' Phyllis had studied at the Chelsea School of Art with Walter Sickert and had also become an expert cartographer: she later drew all the maps for the commentary, including the first of the Andrewes–Dover continuation volumes. They had met during World War 1, probably in London when both were on home leave, for Phyllis was then an ambulance driver in France. The painting is probably set not in their Glasgow apartment but in their house, The Mound, in Long Crendon near Thame — so really a tale of two cities and a village.[14] The Gommes would decamp

---

10 Shortage of paper was evidently a factor: this is noted as a problem in Delegates' minutes as early as April 1940.
11 Sutcliffe 1978, 257.
12 So Kitto 1959, 340; Dover 1994, 75 puts it in 1949 when his manuscript was complete. 1945 seems right. Susan Gomme tells me that Gomme regarded the notes as more serious a loss than the manuscript, and that Andor Gomme remembered meeting him at the station when he arrived. Andor was a schoolboy in London in 1945 but was on national service in 1949.
13 Some other of his notebooks survive, currently on shelves in Professor Ruffell's office: these are not drafts, but notes on articles and some ancient texts. They are meticulously organised, typically with summaries of content on right-hand pages and comments, often trenchant, at appropriate places on the left.
14 This was inherited from his father Sir Laurence Gomme, Clerk to London County Council, and his mother, a notable student of folklore (Kitto 1959, 335). Arnold was one of seven brothers, but the only one with an interest in taking on the property (Susan Gomme, personal communication). A personal touch is felt at Gomme 1962, 4, where he is discussing the physical sense of a town's continuity across the ages of its growth: 'so it is with a cathedral, even with a single

there from Glasgow every year in March and stay until late September,[15] except that Gomme himself would go back to Glasgow for the brief summer term of five weeks or less, and so it is a fair bet that most of the commentary was written there, either at this desk or in the garden summerhouse where he liked to work in all weathers. Their son was born in 1930: this was Andor. His real name was Austin, but Phyllis was so huge during pregnancy that they thought it might be twins, Austin and/or Alison, and the name stuck: he was later a distinguished architectural historian.

Fig. 4: Arnold Wycombe Gomme (reproduced by courtesy of Susan Gomme).

---

house if we are fortunate enough to live in an old one which is still alive in the sense that we can live a modern life in it.'

15 This followed the pattern set by Richard Jebb during the second half of his tenure of the Glasgow chair (1875–89): after purchasing his Cambridge house in 1881 he would decamp there for the summer months (Stray 2005, 16).

I have had the good fortune to talk to Andor's widow Susan and their daughter Hester and to see the first pages of a memoir that Andor had begun to write. Here the cats were not called Thucydides but were named after cricketers — Hobbs, Hammond, Sandham and so on. I wonder if it was quite coincidence that, when the Gommes moved to London during the second war for his work in the Treasury, they took a flat in Hamilton Terrace, just 100 yards or so from Lord's. The garden was a great love: the working pattern was a long morning followed by a late lunch, then gardening, with Gomme often disappearing into an odd corner to work on some horticultural project. The house had its quirky classical aspects too: above the library fireplace there hung during the thirties a head from the Parthenon (Fig. 5).

Fig. 5: Head from the Acropolis (reproduced by courtesy of Susan Gomme).

This had been confiscated by Gomme at the end of the war from a soldier labouring under a suspiciously heavy load. It was in fact one of the heads that were still, so it was said, lying around the acropolis 230 years after the 1687 explosion. It was always going to be returned — there is some talk in correspondence of the

1930s of what would be the right packaging — and it finally was reunited with the Acropolis museum in 1938.

That confiscation came at the end of Gomme's own wartime service, based largely in Salonica and reporting to John Myres, peacetime Wykeham Professor of Ancient History in Oxford but renowned at the time as the 'Blackbeard of the Aegean', with a particular gift for cattle-rustling on the Turkish seaboard. Gomme's role was the collection of political intelligence, and incidentally gets him a mention in a recent book on 'the Real James Bonds'.[16] A rather closer contact with that world came later through the long family friendship with his undergraduate contemporary St John Philby, the noted explorer, Arabist and adviser to Ibn Saud of Saudi Arabia, and his wife. Philby was appointed head of the British Secret Service in Palestine in 1921, working closely with T.E. Lawrence: he had to resign in 1924 after several differences with official British policy (he regarded the Balfour declaration as breaking earlier promises made to the Arabs), but continued to play 'a key role in the oleaginous politics of that region'.[17] Philby's public criticisms of British government policy and his extreme right-wing views led to his being interned for some months early in World War II.[18] The Gommes would have seen the Philbies' dashing son Kim grow up, though Kim's exposure as a spy and his defection to the Soviet Union came only in 1963 after Gomme's death. Philby père may not have been a spy himself, but suspicions were inevitable: one of Kim's first Soviet assignments was to ransack his father's papers for anything of intelligence value.[19]

Gomme's war work demanded a sure grasp of practical economic strengths and weaknesses, and this often comes out in the commentary too; he also had an immense feel for Greek topography, already nurtured during his time before the war as a graduate student in the British School at Athens.[20] His first article was duly on the topography of Boeotia (Gomme 1911–12), but it was in the twenties that he made his name. The important article on 'the position of women in Athens', long a staple of undergraduate reading lists, came in 1925, and he was at the time thinking of writing a social history of Greece.[21] He then went on to publish

---

16 Smith 2011, 177–8.
17 Macintyre 2014, 27.
18 Cf. Trevor-Roper 1968, 30: 'an ex-Indian Civil Servant of impeccable right-wing (not to say, fascist) views'.
19 Macintyre 2014, 43–4.
20 E.g. 1.2.3 n. on Peloponnesian soil quality; 1.103.4 n. on the strategic importance of Pegae. On this as a strength of the commentary see Hornblower 1991–2008, ii. 4–5, giving further examples.
21 Kitto 1959, 340.

his *Population of Athens* in 1933, but it was a series of shorter notes that mark him out more as the future commentator, with titles like 'Notes on Thucydides Book VI' (1920), 'Thucydides and Sphakteria' (1923), 'Notes on the Ἀθηναίων πολιτεία' (1925b and 1926a) and for variety's sake 'Two notes on the Constitution of Athens' (1926b), 'Two notes on Herodotus' (1926), 'The Athenian hoplite force in 431 B.C.' (1927), and 'Thuc. 6.34.7' (1929). It is noticeable that these are not particularly focusing on Book 1, so it was probably more a question of these prompting the OUP commission rather than being prompted by work on the commentary itself, but maybe at some stage the one turned into the other.[22]

Sadly, the OUP file for volume i has not turned up, and so it is unclear whether the idea for it came from the Press or from Gomme himself, but the Delegates' Minutes show that it was approved in May 1936.[23] The preface says that it was finished by 1939, and presumably he had done a fair amount of work, very likely with unofficial encouragement from the Press, before the formal approval. This can reasonably be assumed to have been his major project as soon as he had got *Population* out of the way. So this too fits into the pattern of OUP's thirties interest in commentaries. It was around then that they also commissioned the thirty-year-old Ronald Syme to take over a commentary on Tacitus' *Histories*, something originally assigned in 1931 to W.W. How and then transferred to Syme when How died in 1932; it was in 1932 too that the 'Euripides reds' series was originally envisaged.[24] It is noticeable how ready the Press was to entrust relatively junior scholars — early mid-career, we might say — with these big commissions, though it is true that Gomme was not that young by now (early forties); the same was true a decade later with Walbank, entrusted with Polybius in his early thirties, though already with two books under his belt. They could certainly pick talent, and scholars were duly given jobs that could turn out to last a lifetime — or indeed outlast the lifetime, as with Gomme and later with Bosworth.[25]

It is an easy guess that the Press got more than they bargained for, just as they would have done had Syme fulfilled his commission on the *Histories* rather

---

22 'Some notes on fifth-century history' (Gomme 1930) does have two disquisitions on the *pentekontaetia*, but these are explicitly prompted by the appearance of *CAH* vol. v in 1927: he gave that a lengthy and critical review (1928). One of the surviving volumes of notes (n. 13) is headed 'History 479–32' and clearly dates from the 1920s: it shows a thorough work-through of Busolt's *Griechische Geschichte*, complemented by Gomme's own reflections on the details. Some of the protohistory can be traced here of Gomme's extensive excursus on the *pentekontaetia*, 1945, 361–413; note his (qualified) praise there of Busolt, 392, echoing the tribute in the preface (v).
23 'On the proposal of Mr H.M. Last', Delegates' Order Book, 18 May 1936.
24 Register of Delegates, 11 November 1932 and 24 January 1933: Henderson 2007, 145–6.
25 Vol. iii of Bosworth's Arrian is in the hands of Elizabeth Baynham and Patrick Wheatley.

than getting sidetracked on to *The Roman Revolution*. It is not that massive commentaries were unknown, especially on historical or more particularly archaeological matters: Frazer's 6-volume Pausanias goes back to 1898, and e.g. Wyse's Isaeus of 1904 is not noted for being laconic.[26] Even within Thucydides commentaries, Arnold's in 1830 was advertised as containing 'notes chiefly historical and geographical' — though actually more geographical than historical, and anyway most notes were linguistic — and Jowett kicked off volume 2 of his translation (1881) with a 72-page essay 'on inscriptions of the age of Thucydides'.[27] But the closest analogies with historical texts may be those on Tacitus, not just Furneaux's *Annals* but the disproportionately long commentaries on the shorter texts *Agricola* and *Germania*, again heavily archaeological.[28] Still, length was unlikely to be popular with the OUP editors. Those *Oxford Red* commissions were insistent on cutting back on length in the interest of economy, and it is likely that the model they gave Gomme was How and Wells' *Herodotus*, just as it was in the job-description given to Walbank in 1943[29] and still given to Simon Hornblower (he tells me) in the mid-1980s as a guideline for his own commentary.

If so, we can immediately see what a difference of scale came when Gomme delivered. Vol. i weighed in at 4.31 pages per page of OCT text, and vols ii–iii as 2.83 (more or less the same as the Andrewes-Dover volumes [3.05], though Dover is more succinct than Andrewes). How and Wells average well under one page of commentary per page of text, and Underhill's 1900 commentary on Xenophon's *Hellenica* is not much fuller (309 pages on 266 pages of text). Walbank and Bosworth in fact come much closer to How and Wells, with an overall average of respectively 1.69 and 1.61 pages of commentary per what I calculate an OCT page would have looked like. It is noticeable too how consistent in scale Gomme is over the years from beginning to end, at least if we discount the 50-page excursus on the *pentekontaetia* in vol. i.

---

26 Nor is the Hunter/Handford edition of Aeneas Tacticus, as recently as 1927. Other big oratorical commentaries would include Sandys' edition of *Leptines* (1890) and of Cicero's *Orator* (1885), Clark's *Pro Milone* (1895), the Cope–Sandys three volume Aristotle's *Rhetoric* (1877), and Goodwin's *On the Crown* (1901) and *Meidias* (1906).
27 I owe these points to Christopher Mallan, who suggests that Arnold's geographical emphasis owed a lot to excitement at the advent of steamships to make travel around Thucydides' world so much easier.
28 On *Agricola* see Kraus 2016, noting the differences in emphasis between British editions, with their strong concentration on Roman Britain, and American ones, more interested in the politics and morals.
29 Henderson 2013, 48–50.

[These tables exclude introductions and appendices, but do include excursuses in mid-running commentary such as Gomme's on the *pentekontaetia*, Dover's on the Herms and Mysteries, and Andrewes on the sources for the 411 revolution.]

Tab. 4: Thucydides Commentaries.

	OCT pp.	HCT pp.	Hornblower CT pp.	Rhodes pp.	Rusten pp.
Book 1	88	379 = 4.31 pages per OCT page	230 = 2.61 pages per OCT page		
Book 2	73	251 = 3.43	144 = 1.97	92 = 1.26	152 = 2.08
Book 3	71	185 = 2.51	156 = 2.20	95 = 1.34	
Book 4–5.1–24	102	261 = 2.56	350 = 3.43	134 = 1.31	
Book 5.25–116	49	188 = 3.83 (Andrewes)	216 = 4.41		
Book 6	70	182 = 2.60 (Dover)	279 = 3.99		
Book 7	68	87 = 1.28 (Dover)	205 = 3.01		
Book 8	80	358 = 4.47 (Andrewes)	306 = 3.82		

Tab. 5: Speech and Narrative.

	Speech	Narrative
Gomme	217.5 pp. = 2.57 per OCT page*	888.5 pp. = 3.44 per OCT page
Dover	77.5 pp. = 1.94	191.5 pp. = 1.95
Andrewes (only Melian Dialogue)	34 pp. = 4.85	512 pp. = 4.19
Hornblower	340 pp. = 2.61	1546 pp. = 2.01
Rusten (Bk. 2 g-&-y)	56 pp. = 3.86	96 pp. = 1.64

*Gomme's comm. on funeral speech is unusually full; without that, it would be 2.28 per OCT page.

Tab. 6: Herodotus Commentaries.

	OCT (Wilson) pp.	How–Wells	Green-and-yellow
Book 1	124	102 = 0.82 per OCT page	
Book 2	109	101 = 0.92	
Book 3	98	57 = 0.58	
Book 4	103	67 = 0.65	
Book 5	78	58 = 0.74	(Hornblower) 219 = 2.80 per OCT p.
Book 6	72	66 = 0.91	(Hornblower-Pelling) 218 = 3.02
Book 7	134	110 = 0.82	
Book 8	74	52 = 0.70	(Bowie) 152 = 2.05
Book 9	68	41 = 0.60	(Flower-Marincola) 214 = 3.14

It is interesting too to see how Gomme in fact created a new norm, and in their various series and with various target audiences later commentaries on historical texts are often pretty close to his scale, even the green-and-yellows (often 3 or 4 pages of commentary to one OCT page, sometimes more), or bigger, especially the Cambridge oranges (anything up to 18 pages per OCT page). One further point to which I will return is the greater space Gomme allowed to narrative than to speeches, here contrasting with Dover (scales about the same for both) and particularly with Hornblower and Andrewes, who are distinctly longer on speeches.

This length issue may be one of the reasons for specifying 'historical' commentary, though it is paradoxical that apparently narrowing its scope should justify an extra length. It is not a matter of expertise: we might think of Gomme as an ancient historian, but he became a Professor of Greek and he often comments on linguistic matters with a very sure touch.[30] Comparison with passages in Euripides and Aristophanes is a favourite technique, and his last and posthumous

---

[30] Notice among many examples his succinct and correct point about τυγχάνειν, 1956, 488, discussing the element of chance in Thucydides' treatment of the Pylos campaign: 'τυγχάνειν does not necessarily mean that an event was accidental, but that it was contemporaneous'. Unsurprisingly with Thucydides' Greek, not all issues have been laid to rest: to take just one particularly contentious case, Gomme's understanding of ἀπὸ μέρους at 2.37.1 as 'by rotation' is followed by Hornblower, Rhodes, Rusten, Connor 2018 and in the translations of Lattimore and Hammond, but not by Pope 1988, 192, Harris 1992, Andrews 2004, 546–50, Winton 2004 and 2008, or in Mynott's translation.

book was to be on Menander.³¹ But we have already seen that the nearest classical examples, Frazer and Wyse and the Tacitus volumes, were heavily archaeological and historical; and there were also important models in biblical studies in the German tradition, notably Kalisch's four-volume *Historical and Critical Commentary on the Old Testament* (1875–82). Sir William Ramsay's 'historical commentary' on *Galatians* (1899) ran to 478 pages on 9 pages of text, with an apology on the last page for an accident that prevented him from writing more.³² In Gomme's case the 'historical' does give him more freedom to be much fuller on matters where the main evidence is epigraphic rather than the text itself; that is particularly relevant to Thucydides because of the American publication of the *Athenian Tribute Lists*,³³ on which he draws a good deal and with which he often takes issue — polite issue, more polite than in some of the confrontations in his *Essays* — and several times seem to win.³⁴

---

31 Completed by F.H. Sandbach and published fourteen years after Gomme's death (Gomme–Sandbach 1973).
32 Self-description of classical commentaries as 'historical' is rarer, though in their prefaces Braithwaite characterises his *Vespasian* (1927) in those terms and Butler and Cary say that their commentaries on *Prov. cons.* (1924) are 'in the main, historical' and *Diu. Iul.* (1927) 'almost entirely historical'; Denniston's *Philippics* (1926) has on the title page 'edited with Introduction, Notes (mainly historical) and Appendices'. As early as 1871 J.R. Seeley prefaced his edition of Livy 1 with a promise to give 'a historical as well as a philological commentary', and at that stage planned to continue with similar editions of Books 2–10. How and Wells say that 'our notes are almost entirely on the subject-matter'; perhaps the word 'historical' would have stuck in the throat given some of Herodotus' material. The first volume of the long-running *Sprachlicher und historischer Kommentar zu Ammianus Marcellinus* (de Jonge 1935), in later volumes written in English and retitled 'Philological and Historical Commentary', was in fact almost exclusively *sprachlich*: historical aspects are often just verbatim quotations from *R–E*. The balance in later volumes changed.
33 Meritt, Wade-Gery, and McGregor 1939–53. Gomme's vol. i was effectively finished by 1939 (preface), but he was clearly able to take into account and respond to *A.T.L.* vol. i (cf. esp. pp. 273–80); all four volumes of *A.T.L.* were published in time for Gomme's vols. ii and iii.
34 Especially on the tricky question of the text and interpretation of 2.13.3: the MS text that Gomme defends is retained by Hornblower and Rusten and in Alberti's text, and is supported by Kallet-Marx 1993a, 100–103 with additional arguments, though she differs from Gomme on the interpretation of ὡς ἐπὶ τὸ πολύ. Further examples are the nn. on 2.69 and 3.19, doubting the link of 'money-gathering ships' with reassessments of tribute, and on 4.52.2, sounding caution about the assumption that the '2000 Phocaean staters' correspond to the '8 talents' that they restored in the tribute lists: Kallet-Marx 1993a, 155–9 and 160–64 again reinforces these doubts with extra points, and in each case she is followed by Hornblower, 1991–2008, ii. 7 and 94–5. Gomme also makes some good points against the *A.T.L.* editors in his discussion of the 'reassessment' of 425 BCE, 1956, 500–505, though here Kallet-Marx goes much further, 1993a, 164–70; cf. Hornblower 1991–2008, ii. 93–9. Still, there are other occasions where Gomme was too uncritical of *A.T.L.*:

And 'historical' — as opposed to what? In the biblical cases, at least partly as opposed to homiletic: don't come here for ready-made sermons. In Gomme's case, as opposed to literary and linguistic:[35] this is not going to be the British counterpart to the great works of Krüger and Classen/Steup and Poppo/Stahl, all of them still immensely useful to a commentator on Thucydides. Here he is again striking out in a different direction from How and Wells, who are shameless in how much they take over from their German forebear Stein, and are not too dissimilar from Stein in focus and emphasis. One thing though that he shares with How and Wells and with Underhill's *Hellenica* is the absence of a text, and this is important too.[36] For one thing, it helps to explain the basic title 'Commentary on…': those works that included a text usually just carried the title of the ancient work itself followed by 'edited by', 'erklärt von', or simply 'by', often adding e.g. 'with introduction and notes' or 'with introductory essays and critical and explanatory notes'. But there is more to it than that. It clearly emerges from Henderson's work on the Euripides series and the *Oxford Reds* that the Press was concerned with a school as well as a university market, with an anxious eye to what was likely to be set in the next few years for Higher Certificate.[37] No text means not for schools, and that means the level can be raised higher and the coverage can be fuller, as well, probably, as meaning that there is less pressure to keep the price low. Gomme's target audience is not always easy to pin down, but it is clearly a scholarly one: they are expected to cope not just with untranslated Greek and Latin (nothing unusual there, as that is true of the red series as well, though most of those are more sparing in quoting French and German), but also to recognise a snippet from Plutarch's *Pericles* thrown in without a reference.[38] But sure as can be, it is not a sixth-former.[39] (I did in fact first read vol. i as a sixth-former,

---

Hornblower ii. 6–7. McGregor responds in detail to the disagreements with *A.T.L.* in his reviews (1946 and 1959), but Wade-Gery chose to dwell on other things in his review of vol. i (1949).

35 Similarly Hornblower 1991–2008, ii. 4.
36 On the importance of this for How and Wells cf. Davies 2016, 235–6.
37 Henderson 2006, esp. 44–9, 83, and 156–8; 2007, 149, 150–1, 166.
38 Gomme 1956) 47, quoting Plut. *Per.* 12.6: the previous page had given a hint that this was where the passage came from, but many must have been bemused. Gomme 1937, 249 similarly quotes Plut. *Per.* 13.5 without a reference, and that is in an essay on Menander rather than the fifth century.
39 The OUP file on vols. ii and iii shows that there was by then some thought of producing an abbreviated school edition. Gomme did not find the prospect appealing; by then he was working on vol. iv and on Menander. T.B.L. Webster had similarly raised the possibility of a translation and abbreviated commentary to make it accessible to 'the intelligent layman' (review of vols. ii–iii, *Manchester Guardian* 10 August 1956).

but that was by mistake: it happened to be in the local library. But even then I had a dim awareness that it was not meant for the likes of me.)

So — a Thucydides commentary, but not as we know it: not what we know from Classen/Steup or Poppo/Stahl and not what we would expect from the model of How and Wells. An even greater novelty, one that surely took the Press as well by surprise, is immediately clear from the Contents page to vol. i.

CONTENTS

LIST OF MAPS	viii
BIBLIOGRAPHY OF SHORT TITLES	ix
INTRODUCTION	1
I. WHAT THUCYDIDES TAKES FOR GRANTED	1
A. His Predecessors	1
Note on Chronology	2
B. General Economic Conditions	9
C. Conditions of Warfare	10
D. Constitutional Practice	24
II. THUCYDIDES' SELF-IMPOSED LIMITATIONS	25
His Silence on his own Sources	28
III. SOURCES OTHER THAN THUCYDIDES	29
A. Contemporary Historians	29
B. Official Documents	30
C. Unofficial Documents	35
D. Later Writers	39
i. The Researchers	41
ii. The Others	44
IV. PRINCIPLES OF HISTORICAL CRITICISM	84
COMMENTARY	89
ADDENDA	468
INDEXES	469
1. General	469
2. Authors, and passages discussed	475
3. Greek	479

Fig. 6: Gomme's Commentary, vol. 1 (1945), Table of Contents (reproduced by permission of the Secretary to the Delegates of Oxford University Press).

The content of that introduction is breathtaking for what it includes, and even more for what it does not. Much of it is marvellous stuff. The section on 'sources other than Thucydides' includes 30 pages on Plutarch (pp. 54–84) which was quite easily the best thing written on him, especially his historical methods, when I began research on Plutarch in 1970, and in my own publications I have often bounced points off particular arguments and insights there.[40] But where is the equivalent section on Thucydides himself? There is a lot on what Thucydides doesn't say — what he takes for granted, what he deliberately omits — but what about what he *does* say? Where are the equivalent topics to the 64 pages of Classen/Steup's introduction — Thucydides' life, his attitude to religion, his sharp analysis of human conduct, his division by summers and winters, his treatment of personalities, his style?[41] Never mind 'what Thucydides takes for granted': is all this what Gomme takes for granted too? And why? We saw earlier that he assumes a knowing reader, knowing enough to recognise a Plutarch passage by sight: is the reader so knowing that he or she is assumed to know all this already?

No, I don't think so. A better clue is given by the first paragraph of the Introduction itself:

---

40 E.g. Pelling 1986, 175; 1990, 26; and 1992, 26 = Pelling 2002, 218, 146, and 130. Gomme also has many insights into Plutarch's technique in the body of the commentary, e.g. the brief and confident footnote on Plut. *Per.* 20.4 ('the content may come from Theopompos ... but the style is Plutarch's own: the outlook is too steady, the rhetoric too controlled for the former', 1945, 171, or 1956, 492 on Plut. *Nic.* 6.4–7; more extensively 1945, 284–8 (on Cimon), 378–80 (chronology of the *pentekontaetia*); 1956, 185–9 (attacks on Pericles' friends).
41 'Nowhere does he ask what is Thucydides' own approach, what were his own aims and characteristic techniques, and what limitation these impose on him as a source for the Peloponnesian War', Ellis 1979, 40.

INTRODUCTION

A HISTORICAL commentary on a historian must necessarily derive from two sources, a proper understanding of his own words, and what we can learn from other authorities. The first needs no comment; the second needs a long one, and it is the purpose of this introduction to supply it. As we are dealing with Thucydides, not anyone else, our other authorities serve rather to supplement than to correct him; our first need therefore is to see what gaps there are in his narrative, our second to examine the means of filling these gaps. My introduction is therefore divisible into two parts, *What Thucydides does not tell us* and *An examination of other sources of information*. The former includes both what he deliberately omitted, in accordance with his self-imposed limitations, and what he takes for granted—for example, the work of his predecessors in historiography, normal economic conditions, and normal conditions of land- and sea-warfare. It will readily be seen that this first part of the introduction should be, like most introductions to editions of classical authors, an appendix; for it implies that the author has already been studied. But here this is unavoidable; for the second part, the examination of other sources, depends for its relevance on the first, and throughout the commentary an acquaintance with this second part is assumed.

Fig. 7: Gomme's Commentary, vol. 1 (1945), p. 1 (reproduced by permission of the Secretary to the Delegates of Oxford University Press).

Notice especially that sentence towards the end:

> It will readily be seen that this first part of the introduction [i.e. that dealing what 'What Thucydides does not tell us'] should be, like most introductions to editions of classical authors, an appendix: for it implies that the author has already been studied.

That idea — this would be better coming at the end — repays some thought. It is a familiar point about *writing* a commentary, or anything else: far more often than not, the introduction is what one writes last. But is that true of *reading* it too, in this case reading the material on what Thucydides misses out? The picture would be of building up one's reconstruction of the history first by a painstaking reading of the text, cautiously supplementing or qualifying it from other sources — that is why the material on those other sources does need to come in an introduction — and then filling in the extra bits that Thucydides did not mention. And Gomme was clearly taking the same view of all that other material — life, access to material, world-view etc — that most commentators before and after Gomme have put in their introduction (for this is an area where his successors have not followed him: Walbank's and Bosworth's introductions take much more traditional lines). Gomme is leaving it all to the appendices that he several times promises for the end of what he envisages as vol. iii, and were in fact included, at considerable length, by Andrewes and Dover at the end of the eventual vol. v.[42] That too allowed him scope to revise or deepen his opinions as he continued to engage with the text.[43]

Still, this also reflects a deeper habit of thought, or rather several habits. One is the way he is envisaging that first painstaking reading-through of the text. Of course Gomme does not regard Thucydides as an easy, straightforward author; that is clear from his Sather lectures of 1954, where he finally does give us some of the material that might have figured in those appendices, and is anyway clear enough from the commentary itself. It is still the case that he may see him as easier to come to terms with than we would, and than some of his predecessors would have done — particularly Cornford, whose *Thucydides Mythistoricus* he treats with respect but also with a certain distancing. That ideal procedure of first garnering material from Thucydides and then filling in the gaps might work reasonably well with facts, at least with this author: you accept what Thucydides tells you unless you have good reason not to, then you add some more facts, cautiously, from elsewhere — the missing parts of the jigsaw puzzle. It works much less well with interpretations, not merely the 'what' of history but the 'why'. If as we read we consider, say, whether Thucydides has played down religious considerations when discussing the Herms and Mysteries, the reader might find it very useful already to have an overview along the lines of Classen/Steup's five-page

---

[42] The absence of such material from vols. i–iii prompted the complaint of Ehrenberg 1958, 254: 'Above all, however, we must ask this outstanding expert on Thucydides for a portrait of his mind. We wish to hear of his position in the intellectual development of Greece and of the influences which shaped him. Again we are hoping for the final volume or — still better — for a comprehensive book by G. on Thucydides.' That is over-grumpy, for Gomme's Sather lectures of 1954 had already offered much along those lines, and a fair amount of general material is already there in the body of the commentary (e.g. 1945, 90–91 on Thucydides' thinking about war and about the Athenian empire).

[43] As John Henderson points out to me. He also wonders how far Gomme was taking into account the Oxford tutorial system, given OUP's wary eye to that undergraduate market. Perhaps those broader 'essayistic' topics were to be left for Greats lecturers and tutors to address, and the role of the commentary was to guide students through the nittygritty of the reading.

section on this topic;[44] if we wonder why there is so little on the Megarian Decrees or on the attacks on Pericles' friends, we might well want to ponder Thucydides' combative reticence elsewhere when alternative interpretations or emphases were in the air. What the introduction does not do is help the reader to weigh a particular case against Thucydides' general habits, to *interpretari Thucydidem e Thucydide*.

That preoccupation with facts is there too in that final section of the Introduction on the 'principles of historical criticism'. It is all about what reports one ought to accept and the dangers of taking later and less authoritative sources as correcting or supplementing Thucydides — all very positivist. But he does not take into account the possibility that a later source like, say, Plutarch might supplement Thucydides not on facts but on interpretation, that either from his reading or from the continuous aspects of Greek life Plutarch might have a feeling for fifth-century religion from which we can learn.[45] It is this positivism that Gomme feeds into his preoccupation, very much a feature of his times, with being a 'scientific historian', though he is laudably also insistent on the fact that a historian is or ought to be an artist as well. But his science is about reconstructing *was eigentlich gewesen ist*, the *was* rather than Ranke's *wie*. That positivism feeds over into his general comments on the speeches as well, where his focus is often first on questions of historicity, whether Pericles or Cleon or Hermocrates could really have made those points at the time, what information Thucydides could have had for the speech and when he could have composed it,[46] with rather less on the rhetoric and structure, why it is all put like this.[47] He will often quote parallels

---

[44] Classen–Steup 1900–22, i. xlii–xlvi (not that the views expressed by Classen–Steup are beyond criticism).

[45] Or so I have argued: Pelling 1992, 24 and 31 with n. 58 = 2002, 128 and 134 with n. 63. Hornblower 1991–2008, 10–13 rightly isolates religion as one of Gomme's weak areas. This may be partly a matter of Gomme's never having a chance to expand on religion before getting to those appendices that he never wrote; still, had he chosen he could have constructed that chance, just as he makes himself an opportunity to talk about the attacks on Pericles' friends even though Thucydides ignores them, 1956, 184–9.

[46] See for instance the remarks on Hermocrates' speech at 4.59–64, 1956, 520–2. Notice too his comment on the Mytilenean debate, 1956, 324, noting the absence of any feeling of pity and remorse from Diodotus' argument. That does indeed require an explanation (for various approaches cf. Winnington-Ingram 1965, 77–8, Hornblower 1991–2008, i. 419 and 421, and Pelling 2000, 122), but Gomme concludes only that Thucydides must have composed it some time later than the events.

[47] The Corcyrean debate (1.31–44) is a good example. In the *Essays* (1937, 184) he suggests that there were 'things to be said' about a comparison with Hdt. 8.104 [presumably a misprint for

from Plato and Demosthenes for ideas, but rarely for argumentative strategies or moves. That makes it less surprising that he finds rather less to say about them than his successors do, and that his scale drops when the speeches come along.

This preference for leaving things to the end comes into the commentary too. Later commentators, and indeed earlier ones, usually include some overall comments before a section or, particularly, a speech: Gomme prefers to leave them to the end. A rule of thumb given to green-and-yellow commentators is always to put down first what *you* think, and (if you must) defend that view or state alternatives later.[48] Gomme usually does the opposite, stating the problem first, often summarising what others have said, then developing the discussion so that the answer plops out at the end, sometimes a surprising one.[49] That habit of starting from what others have said prompted one early reviewer to talk of his 'somewhat Housmanesque *odium philologicum*':[50] that phrase would more fairly be applied to the swashbuckling style of his *Essays* (1937 and 1962)[51] than to the commentary, where he tones things down a good deal, but it is true that a lot is delivered 'from the Opposition benches' — Wade-Gery's phrase in another review.[52] In some cases the argument is so intricate that it is easy to lose track of where it is all heading, and several reviewers commented on the difficulty from time to time of knowing what Gomme's own interpretation was.[53] Sometimes indeed he only makes that

---

140]–144, but the commentary does not say them. Perhaps, in fact, the more illuminating comparison would be with the Gelon sequence at Hdt. 7.153–62. But the point should not be overstated: he does for instance allow some space to Thucydides' purposes in including the Mytilenean and Plataean debates (1956, 315, 354–5).

48 For the guidelines to green-and-yellow editors see Gibson in this volume, p. 186.

49 The important note on 1.77.1 is a good example, 1945, 236–44. 'Two possible ways of translating this' are initially aired, with the 'second rendering' signalled as the easier (237); but the long discussion leads him to conclude (243) that 'this second alternative' — which was in fact originally the first, rejected alternative — 'seems after all to be right'.

50 MacKendrick 1946, 498. Similarly in the anonymous *Times Literary Supplement* review of vol. ii, 18 January 1957, looking back to vol. i: 'Professor Gomme ... let himself be frequently sidetracked by scholarly controversy, with all its attendant *odium philologicum*'.

51 Andrewes' obituary (1959) comments that many of those essays 'began in indignation', but adds that this 'pugnacious' style contrasted with his manner in private talk and correspondence; 'N. V. D.' (Nan Dunbar) added a further note to this effect ten days later 'on behalf of a great many of his younger colleagues and friends in Glasgow'. She was by then a lecturer at St Andrews, but would have been taught by Gomme as an undergraduate. 'He was not a contentious man, though he would ruefully admit that he sometimes made that impression' (Kitto 1959, 337).

52 Wade-Gery 1949, 84.

53 Wade-Gery 1949, 85 on vol. i, and cf. e.g. MacKendrick 1946, 498, describing one note as 'tantalizingly inconclusive'; McGregor 1959, 68 on vols. ii and iii, 'at times, because he himself sees so clearly, [he is] obscure to the reader'.

clear in passing,[54] and sometimes he does not say at all.[55] It can easily look as if he is more interested in the debate than the answer.

That contrast with the green-and-yellow, 'say what you think first', approach is interesting. We tend to think of it as the modern or postmodern way to 'empower the reader', and we get bothered by the notion of an authoritarian commentator imposing a viewpoint;[56] but which in fact is the less bossy way? In many ways it is Gomme's manner which is the more pedagogic, leading the student gently in what the writer hopes will be the right direction, and enjoying the journey as much as the destination.

There is so much here that one could talk about. Simon Hornblower has masterfully discussed Gomme's strengths and weaknesses,[57] and I will not go over the same ground here except to emphasise how well-written it is, with such a strong sense of the author's personality as he allows himself to be more exuberant than most commentators:[58]

---

54 E.g. in another bumper note on an important topic, the notorious difficulty of δεκάτῳ ἔτει at 1.103.1, where discussion comes not in 103.1 n. itself but in the excursus on the *pentakontaetia* (1945, 401–8). Gomme's own solution — emend, but it is uncertain what to, with ἕκτῳ as likely as τετάρτῳ, and the period of the helot war was 465/4 or 464/3 to 461, 460, or 459 — is buried away in mid-note at p. 404; this solution is then itself later revised (pp. 410–11) to 465/4–460/59, and πέμπτῳ is thrown into the ring as well.
55 As in the discussion of ἐπιμαθών at 1.138.3: he does not say what it might mean, only what it cannot, 1945, 442. Similarly at 2.40.1 'it is difficult to be happy' about the famous phrase φιλοκαλοῦμεν ... μετ' εὐτελείας, but he does not suggest what he would read instead, nor make it clear whether he is proposing emendation or simply convicting 'Pericles' of misstatement.
56 For such anxiety cf. esp. Goldhill 2000; Kraus 2002, 6 ('How much damage — or influence — do notes, whether in their form or their content, have on the reader's perception of the commented text?'), 9 ('issues of power and authority'); on the possibility that an accumulation of alternative views may liberate rather than constrict cf. Kraus 2002, 22 and 24 ('interactive riches for the creative reader'), Gibson 2002, and Fowler 2000, esp. 436–7, observing for instance that the rigorous selectivity of Dover's *Clouds* (1968) makes it 'a much less interesting and useful commentary than the ragbag of craziness which is W.J.M. Starkie's edition' (1911).
57 Hornblower 1991–2008, ii. 1–19, isolating as strengths (i) his excellent judgement on linguistic points (I agree with Hornblower's reservation that he is over-fond of radical emendation), (ii) his topographical coverage of Greece itself, though he is less strong on Sicily and Asia Minor, and (iii) his financial and other technical coverage; the areas open to improvement are (i) his failure to translate lemmata, (ii) the inevitable out-of-dateness of some of his material by the 1990s, (iii) his coverage of religion, and (iv) his treatment of literary and narratological topics.
58 Cf. Davies 2011, 338: 'to move from Gomme on Thucydides to Walbank on Polybios, as I did as an undergraduate in the late 1950s, was to move from the discursive to the distilled — from Telemann to Brahms.'

> Gorgias is rich and flowing; the river of Thucydides' eloquence is equally abundant, but is obstructed by rocks, and curious eddies are formed. Unlike the other he had something to say. (1956, 131, on 2.42.1)
>
> What dangerous things words are! (1956, 193 on 2.65.9)
>
> Most of this argument has been a waste of time. (1945, 401, discussing some dates in Diodorus)

Admittedly, it is not his own argument to which he is there referring, but still a modern series editor would scrawl 'In that case, OMIT!' Other things too are memorably put, for instance his imagining of what someone may have told Thucydides of the Plataean speech in 427:

> Only the usual things — the Persian wars, the gods and the oaths, the special sanctity of Plataia, the honour of Sparta; but it was very honestly done. (1956, 346)

Nor does he mince his words even at the expense of the revered Pericles (or is it the revered Thucydides himself?): when the advice to war-widows is to be 'as little talked about as possible among men', this is

> not only brief and priggish but advice, not consolation, and advice that is most of it not called for by the occasion. (1956, 143 on 2.45.1)[59]

Two pages towards the end of vol. i capture many characteristic features. This rounds off the long 'excursus', as he is prepared to call it, on Pausanias and Themistocles.

---

[59] But it is possible to see the advice as less priggish and more appropriate than Gomme allows: Kallet-Marx 1993b.

I. 138. 6   COMMENTARY

There is a valuable note in Plutarch, *Them.* 32. 5–6: Διόδωρος δ' ὁ περιηγητὴς ἐν τοῖς περὶ Μνημάτων (fr. 1) εἴρηκεν ὡς ὑπονοῶν μᾶλλον ἢ γιγνώσκων ὅτι περὶ τὸν μέγαν λιμένα τοῦ Πειραιῶς ἀπὸ τοῦ κατὰ τὸν Ἄλκιμον ἀκρωτηρίου πρόκειταί τις οἷον ἀγκών, καὶ κάμψαντι τοῦτον ἐντός, ᾗ τὸ ὑπεύδιον τῆς θαλάττης, κρηπίς ἐστιν εὐμεγέθης, καὶ τὸ ἐπ' αὐτῇ βωμοειδὲς τάφος τοῦ Θεμιστοκλέους. οἴεται δὲ καὶ Πλάτωνα τὸν κωμικὸν (fr. 183) αὐτῷ μαρτυρεῖν ἐν τούτοις·

ὁ σὸς δὲ τύμβος ἐν καλῷ κεχωσμένος
τοῖς ἐμπόροις πρόσρησις ἔσται πανταχοῦ,
τούς τ' ἐκπλέοντας εἰσπλέοντάς τ' ὄψεται,
χὠπόταν ἅμιλλ' ᾖ τῶν νεῶν θεάσεται.

A graceful tribute to the great sailor. Cf. Paus. i. 1. 2; Arist. *H.A.* vi. 15, 569 b 12. Lenschau, *R.E.* xix. 92–3, thinks this tomb may have been set up by Konon in 395–4, as it was unknown to Thucydides; but it may be only later than Thucydides' exile. For its position, see Judeich, 442–3, who adds, "natürlich handelt es sich um eine Legende". Assuming that there is no doubt that Platon was speaking of Themistokles, ὁ σὸς τύμβος is not likely to have been legendary. Diodoros' doubts were like ours—about its identification.[1]

Plutarch adds that descendants of Themistokles continued to his own day enjoying certain privileges and emoluments from Magnesia, and that one of them was a fellow-student with him in Athens. As he says he was Θεμιστοκλῆς Ἀθηναῖος, he was a citizen and presumably inhabitant of Athens.

τὰ μὲν κατὰ Π., κ.τ.λ.: 'Such was the end of Pausanias of Sparta and Themistokles of Athens, the two most eminent men of their day.' λαμπρός means one who stands out among his fellow men, clear for all to see. So λαμπρῶς νικᾶν, to win a decisive victory (cf. 49. 7).

"If Thucydides had always written as he has done in ch. 126–38, no one would ever have called him 'harsh' or 'obscure' or even 'concise'. 'Some, admiring the perspicuity of the narrative about Cylon, have said "here the lion smiled" (λέων ἐγέλασεν ἐνταῦθα)', remarks a scholium on 126–7. The grace and sympathy with which the stories of Cylon, Pausanias, and Themistokles are told, and the manner in which Thucydides strings them on the thread of the negotiations between Athens and Sparta, passing easily from one episode to another without regard to the order of time, remind us of Herodotus"—Forbes (p. 96). The whole excursus on Themistokles is irrelevant to the narrative, and so is the greater part of those on

---

[1] It is possible that Hermippos, fr. 72 (from his Τετράμετρα, not from a play), refers to this place: Θεμιστοκλέους τὸν πρωνός τις ὢν κεβλήπυρις τις ὀνομάζεται. No satisfactory restoration of this has been suggested; but πρωνός itself may be right: what was later called his tomb was at first Θεμιστόκλειος πρών?

COMMENTARY   I. 139. 1

Kylon and Pausanias. Thucydides, besides being impelled, probably, to narrate episodes which he thought had been inadequately or inaccurately dealt with by others—as in the case of the overthrow of the tyrants at Athens—betrays a strong biographical interest, that interest which he so sternly represses, to our great loss and to the detriment of a fuller understanding of the events, in his main narrative.

139. *Further Spartan embassies to Athens*: Plut. *Per.* 29. 7–30 (see 126. 1–2 n.).

1. ἐπὶ μὲν τῆς πρώτης πρεσβείας: 126. 2. It is remarkable that a special embassy should have been sent with this idle demand, however superstitious the Spartans may have been (cf. v. 16. 1 *ad fin.*); the Corinthians must have been made impatient by it. If they wanted simply to weaken the position of Perikles (127. 2), one would have expected the mention of the ἄγος to have been part of more serious negotiations.

ἐπέταξαν: a strong word—'ordered'. See below, 140. 2 n.

φοιτῶντες: more than one ambassadorial journey was made (cf. § 3, *init.*).

Ποτειδαίας τε ἀπανίστασθαι: a proposal not in the least likely to be accepted, as the Spartans must have known.

Αἴγιναν αὐτόνομον ἀφιέναι: a vague, and probably purposely vague demand. Aigina had secretly complained at Sparta that she was not left her autonomy as promised, 67. 2 (see n. there); we do not know of any specific infractions by Athens, but any exercise of pressure could be interpreted as an infraction, including, perhaps, as has been suggested, the order not to allow Megarian wares in the Aeginetan market.

μάλιστά γε πάντων καὶ ἐνδηλότατα προύλεγον τὸ περὶ Μεγαρέων ψήφισμα καθελοῦσι μὴ ἂν γίγνεσθαι πόλεμον: 67. 4. Note the assertive μή for οὐ, as after ὀμόσαι, &c. (Goodwin, *Moods and Tenses*, § 685). In popular opinion, but not in that of Thucydides, this decree was the chief cause of the war: Ar. *Ach.* 515–39; *Pac.* 609. Ephoros, F. 196 (Diod. xii. 38. 1–41. 1), copied popular opinion, and the embroideries of Aristophanes as well, and later writers followed him: Plut. *Per.* 29–31 (see Introd., pp. 69–70).

It is possible that there had been an earlier decree excluding Megarian goods from the Athenian market only, as seems to be implied by *Ach.* 515–22 (so Busolt and others); but, apart from the question of what weight is to be given to a comic narrative, there is a difficulty, for Aristophanes expressly says that the denunciation of Megarian goods (supposed to be a consequence of the decree) was not done by order of the state. If Aristophanes is referring to historical incidents, we may suppose that an earlier

447

Fig. 8: Gomme's Commentary, vol. 1 (1945), Commentary on 1.138.6–139.1 (reproduced by permission of the Secretary to the Delegates of Oxford University Press).

Notice:
- The long and (of course) untranslated passage from Plutarch (top left) on Themistocles' tomb on the sea-shore, 'hailed by merchant sailors and gazing on those who sail in and sail out and watching whenever there is a regatta' — 'a graceful tribute to the great sailor', a lovely turn of phrase that has always lingered in my own memory. One might quibblingly ask whether Themistocles was really so distinctively a sailor: after all, he commanded on land as well, as a *stratēgos* would (Hdt. 7.173.2, Plut. *Them.* 7.2). But that would indeed be curmudgeonly, and Salamis was his great day.
- Then there is the summing up of the Pausanias and Themistocles excursus, typically starting with a long quotation from someone else. The distinctive style of the excursus is mentioned, and it may indeed 'remind us of Herodotus': Gomme has made specific points along those lines in the detailed notes as well. But it is left to us to wonder why this should be. Is it just the 'strong biographical interest' that he goes on to note, with the content imposing a particular manner that Herodotus shared? Is it that these characters are themselves major players in Herodotus, just as there are dangers of waxing Shakespearian when writing about Coriolanus or Cleopatra? Is it the feeling that it was all then a different, simpler world (in which case it would be reasonable to ask whether the beginning of the *pentekontaetia*, with Themistocles tricking Sparta on the building of Athens' walls, is told in the same style)? And how does it tie into the strategy of Book 1? These days we might speculate that the similarities between Themistocles' and Pausanias' stories might qualify the strong differentiation between Athens and Sparta introduced in the Corinthians' speech at 1.69–70; we might wonder too if the difficulties that states find in accommodating their great men might have a particular point right now, just before the first great moment of Pericles. But points along these lines are left for Hornblower to make.[60]
- The narrative resumes, with the Spartans' demand for 'the expulsion of the accursed': for Gomme a bemusingly 'idle demand, however superstitious the Spartans may have been'. Gomme is often at his weakest when religion is in point — Hornblower is right to identify this as a blind spot[61] — and this is not a good note. If he is going to talk about Spartan 'superstition' (there were better words to use) a closer parallel would be 7.18, where Thucydides talks in retrospect about the Spartan bad conscience about their behaviour at the

---

60 Hornblower 1991–2008, i. 211–12.
61 Hornblower 1991–2008, ii. 10–13: above, n. 45.

beginning of the war, and their speculation that this was why things had gone against them in the fighting that followed.

– And then we move towards the Megarian decree — not a topic to pursue here. The linguistic point, though, is interesting: 'Note the assertive μή for οὐ', with a quotation from Goodwin. Gomme knows his Greek, as I said earlier: that detail would have passed many readers and scholars by, though doubtless fewer in 1945 than in 2018. But he is not making things easy for anyone less knowledgeable than himself. 'Assertive'? We might take that to mean 'emphatic', but that is not what Goodwin means; he does not use the word, and simply says that the μή is used in contexts of swearing (cf. Gomme's 'as after ὀμόσαι etc') and hoping, presumably because it carries over into *oratio obliqua* the μή that would be used in a directly expressed oath or hope — μὴ γένοιτο.

What, finally, of the subsequent fate of the 'historical commentary'? The title was taken over by Walbank and Bosworth, the great successors, and by several others,[62] but it has gradually fallen out of fashion.[63] Ogilvie was probably responding to the Gomme and Walbank model in 1965 in writing just 'A Commentary on Livy':

> Inevitably no two readers will ask the same questions, and in consequence I have had to be content with discussing those points which interested me as a reader. I have not, therefore, written it specifically for the needs of the schoolboy or the undergraduate or the scholar but rather for the use of anyone who wants to read Livy.
>
> Ogilvie 1965, vii

Subsequently Briscoe, Oakley and Hornblower similarly called their works just 'Commentaries'. Cambridge green-and-yellows and oranges are not distinctively 'historical', given the nature of their series; the Clarendon Ancient History Series naturally focuses more on historical matters — it is a very different business writing for that than for a green-and-yellow, as I know from experience — but still the series programme is defined as 'to provide authoritative translations, introductions, and commentaries to a wide range of Greek and Latin texts studied by ancient historians'. So the 'history' label is transferred from the subject-matter to the audience.

---

[62] Cf. Ash 2002, 270 and 272 n. 8.
[63] As Ash 2002, 273–4 points out, it is telling that in his first two *Annals* commentaries (1963) Koestermann began by separating material into the 'factual' at the top of each page and the 'linguistic' at the bottom, but then in his third volume (1967) abandoned the experiment.

One reason for the demise of the 'historical commentary' is pinpointed by John Davies: the ancient historian's plight is such that she or he has to squeeze the orange as hard as possible, and approach the evidence from every angle.[64] That includes finding out as much about a writer's habits and mindset as one can. That is fair enough, and chimes with that shift of focus in the Clarendon Series mission statement: the 'study of ancient history' requires not just a 'historical' commentary. But there is a mirroring point to be made from the 'literary' side. If we try to analyse an author's technique, we are asking what that author does with the material, and that means doing our best to work out what the material was that he will have known. That is particularly true of an author like Thucydides, with a reasonable default assumption that even in exile he knew most of what had been going on, or at least what was important. It is a fascinating 'literary' question why Thucydides should have omitted an Athenian alliance with Egesta only two or three years before the Sicilian expedition — but first we have to ask whether there *was* such an alliance and, if so, how much difference it made, and that means getting down there with the historians and epigraphists. And of course literature is itself central to the history of ideas, part of history too. History and literature: whichever is the horse and whichever the carriage, you can't have one without the other, even if some people are more interested in horses and some in carriages.[65] And I am pretty sure that Gomme, whatever he chose to call his book, knew that as well as anyone.[66]

---

[64] Davies 2016, 240–1.
[65] Cf. Moles 1993, 90, quoted by Ash 2002, 269 and 290: Moles' analogy (or rather denial of an analogy) is with icing and cake.
[66] My thanks to Oxford University Press for permission to quote from the commentary and to Karen Raith for providing clean copies of the relevant pages; to Martin Maw, Charlotte Loveridge, and Céline Louasli for tracking down and granting access to OUP files and Delegates' Minutes, and to John Henderson for discussion in the light of his own researches; to the librarians of Balliol College for allowing me to consult Cyril Bailey's unpublished memoir; to Ronald Knox for unearthing some correspondence of Gomme and for sharing Glasgow oral tradition; to Isabel Ruffell for allowing me to see Gomme's notebooks; to Simon Hornblower, Lisa Kallet, and Chris Mallan for Thucydidean points, to Tim Rood for guidance on nineteenth century commentaries, and to Guy Westwood for discussion of monumental commentaries on orators; and particularly to Susan Gomme and Hester Higton for illuminating the family background and especially for sharing the informal memoir begun by Andor Gomme. My general gratitude to Chris Stray for learned conversation is complemented by a debt for particular gleanings from his work on other classical titans.

Bibliography

Alberti, G.B. (1972–2000), *Thucydidis Historiae*, Rome.
Anderson, J.G.C. (1938), *Corneli Taciti: de origine et situ Germanorum*, Oxford.
Andrewes, A. (1959), obituary of Arnold Wycombe Gomme, *The Times*, January 20 1959.
Andrews, J.A. (2004), 'Pericles on the Athenian constitution', *AJPh* 125, 539–561.
Arnold, T.K. (1830), *Thucydides: History of the Peloponnesian War*, Cambridge.
Ash, R. (2002), 'Between Scylla and Charybdis? Historiographical commentaries on Latin Historians', in: Gibson/Kraus 2002, 269–294.
Austin, R.G. (1933), *M. Tulli Ciceronis Pro M. Caelio oratio*, Oxford.
Bailey, C. (1928), *The Greek Atomists and Epicurus: a Study*, Oxford.
Bailey, C. (1932), *Phases in the Religion of Ancient Rome*, London.
Bailey, C. (1935), *Religion in Virgil*, Oxford.
Bailey, C. (1947), *T. Lucreti Cari de Rerum Natura libri sex*, Oxford.
Bailey, C. (c. 1953), *Autobiography*: unpublished, Balliol College library, 81e 10/8.
Bosworth, A.B. (1980–95), *A Historical Commentary on Arrian's History of Alexander i–ii*, Oxford.
Bowie, A.M. (2007), *Herodotus Book VIII*, Cambridge.
Braithwaite, A.W. (1927), *C. Suetoni Tranquilli Diuus Vespasianus*, Oxford.
Briscoe, J. (1973–2012), *A Commentary on Livy* [Books 31–45], Oxford.
Busolt, G. (1893–1904), *Griechische Geschichte bis zur Schlacht bei Chaironeia*, 2nd ed., Gotha.
Butler, H.E./Barber, E.A. (1933), *The Elegies of Propertius*, Oxford.
Butler, H.E./Cary, M. (1924), *M. Tulli Ciceronis de Provinciis Consularibus oratio ad senatum*, Oxford.
Butler, H.E./Cary, M. (1927), *C. Suetoni Tranquilli Diuus Iulius*, Oxford.
Clark, A.C. (1895), *M. Tulli Ciceronis Pro T. Annio Milone ad iudices oratio*, Oxford.
Classen, J./Steup, J. (1900–22), *Thukydides*, 3rd to 5th editions, Berlin.
Connor, W.R. (2018), 'Pericles on democracy: Thucydides 2.37.1', *CW* 111, 165–75.
Cope, E.M./Sandys, J.E. (1877), *The Rhetoric of Aristotle*, Cambridge.
Cornford, F.M. (1907), *Thucydides Mythistoricus*, London.
Davies, G.A. (1907), *Demosthenes: Philippics i, ii, iii*, Cambridge.
Davies, J.K. (2011), 'Frank William Walbank (1909–2008)', *PBA* 172, 325–351.
Davies, J.K. (2016), 'The historical commentary', in: Kraus/Stray 2016, 233–249.
de Jonge, P. (1935), *Sprachlicher und historischer Kommentar zu Ammianus Marcellinus XIV.1–7*, Groningen.
Denniston, J.D. (1926), *M. Tulli Ciceronis Orationes Philippicae I, II*, Oxford.
Denniston, J.D. (1939). *Euripides: Electra*, Oxford.
Dodds, E.R. (1933), *Proclus: the Elements of Theology*, Oxford.
Dodds, E.R. (1977), *Missing Persons: an Autobiography*, Oxford.
Dover, K.J. (1968), *Aristophanes: Clouds*, Oxford.
Dover, K.J. (1994), *Marginal Comment*, London.
Dunbar, N.V. (1959) (as 'N. V. D.'), supplementary obituary of Arnold Wycombe Gomme, *The Times*, January 30 1959.
Ehrenberg, V. (1958), review of Gomme (1956), *Hist.* 7, 251–254.
Ellis, J.R. (1979), 'Characters in the Sicilian expedition', *QS* 10, 39–69.

Flower, M.A./Marincola, J. (2004), *Herodotus Book IX*, Cambridge.
Fordyce, C.J. (1961), *Catullus*, Oxford.
Fowler, D.P. (2000), 'Criticism as commentary and commentary as criticism in the age of electronic media', in: Most 2000, 426–442.
Frazer, J.G. (1898), *Pausanias' Description of Greece* i–vi, London.
Furneaux, H. (1884–91), *The Annals of Tacitus* i–ii, Oxford.
Furneaux, H. (1894), *Cornelii Taciti de Germania*, Oxford.
Furneaux, H./Anderson, J.G.C. (n.d. [1922]), *Cornelii Taciti de vita Agricolae*, Oxford,
Gibson, R.K. (2002): '"Cf. e.g.": a typology of 'parallels' and the function of commentaries on Latin poetry', in: Gibson/Kraus 2002, 331–357.
Gibson, R.K./Kraus, C.S. (eds.) (2002), *The Classical Commentary: Histories, Practices, Theory*, Leiden/Boston/Köln.
Goldhill, S. (2000), 'Wipe your glosses', in: Most 2000, 380–425.
Gomme, A.W. (1911–12), 'The topography of Boeotia and the theories of M. Bérard', *ABSA* 18, 189–210, repr. in Gomme 1937, 17–41.
Gomme, A.W. (1920), 'Notes on Thucydides Book VI', *CR* 34, 81–85.
Gomme, A.W. (1923), 'Thucydides and Sphakteria', *CQ* 17, 36–40, repr. in: Gomme 1937, 125–131.
Gomme, A.W. (1925a), 'The position of women in Athens in the fifth and fourth centuries B.C.', *CPh* 20, 1–25, repr. in: Gomme 1937, 89–115.
Gomme, A.W. (1925b), 'Two notes on the Ἀθηναίων πολιτεία', *CR* 39, 152–154.
Gomme, A.W. (1926a), 'Notes on the Ἀθηναίων πολιτεία (continued)', *CR* 40, 8–12.
Gomme, A.W. (1926b), 'Two notes on the constitution of Athens', *JHS* 46, 171–178.
Gomme, A.W. (1926c), 'Two notes on Herodotus', *CQ* 20, 97–98.
Gomme, A.W. (1927), 'The Athenian hoplite force in 431 B.C.', *CQ* 21, 142–150.
Gomme, A.W. (1928), Review of *Cambridge Ancient History* vols. v and vii, *CR* 42, 183–189.
Gomme, A.W. (1929), 'Thucydides VI.34.7', *CR* 43, 15.
Gomme, A.W. (1930), 'Some notes on fifth-century history', *JHS* 50, 105–108.
Gomme, A.W. (1933), *The Population of Athens in the fifth and fourth Centuries B.C.*, Oxford.
Gomme, A.W. (1937), *Essays in Greek History and Literature*, Oxford.
Gomme, A.W. (1945), *A Historical Commentary on Thucydides* i, Oxford.
Gomme, A.W. (1954), *The Greek Attitude to Poetry and History*, Sather Classical Lectures vol. 27, Berkeley/Los Angeles.
Gomme, A.W. (1956), *A Historical Commentary on Thucydides* ii–iii, Oxford.
Gomme, A.W. (1962), *More Essays in Greek History and Literature*, ed. D.A. Campbell, Oxford.
Gomme, A.W./Sandbach, F.H. (1973), *Menander: a Commentary*, Oxford.
Gomme, A.W./Andrewes, A./Dover, K.J. (1970), *A Historical Commentary on Thucydides* iv, Oxford.
Gomme, A.W./Andrewes, A./Dover, K.J. (1981), *A Historical Commentary on Thucydides* v, Oxford.
Goodwin, W.W. (1904), *Demosthenes: On the Crown*, Cambridge.
Goodwin, W.W. (1906), *Demosthenes: Against Meidias*, Cambridge.
Harris, E.M. (1992), 'Pericles' praise of Athenian democracy: Thucydides 2.37.1', *HSCP* 94, 157–167.
Henderson, J. (2006), *'Oxford Reds': Classic Commentaries on Latin Classics*, London.

Henderson, J. (2007), 'The "Euripides reds" series: best-laid plans at OUP', in: C. Stray (ed.), *Classical Books: Scholarship and Publishing in Britain since 1980*, (*BICS* Supp. 86, London), 143–175.

Henderson, J. (2010), 'A1–Zythum: Domimina Nustio Illumea, or out with the OLD (1931–82)', in: C. Stray (ed.), *Classical Dictionaries: Past, Present and Future*, London, 139–176.

Henderson, J. (2013), '"A piece of work which would occupy some years …": Oxford University Press Archive Files 814152, 814173, 814011', in: B. Gibson/T. Harrison (eds.), *Polybius & His World: Essays in Memory of F.W. Walbank*, Oxford, 37–72.

Hornblower, S. (1991–2008), *A Commentary on Thucydides* i–iii, Oxford.

Hornblower, S. (2013), *Herodotus Histories Book 5*, Cambridge.

Hornblower, S./Pelling, C. (2017), *Herodotus Histories Book VI*, Cambridge.

How, W.W./Wells, J. (1912), *A Commentary on Herodotus* i–ii, Oxford.

Hunter, L.W./Handford, S.A. (1927), *Aeneas on Siegecraft*, Oxford.

Jowett, B. (1881), *Thucydides: translated into English with Introduction, Marginal Analysis, Notes, and Indices* vol. ii, Oxford.

Kalisch, M.M. (1855–72), *A Historical and Critical Commentary on the Old Testament, with a new Translation*, London.

Kallet-Marx, L. (1993a), *Money, Expense, and Naval Power in Thucydides' History 1–5.24*, Berkeley.

Kallet-Marx, L. (1993b), 'Thucydides 2.45.2 and the status of war widows in Periclean Athens', in: R.M. Rosen/J. Farrell (eds.), *Nomodeiktes: Greek Studies in Honor of Martin Ostwald*, Michigan, 133–143.

Kitto, H.D.F. (1959), 'Arnold Wycombe Gomme, 1886–1951', *PBA* 45, 335–344.

Koestermann, E. (1963–8), *Cornelius Tacitus: Annalen* i–iv, Heidelberg.

Kraus, C.S. (2002), 'Introduction: reading commentaries/commentaries as reading', in: Gibson/Kraus 2002, 1–27.

Kraus, C.S. (2016), 'Agricolan paratexts', in: Kraus/Stray 2016, 318–345.

Kraus, C.S./Stray, C. (eds.) (2016), *Classical Commentaries: Explorations in a Scholarly Genre*, Oxford.

Macintyre, B. (2014), *A Spy among Friends: Philby and the Great Betrayal*, London.

MacKendrick, P.L. (1946), review of Gomme (1945), *AJArch* 50, 497–499.

McGregor, M.F. (1946), review of Gomme (1945), *AJPh* 67, 268–275.

McGregor, M.F. (1959), 'Thucydides and A.W. Gomme' (review of Gomme 1956), *Phoenix* 13, 58–68.

Meritt, B.D./Wade-Gery, H.T./McGregor, M.F. (1939–53), *The Athenian Tribute Lists* i–iv, Princeton.

Moles, J.L. (1993), 'Truth and untruth in Herodotus and Thucydides', in: T.P. Wiseman/C. Gill (eds.), *Lies and Fiction in the Ancient World*, Exeter, 88–121.

Monro, W.D. (1929), *Titi Livi liber XXV*, Oxford.

Most, G.W. (ed.) (2000), *Commentaries–Kommentare*, Aporemata 4, Göttingen.

Nisbet, R.G. (1939), *M. Tulli Ciceronis De Domo Sua ad Pontifices oratio*, Oxford.

Oakley, S.P. (1997–2005), *A Commentary on Livy Books VI–X*, Oxford.

Ogilvie, R.M. (1965), *A Commentary on Livy Books 1–5*, Oxford.

Page, D.L. (1938), *Euripides: Medea*, Oxford.

Pease, A.S. (1935), *Publi Vergili Maronis Aeneidos liber quartus*, Cambridge, MA.

Pelling, C. (1986), 'Plutarch and Roman politics', in: I.S. Moxon/J.D. Smart/A.J. Woodman, *Past Perspectives in Greek and Roman Historical Writing*, Cambridge, 159–187, repr. in: Pelling 2002, 207–236.
Pelling, C. (1990), 'Truth and fiction in Plutarch's *Lives*', in: D.A. Russell (ed.), *Antonine Literature*, Oxford, 19–52, repr. in: Pelling 2002, 143–170.
Pelling, C. (1992), 'Plutarch and Thucydides', in: P.A. Stadter (ed.), *Plutarch and the Historical Tradition*, London, 10–40, repr. in Pelling 2002, 117–141.
Pelling, C. (2000), *Literary Texts and the Greek Historian*, London.
Pelling, C. (2002), *Plutarch and History: Eighteen Studies*, London.
Pope, M. (1988), 'Thucydides and democracy', *Hist.* 37, 276–296.
Ramsay, W.M. (1898), *A Historical Commentary on St Paul's Epistle to the Galatians*, London.
Rennie, W. (1909), *The Acharnians of Aristophanes*, London.
Rhodes, P.J. (1988), *Thucydides: History II*, Warminster.
Rhodes, P.J. (1994), *Thucydides: History III*, Warminster.
Rhodes, P.J. (1998), *Thucydides: History IV.1–V.24*, Warminster.
Ross, W.D. (1924), *Aristotle's Metaphysics*, Oxford.
Ross, W.D. (1936), *Aristotle's Physics*, Oxford.
Rusten, J.S. (1989), *Thucydides: The Peloponnesian War Book II*, Cambridge.
Sandys, J.E. (1885), *M. Tulli Ciceronis ad M. Brutum Orator*, Cambridge.
Sandys, J.E. (1890), *The Speech of Demosthenes against the law of Leptines*, Cambridge.
Seeley, J.R. (1871), *Livy, Books 1–10: Book 1*, Oxford.
Smith, M. (2011), *Six: the real James Bonds 1900–1939*, London.
Starkie, W.J.M. (1911), *The Clouds of Aristophanes*, London.
Stray, C. (2005), *The Owl of Minerva: the Cambridge Praelections of 1906*, PCPS Supp. vol. 28.
Stray, C. (2016), 'A Teutonic monster in Oxford: the making of Fraenkel's *Agamemnon*', in: Kraus/Stray 2016, 39–57.
Sutcliffe, P. (1978), *The Oxford University Press: an Informal History*, Oxford.
Trevor-Roper, H.R (1968), *The Philby Affair: Espionage, Treason, and Secret Services*, London.
Underhill, G.E. (1900), *A Commentary on the Hellenica of Xenophon*, Oxford.
Wade-Gery, H.T. (1949), review of Gomme 1945, *JHS* 69, 83–85.
Walbank, F.W. (1957–79), *A Historical Commentary on Polybius* i–iii, Oxford.
Webster, T.B.L. (1932), *M. Tulli Ciceronis Pro L. Flacco Oratio*, Oxford.
Winnington-Ingram, R.P. (1965), 'τὰ δέοντα εἰπεῖν: Cleon and Diodotus', *BICS* 12, 70–82.
Winton, R. (2004), 'Thucydides 2,37,1: Pericles on Athenian democracy', *RhM* 147, 26–34.
Winton, R. (2008), 'Thucydides 2,37,1: a reconsideration', *RhM* 151, 425–426.
Wyse, W. (1904), *The Speeches of Isaeus*, Cambridge.

Christina Shuttleworth Kraus
'Pointing the Moral' or 'Adorning the Tale?' Illustrations and Commentary on Caesar's *Bellum Gallicum* in 19th and Early 20th-century American Textbooks

This paper examines selected editions of classical texts and commentaries published in the 19th and early 20th centuries by the US publishing houses Allyn & Bacon, Appleton, and Harper & Brothers. Since the commentary form is remarkably conservative, and recycling books economical, many of these books are still in use as — or are models for — texts still used to communicate Western literature to students of the Humanities. The relationship of commentator to author has been variously understood over time, but it is abundantly clear that especially when accompanied by diagrams, drawings, and illustration, the interpretation and guidance offered by commentators affects the ways in which a text communicates. The relationship of text (both the 'original' and the commentator's) and image has a great deal to tell us about the use of these books in education, and about their intended audiences.

1 Paratextual Learning

Many different scholarly paratexts accompany a work of Greek or Latin literature as presented to students in a classroom. Here I concentrate on a subset of textbooks, that is works 'designed to teach the elements of an accepted art,'[1] which allowed classical texts to be read and understood by pre-University students:

That I am working in this area is entirely due to Chris's example and encouragement. I am very pleased to be able to offer him this *opus minimum* in return for his endless, generous good cheer — needless to say, his learning has improved this piece immensely. I also thank the anonymous reader for the Press for their rich and detailed comments, which have found their way especially into nn. [4, 7, 62], and record that the deficiencies they point out are entirely my own — I regret especially that I cannot at this point produce the 'deep analysis of primary sources' that they desiderate.

1 The earliest known appearance of the word 'textbook' is in 1830 (Stray 1994, 2); for the definition quoted, Grafton 2008, 19.

https://doi.org/10.1515/9783110719215-011

> A textbook is a book designed to provide an authoritative pedagogic version of an area of knowledge. Other books can be used in teaching, of course: for example, a plain text of Shakespeare's plays. Here pedagogic use is marginal to the intentions of the book's producers. Closer to the textbook is a book produced for use in instructional sequences, but in a less central and constitutive manner. An example would be a school edition of Shakespeare, with notes written to aid comprehension by pupils. This kind of book we can class as *schoolbooks*.[2]

Mostly an exercise in reception, this paper considers selected US teaching materials for Caesar's *Gallic War* in the 19th and early 20th centuries.[3] These books are directed at audiences of pre-university students and used by both genders.[4] Their prefaces are variously explicit about the kinds of pedagogical material included and its purpose — mostly notes, but also other materials to help construe the text: vocabularies, indices historical and geographical, maps, etc. My particular focus is on the pictorial material included in these schoolbooks: how it works with the text, and how it may have shaped students' understanding of Caesar.[5]

Both Caesar and his *Wars* had capacious audiences in the period under discussion. So, for instance, four books of the *Gallic War* were among the requirements for admission both at Bryn Mawr College and at the University of Pennsylvania in 1887.[6] The giant educational publishers of the 19th century — Harper and

---

[2] Stray 1994, 2. Emphasis original.

[3] Specifically, works published first in 1838, 1870, and 1886 and subsequently reissued: see below. Caesar came relatively late to US higher education: see Owen 1936, e.g. at p. 213 'Caesar's conquest of American classical education dates from the days of the Revolution'; his presence in schools goes back somewhat farther (Owen 1936, 214–215). Perhaps not surprisingly for a group of readers far from home, Ovid's *Tristia* was one of the most frequently imported texts in the late 17th century (Owen 1936, 213).

[4] Wyke 2012, 21–46 is fundamental on Caesar in American education from 1900–1914; for 'the Caesar year' see especially 32–37, and for female students, see 29–32 and Winterer 2007. Tetlow 1881 gives select information on 'the five Eastern institutions which offer the higher education to women'; most of them required some Caesar for entrance. On Caesar in North Carolina schools for women see Silkenat 2016, 176. Some of the female audience can be seen in owner's inscriptions; for example, Yale's copy of Harkness 1886 is inscribed by Caroline Duer (its back flyleaf has a list of seven names, all women, headed 1893–1894: a class register?).

[5] Currently available teaching materials, both in paper and online, include 19th and early-20th century commentaries, and the *Bellum Gallicum* is back in the College Board's AP Syllabus for Latin (https://apcentral.collegeboard.org/courses/ap-latin/course/ap-latin-reading-list). Since at least one of these was revised and reissued as recently as 2017 (Stem 2017), this study is relevant to contemporary teaching concerns.

[6] More broadly see Owen 1936, 212–213; he does not include women's colleges. For Caesar in girls' schools see above n. 4. Columbia is the second earliest institution to require Caesar for admittance (1785); see below on Anthon.

Brothers, Appleton (later part of the American Book Company), and John Allyn (later Allyn & Bacon) — commissioned school commentaries by prolific and respected professors of Classics: Charles Anthon (Columbia), Albert Harkness (Brown), and Frances Kelsey (Lake Forest, then Michigan). I will take a slice through these, though there are scores more that one could study.[7] The following table gives the genuinely new *Bellum Gallicum* editions of Anthon, Harkness, and Kelsey (taking copyright data into account; for their complete titles see the entries in the Bibliography):

Tab. 7: Selected editions of Caesar 1838–1918.

Date	Editor	Publisher	Edition
1838	Anthon	Harper	1; 493 pp.
1870	Harkness	Appleton	1; 377 pp.
1882	Harkness	Appleton	'Adapted to the revised standard edition of the author's Latin grammar.'
1886	Kelsey	John Allyn	1, 499 pp.
1886	Harkness	Appleton	'Revised edition, illustrated.'
1897	Kelsey	Allyn and Bacon	[changes detailed in 1896 Preface to the eighth edition]
1901	Harkness and Forbes	American Book Co.	1 (now has co-author; completely new preface)
1918	Kelsey	Allyn & Bacon	1 (now includes *BGall.* 1–4, selections from 5–7 and *BCiv.*; completely new preface)

Each of these texts was published multiple times, including many reprints and revisions, over the period running from 1838, the first appearance of Anthon's Caesar, to 1918, the last of Kelsey's. Anthon was reprinted unchanged by Harper

---

[7] Wyke 2012, 32 on the 'small cottage industry' of Caesar editions, especially of the *Gallic War*. See below for some competitors to Anthon in the period 1838–1870, and for an overview, Owen 1936, 218–221. The 'first American edition' of works ascribed to Caesar was printed in New York in 1802, without notes but with an index of names (Owen 1936, 217, 'a bare list of place names with their modern equivalents'); for details of the very few editions between this and 1838, see Owen 1936, 217–219. An edition of *BGall.* and a Latin grammar were produced by William Bingham in North Carolina in 1863 for use in his own school, and reprinted later in Philadelphia (Bingham 1863, 1864; Weeks 1900, 1152 for the December 1863 actual publication date of the Caesar). It has no illustrations, maps, charts, or other related paratextual material.

approximately three times each decade till 1889, 22 years after Anthon's death,[8] while Harkness and Kelsey were busy improving their editions. That suggests that Anthon's rival presses, Appleton and Allyn (& Bacon), were feeling pressure not just to put out competing scholarly textbooks, but to keep their products saleable by bringing them constantly up-to-date to counter the continuing authority of Anthon 1838, which even to his detractors 'presented a really imposing appearance, which was not altogether deceptive' (Owen 1936, 219; see further below n. 14). The authority was not entirely owing to Anthon's own rather Caesarian majesty (he used a head of Caesar as his seal, for example: Sypher 2014, 112): his books were enormous, the Caesar running to 493 pages and the Virgil to 942 (Anthon 1843a). In the fifty-two years that intervene between Anthon's and Harkness's first editions, presses in Boston, New York, and Philadelphia came out with school texts of the *Gallic War*; but despite prolific reprinting these did not seem to make a dent in Harper's business, and are relatively hard to find today outside of digitized texts.[9] The New York publisher Appleton, too, published a rival edition, by Jesse Ames Spencer, in 1848;[10] that used some of the same illustrative material as Anthon (he speaks of his efforts to render 'a favorite classic' 'attractive': Spencer 1848, 6), but was reprinted only twice.[11]

---

8 Anthon's *Caesar* was reprinted at least in 1839, 1841, 1845, 1848, 1852, 1853, 1855, 1860, 1862, 1868, 1870, 1871, 1876, 1880, 1889. On unchanged reprints see also below n. 22.
9 In Boston, F.P. Leverett (1829) was revised and reprinted a handful of times by Hilliard, Gray, Little and Wilkins; E.A. Andrews (1845) was reprinted 16 times in a dozen years by Crocker and Brewster, who also published a 'New Series of Latin Schoolbooks' including a grammar by Andrews and Stoddard (Andrews 1845, n.p.). In New York, the firm of Pratt, Woodford, & Co. brought out the Rev. Peter Bullions's *Caesar* in 1845, which was reprinted at least five times in at least ten 'editions' up until at least 1860 and keyed to his *Latin Grammar*. In Philadelphia (not treated by Owens 1936), from Eldredge and Brother came 'Chase and Stuart's Classical Series' in 1867/8, with Caesar and Vergil again the first authors (Stuart 1868, reprinted at least seven times through 1892); Lea and Blanchard brought out 'Schmitz and Zumpt's Classical Series,' beginning with Vergil and Caesar (Schmitz and Zumpt 1847, reprinted 1853, 1859; this was pirated from 'Chambers's Educational Course, Classical Section' published in Edinburgh and London; on reprinting books from the UK, see Edelman 2015, 59).
10 Spencer 1848 was reprinted in 1851 and 1859; in Owen's view it was 'a far more competent piece of work than Anthon's and on the whole superior to any of its American predecessors' (1936, 218). Spencer, a divine and Professor of Greek in the College of the City of New York from 1869 to 1879, also began the editing/rewriting of the 'Arnold Series of Greek and Latin Books' (published by Appleton 1846–1856), later overseen by Harkness (below p. 253).
11 D. Appleton & Company began printing in New York City in 1831, after moving from Boston where the founder sold but did not print books. The firm was noted for its educational, travel, reference, historical, and scientific/medical titles; it merged its line of schoolbooks with others in 1890 to form the American Book Company (Wolfe 1981, 262–263). After many mergers and

One reason for Anthon's lead was his publisher's position. Beginning as J & J Harper (1817–1833) and then incorporating as Harper & Brothers (1833–1962), the house was older and bigger than others in New York City, and despite a disastrous fire in 1853 dominated the New York educational market.[12] Anthon, who began publishing commentaries with the New York firm of C. and C.H. Carvill in 1825,[13] was thus backed both by his positions as Professor of the Greek and Latin Languages at Columbia and Rector of the Columbia College Grammar School,[14] and by his contract with Harpers for a whole series of Greek and Latin texts and reference works.[15]

With Albert Harkness, Appleton found a scholar who could front a Latin machine of their own. He began by taking over Spencer's revised version of Arnold's *First Latin Book* (Harkness 1851), and eventually produced Greek instructional textbooks, Latin readers, and a widely used Latin grammar, together with commentaries on Cicero, Sallust, and (leading off) *Caesar's Commentaries on the Gallic War; with Explanatory Notes, a Copious Dictionary, and a Map of Gaul*, which appeared in 1870.[16] Reissues of this edition were fairly frequent.[17] The first substantial revision was done in 1882 to include references to the author's own Latin grammar, whose revised standard edition of 1881 was touted by its publisher as 'the most complete, philosophical, and attractive Grammar ever written'.[18] At the

---

renamings, the firm essentially became defunct in 1999, at which point the only part that retained the original name (Appleton & Lange) was publishing medical textbooks. On the house, see Overton 1925 and Wolfe 1981. The records of the American Book Company are held at Syracuse University (https://library.syr.edu/digital/guides/a/amer_book_co.htm).

12 For the history of the house see Harper 1912, Exman 1965, and Exman 1967; it continues in existence today as Harper Collins. Harper themselves were great self-promoters: see Abbott 1855, an account of the process of publishing from beginning to end with rich illustrative material. They were, however, regarded as unusually conservative, with 'antiquated sales promotion techniques': Wolfe 1981, 294.

13 Anthon 1825a; on this and its subsequent issuings see Sypher 2014, 32.

14 Spencer 1890, 26 describes his experience learning Latin and Greek from Anthon, the 'notorious drill master.' Sypher 2014, 134–154 reprints Samuel Blatchford's 1890 memoir of 'Charles Anthon at College,' which confirms Spencer's emphasis on drills, but also agrees with him on the value of Anthon's pedagogy: 'With all his peculiarities, there was that about Dr. Anthon which the student could not help liking' (Sypher 2014, 152).

15 For the very brief agreement of 1835, see Sypher 2014, 116–117; for the man, see previous note.

16 I have not been able to locate the 1870 edition, but the 1872 seems to have been a simple reprint (WorldCat erroneously lists an 1859 edition). Anthon's death in 1867 will not have hurt sales; though as we have seen, Harper continued to publish the *Caesar* until near the end of the century. For Harkness the man, see Mitchell 1993.

17 Orig. 1870, reprinted 1872, 1873, 1874; revised? 1879 (no new copyright date); revised 1882; revised and illustrated 1886; revised with co-author 1901.

18 See e.g. Lincoln (1882) n.p. (advertising material following p. 372).

same time, the Caesar and other texts edited by Harkness were being billed in publisher's advertisements as 'Professor Harkness's Series of Latin Text-books' and 'Harkness's Books for the Study of Latin' — in direct competition with Anthon's own 'Series of Classical Works for Schools and Colleges.' In Boston, a second center of educational publishing (Tebbel 1972, 386–448), Francis Kelsey's *Caesar's Gallic war with an Introduction, Notes and Vocabulary*, first published in 1886, went through a number of changes before Allyn & Bacon issued his radically revised and reworked commentary in 1918.[19]

2 'Rendered Attractive, Instead of an Object of Aversion'

Both Harkness and Kelsey responded to changing taste and pedagogical theory, and to bibliographical and archaeological developments in renovating their schoolbooks.[20] Anthon did not follow suit. The man himself seems to have been uninterested in revision: his 1843 Virgil, for instance, was published unaltered for decades, though there was a rewritten edition for the British market done by William Trollope, a distant cousin of the novelist.[21] Its notes are lavishly (if unevenly) equipped with woodcuts which range from line drawings to elaborately shaded images, taken primarily from the *Dictionary of Greek and Roman Antiquities* (Smith 1842, pirated by Anthon 1843b; see Stray 2007); of them, Anthon says: 'These illustrations, while they form a very attractive feature in the volume, will be found to exemplify in no slight degree the Horatian precept of speaking to the eye rather than the ear of the student' (Anthon 1843a, vi). Despite this sound pedagogical theory, by the end of the century these woodcuts must have looked very dated. This policy of simple reprinting may have been a Harper habit that Anthon adopted, as his was not the only material that the press put out unaltered during

---

19 Orig. 1886, reprinted 1888, corrected 1889, reprinted 1891, revised and enlarged 1897, reprinted 1898, etc.; new edition with selections published 1918.
20 The epigraph for this section comes from Schmitz and Zumpt 1847, iii (publisher's note). On 'enlivening Caesar's commentaries' in the period see Wyke 2012, 24–27.
21 Anthon and Trollope 1847. Trollope had harsh words for Anthon: 'it will not be denied that in fulness of interpretation the editor has far outstripped the generality of his predecessors; though it is not so clear that his expositions are always correct …. He has done both too much and too little: too much, in the literal translation of almost every line of the poem… and too little, in the scanty supply of verbal and syntactical illustration' (v). For critical reception of Anthon's work in general, including accusations of plagiarism, see Sypher 2014, 70–104.

the century.²² And indeed, Harper did not take advantage of Anthon's death in 1867 to update the illustrations in his editions. Instead, the press apparently ignored, at least in Anthon's case, technological developments in printing.²³

As paper became cheaper and printing technologies developed through the 19th century, books containing illustrations of all types proliferated, especially those featuring natural history, costumes, architectural details, ceramics, and maps. Histories, in particular, and the rapidly developing popular press, used illustration to bring famous faces and actions alive.²⁴ These advances fed the demand for pictorial material, which in turn spurred further technological developments: 'the demand for "pictures"' in a book has undoubtedly stimulated the development of modern methods of engraving.'²⁵ From mid-century the 'democratic art' of colour lithography was widespread and relatively inexpensive,²⁶ and by the end of the 19th century the far more economical photographic reproduction was becoming available.²⁷ For schoolbooks, woodcuts — the cheapest, and

---

22 Harper also reprinted Liddell and Scott's *Greek-English Lexicon* unchanged except for one entry from 1846 into the 1870s (Stray 2019, 14 with n. 29). This procedure was far more economical for the press, which could even recycle plates from another publisher and simply append new material; so Anthon's revision of Lemprière for Duyckinck *et al.* (Anthon 1825b) was reprinted for years until Harper bought and destroyed the plates to make room for a new *Classical Dictionary* by their bestselling classicist (Anthon 1841). See Edelman 2015, 70, and preceding note on Anthon's Virgil.

23 Though inherently conservative (above, n. 12), Harper was certainly aware of these developments: see Abbott 1855 *passim* for their up-to-date shop. Perhaps the issue was a combination of Anthon and the idea of 'the classic'— though as we have seen, both editors and presses were generally keen to update even their ancient material. On the illustration and design (respectively) of Victorian books see Wakeman 1973 and McLean 1972; on woodblock illustrators, De Maré 1980 and Hamilton 1958. These studies include specifically educational works only occasionally; so e.g. McLean 1972, 192 on *The Poultry Book* (1853), 'possibly, the first manual published in Britain on a purely practical, non-artistic subject, containing plates printed in full colour.' A good idea of the range used in schoolbooks can be gleaned from the American Book Company records of illustrations, sorted by subject matter: https://library.syr.edu/digital/guides/a/ABC_4B.xls.

24 On illustrations in works of history, see Mitchell 2000, especially 56–84 on the British history textbook; questioning the utility of uninterpreted faces, Stray 2010 reminds us that 'portraits are not neutral reflections, but artful artefacts.'

25 C.T. Jacobi, quoted in Wakeman 1973, 157. For a case study in 18th–19th century illustrated literature with emphasis on marketing and the culture of reprints, see Jung 2018; and in general, Mainardi 2017, 73–117 on the illustrated press.

26 On chromolithography (not restricted to books), Marzio 1979 and Twyman 2013.

27 Wakeman 1973, 119–145 on the 'photomechanical revolution' through the 1880s, at which point 'photomechanical printing finally triumphed over hand methods' (145). For a detailed description of the various methods of photomechanical reproduction see Cook 2015, 1316–1320.

the quintessentially Victorian, medium — were preferred, as they could be embedded with the text with much less difficulty than other kinds of illustration.[28]

In the great educational reforms of the 18th and 19th centuries, in which the relevance and utility of every feature of pedagogical publishing was hotly debated, it was assumed that each part of a schoolbook should add to a student's comprehension of the material studied.[29] In books designed to teach mathematics or science or language, visual material does not merely adorn the verbal, but presents the information in a manner that may be more easily comprehended (e.g. in a picture of a skeleton or the elements of geometry),[30] or may offer a different approach to the content (e.g. a grammatical paradigm), thus allowing the student more ways to learn.[31] Aside from purely pedagogical considerations, there was another, separate question: how to keep the students interested in their work? For that, one easy approach was to pile on the paratexts, from maps to tables and plans to images of all types. Despite Noah Webster's fear that pictures threatened to 'promote superficial learning,'[32] the anti-illustration camp rapidly lost the battle, not only in successive printings of Webster's *Dictionary*, but everywhere.[33] Despite their popularity, because illustrations were often perceived as simple ornament, even though (or perhaps because) they could help a student think differently about a text, a rationale — even a defence — was required. My title comes from Dr. Johnson,[34] via the preface to the second edition of a schoolbook on *Gallic War* Book 7 (Compton 1892, v):

---

28 Lithography was also a very flexible medium, though perhaps less associated with the Victorian schoolbook: Stray 2006. On boxwood engraving as one of the two period symbols (along with the steam engine) of the entire, long Victorian period, see De Maré 1980, 7.
29 Groves 1995 is particularly interesting on the intersection of book type and educational reforms.
30 For Byrne's *Euclid* and colour organization see Tufte 1990, 84–87; Giocondo 1513, plate 1 (map of northern Europe) is an early use of colour to clarify cartographic design. For anatomical illustrations see Twyman 2013, 254, and for an example see e.g. Steele (1872), one of a set of introductory textbooks ('Steele's Series of the Natural Sciences').
31 Tufte 1990 on 'design strategies that sharpen the information resolution ... of paper' (13) and 2006 on how 'evidence that bears on questions of any complexity typically involves multiple forms of discourse' (9). Both books offer close readings of many different representations of intellectual material.
32 Webster 1843, 309, quoted by Hancher 2010, 2. Children's books in the US (and elsewhere) had had illustrations for decades: *The New England Primer*, an educational publication with woodcuts designed to make learning attractive (first published in the late 1680s), is perhaps the most famous of these in the States (Tebbel 1972, 48–49, 190–195).
33 Hancher 2010 discusses the illustrations throughout the history of the *Dictionary*'s life.
34 'To point a moral, or adorn a tale,' *The Vanity of Human Wishes* (1749) 222.

> Go again, little book, and relieve, if you may, somewhat of the drudgery of the Latin lesson, by showing those who use you that their book is not really uninteresting. ... Tell them ... that you now have a key to explain your pictures, which before may have failed too often to 'point the moral,' however much they may have 'adorned the tale.'

Though this edition does not fall under my rubric of American textbooks, it is one of the clearest statements of the pedagogical dilemmas facing editors and publishers of educational materials, even as late as the early 1890s.

In considering the pedagogical delivery of a literary text, while the novice or even advanced reader may well need grammatical and syntactical help, an illustration of singing shepherds arguably does not help in the understanding of the Latin (though it might create a mood).[35] The *Bellum Gallicum*, which arguably contains both literary and technical prose, is a complex case. Caesar describes physical objects and military activity in ways that are often hard to visualize without help, so including in a school text paratextual material such as maps, battle plans, and illustration of built structures seems unobjectionable. But other images — from military equipment and costume to full colour action scenes — populate the editions we are considering here. While our editors justify their inclusion of illustrative material primarily on the grounds of utility, the arrangement and identification of illustrations in the books themselves can seem to pull instead in the direction of entertainment.[36] And though woodcuts (and the like) cannot match the realism of painting, it is their very nature as 'a formalization, a simplification, an abstraction, a paraphrase of reality' (De Maré 1972, 13) that stimulates creativity, both in the artist and in the viewer.

Anthon's crowded title page advertises his 'English notes, critical and explanatory, plans of battles, sieges, etc., and historical, geographical, and archaeological indexes.'[37] Most of his brief Preface is concerned with the pedagogical

---

[35] So e.g. the illustrations in Thornton 1821, among the 'proper facilities ... enabling youth to acquire the Latin language in the shortest period of time' (title page), are meant to make students 'eager to know the meaning of the different Cuts, and this will surely spur them on to the diligent reading of the original matter to which these allude'; Thornton also adverts to the Horace lines which Anthon mentions (above, p. 254; Thornton 1821, v–vi). From the same period, Leigh Hunt complains about the lack of illustration in Pickering's 1820 Horace: 'we like a few of these trifles thrown in by the bookseller. We are of the school-boy's mind, and are so willing to have our imaginations set at work by the most unassuming of prints, that we never knew but one instance in which they came amiss' (Hunt 1821, 161).

[36] The ability of photographic illustration to 'favor ... empirical knowledge of antiquity' should not be underestimated: Lyons 2005, 39.

[37] The crowding is typical of the period; on title pages see De Vinne 1902, especially 233–267 on the selection of fonts, and more recently, Smith 2000 on the history of the title page; Gehl 2016

suitability of his decision to include the Greek paraphrase of *BGall*. 1, but its final paragraph says: 'The wood-cuts, giving plans of battles, sieges, &c., cannot but prove useful. They are executed with great ability by that talented artist, Mr. A.J. Mason.'[38] These, 13 in all (plus a frontispiece portrait of Caesar and a map of 'ancient France') are full-page woodcuts located in the Latin text near the passage they are meant to illustrate.[39] These are provided with little commentarial guidance for understanding their relationship to the text, apart from some labelled positions. Here, for instance, is 'Arrival of Caesar at the River Sambre, and his Battle with the Belgae' (Anthon 1838, between 42 and 43):

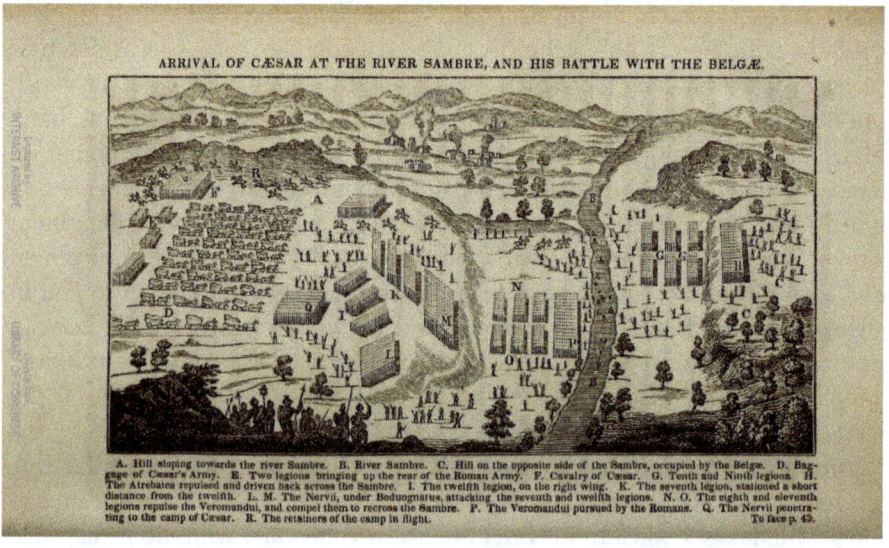

Fig. 9: Arrival of Caesar at the River Sambre, from C. Anthon, *Caesar's Commentaries on the Gallic War* (1838).

The semi-bird's eye view allows a reasonably clear indication of the relative positions of the armies, and the woodcut is detailed in execution. We should note,

---

on title-page advertisements in Renaissance editions of Terence, and Fowler 2017 on the illustrated title-page.

38 Anthon 1838, vi; the preface is not quite a page and a half long.

39 The one exception is the 'Roman Consular Camp according to Polybius,' which is in the 'archaeological index' (Anthon 1838, 482). That index also includes two tables: of dates (488) and of the arrangement of rowers in multi-oared ships (490).

however, that the desire to adorn and entertain shows in the rather exciting labels those plans are given, in which peripeteia ('repulse') and swift action ('pursued,' 'in flight') are suggested.[40]

In 1872 [1870], Harkness advertises on his title page 'explanatory notes, a copious dictionary, and a map of Gaul.' He does have illustrative material, but that is not heralded anywhere; there are two simplified maps (1872, 175, 220), and three schematic diagrams (190, 191), and a plan of Caesar's bridge (241). Not only are these illustrations pared down, they are also located in the commentary, integrated on the page, and discussed by the commentator. But a slight insecurity about the propriety of including any imagistic material may be evident in Harkness's preface, which discusses the sources the editor has drawn on and the excellence of the scholarly work he has been helped by, but mentions only the nature of Caesar's text, not its visual added value:

> The purity of the style, the dramatic interest of the narrative, and the historical significance of the wonderful career of discovery and conquest which they record, all unite to render them at once attractive and valuable. The Notes are intended to guide the faithful efforts of the student, and to prepare him for that course of direct instruction and illustration which belongs exclusively to the teacher.[41]

The language suggests the visual — 'dramatic,' 'wonderful' (which borrow from the language of rhetorical elaboration), 'attractive,' 'illustration' — but Harkness refers to illumination from explication, not from material culture. And when he cites his sources, including several German editions from which pictorial material was regularly drawn for Caesarian editions, it is all the more evident that in 1870, at least, he deliberately avoided such material.[42] Like Anthon, he relies on the strength of his appended material — Anthon has 'historical, geographical, and archaeological indices,' Harkness his friend A.M. Day's 'copious dictionary' — but unlike Anthon, his overall presentation is almost entirely analytic.

The title page for Francis Kelsey's 1886 Boston edition proclaims only that the text comes with 'An introduction, notes, and vocabulary.' But before we even

---

40 I have not been able to find the original of this battle plan, but it perhaps derives, as may other such plates, either from Palladio 1575 (Beltramini 2009) or from Patrizi 1583 (Papy 2004, 124–125); for Palladio's bridge see below, pp. 266–67. In the captions for the illustration of Alesia, Anthon or his engraver have misplaced some of the labels.
41 Harkness 1872 [1870] iii.
42 A rich and entirely other topic is the influence of German commentaries on these 19th-century works; for a start see Harloe 2016 and for the US, Winterer 2002. For Kelsey, see next n.

reach that titular claim we find six full pages of colour plates.⁴³ Other illustrative material is distributed throughout the Latin text (as in Anthon, there are none in the commentary): apart from the introductory plates there is a coloured map and 14 illustrations, all but one of which (the Roman galley, p. 37) are presented as plans. These provide more information than Anthon's bird's-eye view battles or Harkness's schemata, giving as they do the names of contemporary towns, detailed topography, and inset explications of labels, etc., but they require more concentrated attention to understand how they relate to the text, even with distinguishing colour marking out the Roman battle lines (cf. Harkness 1886, iv). Here is Kelsey's version of the battle of the Sambre (Kelsey 1886, between pp. 86 and 87:

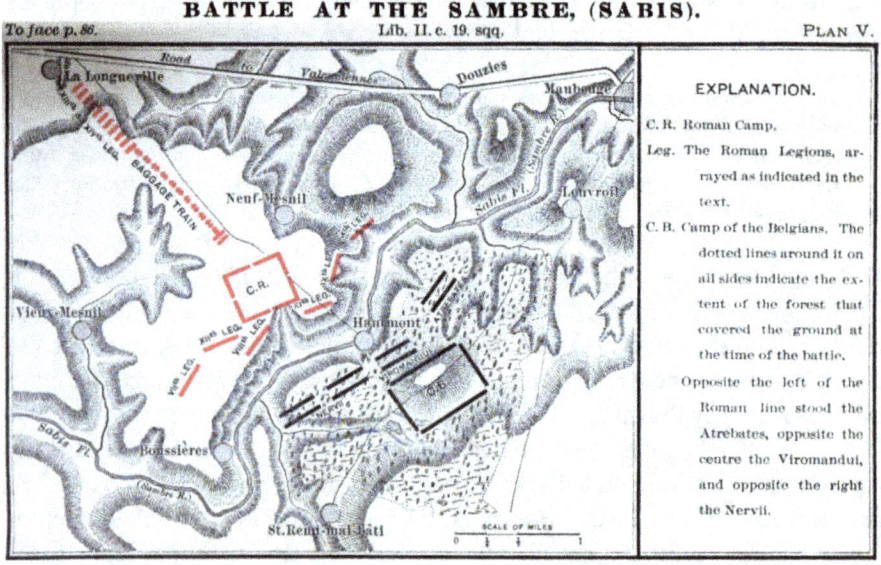

Fig. 10: Battle at the Sambre, from F.W. Kelsey, *C. Iuli Caesaris de bello Gallico libri vii* (1886).

Kelsey's 'Note to teachers' (1886, v–vii) credits his pictorial material to Rheinhard 1883 and (for the plans) to Napoléon III (these are also used by Rheinhard). But Kelsey, though known for his pedagogical strengths, and particularly his interest

---

43 In this arrangement, Kelsey follows his (credited) source, Hermann Rheinhard. He mentions no American editions, either 'critical and text' or 'with explanatory notes,' in his 'Helps to the study of Caesar' (1886, 379–380).

in providing students with context,[44] is primarily concerned with student interest, intellectual grasp, and 'right method of classical study' rather than with helping them read his maps. Preparatory and high school students can be taught with 'the same methods of broad and sympathetic, yet exact and thorough study which characterize college work,' he says, and to that end he emphasizes correct orthography, the proper order in which to read Caesar (his edition allows one to start with either Book II or Book I), and the perennial advantage that comes from the '*systematic* study of a topic or group of topics' (1886, v). He draws attention to his several tables and 'general view of the contents' of the Caesarian books and is the first of our commentators to include an extended bibliography of scholarly works (1886, 379–80). In his 1897 revision, billed as a ten-year anniversary one (1897, vi), he essentially takes the book in the direction it was already heading: more and clearer illustrations, more and more user-friendly bibliography, more help with geography and pronunciation, vowel quantities marked in the Latin text, and notes revised to take account of scholarly developments.

The last revision of Harkness (1886) was published in the same year as Kelsey's first edition. Though the title page announces without more detail that it is a 'revised edition, illustrated,' the preface trumpets its usefulness.[45] In 1870 Harkness claimed to 'admit into my pages only such information as may be made directly serviceable in the actual work of the class-room' (1870, v). In 1886 he opens that claim up to include the value of pictorial illustration:

> To understand and appreciate [the *Commentaries*], the student needs to know something of the Roman mode of warfare, and especially of the organization and movement of armies in the time of Caesar. ... This edition is furnished with colored plates and other illustrations, in the best style of the art. In the plans of battles, the Romans are represented in red, while the hostile lines are in black. The learner thus sees at a glance the relation of the opposing forces to each other (Harkness 1886, iii, iv).

Knowledge of the contemporary military system will enable full understanding of Caesar's particular text; colour in the plans will enable instant comprehension;[46] and everything is 'in the best style of the art' — an expression common in

---

[44] Pedley 2012, 21–22; this is especially noticeable in Kelsey 1918's comparison of the 'two wars in Gaul' (Pedley 2012, 236–237).
[45] On the back cover of Harkness 1887, this revision is announced as 'A New Pictorial Edition of Harkness's Caesar's Commentaries.'
[46] See De Maré 1980, 156 on commercial wood engraving in colours after 1850; it appears as early as 1843 (1980, 168) in Henry Shaw's *Dresses and decorations of the Middle Ages*; on the interest in ethnographic costume illustration see also n. 50.

advertisements for commercial printers, engravers, lithographers, and photographers.[47]

The reason for this new approach is not purely pedagogical, as that explicit advertising language shows. Harkness begins: 'When his first edition was published, the demand for small text-books compelled [the editor] to exclude from his pages much collateral information which, in the interest of the learner, he would gladly have admitted' (1886, iii). Whether 'small' refers to physical size or to the level of its intended readers, one might also posit that Harkness has proven himself a good seller or that his prestige in the market has increased — reasons that would be immodest to put in a preface, but which might account for Appleton's willingness to expand the commentary. Appleton had not in fact been parsimonious in previous editions: in the first big revision, of 1882, there are no alterations to the illustrative material apart from the provision of a slightly altered map,[48] but Harkness went through the Notes substituting section numbers referring to his revised standard grammar; the publishers include a concordance for those who have the pre-1881 *Grammar* (Harkness 1882, 378–384). This did not entail making any changes to the page numbering but cannot have been cost-neutral. In 1886, while retaining the pagination of the Notes, Harkness/Appleton replace woodcuts previously in the Notes with Plates of battle plans in the Latin text, with extended commentary substituted to keep the Notes pagination the same; only the bridge is retained in the same place (Harkness 1872 [1870], 1882, 1886, 241). The big change is a 47-page introductory section on the 'Military System of the Romans,' illustrated both with full-page colour plates and with woodcuts integrated into the pages. This material was published separately the following year, though with the full-page colour illustrations in different order, and with the battle plans from Harkness 1886 inserted at the end. The publisher's note tells us that this was done 'in order that those having the former editions of Caesar may procure this new material in an inexpensive form' (Harkness 1887, n.p.); there were also reduced rates for classes.[49]

This section is the apogee of the particular fascination with the Roman legionary, visible in the materials that appear in illustrated school texts of the *Gallic War* throughout the 19th and into the 20th century. These schoolbooks were certainly not the first to push readers of Caesar in this direction, but their emphasis on generalship, military systems, and ethnography conforms with one — perhaps

---

47 Foy 1984.
48 To my knowledge this first appears in the 1879 'revised edition,' which has the 1870 preface and no other obvious signs of revision.
49 This publication is still available in print, and as a Kindle edition.

the most — typical way of reading Caesar's *Commentaries* in classrooms of any period. We find in this illustrative material scenes both of the metaphoric type (to use Stephen Bann's characterization), where the illustration represents a narrated episode, and of the metonymic type, which relate to the narrative through contiguity — the latter type is represented primarily through drawings of equipment and ships.[50] These illustrations evince a pronounced interest in the legionary's uniforms and accessories, probably cashing in on the continuing 19th-century vogue for costume illustrations, especially in colour.[51] And these figures move: where Anthon gave us bird's-eye views, we now get the legionary integrated into exciting fighting scenes. When Harkness' revised, illustrated edition was itself revised and reissued by the conglomerated American Book Company (Harkness and Forbes 1901), the same images were used, but with a significant improvement in colour and clarity, the result of the new photo-reproductive processes (above, n. 27).

3 'The paragraph on the Rhine Bridge is notoriously obscure'

In this final section, I consider the two described physical structures that are illustrated in these schoolbooks, the Gallic wall in *BGall.* 7.23 and the Rhine bridge in *BGall.* 4.17, allegedly built in 10 days and even more quickly destroyed (4.19.4).[52] Caesar's ekphrastic engineering passages are famously difficult to translate.[53] This is partly owing to the difficulty of technical Latin in general: we do not always understand what the words mean, or how they fit together, even if we can 'translate' them. Furthermore, there is a widespread presumption that descriptions of utilitarian items such as those in Caesar should be capable of understanding in physical terms: that is, that one should be able to draw, or even recreate, a wall or a bridge. This presumption has at times held true even for such

---

50 Bann 1984, 43–47.
51 For costumes as a special subject of colour lithography, see examples illustrated at Twyman 2013, 77–96.
52 The epigraph for this section comes from Dodington 1980, 3.
53 See especially Dodington 1980, Kraus 2007, and for the Rhine bridge see Rice Holmes 1911, 711–724. For the various kinds of Latin and the difficulty of Latin *Kunstprosa* see the chapters by Langslow, Mayer, and Pinkster in Reinhardt, Lapidge, and Adams 2005, and (on Vitruvius) see Oksanish 2019.

manifest fantasies as Achilles' or Aeneas' shield,[54] and may lie behind the now-discredited idea that Vitruvius wrote the architectural passages in the *Bella*.[55] Fitting together the object described, therefore, seems not just helpful but in fact necessary for understanding how the Latin works.

But why should these passages be blueprints for construction? Apart from the *genre* problems such an assumption raises,[56] there are indications in the text itself that these passages are not intended to be tried at home. One such is the Gallic wall in book 7, whose description Caesar prefaces with *Muri autem omnes Gallici hac fere forma sunt* (*BGall*. 23.1 'but all Gallic walls are approximately in this shape'), a sentence which can be paralleled by the typical historiographical disclaimer of the type *orationem huiusce modi habuit* ('he gave a speech of this sort,' e.g. Sall. *Cat.* 20.1). The latter is generally now understood to indicate that the historian has, to a greater or lesser extent, invented the speech he claims to report. I have argued elsewhere that Caesar's wall is a *topos* of a wall, not a real wall (Kraus 2010a, 44). But there is, of course, archaeological evidence for Gallic walls, which certainly did exist (Dehn 1960), and from early on editors have illustrated this one. Anthon's illustration is one of the fullest (1838, 152), and stays firmly in place throughout the publication history of his book.[57]

In his preface, Anthon claims that his paratextual material is artistically as well as pedagogically significant: 'The wood-cuts...are executed with great ability by that talented artist, Mr. A.J. Mason.' But though Abraham John Mason, a British wood engraver working in the United States from 1829 to 1839 (just at the time this edition was published),[58] may well have cut the particular pieces of boxwood used by Harper, he was not ultimately responsible for any of Anthon's illustrations. The title 'Muri Vegetiani' in the plate (and the list of engravings, 1838, xx) gives the game away. This illustration originated in a 16th-century treatise on sieges by Justus Lipsius, via a 17th-century intermediary; the Gallic wall itself may well go back to Palladio.[59] The walls were probably engraved by the Dutch

---

[54] For two different views of ekphrasis (which may be understood as either describing or creating its object) see Fowler 1991.
[55] Dodington 1980, 2 with further bibliography.
[56] We do not know much about the historiographical *commentarius*, but nothing suggests that it was any kind of formal technical writing (Riggsby 2006, 133–150).
[57] Kelsey 1886, Plate VI has a metonymic illustration of the wall (from Rheinhard); Harkness 1886, Plate XIII shows it tucked into the corner of a plan of Avaricum (an image not unique to his commentary or to his press; it derives ultimately from Napoléon 1865–1866, Pl. 30).
[58] On Mason see Hamilton 1958, I.xxxvi, 175–176; 2.114–115. For the interplay between artist and engraver, see Stevens 2019.
[59] Palladio 1575, after p. 138.

artist Pieter van der Borcht the Elder and were in separate, though adjoining, plates in Lipsius' treatise (1596, 176–177). They were put together into one plate in 1661, if not before (Montanus 1661, 293). The illogicality of illustrating Vegetian walls in a 1661 Caesar is just as great as it is in 1838. So Professor Anthon, though crediting a modern artist who was in considerable demand at the time (n. 58), is in fact recycling old material with only minor changes.[60] His battle plans are similarly dated: the illustration of Alesia is also found in Lipsius 1596, 76 (cf. Savorgnan 1599, 83–84 with Beltramini 2008).

Fig. 11: Walls, from C. Anthon, *Caesar's Commentaries on the Gallic War* (1838).

---

60 The backgrounds are different, and some engraver has added more foliage in the foreground. In this case we see illustrations pulled from a scholarly *variorum* edition and moved into a schoolbook.

The case is the same with the Rhine bridge, whose imaginative illustration may ultimately derive from Palladio's *I quattro libri dell'architettura* (1570) but which probably entered the Caesar educational train again via Lipsius' plates.[61]

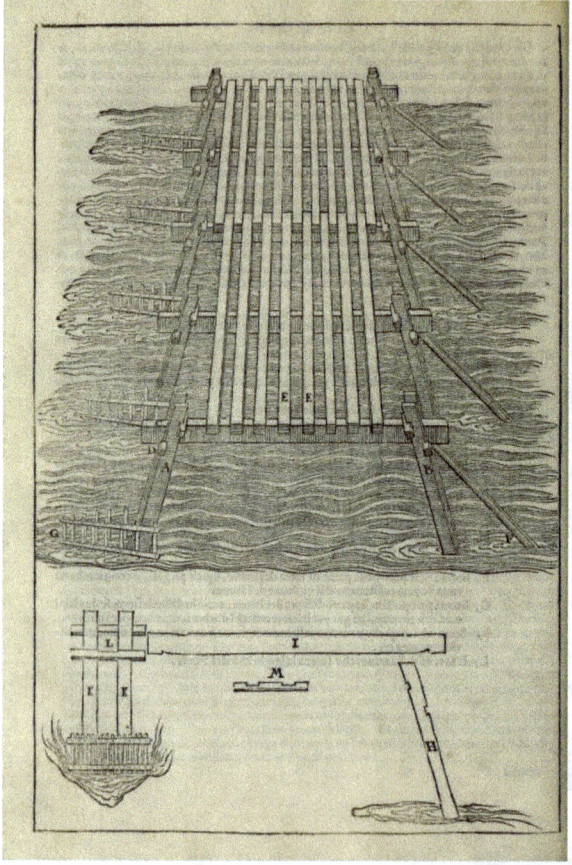

Fig. 12: Bridge over the Rhine, from A. Palladio, *I quattro libri dell'architettura* (1570, 3.14).

---

61 Lipsius 1596, 125. The history of the bridge illustrations is complex and beyond my competence to trace completely. The bridge may have been first imagined by Filarete (Antonio Alverino), 1461–1464, Book XIII, f. 96r; it appears in Giocondo 1513 (Gros and Beltramini 2003, 198) and the Bartoli translation of Alberti 1550 (Gros and Beltramini 2003, 201). Its form in these schoolbooks is to my eye Palladian. On it, with special attention to Giocondo, see Kaiser (2017).

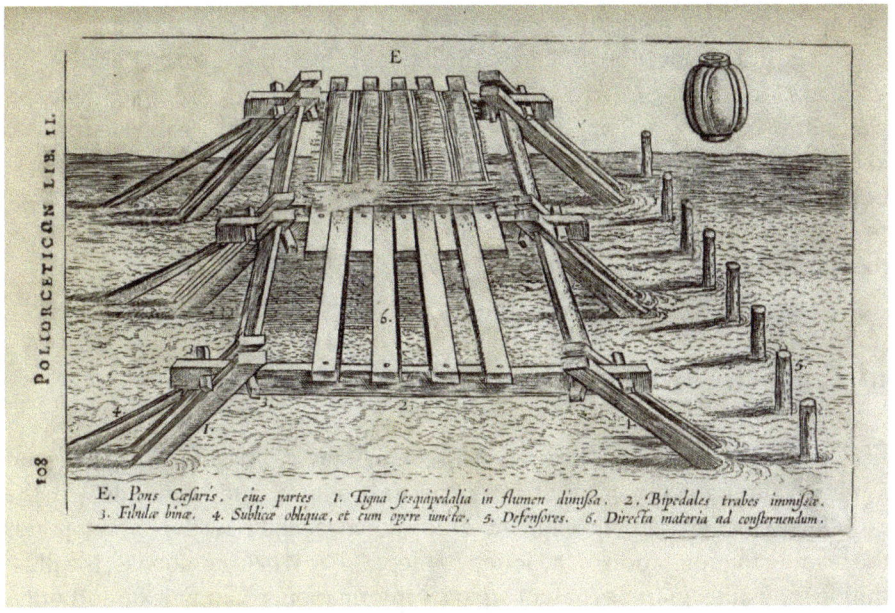

Fig. 13: Bridge over the Rhine, from J. Lipsius, *Poliorcheton* (1596, 108).

It is present in all three of our commentators. Though they wrangle it differently in their texts in terms of position and with slight alterations to the design — Kelsey has used Rheinhard's version (slightly angled, 1886, between 112 and 113), which livens the scene with an adjacent camp, while Anthon (1838, 75) opts for a decorative frieze of mountains — its antiquarian character stands out particularly next to Harkness' schematic battle plans and Kelsey and Harkness' colour plates of busy legionaries, equipment, and siege engines. Most of these last derive ultimately from early drawings of Trajan's column, so have a pedigree as venerable as that of the bridge, but for some reason — perhaps because they have people in them? — receive a more modernizing presentation in our commentaries.[62] Nor is the bridge illustration/plan particularly helpful for understanding the Latin, as

---

[62] Illustrations of Roman costume, equipment, and military activities based on the column are legion; they start appearing as soon as the column was seen as a subject for artistic practice in the early 16th century (Heenes 2014, 1–3; the first known archaeological publication was Du Choul 1557) and continue to this day (https://arts.st-andrews.ac.uk/trajans-column/the-project/the-human-figure-types/). Earlier texts of Caesar were certainly illustrated — e.g. *Die jeeste van Julius Cesar* from the workshop of Govaert van Ghemen, after 1486 (Conway 1884, 153, 298) — but the column was a huge impetus for these representations.

its parts are neither pellucidly labeled nor well explained. The tralaticiousness of the bridge drawing is brought into particular relief by steps taken by Kelsey in his 1918 revision to bring Caesar into the modern world. So, for example, he juxtaposes drawings of the Roman legionary with his World War I equivalent (1918, xiv–xv), and parallels a reconstruction of the siege works at Alesia with wolfholes at Ypres (1918, x). Yet the bridge remains unchanged from its 1886 first appearance. Remarkably, Stem 2017, a substantially revised reprint of Kelsey 1918, reprints the bridge plates exactly.

4 Tralatician teaching

In conclusion, I turn briefly to two typical commentarial procedures that have run implicitly through my discussion here. These are related, and have to do with the question of the relation of commentator to audience, and how the former guides the reading interpretation of the latter. In these *Gallic War* schoolbooks, the illustrations and other graphic content organize information, communicate authority, and regulate the manifold ways in which students consumed this 'classic.' Like any scholarly project, commentaries are both very conservative — we are all familiar with the way each successive commentator builds on the work of predecessors — *and* can differ greatly one from the other: one reader will see things that another does not; or one will solve a problem in a different way from another. Rivalry among commentators on the same text is built into the system. In the examples I have discussed here, we see both the tralatician quality and the rivalry behind choice and inclusion of paratextual elements as well.[63]

Some of this 'intertextuality,' if we can call it that, has to do with the antiquity of the commentary form itself: as possibly our oldest form of scholarly discourse, the commentary — including the school commentary — is by nature exceedingly conservative. Some of it has to do with assumptions about audience: school commentaries, such as the ones we are considering here, guessing that each generation of school children will ask the same questions about the text, tend to give the same answers. That is one reason that Kelsey's 1918 commentary, duly updated, can still be used to teach from in 2021 (other reasons will certainly include avoiding copyright issues and the revision-friendly nature of the original). But the recycling also has to do with economics: Abraham Mason may have redone the woodcuts for Anthon's commentary in 1838, but once you have a stable, reusable

---

63 General discussion: Kraus and Stray 2016b.

set of images, those plates — be they from engravings, woodcuts, or lithographs — can be reproduced from one edition to another, even from one publisher to another; this is especially true once reproduction techniques became cheaper toward the end of the nineteenth century. In the case of the bridge, one might venture that the intractability of the Latin has encouraged commentators to stick with what works — only Rice Holmes, to my knowledge, actually commissioned an architect (E. Stanley Hall) to produce a different blueprint for the structure (Rice Holmes 1914, facing 145).

Robert Brown has analysed Caesar's bridge description as a proper ekphrasis (2013, 45):

> like other engineering feats in the *Commentaries*, [Caesar] presents the bridge less as an exciting visual spectacle than a heroic triumph of will and technology. The description is elaborate in some respects and stylistically striking, but in a way that appeals more to the mind than to the eye. It asks us not so much to 'see' the bridge as a completed artifact as to follow the process of its construction from the bottom up, to grasp the form and function of its separate elements and the strength of the whole. Its technical details place an intellectual demand upon the reader, but the power of the description transcends its technical difficulties. As a statement of mastery over nature, it is unrivalled in the *Bellum Gallicum*.[64]

Wyke, for her part, considers the meta-narrative and pedagogical implications of the bridge's construction:

> Building a small scale replica of the Rhine bridge…operates as a tangible metonymy for overcoming the greater complexity and narrative flow of second-year Latin: it demonstrates physically that a wondrous edifice can be constructed out of interlinked parts, provides a visceral sense of direction and purpose, and offers the excitement clearly absent from drills in accidence and syntax (2012, 32).

Despite the pull toward what one might call literary tradition, however, these illustrations paradoxically bring home our apparently endless appetite for connecting our literary texts with the external, phenomenal world. For many we cannot study in detail here — for example, Filarete and Palladio, or the architects John Soane and Cass Gilbert — the Rhine bridge was a real structure to draw or model as practice and illustration.[65] And even today it is far more common to approach the bridge as the BBC show, 'Secrets of the Ancients,' did: as a wonder, yes, and a matter of fear to the Germans as they watched it advance across the 1300-foot span of the Rhein — but primarily as something that we can understand

---

64 For other material on ekphrasis in Caesar see Kraus 2010b, Brown 2013.
65 Gros and Beltramini 2003; the Soane bridge is illustrated at 64; Gilbert 1910. The American painter Charles Wilson Peale modelled the bridge as a child (Winterer 2007, 58).

only by building it again (Hargreaves 1999). In 2017, the German government announced that they were going to try to reconstruct the bridge in its (putative) original spot, near Nieweid (HEP 2017).

The schoolbooks I have studied here were intended to help pre-college students read, with some enjoyment, a masterwork of Western literature. That reading, in turn, would conduct them 'to a higher knowledge of the power and use of the Latin tongue' (Harkness 1872 [1870], iii), help them be admitted into University (above, p. 250), mold their characters (Wyke 2012, 40–44), and even strengthen their scepticism and critical acumen (Rice Holmes 1914, iv).

Bibliography

Abbott, J. (1855), *The Harper Establishment; or How the Story Books are Made*, New York.
Alberti Leon Battista (1550), *L'Architettura di Leon Battista Alberti tradotta in lingua Fiorentina da Cosimo Bartoli ... Con la aggiunta de Disegni*, Florence.
Andrews, E.A. (1845) *C. Julius Caesar's Commentaries on the Gallic War; with a Dictionary and Notes*, Boston.
Anthon, C. (1825a), *C. Crispi Sallusti opera, omissis fragmentis, omnia; ad optimorum exemplarium fidem recensita animadversionibus illustravit P. Wilson LL.D. Editio quarta recensuit notasque suas adspersit Carolus Anthon*, New York. 4th ed.
Anthon, C. (1825b), *A Classical Dictionary ... by J. Lemprière, D.D. Fifth American edition corrected and improved by Charles Anthon*, New York.
Anthon, C. (1838), *Caesar's Commentaries on the Gallic war; and the First Book of the Greek Paraphrase; with English Notes, Critical and Explanatory, Plans of Battles, Sieges, etc., and Historical, Geographical, and Archaeological Indexes*, New York.
Anthon, C. (1841), *A Classical Dictionary*, New York.
Anthon, C. (1843a), *The Aeneid of Virgil, with English notes, Critical and Explanatory, a Metrical Clavis, and an Historical, Geographical, and Mythological Index*, New York.
Anthon, C. (1843b), *A Dictionary of Greek and Roman Antiquities edited by William Smith, Ph.D. ... First American edition, carefully revised ... by Charles Anthon, LL.D.*, New York.
Anthon, C./W. Trollope (1847), *P. Virgilii Maronis Aeneis. The Aeneid of Virgil, with English notes, Critical and Explanatory, a Metrical Clavis, and an Historical, Geographical, and Mythological Index by Charles Anthon, Ll.D. ... edited, with considerable alterations, and adapted to the use of English schools and colleges, by the Rev. W. Trollope, M.A.*, London.
Bann, S. (1984), *The Clothing of Clio*, Cambridge.
Beltramini, G. (2008), 'Ancient Battles', in: *Palladio* (exhibition catalogue), G. Beltramini/ H. Burns (eds.), London, 342–355.
Beltramini, G. (2009), *Andrea Palladio and the Architecture of Battle*, Venice.
Bingham, W. (1863), *A Grammar of the Latin Language, For the Use of Schools, with Exercises and Vocabularies*, Greensboro, NC.
Bingham, W. (1864), *Caesar's Commentaries on the Gallic War with a Vocabulary and Notes*, Greensboro, NC.

Brown, R.D. (2013), 'Caesar's description of bridging the Rhine (*Bellum Gallicum* 4.16–19): a literary analysis', *CP* 108, 41–53.

Bullions, P. (1845), *The First Six Books of Caesar's Commentaries on the Gallic war, Adapted to Bullions' Latin Grammar; with an Introduction, on the Idioms of the Latin Language; Copious Explanatory Notes; and an Index of Proper Names, etc.*, New York.

Compton, W.C. (1892), *Caesar's Seventh Campaign in Gaul, B.C. 52, De bello Gallico lib. vii. Edited, with Notes, Excursus, and Tables of Idioms*, London.

Conway, W.M. (1884), *The Woodcutters of the Netherlands in the Fifteenth Century*, Cambridge.

Cook, K.S. (2015), 'Reproduction of maps: photomechanical processes', in: M. Monmonier (ed.), *Cartography in the twentieth Century*, 2 vols., Chicago, 1316–1320.

De Maré, E. (1980), *The Victorian Woodblock Illustrators*, London.

De Vinne, T.L. (1902), *A Treatise on Title-Pages*, New York.

Dehn, W. (1960), 'Einige Bemerkungen zum *Murus Gallicus*', *Germania* 38, 43–55.

Dodington, P.M. (1980), *The Function of the References to Engineering in Caesar's Commentaries*, diss. Iowa.

Du Choul, G. (1556), *Discours sur la castramétation et discipline militaire des Romains*, Lyons.

Edelman, H. (2015), 'New wine in old Bottles: Lemprière's Classical Dictionary and the development of scholarly publishing in America', *JRUL* 67, 56–74.

Exman, E. (1965), *The Brothers Harper. A Unique Publishing Partnership and its Impact upon the Cultural Life of America from 1817 to 1853*, New York.

Exman, E. (1967), *The House of Harper. One hundred and fifty years of publishing*, New York.

Filarete. (1461–1464), *Trattato di architettura*. Unpublished, Florence Bib N. Cent. MS II.i.140.

Fowler, A. (2017), *The Mind of the Book: Pictorial Title Pages*, Oxford.

Fowler, D.P. (1991), 'Narrate and describe: the problem of ekphrasis,' *JRS* 81, 25–35, repr. in *Roman Constructions: Readings in Postmodern Latin* (Oxford, 2000), 64–85.

Foy, L. (1984), *In the Best Style of the Art: Commercial and Fine Art Printing in Canada 1850–1950 (exhibition catalogue)*, Ottawa.

Gehl, P.F. (2016), 'Selling Terence in Renaissance Italy', in: Kraus/Stray (eds.) 2016a, 253–274.

Gilbert, C. (1910), 'Construction of Caesar's Bridge across the Rhine / [by] CG Jr,' Library of Congress archives, https://www.loc.gov/item/ade1997000287 (accessed November 2019).

Giocondo, Fra. G. (1513) *Commentatiorum de bello Gallico libri VIII. De bello civili pompeiano libri IIII. De bello Alexandrino liber I. De bello Africano liber I. De bello Hispaniensi liber I*, Venice.

Grafton, A.T. (2008), 'Textbooks and the disciplines', in: E. Campi et al. (eds.), *Scholarly Knowledge: Textbooks in Early Modern Europe*, Paris, 11–35.

Gros, P./G. Beltramini (2003), 'Caesar's bridge on the Rhine', in: A. Maggi/N. Navone (eds.), *John Soane and the Wooden Bridges of Switzerland*, Mendrisio/London, 182–196.

Groves, J.D. (1995), '"Ticknor-and-Fields-Ism of All Kinds": Thomas Starr King, Literary Promotion, and Canon Formation', *New England Quarterly* 68, 206–222.

Hamilton, S. (1958), *Early American book Illustrators and Wood Engravers*, 2 vols., Princeton.

Hancher, M. (2010), 'Illustrating Webster', *Dictionaries* 31, 1–45.

Hargreaves, S. (1999), Transcript and Video of "Secrets of the Ancients, Series 1, Episode 2, Caesar's Bridge", https://search.alexanderstreet.com/view/work/bibliographic_entity%7Cvideo_work%7C2107780 (accessed November 2019).

Harkness, A. (1851), *Arnold's First Latin Book; Remodelled and Rewritten, and Adapted to the Ollendorff Method of Instruction*, New York.

Harkness, A. (1872 [1870]), *Caesar's Commentaries on the Gallic War; with Explanatory Notes, a Copious Dictionary, and a Map of Gaul*, New York.
Harkness, A. (1879), *Caesar's Commentaries on the Gallic War; with Explanatory Notes, a Copious Dictionary, and a Map of Gaul*. Revised edition, New York.
Harkness, A. (1881), *A Latin Grammar for Schools and Colleges*. Revised edition, New York.
Harkness, A. (1882), *Caesar's Commentaries on the Gallic War; with Explanatory Notes, a Copious Dictionary, and a Map of Gaul. Adapted to the Revised Standard Edition of the Author's Latin Grammar*, New York.
Harkness, A. (1886), *Caesar's Commentaries on the Gallic War with Notes, Dictionary, and a Map of Gaul*. Revised edition, illustrated, New York.
Harkness, A. (1887), *The Military System of the Romans*, New York.
Harkness, A./C.H. Forbes (1901), *Caesar's Commentaries on the Gallic War with Introduction, Notes, and Vocabulary*, New York.
Harloe, K. (2016), 'Christian Gottlob Heyne and the changing fortunes of the commentary in the age of Altertumswissenschaft', in: Kraus/Stray (eds.) 2016a, 435–456.
Harper, J.H. (1912), *The House of Harper: A Century of Publishing in Franklin Square*, New York.
Heenes, V. (2014), 'On Sixteenth-Century Copies of the Reliefs from the Column of Trajan – Two New Drawings from an Unknown Rotulus', *RIHA Journal* 0094 (9 July 2014).
HEP (2017), 'Ein Teil von Cäsars Brücke soll entstehen,' *Blick aktuell: Aus Liebe zur Heimat*, 30 June 2017. https://www.blick-aktuell.de/Berichte/Ein-Teil-von-Caesars-Bruecke-soll-entstehen-274309.html (accessed November 2019).
Hunt, L. (1821), 'A new pocket edition of Horace,' *The Indicator* 73, 2/28/1821, 161–162.
Jung, S. (2018), *The Publishing and Marketing of Illustrated Literature in Scotland, 1760–1828*, Lanham, MD.
Kaiser, R. (2017), 'Caesar's Rhine Bridge and its Feasibility in Giovanni Giocondo's *Expositio pontis* (1513),' in: M. Formisano/P. van der Eijk (eds.), *Knowledge, Text and Practice in Ancient Technical Writing*, Cambridge, 68–92.
Kelsey, F.W. (1886), *C. Iuli Caesaris de bello Gallico libri vii. Caesar's Gallic War with an Introduction, Notes, and Vocabulary*, Boston.
Kelsey, F.W. (1897), *C. Iuli Caesaris de bello Gallico libri vii. Caesar's Gallic War with an Introduction, Notes, and Vocabulary*, 8th ed., Boston.
Kelsey, F.W. (1918), *C. Iulii Caesaris Commentarii rerum gestarum. Caesar's Commentaries: the Gallic War, Books I-IV, with Selections from Books V-VII and from the Civil War with an Introduction, Notes, a Companion to Caesar and a Vocabulary*, Boston.
Kraus C.S./C.A. Stray (eds.) (2016a), *Classical Commentaries*, Oxford.
Kraus, C.S. (2007), 'Caesar's account of the battle of Massilia (BC 1.34–2.22): some historiographical and narratological approaches', in: J.M. Marincola (ed.), *A Companion to Greek and Roman Historiography*, Oxford, 371–378.
Kraus, C.S. (2010a), 'Divide and conquer: Caesar, *De bello Gallico* 7', in: C.S. Kraus et al. (eds.), *Ancient Historiography and its Contexts*, Oxford, 40–59.
Kraus, C.S. (2010b), 'Speech and silence in Caesar, *Bellum gallicum*', in: D. Berry/A. Erskine (eds.), *Form and Function in Roman Oratory*, Cambridge, 247–263.
Kraus, C.S./C.A. Stray (2016b), 'Form and content', in: Kraus/Stray (eds.) 2016a, 1–18.
Leverett, F.P. (1829), *Caii Julii Caesaris commentarii de bello Gallico. Accedunt notulae Anglicae atque index historicus et geographicus. In usum scholae Bostoniensis*, Boston.
Lincoln, J.L. (1882), *Livy's Roman History*, New York.
Lipsius, J. (1596), *Poliorcheton sive de machinis, tormentis, telis, libri quinque*, Antwerp.

Lyons, C.L. (2005), 'The art and science of antiquity in nineteenth-century photography: early views of ancient mediterranean sites', in: *eadem et al.* (eds.), *Antiquity and Photography*, Los Angeles, 22–65.
Mainardi, P. (2017), *Another World: Nineteenth-Century Illustrated Print Culture*, New Haven.
Marzio, P.C. (1979), *The Democratic Art: Pictures for a 19th-Century America*, Boston.
McLean, R. (1972), *Victorian Book Design and Colour Printing*, 2nd ed., London.
Mitchell, M. (1993), *Encyclopedia Brunoniana*, Providence, RI. Available online: https://www.brown.edu/Administration/News_Bureau/Databases/Encyclopedia/ (accessed November 2019).
Mitchell, R. (2000), *Picturing the Past. English History in Text and Image 1830–1870*, Oxford.
Montanus, A. (1661), *C. Iulii Caesaris quae extant cum selectis commentariis …*, Amsterdam.
Napoléon III (1865–1866), *Histoire de Jules César,* 3 vols., Paris.
Oksanish, J. (2019), *Vitruvian Man*, Oxford.
Overton, G. (1925), *Portrait of a Publisher and the First Hundred Years of the House of Appleton 1825–1925*, New York.
Owen, E. (1936), 'Caesar in American schools prior to 1860', *CJ* 31, 212–222.
Palladio, A. (1570), *I quattro libri dell'architettura*, Siena.
Palladio, A. (1575), *I commentari di C Giulio Cesare con le figure …*, Venice.
Papy, J. (2004), 'An antiquarian scholar between text and image? Justus Lipsius, Humanist education, and the visualization of Ancient Rome', *Sixteenth-Century Journal* 25, 97–131.
Patrizi, F. (1583), *La militia romana di Polibio, di Tito Livio, e di Dionigi Alicarnaseo*, Ferrara.
Pedley, J.G. (2012), *The Life and Work of Francis Willey Kelsey*, Ann Arbor, MI.
Reinhardt, T./Lapidge, M./Adams, J.N. (2005) (eds.), *Aspects of the Language of Latin Prose*, Oxford.
Rheinhard, H. (1883), *C. Julii Caesaris commentarii de bello gallico zum Schulgebrauch mit Anmerkungen herausgegeben*, 4th ed., Stuttgart.
Rice Holmes, T. (1911), *Caesar's Conquest of Gaul*, 2nd ed., Oxford.
Rice Holmes, T. (1914), *C. Iuli Caesaris commentarii rerum in Gallia gestarum VII A. Hirti commentarius VIII*, Oxford.
Riggsby, A.M. (2006), *Caesar in Gaul and Rome: War in Words*, Austin.
Savorgnan, M. (1599), *Della milizia terrestre e marittima*, Venice.
Schmitz, L./C.G. Zumpt (1847), *C. Julii Caesaris Commentarii de bello Gallico*, Philadelphia.
Silkenat, D. (2016), *Driven from Home: North Carolina's Civil Refugee Crisis*, Athens, GA.
Smith, M.M. (2000), *The Title-Page: its early Development 1460–1510,* London/New Castle, DE.
Smith, W. (1842), *A Dictionary of Greek and Roman Antiquities Edited by William Smith, Ph.D.*, London.
Spencer, J.A. (1848), *C. Julius Caesar's Commentaries on the Gallic War with English Notes, Critical and Explanatory, a Lexicon, Indexes, etc.*, New York.
Spencer, J.A. (1890), *Memorabilia of Sixty-five Years (1820–1886)*, New York.
Steele, J.D. (1872), *Fourteen Weeks in Human Physiology*, New York.
Stem, R./F.W. Kelsey (2017), *Julius Caesar Commentaries on the Gallic War Books 1–5 and 6.11–24. Text, Notes, Companion, and Vocabulary by Francis W. Kelsey. Revised and with a new Introduction by Rex Stem*, Ann Arbor, MI.
Stevens, B. (2019), 'Wood engraving as ghost writing', *Textual Practice* 33, 645–677.
Stray, C.A. (1994), 'Paradigms regained: towards a historical sociology of the textbook', *JCS* 26, 1–29.

Stray, C.A. (2006), 'Paper wraps stone: the beginnings of educational lithography', *Journal of the Printing Historical Society* 9, 13–29.
Stray, C.A. (2007), 'Sir William Smith and his Dictionaries: a study in scarlet and black', in: idem (ed.), *Classical Books: Scholarship & Publishing in Britain since* 1800, *BICS* Supplement 101, 35–54.
Stray, C.A. (2010), Review of A. Craik, *Mr Hopkins' Men: Cambridge Reform and British Mathematics in the 19th Century*, *HoU* 25.1, 219–225.
Stray, C.A. (2019), '*Liddell and Scott* in historical context', in: C.A. Stray/M. Clarke/J.T. Katz (eds.), *Liddell and Scott: The History, Methodology, and Languages of the World's Leading Lexicon of Ancient Greek*, Oxford, 3–24.
Stuart, G. (1868), *Caii Julii Caesaris commentarii de bello Gallico with Notes, and Lexicon*, Philadelphia.
Sypher, F.J. (2014), *Charles Anthon, American Classicist*, Ann Arbor, MI.
Tebbel, J. (1972), *A History of Book Publishing in the United States. Vol. 1: The Creation of an Industry 1630–1865*, New York.
Tetlow, J. (1881), 'The Eastern Colleges for Women: their aims, means, and methods. Part I', *Education* 1, 465–484.
Thornton, R.J. (1821), *The Pastorals of Virgil, with a Course of English Reading, Adapted for Schools*, London.
Tufte, E.R. (1990), *Envisioning Information*, Cheshire, CT.
Tufte, E.R. (2006), *Beautiful Evidence*, Cheshire, CT.
Twyman, M. (2013), *A History of Chromolithography: Printed Colour for All*, London/New Castle, DE.
Wakeman, G. (1973), *Victorian Book Illustration. The Technical Revolution*, Detroit, MI.
Webster, N. (1843), *A Collection of Papers on Political, Literary, and Moral Subjects*, New York.
Weeks, S.B. (1900), *Confederate Textbooks: A Preliminary Bibliography*. Report of the U.S. Commissioner of Education, Washington, D.C.
Winterer, C. (2002), *The Culture of Classicism: Ancient Greece and Rome in American Intellectual Life*, Baltimore, MD.
Winterer, C. (2007), *The Mirror of Antiquity: American Women and the Classical Tradition*, Ithaca, NY.
Wolfe, G.R. (1981), *The House of Appleton: The History of a Publishing House and its Relationship to the Cultural, Social, and Political Events that Helped Shape the Destiny of New York City*, Metuchen, N.J.
Wyke, M. (2012), *Caesar in the USA*, Berkeley.

Part V: **International Connections**

Ward Briggs
The Founding of the American Philological Association

In the decades after Edward Everett, George Bancroft, and others had gone to Germany to acquire a level of learning impossible in their young country, and failed to transplant German methods into American (i.e., Harvard) classrooms, the lustre associated with classical study in Germany began to dim.[1] Only a few American students sought out degrees in Germany in the 1830s and 1840s,[2] but in the decade preceding the Civil War, this thin trickle reached a watershed when students from north and south sought the German doctorates that would enable them to professionalize American classical studies. Among these students were William Dwight Whitney (1827–94), William Watson Goodwin (1831–1912), Basil Lanneau Gildersleeve (1831–1924), George Martin Lane (1823–97), Francis James Child (1825–96), Lewis Richard Packard (1836–84), and James Morgan Hart (1839–1916), men who would have better fortune than the Everett generation in bringing the methods and standards of German study to America.[3]

Beyond German lectures and seminars, these men witnessed the vital role played by philological societies in disseminating research and fostering a sense of community. Philological societies had arisen in Europe following the attention given to the theories of comparative Indo-European linguistics proposed by Franz Bopp (1791–1867) beginning in 1816, supported by Rasmus Kristian Rask (1787–1832), and Jacob Ludwig Karl Grimm (1785–1863) (Evans 1977). Georg Curtius (1820–85) was then instrumental in introducing Bopp's ideas into the schools. The American students at Göttingen, Gildersleeve, Goodwin, Lane, Bonbright, and Allen, who would become the early members of the American Philological Association, not only met great figures at their German universities but may well have seen other worthies perform at the annual meetings of the Versammlung der deutschen Philologen und Schulmänner, founded at Göttingen in 1837. They

---

1 Edward Everett, (1794–1865; Ph.D. Göttingen, 1817), George Bancroft (Ph.D., Göttingen, 1829; Robert Bridges Patton (1794–1835, Ph.D. Göttingen, 1821). See full discussion by Reinhold 1984b.
2 John Lincoln Larkin (1817–91) studied at Halle and Berlin, 1841–3; Thomas Anthony Thacher (1815–86) studied in Germany and Italy 1843–5.
3 William Francis Allen (1830–89) studied at Berlin and Göttingen, 1854–5; Daniel Bonbright (1831–1912) studied at Berlin, Bonn, and Göttingen 1856–8, as did Albert Harkness (1822–1907) in 1853–5; William Elisha Peters (1829–1906) studied at Berlin 1856–8.

https://doi.org/10.1515/9783110719215-012

would likely be familiar with its *Verhandlungen*, published from 1838.⁴ Whitney, who had converted from a medical to a linguistic student while reading Bopp during a youthful illness, would have arrived in Berlin in time to see the 11th Versammlung, held September 30–October 3, 1850, while Gildersleeve, who had departed Göttingen for Bonn in the spring of 1852, might well have attended the 13th in Göttingen on September 29–October 2 of that year (Bindseil).

Britain was introduced to Bopp's theories by Friedrich August Rosen (1805–37), chair of Oriental Literature at London University, but it was not until 1842 that Edwin Guest (1800–1860) proposed the formation of a philological society, whose purpose was 'the Philological Illustration of the Classical Writers of Greece and Rome' along with the study of English.⁵ As president from the first meeting until 1863, Connop Thirlwall (1797–1875) was a steady hand at the helm during the early years. The chief philological interest early on was the lexical work of Grimm and ultimately the major project of the Society was the *New English Dictionary* (1884), edited by James Augustus Henry Murray (1837–1915).⁶

In France the Association pour l'Encouragement des Études Grecques was founded in May of 1867 and led in its early years by Théodore Reinach (1860-1928) and Paul Mazon (1874–1955). After publishing *Actes annuaires* in 1867, it began *Revue des Études grecques* in 1888.

During the bloody disagreement between the Northern and Southern states, some Northerners still went to Germany for study (Southerners were prevented from European travel by a Federal blockade of Southern ports.).⁷ Among them was the son of upstate New York Abolitionists, George Fisk Comfort (1833–1910). He graduated from Wesleyan University in 1857 and taught sufficiently to earn an A.M. in 1860. Impressed at the age of 23 by the European painting and sculpture at the 1853 International Exhibition at New York's Crystal Palace, he wisely spent the years of the Civil War (1860–5) first travelling throughout Italy and Asia Minor for two years, and then passing the next three based in Berlin in order 'to get as

---

4 *Verhandlungen der ersten Versammlung deutscher Philologen und Schulmänner in Nürnberg 1838* (Nürnberg, 1838).
5 Marshall cites a notice in *The Atheneaeum* (1842, 463) that the meeting voted to include other languages besides Greek, Latin, and English, but this did not appear in the final version of the by-laws.
6 On the Philological Society's efforts to begin the dictionary, see Mugglestone 2005, 1–36; Winchester 1998, 107–11, and Gilliver 2018. American classicists maintained an interest in the doings at the Scriptorium at Mill Hill, see Cook 1881 and C.K. Nelson (*Proceedings 1887*, v).
7 E.g., Tracy Peck (1838–1921) studied at Berlin, Jena, and Bonn (1861–4). Clement Lawrence Smith (1844–1909) studied at Göttingen 1865–6.

complete a view as I could of the conditions of art there and the nature of art institutions.'[8] He developed his language skills by hiking everywhere, often, by his own account, covering 20–40 miles per day, visiting every museum and library along the way and versing himself in Western European art from antiquity to the present.[9]

Comfort returned to an America generally ignorant of European languages, much less philology (Sihler 1902, Calder 1966). He was also determined that the newly re-united states should have its own great public museums so that Americans could study the art of the world. When in 1867 Allegheny College, in the far northwestern corner of Pennsylvania, offered him both a professorship in German as well as the first professorship of aesthetics in the country, Comfort landed a position for which he was ideally suited. Allegheny's plan was to establish the first degree-granting course in fine arts and the first teaching museum of art history in the United States, but the economic effects of the 1866 collapse of the Pennsylvania oil boom, upon which these plans depended, finally reached the little college in Meadville, PA, and ended the project.

Comfort summarily left the Pennsylvania hinterland in 1868 for New York, where he lived while a lecturer in Christian Art at the recently (1867) founded Drew Theological Seminary in Madison, NJ. Residence in New York allowed him to mingle freely with the newly moneyed classes and the patrons of the arts who were as educated, well-travelled, and eager as Comfort was to put his newly reformed country culturally and economically on the same footing with Europe at a scale that matched its wealth. While he supplemented his income by producing six German-language instruction books, he still hoped to create a comprehensive museum, such as he had been promised at Allegheny. In the meantime, Comfort felt another pressing need.

In 1868 the only learned associations devoted to a specific field of scholarship were the American Philosophical Society (founded 1743), the American Academy of Arts and Sciences (1780), and the American Antiquarian Society (1812). The American Oriental Society, a Yale-centred organization, was created in 1842 and numbered among its presidents such classicists as Theodore Dwight Woolsey (1801–89) and James Hadley (1821–72). William Dwight Whitney served as its corresponding secretary for 27 years, beginning in 1857. The American Association for the Advancement of Science began in 1848 followed by the American Numismatic Society in 1858 (*Handbook*).

---

8 Howe, 4. For a detailed account of Comfort's travels in Europe, see Tatham 1973, 3–4.
9 George F. Comfort to Ralph M. Comfort, 29 December 1901, Comfort Papers, Syracuse University, see Tatham 1973, 4. See further Comfort 1902.

In the summer of 1868, the 36-year-old Comfort 'opened a correspondence' (*Convention* 1870, 5) that read in part:

> What seems to be adapted to the present wants of America in regard to philological science, is an association which shall be open for membership to all professors of language of respectable standing in our colleges, universities, theological seminaries, and other schools of high education, and to others interested in the promotion of philological studies; which shall hold its sessions annually during the long summer vacation, so that all may be in attendance without being forced to leave the duties of their chairs; and which shall hold its sessions in such different parts of the country as may, from time to time, be found convenient. (Shero 1964, xi)

This letter led to a meeting of over 50 interested parties from the New York area in the white Gothic chapel (long since gone) of New York University on November 13, 1868.[10] The president of the university, the Reverend Dr. Isaac Ferris (1798–1873), was elected president for the meeting and Albert Harkness (1822–1907), professor of Greek at Brown University, was elected secretary. Ferris called on Comfort, who spoke of the many German learned societies that promoted linguistics and philology to the point that Germany was 'the home and centre of modern philology.' (*Convention* 1870, 5) He specifically suggested modelling the new association on the Versammlung der deutschen Philologen und Schulmänner, which held annual summer meetings for the purpose of reading papers that would then be published in learned journals. Comfort then laid out seven areas of interest for the new Association:

1. The science of language and the history of philology
2. Oriental languages and literatures
3. Classical Languages and Literatures
4. Modern European Languages and Literatures
5. English Language and Literature
6. American aboriginal languages
7. Linguistic pedagogy

Comfort was then charged with arranging a full and formal meeting in Poughkeepsie, New York, on July 27, 1869, called 'A Convention of American Philologists.' His proposal to found 'a permanent National Society for the Promotion of Philological Studies and Research in America' was endorsed by over 100 scholars, university presidents, and notable public figures, particularly Massachusetts

---

10 A Sesquicentennial meeting was held at NYU to commemorate the event on November 13, 2018.

Senator Charles Sumner (1811–74), Ohio Congressman James A. Garfield (1831–81), and the Shakespeare scholar Richard Grant White (1822–85).[11]

The group met on the appointed Tuesday afternoon at the Mill Street Congregational Church in Poughkeepsie.[12] Comfort called the meeting to order. A president and secretary for the convention were elected and a nominations committee appointed to supply a slate of officers. While the committee met, Comfort reiterated his goals in virtually the same terms he had used in his proposal, describing the workings of European philological societies.

Rev. Howard Crosby (1826–91), professor of Greek and Chancellor of the University of the City of New York, read a paper sent in by Joseph Henry (1797–1878), the first secretary of the Smithsonian Institution and the second president of the National Academy of Sciences, welcoming the new society with a contribution entitled, 'The Operations of the Smithsonian Institution in regard to Philology.' By describing points of shared interest such as the Institute's devotion to ethnology and thus the philology of indigenous languages realized in its published volumes on archaeology, vocabulary, and dialects of Native American languages, a Library of American Linguistics, and other projects, Henry gave a positive sign that philology was being welcomed into the company of American sciences.

The evening session commenced at 8:00 p.m. The nominations committee reported out the officers: Whitney, currently secretary of the American Oriental Society,[13] as president, Harkness and The Reverend Benjamin Woodbridge Dwight (1816–89), a scholar and educator in Clinton, NY, as vice presidents and, most importantly, Comfort as secretary.[14] Whitney served only one year as president, but his status as a scholar assured that in the early days of the Association,

---

11 As a boy Sumner taught himself enough Latin to recognize a quotation in a speech given by Daniel Webster and repeat it to his father. Impressed, his father agreed to send him to Harvard. 'I felt I too belonged to the brotherhood of scholars.' (Taylor 2001, 28) He became fluent in Spanish, Italian, and German. Garfield was a professor of classical languages and literature and principal at Western Reserve Eclectic Institute (now Case Western University) in Cleveland, OH, before serving in the Civil War. He entered politics in 1863 and was elected 20th president of the United States in 1880. It was popularly said of him, 'He could write Greek with his left hand while writing Latin with his right.' White was a leading musical and literary critic. He completed his 12-volume edition of Shakespeare in 1865 and published *Words and Their Uses* in 1870.

12 For a thorough account of the meeting and synopses of the papers given, see *Proceedings 1869–70*, 8–30.

13 He was corresponding secretary, librarian, and editor of *JAOS*, to which he contributed nearly half the articles in vols. 6–12.

14 As new committees and the Board of Directors were formed, all nominations continued to be made by a committee of three appointed each year by the president which presented a ballot with only one candidate for each office. In 1903 the size of the committee was increased to five,

'Sanskrit still sat upon that towering pedestal.' (Moore 1919, 11) He was regularly elected to the executive committee and was, like Thirlwall for the Philological Society (see further below), a formative influence on the aims and standards of the young Association.

A letter from the indisposed chair of the local committee, Charles Jedediah Buckingham, Esq. (1810–89), who would be treasurer (1875–83), welcomed the attendees to the 'Athens of the Hudson.' In the early days when the attendance was small, interested citizens like Buckingham often gave receptions at their own expense. Once the meetings became larger, local citizens gave teas rather than receptions. Moore comments on the ease with which the disparate members of the 'town and gown' community communicated: 'The eagerness of the professors to talk with people of ordinary education and draw them out, so as to study them, was especially notable.' (Moore 1919, 15–16)

There followed a number of short speeches on language, including one on the proper pronunciation of 'Poughkeepsie,' letters of support from absent members, and a letter of regret for his absence from Samuel F.B. Morse (1791–1872), inventor of the telegraph and founder and benefactor of Vassar College.

The morning session on Wednesday, July 28, commenced at 9:00 a.m. with a session of four papers all devoted to the proper pronunciation of Greek and/or Latin. The authors in this inaugural session were John Baptist Feuling (1838–78), professor of modern languages and English literature at the University of Wisconsin, Samuel Stehman Haldeman (1812–80), then at St. John's College in Annapolis, but at the end of the summer professor of comparative philology at the University of Pennsylvania, and the essayist and translator Charles Astor Bristed (1820–74), who had earlier maintained a protracted disagreement over Greek matters with the Eliot Professor of Greek at Harvard, Cornelius C. Felton (1807–62). A paper sent in by the Greek poet and ambassador to the United States (1867), Alexandros Rizos Rangavis (1809–92), on the pronunciation of ancient Greek was read by Rev. Albert N. Arnold (1814–83) of Madison University (now Colgate). Whitney's comment on Bristed's paper (which he read in Bristed's absence) applied to all the papers: more research was needed before a standard pronunciation could be affirmed. Indeed, we are told that Whitney, Yale's Thomas Day Seymour (1848–1907), and Goodwin could be especially acerbic in criticizing papers, particularly those that advanced new theories (Moore 1919, 10).

The afternoon session was devoted to instruction in classical languages with papers on the topic by Harkness, the Rev. Dr. Henry Martyn Colton (1826–72) of

---

with the retiring president naming his predecessor as the new member. This remained the common practice through the 1960s.

the Yale School for Boys in New York, and E.H. Magill (1825–1907) professor of mental and moral philosophy at the recently opened Swarthmore College. There was discussion of the papers followed by Crosby's presentation of a proposed constitution.[15]

The constitution contained merely six articles ('Name,' 'Officers,' 'Meetings,' 'Members,' 'Sundries,' and 'Amendments'). There would be a president, two vice presidents, a secretary, a curator, and a treasurer. These officers and five others elected from the membership would constitute an executive committee, which would be required to produce a report at each annual meeting and publish the *Proceedings*. No specific time of year was given for the annual meetings though clearly the summer was preferred in an age when educators could not easily take summers abroad.[16] The Constitution also stated that the annual meetings would be held in New York 'or at such other place as at a preceding annual meeting shall be determined upon.'[17] Membership was limited to 'Any lover of philological studies' and each proposed member had to be nominated by an active member and approved by the executive committee. The payment of five dollars in dues ($50 for a life membership) in the first year ensured that the member would be listed evermore as a 'founder' of the Association.

With the constitution swiftly and unanimously approved, the convention agreed to adjourn at noon on the 29th only to re-convene immediately as the American Philological Association.

That evening, Dwight preached to the choir with an inarguable paper, 'The Desirableness of thorough Classical Study to the Attainment of the Ends of the Higher Education.'

The morning session on Thursday the 29th began at 10:00 AM following a visit to Vassar. Crosby began the proceedings by reading a paper by the noted but unreliable archaeologist Heinrich Schliemann (1822–90).[18] (*Proceedings 1869–70*, 18–19) Shero says that Schliemann's paper was 'sent from Paris.' (Shero 1964, xii), but Schliemann was in fact in New York (Chambers 1989, 401–4). Schliemann, who had married an American while he was managing his late brother's gold business in California during 1851–2, interrupted his excavation in Greece (begun in 1868) to come to America to divorce his wife, who was, at the time, in

---

15 For the constitution, see *Proceedings 1869–70*, 16–17.
16 The first winter meeting was held in Ithaca on Dec. 27–29, 1905.
17 The Association did not meet in New York until 1876, then 1899, 1918, 1928, 1935, 1953, 1959, 1970, and most recently there in 1996.
18 For the paper, sent as a letter to the Convention, see Schliemann 1953, 153–7. On Schliemann's divorce, see Traill 1981–2.

Russia. He arrived in New York on March 27, 1869, and moved to Indianapolis, thinking that it would be easier to be divorced in Indiana than New York (see Lilly 1961) He accomplished the divorce on June 30, 1869, and left Indianapolis on July 15. He had hoped to leave New York for France on July 24, which is probably why he wired his paper for Crosby to read on the 29th, but in fact passage for his desired date was fully booked and he could not sail until August 7. Schliemann apparently claimed that the delay allowed him to attend the meeting in Poughkeepsie, but it seems likely that if he had attended, it would have been noticed in the *Proceedings* or by one of the historians. In any case, Schliemann told the about-to-be-formed Association just what it wanted to hear: if half of the collegiate curriculum consisted of language courses then:

> ... this great nation would, in twenty years hence, take the lead of all European nations in philological pursuits and that American genius would perform in philological studies and discoveries just as great wonders as it had until now performed in material arts and in gigantic enterprises. (Chambers 1989, 403)

Schliemann added that American universities should foster the study of Native American languages. In this he was followed the next year when Whitney chose his presidential address to express to all his abhorrence at the government's destruction of the Native American language, culture, and people. In doing so, he set a moral as well as scientific motivation to continue to include studies of Native American languages:

> The philology of the American aboriginal languages...demands, as it has already begun to receive, the most hearty encouragement. Circumstances, and our duty toward the races whom we are dispossessing and destroying, make American philology and archaeology our especial responsibility, and it is our disgrace as a nation that we have been unfaithful to it. (*Proceedings 1871*, 5)

Each of the first nine volumes of *TAPA* contained at least one article on Native American languages. The last paper on the subject was given in 1915 at the 46th meeting of the APA.

Schliemann also sent along the first and only volume of the *Actes annuaires* of the Association pour l'Encouragement des Études Grecques, for which he was thanked in an official resolution. Schliemann was the first foreign member of the APA in 1869 and remained a member until his death in 1890.

The first foreign member to address the association in person was the architect Adolphe Pinart (1849–1915) of Paris, who showed the assembled members photographs of inscriptions and stone statues found on Easter Island.[19] (*Proceedings 1872*, 23).

The second member from outside North America was Edward Wilmot Blyden (1832–1912), a native of the West Indies, who joined in 1879. Unable to be accepted into theological schools in America, he was sent to Monrovia, Liberia, where he was educated, became professor of classics (1862–71) and subsequently president of Liberia College (1880–84) (Lynch 1967).

The first foreign member to publish a paper in *TAPA* and the third foreign member (1879) was a native Swede from Lund, August Hjalmar Edgren (1840–1903). Edgren had served in the Union Army in the American Civil War and afterwards attended Cornell, and was about to leave Yale, where he had been an instructor in French, German, and Sanskrit since 1874, for Lund. His paper was entitled 'The Kindred Germanic Words of German and English, exhibited with reference to their Consonant-Relations'[20] (*Proceedings 1880*, 113–53).

In the next year, Mr. Howard Clarke (ca. 1854–1943), a lecturer at London University and a private tutor based in Notting Hill, London, became the fourth foreign member in 1880. He was also a fellow of Johns Hopkins, but he never published in *TAPA* and did not attend any APA meetings.[21]

Crosby went on to present the abstract of a paper on common grammatical errors sent in by the Rev. Mr. Edwin Otway Burnham (1824–73) from New Ulm, Minnesota. Maximilian Schele de Vere (1820–98), the only member from the University of Virginia, delivered a paper on classical study as the basis of knowing the English language. J. Pierson, principal of Belvidere Academy in Belvidere, NJ, spoke on the study of English in the schools. Discussion followed. The membership endorsed a proposal to establish a standard pronunciation of Greek and Latin.

At 12:00 noon, the Convention adjourned *sine die* and the first meeting of the American Philological Association was immediately called to order. The previous

---

19 Pinart was the second foreign member of the APA but only for 1872.
20 After graduating from Uppsala, Edgren came to America and joined the Federal Army in the American Civil War. He returned to Sweden in 1863 to serve in the Swedish Army (1864–70), then studied at Cornell and Yale in the 1870s, was instructor in French, German, and Sanskrit at Yale (1874–80), lectured in Sanskrit at Lund (1880–4), then modern languages and Sanskrit at the University of Nebraska (1896–1901) when he returned to Sweden and served on the first Nobel Literature Prize Committee.
21 My thanks to Christopher Stray and Rosaline Eyben for information on Clarke.

slate of officers was re-elected with the addition of the private Connecticut historian and scholar of Native American languages,[22] James Hammond Trumbull (1821–97) as Treasurer. Comfort was named Secretary and Curator.

The first paper given at a meeting of the APA was 'The Relation of Phonetics to Philology' by the phonographer James E. Munson (1835–1906) of New York, supporting phonetic spelling.[23] English orthography would be much debated in the ensuing decade and the subject of presidential addresses in 1874 (March), 1875 (Trumbull), 1877 (Haldeman), and 1879 (Sewall). At the 1875 meeting the APA appointed a Committee on the Reform of English Spelling, deleting superfluous letters and using more rational systems of sounds.

The afternoon session was devoted to the value of classical languages in the curriculum with papers by Albert H. Mixer (1822–1908), professor and librarian at the University of Rochester. Rev. Magruder Maury (1836–77) of Cold Spring, NY, defending classical languages, and Comfort, in calling for formal postgraduate study in philology in America, noted that the only postgraduate education in the country was in 'medicine, law, theology, and some branches of natural sciences' (Shero 1964, xvii). Technically Cornell, founded in 1865, began offering a Ph.D. in 1868–9, but when Johns Hopkins University, the first American institution founded on the German model, was finally opened in 1876, the APA celebrated (see below).

Five papers on Native American languages occupied the evening and following morning sessions. In the evening, Trumbull spoke on 'The True Method of Studying the North American Languages' followed by the farmer, missionary to the Cree and Ojibwa tribes, and philologist, the Reverend Thomas Hurlburt (1832–1916) of Caistorville, Canada, 'On the Structure of the Indian Languages' (*Proceedings 1869–70*, 26–7). Hurlburt is the first Canadian to give a paper at an annual meeting, and was a member from 1872 to 1873.

If Comfort's original vision was that 'American' applied only to the United States (though later Canada was fully a part of the organization, see below), the second 'foreign' member (after Schliemann), therefore, would be Hurlburt. Two more Canadians, the ethnologist Horatio Hale (1817–96) and Thomas H. Norton,

---

[22] Trumbull is best known for The Composition of Indian Geographical Names (1870), The Best Methods of Studying the Indian Languages (1871), and Indian Names of Places in Connecticut (1881).

[23] This subject continued to be of interest. In 1905 the APA in concert with the MLA and the National Education Association recommended 'to the makers of dictionaries' the use of a phonetic alphabet and in 1923 the same three associations formed a Joint Committee on Grammatical Nomenclature to regularize grammatical terminology. On March's drive for spelling reform, see Moore 1919, 21–4.

both of Ontario.[24] The first Canadian to publish an article in *TAPA* is William B. Anderson, 'Contributions to the Study of the Ninth Book of Livy' (*Transactions 1908*, 89–103).

The first item read on Friday, July 30, was the abstract by Dr. Frederic Louis Otto Roehrig (1819–1908) professor of Sanskrit and Oriental Languages at Cornell, on the language of the Dakota Indians. Trumbull read a paper by George Gibbs (1815–73) compiler of volumes on Native American vocabularies for the Smithsonian, warning against the destruction of native languages. A paper by the diplomat and editor of the *Washington Chronicle*, Ephraim George Squier (1821–88), on preserving the aboriginal languages of Central and South America was read by Haldeman.

The first meeting concluded with a talk by the new president of Princeton, the Scot Dr. James McCosh (1811–94) 'The Relation of Language to Education.'

The meeting adjourned at 11:30, purposing to reconvene in Rochester, NY, July 26, 1870.

It is clear that the Association began with an earnest desire not only to cover the full range of philology across all languages, but also to pay particular attention to American languages and dialects: Native American (here Trumbull was a leading force), Pennsylvania Dutch, Creole, etc.[25] Over the four days of the first meeting, there were nine sessions, seven of which contained formal paper presentations (four in the Convention; three in the APA). A total of thirteen papers were read, none of them dealing with what we would today consider classical philology. Four papers at the Convention treated the value of classics (Dwight, Schliemann, Schele de Vere, Pierson), an equal number treated the pronunciation of Greek and Latin (Feuling, Haldeman, Bristed, Rangavis), and pedagogy (Harkness, Colton, Magill, Pierson), and one analysed English grammar and spelling (Burnham). Only one speaker was a professor of classics (Harkness). Three were professors of modern languages (Comfort, Feuling, Schele de Vere), and an equal number were schoolmasters (Colton, Dwight, Pierson). The program included professors of comparative philology (Haldeman) and philosophy (Magill), an essayist (Bristed), a diplomat (Rangavis), a clergyman (Burnham), and a banker/archaeologist (Schliemann).

---

24 The next Canadian to join was the Sinologist William Epiphanius Wilson (1845–1916) of Windsor, NS, (1880), D.M. Welton of Toronto (1885), and E.W. Boodle of Montreal (1886). In 1887, sixteen new Canadian members enrolled.

25 Languages of Native Americans were a major interest in the early day of the Association, with two sessions at the first meeting. Each volume of *TAPA* through 1879 contained an article on the subject or a subject related to it. The last paper on Native American language was given in 1889.

The three Association sessions contained nine papers: four on the value of classics (Mixer, Maury, Comfort, McCosh), four on Native American language (Trumbull, Hurlburt, Roehrig, Gibbs). Only one speaker was a professor of Greek (Mixer). The others were clergy (Maury, Hurlburt), professors of modern languages (Comfort, Trumbull), or Sanskrit (Roehrig). There was a phonologist (Munson), an ethnologist (Gibbs), and a college president (McCosh).

In all, five papers were sent in to the meeting (Bristed, Rangavis, Schliemann, Burnham, Gibbs) to be read by others.

The rule was 'small meetings in small places' (Moore 1919, 11). After Poughkeepsie, Rochester, and New Haven (1869, 1870, 1871), the Association met in Providence, RI (1872), Easton, PA (1873), and Hartford, CT (1874), which meeting attracted 74 members. It was thought that a seaside resort not necessarily adjacent to a university might be more appealing to members who might bring their families, so Newport, RI, was selected twice (1875 & 1879) and Saratoga Springs, NY, once (1878), but the meetings also ventured into New York (1876), Baltimore (1877), and Philadelphia (1880). The New Haven meeting set a record with 43% of the members attending (91 out of 210), but between 1878 and 1903 only 4 meetings had more than 60 members present and the Philadelphia meeting was attended by only 24 members. In the second decade the Association began meeting almost exclusively on college campuses: in Burlington, VT, Cambridge, MA, and Amherst, MA.

The second meeting, held in the Brick Presbyterian Church in Rochester, NY, was another four-day gathering, on July 26–9, 1870. (Three-day meetings would start with the third annual meeting.) The meeting welcomed a number of new members, including future presidents Goodwin, Asahel Clark Kendrick (1809–95), and Anglo-Saxon philologist Francis Andrew March (1825–1911) of Lafayette College, as well as one woman, Miss M.B. Flint of Monticello, NY. This meeting established the practice of an address by the outgoing president. Already Whitney saw into the future: 'The classics, of course will occupy the leading place; that department will be most strongly represented, and will least need fostering, while it will call for the most careful criticism' (Shero 1964, xv). For the present, the officers included only one classicist (Harkness); the others were a Sanskritist (Whitney), a schoolmaster (Dwight), and a professor of modern languages (Comfort). Of our first ten presidents, only Goodwin, Kendrick, Harkness, and Gildersleeve were classicists. Only two articles on classics appeared in the first three volumes of *TAPA*. The early volumes rarely reached 200 pages.

Of the sixteen papers read at Rochester, two concerned language in general (Whitney, G.W. Samson of Columbian College, now George Washington University, Washington DC), one was on Indo-European, two on Sanskrit (Whitney), three on Greek (Hadley, Goodwin, Kendrick), one on Latin (Dwight), one on the pronunciation of Greek and Latin (Colton), others on English (Lounsbury), Pennsylvania Dutch (Haldeman), Creole (Van Name) Chinese (Dr. H. McCartee 'of China'), Central American Indian (Porter C. Bliss), Aryan languages (Rev. Annice B. Hyde of Allegheny College) and two on the Algonquin language by Trumbull. Trumbull continued to contribute papers on Native American languages, ultimately publishing 15 articles in *TAPA*, sometimes two or three per volume.

The first full roster of the membership dates to July 1871 (*Proceedings 1869–70*, 27–30) and lists 164 members, with a surprising geographical breadth. The mid-Atlantic region predominated with 54 per cent of the membership: New York (68), Pennsylvania (11), Washington, D.C. (4) New Jersey (4), and Maryland (1). Of the New England representatives Connecticut sent 11, Massachusetts had 10, Maine 4, Rhode Island 3, New Hampshire 2, and Vermont 1. A surprising number came from the middle of the country: Illinois (11), Missouri (6), Michigan (4), Ohio (3), Wisconsin (3), Indiana (2), Minnesota (1). Particularly gratifying for a young association hoping to represent a newly reconstructed nation, seven of the eleven states of the Confederacy were represented: Arkansas (1) Mississippi (1), North Carolina (1), South Carolina (1) Tennessee (2), Texas (2), Virginia (2). One member came from Canada[26] and Schliemann gave his address as 'France.'[27]

Eight women subscribed to the 1868 meeting (Vassar had been founded in Poughkeepsie eight years earlier) but only two of them became members after that first meeting: Mary L. Booth of New York and Alice Robinson Boise [Wood] (1846–1919), the first woman to graduate from the Old University of Chicago.[28] With the growth of women's colleges, there was a consequent growth in female members of the Association. Five years after the Association's founding, there were five women members.[29] There was a growth spurt in 1888 when seven

---

[26] Thomas H. Norton of St. Catherine's. In 1871 there were two Canadian members of the APA. By the 25th meeting (1894) there were three different members. The APA held its first meeting in Canada in 1908. One president, Norman De Witt (1946–7), has been from Canada.

[27] Schliemann listed 'Paris, France' as his address until 1880 when he changed it to 'Athens, Greece.' After 1870 the membership vacillated from year to year, growing to 300 in 1880, nearly 400 in 1894, 500 in 1905, 700 in 1915, 1020 in 1925, 1539 in 1950 and over 3000 in 2000.

[28] Her father, James Robinson Boise (1815–95), was a classicist at Brown (1840–50) and the University of Michigan (1852–68), where he became an advocate for the admission of women (they were admitted first in 1870). Alice informally attended classes at Ann Arbor, but after James moved to the Old University of Chicago (1868–77), she joined the APA as an undergraduate and became the first woman to graduate from that institution (1872). https://dbcs.rutgers.edu/all-scholars/9307-wood-alice-robinson-boise.

[29] Mary C. Dickinson of Northampton, MA, Mrs. M.W. De Munn of Providence, RI, Rebecca S. Lowrey of New York, Julia E. Ward of Mt. Holyoke, and Mrs. A.E. Weston of Antioch College.

women joined the APA and in the next year, two more.³⁰ By 1893 18 of the 378 members of the APA were female. The first female African American member was Helen Maria Chesnutt (1880–1969), the third black graduate of Smith College (1902), who joined in 1920 (Ronnick 2018, 26).

The first woman to give a paper at the annual meeting was Marguerite Sweet, who spoke on the subject of her recent Bryn Mawr dissertation, 'The Third Class of Weak Verbs in Primitive Teutonic, with Special Reference to its Development in Anglo-Saxon.' (*Proceedings 1892*, lii–lvii) It was not until the APA met at Bryn Mawr in 1897 that the first women gave papers on classical topics: Mary Emily Case (1857–1941) of Wells College, 'A Neglected Aspect of Roman Character,' (*Proceedings 1897*, xx–xxi) and Winifred Warren (1870–1958) on the subject of her 1898 Bryn Mawr dissertation, 'A Study of Conjectural Temporal Clauses in Thukydides' (*Proceedings 1897*, lxi–lxv). The first paper published in *TAPA* by a woman was published the year after Abby Leach's presidency: Susan Braley Franklin (1868–1955) of Bryn Mawr on 'Public Appropriations for Individual Offerings and Sacrifices in Greece' (*Transactions 1901*, 72–82).

After inducing Harvard professors to teach women in a separate area known as 'The Annex' (which became Radcliffe College), Abby Leach (1855–1918) taught at Vassar from 1883 and because Harvard would not give women degrees, Vassar awarded her an A.B. in 1885. She was appointed associate professor in 1888, rose to professor of Greek, and worked with several leading lights of the APA while serving on the managing committee of the American School of Classical Studies at Athens (1888–1918). At the 1890 meeting Leach was nominated for the executive committee on an alternate slate proposed by Levi Henry Elwell (1854–1916) of Amherst College (*Proceedings 1890*, xxxii). The slate was not successful, but the executive committee placed her on the slate in 1891. She served on the committee until 1896. In 1897 she was elected second vice president and became the first female president of the APA (1899–1900)³¹ (Briggs 1996–7).

---

30 The Suffragist Eva Channing (1854–1930), the Progressive activist Kate Holladay Claghorn (1864–1938), Mrs. G.W. Field of Brooklyn, NY, Abby Moore Goodwin (1857–1890) of Vassar, Frances Ellen Lord (1835–1920) of Wellesley, Abby Leach (1855–1918) of Vassar, philanthropist and translator of Plato, Ellen F. Mason (1846–1930), Harriett E. McKinstry [Scovill] (1853–1938) of Lake Erie Female Seminary, Painesville, OH, and Helen W. Shute of Smith College.
31 The Modern Language Association, founded 15 years after the APA, did not have a female president until 1954.

In keeping with their European models, the APA produced the first volume of its proceedings in 1871, covering the first two annual meetings,[32] edited officially by the secretary and six anonymous editors 'always screened behind the secretarial veil' (Moore 1919, 19). The secretary would have this responsibility for the first 60 years of the Association's life. The *Proceedings* portion contained minutes and abstracts of papers sent in by members. Presidential addresses were included among the abstracts. The *Transactions* contained full-length articles selected because they were 'real contributions to knowledge' (Moore 1919, 19), fulfilling the promise of Whitney's presidential address, 'Our best welcome, at any rate, will be reserved for actual additions to general knowledge, and such will receive first admission into our published transactions, while more popular and less original papers may be not less acceptable at our meetings.' (*Proceedings 1871*, 5). The 1869–70 volume contained nine articles by seven authors covering the breadth of the philology that the Association considered its purview. Two articles treated classical subjects: Hadley on Greek accentuation and Goodwin on Greek usage. Four of the articles came from Yale: two articles by President Whitney, one on Sanskrit accent and another on the origins of language, one each by English professor Thomas R. Lounsbury (1838–1915) on 16th and 17th-century English, and the librarian Addison Van Name (1835–1922) on the grammar of five dialects of French, Spanish, and Dutch Creole. Trumbull filed two articles on Native American language and Haldeman completed the volume with an article on Pennsylvania Dutch. Either in spite of or because of Whitney's prophecy that Greek and Latin would eventually take over the Association, the number of classics papers was limited to two for the first three volumes, but by volume 4, half the articles were on classical subjects.

When it became clear how selective the anonymous editors were, the members who gave papers at the meeting wrote longer and longer abstracts, which were guaranteed publication. By volume 20, the abstracts covered pages 29–104 of *PAPA*. In 1906 the abstracts were separated from the minutes. In 1894 *TAPA* published two papers in German. Bibliographies of the membership were published annually in 1896 until they, like the abstracts, became too unwieldy.

---

32 The Versammlung der deutschen Philologen und Schulmänner, founded at Göttingen in 1837, published its first *Verhandlung* the following year (see pp. 275–6). The Philological Society would wait 12 years until 1854 to publish its transactions. After publishing its first *Actes annuaires* in 1869, the Association pour l'Encouragement des Études Grecques waited 21 years before publishing *REG* in 1888.

The most notable feature of the third meeting on July 25–27, 1871, in the Representatives' Hall of State House in New Haven, was the since-unmatched proportion of the membership who attended: 91 of 210 members or 43 per cent (Moore 1919, 8).

The fourth meeting was the first held on an academic campus, in the chapel of Brown University in Providence, RI, on July 23–5, 1872.[33] Only 3 of first 12 meetings were held on campuses.[34] To combat the increasingly long-winded papers, it was made a standing rule that papers be limited to 30 minutes (*Proceedings 1877*, 10); extra time would only be allowed 'by unanimous consent.' In time, papers were limited to 20 minutes (Shero, xxi).

From the beginning the APA, though located primarily in the Northeast, aimed to be not only academically but geographically inclusive.[35] When the executive committee met at the Rogers High School in Newport, RI, on July 13–15, 1875, to approve membership, they may have been pleased to see a nomination from the South; of the 204 members in 1875, only 13 came from southern states. When the committee approved the nomination of Harvard-educated Richard Thomas Greener (1844–1922) of the University of South Carolina, it is not clear if they realized that they had accepted the first African American member of the APA.[36]

Greener was born in Philadelphia, educated at Oberlin Preparatory School, Phillips Academy Andover, and after three years at Oberlin College was admitted to Harvard as 'an experiment' and became the first African American graduate of that institution (1870) (Mounter 2002, 17–22). He was a principal of the Institute for Colored Youth in Philadelphia (1870–2), then principal at the Sumner School in Washington, DC, for one semester before joining the University of South Carolina in October 1873 as professor of mental and moral philosophy. The University of South Carolina was the first university in the South to attempt racial integration and Greener was the only African American professor in the states of the Confederacy. He also taught Latin and Greek courses in addition to serving as the

---

[33] The last meeting held at a campus rather than a hotel was at Yale in 1947.
[34] Three of the first ten meetings met in high-school buildings and another in a public library.
[35] Of the first 35 meetings all but five were held in the northeast (Washington to Boston). Exceptions were Cleveland (1881) Charlottesville (1892) Chicago (1893) Madison, WI (1900), and St. Louis (1904) (Benario 1989). The executive committee was asked to consider winter meetings in southern states (*Proceedings 1874*, 35) and in 1876 the Mayor of Greenville, SC, invited the APA to meet in his city, but the executive committee declined citing the 'distance ... from the residences of the large majority of our members' (*Proceedings 1876*, 38).
[36] He might have been known to Harvard classicists, but no one from Harvard was on the executive committee.

university librarian with the task of reorganizing and cataloguing the university's library, which was damaged during the Civil War. His colleague Fisk Parsons Brewer (1832–90) had joined the APA in 1872 while still at the University of North Carolina. He came to the University of South Carolina in 1875 and nominated Greener that year. In 1876, Greener completed his studies in law and was admitted to the South Carolina Bar. Greener proposed a paper for the 1877 meeting in Baltimore which would be presided over by vice-president Basil L. Gildersleeve. The paper was entitled, 'The Library of the University of South Carolina, Its Rare and Curious Books'[37] and was listed on the preliminary program for the meeting, but in the turmoil following the removal of Federal troops from South Carolina in 1877, the subsequent closing of the university by Governor Wade Hampton III (1818–1902), and the threats made to Greener and his family, he fled to Baltimore in June 1877. Even though he was in Baltimore at the time of the meeting on July 10–12, 1877, the upheaval of his life prevented his attendance at the meeting. He became professor of law at Howard University (1877–80), maintaining his APA membership until he became dean (1879–80).[38]

The second African American member of the APA (1880) was Edward Wilmot Blyden (1832–1912), mentioned above. The third African American member (1881) was William Sanders Scarborough (1852–1926), who joined in 1882 and was also the first black member of the Modern Language Association. He was a member for 44 years, participated in person from 1884 to 1907, and gave over 20 papers at meetings (Ronnick 2018, 13).

At the eighth meeting in New York, July 18–20, 1876, half of the papers delivered orally were on Greek and Latin and one-third of the papers in *TAPA* were on these subjects. Classics would not enjoy a complete monopoly until well into the 20th century. Papers on Sanskrit appeared in 1920.

1876 was also the year of the founding of the Johns Hopkins University. Consequently, the university's president Daniel Coit Gilman (1831–1908), its professor of Greek, Gildersleeve, and a student from Gildersleeve's first seminar, Ernst Gottlieb Sihler (1853–1942) were elected to membership. Gildersleeve was immediately elected vice president and the next meeting was set to be hosted by Johns Hopkins.

Baltimore in midsummer is no one's idea of a cool place to relax, but the ninth meeting welcomed the first American university founded on the German model, which would fulfill Comfort's wish at the 1869 Convention that graduate study in philology on the German method be inaugurated in the United States. Samuel

---

37 *TAPA* 7 (1875), 8–9; Columbia *Daily Union Herald* 20 July 1875.
38 On Greener's life, see Mounter 2002.

Hart (1845–1917), who had taken over the duties of Secretary and Curator from Comfort in 1873, had found that the demands of the office had become so onerous that he requested from the executive committee a stipend to allow him to hire 'clerical assistance.'[39]

The association had done its duty to Johns Hopkins and returned for its tenth and eleventh meetings to the vacation zones of the Opera Hall Grand Union Hotel in Saratoga, NY, in July 9–11, 1878 and, for the second time, Newport, RI, on July 15–17, 1879. Only 25 showed up for Saratoga and membership had fallen from a high of 222 in 1873 to 156. Gildersleeve, who had not joined his University of Virginia colleague Schele de Vere as a founding member in 1869, nine years later, as a founding professor of Greek at Johns Hopkins, delivered a memorable presidential address, 'University Work in America and Classical Philology' (Gildersleeve 1878).

At the tenth meeting, the Association was maturing, pursuing the dictates of Whitney, 'the principles by which the study of philology in general and in particular, is to be judged and its value determined' (*Proceedings 1872*, 6). As the Philological Society developed under the leadership of Thirlwall (see above), so the APA had the steady hands of Whitney (*in petto* after the first year), the treasurer Trumbull, and secretary-curator Comfort, who arranged meetings, set the program,[40] and saw each year's *TAPA* through the press until 1873. By 1878 Greek and Latin had begun to predominate on the program with ten of the 16 papers.

As Moore said, 'There were giants whom their admirers wished to see in the flesh.' (Moore 1919, 15), If one were among the 36 members who gathered at Newport, one could have witnessed the Anglicists Albert S. Cook (1853–1927), James M. Garnett (1840–1916), the principal of St. John's College, Annapolis, MD, and F.A. March, the Hebraist Crawford Toy (1836–1919), and the classicists Goodwin of Harvard, Gildersleeve and Charles Rockwell Lanman (1850–1941) of Johns Hopkins, A.C. Merriam (1843–95) and Tracy Peck (1856–1914) of Columbia, L.R. Packard and T.D. Seymour of Yale. One would have heard six papers on Greek (Martin D'Ooge (1839–1915), Merriam, Packard, Anton Sander (1851–81), Seymour, Sihler), two papers on Latin prosody by Milton Humphreys (1844–1928) of

---

39 In 1883 the office of Treasurer was combined with Secretary-Curator and two years later the 'Curator' was dropped (but not dropped from the Constitution until 1933). Early secretary-treasurers tended to have a long tenure: Herbert Weir Smyth (1857–1937) held the job for 15 years (1889–1904), Frank Gardner Moore (1865–1955) for another 13 (1904–16).

40 The executive committee continued to set the program until 1931 when a Program Committee was established comprised of the president, two vice presidents, and chaired by the secretary-treasurer.

the University of Virginia, and deliveries on Latin subjects by Harkness and Robert F. Leighton (ca. 1838–92) of Gloucester, MA. There were two papers on Semitic language by Toy, language by Stephen Pearl Andrews (1812–86) of New York, Chaucer by Goodwin, and other English topics by Haldeman and March. In between papers there was a vacation spirit to the meetings and the ease of access to beloved or idolized colleagues; in Moore's words, (Moore 1919, 22) a 'sense of a family reunion, enlivened by an excursion.'

For the first decade, linguistics and comparative philology were in the foreground, but by 1880 the centre of interest had begun to shift toward antiquity in literature and archaeology. The non-classical philologists found happier homes at the founding of the Modern Language Association in 1883 (see below). English and Sanskrit remained popular until nearly the beginning of the twentieth century.

Slowly a division had developed between the Teutonic or Celtic moderns and the ancient Graeco-Romans (Moore 1919, 12). On the fringe, but still involved, were men interested in comparative philology like the Anglicist March, Native American languages like Turnbull, and Oriental (Semitic or Aryan) philology. Whitney, Goodwin, Seymour, and Gildersleeve were a self-selected 'invisible cult' (Moore 1919, 12). The close-knit group elected three of the first ten presidents to second terms, Goodwin in 1871–2 and 1884–5, March in 1873–4 and 1895–6, and Gildersleeve in 1877–8 and 1908–9. No president since has been accorded that honour.

The membership grew sporadically. From 150 members in 1870, and 164 in 1871, 202 in 1872, the Association reached its decade high with 222 members in 1873, and by 1879 the number was down to 156. The 1875 meeting in Newport drew 64 members, but the 1879 meeting there drew only 36, the Philadelphia meeting the next year, 24. The 1876 meeting in the chapel of Dr. Crosby's New York church drew a decade-high number of 81. The average attendance in this decade was 50.

One feature of the early meetings that can be especially appreciated in the 21st century is the lack of specialized or technical vocabulary: 'The professors in talking English use the plainest possible language, and speak it purely and with that ease which comes from perfect knowledge' (Moore 1919, 15).

The APA showed no interest in supporting its own major projects, as the Philological Society would sponsor the *New English Dictionary (Academy)*.[41] Having in 1901–5 reluctantly invested $1221.88 ($33,800 in 2018 dollars) in Lewis Campbell's never-completed *Lexicon to Plato*, it would be the 1940s before the APA

---

41 On the *NED* see n. 6 above.

sponsored another large project, the 'Harvard Servius' (Moore 1919, 30; Whitaker 2007, 103).

Barely three months after the Poughkeepsie meeting in which he had singlehandedly started the APA, Comfort was the principal guest speaker on November 23, 1869, at a gathering of approximately 300 people at the Union League Club of New York. His topic was his favourite: the need for a great art museum. America already had the Charleston (SC) Museum (1773) and the Pennsylvania Academy of Fine Arts (1805), but no great museum in New York. Comfort's speech, along with others that night, and with some help from the infamous Boss William M. Tweed (1823–78),[42] helped propel fundraising for and construction of 'a Museum of Art, on a scale worthy of this metropolis and of a great nation' (*Proceedings of a Meeting*, 19).

Just as Comfort hoped that the APA would be a comprehensive forum for philology of all languages (especially German), so his plan for the Metropolitan involved art from all over the world, from antiquity to the present.

Comfort was a member of the planning 'Committee of 50' and was a trustee and member of the executive committee (1870–1) all the while he was fulfilling the duties of secretary-curator of the APA. He resigned from the Museum in 1871 to found the College of Fine Arts at the new (1870) Syracuse University, but he remained Secretary and Curator of the APA, along with Trumbull as Treasurer, until 1873.[43]

Just as Comfort knew that the establishment of the Metropolitan would lead to the establishment of smaller museums, so he must have known that eventually the APA would lead to the formation of other specialized organizations. Of his original seven areas of interest for the APA, the science of language and the history of philology was taken over by the Linguistic Society of America (1924), Oriental languages and literatures returned to the AOS, modern European languages and literatures became the purview of the Modern Language Association in 1883

---

[42] Tweed, as the powerful director of the Tammany Hall political machine, virtually controlled New York City after the 1869 elections, and was convicted in 1873 of stealing over $25 million from the New York Treasury. He died in jail.

[43] In 1873 Comfort founded the College of Fine Arts which was almost immediately imperiled but Syracuse provided him a steady income for his growing family; the Panic of 1873, however, threatened the college. In 1891 a college of fine arts in Texas in a new port city near Houston, TX, called La Porte was going to be a centre for arts in the South. Comfort was promised a large salary to direct it. He moved there in 1893 but the next year the plan evaporated. Comfort lost his job and once back in Syracuse in 1894 declared bankruptcy and subsequently lived in a hotel with financial aid from his architect son Ralph. In 1896–1900 he realized his dream by founding a new museum in Syracuse. For a full account of his life, see Tatham 1973.

as did English language and literature. American aboriginal languages became the province of the American Anthropological Association (1902) and linguistic pedagogy was taken over by regional associations like the Classical Association of the Middle West and South (1905), the Classical Association of New England (1906), the Classical Association of the Atlantic States (1907), the Classical Association of the Pacific States (founded in 1908 and affiliated with the APA as its western arm), and the American Classical League (1919). Some historians migrated to the American Historical Association in 1884.

The APA would not have another foreign speaker in person until 1884 when Sir R.C. Jebb (1841–1905), then of the University of Glasgow, spoke at the meeting in Hanover, New Hampshire.[44] In an implicit defence of Goodwin and Gildersleeve, he spoke against the European notion that Americans classicists devoted too much energy to grammar and the publication of supporting statistics. Jebb defended the value of such work as a propaedeutic to a deeper understanding of ancient life and thought. He also spoke of the potential good work of American archaeologists at Assos and that the improvements in photography of manuscripts could allow Americans to make advances in palaeography and text criticism[45] (*Proceedings 1884*, xiv).

TAPA published its first articles in a language other than English following the joint meeting held in 1893 in conjunction with the MLA. The Swiss Wilhelm Streitberg (1864–1925) spoke on 'Ein Ablautproblem der Ursprache' and Hermann Osthoff (1847–1909), who was invited to preside at the meeting with the MLA and the Dialect Society, 'Dunkles und Helles I im Lateinischen' (*Proceedings 1893*, 29–49 & 50–65). Neither Streitberg nor Osthoff were members of the APA.

Frank Gardner Moore designed a seal in 1910, adopted at the 1912 meeting in Washington with the motto ψυχῆς ἰατρὸς τὰ γράμματα, from Philemon frag. 10 K–A, ψυχῆς ἰατρὸν κατέλιπεν τὰ γράμματα. In 1963 a new seal was substituted, the Greek motto was maintained. With the change of name in 2014, the seal was retired.

Little of the intimacy and leisure of the early meetings remains today. Neither does the word 'philology' occur as part of the Association's name (or, for that

---

[44] Jebb had given the commencement address at Harvard and rode to Hanover in a train with Goodwin, Whitney, Seymour, Peck, Lanman, and, making his first appearance at an APA meeting, William Sanders Scarborough (Ronnick 2005, 7).

[45] Thomas D. Goodell, who had just received his Ph.D. from Yale, had the anxious job of speaking after the editor of Sophocles on the subject of his dissertation, 'The Genitive in Sophocles.' After his talk, Jebb rose and graciously complimented the talk and recommended its publication (*Proceedings 1884*, xvi). Goodell went on to be professor of Greek at Yale for nearly 40 years (1888–1920) and president of the APA (1911–12).

matter, 'Association'). In 2014 the membership of the APA found the term 'philological' too narrow to describe the full range of classics in the 21st century and voted to change the organization's name to the Society for Classical Studies. Perhaps they had lost sight of Whitney's early exhortation, 'The special duty of philology is appreciation, full and generous, of every part and parcel of human knowledge.' Change will happen over 150 years, but throughout change and turmoil we are still left with the question raised by President March in the third year of the Association's existence, 'What can philology do for the future? What forces can she supply for improving the estate of man?' These words were echoed by Goodwin in 1885: 'What have we done to justify this long existence, and what do we propose to do to justify a new lease of life in the future?'[46]

Bibliography

Academy = 'The Philological Society's English Dictionary,' *The Academy* (10 May 1879), 413.
Benario, H.W. (1989), 'The APA as a North American organization', in: Culham/Edmunds, 285–94.
Bindseil, H. (1869), *General-Register über die Verhandlungen der ersten fünfundzwanzig Versammlungen deutscher Philologen und Schulmänner 1838–1867*, Leipzig.
Briggs, W. (1996–7), 'Abby Leach (1855–1918)', *Classical World* 90, 7–105.
Calder, W.M., III (1966), 'Die Geschichte der klassischen Philologie in den Vereinigten Staaten,' *Jahrbuch für Amerikastudien* 11, 213–40, repr. in: *Studies in the Modern History of Classical Scholarship* (Naples, 1984), 15–42.
Calder, W.M., III/Cobet, J. (eds.) (1989), *Heinrich Schliemann nach hundert Jahren*, Frankfurt.
Chambers, M. (1989), 'Schliemann and America', in: Calder/Cobet 1989, 397–414.
Comfort, G.F. (1902), 'Biographical sketch', Comfort Family Papers, Syracuse University Archives.
Comfort Family Papers, Syracuse University Archives.
Convention = 'Convention of American Philologists', *Transactions of the American Philological Association* 1 (1870), 8–15.
Cook, A.S. (1881), 'The Philological Society's English Dictionary', *AJPh* 2, 550–554.
Culham, P./Edmunds, L. (eds.) (1989), *Classics: A Discipline and Profession in Crisis?*, Lanham, MD/London.
Evans, R.J.W. (1977), 'Learned societies in Germany in the seventeenth century', *European Studies Review* 7, 129–151.

---

[46] I am grateful to the George Arents Research Library at Syracuse University for access to their George Fisk Comfort Papers, the University Archives at the Rare Book and Manuscript Library at Columbia University for access to APA archives, and to Special Collections of the Thomas Cooper Library, University of South Carolina.

Gildersleeve, B.L. (1878), 'University work in America and classical philology,' *Proc. Am. Phil. Ass.*9: 21–3; expanded version *Princeton Review* 55 (May 1879) 511–536, repr. in: W.W. Briggs Jr. (ed.), *The Selected Classical Papers of Basil Lanneau Gildersleeve* (Atlanta, 1992), 113–132.

Gilliver, P. (2018), *The Making of the Oxford English Dictionary*, Oxford.

Handbook = *Handbook of Learned Societies in America* (1908), Washington.

Howe, W.E. (1934), *George Fisk Comfort*, New York.

Lilly, E. (ed.) (1961), *Schliemann in Indianapolis*, Indianapolis.

Lynch, H. (1967), *Edward Wilmot Blyden, Pan Negro Patriot 1832–1912*, London.

Marshall, F.C., 'History of the Philological Society: The Early Years', available from www.philsoc.org.uk/history.asp

Moore, F.G. (1919), 'A history of the American Philological Association', *TAPA* 50, 5–32.

Mounter, M.R. (2002), *Richard Theodore Greener: The Idealist, Statesman, Scholar, and South Carolinian*, Ph.D. thesis, University of South Carolina.

Muggleston, L. (2005), *Lost for Words: The Hidden History of the Oxford English Dictionary*, New Haven/London.

Proceedings 1869–70 = *Proceedings of the American Philological Association* 1 (1869–1870).

Proceedings 1871 = *Proceedings of the American Philological Association* 2 (1871).

Proceedings 1872 = *Proceedings of the American Philological Association* 3 (1872).

Proceedings 1874 = *Proceedings of the American Philological Association* 5 (1874).

Proceedings 1876 = *Proceedings of the American Philological Association* 7 (1876).

Proceedings 1880 = *Proceedings of the American Philological Association* 11 (1880).

Proceedings 1884 = *Proceedings of the American Philological Association* 15 (1884).

Proceedings 1887 = *Proceedings of the American Philological Association* 18 (1887).

Proceedings 1892 = *Proceedings of the American Philological Association* 23 (1892).

Proceedings 1897 = *Proceedings of the American Philological Association* 28 (1897).

Proceedings 1901 = *Proceedings of the American Philological Association* 32 (1901).

Proceedings of a Meeting Held at the Theatre of the Union League Club, Tuesday Evening, November 23, 1869, New York.

Reinhold, M. (1984a), *Classica Americana*, Detroit, MI.

Reinhold, M. (1984b), 'A new morning': Edward Everett's contributions to classical learning', in: Reinhold 1984, 204–213.

Ronnick, M.V. (ed.) (2005), *The Autobiography of William Sanders Scarborough: An American Journey from Slavery to Scholarship*, Detroit, MI.

Ronnick, M.V. (2018), *Twelve African American Members of the Society for Classical Studies: The First Five Decades (1875–1925)*, New York.

Schliemann, H. (1953), *Briefwechsel aus dem Nachlaß in Auswahl*, E. Meyer (ed.), vol. 1 (1842–1875), Berlin.

Shero, L.R. (1964), *The American Philological Association: An Historical Sketch* (Philadelphia) = *TAPA* 94, x–l.

Sihler, E.G. (1902), 'Klassische Studien und klassischer Unterricht in den Vereinigten Staaten,' *Neue Jahrbücher für das klassische Altertum, Geschichte und deutsche Literatur und für Pädagogik* 10, 458–463, 503–516, 548–556.

Stray, C.A. (ed.) (2007), *Classical Books: Scholarship & Publishing in Britain since 1800*, BICS Supplement 101, London.

Tatham, David (1973), 'George Fisk Comfort' *The Courier* (Syracuse University) 11,1: 3–16.

Taylor, A.-M. (2001), *Young Charles Sumner and the Legacy of the American Enlightenment, 1811–1851*, Amherst.
Traill, D.A. (1981–2), 'Schliemann's American citizenship and divorce', *Classical Journal* 77, 337–342.
Transactions 1901 = *Transactions of the American Philological Association* 32 (1901).
Transactions 1908 = *Transactions of the American Philological Association* 39 (1908).
Verhandlungen der ersten Versammlung deutscher Philologen und Schulmänner in Nürnberg 1838 (1838), Nürnberg.
Whitaker, G. (2007), '*Unvollendetes*: The Oxford Plato Lexicon', in: Stray 2007, 97–112.
Winchester, S. (1998), *The Professor and the Madman: A Tale of Murder, Insanity, and the Making of the* Oxford English Dictionary, New York.

Judith P. Hallett
Gender and the Classical Diaspora

This essay, like the earlier research that I have done with Chris Stray, focuses on women classicists professionally active during the 1930's and 1940's, during an era that witnessed a 'classical diaspora' of scholars who relocated from Nazi-controlled Europe to England, Canada and primarily the United States.[1] Like others, I view this era, and this diaspora, as having transformed the international discipline and profession of classics both demographically and intellectually.[2] Some of these female classicists were Americans, who studied in, and frequently travelled to, Europe, although they spent most of their lives on US soil. Chris and I had the honor and privilege of seeing to publication a biography of Grace Harriet Macurdy (1866–1946), Professor of Greek at Vassar College, written by our late colleague Barbara McManus.[3] Chris' labours have also benefited my own research on Macurdy's contemporary Edith Hamilton (1867–1963), headmistress of the Bryn Mawr School for Girls in Baltimore from 1896 through 1922, who enjoyed acclaim in her post-retirement years as a best-selling author on Greco-Roman antiquity.[4] In referring to Hamilton and Macurdy, the adjective 'American' belongs in quotes. Hamilton was born in Germany, where her mother's family — sugar importers from New York favouring the Confederacy — fled during the U.S. Civil War.[5] Macurdy was born shortly after her family crossed the border from New Brunswick, Canada to Maine, having changed the spelling of their name from M-

---

[1] Although this essay focuses on the women of this 'classical diaspora', it merits attention that there were Jewish male classicists who fled Germanophone Europe and hired by black universities in the USA, such as Ernst Moritz Manasse (Ph.D. Heidelberg in November 1933), who taught German and Latin at North Central University in Durham, NC from 1939–1973 and Ernst Abrahamsohn from Prague, who taught Romance Languages and Latin at Howard University in 1939–1941; see the discussions by Obermayer 2014, 562–593 and 521–561 as well as Edgcomb 1993a and 1993b.
[2] On this 'classical diaspora' and its impact in the UK as well as North America, see Coser 1984, 3–13, and 271; Obermayer 2014; Crawford, Ulmschneider, and Elsner 2017, especially the essays by Crawford and Umschneider, Elsner, Murray, and Stray.
[3] McManus 2017; see also Hallett 2019b. As McManus 2017, 51–54 and 133–134 relates, Macurdy studied in Berlin from 1899–1900, and regularly spent summers and sabbaticals in the UK and on the European continent for nearly two decades.
[4] See, for example, Hallett 2008 and 2016b. Hamilton also studied in Leipzig and Munich on a Bryn Mawr European fellowship from 1895–1896, and often travelled to the UK and on the European continent.
[5] See Hamilton 1943, 24–25.

C-C to M-A-C to improve their employment prospects in the New England of 'no Irish need apply' signs.⁶

Other women I have researched with Chris' invaluable assistance fled to the USA from Germany and Austria after Hitler's rise to power, as part of this classical diaspora. Most were of Jewish ancestry. Among them is the gifted Etruscologist Eva Lehmann Fiesel (1891–1937), who died at age 46, a few months after joining the faculty at the all-female, private, residential Bryn Mawr College, unusual among American women's institutions of higher education for offering graduate as well as undergraduate classics degrees.⁷ Vera Lachmann (1904–1985), who taught in the classics department at Brooklyn College, a co-educational, public, commuter undergraduate institution operating under the aegis of the City University of New York, merits special mention, in part because she taught German at Vassar and enjoyed strong support from Grace Macurdy when she first arrived in the USA in 1941.⁸ Gerda Kroner Seligson (1909–2002), Renata von Scheliha (1901–1967), and Fiesel's protégée Gabriele Schoepflich Hoenigswald (1912–2001) warrant attention as well.⁹ These women relied on scholars based in the UK, native and émigré, to support their escape and immigration.¹⁰ Prominent among them was Eduard Fraenkel, whose life and work during his years at Oxford Chris has illuminated.¹¹ Chris has also helped in my investigations of other British refugees connected with these women, such as Leonie Zuntz, like Fiesel a specialist in linguistics, who came to England from Germany with her brother Gunther in 1935, and died in Oxford in 1942.¹²

---

6 McManus 2017, 15; see also McManus 2016, 198–199.
7 See Hallett 2018; even though Fiesel's parents had converted to Lutheranism around the time of their marriage in the 1880's, and Fiesel's husband Ludolf was a 'pure Aryan' and Nazi supporter, both Fiesel and her daughter Ruth, born in 1921, were nonetheless regarded as 'racially' Jewish. See also Leff 2019, 95–96 and 110–111.
8 For Lachmann, see Hallett and Pearcy 1991, Miller 2014, and Russo 2016, as well as Hallett 2019b.
9 For Gerda M. [Kroner] Seligson, who trained at Kiel, Heidelberg, Goettingen and Berlin, and the University of London (Birkbeck College), and taught at the University of Michigan as Assistant Professor (1961–1965), Associate Professor (1965–1973), and Professor of Latin (1973–1979), see the University of Michigan Faculty History Project 2011. For von Scheliha see 'Renata von Scheliha' 2019 and Hallett 2019b; for Hoenigswald, see Hallett 2019b.
10 According to the University of Michigan Faculty History Project 2011, Seligson fled to the UK from Germany, received a degree from Birkbeck College in London in 1945, and did not arrive in the US until 1947.
11 See Stray 2014 and 2017 as well as Elsner 2017 and Russo 2016.
12 For Leonie Zuntz (1908–1942), and her brother, German refugee classicist Gunther Zuntz (1902–1992), Professor at the University of Manchester, see Baumgarten 2010 and Hallett 2018.

In this paper I will be thinking and theorizing about the role played by gender at this time and during this classical diaspora. My reflections honour the painstaking scrutiny Chris accords individual researchers and particularized contexts in approaching the history of classical scholarship as a human and humanizing enterprise. By employing gender as my lens on this period, by looking at the experiences of specific women classicists as well as by considering how women classicists were affected as a group, I aim to elucidate both the professional lives of women who were themselves forced to relocate, and the lives of those, especially the other women, among whom they relocated.

My ruminations on the challenges of generalizing about women's academic contributions to the field of classical studies in the late nineteenth and twentieth centuries are, I confess, of recent vintage. So, too, these ruminations have so far focused almost exclusively on women classicists who studied and were employed in more than one country over the course of their careers, and on the careers of women classicists that encompassed the turbulent period of the 1930s and 1940s. A study of women classicists who came of age professionally after the second World War, especially those who — like myself — began undergraduate and graduate studies in the 1960s, would be instructive as well. They would, moreover, yield somewhat different results, owing to the increasing number of women who obtained positions in classics departments offering doctoral degrees during those years, and the increased emphasis on research productivity in those departments, and indeed in the field of classics generally.[13]

A 2017 essay by the Swiss classicists Ilse Hilbold, Laura Simon and Thomas Spaeth about 'Miss' Juliette Ernst, in a publication energetically birthed and parented by Lorna Hardwick, *Classical Receptions Journal*, inspired me to start ruminating. Born in Algeria in 1900, educated in Francophone Switzerland until she received the 'licence' degree with highest honours in 1923, Ernst studied and worked in Paris for most of her very long life: after retiring in the early 1990's to a home for senior citizens outside of Lausanne, she died there in 2001, in her 102nd year. For almost sixty years Ernst edited the Paris-based *L'Année Philologique*, a critical and analytical bibliography of scholarly publications on multiple aspects of Greek and Roman antiquity. For a quarter of a century she was secretary-general of FIEC, the *Fédération Internationale des Associations d'Études Classiques / International Federation of Associations of Classical Studies*, estab-

---

13 For demographic details on the female classicists in this category who have been presidents of the American Philological Association/Society for Classical Studies since the 1990s, some of them born or educated or both in the UK, see Hallett 2019a as well as the discussion below.

lished in 1948 under the aegis of UNESCO. Jules Marouzeau, Ernst's Latin professor at the École Pratique des Hautes Études, founded the *APh* in 1926. In his capacity as representative of the Association Guillaume Budé, Marouzeau also played a leading role in the founding of FIEC. The archaeologist Charles Dugas was originally elected its secretary-general, but ill health made it impossible for him to carry out his duties, and Ernst soon assumed them.[14]

The essay on Ernst regards her as exemplifying all women academic classicists whose 'work involved them directly in the production of knowledge' and explores 'the gendered scope of action available to them.' It highlights the praise showered on her loyalty and unselfish dedication to her tasks, including an honorary doctorate at the University of Lausanne at the age of 39, as well as on her crucial and influential role in international institutionalization and worldwide networking. Yet it contrasts this recognition with the accomplishments highlighted in the obituaries for her male colleagues such as Marouzeau, scholarly publications termed 'scientific achievements of lasting value.' What is more, it documents that Ernst, who defined bibliography as a 'servant of humanism', nonetheless saw herself as a 'bibliographical specialist who could meet distinguished academics on equal terms.'[15]

To quote the authors: 'What characterized Ernst that enabled her to gain such influence in a male-dominated social field, and that ultimately enabled her to occupy absolutely central positions within that field? She never submitted a doctoral thesis, nor did she hold a university post. Thus she could not demonstrate any achievements that lead to recognition in the academic field. Judging by her self-assessment, the lack of academic honours represented no shortcoming, nor did it prevent Ernst from comprehensively pursuing an activity that she saw, at least retrospectively, as her life's task. This seemingly contradictory observation gives rise to a hypothesis that future research on Juliette Ernst will need to bear out: two different forms of scientific habitus can be made out in the academic field of twentieth century classical studies. On the one hand stand actors who embark on a university career, who submit the academic work required to gain the necessary formal qualifications, who rise through the ranks, and who thus compete against each other for academic capital — i.e. titles and positions of au-

---

14 See Hilbold, Simon and Spaeth 2017; see also Hilbold, Simon and Spaeth 2016.
15 Hilbold, Simon, and Spaeth 2017, 487–488, 490–491. Among the biographical data they provide about Ernst one might consider in trying to account for the 'global academic influence' that she achieved were her inherited wealth, and her fluency in English, German and Italian, languages that her French colleagues did not command as impressively if at all.

thority. On the other is a sphere of action within the academic field in which actors compete for *social* capital, which they obtain by complying with the rules of this field: they accept a subaltern position vis-à-vis "academic dignitaries", against whom they do not compete, but with whom they can nevertheless enter privileged relationships — not least due to their uncontested subordination — which can develop into broadly based networks. In this way, such actors can take up highly influential positions in the organization of scientific production without holding recognized academic positions. Even if the actors of this subaltern domain within the academic field are by no means exclusively female (just as the actors possessing academic capital are largely, but no longer exclusively male as the twentieth century unfolds), it is obvious that these forms of habitus in the academic field are not gender-neutral in classical studies; the social concepts of masculinity are linked with academic capital and positions of authority, those of femininity with social capital and organizational achievements. Of course, no direct conclusions about the actions of men and women can be drawn from the abstract social concepts attributed to masculinity and femininity — but the scope of action available to men and women in the academic field is shaped by the conformity with these concepts and constrained by the negative evaluation of nonconformist action.'[16]

I would like to pose some challenges to this hypothesis, admittedly described as no more than an assumption arising 'from studying the life and work of a particular individual,' and said to 'raise the question of whether the biographical approach at all permits such general statements about women's scope of action in [twentieth century] classical studies.'[17] These challenges arise from evidence that complicates various assumptions made by this essay, evidence about the different modes of configuring university-level classics study that have long prevailed on the European continent, England and the US. In posing these challenges, I would begin by considering the experiences of such Germanophone female refugee classicists as Fiesel, Lachmann, and Hoenigswald, who found new academic homes in the United States in the 1930's and 1940's. I would urge that we consider, too, the differences between the environments in which they were trained and those to which they were compelled to adjust.

After Hitler's race laws deprived them of their respective academic positions in Munich and Muenster, like other German institutions of higher learning coeducational and state-funded universities, both Eva Lehmann Fiesel and her

---

[16] Hilbold, Simon and Spaeth 2017, 502. Their discussion uses the sociological terms of Bourdieu 1984.
[17] Hilbold, Simon and Spaeth 2017, 503.

younger brother, the art historian Karl Lehmann-Hartleben (1894–1960), were able to find jobs in the USA. He, however, was hired as a full professor at the Institute of Fine Arts at the private New York University, she as a research assistant in the Department of Linguistics at Yale, also a private university: because Yale did not hire female faculty in its all-male undergraduate College or coeducational graduate school. Luckily, efforts spearheaded — and funds donated and raised — by her Yale colleagues enabled Fiesel to obtain her, visiting, associate professorship at Bryn Mawr.[18]

Describing her relocation from Yale to Bryn Mawr to one of her colleagues in the Linguistics Department, Albrecht Goetze, Fiesel pronounced the transition more difficult than the challenge of moving from Munich — and indeed from the University of Florence, where she had relocated after leaving Germany — to Yale.[19] She had ample reason for her pronouncement. Teaching in undergraduate classics programs at women's private, residential liberal arts colleges — such as Macurdy's Vassar (where Lachmann briefly taught German) and Bryn Mawr (where Lachmann subsequently taught Greek and Latin) — was both labor-intensive and time-consuming. Centred on the word-by-word translation and explication of Greek and Latin texts by small classes of intellectually engaged students, rather than lectures to large and not necessarily attentive audiences, it demanded long hours of classroom preparation, as well as constant assessment of students' oral and written performances, by instructors.[20] Vera Lachmann may also have

---

18 See Obermayer 2014 and especially Hallett 2016a and 2018.
19 Letter from Fiesel to Albrecht [misspelled in the Yale library records as Albert] Goetze in Goetze Papers (1936): 'Sie wissen ja, was so eine Umstellung (und die von Yale nach Bryn Mawr ist betdeutend grosser als die von Muenchen oder Florenz nach Yale).' For Goetze (1987–1971), Professor of Semitic Languages at the University of Marburg when Hitler came to power in 1933, who also came to Yale in 1934 under the auspices of Edgar Howard Sturtevant (1875–1952), and eventually became Sterling Professor of Assyriology and Babylonian Literature, see 'Goetze, Albrecht' 2019. My thanks to Michael Frost and the Public Services staff at the Manuscripts and Archives section of the Yale University Library for their valuable assistance during my visit on May 30, 2017, to examine their materials on both Fiesel and her successor as research assistant to Sturtevant, Henry Hoenigswald (1915–2003). Hoenigswald, who married Fiesel's student Gabriele Schoepflich in 1944, had Fiesel's academic papers moved to Bryn Mawr College in the early 1970's.
20 See, for example, McManus 2017, 36–60, describing Macurdy's first, fourteen-hour teaching schedule at Vassar in 1893, of 'three course preparations [each semester], including all the required Greek courses for freshmen and sophomores, plus one elective, a new one-hour course in the Greek New Testament... This was a heavy teaching load, because all the required courses included weekly assignments in which the students rendered English passages into Greek, necessitating careful reading and correction of the Greek.' For Vassar, and its embrace of co-education in 1969, see Hallett 2019b.

met with challenges in adapting to her new teaching environment, as she was clearly charismatic and inspired as well as diligent.[21] Brooklyn College, where she occupied a full-time, tenured post for decades, held its students, mostly from immigrant, working-class families, to high academic standards, no less rigorous than those applied to undergraduates at elite, private, all-male residential institutions such as Yale, which for generations prioritized the social grooming of gentlemen from advantaged backgrounds.[22] Heavy instructional loads and administrative assignments, de rigueur at both public institutions and women's colleges (and other all-male, undergraduate liberal arts colleges), afforded classics faculty members limited time and opportunity for serious research and publication, and for teaching students at a level capable of undertaking serious research assignments.

These teaching expectations, incidentally, were nearly identical to those shouldered by classics faculty at Wellesley College, another women's private, residential liberal arts institution, when I entered in 1962, although most of the Latin and Greek courses did not require 'prose composition' exercises in Latin and Greek, and most faculty members taught at least one course in English translation each year in addition to five courses in the languages themselves, spread over two semesters. My own teaching schedule and assignments at a large public university, the University of Maryland, College Park, were not all that different from those of my Wellesley teachers when I joined its classics department in 1983. This

---

21 Cf. Russo 2016: 'I first encountered Vera Lachmann when she visited my third year Latin class [at Brooklyn College in the 1950's], taught by Professor Ethyle Wolfe, on Catullus and Horace. When we were assigned Catullus 51, we were told that Professor Lachmann would visit our class and recite the Sapphic poem that served as Catullus's model. We knew Professor Lachmann by reputation but most of us had never seen her. And then this small woman appeared, stood in front of the class with her hands clasped and her eyes half closed, and began reciting — almost chanting — in Greek. We knew, from our Catullus, that she was uttering a complaint about jealousy and unattainable love, and she recited with a voice suffused with emotion and had tears welling up in her eyes. We came away from that class feeling as if we had encountered Sappho herself. Eventually I was enrolled with a class with Vera in advanced Greek, a small class reading Aeschylus' *Agamemnon*. We were all in over our heads but loving the challenge, our path through this difficult Greek smoothed by Vera's guiding hand. Our class text was the Oxford edition by Denniston and Page, while Vera had Eduard Fraenkel's commentary from which she drew nuggets of insight to share with us. We were amazed to learn that she knew Professor Fraenkel; in fact, she wrote him a postcard saying that we were enjoying his elucidations of Aeschylus, and had the whole class sign it. We were thrilled when, weeks later, a card came back with the great scholar's gracious reply.'
22 For Brooklyn College, see the *Wikipedia* article 2019 as well as Russo 2016 on his classics courses there during his undergraduate years in the 1950's. For Yale, see Hallett 2016a.

was not, of course, the case at Harvard University, when I entered graduate school there in 1966: faculty in the Department of the Classics there taught at most four courses per year, were not involved in lower-level language teaching, lectured (and did not ask students to actively participate) in their advanced undergraduate language courses, and allocated most of the time in their specialized, graduate seminars to student presentations.

Demographic upheavals caused by World War II significantly impacted American higher education in general as well as the field of classics during that era. Wartime itself wrenched far more men than women from university-level learning, teaching and research, offering women such as Lachmann — and her American-born, Jewish colleagues at Brooklyn, Alice Kober (1906–1950) and Ethyle Wolfe (1919–2010) — opportunities to teach in co-educational, albeit mostly undergraduate and/or public, institutions.[23] More important, the GI bill, subsidizing higher education for military veterans, increased the number of university students nationwide along with the social, ethnic, and religious diversity of the student population.[24]

The careers of American born and trained female classicists such as Macurdy and Hamilton merit notice on this, demographic, front. Although Macurdy died in 1946, the year after World War II ended, from the 1920's onward she had pioneered a major post-war curricular trend in undergraduate classics programs by introducing courses on 'classical civilization' in English translation for Vassar undergraduates who had not studied and did not plan to learn ancient Greek and Latin.[25] During the post-war decades, such courses became standard fare in classics programs outside of the selective, private women's colleges as well, attracting students who needed to fulfill general education humanities requirements for their bachelor's degrees. Among them were male veterans availing themselves of the opportunities afforded by the GI Bill. Such courses often assigned Hamilton's writings on the classical world, aimed at and highly accessible to a non-specialist audience. Yet Hamilton's writings were also of questionable accuracy. While she had begun graduate study in Latin at Bryn Mawr, Hamilton never completed her

---

23 For Kober, a Columbia University PhD 'who played an important role in the classification of remains from Knossos and Pylos and the ultimate decipherment of Linear B', see Briggs 2019; for Wolfe, a New York University PhD 'who chaired the Classics Department at Brooklyn, and — while still chair — was appointed Dean of the School of Humanities and subsequently Provost' — see Clayman 2010. Wolfe was an eminent figure beyond her home institution as well, and awarded the Charles Frankel Prize given by the National Endowment for the Humanities in 1990.
24 For the GI Bill and its impact on higher education in the humanities, see Olson 1973.
25 See McManus 2017, 209–212.

PhD, or taught at the university level, or engaged in serious research.[26] In contrast to Hamilton, Macurdy had earned her PhD at Columbia after she taught at Vassar for several years and studied for a year in Berlin. For the rest of her life she published prolifically, infusing her classes in translation with findings and insights from her specialized scholarly works such as *Hellenistic Queens*, a groundbreaking historical study of 'woman-power in Macedonia, Seleucid Syria and Ptolemaic Egypt,' published by Johns Hopkins University Press in 1932. Yet she did not write for a wider public, nor publish with commercial presses.[27]

But let us return to Juliette Ernst and the gendering of classics during and since the mid-twentieth century, and the relation of both Ernst and other female classicists to the classical diaspora. According to Hilbold, Simon and Spaeth, Ernst's career represents a model of female 'subalternity' applicable to, and helpful in understanding the careers of, other women classical scholars. But I would argue that Ernst's professional experiences, limited to study and employment in Europe, and chiefly in Francophone Switzerland and France, have no counterpart in American academe. Here the pedagogical traditions of undergraduate 'liberal arts colleges', such as the all-female Bryn Mawr or (the once all-female and now co-ed) Vassar, have long held powerful sway, especially for women classicists whose opportunities to study and in particular teach at the university level were for many years largely limited to such institutions, whether at private women's colleges themselves or at public universities such as Brooklyn which followed the curricular practices of liberal arts colleges.

Here in the USA, too, the terms 'academic' and 'social' capital consequently have different valences than those ascribed by Bourdieu. Since the end of World War I, those occupying influential posts, tenured or non-tenured, in university-level classics teaching or administration, even at undergraduate liberal arts colleges and non-elite public institutions, even in professional associations such as the American Philological Association, recently renamed the Society for Classical Studies, have been required to hold the PhD degree. It has been the *sine qua non*, the non-negotiable credential, for women and men classicists alike in the USA and Canada.

Yes, there are exceptions, male exceptions, such as one of my own doctoral dissertation directors at Harvard, Zeph Stewart (1921–2007), who received his BA from Yale in 1942, and then spent several years in the military before returning to academe. Stewart eventually obtained a tenured, full professorial position in the Harvard Department of the Classics, without ever earning a doctorate himself,

---

26 Hallett 2008 and 2016b. See also McManus 2017, 248–250.
27 See McManus 2017, 248–250.

merely on the basis of being named a Harvard Junior Fellow early in his career.[28] He did not, moreover, publish all that much in the way of scholarly research, unlike another PhD-less Harvard Junior Fellow in the Classics, Steele Commager of Columbia University (1932–1984), who produced substantial studies of lasting importance on Augustan poetry.[29] But Stewart's sterling classics training, at an exclusive New England preparatory school, prior to Yale, combined with his aristocratic pedigree (though he attended both prep school and Yale on financial aid) counted a great deal, particularly in the realm of administrative appointments: he was also Master of a Harvard undergraduate residential college, president of the APA, and Director of Harvard's Center of Hellenic Studies.

In the classroom, Stewart was just as erudite and impressive as any of my other Harvard professors, PhD or no PhD: displaying a broad and seemingly effortless command of classical texts in both Greek and Latin, Greco-Roman history, and the scholarship written about both. But he was no more erudite and impressive than any of my female, undergraduate classics professors at Wellesley, the liberal arts undergraduate college for women that I attended, most of whom never had the opportunity to direct a doctoral dissertation. While some of these women did not publish all that much either, owing to heavy teaching loads and administrative responsibilities, all of them held PhD degrees. Truth to tell, Stewart and two of my less-published Wellesley teachers, Barbara P. McCarthy (1904–1988) and Margaret Taylor (1901–1982), knew, and skilfully imparted, far more about Greek and Latin texts, the classical world, and the scholarly elucidation of classical writings than many ostensibly better-credentialed American female and male classicists of my own long acquaintance: some of whom published sufficiently to earn tenure and promotion at major research institutions. Often, moreover, they have extremely narrow fields of specialization, and would never be able to sustain the kind of teaching expected in an undergraduate liberal arts college.

There are, we should emphasize, American female classicists whose professional careers resemble that of Juliet Ernst in that they have produced little in the way of published scholarship but have nonetheless obtained not only highly influential positions in what Hillbold, Simon and Spaeth call the organization of scientific production, but also control over the assessment and professional fortunes of far more productive scholars and teachers than they. Yet in so doing,

---

28 For an assessment of his career, see Coleman, Eck, Gomes, and Thomas 2008.

29 Henderson 2019 lists all of Stewart's publications from 1950–2000, which consist of approximately nine articles, two edited volumes, and several reviews. For Commager and his scholarly publications, see Roots 2019.

they have also achieved a high status that could never be termed 'subaltern'. Furthermore, they differ from Ernst not only in having earned the PhD degree, but also in having worked within the American system of higher education. Its diversely constituted components furnished them with different routes to independent academic influence in the field of classics and beyond, as department chairs and university-level administrators.[30] They also have little in common with Abby Leach, the first female president of the then-American Philological Association in 1900: she did not possess a doctorate, or indeed any undergraduate degrees, and was 'strikingly different from the small number of men who controlled the APA offices — not so much because she was a woman, but rather because, unlike these eminent scholars, she had never published a single article nor delivered a paper at a classics conference until she gave her APA presidential address. She was the "prodigy" of William Watson Goodwin, the Harvard Greek professor whom she had persuaded to give her private tuition. Goodwin had twice served as APA president… To Goodwin and others, Abby Leach was a fine figurehead, an imposing and attractive woman who was a skilled classical linguist but posed no threat to male hegemony in the association.'[31]

It warrants attention that despite the formidable European academic backgrounds and professional survival skills of the female classicists who fled to the US during the classical diaspora, talents that immensely enriched their students and classics community at large, virtually none of them advanced to positions of leadership in their respective institutions, or in the US classics profession itself. Perhaps foreign birth and training as well as gender proved an impediment to female refugee scholars such as Seligson, who, after all, was a full professor at an institution with a top-ranked PhD program, the University of Michigan. While the APA elected its first female president in 1900, only in 1997 did it even elect a woman born and educated abroad: the British Susan Treggiari, who initially held

---

[30] To be sure, scholarly productivity has not been a hard-and-fast requirement for women classicists who attained academic and professional leadership roles either, although the PhD degree and other administrative skills appear to be essential. The record, furnished by Clayman 2019a, of Ethyle Wolfe's impressive academic accomplishments as an administrator at Brooklyn College, only lists two published articles, one from 1952 and the other from 1976. As Toher 2019 attests, my Wellesley college classmate Christina Elliott Sorum (1944–2005), published only six articles after receiving her doctorate from Brown University in 1975, and nonetheless was appointed as Dean of the Faculty from 1994–1999 and then Academic Vice President from 1999 until her death, at Union, a liberal arts college in Schenectady, New York.
[31] McManus 2017, 97–8.

a position at the University of Ottawa in Canada before moving to Stanford.[32] Then, again, only in 2016 did the APA, by then renamed the Society for Classical Studies, even appoint a female as its chief administrative officer: Helen Cullyer, who is also English by birth, although she earned her PhD in the US, from Yale.[33]

Yet males of the classical diaspora did not fare appreciably better. The APA elected its first Jewish president, secondary school headmaster Julius Sachs (1849–1934), in 1891; born in Baltimore, Sachs had also done graduate training in Germany, at the University of Rostock.[34] Nevertheless, plans for the distinguished German (though non-Jewish) émigré scholar Werner Jaeger to serve as APA president at the height of World War II quietly fizzled; the first German-educated, Jewish refugee scholar to hold that post was my Harvard professor Herbert Bloch in 1969.[35] Two Jewish refugees from Germany were elected to the APA presidency in the late 1980s, Martin Ostwald and Thomas Rosenmeyer, but both earned their PhDs at the University of Toronto. Another, the Austrian-born Erich Gruen, elected in 1992, received his degrees from Columbia, Oxford and Harvard.[36]

Several other women attained the APA presidency after Abby Leach in 1900, among them Helen North (1922–2012), the first Roman Catholic to hold the position, in 1976. Like North, who earned her PhD degree, as she had her BA, from

---

32 For Leach, see McManus 2017, 78–96 and 'Leach, Abigail' 2005; for Treggiari (1940–), see her *Wikipedia* entry 2019. As Scott 2019 indicates, Agnes Kirsopp Lake Michels (1909–1993), Professor of Latin at Bryn Mawr College, and APA president in 1972, was born in Holland to British parents, but she came to America in 1914 and took her BA, MA and PhD degrees at Bryn Mawr College. See also Hallett 2019a on other female APA presidents born abroad: Elaine Fantham (1933–2016), president in 2004; Jenny Strauss Clay (1942–), president in 2006; and Kathleen Coleman (1953–) president in 2011. While Clay was born in Egypt, she was adopted and brought to the US as a small child by her uncle, the German refugee political philosopher Leo Strauss, and educated at Reed College and the University of Washington. Fantham, like Treggiari, was educated exclusively in her native England; Coleman, born in what was then Rhodesia, received her BA in South Africa and her doctorate in the UK. In the discussion to follow, I will be drawing on the 'List of Presidents of the American Philological Association' in the *Wikipedia* article on the APA/SCS 2019 in discussing former APA/SCS presidents.
33 For the educational background of Helen Cullyer (1972–), see the announcement of her appointment by her previous employer, the Andrew Mellon Foundation 2016.
34 For Sachs, see Hallett 1994.
35 For the failed presidency of Werner Jaeger (1888–1961), see Hallett 1992; for Bloch (1911–2006), see Brown, Constable, Jones, and Ziolkowski 2008.
36 For Ostwald (1922–2010), president in 1987, see Chopp 2010; for Rosenmeyer (1920–2007), president in 1989, see Mastronarde, Griffith, Long, and Alter 2019; for Gruen (1935–), president in 1982, see his *Wikipedia* article 2019.

Cornell, the seven female APA presidents between Abby Leach and North all received doctoral degrees at prestigious universities in the US, nearly all of them private institutions, and compiled distinguished records as publishing scholars. Yet unlike North and like Abby Leach, all seven women comprising this group were Protestants from middle and upper class social backgrounds. Four, not insignificantly, were employed at Leach's own, private, and at that time all-female institution, Vassar College: Elizabeth Hazelton Haight, president in 1934; Lily Ross Taylor, president in 1942; Cornelia Catlin Coulter, president in 1948; and Inez Scott Ryberg, president in 1962.[37] Two taught at two other all-female private colleges: my own undergraduate professor of Latin Dorothy Robathan, president in 1965; and Agnes Kirsopp Lake Michels of Bryn Mawr College, president in 1972. The seventh, Gertrude Smith, president in 1958, is the exception cited earlier: after receiving BA, MA and PhD degrees from the University of Chicago, a co-educational private institution with a doctoral program in classics, she taught there from 1921 through 1960.[38]

The situation changed in the 1990's, when women began to be promoted to full professorships (and influential administrative positions) at universities with classics PhD programs. Since then the number of women elected to the APA and SCS presidency has risen, in part owing to a commitment to gender balance by the Nominations Committee. Virtually all of these women have held academic and administrative posts at institutions granting the PhD, several of them public institutions. The fourteen women elected since 1995 include the first Jewish woman, Jenny Strauss Clay of the University of Virginia, elected in 2006; she has been succeeded by two other Jewish female presidents: Ruth Scodel of the University of Michigan, in 2007, and Dee Lesser Clayman of the Graduate Center, City University of New York, in 2010.[39]

Furthermore, since Berthold Louis Ullman became the second Jewish APA president in 1935, 44 years after Sachs, all of the Jewish men holding that post — Harry Caplan in 1955; Bloch in 1969; and Ostwald, Rosenmeyer, Gruen, Charles Segal, Robert Kaster, and David Konstan in the late 1980s and 90s — have also taught at prestigious, mostly private PhD-granting institutions as well. So have

---

37 For North, see her Wikipedia article 2019; for Haight (1872-1964), see Lateiner 2019 and McManus 2017, especially 106–107, 120–121, 213–215, 243–244; for Taylor (1886–1969), see Broughton 2019; for Coulter (1885–1960), see Quinn 2019; for Ryberg (1901–1980), see Bacon 2019.
38 For Robathan (1898–1991), see Geffcken 2019; for Michels, see Scott 2019; for Smith (1894–1985), see her *Wikipedia* article 2019.
39 For Scodel (1952–), see her *Wikipedia* article 2019; for Clayman (1945–), see her University of Pennsylvania alumnae profile 2019(b).

the Roman Catholic male APA/SCS presidents; although two chief APA administrative officers have come from Catholic universities, Fordham and Holy Cross, no president has done so: James O'Donnell was not hired at Georgetown until after being elected to the APA presidency.[40] These men and their equally successful female Jewish colleagues claim similar profiles. From all appearances, the achievement of high professional status in the North American classics community, for women as well as men, has always been closely tied to factors including, but not limited to, gender, among them ethnicity and religion, social background, and institutional prestige.

The classical diaspora, as scholars such as William M. Calder, III have argued, visibly increased the number of Jews holding teaching positions in North American university-level classics programs; I would contend that it boosted the numbers of Catholics studying and teaching in non-Catholic university-level classics programs in the US as well.[41] Women classicists on our shores have benefited from the greater ethnic and socio-cultural diversity in these academic hierarchies, on their own and, in recent years, as highly qualified 'spousal hires' partnered with academically high-powered men. But the model of the 'subaltern' Juliette Ernst and her phenomenal accomplishments would seem to have little relevance to the North American academic scene, illustrating the limits of theorizing about women's scope of action in twentieth century classical studies worldwide on the basis of her, singular, life.

Bibliography

Bacon, H.H. (2019), 'Ryberg, Inez Scott', in: the *Database of Classical Scholars*:
    https://dbcs.rutgers.edu/all-scholars/9082-ryberg-inez-gertrude-scott
Baumgarten, A.I. (2010), *Elias Bickerman as a Historian of the Jews: A Twentieth Century Tale*, Tubingen.
Bourdieu, P. (1984), *Homo Academicus*, Paris.
Briggs, W.W. Jr. (2019), 'Kober, Alice Elizabeth', in: the *Database of Classical Scholars*:
    https://dbca.rutgers.edu/all-scholars/8851-kober-alice-elizabeth

---

40 For Ullman (1881–1965), see Den Adel 2019; for Caplan (1896–1980), see North 2019; for Segal (1936–2002), president in 1994, see Reckford 2019; for Kaster (1948–), president in 1996, see his Princeton faculty profile 2019; for Konstan 1940–, president in 1999, see his *Wikipedia* article 2019. For the male Roman Catholic presidents and Secretary-Treasurers headquartering the organization at Roman Catholic institutions, see Hallett 2019a; for O'Donnell (1950–), president in 2003, see his *Wikipedia* article.
41 Calder 1992.

Brooklyn College (2019), *Wikipedia*: https://en.wikipedia.org/wiki/Brooklyn_College
Broughton. T.R.S. (2019), 'Taylor, Lily Ross', in: the *Database of Classical Scholars*: https://dbcs.rutgers.edu/all-scholars/9168-taylor-lily-ross.
Brown, V./Constable, G./Jones, C.P./Ziolkowski, J. (2008), 'Herbert Bloch: Faculty of Arts and Sciences Memorial Minute', in: *The Harvard Gazette*, June 12.
Calder, W. III. (1992), 'The refugee classical scholars in the USA: an evaluation of their contributions', in: *Illinois Classical Studies* 17.1, 153–173.
Chopp, R. (2010), 'Martin Ostwald (1922–2010).' April 12: https://www.swarthmore.edu/profile/martin-ostwald-1922-2010
Clayman, D. (2019a), ' Wolfe, Ethyle Renee', in: the *Database of Classical Scholars*: https://dbcs.rutgers.edu/all-scholars/9247-wolfe-ethyle-ren-e
Clayman, D. (2019b), https://www.classics.upenn.edu/people/dee-clayman
Coleman, K./Eck, D./Gomes, P./Thomas, R. (2008), 'Zeph Stewart, [Harvard] Faculty of Arts and Sciences Memorial Minute', December 11.
Coser, L. (1984), *Refugee Scholars in America: Their Impact and Their Experiences*, New Haven/London.
Crawford, S./Ulmschneider, K. (2017), '"The Bund" and the Oxford Philological Society, 1939–45', in: Crawford/Ulmschneider/Elsner, 133–150.
Crawford, S./Ulmschneider, K./Elsner, J. (eds.) (2017), *The Ark of Civilization: Refugee Scholars and Oxford University, 1930–1945*, Oxford.
'Helen Cullyer Appointed Executive Director of the Society for Classical Studies,' The Andrew Mellon Foundation (2016). https://mellon.org/resources/news/articles/helen-cullyer-appointed-executive-director-society-classical-studies
Den Adel, R.L. (2019), 'Ullman, Berthold Louis', in: the *Database of Classical Scholars*: https://dbcs.rutgers.edu/all-scholars/9192-ullman-berthold-louis
Edgcomb, G.S. (1993a), *From Swastika to Jim Crow: Refugee Scholars at Black Colleges*, forward by John Hope Franklin, Malabar, FL.
Edgcomb, G.S. (1993b), *Displaced German Scholars: A Guide to Academics in Peril in Nazi Germany during the 1930s*, San Bernardino, CA.
Elsner, J. (2017), 'Pfeiffer, Fraenkel, and refugee scholarship in Oxford during and after the Second World War', in: Crawford/Ulmschneider/Elsner, 25–49.
Geffcken, K.A (2019), 'Robathan, Dorothy Mae', in: the *Database of Classical Scholars*: https://dbcs.rutgers.edu/all-scholars/9061-robathan-dorothy-mae
Albert [sic] Goetze Papers, Yale University Library, MS 648. 1.6 Folder 146.
    1936. Letter from Eva Fiesel to Albrecht Goetze, November 7.
Goetze, A. (2019), *Wikipedia*: https://en.wikipedia.org/wiki/Albrecht_Goetze
Gruen, E.S. (2019), *Wikipedia*. https://en.wikipedia.org/wiki/Erich_S_Gruen
Hallett, J.P. (1992), 'The case of the missing President: Werner Jaeger and the American Philological Association', in: W. Calder III (ed.), *Werner Jaeger Reconsidered, Illinois Classical Studies*, supplement 3, 33–68.
Hallett, J.P. (1994), 'Sachs, Julius', in: the *Database of Classical Scholars*: https://dbcs.rutgers.edu/all-scholars/9083-sachs-julius.
Hallett, J.P. (2008), 'The Anglicizing way: Edith Hamilton (1867–1963) and the twentieth century transformation of Classics in the U.S.A', in: J.P. Hallett/C.A. Stray (eds.), *British Classics Outside England: The Academy and Beyond*, Waco (Texas), 149–165.
Hallett, J.P. (2016a), 'Eli's Daughters: female Classics graduate Students at Yale, 1892–1941', in: Wyles/Hall, 260–274.

Hallett, J.P. (2016b), 'Greek (and Roman) ways and thoroughfares: the routing of Edith Hamilton's Classical Antiquity', in: Wyles/Hall, 216–242.

Hallett, J.P. (2018), 'The endeavours and exempla of the German refugee classicists Eva Lehmann Fiesel and Ruth Fiesel', in: Finkmann, S./Behrendt, A./Walter, A. (eds.), *Antike Erzaehl- und Deutungsmuster: Zwischen Exemplaritaet und Transformation. Festschrift Fuer Christiane Reitz zum 65. Geburtstag*, Berlin, 655–693.

Hallett, J.P. (2019a), 'Expanding our professional embrace: the American Philological Association/Society for Classical Studies 1970–2019', *TAPA* 149.2 Supplement (Sesquicentennial Anniversary Issue), 61–88.

Hallett, J.P. (2019b), 'The legacy of the Drunken Duchess: Grace Harriet Macurdy, Barbara McManus and Classics at Vassar College from 1893–1946', *History of Classical Scholarship* 1, 94–127.

Hallett, J.P./Pearcy, L.T. (1991), '*Nunc Meminisse Iuvat*: Classics and Classicists Between the World Wars', *Classical World* 85.1, 1–27.

Hamilton, A. (1943), *Exploring the Dangerous Trades. The Autobiography of Alice Hamilton, M.D.*, Boston.

Henderson, Jeffrey (2019), 'Stewart, Zeph,' in: the *Database of Classical Scholars*: https://dbcs.rutgers.edu/all-scholars/9146-stewart-zeph

Hilbold, I./Simon, L./Spaeth, T. (2016), 'Die Faeden der Altertumwissenschaften in Einer Hand: Mademoiselle Ernst und Die Antike im 20. Jahrhundert', in: *EuGeStA* 6: https://eugesta-revue-univ-lille3.fr/en/issue-6-2016/.

Hilbold, I./Simon, L./Spaeth, T. (2017), 'Holding the reins: Miss Ernst and twentieth-century Classics', in: *Classical Receptions Journal* 9.4, 487–506.

Hurley, D. (2019), 'Gudeman, Alfred', in: In the *Database of Classical Scholars*: https://dbcs.rutgers.edu/all-scholars/8750-gudeman-alfred.

Kaster, R. (2019), Princeton Classics: https://classics.princeton.edu/people/faculty/emeritae-i/robert-kaster

Konstan, D. (2019), *Wikipedia*: https://en.wikipedia.org/wiki/David_Konstan

Lateiner, D. (2019), 'Haight, Elizabeth Hazelton', in: the *Database of Classical Scholars*: https://dbcs.rutgers.edu/all-scholars/8758-HAIGHT-Elizabeth-Hazelton

Leach, A. (2005), in: the *Vassar College Encyclopedia*: http://vcencyclopedia.vassar.edu/faculty/prominent-faculty/abigail-leach.html

Leff, L. (2019), *Well Worth Saving. American Universities' Life-and-Death Decisions on Refugees from Nazi Europe*', New Haven/London.

'List of Presidents of the American Philological Association', (2019), *Wikipedia*. https://en.wikipedia.org/wiki/List_of_Presidents_of_the_American_Philological_Association.

Mastronarde, D./Griffith, M./Long, A./Alter, R. (2019), 'Rosenmeyer, Thomas Gustav', in: the *Database of Classical Scholars*: https://dbcs.rutgers.edu/all-scholars/9074-rosenmeyer-thomas-gustav

McManus, B. (2016), 'Grace Harriet Macurdy (1866–1946): Redefining the Classical Scholar', in: Wyles/Hall, 194–215.

McManus, B. (2017), *The Drunken Duchess of Vassar: Grace Harriet Macurdy, Pioneering Feminist Classical Scholar,* with Introduction by Judith P. Hallett and Christopher Stray, Columbus, Ohio.

Miller, C. (2014), 'Vera Lachmann, the Classics, and Camp Catawba', in: *Amphora*, August 1: https://classicalstudies.org/amphora/vera-lachmann-classics-and-camp-catawba-charles-miller

Murray, O. (2017), 'Arnaldo Momigliano on peace and liberty (1940)', in: Crawford/Ulmenschneider/Elsner, 201–207.
North, H.F. (2019), *Wikipedia*:https://en.wikipedia.org/wiki/Helen_F_North.
North, H.F. (2019), 'Caplan, Harry', in: the *Database of Classical Scholars*: https://dbcs.rutgers.edu/all-scholars/8592-caplan-harry
Obermayer, H.-P. (2014), *Deutsche Altertumswissenschaftler im amerikanischen Exil. Eine Rekonstruktion*, Berlin.
O'Donnell, J.J. (2019), *Wikipedia*: https://en.wikipedia.org/wiki/James_J-O%27Donnell
Olson, K.W. (1973), 'The G.I bill and higher education: success and surprise,' *American Quarterly* 25.5, 596–610.
Quinn, B.N. (2019), 'Cornelia Catlin Coulter', in: the *Database of Classical Scholars*: https://dbcs.rutgers.edu/all-scholars/8627/coulter-cornelia-catlin
Reckford, K. (2019), 'Segal, Charles Paul', in: the *Database of Classical Scholars*: https://dbcs.rutgers.edu/all-scholars/9108-segal-charles-paul
Roots, E.B. (2019), 'Commager, Henry Steele, Jr.', in: the *Database of Classical Scholars*: https://dbcs.rutgers.edu/all-scholars/8621-commager-henry-steele-jr
Russo, J. (2016), 'Vera Lachmann: a personal memoir', document shared on a handout for 'Gendering the Study of Germanophone Refugee Classicists', paper presented by Judith P. Hallett at the 147th meeting of the Society for Classical Studies, San Francisco, CA: https://classicalstudies.org/annual-meeting/147/abstract/gendering-study-germanophone-refugee-classicists
Scodel, R. (2019), *Wikipedia*: https://en.wikipedia.org./wiki/Ruth_Scodel
Scott, R.T. (2019), 'Michels, Agnes Kirsopp Lake', in: the *Database of Classical Scholars*: https://dcbs.rutgers.edu/all-scholars/8937-michels-agnes-kirsopp-lake
Smith, G. (2019), *Wikipedia*: https://en.wikipedia.org/wiki/Gertrude_Smith
Stray, C.A. (2014), 'Eduard Fraenkel: an exploration', in: *Syllecta Classica* 25, 113–172.
Stray, C.A. (2017), 'Eduard Fraenkel (1888–1970)', in: Crawford/Ulmschneider/Elsner, 180–200.
Toher, M. (2019), 'Sorum, Christina Elliott', in: the *Database of Classical Scholars*: https://dbcs.rutgers.edu/all-scholars/9138-sorum-christina-elliott.
Treggiari, S. (2019), *Wikipedia*. https://en.wikipedia.org/wiki/Susan_Treggiari
University of Michigan Faculty History Project, s.v. 'Gerda M. Seligson', 2011. https://www.lib.umich.edu/faculty-history/faculty/gerda-m-seligson
von Scheliha, R. (2019), *Wikipedia:* https://de.wikipedia.org.wiki/Renata_von_Scheliha
Wyles, R./Hall, E. (eds.) (2016), *Women Classical Scholars: Unsealing the Fountain from the Renaissance to Jacqueline de Romilly*, Oxford.

Jaś Elsner
Room with a Few: Eduard Fraenkel and the Receptions of Reception

This paper — in celebration of the remarkable and pioneering work of Chris Stray in writing the history of the discipline of Classics in the United Kingdom — looks at some problems in the changing receptions of that history. I take a poignant and central case, that of Eduard Fraenkel, because it is relatively topical (having hit the newspapers in 2017), and since Chris's own contributions to the Fraenkel story are part of its trajectory.

Eduard Fraenkel (1888–1970) came to Oxford and to Corpus Christi College as Corpus Professor of Latin in 1935, having been dismissed from his chair in Freiburg in 1934 because he was a Jew. He served with immense distinction in that role until his retirement in 1953, and was in particular responsible for the creation of a German style academic seminar in Oxford which transformed the gentlemanly amateur model of Classics as a discipline forever. Thereafter he continued to give lectures and seminars, and Corpus (exceptionally) allowed him to retain an office in the college, part of which was to become the Fraenkel Room, as acknowledged in the dedication of his 1957 book, *Horace*. He died by his own hand in a College house close to the main site on 5th February 1970, a few hours after the natural death of his wife Ruth.[1]

Nearly half a century later, the series of events occurred which forms the subject of this paper. On Sunday November 26, 2017, at its last meeting of the Michaelmas Term, the Junior Common Room (JCR, the official voice of the College's undergraduates) at Corpus voted by 35 (with 1 vote against and 1 abstention) to press the College to rename the Fraenkel Room, in response to allegations of sexual harassment made against its honorand. They mandated the JCR President and Equal Opportunities Officer to 'lobby the College to change the name of the Fraenkel Room' and to remove Eduard Fraenkel's portrait photograph from the room. They also supported a boycott of the existing name — applied to the room, which was a vestige of Fraenkel's own office, in the 1970s, after his death — ruling that JCR committee members should now refer to it officially by a neutral name (such as the 'Corridor Room') until negotiations with the College were concluded. By the next day, these proceedings had reached the *Cherwell* (student) newspaper,[2] whence — by

---
1 The most important accounts are Stray 2014, Stray 2016, and Stray 2017.
2 http://cherwell.org/2017/11/27/corpus-votes-rename-room-after-allegations-of-sexual-misconduct/

https://doi.org/10.1515/9783110719215-014

Tuesday 28th November — the news was picked up with gusto by the national press in the form of the *Daily Telegraph*,[3] followed on the Wednesday by the *Times*, the *Daily Mail* and more locally the *Oxford Mail*.[4] In immediate response to the Cherwell report (and before any direct representations had been made by the students), the then President of the College, Steve Cowley, called a meeting of Fellows most directly concerned on the 28th to devise a way forward ahead of the last Governing Body of term on Wednesday 29th.[5] As the upshot of that meeting, the President urged that the College should make the whole issue a small part of the much bigger question of whether and to what extent varieties of abuse are still happening today in universities and how we might work with students, graduates as well as undergrads, to stop them. It was acknowledged that the students did not realize that talking to *Cherwell* meant instant attention from the national press. Meanwhile, Governing Body — conscious that there was no time for extended consultation before the Oxford interviewing season began the following week, no time for the Middle Common Room (MCR, the official organizing body of graduate students) to meet to offer a view, and that already representations from former students and alumni in response to Press coverage had begun to arrive — resolved to consider the case the following term and put out a public statement that its discussions would be within the College community and in private.[6]

In the course of the next three months, a steady stream of letters from more than twenty extremely distinguished Classicists, philosophers and others — both

---

[3] https://www.telegraph.co.uk/education/2017/11/28/oxford-college-rename-room-dedicated-renowned-classicist-following/

[4] http://www.oxfordmail.co.uk/news/15690265.Students_vote_to_rebrand_room_named_after__sex_pest__professor/

[5] For the record, those invited were the Senior Tutor, the Vice-President, the Domestic Bursar, the Academic Registrar, two Classical Fellows (Constanze Güthenke, the E.P. Warren Praelector, and myself) as well as Sam Gartland, the College Lecturer in Ancient History. Stephen Harrison, the Latin Tutor, was away in Italy at the time. I do not recall who could not make the meeting out of those invited, but I was present myself.

[6] This is the text sent to old members: 'As may have been seen in the press, we have been asked by the JCR to look again at the naming of one of the College teaching rooms — the Fraenkel Room — in the context of allegations made against Eduard Fraenkel, the distinguished philologist, after his death. When the JCR raises a concern of this kind, the College always takes it seriously and will consider the matter alongside any representations made by other sections of the College community and the likely impact on its wider reputation. In this case, the College is actively engaged in discussions with representatives of the JCR and senior members of governing body, especially those from within the Classics Faculty. So that we may reach an acceptable consensus, we will be conducting these discussions in private and will not be making any further comment until the outcome has been determined.'

old members of the College and former students of Fraenkel from other Colleges — were sent to the President. I find myself in the strange position of having access to this correspondence but being unable to make attributed quotations from it, since it is not clear that any one of the writers wrote in the expectation of being publicly quoted and at least one specifically asked not to be outed. So, in due deference to Thucydides' famous comments on speeches (I.22.1), I will summarize as fairly as possible the sentiments expressed (the reader will have to trust me) but refrain from making up what ought to have been said...

Meanwhile, a 'town hall' meeting was called between students concerned over the Fraenkel issue and the Classical Fellows of the College for the evening of Tuesday 6th February.[7] This was a constructive, open and robust conversation; here is what I wrote in an email to the other Fellows present on the following day:

> The results of yesterday's meeting make me feel as if there is no way we can keep the name or the picture. However, we may judge the students' arguments in many cases, two things cannot be gainsaid: they are pretty united and their basic point that the College cannot be seen to condone or honour abuse in any form is very strong.

Now before continuing with the recent narrative, it is worth pausing to look at the issues. The question of Fraenkel's inability to keep his hands off young women was not fresh news in the winter of 2017. Indeed, in the recent scholarly revival of interest in Fraenkel's work and career, notably in the work of Chris Stray,[8] it has been aired and discussed.[9] The more substantive question, therefore, in relation to the challenge put to the College by the JCR, was how that element in his behaviour should play in terms of later reputation and official commemoration.[10] Several of the correspondents to the President argued that, in the case of whether Fraenkel should remain worthy of commemoration, the key issue turns on balance. Here is a clear formulation by a distinguished male philosopher:

---

7 The Corpus Classical Fellows present were: Constanze Güthenke, Anna Marmodoro, Tobias Reinhardt and myself; also present were Sam Gartland as Lecturer in Ancient History and Ursula Coope, who had been Fellow in Ancient Philosophy until September 2017, when she moved to the Chair at Keble. Stephen Harrison was again away, this time in the USA. According to my memory there were some 15 students, mainly undergraduates but also some from the MCR, all Classicists. See the official record of the meeting at Appendix 1.

8 Key pieces include Stray 2014, Stray 2016, Stray 2017; also Elsner 2017.

9 Most recently and notably by Stray 2014, 144–8 and by Charles-Edwards and Reid 2017, 374.

10 As Mary Beard points out, the question of what counts as balance in these matters and 'what gets left out' is at least as important in written memorials like biographies as it is in material ones like room names and pictures. See Beard 2013, 265.

> My own view is that in naming rooms, or putting up pictures, we mark our respect for scholarship and/or contribution to the College more generally. We do not endorse every aspect of the lives of those honoured in this way, nor need we do so either explicitly or implicitly. Of course there is a balance in this, but in Fraenkel's case I think the balance is clearly in favour of sticking with the status quo... Unless we take the view that transgressions of this sort are an absolute bar to any academic recognition I think the balance is clearly on Fraenkel's side.

One view of the JCR's position may be to see it as disagreeing specifically with this view of the balance. Moreover — if we allow the question of balance to weigh — insofar as honouring a person in a University context is a matter of role models, then whatever one thinks of the model of Fraenkel as scholar the fact is that the anti-model of Fraenkel as abuser (in an age that stresses equality, diversity and inclusivity) tips the balance rather decisively to the side of the JCR.

Here there seems to be a watershed of changing attitudes that clearly define different generations, responding to the same historical evidence. There is what the President of the College (a physicist) described as 'an algorithm' by which anyone over 50 (that is, mainly people from the sixties and immediately post-sixties generations) was much more likely to take a forgiving view of Fraenkel's activities (edging the 'balance' in favour of his academic distinction and influence), and anyone younger than 50 was much more likely to be strongly condemnatory (weighing the problem of sexual abuse more heavily). It may indeed be that there is a relatively recent move in what Kenneth Dover called 'popular morality' which tends to the view that any 'transgression of this sort' constitutes an 'absolute bar' to recognition of the kind implied by a name like the 'Fraenkel Room' and a photograph of the honorand. What is in no doubt is that the students' agitation follows, and is part of, the explosion of the *#MeToo* movement in the wake of the allegations made by many women against the movie mogul Harvey Weinstein as a sexual predator, which spread virally in October 2017, and occurs in the context of a near-overwhelming and relentless flood of compelling evidence about sexual abuse and institutional cover-up by older people in positions of power across churches, schools, universities, care homes and many other institutions of supposed responsibility and trust.

In certain ways, the student energy was not unlike that of the 2015/6 *Rhodes Must Fall* campaign to remove the statue of Cecil Rhodes on the High Street elevation of Oriel College,[11] which did not succeed at the time, only to revive with much

---

11 Some Press accounts include:
- https://www.independent.co.uk/student/news/oxford-university-students-call-for-greater-racial-sensitivity-at-the-institution-and-say-it-must-be-10332118.html;

greater force in the worldwide protests of the *Black Lives Matter* movement after the death of George Floyd by police hands in the US on 25 May 2020 during the Covid-19 lockdown.[12] Another contextual spur was the rise of a passion for renaming university buildings, occasioned by the removal of their dedications to famous alumni or scholars, whose reputations had become tarnished by virtue of intellectual positions held or activities conducted that have become controversial by the second decade of the twenty-first century.[13] In the immediate chronological vicinity of the row about the Fraenkel Room, pressure from students and others had caused Yale University to rename Calhoun College (so called after an alumnus, John Calhoun, former Vice-President of the United States and strong white supremacist), a decision made in February 2017 and enacted in a formal ceremony in early September.[14] At UCL, since 2014, there was a campaign to rename the buildings commemorating the distinguished eugenicists Francis Galton and Karl Pearson,[15] which led to a long official review and much soul searching about the College's links with eugenics as a discipline and an ideology, but as yet (in mid 2020) no final decision on changing the dedications.[16] By the bye, it probably did not help the claims for keeping the Fraenkel name that the room was not any old room named after a famous scholar:

- https://www.thetimes.co.uk/article/the-statue-of-cecil-rhodes-like-that-of-saddam-must-fall-sqtptnrrvbl;
- https://www.telegraph.co.uk/education/educationopinion/12073349/Its-time-to-say-No-to-our-pampered-student-emperors.html;
- https://www.timeshighereducation.com/features/must-rhodes-fall;
- https://www.theguardian.com/uk-news/2016/mar/16/the-real-meaning-of-rhodes-must-fall.

12 For some press accounts:
- https://www.mirror.co.uk/news/uk-news/hundreds-attend-rhodes-must-fall-22164728;
- https://www.theguardian.com/world/2020/jun/09/protesters-rally-in-oxford-for-removal-of-cecil-rhodes-statue.

13 Indeed at the time the fad for renaming extended well beyond academia. See for example the renaming of Colston Hall in Bristol (announced in April 2017): https://www.theguardian.com/world/2017/apr/29/renamed-and-shamed-taking-on-britains-slave-trade-past-from-colston-hall-to-penny-lane; or the renaming of the airport in the Republic of Macedonia (https://www.independent.co.uk/travel/news-and-advice/macedonia-airport-rename-alexander-the-great-greece-feud-zoran-zaev-a8179601.html), before that state changed its name to North Macedonia, https://en.wikipedia.org/wiki/Macedonia_naming_dispute.

14 E.g. https://www.nytimes.com/2017/02/11/us/yale-protests-john-calhoun-grace-murray-hopper.html; https://www.nytimes.com/2017/09/03/nyregion/yale-calhoun-college-grace-hopper.html.

15 https://profjoecain.net/rename-galton-lecture-theatre-ucl/.

16 https://www.ucl.ac.uk/news/2020/feb/ucl-announces-action-acknowledge-and-address-historical-links-eugenics; https://www.independent.co.uk/news/education/education-news/eugenics-university-college-london-ucl-secret-conference-francis-galton-a9365036.html.

it was actually what remained (after adaptation in the 1970s) of Fraenkel's own office. From the point of view of those distressed by its associations, it not only celebrated what the Press happily called a 'sex pest' but it was the site of the act.[17] As was remarked in the town hall meeting, the Fraenkel Room was normally used for the College's women's welfare events, to which (as a site that commemorated a harasser) it could not be less suited.

Let us turn to the evidence. The key item, Mary Warnock's memoir published in 2000, is explicit — describing how Iris Murdoch had been warned by her own tutor Isobel Henderson that Fraenkel would 'probably "paw her about a bit"',[18] and then describing her own personal experience, that of her friend, Imogen Wrong (later Imogen Rose), who was a student in Cambridge but whose family home was in Oxford, and that of one other unnamed female student from Lady Margaret Hall (LMH),[19] of being taught by him in one-to-one meetings in his office:

> He also and increasingly, as he opened my eyes to the nature of scholarship, indulged in 'pawing about'. I was sexually innocent to a degree that is nowadays almost impossible to imagine, and at first I was disconcerted and embarrassed, even disgusted by his attentions... There was undoubtedly an extremely comic side to the difficulties we found ourselves in. But it never occurred to us for a moment that there was anything we could possibly make a public fuss about; nor that Fraenkel wanted more than kisses and increasingly constant fumblings with our underclothes...[20]

Warnock's account has been much discussed,[21] but it needs stressing that this is a deeply disturbing text, combining the disconcertedness with reference to comedy and to a breathless attraction to the 'extraordinary excitement' of Fraenkel's

---

17 In fact, between 1935 and 1952 Fraenkel is recorded as being in a different room: 'Fellows Building Staircase 1, Second Floor Left'. Only after 1952 did he move to 'Staircase 5, Ground Floor Left', which became, in an adapted form, the Fraenkel Room. So the activities of the 1940s did not take place in the room named for Fraenkel, but at the time of the crisis about the room's naming neither students nor Fellows were aware of this.
18 Warnock 2000, 79.
19 Warnock 2000, 82
20 Warnock 2000, 79–81.
21 E.g. Beard 2013, 264–71; Stothard 2006; Stray, 2014, 145–8. It transpires that Warnock's personal diaries for the relevant period in the 1940s have survived in her private papers after her death. Philip Graham, who is in the process of writing her biography, tells me that these reveal she was far more tortured at the time by feelings of sin and guilt than one would have imagined from the way she wrote about his behaviour in later years.

teaching.[22] That is, Warnock pin-points and indeed, in the literary texture of her account, rather eloquently enacts that highly problematic impossibility fully to segregate attractions (physical and intellectual) within education, which has been described as the 'erotics of paedagogy',[23] and has been fundamental to *paideia* in Classics at least since Plato's *Symposium*.[24] Warnock writes of 'the best teacher I ever had', and of 'the great power he had to excite one's imagination with the feeling ... of the infinite horizons of the world of scholarship'.[25] She comments:

> In one way, the impropriety of his sexual behaviour seemed utterly trivial compared with the riches he offered us, and the vast horizons he opened up. In another way, the conjunction of the physical and the intellectual seemed the most natural thing in the world, a conjunction of mind and body which it would have been silly and ungrateful to attempt to disjoin, and which indeed may have shown a glimpse, however faint and indeed absurd, of some sort of ideal...[26]

She quotes John Bayley's account of Iris Murdoch:

> She had already told me how fond she had been of Fraenkel, both fond and reverential. In those days there had seemed to her nothing odd or alarming when he caressed her affectionately as they sat side-by-side over a text, sometimes half an hour over the exact interpretation of a word, sounding its associations in the Greek world as he explored them, as lovingly keen on them as he seemed to be on her. That there was anything dangerous or degrading in his behaviour, which would nowadays constitute a shocking example of sexual harassment, never occurred to her.[27]

---

22 Cf. Warnock 1991, 53: 'Fraenkel picked his pupils from among those who attended his lectures in scholars' gowns. They were all girls (but as it was wartime there were lots of girls and few boys). Nowadays this would count, I fear, as sexual harassment. But to have removed his pupils from him or had him reprimanded would have deprived us of an intellectual excitement without parallel.'
23 Stray 2014, 144; cf. Beard 2013: 'the erotic dimension of pedagogy'.
24 For a deep historical discussion of 'feeling and philology' with trenchant thinking on questions of eros and charisma, see Güthenke 2020.
25 Warnock 2000, 82, 85.
26 Warnock 2000, 84.
27 Warnock 2000, 84, from Bayley 1998, 49; cf. Conradi 2001, 115. Murdoch's own relations with Fraenkel remained extremely warm throughout his life (see the correspondence in Corpus under MS 551, A II, 7). Here is some of her letter to him of February 7, 1966: 'You are something very precious and permanent in my life, and I felt all the time, even when I idiotically didn't write to you (forgive that). You have always given me, ever since the days of the Agamemnon class, a vision of excellence. More simply, I love you...' On April 30 of that year she wrote to ask Fraenkel if she might dedicate a novel to him: this was done in *The Time of the Angels*, published in the

At the same time, and with real relevance to the issues raised by the students in 2017, Warnock notes that her friend 'Imogen... did not altogether share my feelings about Fraenkel. She found his behaviour, though comic, genuinely disgusting, and she told me recently that she thought it had had a lasting and bad effect on her attitude to sex, which I deeply hope was not true...'[28] This last is potent testimony.

Now it is the case that these accounts are (at any rate, from a legal point of view) no more than allegations. As one of the male correspondents to the President writes, they were 'published long after Fraenkel's death in 1970. He was in no position to defend himself'. But no one seriously questions the evidence of Mary Warnock both about her own story and about those of others which she witnessed first-hand. Certainly none of the defenders of keeping Fraenkel's name on his room went so far as to doubt what Warnock describes as taking place: in the words of the College's own *History*, written in the last few years and published in 2017 for the Quincentennial, 'Fraenkel was a habitual groper'.[29] And while it seems likely that he reformed after he was confronted by Imogen Wrong's Cambridge tutor, Jocelyn Toynbee,[30] and by Martha Kneale from LMH,[31] this does not alter the fact of the earlier transgressions, nor their effects on his victims.

The rich range of defences of Fraenkel, sent to the President, which I will summarize, reflect positions held by an older generation, mainly retired, by contrast with the views of the young. Not one letter or email received by the President supported the JCR's proposal, although other Fellows did receive representations in support of the students' case. The defences include an emphasis on Fraenkel's exceptional scholarship and influence, and an insistence on him being a victim of Nazi persecution (all of which is true, but irrelevant to the problem at hand). A

---

same year. Fraenkel is also the model for Max Lejour in her novel *The Unicorn* (1963) and for Levquist in *The Book and the Brotherhood* (1987) — see e.g. Spear 2007, 1.

28 Warnock 2000, 84.
29 Charles-Edwards and Reid 2017, 374.
30 Stray 2014, 145: Chris tells me the source of this story (involving a letter, later burnt by the recipient, from Fraenkel to Toynbee) is a verbal account given by Imogen Wrong to him over lunch with Mary Warnock (pers. comm.). The story has been confirmed to me by Mary Warnock (pers. comm.). It should be added that the surviving correspondence at the Corpus archives (Ms 551, A II, 12) between Toynbee and Fraenkel, including letters on matters political (the teaching of Roman archaeology in Oxford) and intellectual (the dates of Seneca's *Apocolocyntosis* and Calpurnius Siculus), is very warm and dates from precisely this period (1943–45)
31 Mary Warnock (pers. comm.) tells me that the other girl from LMH complained to her moral tutor, the philosopher Martha Kneale (because their Mods don A.M. Dale was at Bletchley), and that Kneale confronted Fraenkel as well as Warnock herself, cf. Warnock 2000, 82.

collective letter signed by a string of immensely distinguished figures (all male) contains this comment:

> Regarding the frequency and extent of such actions, and the question of how far they were consensual, or coercive, the evidence which has recently been publicised, after an interval of seventy or more years, appears insufficient to establish the facts with any degree of certainty.

This is true — but even in cases of very recent sexual harassment it is all too often difficult 'to establish the facts with any degree of certainty', in the sense demanded by a court of law, as long as the issues turn on whose word we choose to believe (as opposed to, say, the presence of DNA). There is a worrying apologetic in the option of 'consensual or coercive' which, from a contemporary perspective in relation to the power structures involved, seems artificial.

One correspondent, female, writes:

> I do not doubt that many of the men whose portraits hang in Oxford colleges behaved towards women in a manner that was considered normal in that time but is rightly regarded as reprehensible today. In most cases, this behaviour will never come to light: taking a portrait away and renaming a room will not, alas, undo the sins of the past.

There is substance here. Of all the people one might condemn for a crime systematically committed over generations by men with power in relation to the young (both female and male), it does make one slightly queasy that it be the refugee, the Jew with the withered arm,[32] the outsider, who takes the rap. Here Fraenkel is an easy and alien scapegoat for a culture of abuse that was widespread and homegrown. But this does not exonerate his transgressions. There is moreover a real problem in the terminology of 'was considered normal in that time but is rightly regarded as reprehensible today'. It is right that it is very difficult to assess past and present cases in the same way because in the past different kinds of criteria will have been in play. Nonetheless, however 'normal', widespread or widely condoned sexual harassment may have been (in Germany in the early twentieth century or in England), it was never considered at any time, or by any party, to be right.

One form of defence is attack — and two more aggressive arguments against the JCR position are worth repeating here. One male correspondent (perhaps anticipating the woes of the Labour Party in the Summer of 2018)[33] writes of 'the

---

32 On the withered arm, see Horsfall 1990, 61; Beard 2013, 264–5; Stray 2014, 145.
33 As I write, we are not sufficiently out of the mess for the crisis to have found a historian. Suffice it for the interested reader to put 'Jeremy Corbyn' and 'antisemitism' into any search browser and then review the long cocktail of apologetic and polemic.

whiff of anti-semitism'. He is unfair to the Corpus JCR in potentially imputing antisemitism to them, at any rate in the matter of their proposal about the Fraenkel Room, but not perhaps entirely wrong to say that some 'now seem to regard anti-semitism as a tiresome preoccupation of older people, to be ignored on principle'.[34] The second attack from more than one correspondent — which cuts to the heart of what we think history is and how it should be used — is on the 'uninformed and ahistorical viewpoint' of those who cannot recognize the '*mores* of the time*'*, or who betray 'a lack of awareness of changing *mores*', resulting in 'a blinkered lack of historical perspective'. It is true — but is it not always true? — that the young are impatient with the compromises and attitudes of an earlier generation, and the old (in feeling misunderstood or not sufficiently empathetically regarded) are often critical of a youthful impatience with the complex nuances of history. But here — and this cuts to the quick of old 'Greats' (combining ancient history and philosophy) as the traditional culmination of Lit. Hum. as the great Oxford Classics degree — the question of historical nuance clashes with that of philosophical clarity. Whatever the historical position and to whatever extent 'the past is another country' as one correspondent writes, quoting L.P. Hartley, it remains the case that harassment is harassment, always was and always will be. No amount of history can get away from this, and here — on purely philosophical grounds of principle — the students' objection to the honouring of 'a groper' had its strongest force. Moreover, one need not disregard changing *mores* to say that this kind of activity is nonetheless unacceptable in a figure who continues to be honoured in the present.

I now turn, finally, in this consideration of the case made in Fraenkel's defence, to a letter whose authorship I had better reveal, but do so with permission. On 23 January 2018, Mary Warnock herself wrote to the President. Here is what she said:

> I was horrified to see last week that undergraduates at Corpus were agitating to have the Fraenkel room dismantled, and memorials of him removed, on grounds of sexism. I feel extremely guilty to think that it was partly my pages about Eduard Fraenkel that have been responsible for this nonsense. I have never in my life gained so much as I gained from being 'picked up' by Fraenkel from his Agamemnon lectures and taught especially about early Latin, and other things as well. It was my introduction to scholarship and learning and represented what was the most exciting and amazingly eye-opening experience I could ever

---

[34] On the anti-semitism issue re-Fraenkel, Mary Warnock comments (pers. comm.): 'I suppose now there might be a question of anti-Semitism in the judgement of Fraenkel — but not then (except possibly among some of the older Mods dons, those whose lives consisted in setting and returning proses and unseens).'

have had. Of course, I complained of his mild mauling <u>but</u> I need not have gone on going to him if I thought it worse than mildly awful (and a subject for a lot of jokes). I do very much hope that you can get some sense of proportion into the undergraduates — who seem to me to have no sense of history apart from anything else.

Please forgive my terrible handwriting.

Yours very sincerely

Mary Warnock

Now, apart from the importance of this as a considered view in the light of the various later responses to her original memoir, this letter seems to me to offer some significant considerations on the ethical front. Warnock's underlined 'but' and the phrase 'I need not have gone on going to him if I thought it worse than mildly awful' implies that she believes herself to have had some agency in the situation and was able to make choices for which she held herself responsible. Effectively she tolerated, even condoned, a certain set of activities on whose ridiculous side she insists, did not see them at the time as abuse and did not act to stop them. The perpetrator's acts are seen here as 'ridiculous', 'comic', 'utterly trivial' rather than as aggressive. Modern responses, such as those implied by the JCR, certainly do not share these attitudes because they would never see a student victim of a senior academic as having the power or agency to say no, at least without significant risk. The issues recall the debate within feminism between those who expect the culture, and indeed the law, to protect women and hence condemn any act that infringes the integrity of the body, on the one hand, and those who (perhaps more like Mary Warnock) take the view that women should be empowered to act with free agency, to take full responsibility for their lives and bodies and be able to repel any potential infringement if they wish, on the other. At the same time, arguably Warnock concedes the point that she had no options but an either/or choice of accepting harassment or giving up the best opportunities of a brilliant education in her life (on her own account). There was, at any rate in her time as a student, no viable alternative move (such as telling him to stop, for instance), and that constitutes a very strange definition of freedom or agency. Whatever position one takes on the issue of responsibility and agency in contexts of harassment, it remains the case that this does not exonerate a serial instigator of abuse in what was serially an uneven balance of power.

I should put it on record that the correspondence sent to the College, all of it in defence of Fraenkel and in favour of keeping the name on his room as a memorial, while initially substantially raising the stress-levels of those trying to contain and resolve the situation, was in fact extremely helpful. It set out a range of positions, some carefully considered, and showed the strength of feeling among old members and the community of emeriti. But the question remained, what was the College to do? An Oxford Governing Body as such — a democratic medley of competing voices — is singularly ill-equipped to think through a barrage of competing positions and to argue consistently for a correct ethical and public stance. Perhaps two considerations above all stood out. First, a number of the correspondents had warned us against *damnatio memoriae*, and there was no appetite in Governing Body for a systematic condemnation of everything Fraenkel stood for. Second, the key issue the students had highlighted — despite the fact that it had long been swept under the carpet, or belittled, or deemed irrelevant — remained potent: Fraenkel had, at a period in his Oxford career, harassed students sexually, in a manner that has never been appropriate, that he and his victims knew was inappropriate,[35] and that in certain cases may have caused real damage, as was suggested by Imogen Wrong's comment to Warnock that her attitude to sex may have been permanently affected. There is no way that any institution of higher education can possibly condone such activity or be seen to do so, however elevated, distinguished or inspiring in other respects the harasser may be.

Let us return then to the 'town hall' meeting with members of the JCR on 6 February 2018, in the middle of the 4th week of the eight-week Oxford term. In the course of that conversation, and as part of the process of presenting the students with some of the positions articulated in the correspondence I have been discussing, a potential solution arose. Was there a way of removing Fraenkel's picture and his name from the room, but not condemning him entirely to oblivion? It happens that 2018, in addition to being the 501st year of the life of the College, is the centenary of a very specific and at the time probably quite a small event in the history of refugee scholars in Oxford. It was the year in which Mikhail Rostovtzeff (1870–1952), perhaps the greatest ancient historian of the first half of the twentieth century, arrived in Oxford fleeing the Russian Revolution.[36] In 1919, Sir Paul Vinogradoff (the immensely distinguished Corpus Professor of Jurisprudence from 1903 and himself a refugee from Tsarist Russia)[37] persuaded the College to take Rostovtzeff as a member and (alongside Christ Church) to supply some financial support.[38] As it turned out, Rostovtzeff superbly fulfilled the two

---

35 The fact that Fraenkel stopped when privately outed and challenged by Toynbee's letter implies he acknowledged his behaviour was wrong.
36 On Rostovtzeff in England, see Bongard-Levin 1999.
37 See Stein 2004.
38 Charles-Edwards and Reid 2017, 358; Crawford, Ulmschneider and Elsner 2017b, 2.

key obligations of a temporary guest: he was exceptionally brilliant and he did not outstay his welcome. In 1920 he moved to Wisconsin and thence in 1925 to Yale. His tenure in Corpus became much more important than his individual case because fifteen years later, in the turmoil of Hitler's takeover of Germany, the precedent of giving succour to refugee scholars of exceptional ability, including Fraenkel of course, would be remembered and emulated with incalculable positive consequences both for those rescued and for the University as a whole in all disciplines.

The proposal that emerged at the town hall meeting was to honour all the distinguished refugee scholars associated with Corpus in the last century, by renaming the Fraenkel Room as the Refugee Scholars Room. It would be a move that would incorporate Fraenkel and keep his name alongside a list of exceptional figures, whose distinction was not less than his own. The photograph would be removed and a plaque would go up commemorating all those honoured in this way. Armed with consensus, Constanze Güthenke, representing the Fellows present at the 'town hall' meeting, was able to bring the proposal to Governing Body at the end of Hilary term on 7 March 2018 (see Appendix 1 which represents the minutes of the meeting of the 6th of February as well as the starting point of the conversation in Governing Body on 7th March). In the event, Governing Body was relieved that the most difficult discussions had already taken place and that the kernel of a way forward had been presented for it to discuss (see Appendix 2 for the relevant GB Minute of the meeting of 7 March). It acknowledged the sensitivity of the issues, as well as the range and diversity of competing views across the generations (from people in their nineties to current undergraduates) and the great difficulty of finding a solution that could satisfy all. A clear majority voted to accept the change of name to the Refugee Scholars Room, although there was concern (not mentioned in the Minute) about the tendentious writing and re-writing of history as well as the fact that there remains a refugee crisis among scholars from a number of countries in the Middle East and Africa. A meeting was subsequently arranged with representatives of CARA (the Council for At-Risk Academics),[39] itself the successor of the Academic Assistance Council and the Society for the Protection of Science and Learning, which were the British organizations primarily responsible for bringing Jewish scholars out of Nazi Germany in the 1930s,[40] to explore how the College might continue to support refugee

---

39 See https://www.cara.ngo/
40 E.g. https://www.cara.ngo/who-we-are/our-history/; the archives of the AAC and SPSL are held at the Bodleian under the title MS. SPSL. See e.g. Bentwich 1953, Seabrook 2013, 13–91, and Davies 2017.

scholars in the current era. The Governing Body committed to take on the responsibility for housing and feeding such a person, should they be accepted by a Faculty and should there be a Fellow in a related field within the College.

The list of the others alongside Fraenkel to be honoured in the room is impressive (see Appendix 3 for the proposed text of the plaque to go in the newly named room). Alongside Vinogradoff, Rostovtzeff and Fraenkel himself, it includes Rudolf Pfeiffer, the great editor of Callimachus and historian of Classical Scholarship,[41] and Isaiah Berlin, who was an undergraduate and later Honorary Fellow of the College. Three of these were Russians (Vinogradoff, Rostovtzeff and Berlin), two were Jews (Fraenkel and Berlin), two were refugees from Nazi Germany (Fraenkel and Pfeiffer). Only Vinogradoff and Fraenkel were ever actually Fellows, though both Berlin and Pfeiffer were elected to Honorary Fellowships. Rostovtzeff was a guest.

In the term following the Governing Body meeting, the President would both circulate the junior members by email (see Appendix 4 for the text) and write to his many correspondents on the issue (see Appendix 5), informing them of the College's decision.

Let me conclude with some reflections on all this. I am broadly happy with the solution. It has kept the many generations of the College community together and it has answered some of the key demands of both parties — not to exact a *damnatio memoriae*, on the one hand, but to establish a line that absolutely refuses to condone harassment or abuse in the academic workplace. But beyond this, there is a bigger picture. Especially in relation to the different assessments of what one correspondent called 'balance' and Mary Warnock called 'a sense of proportion' in the various matters concerning Fraenkel's reputation, there has clearly been a sea-change in attitudes between generations. The same evidence, even when accepted, has prompted different conclusions and entailments largely on grounds of age or what we might call differential historical life-experience (not so much, interestingly, on grounds of gender — 5 letters or emails to the President came from women, 8 from men, although one of these had 11 signatures all from men).

---

41 Of Pfeiffer, Mary Warnock writes (pers. comm.): 'It is interesting to compare Fraenkel with that other great scholar, Rudi Pfeiffer, by whom I was also, occasionally taught on my own — not because he 'picked me up' but because I was doing Greek Lyric Poetry as one of my special subjects in Mods and in fact [he] was the main reason to be doing it. I adored him — he was a gentle, subtle, brilliant man — very conscious of his debt to Oxford, and therefore inhibited from being as rude about the text we had to use (the Oxford Book of Greek Verse, which had been largely written by Maurice Bowra) as he would otherwise have been.' I know of no other tribute to Pfeiffer's teaching at Oxford, so this exceptional testimonial deserves publication.

Yet the contemporary and live issue of continuing sexual harassment by people in power, which underlay the JCR's position, is an entirely different question from 'balance' about how much wrong-doing can tip someone out of a position that merits a memorial. Universities are not neutral spaces, but ones in which hierarchies of power that enable abuse are still present (many of the younger generation might say endemic). The real point about the College's decision was not to engage in a game of adjusting the balance of honour paid directly to Fraenkel or in moving the pointer to a different slot on a scale whose extremes are represented by the JCR (or even a 'Fraenkel must fall' model) and the arguments of the distinguished persons who wanted to preserve the *status quo*. Rather, the College decided to abandon that scale altogether and to shift the direct focus of celebration to the tradition of sheltering refugee scholars, revived in the present with the CARA initiative. This shift in criteria had the advantage of not excluding Fraenkel (on the grounds of being a distinguished refugee scholar), but at the same time of specifically stepping away from any commemoration of his person, including and because of his history of sexual harassment. When the room was first named for Fraenkel in the 70s it is not clear if anyone in the College knew of the events in the 30s and 40s on which the JCR's position is based.[42] At the conference from which this volume arises, some who were a living part of the College or University in the 70s, 80s and 90s said that they were not aware of anything, others said that *sotto voce* rumours did circulate.[43] The harassment story only became public knowledge in 1991 after Mary Warnock published a piece called 'My Old Teacher' in the *Independent on Sunday* in which she is unspecific but mentions 'sexual harassment'.[44] Much more direct information emerged after 1998, when John Bayley published his memoir based on the memories of Iris Murdoch, by then already lost to Alzheimer's and then her death a year later. But they were powerfully confirmed by Mary Warnock's memoir of 2000. Neither of these texts was intended to bury Fraenkel but rather to praise him. Both Warnock and Murdoch report their compelling attraction and fascination for Fraenkel, adding to the record the sense

---

42 Accounts by more recent students of Fraenkel, e.g. Horsfall 1990 and West 2007, 203–18, or Clemence Schultze (speaking to me during the conference at which this paper was given) make no mention of the groping issue. According to Stray 2014, 146–8, this is probably because the activity stopped after the early 1940s and there was no record or even much gossip until Bayley and Warnock published. However, see n. 43.
43 I do wonder whether the failure to award Fraenkel a knighthood when his academic distinction deserved it and when other refugee scholars did receive this accolade (i.e. it was not kept from foreigners) may have its roots in a black mark over his 'pawing' activities.
44 See Warnock 1991, 53, the key passage is cited at n. 22.

that beyond exceptional philological exactitude and vast knowledge his charisma extended to the frisson of 'the conjunction of the physical with the intellectual', as Warnock puts it (p. 84). That openness to telling the complete story was itself part of the moment when these texts were written. After 2000, that information — in the public sphere — effectively sat alongside the traditional reasons for honouring Fraenkel, and it could be argued that it was ignored or denied in the routine commemoration that constituted the daily use of a room named for him. In 2017 a new generation, basing its judgments on the same evidence known since 2000, but drawing different conclusions challenged the institution on what some might describe as stringent grounds (in relation to evaluating the long and complex life-history of a human being), but ones that are nonetheless unassailable in the context of questions of harassment and abuse.

The results of the change in the sociology of what can and cannot be tolerated, and of how reputations will last, are impossible to assess. We are entering an era in which transgressions in the sexual arena constitute abuse and are therefore an 'absolute bar' to any possibility of commemoration. This is quite different from the world of the post-sixties, where what was perceived as right and wrong was much more fluid and uncertain. It may also be added we are now in an period where, for very good reasons, much less respect and deference is granted to institutions of privilege and distinction, and to their decisions, than was the case even twenty years ago — largely I suspect because of the shocking legacy especially of sexual abuse and cover-up which has been made public across the world. I should stress here (as the College recognised in its first meeting after the JCR resolution) that the issue at stake, to which different generational judgements are being brought, is anything but neutral in itself and remains — sadly but strongly — live. One huge difference between, say, the 1930s and 40s when Warnock and Murdoch experienced Fraenkel's harassment and today (including the late 1990s, when the accounts of this were written) is that we can clearly *name* the activity: the terminology of 'harassment' only came into being in the 1970s.[45] The sense of guilt, consternation, crossed boundaries but unclarity about how to respond in victims is much increased when the transgressions are unnameable (as implied by John Bayley's comments in relation to Murdoch).

---

45 The terminology appears to have been created in America in the 1970s, notably in the work of Mary Rowe at MIT, where the problems are well described and called 'harassment'. See Rowe 1973 and later papers; and MacKinnon 1979.

The reception histories of Fraenkel have played a different role in this from that perhaps intended by their authors; as have the first-hand accounts by Murdoch, as reported by Bayley, and by Warnock.[46] The airing of information and the willingness, in a generation deeply marked by the changes of attitudes in the sixties, to mention what might once have been excluded have clearly provided the evidential basis on which the students could make up their own minds. But the swiftness by which an allegation and the decisions of a group like the JCR can go viral, or attract national publicity, makes questions of good judgment much more difficult since no one can think clearly or assess all the issues and options in an atmosphere of public pressure. History, we may worry, nowadays lies less in the evidence, painstakingly adduced, than in the conclusions and judgments drawn from it, whose dissemination may be at lightning speed. The reception of receptions of the past, in the context of a major social change away from the behavioural laissez-faire of the post-sixties, have consequences that are unforeseen.

1 Coda: The Gentleman and the Captive

The years of Fraenkel's harassment can be accurately dated to before 1938–40, when Iris Murdoch was in her first and second years at Oxford, studying for Mods, and 1942–44, when Mary Warnock read for Mods. We know he must have embarked on this kind of activity in England before 1938 (because Murdoch was warned by her tutor that she might be pawed) and he had likely done so in Germany,[47] but if he stopped when confronted publicly by Jocelyn Toynbee and Martha Kneale, then the abuse of young female undergraduates ended in 1944.[48] The

---

46 The relevant sections of Warnock 2000, including her quotation from Bayley, and Stray 2014 were circulated to all members of Governing Body and among the students in the course of the internal discussions within College. The students first discovered the harassment issue from Beard 2013 and on Fraenkel's Wikipedia page, which has a paragraph referring to both Beard and Warnock: https://en.wikipedia.org/wiki/Eduard_Fraenkel.
47 There is anecdotal evidence that Ruth, Fraenkel's wife, was unhappy at her husband's behaviour with young female students from his years in Göttingen (1928–31) and then Freiburg (1931–34): see Warnock 2000, 85; Stray 2014, 146–7. The key archival document is a family history of 2007 by Fraenkel's eldest son Gustav, in the archives of Flinders University, Adelaide, cited by Stray.
48 But the 'if' in this sentence is significant. Charlotte Roueché, who was an undergraduate in Cambridge in the mid 60s, reports that she invited the then retired great man to speak to the student society known as the Herodoteans. He could not come but invited her to visit him in

dates in England coincide with the trajectory of the *Agamemnon* seminar (which ran from 1936–1942) and then with the writing up of the commentary (from 1942–46).[49] I have argued elsewhere that the commentary was about far more than Aeschylus' play — that it was effectively a profound and extended response, through the prism of German Classical philology and its commentarial tradition but enacted in exile and in English, to the experience of persecution as a German Jew, of being a refugee and ultimately to the Holocaust. The seminar and writing of the commentary ran concurrently with these events in the wider world beyond Oxford, took almost as long as they did and quite as long as Agamemnon took to win the Trojan War.[50] I want now to supplement that suggestion with the further argument that, in the tradition of personal self-revelation that underlies the infusion of feeling in German Classical philology, discussed so well in Constanze Güthenke's new book,[51] Fraenkel's *Agamemnon* offers a strange and disturbingly delusory reflection on his relations with young women and that the circumstances of his behaviour in one-on-one tutorials during the period explain, or at least set in context, some of the most peculiar and incomprehensible aspects of his interpretation of the play. These are primarily his attitude to the character of Agamemnon, which may be characterised as reflecting an extraordinary level of identification,[52] and to the relations of the conquering monarch with his captured maidservant and sex slave, Cassandra.

Scholarship on the *Agamemnon*, after Fraenkel, has seized on the absurdity of his interpretation of the king as 'a great gentleman',[53] a view from which

---

Oxford: 'When I did so he gave me some offprints, which I still have; he also showed an inclination to knee-patting, which was easily dealt with by moving away a bit. I wasn't under his authority, so there was not too much of a problem...' (pers comm.).
49 See Stray 2016 and Elsner 2017, 34–5.
50 See Elsner 2017, 35–45.
51 Güthenke 2020. I am most grateful to Constanze for discussing the issues with me and for letting me read her manuscript in advance of publication.
52 Elsner 2017, 42–3.
53 Fraenkel 1950, vol. 2, 425 and 441. The critiques began immediately and include, for instance: Murray 1951; Winnington-Ingram 1951, 150: 'I must confess I am confirmed in a theory that the better the scholar, the worse he argues a bad case' (cf. Winnington-Ingram 1983, 88: 'the eccentricity of a distinguished scholar'); Denniston and Page 1957, 151; Dodds 2007, 261, n. 41; Lloyd-Jones 1962, 195–6 ('not convincing'); Lebeck 1971, 76: 'This is not the Agamemnon of Aeschylus but a figure created by Fraenkel'; Buxton 1982, 106: 'Unfortunately there is nothing in the Greek to support...this interpretation'; Goldhill 1984, 69–70; Goldhill 1997, 327; Garland 2004, 131; Goward 2005, 80–1; Goldhill 2007, 111. Some discussion by Gaskin 2018, section 31.

Fraenkel is said later to have distanced himself.⁵⁴ It has said less about Fraenkel's very peculiar account of the relationship between Agamemnon and Cassandra.⁵⁵ He writes at v. 954ff (of Agamemnon's description of Cassandra, when he walks into the house over the purple carpets, as 'the flower chosen especially for me from among much wealth, the army's gift'):⁵⁶

> Not with a single word does Aeschylus indicate whether the king has any other feeling towards his captive beyond that of pity for her fate. There is no room in this tragedy for the idea ἔρως ἐτόξευσ' αὐτόν (Agamemnon) ἐνθέου κόρης (Euripides, *Tro.* 255), *arsit Atrides medio in triumpho virgine rapta* (Horace *Odes* 2.4.7 f.). It is quite hopeless to attempt to convince those who are in the habit of reading into any work of poetry what they want to find there and, when challenged to produce some evidence from the text, will fall back on the argument 'but is it not simply human nature.....?' Unless we allow a great poet to draw a line precisely where he chooses, we shall never be able to understand his work.⁵⁷

He expressly rejects any sexual appropriation of Cassandra (such as he recognises is present in the versions of both Euripides and Horace, whose positions he does not name or summarize in English but leaves in quotation).

Clytemnestra, revelling over the slaughtered bodies of the king and Cassandra later in the play, speaks some tellingly brutal verses against the Trojan princess:

> καὶ κοινόλεκτρος τοῦδε, θεσφατηλόγος
> πιστὴ ξύνευνος, ναυτίλων δὲ σελμάτων
> †ἰστοτρίβης†.⁵⁸
>
> ...this soothsayer, this chanter of oracles who shared his bed, this faithful consort, this cheap whore of the ship's benches. (vv. 1440–1443).⁵⁹

---

54 Lloyd Jones 1982, 222 n. 8 reports Fraenkel as saying: 'In the case of Aeschylus' Agamemnon, an interpreter who had learned so much from Tycho's book ought not to have let himself be tempted into trying to find out by psychological speculations why the king finally gives in to Clytemnestra's flattering entreaties and walks into the house where murder awaits him over the purple tapestry that is too precious to be trod by human feet'. The reference is to (Tycho von) Wilamowitz-Moellendorff 1917. My thanks to Chris Pelling for this information.
55 This silence among later scholars (who are so vocal on the 'gentleman' question) is odd. It is perhaps, in the space of scholarly critical practice, a symptom of the phenomenon that delayed (or turned a blind eye to) condemnation of Fraenkel's activities for so long.
56 Fraenkel's translation: Fraenkel 1950, vol. 1, 147.
57 Fraenkel 1950, vol. 2, 433.
58 Text obelized as edited by Denniston and Page 1957.
59 Sommerstein 2008, 175; Fraenkel prints: '...this captive here and auguress, the prophesying bedfellow of this man, a faithful concubine, and ... of (?) the benches of the ship'.

I here give Alan Sommerstein's new Loeb version, since Fraenkel neglects to translate the crucial and deeply demeaning word ἱστοτρίβης, which — after an immensely long discussion — he describes as 'completely obscure'.⁶⁰ It literally means 'rod-rubber' — about as aggressive an assault on Cassandra's sexual availability (across the rowers' benches) on the journey home from Troy as Clytemnestra could conceive; and it is not awfully difficult to construe (as a group of articles in the 1980s showed) so long as you allow a great artist like Aeschylus to 'stoop', for excellent dramatic reasons, to the obscene.⁶¹ Instead, protecting Cassandra's propriety, Fraenkel claims:

> Clytemnestra exaggerates here, for the purpose of her self-justification, the insult done to her by Agamemnon's relations with Chryseis and Cassandra. Actually this, as the prophetess contends (1260 f.), merely adds a flavour to the draught of her revenge...'⁶²

Developing the line that Clytemnestra's claims are all abuse with no substance, he described her 'mockery' as 'particularly vitriolic: the dedicated prophetess of the god should give herself to no man'.⁶³

Fraenkel's reading of the characters of Agamemnon and Cassandra in Aeschylus rests on two implausibilities, both rooted in powerful identification.⁶⁴ The first is that the king, although weary, is always a gentleman (never the 'abuser', λυμαντήριος, of Clytemnestra's claim in v. 1438), and the second is that his relations with his captive are at all points entirely honourable, despite the power-

---

60 Fraenkel 1950, vol. 3, 680–83, quotation 683. On the accentuation of this unique word, see Fraenkel 1950, vol. 3, 680 n. 5.
61 The word (Fraenkel accepts it may be 'coarse', 683) has since been subjected to significant and sane scholarly discussion: See Koniaris 1980; Tyrrell 1980; Borthwick 1981; now Willi 2002, 155–7: 'If, as the comic parallels suggest, ἱστοτριβής [accent sic] would be taken as meaning approximately "one who gives hand jobs", then on the one hand the princess and prophetess Kassandra (to whom Klytaimestra was so elaborately sympathetic in 1035–46) is being downgraded to the level of the meanest slave in a Peiraeus brothel, and on the other hand it is being insinuated that Agamemnon had been suffering from erectile dysfunction and had needed manual assistance to overcome it' (156); Steiner 2016, 179–80.
62 Fraenkel 1950, vol. 3, 679.
63 Fraenkel 1950, vol. 3, 680. We may add that Clytemnestra calls Cassandra Agamemnon's φιλήτωρ at v. 1446, 'lover', in Fraenkel's version with his comment: 'It may be a really subtle touch that a word which properly denotes the ἐραστής is here used of the woman. Headlam's conjecture, 'perhaps by the active word she wishes to imply that the woman was the seducer' is worth considering'; cf. Willi 2002, 156.
64 Further on identification with Cassandra, see Elsner 2017, 38–9, 42–3.

dynamics of the situation, despite how other ancient writers construed Cassandra's 'yoke of slavery' (as Agamemnon calls it, v. 953, in Fraenkel's version)[65] and despite how Clytemnestra portrays it. It is the second of these idealizing implausibilities that resonates not with the Second World War or the exilic context, but with the facts of Fraenkel's own behaviour in respect of the brilliant and attractive young women (as Cassandra is) that he 'picked up', like Iris Murdoch and Mary Warnock. It may be a case of excessive reading-in on my part — quite as excessive as that which Fraenkel's own commentary perpetrates on Aeschylus' play — to see a strange self-reflection on what he imagined was going on as he fumbled with young women's underwear while he taught them the *Agamemnon*, in his account of the doomed gentleman and the young woman in his service. I submit that in the most eccentric part of his interpretation of the great tragedy that occupied his mind throughout the period of the Nazi government in Germany and the war, as well as that of his documented molestation of female students, Fraenkel conducted a remarkable whitewash of the negative aspects of the power relations of older men and younger women, including especially his own, through the prism of scholarly commentary on Aeschylus, by elevating an idealised model of their propriety onto the level of tragic paradigm. The mix of a kind of desire for honesty in reflecting on what he was doing through the vicarious means of philological commentary, combined with a strong reflex to self-justification and some spectacular self-delusion,[66] in the course of an entirely private conversation between himself, his conscience and Aeschylus' play, explains why he could produce so gratuitous an interpretation of Agamemnon's noble character and his pure relations with Cassandra, which no other reader has been able to understand (or take seriously) and which is in fact unnecessary for the larger thrust and scope of his reading of the drama. Moreover, as Fraenkel sublimates and aestheticizes the noble relations of gentleman and concubine, he projects all condemnation away from himself, as identified with Agamemnon, onto the vindictive and murderous wife, Clytemnestra.

The result, for all its weirdness as the exegesis of drama, is a testament to the role of classical philology in its time and in Fraenkel's great Prussian tradition,

---

[65] Fraenkel 1950, 147.

[66] A good parallel for this kind of self-justification and self-delusion might be the issues dramatized in Alan Bennett's play *The History Boys* (2004), which turns in part on the sexual harassment of boys in a school. In Act Two, the male teacher concerned claims: 'I didn't actually do anything. It was a laying-on of hands, I don't deny that, but more in benediction than in gratification or anything else', to which his interlocutor, a female teacher, responds 'A grope is a grope. It is not the Annunciation': see Bennett 2004, 95.

as a mode through which much larger and very personal truths could be reflected, as well as rather interesting evidence for his self-awareness and internal defensiveness about the activity by which in the end his memory has been tarnished. Fraenkel's take — personal and scholarly — on the canonical tragedy of his principal focus is a universalist and humanist reading of epic proportions. In the course of this, his blindness to the abuse of Cassandra — raped twice in the imaginary world of the play (first by Apollo, to cause her madness, and then we may presume repeatedly, by Agamemnon, in a relationship which will ultimately cause her death) raises with bitter irony to epic and tragic proportions both the question of sexual abuse and the strange knowingness of its insistent denial by its perpetrators. The witnessing of Warnock and Murdoch that outed the abuse was itself as strange as Fraenkel's reading of the play — replete as it is with repeated expressions of praise, affection, even love for the perpetrator. We owe it to the Warnock and Murdoch memoirs, to Chris Stray's balanced discussion and to the Corpus undergraduates in the #MeToo movement to have thrown light not only on an issue of scholarly biography and the implications of commemoration, but also on a notoriously eccentric twist in scholarly interpretation.

2 Acknowledgments

I am grateful to Philip Graham, Chris Stray and Mary Warnock for help with the research and the factual basis of several aspects of this history. A number of readers of all generations and genders, several close to the events described, have been kind enough to respond with critiques both gentle and stringent: I thank the editors and anonymous readers for their many suggestions and especially (in reverse alphabetical order) Alexia Petsalis-Diomidis, Katherine Harloe, Constanze Güthenke, Silvia Frenk, Maia Elsner and Freya Chambers.

3 Appendix 1

Note to Governing Body on the Classics Townhall meeting regarding the Fraenkel Room, 6. February 2018:

> At its last meeting of Michaelmas term 2017, the JCR approved a motion (35 in favour, 1 against, 1 abstention) to 'mandate the JCR President and Equal Opportunities Officer to lobby College to change the name of the Fraenkel Room; to remove the picture of Eduard Fraenkel from the room; and to remove the plaque from the door of the room'.

In response to this motion, the Classics tutors felt it was useful and appropriate to hold a townhall-style meeting open to all classicists in College, to create a forum for respectful debate and for hearing opinions and arguments. We called such a meeting on Tuesday of 4th week this term (6. February), and circulated in advance to all undergraduates, graduates and teaching and research staff in Classics at Corpus the materials that are available in the public domain and that had, in part or in full, also been made available to Governing Body: the relevant excerpt from Mary Warnock's published memoir (2000); Mary Beard's 2005 *TLS* review of a biographical dictionary of British Classical scholars, that had at the time made Mary Warnock's testimony more prominently known within the public sphere and among classicists; the long and careful research article on Eduard Fraenkel's life, scholarship, and career by Christopher Stray, published in *Syllecta Classica* (2014); and the relevant sections on Fraenkel from the recently published College history (2017), ed. Julian Reid and Thomas Charles-Edwards.

The meeting was attended by ca 15 students, of all year groups and including both Freya Chambers, the 2nd year Classics student who had brought the original motion and the current JCR president, Shiv Bhardwaj (a classicist), as well as several senior members (Constanze Güthenke, Sam Gartland, Jaś Elsner, Tobias Reinhardt, Ursula Coope, and Anna Marmodoro). There were a good number of students who were unable to attend the meeting but who had let us know their opinions in advance or had delegated some of the students present.

In the discussion, which was throughout well-informed, respectful, careful, open, and open-ended, neither of the constituencies spoke with absolute unanimity; that said, there was a strong sense that a significant majority of undergraduate classicists present (or represented) supported in broad terms the original JCR motion brought last term.
In probing discussion, there emerged broad consensus about a range of points:

– that maintaining the status quo (keeping the Fraenkel Room in place as stands) without further debate or discussion within College was problematic;

– a strong appreciation of the willingness of College and Governing Body to discuss the matter in depth and with care; as well as an appreciation of the range of interests, constituencies, and factors at play in any such debate an awareness that the historical case of Fraenkel was and should be separate from the need to address current forms of harassment and inequality in the academy; but that, at the same time, any present responses also resonate within and reflect more contemporary debates and responsibilities.

It is fair to say that it was evident that the students present (and the students whose views were represented) were explicit about not wanting to be seen as historically naïve. There was strong support for acknowledging multiple and at times conflicting forms of historical memory: Fraenkel as important scholar and inspiring teacher; Fraenkel as a teacher whose behaviour, judging by the documentation available, caused concern and upset; and Fraenkel as a refugee scholar from Nazi Germany who found a home in Oxford and at Corpus Christi, and was seminal, as one of a generation of scholars, in changing academic practices and formats (especially the seminar) in Oxford.

There was no wish on the students' part to 'expunge' Fraenkel's name from College; there was, in fact, a strongly endorsed suggestion on part of the students that the College community of classicists ought to find, in addition to any other solution, ways of publicizing more widely, through workshops, academic events, and lectures, the relevance of Fraenkel's own work, as well as the history of Classics at Corpus and within the university, with an additional welcome emphasis on making this a more inclusive and diverse history.

Nonetheless, there was strongly felt concern over the meaning and significance of continuing to name a room that is specifically designated and very regularly used for teaching after Fraenkel, in light of the documentation that is available and now widely known to students and members of the Classics and College community. It was pointed out that naming signals less a one-time act of the past, but also an active, on-going process whose maintenance requires continued choices, and reflects changing and evolving circumstances.

There was acknowledgement of historical circumstance, as well as of the insistence that has been voiced by some of those who were historically directly or indirectly affected (including Mary Warnock), arguing that personal behaviour should be considered as entirely separate from scholarly and pedagogical achievement. But there was equal unease over what it might mean now, and within a teaching community, to consider behaviour that even at the time was perceived as inappropriate and problematic to be an integral part of pedagogy and of the intellectual communities in which we live and which we shape.

In sum, two priorities seemed to emerge from the discussion:

– to find, in a spirit of collaboration, a way forward that strives to mark historical complexity (including that of the present), instead of shying away from it; and

– to acknowledge that the College, as a community and as an institution, should consider ways to make a statement about its own stance on forms of harassment and inequality.

One possible proposal that was voiced as a result of the meeting is included here. It might offer an integrating approach that combines current needs with avoidance of a *damnatio memoriae*. This is to reconceive of and rename the room as the Refugee Scholars Room, to honour a number of refugee scholars to whom Corpus Christi College offered help and an intellectual home, and among whom Fraenkel is included. This would mean a recontextualisation of his importance as a scholar that opens the view onto a feature of Corpus' history that, maybe more than ever, resonates with our current moment.

Constanze Güthenke 23.ii.2018

4 Appendix 2

Governing Body Minute, 7 March 2018

Fraenkel Room discussion

Following the JCR's decision to lobby the College to change the name of the Fraenkel Room (following known historic harassment claims) a meeting of the College's Classics community was held on 6 February. Professor Güthenke's paper setting out the discussion that had taken place at that meeting was received and a lengthy discussion followed.

It was noted that there were many differing views on the matter from a wide constituency — junior members, senior members, emeriti and alumni.

It was further noted that the junior members were appreciative that the College was taking the matter seriously and that discussions were being held which included their views. A number of emeriti had written to the President indicating their reluctance to change the name as had a number of alumni; however, it was acknowledged that the matter is sensitive in different ways to different constituencies and all views should be considered.

The proposal that came out of the Classics meeting – to rename the room as the Refugee Scholars' Room – was discussed. The renaming would honour a number of refugee scholars who fled persecution in their home countries during the 20th C and were offered refuge in Corpus. It was argued that this could include Fraenkel (who fled from Nazi persecution) amongst others. It was also suggested that a display or plaque recording the history of the room and conflict of views could be installed to contextualize the renaming (if this was approved). There was general support for the proposal; however, a number of Fellows were concerned that renaming the room as suggested might have an impact in the future and would not acknowledge that there are currently many refugee scholars from contemporary conflicts whom the College is not seen to be assisting.

Following the discussion a vote was held on two matters:
- Should the name of the room be changed? There was a majority view that this should be the case;
- Should there be further work on what the change should be and how it should be implemented by creating a working group? It was unanimously agreed that this should take place.

5 Appendix 3

Text of the plaque in the new Refugee Scholars Room

The Refugee Scholars Room
Since its foundation Corpus has had a history of welcoming refugee scholars, from the arrival of the Jewish *converso*, Juan Luis Vives (1493–1540), the great humanist in exile from Habsburg Spain, who was among the earliest scholars to lecture at the College. This room was named for Eduard Fraenkel after his death in 1970. In 2018, the 501st year since the foundation, it was renamed in honour of all the Refugee Scholars who fled persecution and were given a home in Corpus during the 20th century.

Five figures stand out:
- Paul Gavrilovitch Vinogradoff (1854–1925), Liberal refugee from Tsarist persecution, Corpus Professor of Jurisprudence in Oxford from 1903, major medieval and legal scholar.

- Mikhail Ivanovich Rostovtzeff (1870–1952), Liberal refugee from the Bolshevik Revolution, perhaps the greatest historian of the Hellenistic and Roman worlds of the first half of the 20th century, who was supported by Corpus from 1919–1920 before he moved to the USA.
- Eduard Fraenkel (1888–1970), Jewish refugee from Nazi persecution, Corpus Professor of Latin (1934–1953), one of the greatest Classical philologists of the 20th century, a revered and hugely influential scholar at Oxford.
- Rudolf Pfeiffer (1889–1979), opponent of Nazism, great historian of Hellenistic poetry and of ancient scholarship, who lived in Oxford sponsored by Corpus from 1937–51 before returning to Germany.
- Isaiah Berlin (1909–1997), child of bourgeois Jewish refugees from the Bolshevik Revolution, undergraduate of Corpus and Honorary Fellow, philosopher, historian of ideas, President of the British Academy (1974–1978), founding President of Wolfson College (1966–1975).

6 Appendix 4

Text of the announcement of the College's decision on the re-naming of the Fraenkel Room, circulated to Junior Members in Trinity Term 2018.

> At a meeting on 7. March 2018, Governing Body approved a proposal to change the name of the Fraenkel Room, one of the College's teaching rooms. His former study, it had been named for Eduard Fraenkel, German émigré scholar and Corpus Professor of Latin from 1934–1953, after his death in 1970. As the Refugee Scholars Room, it will reflect a more inclusive understanding of the lives and work of refugee scholars, and the contributing role of the College, past and present; it will also be a reminder of the continuing responsibility which the College bears, as a place of learning and as a scholarly community, for creating environments that are diverse and that offer a refuge from harassment for all its members. The College aims to reconceive the room's layout over the summer to be able to chart more clearly the history of dispossessed scholars at Corpus, from one of its very first members, the Jewish converso Juan Luis Vives (1493–1540), up to the considerable number of scholars who fled persecution in the 20th century and were given support by the College, among whom was Fraenkel.

7 Appendix 5

Text of the letter sent by the President at the end of Trinity term 2018 to all those who had written to him on the Fraenkel issue.

Dear X,

Thank you very much for writing to me with your views on the naming of the Fraenkel teaching room in Corpus Christi. I have received a number of letters, expressing various views on the matter, and all have been useful in informing our College discussions. I and the Governing Body appreciate the care and time that all those who corresponded with us on this matter have expended, and we are grateful for the warm interest in the College that they express.

We have undertaken a careful and nuanced process of listening and discussion in College and have now reached a decision on the future of the room, which I am writing to share with you. At its meeting on 7th March 2018, Governing Body approved a proposal to change the name of the teaching room to the Refugee Scholars Room. Bearing this name, it will reflect an inclusive understanding of the lives and work of refugee scholars, and the contributing role of the College, past and present; it will also be a reminder of the continuing responsibility which the College bears, as a place of learning and as a scholarly community, for creating environments that are diverse and that offer a refuge from harassment for all its members. The College aims to reconceive the room's layout over the summer to be able to chart more clearly the history of dispossessed scholars at Corpus, from one of its very first members, the Jewish converso Juan Luis Vives (1493–1540), up to the considerable number of scholars who fled persecution in the 20th century and were given support by the College, among whom Eduard Fraenkel is numbered. Since its foundation, Corpus has had a history of welcoming dispossessed and émigré scholars, and the intention is to recognise these connections with those who have experienced the hardships of the refugee or dispossession including, amongst others, Paul Vinogradoff (Professor of Jurisprudence), the ancient historian Mikhail Rostovtzeff, the Hellenist Rudolf Pfeiffer and the renowned philosopher Isaiah Berlin.

Thank you again for your time in writing to me on this matter.

Best wishes

Steve Cowley
President

Bibliography

Bayley, J. (1998), *Iris: A Memoir of Iris Murdoch*, London.
Beard, M. (2013), *Confronting the Classics: Traditions, Adventures and Innovations*, London.
Bennett, A. (2004), *The History Boys*, London.
Bentwich, N. (1953), *The Rescue and Achievement of Refugee Scholars*, The Hague.
Bongard-Levin, G.M. (1999), 'M.I. Rostovtzeff in England: A Personal Experience of West and East', in: Gocha Tsetskhladze (ed.), *Ancient Greeks East and West*, Leiden, 1–45.
Borthwick, E.K. (1981), 'ἱστοτρίβης: An Addendum', *American Journal of Philology* 102, 1–2.
Buxton, Rd. (1982), *Persuasion in Greek Tragedy*, Cambridge.
Briggs, W./Calder, W.M. III (eds.) (1990), *Classical Scholarship: A Biographic Encyclopedia*, New York.
Cazzato, V./Obbink, D./Prodi, E. (eds.) (2016), *The Cup of Song*, Oxford.
Charles-Edwards, T./Reid, J. (2017), *Corpus Christi College Oxford: A History*, Oxford.
Conradi, P. (2001), *Iris: The Life of Iris Murdoch*, New York.
Crawford, S./Ulmschneider, K./Elsner, J. (2017a), 'Oxford's ark: Second World War refugees in the Arts and Humanities', in: Crawford/Ulmschneider/Elsner 2017b, 1–21.
Crawford, S./Ulmschneider, K./Elsner, J. (eds.) (2017b), *Ark of Civilization: Refugee Scholars and Oxford University, 1930–1945*, Oxford.
Davies, P. (2017), 'Out of the Archives: Oxford, the SPSL and *Literae Humaniores* refugee scholars', in: Crawford/Ulmschneider/Elsner 2017b, 77–95.
Denniston, J.D./Page, D. (eds.) (1957), *Aeschylus: Agamemnon*, Oxford.
Dodds, E.R. (2007), 'Morals and Pollution in the *Oresteia*' (1960), in: Lloyd 2007, 245–264.
Easterling, P. (ed.) (1997), *The Cambridge Companion to Greek Tragedy*, Cambridge.
Elsner, J. (2017), 'Pfeiffer, Fraenkel, and Refugee Scholarship in Oxford during and after the Second World War', in: Crawford/Ulmschneider/Elsner 2017, 25–49.
Fraenkel, E. (1950), *Aeschylus, Agamemnon*, 3 vols., Oxford.
Garland, R. (2004), *Surviving Greek Tragedy*, London.
Gaskin, R. (2018), *Tragedy and Redress in Western Literature: A Philosophical Perspective*, London.
Goldhill, S. (1984), *Language, Sexuality, Narrative: The Oresteia*, Cambridge.
Goldhill, S. (1997), 'Modern Critical Approaches to Greek Tragedy', in: Easterling 1997, 324–347.
Goldhill, S. (2007), *How to Stage a Greek Tragedy*, Chicago.
Goward, B. (2005), *Aeschylus: Agamemnon*, London.
Güthenke, C. (2020), *Feeling and Classical Philology: Understanding Antiquity in German Scholarship, 1770–1920*, Cambridge.
Horsfall, N. (1990), 'Eduard Fraenkel 17 March 1888–5 February 1970', in: Briggs/Calder 1990, 61–67.
Koniaris, G. (1980), 'An obscene word in Aeschylus I', *American Journal of Philology* 101, 42–44.
Kraus, C.S./Stray, C. (eds.) (2016), *Classical Commentaries*, Oxford.
Lebeck, A. (1971), *The Oresteia: A Study in Language and Structure*, Washington DC.
Lloyd, M. (ed.) (2007), *Aeschylus*, Oxford.
Lloyd-Jones, H. (1962), 'The guilt of Agamemnon', *Classical Quarterly* 12, 187–199.
Lloyd-Jones, H. (1982), *Blood for the Ghosts: Classical Influences in the Nineteenth and Twentieth Centuries*, London.

MacKinnon, C. (1979), *Sexual Harassment of Working Women*, New Haven.
Murray, G. (writing as GM) (1951), 'A learned commentary', *Oxford Magazine*, 8 March, 331–333.
Rowe, M. (1973), 'The Saturn rings phenomenon' (http://mitsloan.mit.edu/shared/ods/documents/?DocumentID=3986)
Seabrook, J. (2013), *The Refuge and the Fortress: Britain and the Persecuted 1933–2013*, Basingstoke.
Sommerstein, A. (tr.) (2008), Aeschylus, *Volume 2: The Oresteia*, Cambridge, Mass.
Spear, H. (2007), *Iris Murdoch*, Basingstoke.
Stein, P. (2004) 'Vinogradoff, Sir Paul Gavrilovitch [Pavel Gavriilovich Vinogradov] (1854–1925)' *Oxford Dictionary of National Biography* 2004, https://ezproxy-prd.bodleian.ox.ac.uk:2095/10.1093/ref:odnb/36664
Steiner, D. (2016), 'Parting shots: Aeschylus, Agamemnon 1384–98 and symposia in the visual repertoire', in: Cazzato/Obbink/Prodi 2016, 159–183.
Stothard, P. (2006), 'Pawed about a bit' (https://www.the-tls.co.uk/pawed-about-a-bit/)
Stray, C. (ed.) (2007), *Oxford Classics: Teaching and Learning 1800–2000*, London.
Stray, C. (2014), 'Eduard Fraenkel: an exploration', *Syllecta Classica* 25, 113–172.
Stray, C. (2016), 'A Teutonic monster in Oxford: the making of Fraenkel's *Agamemnon*', in: Kraus/Stray 2016, 39–57.
Stray, C. (2017), 'Eduard Fraenkel (1888–1970)', in: Crawford/Ulmschneider/Elsner 2017b, 180–195.
Tyrrell, W.B. (1980), 'An obscene word in Aeschylus II', *American Journal of Philology* 101, 44–46.
Warnock, M. (1991), 'My old teacher', *The Independent*, 2 June, 1991, 53.
Warnock, M. (2000), *A Memoir: People and Places*, London.
West, S. (2007), 'Eduard Fraenkel recalled', in: Stray 2007, 203–218.
Willi, A. (ed.) (2002), *The Language of Greek Comedy*, Oxford.
Winnington-Ingram, R.P. (1951), 'Fraenkel's *Agamemnon*', *Classical Review* n.s. 1, 147–151.
Winnington-Ingram, R.P. (1983), *Studies in Aeschylus*, Cambridge.

Part VI: **Academic Practices**

Graham Whitaker
Congratulations and Celebrations: Unwrapping the Classical Festschrift

1 Introduction

In 1936 the Clarendon Press published a volume of essays under the title *Philosophy & History*, presented to the exiled German philosopher Ernst *Cassirer (1936),[1] and it was this volume that first awakened my interest in Festschriften. Books, in one form or another, have been exchanged and presented since ancient times, but the concept of the Festschrift as currently understood has a relatively recent history.[2] As the word suggests, its root lies firmly in the soil of German scholarship, and this is perhaps especially true for the study of the ancient Greek and Roman civilizations.

Friedrich Thiersch was one of the most important educationalists in Germany in the first half of the nineteenth century. He reformed the school curriculum in Bavaria, and produced several textbooks, one of which, his Greek grammar, was translated into English by Daniel Keyte Sandford, Professor of Greek at Glasgow.[3] On Thiersch's initiative the first *Versammlung deutscher Philologen und Schulmänner* took place at Nuremberg in 1838. This was designed to bring representatives of the universities and *Gymnasien* together at a time when educational reform in the

---

Festschriften mentioned in the text or footnotes are indicated by an asterisk against the honorand's surname, followed by the date(s) of publication in parentheses, and are listed in the bibliography following this chapter. Festschriften relating to universities, publishing houses, or other institutions are generally omitted. A few examples that are not strictly classical are included. The broad reach of the topic necessitates some generalization and guesswork. I am grateful for access to libraries in Scotland, London, and elsewhere, and in particular to the staff at the Institute of Classical Studies, School of Advanced Studies, London. Other libraries, notably the Bavarian State Library, Munich, have been generous in lending obscure Festschriften.

1 See Whitaker 2017, 346–349; 2018, 80–107. In addition to paying homage to Cassirer, the book was designed to promote the Warburg Institute, which had arrived in London from Hamburg in December 1933, and opened to the public in 1934.
2 As currently understood: a collection of essays in honour of someone or something, often to celebrate a particular occasion. There is, however, an earlier line traceable through emblem books, some of which were also published to honour special occasions.
3 Thiersch 1830.

various German states was under discussion and often in conflict. With some exceptions, meetings were held regularly thereafter in different cities,[4] the proceedings (*Verhandlungen*) being published, and it was for the twentieth meeting, held at Frankfurt am Main in September 1861, that Alfred Fleckeisen issued a pamphlet on Latin orthography respectfully dedicated (*ehrerbietig gewidmet*) to the Assembly.[5] Four years later, at Heidelberg, a substantial volume including in its title the word *Festschrift*, and more recognizable as such, was issued for the twenty-fourth meeting by the *Historisch-Philosophischer Verein*. It was edited by Wilhelm Oncken,[6] and included contributions from Eduard Zeller and Alexander Riese; Zeller had already published his *Die Philosophie der Griechen in ihrer geschichtlichen Entwicklung*, and Riese was to become celebrated for his work on Latin literature, in particular the *Anthologia Latina*.[7] Festschriften were issued intermittently to honour subsequent meetings of the *Versammlung*; occasionally, as in 1887, when the thirty-ninth meeting was held in Zürich, there were two offerings.

To honour an occasion or institution is one thing; honouring an individual or individuals is another, because of the necessary change of emphasis. This is seen in the Festschriften that were published during the 1860s and 1870s, notably those for Friedrich *Ritschl (1864, 1867), Johan Nikolai *Madvig (1876), and Theodor *Mommsen (1877).[8] There is a marked difference between the latter two: Madvig's contains essays in Danish and Latin, the Danish language acting as a bar to a wide readership. Mommsen's can be considered as the first international classical Festschrift; apart from contributions in German (fifty) and Latin (fifteen), it includes eleven contributions in Italian, and one each in French and

---

4 The exceptions were 1848/49, 1853, 1859, 1866, 1870/71, 1873, 1881, 1883; from 1885 meetings were held in alternate years. During the years 1846 to 1860 Orientalisten was added to the title.
5 Fleckeisen 1861.
6 In 1865 Oncken was a private teacher (Privatdocent) at the University of Heidelberg; he became a professor in 1866. His introduction reveals that the Festschrift originated in 1863 from a seminar held at the University. Oncken's own contribution was an essay on the revival of Aristotle's *Politics* in western culture and literature.
7 Zeller 1844, 1846: first edition; Riese 1869: first edition.
8 The Festschrift for Ritschl is the first major classical Festschrift for an individual; it was issued by Teubner in two parts, the first in 1864, the second in 1867. Contributions are in German or Latin, and there is an emphasis on textual criticism. A joint Festschrift for Franz *Buecheler and Hermann Usener (1873) is in Latin throughout. Joint Festschriften are not uncommon, particularly if the honorands share a common discipline, have the same age, or have worked in the same institute or university. As many as four are squeezed into *De Regibus (1966), a volume celebrating the careers of Luca De Regibus, Paolino Mingazzi, Aldo Neppi Modona, and Enrico Turolla; all receive equal treatment in terms of bibliographical listing and portraiture.

English.⁹ It also served as a model in the variety of its subject matter, however; this aspect became problematic later on, and was one cause why the genre became a target for disdain.¹⁰

Discussion as to the nature and value of Festschriften as a genre came to the fore in 1929. Two articles were published in the *Philological Quarterly*, the first by Sylvanus Griswold Morley and the second by Alfred Gudeman. The starting point for Morley, Professor of Spanish at the University of California, Berkeley, was an invitation to contribute to a Festschrift for an honorand¹¹ of whom he had no knowledge, and a feeling accordingly that anything he wrote would be merely a superfluous academic exercise. He prescribed guidelines for the publication of Festschriften towards the end of his survey. Gudeman's article offers additions and corrections to the rather thin data that Morley supplied; writing from Munich, he was able to add a German perspective on various aspects of problems associated with the genre. Twenty-five years later, in 1954, a more substantial survey was published by Dorothy Rounds and Sterling Dow; it included statistical information for the statistically-minded, offered more detailed arguments for and against Festschriften, and was also prescriptive.¹² In 1962 Rounds published an index of Festschriften from the date of the Festschrift for Friedrich *Haase (1863)

---

9 The contribution in English was by John Collingwood Bruce, 'The fountain of Coventina, at Procolitia, on Hadrian's Wall, England', *Mommsen (1877), 739–746. Mommsen was not a Festschriften enthusiast; in an undated letter (early 1899) to Ulrich von Wilamowitz-Moellendorff, discussing the Festschrift planned for Wolfgang *Helbig (1900), he described them as fashionable potpourris ('Helbigs 60. Geburtstag soll nun einmal gefeiert werden durch eines der leider beliebten Schriftsteller-Potpourris ...'), Calder III and Kirstein 2003, II, 685. Wilamowitz had already taken a similar view in 1877, according to his memoirs: Wilamowitz-Moellendorff 1929², 180–181.

10 Particularly by R.G. Collingwood: 'And if there are any who think my work good, let them show their approval of it by attention to their own. So, perhaps, I may escape otherwise than by death the last humiliation of an aged scholar, when his juniors conspire to print a volume of essays and offer it to him as a sign that they now consider him senile.' Collingwood 1939, 118–119.

11 Honouree is preferred in the *Oxford English Dictionary* and, more recently, in library catalogues; not by me.

12 Morley 1929, 61–68; Gudeman 1929, 335–338; Rounds and Dow 1954, 283–298, reprinted with additions and corrections in Rounds 1962, 551–560. In addition, more subject-specific bibliographies have been published. A good example is *A Bibliography of Legal Festschriften* by Lilly Melchior Roberts, who was the bibliographer at the University of Michigan Law Library from 1945 until her death in 1966. It was continued thereafter to December 1968, and published in 1972.

up to the end of 1954, and including those on Byzantine and Old Testament studies.¹³

Editors of Festschriften are divided in the way that they perceive their task, and its significance. For some, the recipient is self-selecting, as exemplified by the Festschrift for the ecclesiastical historian Owen *Chadwick (1985), of which the editors wrote [Preface, ix] that 'The production of this volume was *demanded* [my italics] by the fame and stature of the historian to whom it is presented …'. For others, it is to recognize a significant point in the honorand's life, for example a sixtieth anniversary, as in the Festschrift for Eric *Birley (1966).¹⁴ A further variation occurs when editors are aware of an honorand's dislike of Festschriften, but decide to circumvent this potentially fatal drawback.¹⁵ To excuse this disparity of function or purpose, some have resorted to metaphor. A Festschrift may be seen as a ritual,¹⁶ and indeed there are elements — gathering the contributions, ordering and editing them, creating a *tabula gratulatoria*, and presenting the finished product to an astonished and delighted recipient — that suggest as much. Because of the division mentioned earlier and the varying elements, reviewed in the next section, it would however be wrong to overemphasize ritual as a necessary component of the process.¹⁷ Despite all this soul-searching, the genre does

---

13 *Haase (1863) is little more than a pamphlet; its fifty-four pages include eleven contributions, on grammatical aspects or textual criticism. See n.68 for online access.
14 Eric *Birley (1966), Preface, v: 'The occasion, his sixtieth birthday, is chosen to avoid the confusion of this modest and intimate tribute with whatever may seem fitting to his colleagues and fellow-scholars at a later date … It does not imply his retirement from either research or teaching; to those who know him, such a retirement is inconceivable.'
15 Two examples: (1) Ronald *Stroud (2015), I, Preface, 14: 'The second problem was Stroud's well-known aversion to Festschrifts, which acted as a serious deterrent to several of the potential contributors … We therefore insisted from the beginning that the thematic scope of the present volume was to be Epigraphy and Historical Topography … This choice, we feel, reflects Stroud's real interests, and hopefully helps alleviate his anti-Festschrift sentiments.' (2) The art historian Erwin *Panofsky (1961), I, Preface, vii: 'We were convinced at the outset that the book would be peculiarly incomplete without one paper, that of a scholar who from time to time has been a collaborator of Panofsky: Dora, his wife. But to invite her participation and ask for secrecy would … have put a heavy burden on her. Not to request secrecy, on the other hand, would have given Panofsky an opportunity to nip the enterprise in the bud … So at last we reluctantly decided we preferred a book without Dora to no book at all.'
16 Werner *Suerbaum (2003), 9–10 where the editors discuss the place of ritual in Festschriften.
17 How easy it is to do this is demonstrated in a bizarre essay by Ender and Wälchli 2012, 143–167. Another approach is to suggest that the Festschrift is a game, as in the title of the book *Shall we Play the Festschrift Game?* by Santos, Linden, and Ng'ang'a, 2012. Not surprisingly the answer is yes. This, and the book edited by Ender, Leemann, and Wälchli, deal with linguistic theory. For a Festschrift which subverts the ritual idea, see Anthony R. *Birley (2008).

have its supporters. In reviewing a Festschrift containing essays on the Black Sea region, Stanley Burstein wrote that

> No genre of scholarly literature is more maligned than the Festschrift. Throughout my career I have repeatedly heard Festschrifts condemned as incoherent collections of and repositories for rejected papers rescued from dusty files ... A well designed and edited Festschrift, however, can be a valuable contribution to scholarship that will be consulted for years to come.[18]

While this might suggest that poorly designed or edited ones are destined to fade into oblivion, it is not the only matter to consider. Large-scale Festschriften are still published, with the likelihood that they will receive limited circulation, owing to such factors as language or cost; an example of the former is the Festschrift for Manuel *García Teijeiro (2014), which — according to the union catalogues I was able to consult — is held in fewer than thirty libraries worldwide.[19]

There are also 'discreet' Festschriften; these may behave like a Festschrift, including at least some of the furnishings, but keep the fact hidden. An example of this is *Metaphysics, Soul, and Ethics in Ancient Thought*, based on a conference in México City in March 2001 to honour Richard *Sorabji (2005). The resulting book naturally has a high level of engagement with the honorand's thought and his published work; it also includes a lengthy autobiographical essay by way of an introduction, a full bibliography for the years 1964–2004, with a separate listing of the books in the *Ancient Commentators on Aristotle* series, to 2003.[20] Another example is a book on Heraclides of Pontus, where — more seriously —

---

18 Burstein 2004. Juliette Ernst, *Directrice* of *L'Année philologique* for many years, was formidably opposed to Festschriften: Ernst 1957, 28–38. Reviewing Festschriften may, it seems, be a thankless task. Should the reviewer plod dutifully through each contribution, and then perhaps speed up for the last few (Westlake 1992, 416–418), or pick out a few plums and hope that they provide a sufficient account of the book, while annoying other contributors who might have hoped for, if not praise, at least a mention? The problem is not confined to Festschriften.
19 *García Teijeiro (2014). The book contains 1319 pages, of which 1240 are given over to 130 academic essays, divided into thirteen subject sections. The majority of the essays (121) are in Spanish, including brief abstracts in English, with one essay each in Catalan, French, Greek, Italian, and Portuguese; the remaining four are in English. The Festschrift is well-presented, but the organization necessary for such a large enterprise, and slender result in terms of its likely readership, is only too obvious from its opening pages. The question of multilingualism in classical studies, raised by Alexander Rubel (Rubel 2019) and pertinent here, is answered — to some extent — by journals, such as *History of Classical Scholarship*, that are willing to accommodate multiple languages.
20 The Institute of Classical Studies library classifies it as a Festschrift in the relevant sequence (202). See also R. Sorabji 2016².

the reader learns only in the Preface, (v) that it is a memorial tribute to H.B. *Gottschalk (2009), and at (x) that the book is based on a conference at the University of Leeds in 2003, attended by Gottschalk, which took as its starting point his own 1980 book on Heraclides. This has had the unfortunate result that most library catalogues fail to add an entry under his name. In other instances, editors have denied Festschrift status to a book that might, at first glance, look like one.[21]

No limits seem to apply as to the number of Festschriften that an individual may receive, nor to the number of volumes that Festschriften may occupy. The eminent scholar of Renaissance Humanism, Paul Oskar Kristeller, was given no fewer than six between 1975 and 1987. This is exceptional, but the award of two is not uncommon, sometimes in close proximity, as was the case with Gilbert *Murray (1936) on the occasion of his seventieth birthday.[22] One of the two Festschriften for Pierre *Lévêque (1988–1995), the French historian of Greece, was published in eight volumes together with a separate index. The volumes hover between religion, and anthropology or social history in their contents.

2 Furnishing a Festschrift

Difficulties arise in establishing a single typology for Festschriften, owing to the number of possible elements and — more importantly — the varying circumstances and methods that lead to their publication. Is the honorand living or deceased?[23] If the former, an element of *gratulatio* or *laudatio* can be added to that of pietas, the element common to all Festschriften.[24] How is it to be published —

---

21 *Syme (1984) is an example. In their preface the editors, Fergus Millar and Erich Segal, wrote that 'The volume is not, however, intended as a *Festschrift*, a literary sub-species of which Sir Ronald is known to disapprove.' — Preface, v.
22 *Essays in Honour of Gilbert Murray* (1936a) mainly celebrated his public persona and achievements, whereas *Greek Poetry and Life* (1936b) celebrated the Greek scholar and translator, with most of the contributors drawn from Oxford colleges.
23 The word *Gedenkschrift* indicates a memorial volume in German usage. A further distinction, now less often observed, was made between a *Festgabe* and *Festschrift*, the former being of more limited scope. Franz Zimmermann, editor of the Festschrift for Franz *Poland (1932), lamented the growth of what he had planned as a *Festgabe* into a more impressive (*stattlich*) volume. The adjective can also mean portly.
24 The editors of the memorial volumes for T.B.L. *Webster (1986, 1988) demonstrate this: 'Despite the lapse of a dozen years since Tom Webster's death and his own expressed disdain for hefty *Festschriften* and Memorial Volumes, we have nonetheless felt the compilation of this collection a pleasurable act of *pietas*.' — Preface to vol. 1, vii; repeated in vol. 2, v. Whether such

as a separate volume, as part of a periodical, or exclusively online?[25] Do the contributions to a Festschrift stem from a conference, a starting point that has grown in favour since the 1970s, as conferences, and the accompanying air miles to reach them, have multiplied? There are drawbacks both to periodical publications and to conferences. In the first, the inclusion of unrelated material such as book reviews, or annual reports if the periodical is linked to a society, tends to dim the focus of the Festschrift contributions. Similarly, and assuming that the honorand attends the conference, any element of surprise — if this is a factor — is naturally diminished, unless the time lapse between conference and publication is so prolonged that the honorand has forgotten all about the former.

The task of establishing some sort of typology was made a little easier by Alan G. Soble,[26] at the time (2003) Research Professor of Philosophy at the University of New Orleans, who, in his review of a Festschrift for the American philosopher Judith Jarvis Thomson, drew up a wish list of thirteen criteria for any similar volume that might be proposed for himself. Although his list varies between the sensible or practical, and the preposterous, there is an underlying insistence on engagement with the honorand's own writings, natural in a philosophical context, but not always found elsewhere. Engagement has, however, become more regular with the gradual change during the last century away from Festschriften burdened with contents of disparate length, subject matter, or value, to those that have a sharper thematic focus.

The components of a Festschrift will include at least some of the following: a title; a portrait of the honorand, often facing the title page; an epigraph; a list of contents and, where appropriate, a similar list of abbreviations and/or illustrations; a *tabula gratulatoria*; a preface, often justifying the publication; details of the contributors; a career résumé and bibliography of the honorand's publications; the individual contributions, occasionally with abstracts; one or more indexes; illustrations (plates). Few include all of these, although, depending on the subject, some would clearly be redundant. The choice of title by the editor(s) may indicate the scope of the book (*Studies in ...*), be creative in various ways, or abstruse. Food, drink, and banqueting have been regular themes, both as a title and as a metaphor to describe the varied contents. French publications are likely

---

volumes are justified when it is known that the deceased honorand would have disapproved is open to question.

25 A Webfestschrift published in October 2003 for the archaeologist Boris *Marshak (2003), who excavated at Panjakent in Tajikistan, was claimed by its editors to be the first use of that term. A printed edition was published in 2006.

26 Soble 2003. Soble has written extensively on the philosophy of sex, and founded the Society for the Philosophy of Sex and Love in 1977.

to include the word *mélanges*, which might in another context refer to the blending of wine grapes. *Lanx* and *satura* are found together, suggesting that the banquet might be substantial. An unexpected banquet reference is to be found in the Festschrift for Henri *Weil (1898), where Lewis Campbell, in concluding his essay on Greek tragedy, referred to the collection as a contributory feast (ἔρανος).²⁷ Other titles, such as *Antidoron* or *Apophoreta*, concentrate on the act of giving, or giving back. Editors occasionally indulge in wordplay on the name of the honorand, or offer something obscure, while *Vir bonus* ... has been treated as an expanding trope.²⁸

The earliest portrait in a classical Festschrift — or in this instance a memorial volume — is probably that of Charles Henri *Graux (1884). Graux died of typhoid at the age of only 29, but managed to produce a substantial amount of work in such a short lifespan, including editions of Xenophon's *Oeconomicus* and Plutarch's lives of Demosthenes and Cicero, and the documentation of manuscripts in Spain, Denmark, and Sweden.²⁹ The oval portrait used as a frontispiece is from a photograph taken in Madrid in December 1875, and shows the sitter wrapped in an overcoat and scarf against the cold. This is less formal than many subsequent portraits, where the honorand is depicted in profile, or looks sternly at the camera in dignified silence. An unusual example is the medallic portrait used for the frontispiece in the Festschrift for Harold *Mattingly (1956). It was made by the Hungarian emigré medallist Paul Vincze, and is entirely appropriate for Mattingly's career as a distinguished numismatist, but has the effect of distancing him from the reader.

---

27 Lewis Campbell, 'Le point culminant dans la tragédie grecque', *Weil (1898), 17–24, at 24. Eleven years earlier, in his contribution to the Festschrift for Léon *Renier (1887), 1–8, Henri Gaidoz had anticipated Campbell, in his essay on cakes with writing ('Les gâteaux alphabétiques'), which he traced back to an Irish legend relating to St. Columba. Gaidoz was a folklorist with a particular interest in Celtic studies, religion, and mythology. Banqueting is a feature, as well as part of the title, of the Festschrift for Pauline *Schmitt Pantel (2012). The history of food and banquets, and their social aspects, has played a significant part in her writings.
28 Wordplay: Hans Armin *Gärtner (2000); the editors refer to the collection as providing the colourful profusion of a well-cultivated garden, comparable to the honorand's broad interests ('Das thematische Spektrum der hier versammelten Aufsätze ... bietet die bunte Fülle eines wohlbestellten Gartens und entspricht so den weitgespannten wissenschaftlichen Interessen des Jubilars ... '). Obscurity: The title of the Festschrift for Martin Persson *Nilsson (1939) is *Drágma* — a handful, or sheaf. Perhaps this refers indirectly to the Swedish countryside, where he was born. *Vir bonus* has been used in Festschriften for Otto *Skutsch (1988: *Vir bonus discendi peritus*), Alfons *Weische (1997: *Vir bonus dicendi peritus*), and Arnaldo do *Espírito Santo (2013: *Vir bonus peritissimus aeque*). Several of the contributions to Weische explore the trope further.
29 A detailed account of Graux's life and work is given by Ernest Lavisse, *Graux (1884), xi–l.

Fig. 14: Charles Henri Graux (1852–1882); photograph (Mun, Madrid, December 1875).

Just as Festschriften have tended to be more focused in subject matter, so honorands — and particularly archaeologists — have been depicted in less formal surroundings. The editors of the Anthony *Birley Festschrift (2008, n.17) decided to reverse the process, and encourage the contributors to accompany their essays with memories of meeting or working with Birley, and to include photographs of themselves. Most of the photographs used are also informal — one cat and two horses participate — but somehow enhance the link between contributor and honorand.

Portraits may also hide secrets. The publication of Alan Kaiser's book in 2015 revealed that the eminent American archaeologist David Moore Robinson, who led the excavations at Olynthus between 1928 and 1938, plagiarized the work of Mary Ross Ellingson,[30] and possibly others who worked on the excavations. Kaiser points in particular to the seventh and fourteenth volumes of *Excavations at Olynthus* (1933, 1952), containing the publication of the terracotta figurines, for which Robinson used Ellingson's 1932 master's thesis *The Terra Cotta Industry at Olynthus*, and her 1939 Ph.D. dissertation, *Terra-cotta Figurines of Macedonia and Thrace*,[31] both of which remained unpublished. In neither case did he fully acknowledge her authorship when publishing the two volumes. The relevance of this lies in the different frontispiece portraits used in the two-volume Festschrift for *Robinson (1951, 1953). In the first volume this is a photograph, with Robinson's signature beneath. In the second, however, a painting by the Polish-born portrait artist Stanislav Rembski is used. Kaiser devotes part of his sixth chapter[32] to an analysis of the portrait, in particular the open book in Robinson's lap, which is identifiable as the seventh volume of the *Excavations*, the volume from which he had most extensively used Ellingson's work. He had a card made from the portrait, and sent it to Ellingson at Christmas 1952, more or less simultaneously with the unveiling of the portrait on 20 December at the University Club of Baltimore, where Robinson had been a former president. Kaiser suggests that this was by way of an apology and recognition of his failure to give Ellingson due credit.

There is a further opportunity for editors to be creative when it comes to choosing an epigraph. The epigraph in the *Cassirer (1936) Festschrift, my starting point, provides an apt description of the honorand's character and philosophical aims, while also suggesting the uneasy background of the 1930s and concomitant difficulties faced by refugee scholars.[33] The editors of *Supplementum festivum*, the last of six Festschriften which *Kristeller (1987) was given during his lifetime, reprinted a poem by him, *Nachmittag des Lebens*, that Kristeller had included in

---

30 Ellingson married Rudolph Conrad Ellingson in August 1939. Her given names were Helen Madeline Mary Ross: Kaiser 2015, xii.
31 Thesis: Kaiser 2015, 142–144 — this conflicts with the date and title given on 105. Dissertation: 108–109.
32 Kaiser 2015, 164–168. The book also explores more generally the difficulties faced by women archaeologists in achieving recognition for their work.
33 Whitaker 2018, 104–105. It is unclear who was responsible for choosing this particular Euripides fragment (Loeb Classical Library 504, Euripides, vol. 7, *Fragments: Aegeus-Meleager* [2008] 226–227), although I suspect it was Raymond Klibansky, one of the two editors.

the first volume of his *Iter Italicum* in 1963. Other epigraphs may be commissioned, and therefore include a direct reference to the honorand; examples of these can be found in the Festschriften for Walter *Burkert (1998) and Felix *Jacoby (1956).³⁴

It is clearly impossible within a single essay to convey the variety of contributions to Festschriften, but there are some points worth noting. A few subjects are self-contained and this applies particularly to numismatics. Most of the Festschriften in this area are written by specialists for specialists, and to honour specialists, but may also include contributions on allied aspects such as archaeology and art history. Some are published as limited editions.³⁵ Occasionally, buried in a Festschrift, there is a surprise in the biographical detail which an introduction or essay may provide. In her biographical note for the memorial volume to Margaret Head *Thomson (1998), Catherine Rubincam noted that Thomson resigned from her post at McMaster University in 1955.

> Various factors apparently contributed to her decision. She made no secret of her feeling that the atmosphere in the department and the university as a whole was unfriendly to her as a woman, and particularly to her aspirations to promotion. Her inclination to go back to high school teaching was strengthened when she discovered that the financial rewards would also be greater.³⁶

Editors need not necessarily contribute to the Festschrift they edit, although most choose to do so. Conversely, honorands may make an appearance in their own Festschrift, in a variety of ways. Jocelyn *Toynbee (1997) contributed an essay on Greek mythology and Roman numismatics to her Festschrift, which celebrated her eightieth birthday. Lewis Ayres, the editor of the Festschrift for Ian *Kidd (1995), included Kidd's 1978 inaugural lecture ('The Greeks and the Passionate

---

34 For the Burkert Festschrift Martin West contributed an epigraph in Greek, which includes wordplay on Burkert's name, as well as referencing his work on religion. The epigraph for Jacoby is in Latin and was written by Andreas Thierfelder. It serves a double purpose, as the Festschrift was in honour of Jacoby's eightieth birthday, and 1956 was also the year in which Jacoby returned to Germany. Its title, *Navicula Chiloniensis*, refers to the port and city of Kiel where Jacoby had been a Professor from 1906 until his enforced retirement in 1935 by the Nazi regime.

35 *Witschonke (2015), for example, published by the American Numismatic Society in a limited edition of 150 copies.

36 *Thomson (1998) 6–7. As Rubincam also notes, Thomson studied at the Sorbonne under Alphonse Dain. 'The development of these friendships [made with other students at the Sorbonne] was facilitated by her residence at the Association Fénélon, an institute founded in 1911 to promote higher education for women, and heavily endowed by Yvonne [Frédy] de Coubertin, daughter of Baron Pierre de Coubertin, best known to posterity as a leader in the campaign to establish the modern Olympic Games, but active throughout his life in educational causes.'

Intellect') as Professor of Greek at St Andrews.³⁷ Edith *Porada (1987), the distinguished art historian, archaeologist, and expert on ancient cylinder seals, contributed an introduction to the second of her two Festschriften, *Monsters and Demons in the Ancient and Medieval Worlds*.³⁸ The Festschrift for Arthur *Adkins (1996) includes responses to the six main papers, which derive from an April 1994 symposium in his honour. It also contains Adkins' last paper, 'The "Speech of Lysias" in Plato's *Phaedrus*';³⁹ he died in February 1996 before publication of the Festschrift.

The most startling literary selfie, however, occurs in the Festschrift for Herbert *Hoffmann (2010). In three deftly-written pages, Hoffmann relates how he came under suspicion for the theft of the Nike chariot earring (accession no. 98.788) in the Museum of Fine Arts in Boston, which took place in September 1963.⁴⁰ From a previous post at the Metropolitan Museum of Art in New York he had joined the staff of the Museum in autumn 1962 as Associate Curator of Classical Art, the department headed by Cornelius Clarkson Vermeule III, but fell out with the senior administration over the purchasing policies of the Museum. In fact the earring had been buried in a soup can on the Fenway, near to the Museum, by a young thief who confessed after being arrested for a second theft from the Museum. The ground had since frozen over and it was mid April 1964 before any attempt to trace and recover the can and its contents could be made. Emily Vermeule led one of her graduate classes from Boston University on a retrieval dig, ultimately successful when Florence Wolsky, one of her mature students, rediscovered it.

Although exonerated, Hoffmann felt he needed to get away from the poisonous atmosphere of the Museum; he resigned and moved to Germany in May 1964. *Life* magazine, which had covered the original theft, was drafted in to report on the retrieval. The article appeared under the byline of Jane Howard, an assistant editor, in the issue for 1 May 1964 under the catchpenny title *Big Dig for the Lost Earring*;⁴¹ it is sandwiched between fossilized adverts for beds, diamonds, and

---

37 Many of the essays were supplied by Kidd's colleagues, or former students at St Andrews.
38 For an account of Porada's life and work see the obituary notice by Collon 1994.
39 *Adkins (1996) 224–240.
40 *Hoffmann (2010) 394–397. See also n.42.
41 Howard is also known for her 1984 biography of the American anthropologist Margaret Mead (1901–1978).

motorcycles ('You meet the nicest people on a Honda').⁴² Howard wrote it in gossipy journalese; it also features what might be considered an unflattering photograph of Emily Vermeule.

The final furnishing that requires some notice is the *tabula gratulatoria*. In bygone days the issuing of a separate Festschrift (as opposed to one in a periodical) would almost certainly have been on subscription, with the subscribers duly listed, and this would make the difference between a viable book and an unviable one for the publisher. An example of this is the Festschrift to mark the retirement of Barclay Vincent *Head (1906), a former Keeper of Coins in the British Museum. The preface records that 'An appeal for subscriptions to defray the cost of publication was circulated, and met with a most generous response from numismatists and personal friends in all parts of the world.' The book, which contains eighteen collotype plates, a frontispiece portrait, in-text illustrations, and required both Greek and Hebrew typesetting, would have been expensive to produce, hence the requirement to find wealthy subscribers.⁴³ It is more than likely now that a Festschrift will be financed by other means, such as charitable foundations, government departments (particularly so in German-speaking countries),⁴⁴ or universities, to which the honorand or the editors have some connection. Alternatively, if the contents are sufficiently focused to ensure a wide readership, or can be issued as part of a series to which libraries regularly subscribe, the publisher might take on the expense and expect not to make a loss.

---

42 The theft: *Life* 55, no. 15 (11 October 1963) 86, 88, 94a; the recovery: *Life* 56, no. 18 (1 May 1964) 75–76, 78. The story as told by Hoffmann is disturbing, and reveals the murkier side of museum acquisitions and administration. It is repeated in an abbreviated form by Lambert Schneider in his obituary of Hoffmann: Schneider 2012, 177–181. There are discrepancies, however, between Hoffmann's and Jane Howard's accounts. Hoffmann's dates here are incorrect, and his account of contacting Cornelius Vermeule after the theft was discovered disagrees with Howard's. The final sentence by Hoffmann is also suspect. A more accurate account is provided in Hoffmann and Davidson 1965, 76–83, where the exact dates of the theft (7 September 1963) and recovery (16 April 1964) are given. The theft and recovery came to public attention again with a film on Florence Wolsky made by the independent filmmaker Karen Audette in 2015 (available at the time of writing [May 2020] on https://vimeo.com/129969514: last viewed 22 April 2020). Hoffmann is not mentioned.

43 The book was printed by Oxford University Press and sold under the imprint of Henry Frowde, publisher to OUP from 1883 to 1913. Keith Rutter contributed an essay on Head, together with a bibliography, to yet another Festschrift, for Staffan *Fogelmark (2004) 418–434.

44 As an example, the Festschrift for Peter W. *Haider (2006) was financed by the Austrian Bundesministerium für Wissenschaft und Forschung, the cultural and educational offices of the Tirol and Vorarlberg regions, and Haider's own university at Innsbruck.

In contrast to this, the *tabula gratulatoria* has gradually become an offshoot from the subscriber list, a means by which friends and colleagues of the honorand are freed from the necessity to subscribe, or even to buy the book, and where the concepts of pietas and ritual are most likely to interact. There is a risk, however, that the list of names, sometimes prolonged, may give little idea of the relationship, if any, between the honorand and individuals listed. In an attempt to avoid this, the unnamed editor(s) of the Festschrift for *Jacoby (1956) restricted both the contributions and the *tabula* to former students, and former or contemporary academic staff, with the relevant dates. Very occasionally, there is some information to be derived for historians from such lists, but most readers of a Festschrift will turn the pages quickly.[45]

3 *Cui donamus ... ?*

My misquotation from Catullus I[46] suggests a further problem: who receives what, and when, as an honorand is unpredictable. One might have supposed that Wilamowitz would receive a substantial volume in view of his eminence, and, although his dislike of the Festschrift genre was well-known (n.9), the only one that honoured him, on his eightieth birthday, was the seventh fascicle of the Norwegian periodical *Symbolae Osloenses*.[47] Even this raises the question of engagement, as only some of the contributors referred to Wilamowitz's writings. The two editors of the periodical, Samson Eitrem and Gunnar Rudberg, did so, the latter discussing the Platonic Socrates with reference to Wilamowitz's *Platon*. On the other hand the numismatist Hans Holst merely contributed one in a series of numismatic essays which he had begun in the previous fascicle of *Symbolae Osloenses* and continued in the following one. At the opposite end of the scale, Jacqueline de Romilly contributed to at least twenty, but seems not to have received one in her lifetime; in 2011, the year after her death, a colloquium was held in her honour at the École Normale Supérieure and the Académie des Inscriptions

---

[45] This is not a problem with *García Teijeiro (2014), in which the *tabula* is relegated to the back of the book.

[46] Catullus I provides as useful a prop for book-related essays, as it does for imitation and parody. *Cui donamus ... ?* is used in the 2008 Festschrift for Anthony *Birley, instead of a foreword.

[47] *Wilamowitz-Moellendorff (1928).

et Belles-Lettres, although the memorial volume derived from it was not published until 2014.[48] Other honorands have a long wait before Festschrift recognition, and it is not uncommon for recipients to have reached their eightieth birthday. For some the wait is even longer, until their ninetieth, which might be regarded as an unnecessary actuarial risk.[49]

Women honorands are few before the 1960s and, even afterwards, there are only one or two each year until the 1980s. This is in line with other aspects of the lack of recognition afforded to women scholars. Ida *Kapp (1954) was honoured with a Festschrift, although hers is unlikely to have been the earliest such token of recognition. Kapp worked for nearly 50 years on the *Thesaurus Linguae Latinae* in Munich, which is reflected in the title of her Festschrift, *Thesaurismata*. She had a difficult life in many ways. At the University of Berlin, she was admitted to Wilamowitz's seminar, at a time when this was still unusual for women students. She graduated in 1915, as the first woman doctorand to have studied with Wilamowitz, with her dissertation on the fragments of the *Hecale* of Callimachus. The following year, she joined the staff of the *TLL* in Munich, and continued to work there until the end of March in 1962. Her principal contribution to the *TLL* was as editor of the alphabetical volume for the letter E, begun in 1931 as volume five part two of the *Thesaurus*, on which she had worked with the Swiss scholar Gustav Meyer; it was the first volume to be completed after the Second World War. Meyer was called back to Switzerland in September 1939 and was unable to return after the war ended, a fact recorded in her preface to the whole volume. This caused Kapp much disappointment.

In a Festschrift for Ernst *Vogt (1993), Otto Hiltbrunner, who was able to join the *TLL* staff in 1940 and became her co-editor, described the care which Kapp

---

48 *Romilly (2014). Her contributions to Festschriften included those for E.R. *Dodds (1973), Albin *Lesky (1966), Claire *Préaux (1975), and Mary Estelle *White (1974). In the case of Lesky, her essay, 'La condamnation du plaisir dans l'œuvre de Thucydide', concluded with a tribute to his work: 'It is accordingly fitting that these brief remarks find their place in a collection intended to honour the scholar who has, by himself, known how to make clear for so many readers the uninterrupted succession of Greek literature in its continuity; they will be in any case a testimony of our admiration for his work, and of our gratitude.' ('Ainsi se justifie que ces brèves remarques prennent place dans un ensemble destiné à honorer le savant qui a su, à lui seul, déployer pour tant de lecteurs, la suite ininterrompue de la littérature grecque dans sa continuité: elles y seront en tout cas un témoignage de notre admiration pour son oeuvre et de notre reconnaissance.') — *Lesky (1966), 142–148. Romilly dedicated one of her later books, «*Patience, mon cœur*», 1984, to the memory of Lesky, who had died in 1981.
49 An example is provided by *Wimmel (2013). The editors' choice of an ambiguous title, which could be translated in one way as 'On the Long Haul of Old Age', might seem a little tactless. Fortunately, Wimmel had previously received a seventy-fifth birthday Festschrift.

brought to her work, and the encouragement she gave to the staff working with her; problems were discussed individually or in editorial meetings, often at length.⁵⁰ She retained links with the Thesaurus after her retirement, and was awarded the medal *bene merenti* by the Bavarian Academy on the seventy-fifth anniversary of the Thesaurus, for her long service and achievements. The Festschrift for her seventieth birthday was edited by Hiltbrunner together with Franz Tietze, and Hildegard Kornhardt, who had joined the *TLL* in 1936, and is the only woman contributor. Other contributors, apart from the editors, included Gustav Meyer, Bruno Snell and Rudolf Pfeiffer, who engaged directly with Kapp's earlier work on Callimachus.⁵¹ Unfortunately the actual appearance of the Festschrift suggests that it was produced cheaply from typescript, with print added for the chapter headings and pagination. Nor is it free from errors: one of the essays is clearly missing at least one sentence, possibly more. This seems doubly unfortunate, when the honorand had spent her working years in achieving high standards, through keen attention to detail.

There are two distinguished recipients who stand apart by their status, but who also contributed in different ways to the study of the ancient world. The first of these is *Gustaf Adolf (1932), Crown Prince of Sweden from 1907 to 1950, and thereafter Gustaf VI Adolf, King of Sweden.⁵² His interests in archaeology and art were wide, and he had taken part in the excavations at Asine in 1922. He was also responsible with others for the founding of the Swedish Institute at Athens after the Second World War. In 1932 he received two Festschriften to mark his fiftieth birthday. The first is wholly in Swedish and includes essays on archaeological research in Sweden, Central Asia and China, as well as at Greek and Roman sites. The second is devoted to Greek and Roman archaeology. Some of the essays in it were recycled from the Swedish periodical *Eranos*, although revised and extended. Another, by Einar Gjerstad, is a revised version in English, with additional material, of his Swedish contribution to the first Festschrift. Two of the contributions refer to the Crown Prince's visit in October 1930 to Cyprus, where the Swedish Cyprus Expedition was carrying out excavations at Soli, and to the agreement drawn up with the Cyprus authorities, to enable continuation of the work on that site.⁵³ Erik Sjöqvist recorded that

---

50 Otto Hiltbrunner, 'Ida Kapp (1884–1979)', *Vogt, E. (1993), 233–237.
51 Rudolf Pfeiffer, 'Morgendämmerung', *Kapp (1954), 95–104.
52 *Gustaf Adolf (1932a; 1932b). His full name was Oscar Fredrik Wilhelm Olaf Gustaf Adolf. Both Festschriften refer to the Crown Prince as the founder and sponsor of archaeological research in Sweden.
53 The agreement stipulated that all finds from the site were to go to the Cyprus Museum. 'Thanks to the keen interest which the Crown Prince took in the new discoveries at Soli and to

During our work we had the great advantage not only of the personal presence of H.R.H. the Crown Prince of Sweden, but also of his active assistance, which benefited the result in various ways. Thanks to his technical skill and great archaeological experience the observations on the very badly damaged skeleton material have obtained their present exactness, and it is needless to say in how great a degree His Royal Highness' help contributed to the success of the work as a whole.[54]

The second such honorand is Léopold Sédar *Senghor (1977, 1979), the first President of Senegal, from 1960 to 1980. Senghor was one of the three intellectuals and poets, the others being Aimé Césaire and Léon-Gontran Damas, who from the 1930s onwards developed Négritude, variously described as a movement or framework. It included aesthetic, social, and political strands in its aim to advance the appreciation of African and African diaspora civilization and cultures, and their distinct history, against the dominant forms of white colonization.[55] The breadth of this aim led to different interpretations in practice, and Senghor balanced his own with an acknowledgement of the need to see 'western' ancient civilizations as interacting, however harshly, in the history of the continent. During the 1970s, and coinciding with the expansion of universities in West Africa, Senghor hosted several conferences in Dakar, including the *Colloque sur l'Afrique noire et le Monde méditerranéen* during January 1976, and, a year later in April 1977, the fourth meeting of the International Conference for the Promotion of Latin Language and Literature (*Omnium gentium ac nationum Conventus Latinis litteris linguaeque fovendis*).

At the opening of the conference on 13 April Robert Schilling presented Senghor with a Festschrift,[56] which included contributions on Latin and Greek literature, and history.

---

the amiable courtesy of H.E. Sir Ronald Storrs, the Governor of Cyprus, an agreement with the Cyprian authorities was drawn up, to the effect that the bulk of the expenses for the excavations of the site was to be paid by the Cyprus Museum. All the finds made in the course of the excavation were to be delivered afterwards to the museum without any division', Alfred Westholm 1932, 'Sculptures from the Temple Site at Soli-Holades: Preliminary Notes', *Gustaf Adolf (1932b), 172–188, at 172–173.

54 Erik Sjöqvist, 'Some Cypriote Iron Age Tombs', *Gustaf Adolf (1932b), 189–207, at 189.
55 Souleymane Bachir Diagne provides a useful overview of the movement: Diagne (2018), https://plato.stanford.edu/archives/sum2018/entries/negritude/ (accessed 24 May 2020). For details of Senghor's writings, and particularly his poetry, see the African Studies Centre, Leiden, site: https://www.ascleiden.nl/content/webdossiers/leopold-sedar-senghor (accessed 24 May 2020).
56 *Senghor (1977). It includes a speech made in honour of Senghor by Schilling in December 1969 [xxi–xxx]; the President returned the favour by writing a foreword to the Festschrift for *Schilling (1983), 23–24.

Fig. 15: Paolo Brezzi (left), Léopold Sédar Senghor (centre), Robert Schilling (right); presentation of Festschrift, Dakar, 13 April 1977. Reproduced with the permission of L'Erma di Bretschneider, Rome.

Other contributions, though fewer in number, pay more attention to specific African topics.[57] The bibliography at the beginning of the Festschrift lists Senghor's writings between 1962 and 1975 on the teaching of classical languages and the relationship of the ancient world to Africa. The conference volume is also dedicated to Senghor,[58] and is exclusively focused on relations between Africa and Rome, as its title suggests; it opened with a speech by the President and, over the next three days, included papers on historical themes (trade, exploration, demography), Latin language (grammar, aspects of teaching in Senegal and in other African states), and literature (Latin authors born in Africa, or others who made reference to Africa in their writings, and reception studies).

---

57 In particular François-Régis Chaumartin, 'Le rapport de l'homme au monde dans les cultures négro-africaine et gréco-romaine', *Senghor (1977), 55–78; P. Ngandu Nkashama and V.Y. Mudimbe, 'Remarques synthétiques sur la contribution africaine à la fondation de la pensée et de la littérature latines chrétiennes', *Senghor (1977), 355–374; Jean-Georges Texier, 'Sparte et l'Afrique: réflexions à propos d'un thème historiographique', *Senghor (1977), 465–477.
58 *Senghor (1979). His speech is entitled 'Les Noirs dans l'antiquité romaine', 36–52.

4 Editorial Control

For about twenty years, the claim for the most extravagant Festschrift was retained by the two-volume set in honour of David Moore Robinson.[59] In June 1970, however, the distinguished Roman historian, Joseph Vogt, celebrated his seventy-fifth birthday. In honour of the occasion, a booklet was prepared as a *Festgabe*, containing a portrait of Vogt, an appreciation by Victor Ehrenberg, and a full bibliography of Vogt's writings from 1924 onwards, compiled by Ursula Vogt, his daughter.[60] This heralded the beginning of the vast, international *Aufstieg und Niedergang der römischen Welt (ANRW)* project, which began development in 1968, and was published from 1972 onwards; the first volume included the booklet. Contributions are in four main languages, English, French, German, and Italian. The title, together with the subtitle, *Geschichte und Kultur Roms im Spiegel der neueren Forschung*, revealed the essential aim of the work, though not the lavish and protracted way in which it was to be carried out.[61] There were three main strands in the contents: bibliographies, surveys of individual topics or persons, and essays generally based on recent research, as indicated in the surveys. Similarly there were three projected chronological parts: Early Rome down to the end of the Republic; the Principate; Late Antiquity. These were divided into six broad subject areas, and, in the second part, spread over multiple volumes. The third part remains unpublished, together with continuing gaps in the second part.

In her introduction, the first editor of *ANRW*, Hildegard Temporini, denied that the project was a Festschrift in the normal sense of the word (before going on to criticize 'normal' Festschriften), yet, in my opinion, it contains enough of the furnishings mentioned in the second part of this chapter to qualify. Her denial was also undermined by the repeated dedication to Vogt as each new subject area

---

59 *Robinson (1951, 1953). One afternoon, with nothing better to do, I carried my copy of the second volume to my local post office and had it weighed. Its weight is 3.886 kg. Allowing for a share of the binding, preliminaries, and plates, I was able to calculate the average weight of the 149 contributions as 26.08 g. I owe the idea to Dionysos and Aristophanes.
60 On Vogt, see Ehrenberg 1970, 5*–13*; Christ 1990, 63–124; Königs 1995, *passim*. Ehrenberg only hints at the break in their friendship, after Vogt joined the Nazi party in 1933. Vogt's bibliography for the following years includes a number of essays in Nazi-influenced publications.
61 *Vogt, J. (1970–[98]). Ninety separate volumes were published between 1972 and 1998. It has been available online since 2016.

began.⁶² While no-one would doubt that *ANRW* contains a great number of important essays and useful surveys, though the usefulness of these naturally tends to lessen with the passing years, there are some imbalances in the coverage. The four large volumes, together with a separate volume of plates, that constitute the first part are necessarily unbalanced in coverage against the eighty-five accorded to the second part. In this, essays on the writings of Tacitus occupy over 2,700 pages, across three volumes and part of a fourth; in part one the writings of Cicero make do with 179 pages.⁶³ Geographical coverage too is uneven, and, given its date span, *ANRW* largely missed out on developments such as reception or women's studies.

Whether *ANRW* became something of a vanity project, particularly after Vogt's death in 1986, is open to dispute. There are, however, other problems associated with the project, not least its cost. A colleague in the University of Glasgow Library made the original accession cards available to me, so that I could discover the actual cost of the whole set, at the time of publication. Even allowing for exchange rate fluctuations, it amounted to £13,100.⁶⁴ Inflation and diminished acquisitions budgets during the late 1980s and 1990s meant that some libraries had to close their standing orders for the series. One curious effect of such a large-scale project is that, from the condition of the bound volumes, it is possible to see which ones are popular, and which neglected.⁶⁵ Roman law and the philosophy/medicine/technology volumes find little favour. As might be expected, the history volumes and those concentrating on individual authors find more. To judge from the overall condition of the volume and the high level of student marginalia, any award for the most popular contribution would have been achieved locally in Glasgow by Ernst Badian's chapter on Tiberius Gracchus.⁶⁶

Festschriften, I suspect, suffer more than other genres from errors, especially if they are rushed out to coincide with a particular date and lack a final editorial

---

62 *ANRW* = *Vogt, J. I.1 (1972), Vorwort, xi. The dedication (re)appears in I.1–4.1 and II.1–5.1, 6, 8, 9.1, 12.1, 13, 15, 16.1, 29.1.
63 Tacitus: *ANRW* II.33.2–II.33.5 1990–91. Cicero: *ANRW* I.3 1973, 60–238.
64 My thanks to Stuart Sharp, who provided this information. The cards give the price of each volume in Deutsche Mark, as the most recent volume (II.34.4) was published in 1998, and the euro was not fully adopted in Germany until the beginning of 2002. Inflation over the years drove up the price of *ANRW* I.1 from DM. 180 in 1972 to DM. 710 in 1996, the price given in the separate contents and author list published that year.
65 This is inevitably influenced by the university courses on offer at any given time.
66 Ernst Badian, 'Tiberius Gracchus and the Beginning of the Roman Revolution', *ANRW* = *Vogt, J. I. 1 (1972), 668–731.

touch. There have been some horrors: the name of the honorand misspelt on the title page and spine; contents lists that are incomplete, or at variance with chapter headings (a problem for bibliographic indexers, but by no means uncommon elsewhere); a Festschrift with an errata list inserted, the list also containing an erratum; failure to describe plates adequately, or link them to the appropriate texts. The worst omission is the lack of an adequate index, or indeed any index, thereby reducing the usefulness of the book.[67] Not all Festschriften are, or are likely to be, available online even for keyword searching and, while there may be linguistic problems in providing subject terms for an index, the least that an editor should provide is an index of names, and, where appropriate, an index of passages cited from authors, inscriptions or whatever source. The larger the Festschrift, the less likely it is to be indexed — a strong argument against behemoths.

5 Conclusion

All this is a long way from the 1860s and the world of Friedrich Haase (n.13), though he too has entered the digital era.[68] When new Festschriften are created and published, perhaps freely and uniquely available online, there is a new set of considerations that apply. How easy is it to discover their existence? What are the economics of born-online publication, and do they prevent a subsequent print edition? Will availability be enduring? Online publications facilitate word searching, although keywords are often a primitive approach to finding answers and gaining knowledge. As with other aspects of the Festschrift 'game' or 'ritual', nothing is fixed. If, however, a future honorand were offered only a text message with a request to 'download your very own Festschrift in the comfort of your own home', something would be amiss, like flat champagne. People may need congratulations from time to time. Celebrations need some fizz.

---

67 As Jacob Bernays pointed out, in connection with the *Mommsen Festschrift (1877): Wilamowitz-Moellendorff 1929², 181.
68 Available at: http://resolver.sub.uni-goettingen.de/purl?PPN1667654950 (accessed 24 May 2020).

Festschriften Mentioned in the Text and Notes

[Adkins] Louden, R.B. and Schollmeier, P. (eds.) (1996), *The Greeks and us: Essays in Honor of Arthur W.H. Adkins*, Chicago, IL.
[Birley, A.] Schellenberg, H.M. *et al*. (eds.) (2008), *A Roman Miscellany: Essays in Honour of Anthony R. Birley on his Seventieth Birthday*, Gdańsk.
[Birley, E.] Jarrett, M.G. and Dobson, B. (eds.) (1966), *Britain and Rome: Essays Presented to Eric Birley on his Sixtieth Birthday*, Kendal.
[Buecheler & Usener] (1873), *Commentationes in honorem Francisci Buecheleri, Hermanni Useneri editae a Societate Philologa Bonnensi*, Bonn.
[Burkert] Graf, F. (ed.) (1998), *Ansichten griechischer Rituale: Geburtstags-Symposium für Walter Burkert*, Stuttgart.
[Cassirer] Klibansky, R. and Paton, H.J. (eds.) (1936), *Philosophy & History: Essays Presented to Ernst Cassirer*, Oxford.
[Chadwick] Beales, D. and Best, G. (eds.) (1985), *History, Society and the Churches: Essays in Honour of Owen Chadwick*, Cambridge.
[De Regibus] (1966), *Tetraonyma: miscellanea græco-romana [In Honour of Luca de Regibus, Paolino Mingazzini, Aldo Neppi Modona, and Enrico Turolla]*, Genoa.
[Dodds] (1973), *Volume in Honour of E.R. Dodds*, Journal of Hellenic Studies, vol. 93, London.
[Espírito Santo] Pimentel, M.C. and Alberto, P.F. (eds.) (2013), *Vir bonus peritissimus aeque: estudos de homenagem a Arnaldo do Espírito Santo*, Lisbon.
[Fogelmark] Sandin, P. and Wifstrand Schiebe, M. (eds.) (2004), *ΔΑΙΣ ΦΙΛΗΣΙΣΤΕΦΑΝΟΣ: Studies in Honour of Professor Staffan Fogelmark, Presented on the Occasion of his 65th Birthday, 12 April 2004*, Uppsala.
[García Teijeiro] Martínez Fernández, Á. *et al*. (eds.) (2014), *Ágalma: ofrenda desde la filología clásica a Manuel García Teijeiro*, Valladolid.
[Gärtner] Haltenhoff, A. and Mutschler, F.-H. (eds.) (2000), *Hortus litterarum antiquarum: Festschrift für Hans Armin Gärtner zum 70. Geburtstag*, Heidelberg.
[Gottschalk] Fortenbaugh, W.W. and Pender, E. (eds.) (2009), *Heraclides of Pontus: Discussion*, New Brunswick, NJ.
[Graux] (1884), *Mélanges Graux: recueil de travaux d'érudition classique dédié à la mémoire de Charles Graux, maître de conférences à l'École pratique des hautes études et à la Faculté des lettres de Paris, bibliothécaire à la Bibliothèque de l'Université ...*, Paris.
[Gustaf Adolf] Thordeman, B. (ed.) (1932a), *Arkeologiska studier tillägnade H.K.H. Kronprins Gustaf Adolf utgivna av Svenska Fornminnesföreningen*, Stockholm.
[Gustaf Adolf] (1932b), *Corolla archaeologica principi hereditario Regni Sueciae Gustavo Adolpho dedicata*, Lund.
[Haase] (1863), *Viro summe reverendo Friderico Haase ... pie gratulatur Societas Latina Vratislaviensis*, Breslau/Wrocław. [online: http://resolver.sub.uni-goettingen.de/purl?PPN1667654950]
[Haider] Rollinger, R. and Truschnegg, B. (eds.) (2006), *Altertum und Mittelmeerraum: die antike Welt diesseits und jenseits der Levante: Festschrift für Peter W. Haider zum 60. Geburtstag*, Stuttgart.
[Head] Hill, G.F. (ed.) (1906), *Corolla numismatica: Numismatic Essays in Honour of Barclay V. Head*, London.

[Helbig] (1899), *Strena Helbigiana sexagenario obtulerunt amici a.d. IIII. non. Febr. a. MDCCCLXXXVIIII*, Leipzig.
[Hoffmann] Metzler, D. (ed.) (2010), *Mazzo di fiori: Festschrift for Herbert Hoffmann*, Wiesbaden.
[Jacoby] (1956), *Navicula Chiloniensis: studia philologica Felici Jacoby professori Chiloniensi emerito octogenario oblata*, Leiden.
[Kapp] Hiltbrunner, O. et al. (eds.) (1954), *Thesaurismata: Festschrift für Ida Kapp zum 70. Geburtstag*, Munich.
[Kidd] Ayres, L. (ed.) (1995), *The Passionate Intellect: Essays on the Transformation of Classical Traditions Presented to Professor I.G. Kidd*, New Brunswick, NJ.
[Kristeller] Hankins, J. et al. (eds.) (1987), *Supplementum festivum: Studies in Honor of Paul Oskar Kristeller*, Binghamton, NY.
[Lesky] Hanslik, R. and Kraus, W. (eds.) (1966), *Donum natalicium Albin Lesky zum 7. Juli 1966, Wiener Studien*, Bd. 79, Vienna.
[Lévêque] Mactoux, M.-M. and Geny, E. (eds.) (1988-1995), *Mélanges Pierre Lévêque*, Paris.
[Madvig] (1876), *Lykønskningsskrift i Anledning af Johan Nicolai Madvigs halvtredsindstyveaarige Jubilæum som Lærer ved Kjøbenhavns Universitet fra hans Disciple = Opuscula philologica ad Ioannem Nicolaum Madvigium per quinquaginta annos Universitatis Hauniensis decus a discipulis missa*, Copenhagen.
[Marshak] Compareti, M. et al. (eds.) (2003), *Ērān ud Anērān: Studies Presented to Boris Il 'ich Marshak on the Occasion of his 70th Birthday*, Transoxiana Webfestschrift Series, 1. Printed edition (2006), Venice.
[Mattingly] Carson, R.A.G. and Sutherland, C.H.V. (eds.) (1956), *Essays in Roman Coinage Presented to Harold Mattingly*, Oxford.
[Mommsen] (1877), *Commentationes philologae in honorem Theodori Mommseni, scripserunt amici*, Berlin.
[Murray] Thomson, J.A.K. and Toynbee, A.J. (eds.) (1936a), *Essays in Honour of Gilbert Murray*, London.
[Murray] Bailey, C. et al. (eds.) (1936b), *Greek Poetry and Life: Essays Presented to Gilbert Murray on his Seventieth Birthday, January 2, 1936*, Oxford.
[Nilsson] Hanell, K. et al. (eds.) (1939), *ΔΡΑΓΜΑ: Martino P. Nilsson a.d. IV Id. Iul. anno MCMXXXIX dedicatum*, Lund.
[Panofsky] Meiss, M. (ed.) (1961), *De artibus opuscula XL: Essays in Honor of Erwin Panofsky*, New York, NY.
[Pelling] Ash, R., Mossman, J., and Titchener, F.B. (eds.) (2015), *Fame and Infamy: Essays for Christopher Pelling on Characterization in Greek and Roman Biography and Historiography*, Oxford.
[Poland] Zimmermann, F. (ed.) (1932), 'Franz Poland zum fünfundsiebzigsten Geburtstag', in: *Philologische Wochenschrift* Jg. 52, No. 35-38 = 25 August, col. 1/945-296/1240.
[Porada] Farkas, A.E. et al. (eds.) (1987), *Monsters and Demons in the Ancient and Medieval Worlds: Papers Presented in Honour of Edith Porada*, Mainz.
[Préaux] Bingen, J. et al. (eds.) (1975), *Le monde grec: pensée, littérature, histoire, documents: hommages à Claire Préaux*, Brussels.
[Renier] (1887), *Mélanges Renier: recueil de travaux publiés par l'École pratique des hautes études (Section des sciences historiques et philologiques) en mémoire de son président Léon Renier*, Paris.

[Ritschl] (1864, 1867), *Symbola philologorum Bonnensium in honorem Friderici Ritschelii collecta*, Leipzig.
[Robinson] Mylonas, G.E. (ed.) (1951), *Studies Presented to David Moore Robinson ... on his Seventieth Birthday*, Vol. 1, Saint Louis, MO.
[Robinson] Mylonas, G.E. and Raymond, D. (eds.) (1953), *Studies ...* Vol. 2, Saint Louis, MO.
[Romilly] Fumaroli, M. *et al.* (eds.) (2014), *Hommage à Jacqueline de Romilly: l 'empreinte de son œuvre*, Paris.
[Schilling] Zehnacker, H. and Hentz, G. (eds.) (1983), *Hommages à Robert Schilling*, Paris.
[Schmitt Pantel] Azoulay, A. *et al.* (eds.) (2012), *Le banquet de Pauline Schmitt Pantel: genre, mœurs et politique dans l'antiquité grecque et romaine*, Paris.
[Senghor] (1977), *Mélanges offerts à Léopold Sédar Senghor: langues, littérature, histoire anciennes*, Dakar.
[Senghor] Farenga Ussani, G. (ed.) (1979), *Africa et Roma: acta omnium gentium ac nationum conventus Latinis litteris linguaeque fovendis, a die XIII ad diem XVI mensis Aprilis a MDCCCCLXXVII Dacariae habiti [Leopoldo Sedar Senghor humanissimo Senegalensium rei publicae principi grato animo Academia latinitati inter omnes gentes fovendae hunc librum d.d.d.]*, Rome.
[Skutsch] Horsfall, N. (ed.) (1988), *Vir bonus discendi peritus: Studies in Celebration of Otto Skutsch 's Eightieth Birthday*, London.
[Sorabji] Salles, R. (ed.) (2005), *Metaphysics, Soul, and Ethics in Ancient Thought: Themes from the Work of Richard Sorabji*, Oxford.
[Stroud] Matthaiou, A.P. and Papazarkadas, N. (eds.) (2015), *ΑΞΩΝ: Studies in Honor of Ronald S. Stroud*, Athens.
[Suerbaum] Schauer, M. and Thome, G. (eds.) (2003), *Altera ratio: klassische Philologie zwischen Subjektivität und Wissenschaft: Festschrift für Werner Suerbaum zum 70. Geburtstag*, Stuttgart.
[Syme] Millar, F. and Segal, E. (eds.) (1984), *Caesar Augustus: Seven Aspects ... [in Honour of the 80th Birthday of Sir Ronald Syme]*, Oxford.
[Thomson] (1998), *[Hommages Margaret Head Thomson (1907-1993)]*, Cahiers des études anciennes, no. 34, Trois-Rivières, QC.
[Toynbee] Munby, J. and Henig, M. (eds.) (1977), *Roman Life and Art in Britain: a Celebration in Honour of the Eightieth Birthday of Jocelyn Toynbee*, Oxford.
[Vogt, E.] Suerbaum, W. and Dubielzig, U. (eds.) (1993), *Festgabe für Ernst Vogt zu seinem 60. Geburtstag am 6. November 1990: Erinnerungen an Klassische Philologen*, Eikasmos: Quaderni Bolognesi di Filologia Classica, 4, Bologna.
[Vogt, J.] Temporini, H. *et al.* (1970-[98]), *Aufstieg und Niedergang der römischen Welt: Joseph Vogt zum 23.6.1970*, Berlin.
[Webster] Betts, J.H. *et al.* eds. (1986, 1988), *Studies in Honour of T.B.L. Webster*, Bristol.
[Weil] (1898), *Mélanges Henri Weil: recueil de mémoires concernant l 'histoire et la littérature grecques dédié à Henri Weil ... à l 'occasion de son 80ᵉ anniversaire*, Paris.
[Weische] Czapla, B. *et al.* (eds.) (1997), *Vir bonus dicendi peritus: Festschrift für Alfons Weische zum 65. Geburtstag*, Wiesbaden.
[White] (1974), *Studies Presented to Mary [Estelle] White on the Occasion of her Sixty-Fifth Birthday*, Toronto, ON.
[Wilamowitz-Moellendorff] Eitrem, S. and Rudberg, G. (eds.) (1928), *Ulrich von Wilamowitz-Moellendorff zum 80. Geburtstage gewidmet, 22. Dezember 1928*, Symbolae Osloenses, fasc. 7, Oslo.

[Wimmel] Dunsch, B. and Prokoph, F.M. (eds.) (2013), *Am langen Seil des Altertums: Beiträge aus Anlass des 90. Geburtstags von Walter Wimmel*, Heidelberg.
[Witschonke] Van Alfen, P.G. *et al.* (eds.) (2015), *Fides: Contributions to Numismatics in Honor of Richard B. Witschonke*, New York, NY.

Bibliography

Burstein, S.M. (2004), Review of P. Guldager Bilde *et al.* (eds.), *The Cauldron of Ariantas: Studies Presented to A.N. Ščeglov on the Occasion of his 70th Birthday* [Aarhus, 2003], in: *BMCR* 2004.11.06.
Calder III, W.M./Kirstein, R. (eds.) (2003), *«Aus dem Freund ein Sohn»: Theodor Mommsen und Ulrich von Wilamowitz-Moellendorff, Briefwechsel 1872–1903*, Bd. 2, Hildesheim.
Christ, K. (1990), *Neue Profile der Alten Geschichte*, Darmstadt.
Collingwood, R.G. (1939), *An Autobiography*, Oxford.
Collon, D. (1994), Obituary: 'Professor Edith Porada', *The Independent*, Monday 4 April 1994.
Crawford, S. *et al.* (eds.) (2017), *Ark of Civilization: Refugee Scholars and Oxford University, 1930–1945*, Oxford.
Despoix, P./Tomm, J. (eds.) (2018), *Raymond Klibansky and the Warburg Library Network: Intellectual Peregrinations from Hamburg to London and Montreal*, Montreal, QC.
Diagne, S.D. (2018), 'Négritude', in: Zalta, E.N. (2018). [online: https://plato.stanford.edu/archives/sum2018/entries/negritude/]
Ehrenberg, V. (1970), 'Joseph Vogt', in: *Beilage zu Aufstieg und Niedergang der römischen Welt*, 5*–13* [issued with Temporini, H. (ed.) (1972), *Aufstieg und Niedergang der römischen Welt*. Bd. I.1, Berlin].
Ender, A./Wälchli, B. (2012), 'The Making of a Festschrift. Is it a Ritual?', in: A. Ender *et al.* (eds.), *Methods in Contemporary Linguistics*, Berlin, 143–167.
Ernst, J. (1957), 'Actualités philologiques: réflexions d'une bibliographe', *Bulletin de l'Association Guillaume Budé*, n°3 (octobre), 28–38.
Fleckeisen, C.F.W.A. (1861), *Fünfzig Artikel aus einem Hülfsbüchlein für lateinische Rechtschreibung der zwanzigsten Versammlung deutscher Philologen, Schulmänner und Orientalisten ehrerbietig gewidmet*, Frankfurt am Main.
Gudeman, A. (1929), 'The Homage-Volume Once More', *Philological Quarterly* 8, 335–338.
Hoffmann, H./Davidson, P.F. (1965), *Greek Gold: Jewelry from the Age of Alexander*, Mainz.
Kaiser, A. (2015), *Archaeology, Sexism, and Scandal: the Long-Suppressed Story of One Woman's Discoveries and the Man Who Stole Credit for Them*, Lanham, MD.
Königs, D. (1995), *Joseph Vogt: ein Althistoriker in der Weimarer Republik und im Dritten Reich*, Basel.
Kristeller, P.O. (1963), *Iter Italicum: a Finding List of Uncatalogued or Incompletely Catalogued Humanistic Manuscripts of the Renaissance in Italian and Other Libraries*, vol. 1, London.
Morley, S.G. (1929), 'The Development of the Homage-Volume', *Philological Quarterly* 8, 61–68.
Oncken, C.F.G.W. (ed.) (1865), *Festschrift zur Begrüßung der vierundzwanzigsten Versammlung deutscher Philologen und Schulmänner …*, Leipzig.

Riese, A. (ed.) (1869–70), *Anthologia Latina, sive Poesis Latinae Supplementum*. Pars prior, *Carmina in Codicibus Scripta*, Leipzig.

Roberts, L.M. (1972), *A Bibliography of Legal Festschriften*, The Hague.

Robinson, D.M. [and Ross, H.M.M.] (1933), *Excavations at Olynthus*. Part 7, *The Terra-cottas of Olynthus Found in 1931*, Baltimore, MD.

Robinson, D.M. [and Ellingson, M.R.] (1952), *Excavations at Olynthus*. Part 14, *Terracottas, Lamps, and Coins Found in 1934 and 1938*, Baltimore, MD.

Romilly, J. de (1984), *«Patience, mon cœur»: l'essor de la psychologie dans la littérature grecque classique*, Paris.

Rounds, D./Dow, S. (1954), 'Festschriften', *Harvard Library Bulletin* 8:3, 283–298.

Rounds, D. (ed.) (1962), *Articles on Antiquity in Festschriften ... an Index*, Cambridge, MA.

Rubel, A. (2019), 'Quo Vadis *Altertumswissenschaft*? The Command of Foreign Languages and the Future of Classical Studies', *Classical World* 112, 193–223.

Santos, D. et al. (eds.) (2012), *Shall we Play the Festschrift Game? Essays on the Occasion of Lauri Carlson's 60th Birthday*, Berlin.

Schneider, L. (2012), 'Herbert Hoffmann (1930–2012): Erinnerungen an den Freund und Wegbegleiter', *Hephaistos* 29, 177–181.

Soble, A.G. (2003), Review of A. Byrne et al. (eds.), *Fact and Value: Essays on Ethics and Metaphysics for Judith Jarvis Thomson*, *Essays in Philosophy* 4.1, article 5 [online: https://commons.pacificu.edu/work/ee5348e2-19fe-4bef-bfc5-22e258980f9b].

Sorabji, R. (ed.) (2016), *Aristotle Transformed: the Ancient Commentators and their Influence*, London. Second edition.

Thiersch, F.W. (1830), *The Greek Grammar of Frederick Thiersch, Translated from the German* [by Daniel Sandford], *with Brief Remarks*, Edinburgh.

Westlake, H.D. (1992), Review of M.A. Flower/M. Toher (eds.), *Georgica: Greek studies in honour of George Cawkwell*, *Classical Review* N.S. 42:2, 416–418.

Whitaker, G.H. (2017), 'Philosophy in Exile: the Contrasting Experiences of Ernst Cassirer and Raymond Klibansky in Oxford', in: S. Crawford et al. (eds.) 2017, 341–358.

Whitaker, G.H. (2018), 'The Warburg Institute Reaches Out: Raymond Klibansky and his British Contacts', in: Despoix/Tomm 2018, 80–107.

Wilamowitz-Moellendorff, U. von (1919), *Platon*, Berlin.

Wilamowitz-Moellendorff, U. von (1929), *Erinnerungen, 1848–1914*, Leipzig. Second edition.

Zalta, E.N. (ed.) (2018), *The Stanford Encyclopedia of Philosophy* (Summer 2018 Edition). [online: https://plato.stanford.edu/archives/sum2018/entries/negritude/]

Zeller, E. (1844, 1846), *Die Philosophie der Griechen: eine Untersuchung über Charakter, Gang und Hauptmomente ihrer Entwicklung*, Tübingen.

Christopher Stray
Working Together: Classical Scholars in Collaboration

This paper is about groups of classical scholars who work together.[1] My main focus will be on Britain, but there will be excursions to France, Germany and the US.[2] The groups vary widely in size, from two upwards.[3] My concern is thus not with categories, that is, sets of scholars with shared characteristics, but with groups of people who interact in some way. That interaction has usually been collaborative, but collaboration does not rule out the possibility of disagreement: friends fall out and groups split, sometimes into smaller groups or even individuals. W.S. Watt and D.R. Shackleton Bailey, who in 1956 agreed to collaborate on an Oxford Classical Text of Cicero's *Epistulae ad Atticum*, were temperamentally and intellectually incompatible. The relationship soon broke down amid mutual recrimination, and their texts were published separately.[4] A similar fate met the collaboration of Thomas Stangl and Paul Hildebrandt on an edition of the Scholia Bobiensia: 'the two men had a bitter falling out' (Zetzel 2018, 258). Even when collaboration does not break down, its product may bear signs of tension between the parties concerned. At some point in the 1920s Robert Rattenbury and Thomas Lumb agreed to work together on an edition of Heliodorus' *Aethiopica*, but often disagreed about textual readings. Their edition has notes signed by one editor or the other, to show that they could not reach agreement on them.[5]

When we talk of classical communities, we are usually thinking of academic societies, whether general or specialized (the Oxford Philological Society, the Hellenic Society, the Association for Roman Military Equipment Studies), or of

---

[1] This paper has its origin in a talk on the subject given at Corpus Christi College, Oxford on 12 October 2016, at the invitation of Constanze Güthenke. My thanks to her, and to the audience for helpful questioning.
[2] For recent non-British work which focuses largely on continental Europe, see Güthenke 2018, 4 n. 12.
[3] We would not normally speak of a group of two, but for the purpose of analysis, I am operating with a stipulative definition of a group as n+1 persons.
[4] Bailey's OCT of the letters to Atticus books 9–16 was published in 1963, Watt's of books 1–8 in 1965. For a detailed account, see Stray 2015.
[5] Héliodore, *Les Éthiopiques : Théagène et Chariclée: texte établi par R.M. Rattenbury et T.W. Lumb et traduit par J. Maillon* (Paris, 1935). Rattenbury, a fellow of Trinity College, Cambridge, moved into college and then university administration. Lumb, educated at Jesus College, Oxford, taught at Charterhouse before becoming a clergyman. In 1948, aged 65, he married an 18-year old parishioner, was denounced and ridiculed, and committed suicide by jumping into a well.

https://doi.org/10.1515/9783110719215-016

cultural and educational bodies (the Classical Association, the American Classical League). But if we go back to the early nineteenth century, we can find almost nothing of this sort. The obvious exception is the Society of Dilettanti, founded in the 1730s by aristocrats and gentlemen who had been on the Grand Tour in Italy and less commonly in Greece.

Fig. 16: *The Dilettanti Society* (1777–8), print after oil by Sir Joshua Reynolds: public domain.

In 1743 Horace Walpole condemned its affectations and described it as '…a club, for which the nominal qualification is having been in Italy, and the real one, being drunk' (letter to Sir Horace Mann, 14 April 1743: Dover 1833, 269). Reynolds' painting shows dilettanti gathered round a decanter, which is in fact an ancient vessel. This is turn is illustrated in the book which lies open before them. Drink and sociability are nicely linked to the serious aspects of their shared activities. To this day at the society's dinners, members raise their glasses to the toast 'seria ludo', 'to take serious matters in a lighthearted spirit'.[6] Reynolds's pictures are themselves a visual demonstration of this spirit, for in them he parodies the Venetian master Paolo Veronese's 'Feast in the House of Levi', transforming the depiction of a solemn occasion at which Christ was present into a raucous gathering of hard-drinking libertines. The Society's more lasting achievements include the funding of travel to Greece which led to the publication of pioneering books on Greek architecture, underpinning the Greek revival in Britain.[7] The other eighteenth-century community which needs to be mentioned is one of a very different kind, the longstanding *res publica litterarum*: the European community of scholars who communicated with one another in Latin (Masseau 1994). But by the early nineteenth century this community was on its last legs, weakened by nationalism, vernacular publishing and war.

The first academic community I want to mention is the loose-knit group of pupils and admirers of the Cambridge classical scholar Richard Porson, who died in 1808 (Stray 2018a, 82–107). Porson was a heavy drinker, like many of the Dilettanti, but unlike them he never left Britain. The Porsonians based their identity on their shared worship of their hero and on their commitment to his scholarly style, which focused on the detailed linguistic study of Greek texts and paid little attention to their literary merits. Their activities also had an institutional base in Trinity College Cambridge, where Porson had been a student, a fellow and finally held the Regius chair of Greek. The leading tenders of the Porsonian flame were two younger fellows of the college, James Monk, who succeeded Porson in the Greek chair and eventually became Bishop of Gloucester, and his friend Charles Blomfield, the future Bishop of London. They were also the editors of a new classical journal, the *Museum Criticum, or Cambridge Classical Researches*, launched

---

[6] In the late nineteenth century a similar spirit animated the Sidgwick brothers, Arthur, Henry and Alfred, whose tendency to introduce joking remarks into serious discussions was labelled 'Sidgwickedness' (Stray 2019a, 144).

[7] For the Dilettanti, see Redford 2008, Jason 2009. The Society of Dilettanti still exists, and provides grants for travel to Greece and Italy, as well as supporting the British Schools at Athens and Rome.

in 1813 (Stray 2018a, 146–70). This promoted work in the Porsonian style, by the editors and others; its subtitle, disapproved of by Oxford men, also proclaimed their institutional affiliation. Even an account of the Porsonians as brief as this demonstrates that institutions and publications played an important part in the maintenance of their identity as a community.

It also highlights the role of the past in creating communities, the Porsonians' identity being based on their reverence for a dead scholar. By the twentieth century Porson had become the central figure in a triptych of scholarly heroes: Bentley, Porson and Housman. All three were famous for their mastery of the minutiae of classical texts, while the differences between them encapsulated the history of classical scholarship. Bentley's broad vision of the ancient world took in both Greek and Latin; Porson's focus on Greek alone represented the beginnings of professionalization and specialization; Housman's concentration on Latin continued this in an era when Latin scholarship was emerging from of the shadow of Greek. The trio of Bentley, Porson and Housman has formed the backbone of the dominant tradition of the historiography of British classical scholarship.[8] This has focused on the lives of individual scholars, leaving almost unexamined the role of institutions, communities and publications.[9] The example of the Porsonians shows how a tradition of historical writing focused on individuals can allow for community, by recognising the genealogical links between individuals, in this case between Porson and his pupils and disciples. In fact the tradition not only recognises the existence of the community, it is liable to reify it by treating membership as monolithic. A close look at the Porsonians, however, makes it possible to distinguish between degrees of commitment and membership, including 'inside outsiders' and 'outside insiders' (Stray 2018a, 95).

A striking contrast with the Porsonians comes from the other end of the nineteenth century, with the so-called Cambridge Ritualists. Here the individuals concerned are Jane Harrison, Francis Cornford, and Gilbert Murray (Robinson 2002; Gold 2003, 180–210; Gerson 2004, 137–50; Lubenow 2009). Often referred to and reified as a group, they were in fact a set of individuals whose interests and scholarly approaches converged and interacted in the 1890s and 1900s. Drawing on the work of Durkheim and early British anthropologists, they analysed Greek drama as an art form based on ritual practice, subverting the received emphasis

---

[8] Monk wrote the standard life of Bentley, whose style of scholarship was very different from Porson's (Monk 1830); but then Bentley was a local hero, having been, however controversially, master of Trinity 1700–42.

[9] Examples of this tradition include Sandys 1903–8, Wilamowitz-Moellendorff 1921, Pfeiffer 1968–76, and Brink 1986, all of which are discussed in Stray 2016a.

on literature as an autonomous realm, and confronting the dominant Victorian emphasis on the serene Olympian deities with a stress on the gods of the underworld. In a curious way this non-group contained its own hero-figure, since the moving spirit was Jane Harrison, the first woman to make a name as a professional classical scholar in Britain. She was older than the two men, having been born 16 years before Murray and 24 years before Cornford, so might also be seen as a past hero. When Cornford married one of her pupils, the couple referred to her as 'Aunt Jane'. We might see the Ritualists as a cultural atom, with Harrison as its nucleus and the two men circling her like electrons. As this suggests, we need a historiography which runs parallel to quantum physics in de-reifying its subjects. Referring to such phenomena as 'groups' is both convenient and hard to avoid, and reinforces the desire of historians to identify and categorize. Looking back at heroic pasts not only creates and reinforces disciplinary identities, it gives firm descriptive contours to past realities which were often shifting and fluid. Some group identities are firmly based on mutual recognition, as with the X-Club of nine liberal scientists in the period 1864–93, who dined together and corresponded regularly (Barton 2018). The ontological status of the 'Cambridge Network', a collection of scientists and liberal churchmen in the period 1810–50, is more dubious. The term was coined by the historian of science Walter F. Cannon, who identified different 'nodes' in the network; for him, 'This group ... was a loose convergence of scientists, historians, dons, and other scholars' (Cannon 1964, 66). The term was later taken over in a study of the Cambridge philosopher John Grote, where the 'Network' was described as 'a straggling conglomeration of personalities and movements' (Gibbins 1987, 2.287; cf. Gibbins 2007, Snyder 2012). Such characterizations suggest that we need to be very careful in assigning terms like 'group' and network' to historical patterns of interaction.[10]

The Porsonians and Ritualists were both Cambridge-based, though both had Oxford links: Peter Elmsley in the former case, Gilbert Murray in the latter. What does this tell us about the kind of environments in which such communities take form? In 1805 Thomas Gaisford, soon to become a long-serving Regius Professor of Greek at Oxford, wrote to Charles Burney:

---

10 An interesting case which I have no space to pursue here is the Seminar Boreas set up in the late 1960s at Newcastle by David West, which was then continued by Francis Cairns as the Liverpool Latin Seminar. This in turn moved to Leeds as the Leeds Latin Seminar, and eventually to Florida State University as the Langford Latin Seminar. The Seminar might be seen as the classical equivalent of 'the longest-established permanent floating crap game in New York' in *Guys and Dolls*. (My thanks to Iain Du Quesnay and Tony Woodman for information.)

> ...In Oxford, as you will know, there are very few who have studied the classics critically, and still fewer who have read the Greek poets with that care and accuracy which they deserve, so that on nice points I can expect neither advice nor assistance from any persons here. (Christ Church Library, MS 436, letter of 18 January 1805)

Christ Church was the largest college in Oxford, as Trinity, home of the Porsonians, was in Cambridge, but their relations with their universities differed. The dominance of Classics at Christ Church reflected a similar dominance in the university, whereas Trinity's focus on Classics in the years after Porson's death in 1808 contrasted sharply with the emphasis on mathematics of both the university as a whole and of its neighbour and rival St John's.[11] A complicated matrix of local institutional politics thus provided favourable soil for the growth of the Porson cult in Trinity, while it was a fellow of St John's, the future headmaster and bishop Samuel Butler, who teasingly labelled the cult 'Porsoniasm' (Stray 2018a, 83).

If we stay in Cambridge but fast-forward to the end of the century, the era of the 'Ritualists', we find that the academic environment had changed in several respects: the small colleges in Cambridge had grown larger, and women's colleges had been founded – Girton in 1869, Newnham in 1871. Francis Cornford's alliance with Jane Harrison belonged to a recent history in which liberal dons from Trinity, in particular, supported the new female undergraduates by teaching them in small groups, allowing them into university lectures and marking their Tripos papers. In some cases they also married them (college fellows were allowed to marry from 1882), and Cornford married a Newnham graduate, as his colleague Arthur Verrall had done earlier. Verrall, a friend of both Cornford and Murray, was well known, indeed notorious, for his radical and eccentric readings of Euripides (Lowe 2005). It is an interesting question, and one that has not been asked, why Verrall did not go down the Ritualist path: but he stuck firmly to literature, gave lectures on Jane Austen, and in 1911 became the first holder of the Cambridge chair of English literature.[12]

A striking evidence of the close relationship between Harrison, Murray and Cornford is that they contributed chapters to each other's books, something that rarely happened in academic life in that period.[13] If we take such collaboration as a manifestation of community, then we might see community in earlier joint

---

[11] The Classical Tripos was not founded till 1822, and was not independent of the Mathematical Tripos till 1854.

[12] For Verrall see Lowe 2005. Verrall was strongly antichristian, something which perforce was veiled in publications.

[13] Perhaps this phenomenon might be claimed as a legitimating forerunner of the inclusion in the present volume of a chapter on Festschriften and another contributed by the honorand.

work, such as that of Monk and Blomfield in the 1810s. Their joint editing of the *Museum Criticum* stemmed not just from their shared reverence for Porson but from their lifelong friendship, which led them to name their sons after each other. Later examples of such joint editing of journals can be found in the nineteenth century, as we shall see, and it is in fact one of two genres where such collaboration was most common. Its focus on the organization of texts written by others perhaps helps to explain why this was so, since the authorial ego was to a degree marginalized within the role of editor. The same point could be made about the best-known classical collaboration of the century in the second genre, lexicography. This is the joint editorship of the Oxford classical scholars Henry Liddell and Robert Scott, whose famous Greek-English lexicon first appeared in 1843 (Stray, Clarke, and Katz 2019). Here again we are dealing with a pair of close friends, in this case dividing the work between them and meeting daily for several years to compare notes. They belonged to different Oxford colleges, but Balliol and Christ Church were only a few minutes' walk apart.[14] These collaborations were of different kinds, since Murray, Cornford and Harrison contributed discrete texts with their names attached, whereas Liddell and Scott's lexicon was a joint effort throughout; we know that the two men took different authors to work through, but not who read what. Similarly, some of the standard sources on nineteenth-century India, such as the dictionary of Anglo-Indian colloquialisms *Hobson-Jobson*, have been co-authored in a way which has been seen as reflecting a dialogue between British and Indian sources (Majeed 2011).

One of the consequences of the influence of German scholarship on Britain in the first half of the nineteenth century was the emergence of a dictionary tradition that encompassed a wider field than that of language. In this case we can see the transition from single to plural authorship. In the decade before Liddell and Scott were commissioned to make their Greek-English lexicon, John Wordsworth of Trinity College, Cambridge, contracted with the publisher John Murray to assemble a replacement for Lemprière's *Bibliotheca Classica*.[15] Wordsworth's progress and methodology can be glimpsed in his papers, now in the Bishops Wordsworth collection at Lancaster University Library.[16] After his death, Murray

---

14 Eight minutes according to Google; the record is held by Chris Pelling (six minutes).
15 Wordsworth was the eldest son of Christopher Wordsworth, master of Trinity 1820–41 and brother of the poet. John was saved from an ecclesiastical career by his premature death in 1839. His younger brothers Charles and Christopher became bishops and wrote parallel Latin and Greek grammars: see Stray 2016b. Lemprière's readable but unreliable classical dictionary had been first published in 1788.
16 Wordsworth's plan for his dictionary are in this collection, A3.

asked a younger Trinity don, John William Donaldson, to complete the dictionary. Donaldson replied that it was 'too large a work for one man to finish. But in collaboration it might be done.'[17] He probably knew of the dictionary edited by August von Pauly which had been issued in parts in Germany since 1837.[18] In the event, a similar project was organised by the London-based scholar William Smith, later famous as Dr (then Sir) William 'Dictionary' Smith.[19] Smith ran teams of contributors for his several classical dictionaries, which together made up an encyclopaedia that rivalled Pauly's for authority and coverage in its early years. In the twentieth century it was replaced as a standard English-language source by the *Oxford Classical Dictionary*, whose first edition (1949) had nine editors and 161 contributors.[20]

The genres of journal-editing and dictionaries were joined toward the end of the nineteenth century by editions of and commentaries on texts. Editors tended to hunt in pairs, as did Liddell and Scott. Some were of equal status, precedence on the page being merely alphabetical, as with How and Wells (Herodotus). Any other order often stemmed from a teacher-pupil relationship (Tyrrell and Purser on Cicero's letters) or from chronological order, as where one editor died and another completed the task, as with Kiessling-Heinze on Horace, and the Gomme-Dover-Andrewes commentaries on Thucydides.[21]

The pleasure scholars take in collaboration with friends and colleagues has to be assessed, in nineteenth-century cases, in relation to external factors such as persistence in joint publishing, or from posthumous references in biographical memoirs. More recently, however, collaborators have been bold enough to admit or declare their pleasure. Meiggs and Lewis on Greek historical inscriptions: 'We should ... compliment one another, for we have found a surprising measure of agreement and our few differences of opinion have never escalated' (Meiggs and Lewis 1969, viii), quoted and repeated by Rhodes and Osborne in their updated collection ('Like Meiggs and Lewis, 'we compliment one another...', Rhodes and

---

17 Donaldson to Murray, 16 April 1840. John Murray archive, National Library of Scotland. A collaborative project is under way to explore Donaldson's work.
18 A. von Pauly (ed.), *Real-Encyclopädie der classischen Alterthumswissenschaft*, 6 vols. in 7, Stuttgart 1839.
19 For Smith and his dictionaries, see Stray 2007c.
20 Stray 2007c, 53. First projected in 1933, the *Dictionary* was delayed by World War II, but drew on the contributions of refugee German scholars.
21 On Kiessling-Heinze see Harrison 2016, which also discusses Nisbet-Hubbard and Nisbet-Rudd on Horace. For the Gomme-Dover-Andrewes Thucydides, see Pelling's chapter in this volume.

Osborne 2007, vii). The pleasure here is perhaps rather cerebral; not so in Rhiannon Ash's dedication of her commentary on Tacitus, Annals 15 to 'the genial and unique triumvirate' of Ted [Kenney], Tony [Woodman] and Chris [Pelling]' (Ash 2018, vii); though her dedicatees were not precisely collaborators on that volume.[22]

The appearance of vernacular dictionaries of Greek belonged to the age of romantic nationalism. The preface to the first edition of Liddell and Scott's lexicon, in 1843, contained a ringing endorsement of the use of Anglo-Saxon vocabulary rather than Latin in translating Greek terms. English, they declared, is far better equipped to render the 'richness, boldness, freedom, and variety of Greek words ... A Frenchman may have reason for using a Greek-Latin lexicon; an Englishman can have none' (Liddell and Scott 1843, iii). The preface belongs to a moment in British history when Anglo-Saxon language and literature were beginning to be asserted as cultural exemplars independent of Classics, models which could inspire a new sense of Englishness. Here again, as with Porson but on a much larger scale, we have a specific past invoked to promote a sense of community — in this case, a national community (Stray 2019b, Williamson 2019).

Liddell and Scott supported their position by identifying an Other — the French were widely seen as an alien threat in the 1840s and 50s, when invasion scares were common (Stray 2018b). In France itself an even more explicitly nationalist agenda operated. In the late 1820s the Parisian publisher Ambroise Firmin-Didot commissioned a new edition of the *Thesaurus Graecae Linguae* of the sixteenth-century French scholar Henri Estienne, usually known as Stephanus (and in England as 'Henry Stephens'). The intention was to subvert more recent German scholarly supremacy by going back beyond it to the Renaissance, hailing Estienne as a heroic founder and retaining his use of Latin for the Lexicon's glosses. Liddell and Scott's reference to the French was presumably to Didot's lexicon. Unfortunately the French team which began work on revising the Lexicon made such slow progress that Didot was obliged to seek help from a scholar and teacher in Paris, Charles Benoît Hase. Hase had in fact been born Karl Benedikt Hase in Germany, but had established himself at the École Royal in Paris, and in 1812 was put in charge of the education of Napoleon's nephews. Hase brought in two other German classicists, the brothers Karl and Ludwig Dindorf of Leipzig, to work on the project, and the rate of production accelerated, though the last of the lexicon's nine folio volumes did not appear till 1865 (Petitmengin

---

[22] I myself am happy to report the pleasure I have gained from fruitful and genial collaboration with the editors of this volume (for example, Harrison and Stray 2012 = Stray 2012; Stray, Pelling and Harrison 2019 = Stray 2019c and d).

1983, Maufroy 2009). The case of the *Thesaurus* shows how the history of fields of study is inflected by the cultural dynamics of nationalism; Hase's career was investigated in the early work of Michel Espagne and his colleagues in Paris, who have now been exploring Franco-German and other cultural transfers for over 30 years (Espagne and Werner 1988). For Didot's project a community of scholars was set up with a mixture of intellectual, economic and patriotic motives, but its personnel changed in a way that undermined Didot's nationalist agenda.

The power of German scholarship was also felt in England. In the second half of the nineteenth century Oxford and Cambridge were gradually forced to change as a result of state intervention. The example of the German universities played an important part in these changes, offering a new vision of scholarship and organisation. Oxford and Cambridge were unique in Europe: they were confessional, being the educational wings of the Church of England, and dominated by colleges rather than faculties, and had changed little in the period of the French revolution, when continental universities had been either destroyed or reconstructed (Brockliss 1997, Anderson 2004). From the 1840s on, the Teutonic system of systematic research by professors, organized in faculties and teaching in seminars, offered an alternative vision, which gained support especially in Oxford. The supporters of research challenged the rule of college tutors, the two positions symbolised by their leaders: for the tutors, Benjamin Jowett, for the researchers, Mark Pattison. Each side had a vision of community, but they differed profoundly.[23] A series of royal commissions took money from the colleges to found chairs in a wide range of subjects. The Latin chair, established in 1854, was named for Corpus Christi, the college whose finances were drawn on to support it.[24]

The characteristic pedagogic institution of the nineteenth-century German university, the seminar, had begun as doubly pedagogic, a device for training teachers, but was taken over by philologists, scientists, and historians from the late eighteenth century (La Vopa 1990; Clark 2003, 158–82; Wellmon 2015, 235–44). This development belonged to the contemporary romantic reaction against Enlightenment rationalism and protestant humanism in Germany. Its first appearance in Britain, as far as I know, was in Oxford in 1879, when the Corpus professor of Latin, Henry Nettleship, ran what he called a 'class' on textual criticism. Nettleship had been to lectures and seminars in Berlin in 1865, and had

---

[23] Stuart Jones's recent study of Pattison has a good account of the debate (Jones 2007).
[24] The long tradition of using Latin as a communicative medium rather than an object of study explains why Latin chairs were founded so much later than Greek. The Regius chair of Greek at Oxford had been founded in 1546. At Cambridge the dates are 1540 for Greek and 1869 for Latin.

been impressed by the teaching of Theodor Mommsen, Emil Hübner, Jacob Bernays and Moriz Haupt.[25] Other German-style seminars in Oxford similarly came from individual initiative. The theologian William Sanday ran a New Testament text-criticism seminar from 1894, and in the following decade a law seminar was also set up by Paul Vinogradoff, who established a supporting library and a publication series. Vinogradoff came to Oxford from Moscow, but as with Nettleship the inspiration for his seminar came from Berlin, where he had attended the seminars of Mommsen and others in 1875. The only classical seminar of this period other than Nettleship's was conducted for three years just before the First World War by the Scottish classical archaeologist Sir William Ramsay, who had retired to Oxford in 1911 (Stray 2016a, 122). Oxford remained in essence, as it did up to the Second World War and beyond, a university dominated by the humanities and by college tutors (Morrell 1997). Faculties had been founded in 1912, but the faculty of Literae Humaniores was a community with both internal and external tensions. Externally, it often had a difficult relationship with the Mods tutors, since for some Greats tutors, as Donald Russell, himself a Mods don, remembered, 'the subspecies Mods don was an inferior breed, not up to handling the more mature minds and capable only of donnish games and a kind of sophisticated proof-reading. That was offensive, and bred much ill-will' (Russell 2007, 237).[26] Internally, Literae Humaniores was split between historians and philosophers, with the added complication that modern philosophy had come to loom large. In the nineteenth century the study of modern philosophy had been officially 'admitted but not required', but as E.R. Dodds put it in his autobiographical memoir *Missing Persons*, 'cuckoos had laid strange eggs in the traditional nest', and Greats in the 1950s had been 'on the way to becoming in effect a bizarre combination of two wholly unrelated subjects, epigraphically based history and modern logic' (Dodds 1977, 177). The cuckoos of course were the philosophers.

The third party in these quarrels — one can hardly call it a community — was the professoriate. Discussing Dodds's attempt to reform the Greats syllabus in the 1950s, Kenneth Dover wrote that Dodds was supported by Eduard Fraenkel, but

---

25 On Nettleship see Harrison 2007.
26 The Oxford classical course was in two parts, the first based on language and literature and leading to an examination in Honour Moderations (Mods), the second dominated by history and philosophy (Literae Humaniores or 'Greats'). In 1938 Kenneth Dover, then an undergraduate at Balliol, referred in a letter to his parents to '... a wrong reasoning on my part that because we take Mods two years before Greats a Mods tutor is ipso facto inferior in intellect and salary to a Greats tutor. That ... is quite wrong, because Mods and Greats involve different subjects. Importance and pay among the Fellows of a College is graded solely by the numbers of years of service as a Fellow....' (letter of 10 October 1938: Dover family papers).

that this was 'the kiss of death, because so many of the older members of the Subfaculty (notably Maurice Bowra) resented any criticisms that came from him, and huddling together to protect themselves against interference from professors was second nature to Mods tutors' (Dover 1994, 82–3). It did not help, of course, when a new professor was a stranger in more senses than one. Eduard Fraenkel, elected to the Corpus chair of Latin in 1934, was a German Jew, a leading representative of the tradition of Altertumswissenschaft (West 2007, Stray 2014). E.R. Dodds, elected Regius professor of Greek in 1936, was an Irishman who as an Oxford undergraduate had been asked to leave because of his support for the Easter Rising, though he was allowed to return to take his degree (Stray, Pelling and Harrison 2019). Fraenkel's seminars are famous, especially that on the *Agamemnon*, which he ran in Corpus from 1936 to 1942. One of the later participants in the 1960s, Martin West, conjured it up vividly:

> Here we saw German philology in action; we felt it reverberate through us as Fraenkel patrolled the room behind our chairs, discoursing in forceful accents. As he spoke of his old teachers and past colleagues — Leo and Norden, Wilamowitz and Wackernagel — it was like an *apparition de l'Église éternelle*. We knew, and could not doubt, that this was what Classical Scholarship was, and that it was for us to learn to carry it on. (quoted by S. West 2007, 211)

I quote this partly to make the point that once again we have heroic exemplars on display. With West's list we might compare that given by Louis MacNeice in his poem *Autumn Journal*, writing of his time in Oxford reading Classics in the late 1920s: 'Oxford crowded the mantelpiece with gods — Scaliger, Heinsius, Dindorf, Bentley and Wilamowitz — as we learned our genuflections for Honour Mods' (MacNeice 1939, 51).

The only name common to both lists is that of Wilamowitz; but in both cases a community of sorts is being invoked, a community over time, but in rather different ways. The undergraduate MacNeice wrote of genuflecting, and one senses that it was seen as good technique for candidates to press examinatorial buttons by mentioning some great names. The Wilamowitz-reference, then, was the student precursor to the Wilamowitz footnote, the ritual marker of authority in scholarly articles which, Steve Nimis has argued, constituted a rhetorical claim to membership of the academic community.[27] Fraenkel, on the other hand, was working

---

[27] Nimis 1984. Nimis himself belonged to an academic community founded to provide critical evaluations of current academic practice, the Society for Critical Exchange (Nimis 2007; cf. Stray 2016a, 113–14).

a full seminar room, invoking the scholarly tradition maintained by the community which had nurtured him and which he was carrying on with every word and every step. As with the German seminar tradition, we also have tensions between the horizontal community of shared reading and discussion and the vertical hierarchy of teacher and taught — a verticality sharpened in this case by its being between German professor and British pupils, some of them in fact senior academics. In his edition of the *Agamemnon* Fraenkel wrote that 'My favourite reader, whose kindly and patient face would sometimes comfort me during the endless hours of drudgery, looked surprisingly like some of the students who worked with me for many years at Oxford in our happy seminar classes on the Agamemnon' (Fraenkel 1950, I.viii). Others had a less rosy picture than Fraenkel gave in his sketch of his imagined reader. In his obituary of Fraenkel, Colin Macleod referred to his 'occasional outbursts of rage', and declared that 'he never realized what terror he could strike into his students'. One of them, Iris Murdoch, said later that 'the day when she had to prepare a bit [of text] for the class was beyond question the most terrifying of her undergraduate life'. Another participant, admittedly with tongue in cheek, described it as 'a circle of rabbits addressed by a stoat' (Stray 2014, 143).

If we compare the two groups or tendencies with which we began, the Porsonians of the 1810s and the Cambridge Ritualists almost a century later, the contrast is marked between the dominance of linguistic work for the former and the immersion of the latter in archaeology, ancient history and anthropology. To some extent this is the product of institutional change. The Cambridge classical degree course, first examined in 1824, included almost nothing except language and literature till 1850, when questions on history and philosophy were included. Further reform in this direction took place in the late 1860s, but the major reform came around 1880, when the course was divided into two parts. The first consisted of the traditional mixture of language and literature; the second part contained five optional sections, on literature, philosophy, history, archaeology and philology. A different situation obtained in Oxford. Here too the degree course had two parts, first Moderations, like the Cambridge part 1 a language and literature course, and then Literae Humaniores or Greats, which was dominated by ancient history and philosophy — I have already mentioned Dodds's comments on this. Attempts to insert archaeology into Greats failed for several decades, and classical literature was only added at the end of the 1960s. All these changes have had implications for community boundaries and interactions.

Some of these curriculum reforms were aided or sparked off by collaboration. In Trinity College Cambridge, in the late 1860s, a group of young fellows, including Richard Jebb, James Stewart, Henry Jackson and William Currey, introduced a new system of college teaching, their aim being to render redundant the extensive informal system of coaching (private tutoring) which was then dominant (Winstanley 1947, 254–5; Rothblatt 1968; 205–7; Stray forthcoming). This initiative was paralleled by a campaign of two senior fellows, William Clark and Robert Burn, to reform the Classical Tripos; the flysheet they issued in 1867 provoked over a dozen responses, and led a few years later to significant change. (Winstanley 1947, 212–23). In twentieth-century Oxford, similarly, a pair of reform-minded friends, Robin Nisbet and Donald Russell, put forward a proposal for the reform of Greats in the 1960s; this led to the integration of literature into a course previously dominated by philosophy and history (Russell 2007). Nisbet and Russell's initiative thus achieved a reform which Gilbert Murray (Regius Professor of Greek 1908–36) and his successor E.R. Dodds (1936–60) had argued for in vain.

Some of the changes I have mentioned led to the rise of new institutional forms. Most important of these was the museum, which came to provide a home and a focus for a community in the emerging field of classical archaeology. The classical collections of the Ashmolean Museum were expanded rapidly by Arthur Evans after his appointment as curator in 1884. In the same year, a museum of classical archaeology was founded in Cambridge, responding to the recent setting up of the optional Part 2 archaeology course I mentioned earlier. More significant than either of these, in some ways, was the development of the department of Greek and Roman Antiquities at the British Museum. This was founded in 1860, and its first keeper was Sir Charles Newton, who had excavated in Asia Minor and brought artefacts back to London for the Museum (Cook 1997). Its position rested on its collections, its staff, and the Museum's library (now the British Library). Together with the University of London, founded in 1836, it belonged to a metropolitan academic and cultural world which constituted a significant third force in relation to Oxford and Cambridge.[28] In a review of the first volume of the Hellenic Society's *Journal of Hellenic Studies*, the Oxford Homerist D.B Monro had remarked that 'The society was brought into existence in London, which is, for obvious reasons, the centre of archaeological study; hence it is dominated by the spirit of the British Museum rather than that of the Oxford and Cambridge lecture-rooms.'[29] This world later became the British home of the archaeological schools established in Athens in 1886 and in Rome in 1900. Those schools, especially as they were residential, functioned as communities, but in turn belonged to the

---

28 The University was a teaching institution which incorporated two earlier foundations, London University (renamed University College, London) and King's College, London.
29 D.B. Monro, review of *JHS* 1, *The Academy* 454, 15 Jan. 1881, 38–39, at 38; cf. Stray 2019b, 55–57.

larger communities made up of the foreign schools in each city. The mixture of collaboration and competition in these larger communities has been very well explored by Frederick Whitling.[30]

Tab. 8: British classical societies and archaeological schools.

1870 Oxford Philological Society
1871 Cambridge Philological Society
1879 Society for the Promotion of Hellenic Studies
1886 British School at Athens
1900 British School at Rome
1902 Classical Association of Scotland
1903 Classical Association of England and Wales
1910 Society for the Promotion of Roman Studies

The new realm of classical archaeology was also supported by the Hellenic Society, founded in London in 1879. The earliest classical societies were based in universities, beginning in Oxford, but the Hellenic Society was the first national body to be founded. It combined the growing appeal of archaeology with the dominance of Greece over Rome in British culture since the later eighteenth century (Turner 1989). The expectations it set up for a parallel Roman society were not satisfied till 1910; the same pattern as we have just seen with the archaeological schools. The Hellenic Society's broad cultural appeal came with a price: its non-academic supporters expected to be entertained and to get something for their money, and some of its academic supporters wanted more than just archaeology. This became clear once it had launched its journal (the *Journal of Hellenic Studies*) in 1880 (Stray 2018a, 231–32).

Having located the Hellenic Society in a British context, I should like to widen the scope even further and consider the continental scene, especially that in Germany. The first years of the Hellenic Society coincided with the emergence in Germany of what Theodor Mommsen in 1890 was to call *Grosswissenschaft*, big scholarship (Marchand 1996, 75–77). This was the age of large-scale collaborative projects like the *Corpus Inscriptionum Graecarum*, the *Monumenta Germaniae Historica* and the *Thesaurus Linguae Latinae*. These were the grand enterprises

---

[30] Whitling 2018. For a different perspective on 20th-century archaeology, via self-presentation and publication, see Thornton 2019.

referred to by Wilamowitz in a letter to his friends Hermann Diels as 'DMWissenschaft'. This term was interpreted by the editors of their correspondence, doubtless thinking of the inscriptional abbreviations on tombs, 'Dis manibus sacrum', sacred to the spirits of the dead, as 'Dis manibus wissenschaft'. The problem was that this made very little sense. Much better sense was offered by a reviewer of the edition: *Dampfmaschinewissenschaft*, steam-engine scholarship (Fowler 1997). These enterprises, as Suzanne Marchand has pointed out, involved specialisation and hierarchy, and thus the suppression of the individual personality whose cultivation lay at the heart of the older ideal of *Bildung*, aesthetic self-formation. The new modern form of classical scholarship threatened to destroy the Humboldtian basis on which it had built. As Marchand comments, 'If *Bildung* was about the cultivation of the individual personality, *Grosswissenschaft* was about its suppression' (Marchand 1996, 75–115, at 76). It was this ethos that Housman denounced when he referred to the home of the *Thesaurus Linguae Latinae* as 'the ergastulum in Munich'.[31]

It may seem grotesque and bathetic to compare this vast German phenomenon with what was happening in Britain, but the causes were similar, though the British developments, in Cambridge and in London, were on a much smaller scale, particularly as the state hardly intervened at all, as it did on a large scale in Germany. When Richard Jebb was conducting his campaign for the foundation of a British archaeological school in Athens, he wrote to William Gladstone, then Prime Minister, for support. In his reply Gladstone commented on

> ... the relation of the scheme to the Government and to the Universities. The great endowments existing in England create a broad difference between our case, and that of France or Germany. This you have frankly recognised in contemplating public subscription as your main resource.[32]

The outstanding example of organised scholarly collaboration on a national scale in Britain came in the 1870s, with the revised translation of the Bible. This was carried out by two 'companies' of revisers, the New Testament being published in 1881 and the Old Testament in 1885. The whole scheme had begun in 1870, after the two Convocations of the Church of England, Canterbury (south) and York

---

31 'That was enough for the chain-gangs working at the dictionary in the ergastulum at Munich: theirs not to reason why.' Housman 1969, 42. 'Theirs not to reason why' echoed Tennyson's poem on the charge of the Light Brigade at Balaclava (1854), when 300 lightly-armed cavalry rode against Russian artillery and sustained heavy casualties.
32 Gladstone to Jebb, 3 February 1833: Stray 2013, 115.

(north), had been asked to approve the project. York refused, Canterbury accepted, and established a New Testament revision company of 29 men. Their theological opinions ranged from High Anglicanism to Dissent and even Unitarianism, their views of the original texts from conservatism to liberalism. The Company met for a total of 407 days across ten and a half years, and the proceedings can in many cases be reconstructed from official documents and private diaries (Cadwallader 2019). The whole enterprise could be called national, though set up by only one of the two Anglican Convocations, but the state was not involved.[33] The next large-scale biblical translation project followed the expiry of the revised version's copyright in 1935. The two ancient university presses proposed a revision of the Revision, but in 1946 it was decided that a fresh translation should be produced, and a series of small committee was set up. The result was published in 1970 as *The New English Bible*.

The final carrier of classical communities I want to consider, scholarly journals, constitute an important and (in my view) neglected basis for disciplinary solidarity, one that we now take for granted. One of them, the Porsonian *Museum Criticum*, has already been mentioned.[34] Some of them are the products and reflections of communities, while others have themselves created communities. For example, the first scholarly journal was the French *Journal des sçavans*, whose first issue appeared in 1665, just two months before the first of the *Philosophical Transactions of the Royal Society*. The former aimed to create a community of scholars; the latter derived from an existing community. Some nineteenth-century journals tried to establish a supportive community by securing subscribers, who were then listed in print to demonstrate the size and nature of the community: this was done, for example, by the editors of the *Classical Museum* (1843-9). The founders of the *Classical Review* (1887–) set out to establish a support group of scholars who would not only subscribe to the journal but write reviews for it (Stray 2018a, 171–86). In the twentieth century, a Classical Journals Board was set up by the Classical Association in 1910, after it purchased the *Classical Review* and *Classical Quarterly* from their publisher David Nutt in the previous year. The Board became a semi-autonomous community, operating for several decades independently of the Classical Association, until in the 1990s an inquisitive Association treasurer investigated its accounts. It was this Board, as constituted in 1931,

---

33 An American committee was also formed; relations between its members and the English companies were at times strained. For the US context, see Thuesen 2002.
34 The treatment here is relatively brief, as I have dealt with the topic in detail elsewhere: Stray 2016a, 2018a, 146–86.

that voted 4–3 not to publish A.E. Housman's 'Praefanda'.³⁵ Finally, the editorial committee of the *Journal of Roman Studies* was in the late twentieth century a very hands-on body. Articles submitted to it were passed from one member to another, each writing a comment on the submission, so that a kind of linear discussion was built up in which (for example) a comment by Fergus Millar might be followed by one from the hand of Arnaldo Momigliano, giving his opinion not only on the article itself, but also on previous comments.³⁶ The examples I have given show the variety of kinds of community involved in the running of classical journals.

I should like to end by looking at a pair of books deliberately aimed at a wider audience, written by a scholar who was very conscious of the widening gulf between the academic community and amateurs: John Clarke Stobart's *The Glory that was Greece*, published in 1911, and the sequel, *The Grandeur that was Rome*, which followed the next year.³⁷ Both books were themselves the products of a collaboration between Stobart and his publisher Frank Sidgwick. Stobart provided the text, Sidgwick scoured the photographic libraries of Britain, Germany, Italy and Greece for illustrations and commissioned photographs and drawings from the Department of Greek and Roman Antiquities at the British Museum. The *Glory* and the *Grandeur* appeared at the moment referred to, and were designed to bridge the fissures which were opening up in British Classics. Stobart, like his books, can be situated at the moment when classical scholarship was becoming professionalized and internally specialized; when Classics was becoming marginalised in British high culture, while some of its devotees held to a post-religious spiritual mission to educate a Greekless population. Stobart very much fits this pattern. He was a vicar's son who graduated in Classics at Trinity College Cambridge (Stray 2004). He became a schoolmaster, and was briefly a history lecturer at Trinity. He then became an inspector of schools, and finally, in the 1920s, the first director of education for the BBC. His proposal for a cultural radio network called Minerva was turned down, but realised after World War II as the Third Programme, now Radio 3 (Lambert 1940, 49–50; Briggs 1961, 184).

---

35 Stray 2003, 110–13; for 'Praefanda', see 112. Housman's discussion of ancient obscenity, written in Latin, was later published in *Hermes* 66 (1931), 402–12. An English translation was published in the journal *Arion* (Housman 2001).
36 The articles and comments were loaned to me by the late Simon Price; the copies I took of them are now in the Roman Society archive. The review procedure for the *Journal of Hellenic Studies* was very different, each submission being read by a single member of the editorial committee before it went to an external reviewer. The *JRS* committee, in contrast, was self-sufficient, and did not use external reviewers. (My thanks to Averil Cameron for information.)
37 Stobart 1911, 1912. For a fuller account of Stobart's project, see Stray 2019a.

In the preface to *The Glory that was Greece*, Stobart wrote:

> With the progress of research, classical scholarship tends more and more towards narrower fields of specialisation. Real students are now like miners working underground each in his own shaft, buried far away from sight of the public, so that they even begin to lose sight of one another. (Stobart 1911, v)

Stobart's project was to take classical civilisation to readers who knew no Latin or Greek, and he did this by means of a clearly-written text profusely illustrated by photographs. The illustrations were crucial to his project, and in his preface he declared that his text supported them, not the other way round. His project can be compared with the exactly contemporaneous launching of the Loeb Classical Library (planned in 1911, launched in 1912), which provided classical texts with facing English translations (Henderson and Thomas 2020). Stobart's books were very successful, went into over a dozen editions and were still in print 50 years later. Stobart's project gives us a glimpse of the boundaries of his field of study, its internal organisation, and its situation at a historical moment when its status and its relationship to school and university curricula were in transition. His two books were designed to reach out to a wide readership, his BBC work to an even wider audience of a new kind. Stobart's career took him from school teaching to university teaching and from school inspecting to the BBC. He belonged to a generation in which the boundaries between these occupational sectors had not hardened as they would later on. His publisher Frank Sidgwick's father Arthur Sidgwick had similarly moved from school teaching (at Rugby) to university teaching (at Oxford). Frank Sidgwick represented another contemporary cultural shift in his move from a classical training to a focus on English literature. In the twenty-first century, occupational boundaries have shifted again, with significant rapprochements between universities and both schools and communication media.[38]

Conclusion

In this essay I have tried to look at the varieties of classical communities, from those at national level down to those so small (n+1 members, where n=1) that one would not normally call them communities at all. I have done that in order to bring a wide range of relationships into the picture. What has emerged, I think,

---

[38] The most notable example of the latter can be seen in the career of Dame Mary Beard.

is that classical communities owe their inception and maintenance to a variety of different forces: shared material environments, overlapping interests, shared institutional experience, communicative fora and mechanisms such as journals and reviewing: and sometimes, friendship, exemplified by the relationship between Liddell and Scott.[39] As I come to the end of this essay, I am glad to welcome a discussion of collaboration by a scholarly collective set up explicitly to practise a collaborative discussion of the future of Classics.[40]

Bibliography

Anderson, R.D. (2004), *European Universities from the Enlightenment to 1914*, Oxford.
Ash, R. (ed.) (2018), *Tacitus: Annals XV*, Cambridge.
Barton, R. (2018), *The X Club: Power and Authority in Victorian Science*, Chicago.
Bollack, M./Wismann, H./Lindken, T. (eds.), *Philologie und Hermeneutik im 19. Jahrhundert II*, Göttingen.
Briggs, A. (1961), *The History of Broadcasting in the United Kingdom. Vol. I, The Birth of Broadcasting*, Oxford.
Brink, C.O. (1986), *English Scholarship: Historical Reflections on Bentley, Porson and Housman*, Cambridge.
Brockliss, L.W.B. (1997), 'The European university in the age of revolution, 1789–1950', in: M.G. Brock/M.C. Curthoys (eds.), *The History of the University of Oxford VI: Nineteenth-century Oxford, Part 1*, Oxford, 77–133.
Cadwallader, A. (2019), *The Politics of the Revised Version: A Tale of Two New Testament Revision Companies*, London.
Cannon, W.F. (1964), 'Scientists and Broad Churchmen: An early Victorian intellectual network', *Journal of British Studies* 4, 65–88.
Clark, W. (2003), *Academic Charisma and the Origins of the Research University*, Chicago.
Dodds, E.R. (1977), *Missing Persons: An Autobiography*, Oxford.
Dover, K.J. (1994), *Marginal Comment: A Memoir*, London.
Dover, L. (ed.) (1833), *Letters of Horace Walpole, Earl of Orford, to Sir Horace Mann*, 2nd ed., London.
Espagne, M./Werner, M. (1988), *Transferts: les Relations Interculturelles dans l'Espace Franco-Allemand (XVIIe et XIX siècle)*, Paris.

---

[39] At the end of the oral paper on which this piece is based, I added, 'And we should not forget the shared experience of occasions like this seminar.' To which I can now add that we should also take account of the communal activity represented in the present volume. This essay has benefited greatly from comments by Gian Mario Cao, Stephen Harrison, Chris Kraus and Chris Pelling.
[40] The Postclassicisms Collective 2020, 201–4.

Fowler, R.L. (1997), Review of M. Braun, W.M. Calder III, and D. Ehlers (eds.), *Philology and Philosophy. The Letters of Hermann Diels to Theodor and Heinrich Gomperz*, Bryn Mawr Classical Review 97.03.13 https://bmcr.brynmawr.edu/
Fraenkel, E.D.M. (1950), *Aeschylus, Agamemnon*, 3 vols., Oxford.
Gerson, G. (2004), *Margins of Disorder: New Liberalism and the Crisis of European Consciousness*, Albany, NY.
Gibbins, J.R. (1987), 'John Grote, Cambridge University and the development of Victorian ideas', PhD thesis, University of Newcastle.
Gibbins, J.R. (2007), *John Grote, Cambridge University and the Development of Victorian Thought*, Exeter.
Gold, D. (2003), *Aesthetics and Analysis in Writing on Religion: Modern Fascinations*, Berkeley, CA.
Güthenke, C. (2018), 'Introduction: "A mirror does not develop": The history of classical scholarship as reception', in: Stray 2018a, 1–9.
Harrison, S.J. (2007), 'Henry Nettleship and the beginning of modern Latin studies in Oxford', in: Stray 2007a, 106–116.
Harrison, S.J. (2016), 'Two-author commentaries on Horace: Three case studies', in: Stray 2016a, 71–83.
Harrison, S.J./Stray, C.A. (2012), *Expurgating the Classics: Editing Out in Greek and Latin*, London.
Henderson, J./Thomas, R.F. (eds.) (2020), *The Loeb Classical Library and Its Progeny* (Loeb Classical Library Monographs, 18), Cambridge MA.
Housman, A.E. (1969), *The Confines of Criticism. The Cambridge Inaugural 1911. The Complete Text, With Notes by John Carter*, Cambridge.
Housman, A.E. (2001), 'Praefanda', trans. J. Jayo, Arion 9.2, 180–200.
Jason, M. (2009), *The Society of Dilettanti: Archaeology and Identity in the British Enlightenment*, New Haven.
Jones, H.S. (2007), *Intellect and Character in Victorian England: Mark Pattison and the Invention of the Don*, Oxford.
La Vopa, A.J. (1990), 'Specialists against specialization: Hellenism as professional ideology in German classical studies', in: G. Cocks/K.H. Jarausch (eds.), *German Professions 1800–1950*, Oxford, 27–45.
Lambert, R.S. (1940), *Ariel and All his Quality: An Impression of the BBC from Within*, London.
Liddell, H.G./Scott, R. (1843), *A Greek-English Lexicon*, Oxford.
Lowe, N.J. (2005), 'Problematic Verrall: the sceptic at law', in: Stray 2005, 142–160.
Lubenow, W.C. (2009), 'The Cambridge Ritualists 1876–1924: A study of commensurability in the history of scholarship', *History of Universities* XXIV/1–2, 280–308.
MacNeice, L. (1939), *Autumn Journal*, London.
Majeed, J. (2011), 'What's in a (proper) name? Particulars, individuals, and authorship in the Linguistic Survey of India and colonial scholarship', in: I. Sengupta/D. Ali (eds.), *Knowledge Production, Pedagogy, and Institutions in Colonial India*, London, 19–39.
Marchand, S.L. (1996), *Down from Olympus: Archaeology and Philhellenism in Germany, 1750–1970*, Princeton.
Masseau, D. (1994), *L'Invention de l'Intellectuel dans l'Europe du XVIIIe siècle*, Paris.
Maufroy, S. (2009), 'Pour une etude du philhellènisme Franco-Allemand. Une approche de la question à partir des cas de Karl Benedikt Hase et de Friedrich Thiersch', *The Historical Review/La Revue Historique* 6, 99–127.

Meiggs, R./Lewis, D.M. (1969), *A Selection of Greek Historical Inscriptions to the End of the Fifth Century BC*, Oxford.
Monk, J.H. (1830), *The Life of Richard Bentley, D.D., with an Account of his Writings, and Anecdotes of Many Distinguished Characters during the Period in which he Flourished*, London.
Morrell, J. (1997), *Science at Oxford: Transforming an Arts University 1914–1939*, Oxford.
Nimis, S. (1984), 'Fussnoten: der Fundament des Wissenschaft', *Arethusa* 17, 105–134.
Nimis, S. (2007), 'The Society for Critical Exchange at Miami University', *Works and Days* 25/1–2, 135–136.
Petitmengin, P. (1983), 'Deux têtes de pont de la philologie allemande en France: Le *Thesaurus Linguae Graecae* et la *Bibliothèque des auteurs grecs* (1830–1867)', in: Bollack et al. 1983, 76–107.
Pfeiffer, R. (1968–76), *History of Classical Scholarship*, 2 vols., Oxford.
Postclassicisms Collective, The (2020), *Postclassicisms* (Chicago).
Redford, B. (2008), *Dilettanti: The Antic and the Antique in Eighteenth-Century England*, Los Angeles.
Rhodes, P.J./Osborne, R. (eds.) (2007), *Greek Historical Inscriptions: 404–323 BC*, Oxford.
Robinson, A. (2002), *The Life and Work of Jane Ellen Harrison*, Oxford.
Rothblatt, S. (1968), *The Revolution of the Dons: Cambridge and Society in Victorian England*, London.
Russell, D.A. (2007), 'The study of classical literature at Oxford, 1936–1988 II: Times change', in: Stray 2007a, 225–238.
Sandys, J.E. (1903–8), *A History of Classical Scholarship*, 3 vols., Cambridge.
Snyder, L.J. (2011), *The Philosophical Breakfast Club: Four Remarkable Friends Who Transformed Science and Changed the World*, New York.
Stobart, J.C. (1911), *The Glory That Was Greece*, London.
Stobart, J.C. (1912), *The Grandeur That Was Rome*, London.
Stray, C.A. (ed.) (2003), *The Classical Association: The First Century, 1903–2003. Greece & Rome*, supplementary volume, Oxford.
Stray, C.A. (2004), 'John Clarke Stobart', in: R.B. Todd (ed.), *Dictionary of British Classicists*, 3 vols., Bristol, 926–927.
Stray, C.A. (ed.) (2005), *The Owl of Minerva: The Cambridge Praelections of 1906. Reassessments of Richard Jebb, James Adam, Walter Headlam, Henry Jackson, William Ridgeway and Arthur Verrall. Proceedings of the Cambridge Philological Society* Supp. vol. 28, Cambridge.
Stray, C.A., ed. (2007a), *Oxford Classics: Teaching and learning 1800–2000*, London.
Stray, C.A. ed. (2007b), *Classical Books: Scholarship and Publishing 1800–2000* (Bulletin of the Institute of Classical Studies, Supp. Vol. 101).
Stray, C.A. (2007c), 'Sir William Smith and his dictionaries: a study in scarlet and black', in: Stray 2007b, 35–54.
Stray, C.A. (2013), *Sophocles' Jebb: A Life in Letters. Cambridge Classical Journal*, Supplement 38, Cambridge.
Stray, C.A. (2014), 'Eduard Fraenkel: an exploration', *Syllecta Classica* 25, 113–172.
Stray, C.A. (2015), 'A divided text: Shackleton Bailey, W.S. Watt and Cicero's *Epistulae ad Atticum*', in: Stray/Whitaker 2015, 115–128.
Stray, C.A. (2016a), 'Disciplinary histories of Classics', *History of Universities* XXIX/1: 112–134.
Stray, C.A. (2016b), 'A semi-sacred monster: Charles Wordsworth's *Graecae Grammaticae Rudimenta*', *Philologia Classica* [St Petersburg] 11, 98–115.

Stray, C.A. (2018a), *Classics in Britain: Scholarship, Education, and Publishing, 1800–2000*, Oxford.
Stray, C.A. (2018b), 'From *odium* to *bellum*: classical scholars at war in Europe and America, 1800-1924', *Classical Receptions Journal* 10.4, 356–375.
Stray, C.A. (2019a), 'The Glory and the grandeur: John Clarke Stobart and the defence of high culture in a democratic age', *History of Classical Scholarship* 1, 135–173.
Stray, C.A. (2019b), 'Brexit as banquet: A.E. Housman on the history of classical scholarship', *The Housman Society Journal* 45, 40–64.
Stray, C.A. (2019c) [with C. Pelling], 'Introduction: a missing person?', in: Stray/Pelling/Harrison 2019, 1–9.
Stray, C.A. (2019d), 'An Irishman abroad', in: Stray/Pelling/Harrison 2019, 10–35.
Stray, C.A. (forthcoming), 'Teaching and learning', in: A.J.B. Hilton/E.S. Leedham-Green (eds.), *History of Trinity College, Cambridge*, vol. 2.
Stray, C.A./Clarke, M.J./Katz, J.T. (eds.) (2019), *Liddell and Scott: The History, Methodology and Languages of the World's Leading Lexicon of Ancient Greek*, Oxford.
Stray, C.A./Harrison, S.J. (eds.) (2012), *Expurgating the Classics: Editing Out in Greek and Latin*, London.
Stray, C.A./Pelling, C./Harrison, S. (eds.) (2019), *Rediscovering E.R. Dodds: Scholarship, Poetry, and the Paranormal*, Oxford.
Stray, C.A./Whitaker, G. (eds.) (2015), *Classics in Practice: Studies in the History of Scholarship*, BICS Supp. 128, London, 115–128.
Thornton, A. (2019), *Archaeologists in Print: Publishing for the People*, online at https://www.uclpress.co.uk/products/107948
Thuesen, P.J. (2002), *In Discordance with the Scriptures: American Protestant Battles over Translating the Bible*, New York.
Turner, F.M. (1989), 'Why the Greeks and not the Romans in Victorian Britain?', in: G.W. Clarke, (ed.), *Rediscovering Hellenism: The Hellenic Inheritance and the English Imagination*, Cambridge, 61–81.
Wellmon, C. (2015), *Organizing Enlightenment: Information Overload and the Invention of the Modern Research University*, Baltimore.
West, S. (2007), 'Eduard Fraenkel recalled', in: Stray 2007a, 203–218.
Whitling, F. (2018), *Western Ways: Foreign Schools in Rome and Athens*, Berlin/Boston.
Wilamowitz-Moellendorff, U. von (1921), *Geschichte der Philologie*, Leipzig.
Williamson, M. (2019), 'Dictionaries as translations: English in the Lexicon', in: Stray/Clarke/Katz 2019, 25–44.
Winstanley, D.A. (1947), *Later Victorian Cambridge*, Cambridge.
Zetzel, E.G. (2018), *Critics, Compilers, and Commentators: An Introduction to Roman Philology, 200BCE–800CE*. Oxford.

Complete List of Publications of Christopher Stray

[* = reprinted in Stray, *Classics in Britain* — see **2018** below]

1977
- 'Classics in Crisis: The Changing Forms and Current Decline of Classics as Exemplary Curricular Knowledge, with Special Reference to the Experience of Classics Teachers in South Wales.' MScEcon thesis, University of Wales.

1985
- 'From monopoly to marginality: Classics in English education', in: I.F. Goodson (ed.), *Social Histories of the Secondary Curriculum*, Beckenham, 19–52.

1986
- 'Culture or discipline? The redefinition of classical education', in: M.H. Price (ed), *The Development of the Secondary Curriculum*, London, 10–48.

1988
- 'England, culture and the 19th century', *Liverpool Classical Monthly* 13.6, 85–90.

1989
- 'Paradigms of social order: the politics of Latin grammar in 19th-century England', *Bulletin of the Henry Sweet Society* 13, 13–24.

1990
- 'Beyond classification: Bernstein and the grammarians', *History of Education* 19, 267–268.
- 'A cellarful of ghosts? The library of the Educational Division of the South Kensington Museum', *Paradigm* 3, 13–15.
- Review of P.G. Naiditch, A.E. Housman at University College, London, *Classical Philology* 85, 244–248.

1991
- *'Locke's system of classical instruction', *The Locke Newsletter* 2, 115–121.
- Review of C. Shrosbree, *Public Schools and Private Education*, *English Historical Review* 106, 225–226.
- Review of S. Peacock, Jane Ellen Harrison, *Liverpool Classical Monthly* 16.7, 103–111.

1992
- *The Living Word. W.H.D. Rouse and the Crisis of Classics in Edwardian England*, Bristol.
- 'Digs and degrees: Jessie Crum's tour of Greece, Easter 1901', *Classics Ireland* 2, 121–131.

1993
- 'Zulu and Zuleika', *The Book Collector* 42, 429–431.
- Review of M. McCrum, *Thomas Arnold, Headmaster. A Reassessment*, *English Historical Review* 108, 737.

1994
- (edited with Robert A. Kaster) *Reinterpreting the Classics* (special issue of *Annals of Scholarship*, vol. 10.1).
- 'Ideology and institution: English classical scholarship in transition', in: Stray/Kaster 1994, 111–131.
- 'Paradigms regained: towards a historical sociology of textbooks', *Journal of Curriculum Studies* 26, 1–29.

- *'The smell of Latin grammar: contrary imaginings in English classrooms', *Bulletin of the John Rylands Library* 76, 201–222.
- 'Culture and Discipline: The Reconstruction of Classics in England 1830–1930'. PhD thesis, University of Wales. Published in revised form as Stray, *Classics Transformed* (1998, below).

1995
- (edited with an introduction) *Grinders and Grammars: A Victorian Controversy. The Text of Thirty-Six Letters Printed in The Times following the Publication of Kennedy's Public School Latin Primer in September 1866, with an Introduction and Notes*, Reading.
- 'On first looking into Kennedy's Latin Primer', in: Stray 1995, 7–12.

1996
- (edited with an introduction) *The Mushri-English Pronouncing Dictionary. A Chapter in 19th- century Public-School Lexicography*, Reading.
- 'Idiosyncrasy and idiolexis in Victorian public schools', in: Stray 1996, 2–36.
- *'Primers, publishing and politics: the classical textbooks of Benjamin Hall Kennedy', *Papers of the Bibliographical Society of America* 90, 451–474.
- 'Scholars and gentlemen: towards a historical sociology of classical scholarship', in: H.D. Jocelyn (ed.), *Aspects of Nineteenth-century British Classical Scholarship*, Liverpool, 13–27.
- Review of K.J. Dover, *Marginal Comment. A Memoir*, *Classical Review* 46, 195–196.

1997
- 'Contestation and change in Cambridge Classics, 1822–1914', *Dialogos* 4, 1–16.
- *'John Taylor and Locke's Classical System', *Paradigm* 20, 26–38.
- 'Thucydides or Grote? Classical disputes and disputed classics in 19th-century Cambridge', *Transactions of the American Philological Association* 127, 363–71.
- Review of P. Hummel, *Humanités normaliennes. L'enseignement classique et l'erudition philologique dans l'Ecole normale supérieure du XIXe siècle*, *Classical Review* 47, 405–407.
- Review of M. Lefkowitz, *Not out of Africa* and M. Lefkowitz and G. Rogers, *Black Athena Revisited*, *Journal of Hellenic Studies* 117, 229–231.

1998
- *Classics Transformed: Schools, Universities, and Society in England*, 1830–1960, Oxford.
- (edited, with an introduction) *Winchester Notions: The English Dialect of Winchester College*, from an unpublished glossary by C.G. Stevens, London.
- 'Introduction', in: Stray 1998 [*Winchester Notions*], 1–20.
- 'Attractive and nonsensical Classics': Oxford, Cambridge, and elsewhere', *CUCD Bulletin* 27, 3–8.
- *'Renegotiating Classics: the politics of curricular reform in late-Victorian Cambridge', *Echos du Monde Classique/Classical Views* 42, 449–470.
- 'Schoolboys and gentlemen: classical pedagogy and authority in the English public school', in: N. Livingstone/Y.L. Too (eds.), *Pedagogy and Power: Rhetorics of Ancient Learning*, Cambridge, 29–46.
- 'Unseen university. Remembering and forgetting Cambridge', *Cambridge Review* 2331, November, 1–8.

1999
- *Classics in 19th and 20th Century Cambridge: Curriculum, Culture and Community*. Proceedings of the Cambridge Philological Society, Supp. vol. 24, Cambridge.

- 'The first century of the Classical Tripos: high culture and the politics of curriculum', in: Stray 1999, 1–14.
- Review of J. Hallett/T. van Nortwick (eds.), *Compromising Traditions: The Individual Voice in Classical Scholarship*, *Journal of Roman Studies* 88, 225–226.
- Review of E.C. Kopff, *The Devil Knows Latin – Why America Needs the Classical Tradition*, *Times Literary Supplement* 5005, 5 March, 32.

2001
- (edited with Jonathan Smith) *Teaching and Learning in 19th-century Cambridge*, Woodbridge.
- * 'Curriculum and style in the collegiate university: Classics in nineteenth-century Oxbridge', *History of Universities* 16, 183–218.
- 'A parochial anomaly: the Classical Tripos 1822–1900', in: Smith/Stray, 31–44.
- * 'Purity in danger: the contextual life of savants', in: S.J. Harrison (ed.), *Texts, Ideas, and the Classics*, Oxford, 265–284.
- 'The shift from oral to written examination: Cambridge and Oxford, 1700–1914', *Assessment in Education* 8, 35–51.

2002
- Introduction to Kiddle, H. and Schem. A.J., *Cyclopaedia of Education* [1887], 2 vols., Bristol, I.v–viii.
- Introduction to [various authors], *English Slang in the Nineteenth Century*, 5 vols., Bristol, I.v–xviii.
- Introduction to Carlisle, N., *Concise Description of the Endowed Schools of England and Wales* [1818], 6 vols., Bristol, I.v–xiii.
- 'A pedagogic palace: the Feinaiglian Institution and its textbooks', *Long Room* [Trinity College Dublin] 47, 14–25.
- 'The pen is mightier than the spade: archaeology and education in nineteenth-century England', *Pharos* [Netherlands Institute in Athens] 10, 121–32.

2003
- * *Promoting and Defending: Reflections on the History of the Hellenic Society (1879) and the Classical Association (1903)*, London.
- (edited with Jonathan Smith) *Cambridge in the 1830s: The Letters of Alexander Chisholm Gooden, 1831–1841*, Woodbridge.
- (edited) *The Classical Association: The First Century, 1903–2003*. Greece & Rome supplementary volume, Oxford.
- 'The foundation and its contexts' (3–22), 'Getting under way: challenge and response, 1904–22' (23–37), 'A lull between two storms: from the 1920s to the 1950s' (38–42), 'The CA's publications' (112–21), 'The CA archive' (292), all in: Stray 2003 [*The Classical Association*].
- Introduction to Watson, F., *Encyclopedia and Dictionary of Education* [1921–2], 4 vols., Bristol, I.v–vii.
- 'Introduction' in: Smith and Stray 2003, 1–17.
- (with Margaret Harris) 'Charles Waldstein waits upon George Eliot', *George Eliot-George Henry Lewes Studies* 44–5, 12–25.
- 'Classics in the curriculum up to the 1960s', in: J. Morwood (ed.), *The Teaching of Classics*, Cambridge, 1–5.
- 'Mrs Gladstone's drawers: language and identity in Victorian families', *Australasian Victorian Studies Journal* 9, 1–16.

- *'Sexy ghosts and gay grammarians: Kennedy's Latin Primer in Britten's Turn of the Screw', *Paradigm* 2.6, 9–13.
- Review of W.M. Calder, R. Scott Smith, J. Vaio (eds.), *Teaching the English Wissenschaft. The Letters of Sir George Cornewall Lewis to Karl Otfried Müller (1828–1839)*, Classical Review 53, 262.
- Review of S. Goldhill, *Who Needs Greek? Contests in the Cultural History of Hellenism*, Journal of Hellenic Studies 12, 262–3.

2004
- Articles on E.H. Barker, Marion and Julia Kennedy, T.H. Key, E.D.A. Morshead, Gilbert Murray, J.P. Postgate, W.H.D. Rouse, H.J. Roby, and E.A. Sonnenschein, for *Oxford Dictionary of National Biography*, 60 vols., Oxford, and online at https://www.oxforddnb.com/
- Articles on E.A. Abbott, J.B. Allen, E.V. Arnold, Thomas Arnold, T.K. Arnold, E.H. Barker, M.A. Bayfield, C.G. Botting, G.G. Bradley, Samuel Butler, H.M. Butler, Janet Case, John Coleridge, A.M. Cook, Ronald Knox, R.W. Livingstone, Henry Malden, H.C.F. Mason, J.E. Millard, Edward Miller, E.D.A. Morshead, J.A. Nairn, M.A. North, T.E. Page, W.C. Perry, Agnata Ramsay, F.T. Rickards, H.J. Roby, W.H.D. Rouse, W.G. Rutherford, Leonhard Schmitz, John Sergeaunt, Walter Shewring, Isaac Smedley, E.A. Sonnenschein, J.C. Stobart, Edmond Warre, Francis Warre-Cornish, J.S. Watson, S.E. Winbolt, Charles Wordsworth, and Christopher Wordsworth, for *Dictionary of British Classicists*, 3 vols., ed. R.B. Todd, Bristol.
- * 'Edward Adolf Sonnenschein and the politics of linguistic authority in England 1880–1930', in: A. Linn/N. McLelland (eds.), *Flores Grammaticae: Essays in Memory of Vivien Law*, Münster, 211–19.
- * 'From one Museum to another: the *Museum Criticum* (1813–26) and the *Philological Museum* (1831–3)', *Victorian Periodicals Review* 3, 289–314.
- Review of S. Dyson, Eugenie Sellers Strong: Portrait of an Archaeologist, *New England Classical Journal* 31, 333–335.

2005
- (edited) *The Owl of Minerva: The Cambridge Praelections of 1906. Reassessments of Richard Jebb, James Adam, Walter Headlam, Henry Jackson, William Ridgeway and Arthur Verrall*. Proceedings of the Cambridge Philological Society Supplementary volume 28, Cambridge.
- (edited) Lord Lyttelton, *Contributions towards a Glossary of the Glynne Language [1851]*, Newcastle.
- 'Flying at dusk: the 1906 praelections' and 'Reading Jebb: life and afterlife', in: Stray 2005 [*Owl of Minerva*], 1–12, 13–24.
- 'The Glynnese Glossary: language and identity in Victorian families', in: Stray 2005 [*Glynne Language*], vii–lv.
- (with Mary Beard) 'The Academy abroad: the nineteenth-century origin of the British School at Athens', in: M.J. Daunton, (ed), *The Organization of Knowledge in Victorian Britain*, Oxford, 371–387.
- 'Charles Astor Bristed', *Oxford Dictionary of National Biography* (online at https://www.oxforddnb.com/)
- 'From oral to written examination: Oxford, Cambridge and Dublin 1700–1914', *History of Universities* 20, 76–130.
- *'Scholars, gentlemen and schoolboys: the authority of Latin in nineteenth and twentieth-century England', in: C. Burnett/N. Mann (eds.), *Britannia Latina: Latin in the Culture of Great Britain from the Middle Ages to the Twentieth Century*, Oxford, 194–208.

2006

- (edited) *Travellers to Greece*, Oxford.
- 'The history of the discipline', in: E. Bispham/T. Harrison/B. Sparkes (eds.), *Edinburgh Companion to Ancient Greece and Rome*, Edinburgh, 3–8.
- Introduction to Smith, W. (ed.) *Dictionary of Greek and Roman Geography* [1878], 2 vols., London, I. vi–xvi.
- 'Marshall's Cambridge', in: T. Raffaelli/G. Becattini/M. Dardi (eds.), *The Elgar Companion to Alfred Marshall*, Cheltenham, 99–104.
- *'Paper wraps stone: the beginnings of educational lithography', *Journal of the Printing Historical Society* n.s. 9, 13–29.
- 'Teaching and learning the classics', in: C. Kallendorf (ed.), *Handbook of the Classical Tradition*, Oxford, 5–14.
- (with Robert Ackerman) 'An unknown contemporary review of K.O. Müller's 'History and Antiquities of the Doric Race', *Illinois Classical Studies* 50, 181–218.

2007

- (edited) *Classical Books: Scholarship and Publishing 1800–2000*. Bulletin of the Institute of Classical Studies, Supp. Vol. 101, London.
- (edited) *Gilbert Murray Reassessed: Hellenism, Theatre, and International Politics*, Oxford.
- (edited) *Oxford Classics: Teaching and Learning 1800–2000*, London.
- (edited) *Remaking the Classics: Literature, Genre and Media in Britain 1800–2000*, London.
- 'Classics', in: L. Howsam *et al.*, 'What the Victorians learned', *Journal of Victorian Culture* 12, 263–267.
- 'Introduction; a neglected genre', in: Stray 2007 [*Classical Books*], 1–6.
- * 'Sir William Smith and his dictionaries: a study in scarlet and black', in: Stray 2007 [*Classical Books*], 35–54.
- *'Jebb's Sophocles: an edition and its maker', in: Stray 2007 [*Classical Books*], 75–96.
- 'Introduction', in: Stray 2007 [*Gilbert Murray*], 1–16.
- * 'Non-identical twins: Classics in nineteenth-century Oxford and Cambridge', in: Stray 2007 [*Oxford Classics*], 1–13.
- 'Preface', in: Stray 2007 [*Remaking the Classics*], ix–xii.
- * 'Politics, Culture, and Scholarship: Classics in the *Quarterly Review*', in: J. Cutmore (ed.), *Conservatism and the Quarterly Review*, London, 87–106, 233–238.
- * 'The rise and fall of Porsoniasm', *Cambridge Classical Journal* 53, 40–71.
- Introduction to Smith, W. (ed.) *Dictionary of Greek and Roman Biography and Mythology* [1880], 3 vols., London, 1. v–xvi
- Introduction to W. Smith (ed.), *Dictionary of Greek and Roman Culture* [1890], 2 vols., London, I.v–xviii.
- Review of J. Henderson, *'Oxford Reds': Classic Commentaries on Latin Classics*, *Journal of Roman Studies* 97, 309–310.

2008

- (edited) *An American in Victorian Cambridge: Charles Astor Bristed's Five Years in an English University (1852)*, Exeter/Chicago.
- 'Introduction', in: Stray 2008 [*An American*], xiii–xxxiv.
- (edited with L.P. Hardwick) *A Companion to Classical Receptions*, Oxford.
- (with Gillian Sutherland) 'Educational publishing', in: D.J. McKitterick (ed.), *Cambridge History of the Book in England vol. 6: 1830–1914*, Cambridge, 359–381.

- 'Introduction' to reprint of *Quarterly Journal of Education* [10 vols., 1831–5], London, v–xvii.
- Review of A. Burnett (ed.), *The Letters of A.E. Housman*, *Journal of Hellenic Studies* 128, 298.
- Review of V. Coltman, *Fabricating the Antique: Neoclassicism in Britain, 1760–1800*, *American Historical Review* 113, 1597–1598.

2009
- (edited with D.J. Butterfield) *A.E. Housman, Classical Scholar*, London.
- (edited with Judith P. Hallett) *British Classics Outside England: The Academy and Beyond*, Waco, TX.
- 'Introduction', in: Butterfield/Stray 2009, 1–10.
- (with Judith P. Hallett) 'Introduction', in: Hallett/Stray 2009, 1–11.
- 'Housman and R.C. Jebb: intellectual styles and the politics of metre', in: Butterfield/Stray 2009, 155–174.
- Review of N. Aldridge, *GB: Master or Monster? A Biography of Geoffrey Bolton*, *Classical Review* 59, 642.

2010
- (edited) *Classical Dictionaries: Past, Present and Future*, London.
- '"Patriots and professors": a century of Roman studies, 1910–2010', *Journal of Roman Studies* 100, 1–31 = *Britannia* 41, 1–31.
- 'Liddell and Scott: myths and markets', in: Stray 2010, 94–118.
- Review of A. Craik, *Mr Hopkins' Men: Cambridge Reform and British Mathematics in the 19th Century*, *History of Universities* 25, 219–225.
- Review of L. Mitchell, *Maurice Bowra: A Life*, *Classical Review* 60, 296–298.

2011
- 'On first looking into Liddell & Scott', *Classical Association News* 45, December, 1–2.
- (with Arthur Burns), 'The Greek-play bishop: polemic, prosopography and nineteenth-century prelates', *Historical Journal* 54, 1013–1038.
- Introduction to Sandys, J.E., *A History of Classical Scholarship* [1903–8], London, I.vii–xvii.
- 'Lex Wrecks: a tale of two Latin dictionaries', *Dictionaries* 32, 66–81.
- 'Reading silence: the books that never were', in: A. Verlinsky et al. (eds.), *Variante loquella. Alexandro Gavrilov septuagenario*, St.Petersburg [=*Hyperboreus* 16–17], 527–538.
- 'T.B. Macaulay', in: A.T. Grafton/G. Most/S. Settis (eds.), *The Classical Tradition*, Cambridge, MA, 551–2.

2012
- (edited, with Stephen Harrison) *Expurgating the Classics: Editing Out in Greek and Latin*, London.
- (with Stephen Harrison) 'Introduction', in: Harrison/Stray 2012, 1–7.
- 'The Oxford Latin Dictionary: A historical introduction', in: P.G.W. Glare (ed.), *The Oxford Latin Dictionary*, 2nd ed., Oxford, x–xvii.
- 'Rank (dis)order in Cambridge 1753–1909: the Wooden Spoon', *History of Universities* 26, 163–201.
- 'Virgil in English education', in: R. Thomas/J. Ziolkowski (eds.), *The Virgil Encyclopedia*, Oxford/Malden MA, 1131–1132.

2013
- *Sophocles' Jebb: A Life in Letters*. Cambridge Classical Journal, Supplement 38, Cambridge.
- 'The absent academy in 19th-century Britain', *Hyperboreus* 19, 214–226.
- 'Classics', 'Education', and 'History and law', in: S. Eliot (ed.), *History of Oxford University Press 2: 1780–1896*, Oxford, 435–470, 472–510, 559–582.
- 'Classics' in: W.R. Louis (ed.), *History of Oxford University Press 3: 1896–1970*, Oxford, 423–440.
- 'Women and Classics in Victorian Oxbridge: parallels and contrasts', in: D. Lateiner/B. Gold/J. Perkins (eds.), *Roman Literature, Gender and Reception: Domina Illustris*, London, 252–266.
- Review of M.M. Augello/M.E.L. Guidi (eds.), *The Economic Reader. Textbooks, Manuals and the Dissemination of the Economic Sciences during the Nineteenth and Early Twentieth Centuries*, European Journal of the History of Economic Thought 20, 672–677.

2014
- (with Stuart Wallace) '"The Earl and the Doctor": Richard Jebb, James Donaldson and university politics in Victorian Scotland', *The Scottish Historical Review* 93, 109–141.
- 'Eduard Fraenkel: an exploration', *Syllecta Classica* 25, 113–172.
- Review of S. Lewis, *Boundless Life: A Biography of Andrew Joseph Armstrong*, Carlyle Studies Annual 30, 185–188.
- Review of E. Richardson, *Classical Victorians: Scholars, Scoundrels and Generals in Pursuit of Antiquity*, Bryn Mawr Classical Review 2014.6.5. https://bmcr.brynmawr.edu/

2015
- (edited, with Graham Whitaker) *Classics in Practice: Studies in the History of Scholarship*. Bulletin of the Institute of Classical Studies, Supp. 128, London.
- 'A divided text: Shackleton Bailey, W.S. Watt and Cicero's *Epistulae ad Atticum*', in: Stray/Whitaker 2015, 115–128.
- 'Classics and social closure', in: H. Stead/E. Hall (eds.), *Greek and Roman Classics in the British Struggle for Social Reform*, London, 116–137.
- 'Education and reading', in: N. Vance/J. Wallace (eds.), *Oxford History of Classical Reception in English Literature*, Vol. 4: 1790–1880, Oxford, 79–102.
- Review of S. Butler (ed.), *Deep Classics: Rethinking Classical Reception*, Classics Ireland 21–22, 169–72.

2016
- (edited, with Christina S. Kraus), *Classical Commentaries: Explorations in a Scholarly Genre*, Oxford.
- 'A Teutonic monster in Oxford: the making of Fraenkel's *Agamemnon*', in: Kraus/Stray 2016, 39–57.
- 'Disciplinary histories of Classics', *History of Universities* 29, 112–134.
- 'Greek in nineteenth-century Britain', in: A. Karanapou (ed.), *British-Greek Relations: Aspects of their Recent History*, Athens, 43–54.
- 'Kenneth Sisam', *Oxford Dictionary of National Biography* https://www.oxforddnb.com/
- 'A semi-sacred monster: Charles Wordsworth's *Graecae Grammaticae Rudimenta*', *Philologia Classica* [St Petersburg] 11, 98–115.

2017
- 'Eduard Fraenkel (1888–1970)', in: S. Crawford/K. Ulmschneider/J. Elsner (eds.), *Ark of Civilization: Oxford and Refugee Academics in the Arts during World War II*, Oxford, 180–197.

2018
- *Classics in Britain: Scholarship, Education, and Publishing, 1800–2000*, Oxford.
- 'From *odium* to *bellum*: classical scholars at war in Europe and America, 1800–1924', *Classical Receptions Journal* 10, 356–375.
- 'Ian Jackson, 1951–2018: the moment of Mushri', *The Book Collector* 67, 238–239.

2019
- (edited, with M.J. Clarke and J.T. Katz), *Liddell and Scott: The History, Methodology and Languages of the World's Leading Lexicon of Ancient Greek*, Oxford.
- (edited, with Christopher Pelling and Stephen Harrison), *Rediscovering E.R. Dodds: Scholarship, Poetry, and the Paranormal*, Oxford.
- 'A note on the history of the Lexicon', in: Stray/Clarke/Katz 2019, xvii–xviii.
- '*Liddell and Scott* in historical context: Victorian beginnings, twentieth-century developments', in: Stray/Clarke/Katz 2019, 3–24.
- (with Christopher Pelling), 'Introduction: a missing person?', in: Stray/Pelling/Harrison 2019, 1–9.
- 'An Irishman abroad', in: Stray/Pelling/Harrison 2019, 10–35.
- 'Stereotactic: a note on the lexicography of radiotherapy', online at *www.academia.edu*.
- 'The Glory and the Grandeur: John Clarke Stobart and the defence of high culture in a democratic age', *History of Classical Scholarship* 1, 135–73, online at https://www.hcsjournal.org/ojs/index.php/hcs
- 'Brexit as banquet: A.E. Housman on the history of classical scholarship', *The Housman Society Journal* 45, 40–64.

2020
- *Sophocles' Jebb: A Life in Letters*. Cambridge Classical Journal, Supplement 38, Cambridge. Ebook version of 2013a.
- 'Housman and W.H. Semple: a newly-discovered correspondence', *The Housman Society Journal* 46, 8–20.
- Review of A. Nash/C. Squires/I.R. Willison (eds.), *The Cambridge History of the Book in Britain Vol. VII: The Twentieth Century and beyond*, *The Library: Transactions of the Bibliographical Society* 21, 251–253.

2021 [all forthcoming]
- 'De Morgan as commentator on education', in: K. Attar/A. Rice/C.A. Stray (eds.), *Augustus De Morgan, Polymath: A Reassessment at 150*, Cambridge.
- 'Eduard Fraenkel in Germany, England, Italy, and almost in the US', in: Danuta Renu Shanzer/ Ward W. Briggs/Sonja Schreiner (eds.), *Qui Trans Mare Currunt: Classicists in Transit(ion) between the German-Speaking World, the UK, and North America: 1850–1985*, Berlin/Boston.
- 'The education of Robert Leslie Ellis', in: L. Verburgt (ed.), *A Prodigy of Universal Genius: Robert Leslie Ellis, 1817–1859*, Heidelberg.
- 'Hunting the scholar: Adventures in archives', in: C. Serracino (ed.), *Ardet Amans* (Festschrift for Horatio Vella), Santa Venera, Malta.
- 'A riotous Commencement: Degree Day 1831', *The Eagle* (St John's College, Cambridge).
- 'Towards a sociology of scholarly forgetting', *History of the Humanities* 5.

- 'Working together: classical scholars in collaboration', in: S.J. Harrison/C.B.R. Pelling (eds.), *Classical Scholarship and its History from the Renaissance to the Present: Essays in Honour of Christopher Stray*, Berlin/Boston, 377–99.
- Review of S. Ogilvie/G. Safran (eds.), *The Whole World in a Book: Dictionaries in the Nineteenth Century*, The Library: Transactions of the Bibliographical Society 21, 102–4.
- Review of K.S. Staikos, *Intellectual Routes of the Greeks: Through the Manuscript and Printed Book. Volume 1: 13th to Mid-16th Centuries*, The Library: Transactions of the Bibliographical Society, 21 [forthcoming]

2022 [forthcoming]
- *Success and failure in early nineteenth-century Cambridge: J.M.F. Wright's Alma Mater (1827)*. Edited with an introduction and annotations. University of Exeter Press.
- 'The slaughter of 1841: Mathematics and Classics in early Victorian Cambridge', *History of Universities* 34.

List of Contributors

Ward Briggs is Carolina Distinguished Professor of Classics and Louise Fry Scudder Professor of Humanities, emeritus, at the University of South Carolina.

David Butterfield is Senior Lecturer in Classics at the University of Cambridge and Fellow and Director of Studies in Classics at Queens' College.

James Clackson is Professor of Comparative Philology at the University of Cambridge and Fellow and Director of Studies in Classics at Jesus College.

Michael Clarke is Established Professor of Classics at NUI Galway.

Jaś Elsner is Professor of Late Antique Art at the University of Oxford and Senior Research Fellow at Corpus Christi College.

Roy Gibson is Professor in the Department of Classics and Ancient History at the University of Durham.

Edith Hall is Professor of Classics at King's College London.

Judith P. Hallett is Professor of Classics and Distinguished Scholar-Teacher Emerita at the University of Maryland, College Park.

Lorna Hardwick is Professor Emerita of Classical Studies at the Open University.

Stephen Harrison is Professor of Latin Literature at the University of Oxford and Senior Research Fellow at Corpus Christi College.

Robert A. Kaster is emeritus Kennedy Foundation Professor of Latin Language and Literature and emeritus Professor of Classics at Princeton University.

Christina Shuttleworth Kraus is Thomas A. Thacher Professor of Latin at Yale University.

Christopher Pelling is emeritus Regius Professor of Greek at the University of Oxford and emeritus Student of Christ Church.

Christopher Stray is Honorary Research Fellow in the Department of History and Classics at Swansea University.

Graham Whitaker is Honorary Research Fellow in the School of Humanities at the University of Glasgow.

Index

Aberdeen University 145
Aberystwyth: University College of Wales, Aberystwyth 132
Academic Assistance Council 331
Achilles Tatius 212
Adam, James 142
Adams, John 92
Addison, Joseph 51
Adkins, Arthur 362
Aeschines 109
Aeschylus 26 n. 29, 50, 123, 133 n. 15, 156–8, 209, 212, 213, 214, 307 n. 21, 325 n. 27, 328, 336–9, 388–9
Aesop 35, 73 n. 42
Agricola, Rodolphus 73–4
Ainsworth, Robert 49
Alan of Lille 88
Alba, Duke of 66
Albanus Torinus (Alban Thorer) 89
Alesia 265, 268
Allan, William 188 n. 50, 195 n. 59, 211–12
Allegheny College 279
Allen, W. Sidney 133 n. 15
Allen, William Francis 277
Allyn & Bacon (publishers) 249, 251–2, 254
Allyn, John 251 *see also* Allyn & Bacon
American Academy of Arts and Sciences 279
American Anthropological Association 297
American Antiquarian Society 279
American Association for the Advancement of Science 279
American Book Company 251, 255 n. 23
American Classical League 297, 378
American Historical Association 297
American Numismatic Society 279
American Philological Association 5, 277–300, 303 n. 13, 309, 311
American Philosophical Society 279
Amis, Kingsley 194 n. 65
Anacreontea 46
Anderson, J.G.C. 219 n. 1

Anderson, William B. 287
Andrewes, Antony 221, 226–8, 234, 384
Andrews, Stephen Pearl 295
Anthon, Charles 251–70
Antiphon 210
Antwerp 66
Apollonius of Rhodes 189, 209, 211
Apostles 134–5
Appleton (publishers) 249, 251–3, 262
Apuleius 200, 209
Arion 42
Aristophanes 118, 177, 228
Aristotle 47, 123, 128 n. 75, 226 n. 26, 352 n. 6, 355
Armenian 144
Arnold, Albert N. 282
Arnold, Matthew 162
Arnold, Thomas 106, 155, 226
Ash, Rhiannon 199, 211–12, 214 n. 113, 385
Ashmolean Museum, Oxford 390
Association for Roman Military Equipment Studies 377
Association pour l'Encouragement des Études Grecques en France 278, 284, 291 n. 32
Athenaeus 118
Athenian Tribute Lists 229
Atkinson, Basil Ferris Campbell 145
Audette, Karen 363 n. 42
Aufstieg und Niedergang der römischen Welt 369–71
Augustine, St 38, 192, 193, 194, 200, 210, 212
Augustus 192
Aurelius Victor, Sextus 41
Aurelius, Marcus 38
Ausonius 200
Austen, Jane 382
Austin, R.G. 178 nn. 11–12, 220
Ayres, Lewis 361

Babington, Churchill 122
Bacchylides 210

Badian, Ernst 370
Bailey, Cyril 219, 220
Bailey, Harold 146
Baker, Mona 23–4
Balliol College, Oxford 383
Bancroft, George 277
Banks, Jonathan 39
Bann, Stephen 263
Barber, E.A. 219 n. 1
Barsby, John 206
Batrachomyomachia 46
Battezzato, Luigi 188 n. 50, 212
Baudri de Bourgeuil 85
Bayley, John 325, 333, 335
Beard, Dame Mary 321 n. 10, 341, 395 n. 38
Bedford Modern School 145
Bendall, Cecil 132 n. 12, 139
Benfey, Theodor 139
Bennett, Alan 339 n. 66
Benoît de Sainte-Maure 86–8
Bentley, Richard 158, 380, 388
Berlin, Sir Isaiah 332, 344, 345
Bernays, Jacob 371 n. 67, 387
Betts, John 181 n. 19
Bhardwaj, Shiv 341
Bible: New English Bible 393
Bible: Revised Standard Version 392–3
Bingham, William 251 n. 7
Birley, Anthony R. 354 n. 17, 359
Birley, Eric 354
Black Lives Matter 26, 323
Blackie, J.S. 158
Blair, Hugh 82
Blatchford, Samuel 253 n. 14
Bliss, Porter C. 289
Bloch, Herbert 312, 313
Blomfield, Charles 379, 383
Blyden, Edward Wilmot 285, 293
Boccaccio, Giovanni 94 n. 55
Boise, Alice Robinson 289
Boise, James Robinson 289 n. 28
Bonbright, Daniel 277
Bond, Godfrey W. 188 n. 50
Boodle, E.W. 287 n. 24
Booth, Mary L. 289
Bopp, Franz 133, 277–8

Boston Museum of Fine Arts 362
Bosworth, A.B. 221, 225–6, 234, 242
Bourdieu, Pierre 309
Bowie, Angus 195 n. 69, 196–7, 199 n. 89, 211–12, 228
Bowie, Ewen 191, 200, 212
Bowra, Maurice 219, 332 n. 41, 388
Boyer, Abel 46
Braithwaite, A.W. 219 n. 1, 229 n. 32
Braund, Susanna Morton 210, 214
Braunholtz, E.G.W. 133 n. 14
Braunholtz, G.E.K. 133 n. 14, 146
Brewer, Fisk Parsons 293
Brezzi, Paolo 368
Brink, Charles Oscar 176–7, 180, 185 n. 36
Briscoe, John 212, 242
Bristed, Charles Astor 282, 287, 288
Bristol 24–6; *see also* Colston Hall
British Broadcasting Corporation 394–5
British Museum 145, 363, 390, 394
British School at Athens 391
British School at Rome 391
Brocklebank, Thomas 113 n. 35
Brooklyn College 307–9
Brown, Andrew 19
Brown, Robert 269
Bruce, John Collingwood 353 n. 9
Brugmann, Karl 141–2, 145, 147
Bryn Mawr College 143, 250, 290, 302, 306, 308, 309, 313
Buckingham, Charles Jedediah 282
Budelmann, Felix 196 n. 75, 202 n. 95, 212
Budgell, Eustace 49
Buecheler, Franz 352 n. 8
Bullion, Revd. Peter 252 n. 9
Burkert, Walter 361
Burn, Robert 390
Burney, Charles 381
Burnham, Revd. Edwin Otway 285, 287, 288
Burrow, Thomas 145
Burstein, Stanley 355
Butcher, Samuel 125
Butler, H.E. 219 n. 1, 229 n. 32
Butler, Henry Montagu 110

Butler, Samuel 110, 122 n. 56, 382
Butler, Samuel senior 103
Byrne, Oliver 256 n. 30

Caesar, Julius 4–5, 37, 43, 52, 249–74
Calcutta 139
Calder III, William M. 313
Calhoun College, Yale 323
Calhoun, John 323
Callimachus 41, 332, 365, 366
Calpurnius Siculus 326 n. 30
Cambridge Greek and Latin Classics ('green-and-yellow') 4, 175–217, 236, 242
'Cambridge Network' 381
Cambridge Philological Society 139, 141–4, 391
Cambridge, University of 3, 4, 49, 53, 54, 101–30, 131–54, 169, 177, 201, 204, 326, 386, 389–90, 392; *see also* names of individual colleges
Cameron, David 20
Campbell, Lewis 295, 358
Cannon, Walter F. 381
Canterbury 70
Caplan, Harry 313
CARA (Council for At-Risk Academics) 331
Cardiff: University College of Wales, Cardiff 145
Carey, Chris 188 n. 48, 202 n. 95, 205, 209
Carlyle, Thomas 169
Carnegie, Jim 220
Carvill, C. and C.H. (publishers) 253
Cary, Max 219 n. 1, 229 n. 32
Casaubon, Isaac 46
Case, Mary Emily 290
Cassirer, Ernst 351, 360
Catullus 168, 178 n. 12, 195, 307 n. 21, 364
Cavendish, William, 7th Duke of Devonshire 123
Caxton, William 162
Celtic 132, 147
Césaire, Aimé 367
Chadwick, Owen 354
Chalk, Henry 220

Channin, Eva 290 n. 30
Chapman, Matthew 104
Charlemagne 85–6
Charles I of England 37
Charterhouse 47, 115
Cheltenham College 145
Cheltenham Ladies College 143
Chesnutt, Helen Maria 290
Chesterfield, Earl of 46, 49
Chèvre d'Or, Simon 85
Child, Francis James 277
Christ Church, Oxford 46, 54, 158, 382–3
Christ's College, Cambridge 124, 139
Christenson, David 195 n. 69, 210, 212
Churchill, A. & J. 42
Cicero 35, 40, 41, 42, 47, 53, 83, 183, 205, 209, 210–11, 213, 220, 253, 358, 370, 377, 384
Claghorn, Kate Holladay 290 n. 30
Clare College, Cambridge 124
Clarendon Ancient History Series 242–3
Clark, A.C. 226 n. 26
Clark, Gillian 193–4, 200
Clark, John Willis 117
Clark, William 390
Clarke, Howard 285
Classical Association 3, 177 n. 10, 378, 391, 393
Classical Association of Scotland 391
Classical Association of the Atlantic States 297
Classical Association of the Middle West and South 297
Classical Association of the Pacific States 297
Classical Museum 393
Classical Quarterly 393
Classical Review 393
Claudian 200
Clay, Jenny Strauss 312 n. 32, 313
Clayman, Dee Lesser 313
Cleland, Max 14
Cleon 114, 235
Cobet, Carel Gabriel 127
Cockerill, Thomas 42
Coffey, Michael 209, 214 n. 112
Coleman, Kathleen 312 n. 32

Coleman, Robert 184, 205, 209, 213
Collinge, N.E. 133 n. 15
Collingwood, R.G. 353 n. 10
Colston Hall, Bristol 24–5, 323 n. 13
Colston, Edward 25–6
Colton, Revd. Dr Henry Martyn 282–3, 287, 289
Columbia College 250 n. 6, 253
Colvin, Sir Sidney 111 n. 27
Comfort, George Fisk 5, 278–81, 286–8, 293–4, 296
Comfort, Ralph 296 n. 43
Commager, Steele 310
Comparative Philology 131–54
Conington, Francis Thirkill 159
Conington, John 4, 155–72
Conington, Revd. Richard 155 n. 3
Conington, Sarah 155 n. 3
Constantine 192
Conti, Natale 95
Conway, Robert Seymour 132 n. 13, 140–3, 145
Cook, Albert S. 294
Coope, Ursula 321 n. 7, 341
Cope, Edward 123, 226 n. 26
Corbyn, Jeremy 327 n. 33
Cornell University 159 n. 22, 313
Cornford, Francis 234, 380–3
Corpus Christi College, Oxford 5, 24–5, 158–60, 319–47, 386
Corpus Inscriptionum Graecarum 391
Cory, William 122
Coulter, Cornelia Caitlin 313
Covent Garden 46, 52
Cowell, Edward Byles 139, 147
Cowley, Sir Steve 320, 322, 345
Cowper, William 165
Creech, Thomas 168
Crosby, Revd. Howard 281, 283–5
Cullyer, Helen 312
Curio, Celio Secondo 75
Currey, William 389
Curtius, Georg 140, 142, 277
Curtius, Quintus 42

D'Ooge, Martin 294
Dacier, André 46
Dacier, Anne 40–41, 43, 46
Dale, A.M. 326 n. 31
Damas, Léon-Gontran 367
Damon, Cynthia 210
Danet, Pierre 42, 46
Darbishire, Herbert Dukinfield 143–4
Dares Phrygius 4, 41, 81–98
Davidson, Charles 103
Davies, Gilbert 220
Davies, John K. 243
Dawe, R.D. 182 n. 22, 183 n. 27, 184 n. 31, 205, 209–10
Dawkins, Richard MacGillivray 145
Day, A.M. 259
De Coubertin, Baron Pierre 361 n. 36
De Coubertin, Yvonne 361 n. 36
De Jong, Irene 211, 214 n. 114
De Munn, Mrs M.W. 289 n. 29
De Regibus, Luca 352 n. 8
De Romilly, Jacqueline 364–5
De Saint-Maure, Charles *see* Montausier, Duc de
De Witt, Norman 289
Defoe, Daniel 51
Deighton Bell 109
Delphin series 4, 37, 40–6, 91, 177
Demosthenes 40, 108–9, 188 n. 48, 299–10, 212, 220, 236, 358
Denniston, J.D. 219, 229 n. 32
Denyer, Nicholas 202 n. 95, 210–12
Desprez, Louis 42
DiAngelo, Robin 17
Dickinson College Commentaries 197
Dickinson, Mary C. 289 n. 29
Dictys 41, 83, 91
Didot *see* Firmin-Didot, Amboise
Diels, Hermann 392
Dilettanti *see* Society of Dilettanti
Dindorf, Karl 385, 388
Dindorf, Ludwig 385
Dio Chrysostom 209, 214 n. 112
Diodorus Siculus 238
Dionysius of Halicarnassus 40, 43
Disraeli, Benjamin 127
Dobson, William 105
Dodds, E.R. 78, 219 n. 1, 364 n. 48, 387–90

Donaldson, John William 120-1, 136, 156-7, 384
Dover, Sir Kenneth 205-6, 209, 213, 221, 226, 227-8, 234, 237 n. 55, 322, 384, 387-8
Dow, Sterling 353
Dresemius, Samuel 91
Drew Theological Seminary 279
Drury, Henry 116 n. 41
Dryden, John 4, 40 n. 19, 44, 45, 49, 165
Du Guernier, Luc 46
Dugas, Charles 304
Dunbar, Nan V. 236 n. 51
Durham University 121
Durkheim, Émile 380
Dwight, Revd. Benjamin Woodbridge 281, 283, 287, 288, 289
Dyck, Andrew 210, 211
Dyer, George 43

Easterling, P.E. 176, 178 n. 14, 179-89, 190 n. 53, 191 n. 57, 200, 201 n. 93, 209
Eden, P.T. 196 n. 73, 209
Edgren, August Hjalmar 285
Edict of Nantes 46
Edinburgh University 104, 132, 166, 167, 169
Edleston, Joseph 113 n. 35, 122
Edward III of England 37
Edwards, Catharine 212
Edwards, Revd. John 121
Ehrenberg, Victor 369
Eitrem, Samson 364
Eleanor of Aquitaine 86
Ellingson, Mary Ross 360
Elmsley, Peter 381
Elwell, Levi Henry 290
Ely Cathedral 123
Emmanuel College, Cambridge 140, 146-7
Ennius 73 n. 42, 88, 167, 195
Erasmus 38, 63, 66-76
Ernst, Juliette 303-4, 309-10, 314, 355 n. 18
Espagne, Michael 386
Espirito Santo, Arnaldo do 358 n. 28
Estienne, Henri (Stephanus) 385
Eton College 116 n. 41, 121

Euclid 256 n. 30
Euripides 178 n. 11, 188, 205, 210-12, 219, 225, 228, 230, 337, 360 n. 33, 382
Eutropius 39-41
Evans, Sir Arthur 390
Evans, Thomas 122
Everett, Edward 277

Fantham, Elaine 201, 202, 203-4, 209-10, 312 n. 32
Fédération Internationale des Associations d'Études Classiques 303
Felton, Cornelius C. 282
Felton, Henry 47-8
Fénelon, François 53
Fennell, Charles Augustus Maude 144 n. 67
Ferris, Dr Isaac 280
Festschriften 351-76
Feuling, John Baptist 282, 287
Field, Mrs G.W. 290 n. 30
Fielding, Henry 50, 51
Fiesel, Eva Lehmann 302, 305-6
Fiesel, Ludolf 302 n. 7
Filarete (Antonio di Pietro Averlino) 269
Finley, Sir Moses 11
Firmin-Didot, Amboise 385-6
Fitzpatrick, W.J. 119 n. 50
Fleckeisen, Alfred 352
Flint, Miss M.B. 288
Florus 41, 43
Flower, Michael 197 n. 76, 199 n. 89, 210, 228
Floyd, George 323
Forbes, C.H. 251
Fordyce, C.J. 178 n. 12, 220
Fraenkel, Eduard 5, 24-5, 219 n. 3, 302, 307 n. 21, 319-47, 387-9
Fraenkel, Ruth 319, 335 n. 47
France, Francis 122
Franklin, Susan Braley 290
Fraser, John 145
Frazer, Sir James 226, 229
Fribourg 143
Froben, Johann 63, 71-2
Furneaux, H. 226

Gagarin, Michael 210
Gaidoz, Henri 358 n. 27
Gaisford, Thomas 54, 127, 158–9, 381–2
Galen 200
Galton, Francis 323
Garcia Teijeiro, Manuel 355, 364 n. 45
Garfield, James A. 281
Garnett, James 294
Gartland, Sam 320 n. 5, 321 n. 7, 341
Gärtner, Hans Armin 358 n. 28
Garvie, A.F. 198, 210, 214
Gellius, Aulus 38, 40
Geoffrey of Monmouth 87
George Bell (publishers) 160
Gertz, M.C. 59, 60 n. 4, 79
Gibbs, George 287, 288
Gibert, John C. 212
Gilbert, Cass 269
Gildersleeve, Basil Lanneau 142, 277, 278, 293–5
Giles, Peter 140, 142
Gilman, Daniel Colt 293
Girton College, Cambridge 382
Gjerstad, Einar 366
Gladstone, William Ewart 156, 161, 392
Glasgow University 105, 220–2, 236 n. 51, 297, 351, 370–1
Goetze, Albrecht 306
Goldberg, Sander 211
Gomme, A.W. 4, 219–47, 384
Gomme, Andor 221 n. 12, 222–3
Gomme, Phyllis 221
Gomme, Sir Laurence 221 n. 14
Gomme, Susan 222–3
Gonville and Caius College, Cambridge 66, 124, 139
Goodell, Thomas D. 297 n. 45
Goodwin, Abby Moore 290 n. 30
Goodwin, William Watson 142, 226 n. 26, 242, 277, 282, 288–9, 291, 294–5, 297, 298, 311
Gorgias 238
Gothofredus (Denis Godefroy) 64
Göttingen 134, 139, 161, 277, 278, 291 n. 32, 335 n. 47
Gottschalk, H.B. 356
Gow, James 119 n. 49

Gowers, Emily 196, 211, 214 n. 114
Graevius (Johann Georg Greffe) 43
Gransden, K.W. 183 n. 28, 207 n. 107, 209, 213 n. 111
Gratwick, A.S. 209
Graux, Charles Henri 358
Graves, Revd. C.E. 119
Gray, Thomas 165
Gray, Vivienne 202 n. 95, 210
Graziosi, Barbara 195 n. 69, 211, 214
Greener, Richard Thomas 292–3
Griffin, Jasper 188, 190, 201–2
Griffith, Mark 182 n. 22, 205, 209–10, 213
Grimm, Jacob Ludwig Karl 133–4, 277
Grimm, Wilhelm 133–4
Gronovius (Johann Friedrich Gronow) 43, 59, 64, 69, 76–8
Grote, George 114–7
Grote, John 115, 381
Gruen, Erich 312, 313
Gruter, Jan (Janus Gruterus) 64–8, 69, 76–9
Gudeman, Alfred 353
Guest, Edwin 278
Guido de Columnis 86
Gunning, Henry 113–4
Gunson, William 122
Gurney, Ivor 13 n. 4
Gustaf VI Adolf of Sweden 366–7
Güthenke, Constanze 320 n. 5, 321 n. 7, 331, 336, 341

Haase, Friedrich 59, 78, 353, 371
Habermas, Jürgen 49
Hadley, James 279, 289, 291
Haider, Peter W. 363 n. 44
Haight, Elizabeth Hazelton 313
Haldeman, Samuel Stehmann 282, 286, 287, 289, 291, 295
Hale, Horatio 286
Hallett, Judith P. 12
Hamilton, Edith 301, 308–9
Hampton, Wade 293
Handford, S.A. 219 n. 1, 226 n. 26
Hannibal 52
Harcourt, Sir William 110, 127

Hardie, Philip 189, 190, 199–200, 210
Hardwick, Lorna 303
Hardy, Thomas 43
Hare, Julius Charles 135
Harkness, Albert 251–70, 277 n. 3, 280–2, 287–8, 295
Harper & Brothers (publishers) 249, 250–5, 264
Harper, J.J. 253 *see also* Harper & Brothers
Harrison, Jane 380–3
Harrison, Stephen 214, 320 n. 5, 321 n. 7, 385 n. 22
Harrow School 106, 116
Hart, James Morgan 277
Hart, Samuel 293–4
Hartley, L.P. 328
Harvard University 20, 277, 281 n. 11, 282, 285, 286, 291 n. 44, 308–12
'Harvard Servius' 296
Hase, Charles Benoît 385–6
Haubold, Johannes 195 n. 69, 211, 214
Haupt, Moriz 161, 387
Hawtrey, Edward 121 n. 53
Hays, John 113 n. 35
Head, Barclay Vincent 363
Heaney, Seamus 27
Heidelberg 66
Heinsius, Daniël 388
Heinze, Richard 160 n. 25, 384
Heitland, William 111, 123, 125, 128–9
Helbig, Wolfgang 353 n. 9
Heliodorus 377
Henderson, Isobel 324
Henderson, John 219–20, 230
Henry II of England 85
Henry, Joseph 281
Heraclides of Pontus 355–6
Hermann, Gottfried 156–7, 161
Hermocrates 235
Herodotus 83, 189, 196–7, 199, 210–12, 225, 226, 228, 229, 241, 384
Herrman, Judson 212
Hesiod 43, 122 n. 56
Heyworth, Stephen 201, 212
Hilbold, Ilse 303–4, 309–10
Hildebrandt, Paul 377

Hildyard, James 106–8
Hill, Aaron 45
Hiltbrunner, Otto 365–6
Hind, John 112
Hire, Pauline 190, 200
Hoenigswald, Gabriele Schoepflich 302, 305, 306 n. 19
Hoenigswald, Henry 306 n. 19
Hoffmann, Herbert 362–3
Hogarth, W.D. 219
Holmes, Arthur 122–4
Holmes, T. Rice 269
Holst, Hans 364
Homer 4, 14, 16 n. 5, 35, 40, 43, 49, 53, 81–98, 127, 161, 162, 189, 195 n. 69, 198, 205, 209, 211–12, 214
Hopkinson, Neil 190, 192 n. 61, 200, 202 n. 95, 207 n. 107, 209–12, 214 n. 112
Horace 4, 43, 48, 118, 127, 164–70, 193–4, 196, 202, 209, 210–12, 214 n. 114, 254, 257 n. 35, 307 n. 21, 337, 384
Hornblower, Simon 199 n. 89, 211–12, 221, 226, 227–8, 237, 241, 242
Horton-Smith, Lionel 143
Housman, A.E. 110 n. 22, 185, 236, 380, 392, 393–4
How, W.W. 225, 229 n. 32, 230, 384
Howard, Jane 362–3
Hübner, Emil 387
Hudson, Richard 133 n. 15
Huet, Pierre-Daniel 41–2
Huitink, Luuk 212
Humboldt, Wilhelm von 157, 392
Humphreys, Milton 294
Hunter, L.W. 219 n. 1, 226 n. 26
Hunter, Richard 188 n. 50, 189, 190–1, 199–200, 202 n. 95 206, 209–12, 214
Hurlburt, Revd. Thomas 286, 288
Hurley, Donna 191 n. 56, 199, 210
Hussein, Sadaam 25
Hutchinson, Gregory 210
Huxley, T.H. 118
Hyde, Revd. Annice B. 289

Identity and scholarship 9–31
Isaeus 226
Isidore of Seville 84, 87

Jackson, Henry 110, 112, 125, 127, 133, 389
Jacoby, Felix 361, 364
Jaeger, Werner 312
Jebb, Sir Richard 21, 110, 125, 182 n. 22, 222 n. 15, 297, 389, 392
Jefferson, Thomas 4, 81–2, 84, 91–5
Jerome, St 69–70, 73, 200
Jesuits 36, 41, 45
Jocelyn, H.D. 188 n. 47
Johnson, Samuel 48, 256
Johnson, William (later Cory) 122
Joint Association of Classical Teachers (JACT) 177–82, 186, 188, 197
Jones, Sir William 133, 135 n. 26, 149 n. 93
Jopson, Norman Brooke 145–7
Joseph of Exeter 87–95
Journal des sçavans 393
Journal of Hellenic Studies 394 n. 36
Journal of Roman Studies 394
Jowett, Benjamin 226, 386
Juvenal 42, 214

Kaiser, Alan 360
Kalisch, M.M. 229
Kapp, Ida 365–6
Kaster, Robert 313
Kells, J.H. 182 n. 22, 183, 184 n. 31, 187 n. 43, 206, 208
Kelsey, Francis 251–4, 259–61, 264, 267–8
Kemble, John Mitchell 134–6
Kendrick, Asahel Clark 288, 289
Kenna, Margaret 2
Kennedy, Benjamin Hall 103, 110, 116, 122–3, 135–6, 143
Kennett, Basil 46
Kenney, E.J. 176, 179–89, 190 n. 53, 191 n. 57, 194 n. 65, 195–6, 200, 201 n. 93, 205, 208–11, 213, 385
Key, Thomas Hewitt 132 n. 12, 135
Keynes, Simon 134
Kidd, Ian 361–2
Kiessling, Adolf 160 n. 25, 384
King Edward's School, Birmingham 145

King's College, Cambridge 70, 106, 110, 112, 116, 124
King's College, London 145, 390 n. 28
Klibansky, Raymond 360 n. 33
Kneale, Martha 326, 335
Knox, Peter 189, 210
Kober, Alice 308
Konstan, David 313
Kornhardt, Hildegard 366
Kovacs, David 188 n. 50
Kraus, Christina 199, 202, 202, 209, 211, 214
Kristeller, Paul Oskar 356, 360–1

Lachmann, Karl 159
Lachmann, Vera 302, 305–8
Lady Margaret Hall, Oxford 324, 326
Laemmle, Rebecca 188 n. 50, 212
Lane, George Martin 277
Lanman, Charles Rockwell 294, 297 n. 44
Latham, Henry 113 n. 35
Lausanne, University of 304
Lawrence, T.E. 224
Layamon 87
Le Fèvre, Anne *see* Dacier, Anne
Le Fèvre, Tanneguy 41
Le Tellier, Michel 42
Leach, Abby 290, 311–3
Lectrix 197–8
Lehmann-Hartleben, Karl 306
Leibniz, Gottfried Wilhelm 42
Leiden 66
Leighton, Robert F. 295
Leipzig 140, 142, 143 n. 63, 156, 301 n. 4, 385
Lemprière's Classical Dictionary 255 n. 22, 383–4
Leo, Friedrich 167, 388
Lesky, Albin 364–5 n. 48
Lévêcque, Pierre 356
Lewis, David M. 384
Liapis, Vayos 188 n. 50
Liddell, Henry 383–5
Lincoln's Inn Fields 46
Linguistic Society of America 296
Linwood, Revd. William 156, 159

Lipsius, Justus (Joest Lips) 64, 66, 76–8, 264–7
Livy 209, 212
Locke, John 48
Loeb Classical Library 395
London University 132 *see also* names of colleges
London: School of Slavonic Studies 146
Long Crendon 221–2
Long, George 160
Longinus 38, 47
Longus 191, 200, 212
Lonsdale, James 121 n. 53, 122, 126–7
Lord, Frances Ellen 290 n. 30
Lorsch 60
Louis XIV of France 37, 40–2
Lounsbury, Thomas R. 289, 291
Lowrey, Rebecca S. 289 n. 29
Lowther, Sir John 40
Lucan 37, 180 n. 15, 200, 209–12, 214 n. 114
Lucian 211
Lucilius 168
Lucretius 118, 159, 167–8, 180, 184, 187 n. 43, 195–6, 205, 208, 211, 213, 219 n. 3
Lumb, Thomas 377
Lusher, Mr, of Pembroke College, Oxford 44
Lushington, Edward Law 105
Lyly, William 39
Lyons, Sir John 133 n. 15
Lysias 205, 209
Lyttelton, Lord 110

MacCary, W.T. 209
Macedonia 323 n. 13
Macleane, Arthur 160
Macleod, Colin 184 n. 33, 198, 205, 209, 389
Macmillan (publishers) 177, 180
MacNeice, Louis 388
Macpherson, James 82
Macurdy, Grace Harriet 301–2, 306, 308–9
Madvig, Johan Nikolai 352
Maehler, Herwig 202 n. 95, 320
Magdalen College, Oxford 155

Magdalene College, Cambridge 47
Magill, E.H. 283, 287
Maidwell, Lewis 40
Maittaire, Michel 46
Malik, Kenan 18
Maltby, Edward 122 n. 56
Manchester University 132
Mankin, David 193–4, 210–11, 214 nn. 113–4
Mann, Sir Horace 379
Manuwald, Gesine 191, 212, 214 n. 114
March, Francis Andrew 288, 294, 295, 298
Marchand, Suzanne 392
Marincola, John 197 n. 76, 199 n. 89, 210, 228
Marlborough, 1st Duke of 47
Marmodoro, Anna 341
Marouzeau, Jules 304
Martial 44, 214
Martin, Francis 104
Martin, R.H. 197, 205
Martin, Theodore 164
Maryland, University of 307
Mason, Abraham John 258, 264, 268
Mason, Ellen F. 290 n. 30
Mastronarde, Donald 188 n. 50, 205
Matthews, Peter 133 n. 15
Mattingly, Harold 358
Maury, Revd. Magruder 286, 288
Maury, Revd James 91–2
May, Thomas 37
Mayer, Roland 202, 214 n. 112
Mayor, J.E.B. 110, 122, 136
Mazon, Paul 278
McCain, John 14
McCartee, Dr H. 289
McCarthy, Barbara P. 310
McCosh, James 287, 288
McGill, Scott 183 n. 28
McKinstry, Harriett E. 290 n. 30
McManus, Barbara 301
McMaster University 361
Meiggs, Russell 384
Memory studies 26–7
Menander 211, 229, 230 nn. 38–9
Merriam, A.C. 294

#MeToo 5, 322, 340
Metropolitan Museum of Art 5, 296, 362
Meyer, Gustav 365, 366
Michels, Agnes Kirsopp Lake 311–2 n. 32, 313
Mill, John 158
Millar, Sir Fergus 394
Miller, Nancy 12
Miller, Norma 178
Milton, John 163
Mingazzi, Paolino 352 n. 8
Mixer, Albert H. 286, 288
Modern Language Association 290 n. 31, 293, 295, 296
Modona, Aldo Neppi 352 n. 8
Molière 41
Momigliano, Arnaldo 394
Mommsen, Theodor 142, 352–3, 371 n. 67, 387, 391
Monk, James 379, 383
Monro, D.B. 390
Monro, W.D. 219 n. 1
Montausier, Duc de 40–41, 42
Monumenta Germaniae Historica 391
Moore, Frank Gardner 282, 294–5, 297
Moorhouse, A.C. 145
Morauus, Mathias 60
Morley, Sylvanus Griswold 353
Morse, Samuel F.B. 282
Moulton, James Hope 132 n. 13, 140–2
Müller, Karl Ottfried 157
Munro, H.A.J. 113 n. 35, 125, 136, 167–9
Munson, James E. 286, 288
Murdoch, Iris 324–5, 333–5, 339–40, 389
Muretus (Marc-Antoine de Muret) 63–4, 66, 67, 69, 75–6
Murray, Gilbert 356, 380–3, 390
Murray, Sir James Augustus Henry 278
Murray, John (publisher) 383–4
Murray, Penelope 202 n. 95, 210
Museum Criticum 379–80, 383, 393
Myers, F.W.H. 118
Myers, K. Sara 211
Mynott, Jeremy 181–2, 190
Myres, Sir John 224

Nathaniel 15–16
Négritude 367
Neil, Robert Alexander 139
Nepos, Cornelius 54, 83, 89
Nesen, Wilhelm 70–3
Nettleship, Henry 160, 161, 168, 170, 386–7
New Baskerville 207 n. 109
New English Dictionary 295
New Hellenic 207
New Testament 45, 46, 70, 84, 92 n. 50, 158, 306 n. 20, 387, 392–3
New York 5, 252–3, 278–84, 288, 289, 293, 295, 296, 301, 302, 306, 381 n.10
 see also Metropolitan Museum of Art
Newlands, Carole 211, 214 n. 114
Newnham College, Cambridge 382
Newton, Sir Charles 390
Nicholson, John 42–4
Nicolò delle Valle 90
Nilsson, Martin Persson 358 n. 28
Nimis, Steve 388
Nind, William 113 n. 35
Nisbet, R.G. 220
Nisbet, R.G.M. 178 n. 12, 220, 390
Noble, Peter Scott 145
Norden, Eduard 388
North, Helen 312
North, Sir Dudley 38
Norton, Thomas H. 286, 289 n. 26
Norwich 66
Nottingham High School 119 n. 49
Nudge theory 20–22

O'Donnell, James 194, 314
Oakley, Stephen 190, 199, 221, 242
Obama, Barack 20
Ogilvie, R.M. 198, 242
Old Testament 392–3
Oldenburg, Henry 41, 42
Oncken, Wilhelm 352
Oriel College, Oxford 322
Origen 41
Osborne, Robin 384–5
Ossian 82
Osthoff, Hermann 141, 297
Ostwald, Martin 312, 313

Otele, Olivette 26 n. 26
Ovid 35, 42, 44, 45, 95 n. 57, 181, 189, 192, 201, 202 n. 97, 210–12, 250 n. 3
Owen, Wilfred 13
Owens College, Manchester 132
Oxford Classical Dictionary 384
Oxford Greek and Latin College Commentaries 197
Oxford Philological Society 377, 391
'Oxford reds' 178, 180, 181 n. 19, 188, 206, 219, 230, 238
Oxford, University of 3, 4, 49, 53, 132, 155–72, 177, 204, 386–90; *see also* names of individual colleges
Oxford University Press 219–21, 225–6; *see also* Clarendon Ancient History Series, 'Oxford reds'

Packard, Lewis Richard 277, 294
Page, Sir Denys 184 n. 34, 219
Paley, F.A. 126
Paley, William 104
Palladio, Andrea 259 n. 40, 264, 266–7, 269
Panofsky, Dora 354 n. 15
Panofsky, Erwin 354 n. 15
Parker, L.P.E. 188 n. 50
Pattison, Mark 170 n. 49, 386
Paul, Hermann 142
Paul, St 38
Pauly, August von 384
Pausanias (author) 226
Pausanias (Spartan regent) 238, 241
Pearson, Alfred Chilton 142, 146
Pearson, Karl 323
Pease, A.S. 220
Peck, Tracy 278 n. 7, 294, 297 n. 44
Peel, Sir Robert 113
Peile, John 139, 140, 142–3, 145, 148 n. 86, 157 n. 8
Pelling, Chris 191 n. 56, 199 nn. 88–9, 200, 209, 212, 383 n. 14, 385 n. 22
Pembroke College, Cambridge 124, 139
Pennsylvania, University of 250
Pericles 235, 238, 241
Perkins, William 38
Perrault, Charles 54

Persius 42, 168–9
Personal voice scholarship 9–31
Peterhouse, Cambridge 123–5, 129
Peters, William Elisha 277 n. 3
Petronius 181 n. 19
Pfeiffer, Rudolf 332, 344, 345, 366
Phaedrus 35, 42
Phaer, Thomas 162
Philby, Kim 224
Philby, St John 224
Philological Society 278 n. 6, 282, 291 n. 32, 294, 295
Philosophical Transactions of the Royal Society 393
Philostratus 84, 94 n. 55
Pierson, J. 285, 287
Pinart, Adolphe 284–5
Pincianus (Hernán Núñez de Toledo y Guzmán) 63, 65, 68, 75–8
Pindar 90, 123, 210
Pitt Press 179–181, 182 n. 20
Plato 83, 159, 123, 159, 205, 207 n. 108, 209, 210–12, 236, 295, 325, 362, 364
Plautus 159, 208, 210, 212
Pliny the Elder 38, 43
Pliny the Younger 38, 196, 211, 214 n. 114
Plutarch 40, 43, 46, 54, 199, 200, 209, 219 n. 2, 230, 232, 235, 241, 358
Pointer, John 48
Poland, Franz 356 n. 23
Polybius 237 n. 58, 258 n. 39
Pope, Alexander 4, 49, 90, 165
Porada, Edith 362
Porson, Richard 101, 102, 117, 123 n. 57, 126, 128, 157, 159, 169, 207, 211, 379–83, 385, 393
Porter, James 113 n. 35
Postgate, John Percival 132 n. 12, 140, 148–50
Potter, John 43, 46
Poughkeepsie 280–4, 289, 296
Powell, Enoch 219 n. 2
Préaux, Claire 364 n. 48
Prien, Carl 156 n. 5
Priestley, Joseph 81, 92
Propertius 210
Proust, Jean 42

Prudentius 200
Pucci, Pietro 183
Purdle, Eleanor 143
Purser, Louis Claude 384

Quincy, Massachusetts 92
Quintilian 47

Radcliffe College 290
Rafaello Volterrano 89
Ramsay, Sir William 229, 387
Ramsey, John 210
Rangavis, Alexandros Rizos 282, 287, 288
Ranke, Leopold von 235
Rapson, Edward James 132 n. 12, 139, 142, 145, 146
Rask, Rasmus Kristian 277
Rattenbury, Robert 377
Reeve, Michael 190
Reid, James Smith 146
Reid, Richard 188 n. 48, 202 n. 95, 209
Reinach, Théodore 278
Reinhardt, Tobias 321 n. 7, 341
Rembski, Stanislav 360
Renier, Léon 358 n. 27
Rennie, William 220
Repton 103
Reynolds, David 13
Reynolds, Sir Joshua 378–9
Rheinhard, Hermann 260 n. 43, 264 n. 57, 267
Rhenanus, Beatus (Beatus Bild) 70–3
Rhine bridge 263–70
Rhodes, Cecil 25, 322
Rhodes, Peter J. 227, 384–5
Richardson, Nicholas 187, 202 n. 95, 211
Richardson, Samuel 50
Richmond, Sir Ian 198
Rickards, F.T. 119 n. 49
Riddell, James 122–3
Ridgeway, Sir William 140–1, 146
Riese, Alexander 352
Ritschl, F. W. 159, 166 n. 39, 170 n. 49, 352
Robathan, Dorothy 313
Roberts, Ernest Stewart 139

Robinson, David Moore 360, 369
Roche, Paul 212, 214 n. 114
Roehrig, Frederic Louis Otto 287, 288
Rogerson, Anne 160
Romilly, Joseph 112–3, 122, 128 n. 75
Rood, Tim 212
Rose, Imogen *see* Wrong, Imogen
Rosen, Friedrich August 278
Rosenberg, Isaac 13 n. 4
Rosenmeyer, Thomas 312, 313
Ross, Sir David 219 n. 1
Rostovtzeff, Mikhail 330, 332, 344, 345
Roueché, Charlotte 335–6 n. 48
Rounds, Dorothy 353
Rouse, William Henry Denham 142, 145
Rousseau, Jean-Jacques 48
Routh, Edward 113
Rowe, C.J. 209
Roy, Arundhati 23–4
Rubel. Alexander 355 n. 19
Rubens, Sir Peter Paul 92–5
Rubincam, Catherine 361
Rudberg, Gunnar 364
Rudd, Niall 209
Rugby School 106, 122, 155, 395
Ruhkopf, F.R. 59
Russell, D.A. 186 n. 73, 200, 202 n. 95, 209, 211, 214 n. 112, 387, 390
Rusten, Jeffrey S. 209, 214 n. 113, 227
Ruthall, Thomas 69
Rutherford, Richard B. 195 n. 69, 198, 209, 212
Rutland, 2nd and 3rd Dukes of 47
Ryberg, Inez Scott 313

Sachs, Julius 312
Said, Edward 23
Sallust 43, 89, 91, 253
Salutati, Coluccio 91
Sambre, River 258, 260
Samson, G.W. 288
Sancroft, Revd. William 38
Sanday, William 387
Sander, Anton 294
Sandys, Sir John Edwin 110, 125, 146, 226 n. 26

Sanskrit 132–4, 136–40, 145–7, 282, 285, 287, 288, 291, 293, 295
Sansone, David 212
Sassoon, Siegfried 13
Saussure, Ferdinand de 141
Scaliger, Joseph 46, 388
Scarborough, William Sanders 293, 297 n. 44
Schein, Seth 183, 211
Schele de Vere, Maximilian 285, 287, 294
Schilling, Robert 367
Schlegel, Friedrich 133
Schleicher, August 140, 142
Schliemann, Heinrich 283–4, 286–9
Schmitt-Pantel, Pauline 358 n. 37
Schultze, Clemence 333 n. 42
Scodel, Ruth 313
Scott, Alexander John 132 n. 6
Scott, Charles 122
Scott, Revd. Robert 103, 383–5, 396
Scott, Sir Walter 119, 162
Seaford, Richard 188 n. 50
Seeley, J.R. 229 n. 32
Segal, Charles 313
Seligson, Gerda Kroner 302, 311
Sellar, William Young 167, 169
Seminar Boreas 381 n. 10
Seneca 4, 43, 35, 59–80, 166–7, 209–10, 212, 214 n. 112, 326 n. 30
Senghor, Léopold Sédar 367–9
Sens, Alexander 212
Servius 83, 94 n. 55, 296
Servius Tullius 37–8
Sevenoaks School 115
Sewall, Jotham B. 286
Seymour, T.D. 294, 295, 297 n. 44
Shackleton Bailey, D.R. 205, 209, 213, 377
Shaftesbury, 3rd Earl of 48
Shakespeare, William 39, 84, 87, 116 n. 41, 149, 163, 241, 250, 281
Sharp, Michael 190, 207–8
Shaw, George Bernard 131
Shaw, Samuel 48
Shay, Jonathan 13–14, 20, 23, 24
Shilleto, Arthur 105, 128 n. 75
Shilleto, Catherine 105
Shilleto, Edward 105, 119
Shilleto, Ellen 105
Shilleto, Isabella *see* Snelgar, Isabella
Shilleto, Isabella junior 105
Shilleto, John junior 105, 128 n. 75
Shilleto, John senior 103
Shilleto, Mary 105
Shilleto, Richard 4, 101–30
Shilleto, Richard junior 105, 128 n. 75
Shilleto, William 105, 119, 125, 128 n. 75
Shrewsbury School 103, 105, 108, 116, 117, 122, 123
Shute, Helen W. 290 n. 30
Sickert, William 221
Sidgwick, Arthur 395
Sidgwick, Frank 394–5
Sidonius Apollinaris 200
Sihler, Ernst Gottlieb 293, 294
Silius Italicus 191
Simon, Laura 303–4, 309–10
Sisam, Kenneth 219
Sjöqvist, Erik 366–7
Skutsch, Otto 358 n. 28
Smith, Clement Lawrence 278 n. 7
Smith, Gertrude 313
Smith, Goldwin 159
Smith, Neil 133 n. 15
Smith, Sir William 384
Smithsonian Institution 281
Smollett, Tobias 50
Snelgar, Isabella 105
Snelgar, Isabella senior 105
Snelgar, Jacob 105
Snelgar, Jacob junior 105
Snell, Bruno 366
Soane, Sir John 269
Soble, Alan G. 357
Society for the Promotion of Hellenic Studies 377, 391
Society for the Promotion of Roman Studies 391
Society for the Protection of Science and Learning 331
Society of Dilettanti 378–9
Society of Jesus 36
Sommerstein, Alan H. 195 n. 69, 209, 211, 212, 214, 338

Sonnenschein, Edward Adolf 10
Sophocles 9, 21, 164, 179, 180, 182–4, 187–9, 192–3, 200, 205, 206, 208–10, 213 n. 111, 297 n. 45
Sorabi, Richard 355
Sorum, Christina Elliott 311 n. 30
Spaeth, Thomas 303–4, 309–10
Spateman, Thomas 52–4
Spencer, Jesse Ames 252–3
Spondanus, Johannes 90–5
Squier, Ephraim George 287
St Andrews 44
St Bartholomew's Church 52
St Botolph's, Cambridge 106
St Edmund Hall, Oxford 47, 158
St John's College, Cambridge 124, 135, 143, 382
St Leonard's College, St Andrews 44
St Paul's Cathedral 52
Stanford University 182 n. 23, 204, 312
Stanford, W.B. 177
Stangl, Thomas 377
Stanley, Lord, later 15th Earl of Derby 111 n. 27
Starkie, W.J.M. 237 n. 56
Statius 94, 167, 191, 200, 211
Steele, Sir Richard 45, 51
Steiner, Deborah 198, 211
Stewart, James 389
Stewart, Zeph 309–10
Stirling, John 48
Stobart, John Clarke 394–5
Strachan, John 132 n. 13, 140, 142, 145
Strauss, Leo 312 n. 32
Streitberg, Wilhelm 143, 297
Stroud, Ronald 354 n. 15
Suerbaum, Werner 354 n. 16
Suetonius 62–3, 191, 199, 210
Sumner, Charles 281
Sunstein, Cass 20–21
Swansea University 3, 145
Sweet, Henry 131, 136, 148–9
Sweet, Marguerite 290
Swift, Jonathan 49
Swinburne, Algernon 116–7 n. 43
Syme, Sir Ronald 225–6, 356 n. 21

Tacitus 44, 178 n. 14, 197, 198–9, 205, 209–12, 214 nn. 113–4, 225–6, 229, 370, 385
Tamworth 48
Tarrant, Richard 202–3, 211, 214 n. 114
Tate, Nahum 39–40
Taylor, Lily Ross 313
Taylor, Margaret 310
Temporini, Hildegard 369
Terence 205, 206, 208, 210–11, 213, 258 n. 37
Tertullian 200
Thaler, Richard 21
Themistocles 238, 241
Theocritus 118, 145, 206, 210, 214
Thesaurus Linguae Latinae 365–6, 391
Thierfelder, Andreas 361 n. 34
Thiersch, Friedrich 351
Thirlwall, Connop 135, 278, 294
Thomas, Frederick William 132 n. 12, 139, 140, 142, 145
Thomas, Richard 202, 205, 209, 211, 214 n. 114
Thompson, W.H. 101, 105, 121, 123, 136
Thomson, Judith Jarvis 357
Thomson, Margaret Head 361
Thucydides 4, 43, 114–6, 125–7, 209, 214 n. 112, 219–47, 321, 384
Tietze, Franz 366
Tissol, Garth 211
Tooke, Benjamin 42
Toy, Crawford 294, 295
Toynbee, Jocelyn 326, 330 n. 35, 335, 361
Trajan's column 267
Trapp, Michael 190 n. 54, 196 n. 73, 210, 213 n. 111
Treggiari, Susan 311, 312 n. 32
Trinity College, Cambridge 103–5, 123, 134, 135–6, 145, 148, 377 n. 5, 379, 380 n. 8, 382, 384, 389, 394
Trinity Hall, Cambridge 124
Trollope, William 254
Trudgill, Peter 133 n. 15
Trumbull, James Hammond 286–9, 291, 294, 296
Tucker, Thomas George 133, 177
Turulla, Enrico 352 n. 8

Tweed, William M. 296
Tyrrell, Robert Yelverton 384

Ulleskelf 103
Ullman, Berthold Louis 313
Underhill, G.E. 226, 230
University College London 132, 135, 323
University College, Oxford 155–6, 158 n. 18, 159
Usener, Hermann 352 n. 8

Valerius Flaccus 191, 211, 214 n. 114
Valpy, A.J. 43, 91
Van der Borcht, Pieter, the elder 265
Van Name, Addison 289, 291
Vansittart, Augustus Arthur 136
Vassar College 282–3, 289, 290, 301–2, 306, 308–9, 313
Vermeule III, Cornelius Clarkson 362, 363 n. 42
Vermeule, Emily 362–3
Verner's Law 141
Veronese, Paolo 379
Verrall, Arthur 382
Versammlung deutschen Philologen und Schulmänner 277–8, 280, 291 n. 32, 351–2
Victoria, Queen 113
Vincentius Opsopoeus (Vinzenz Heidecker) 90
Vincze, Paul 358
Vinogradoff, Sir Paul 330, 332, 343, 345, 387
Virgil 4, 35, 43, 44, 49, 61, 83, 157 n. 12, 159–70, 184, 189, 192, 201, 202, 205, 209, 211–12, 252, 254
Vitruvius 264
Vives, Juan Luis 344, 345
Vogel, E.J. 59, 69
Vogt, Ernst 365–6
Vogt, Joseph 369–70
Vogt, Ursula 369
Von Scheliha, Renata 302

Wace 87
Wackernagel, Jacob 388
Wade-Gery, H.T. 236

Walbank, F.W. 221, 225–6, 234, 237 n. 57, 242
Walcott, Derek 27
Walford, Edward 120
Walpole, Horace 379
Ward, Julia E. 289 n. 29
Ware, Herts., UK 106
Warnock, Baroness Mary 324–35, 339–40, 341–2
Warren, Winifred 290
Waterland, Daniel 47
Watson, David 44
Watson, Lindsay 210–11, 214
Watson, Patricia 210–11, 214
Watt, W.S. 377
Webster, Noah 256
Webster, T.B.L. 182–3, 187, 204, 208, 227 n. 1, 230 n. 39, 356
Weil, Henri 358
Weinstein, Harvey 322
Weisch, Alfons 358 n. 28
Welford, Alfred 143
Wellesley College 307, 310
Wellington, 1st Duke of 113
Wells, John 133 n. 15
Wells, Joseph 226, 229 n. 32, 230, 384
Welton, D.M. 287 n. 24
West, Martin 361 n. 34, 388
Westminster School 46, 49, 122
Weston, Mrs A.E. 289 n. 29
Wheatley, T.F. 179–81
Whewell, William 135
White, Mary Estelle 364 n. 48
White, Peter 192 n. 68, 194, 212
White, Richard Grant 281
Whitling, Frederick 391
Whitmarsh, Tim 191, 212
Whitney, William Dwight 277–9, 281–2, 284, 288, 291, 294, 295, 297 n. 44, 298
Whitton, Christopher 196, 211, 214 n. 114
Wickham, E.C. 168
Wilamowitz-Moellendorff, Tycho von 337 n. 54
Wilamowitz-Moellendorff, Ulrich von 353 n. 9, 364, 365, 388, 392
Wilkins, Augustus Samuel 132 nn. 6, 13
Wilkins, John 188 n. 50

Willcock, M.M. 202 n. 95, 209, 210
William and Mary College 91
William III of England 43
Williams, Gareth 210, 214
Williams, R.D. 178 n. 12
Willink, Sir Charles 188 n. 50
Wilson, William Epiphanius 287 n. 24
Wimmel, Walter 365 n. 49
Witschonke, Richard B. 361 n. 35
Wittenberg 66
Wolfe, Ethyle 308, 311 n. 30
Wolsky, Florence 362, 363 n. 42
Woodman, Tony 191 n. 56, 197, 198–9, 205, 209, 211, 214 n. 114, 385
Woolsey, Theodore Dwight 279
Wordsworth, Revd. Charles 383 n. 15
Wordsworth, Revd. Christopher 104 n. 7, 383 n. 15
Wordsworth, John 383 n. 15
Wordsworth, William 383 n. 15

Wrong, Imogen 324, 326, 330
Wyke, Maria 269
Wyse, W. 226, 229

X-club 381
Xenophon 43, 202 n. 95, 210, 212, 226, 358

Yale University 306–7 *see also* Calhoun College
Young, Thomas 134
Ypres 268
Yunis, Harvey E. 210–11

Zeller, Eduard 352
Zetzel, James E.G. 210
Zimmermann, Franz 356 n. 23
Zuntz, Gunther 302
Zuntz, Leonie 302
Zupitza, Julius 142

www.ingramcontent.com/pod-product-compliance
Lightning Source LLC
Chambersburg PA
CBHW052055230426
43662CB00037B/1801